Consent to Treatment

Consent to Treatment
A Practical Guide
Second Edition

Fay A. Rozovsky, J.D., M.P.H.
Member, Massachusetts and Florida Bars

President, LEFAR Health Associates, Inc.
Providence, R.I.
Halifax, N.S.

Visiting Lecturer in Health Law
Harvard University
School of Public Health

Little, Brown and Company
Boston   Toronto   London

Library of Congress Catalog Card No. 89-085547

ISBN 0-316-76057-9

Second Edition

MV NY

*Published simultaneously in Canada
by Little, Brown & Company (Canada) Limited*

Printed in the United States of America

To my boys, Lorne, Joshua, and Aaron, with love

Summary of Contents

Table of Contents   ix
Foreword   xxxi
Preface   xxxv

ONE   The Rules for Consent to Treatment   1
TWO   Exceptions to the Rules   99
THREE   Women and Reproductive Matters   135
FOUR   Prisoners and Detainees   215
FIVE   Minors   255
SIX   Mental Illness, Mental Retardation, and Consent   361
SEVEN   The Right to Refuse Treatment   437
EIGHT   Human Research and Experimentation   527
NINE   Organ Donation and Autopsy   613
TEN   The Elderly and Consent   671
ELEVEN   AIDS and Consent   689
TWELVE   Documentation of Consent and Practical Rules
           for Consent   707

Appendix A   Long Consent Form   743
Appendix B   Short Consent Form   745
Appendix C   Detailed Note in Medical Record   747
Appendix D   Consent Checklist Form   751
Appendix E   Jehovah's Witness Cards and Release Forms   753
Appendix F   Uniform Brain Death Act   761
Appendix G   Uniform Anatomical Gift Act   763
Appendix H   Proposed Uniform Donation Card   769
Table of Cases   771
Table of Statutes   781
Index   801

Table of Contents

Foreword   *xxxi*
Preface   *xxxv*

ONE

The Rules for Consent to Treatment

A. The Law of Consent in Perspective   3
    §1.0   What Is Consent to Treatment?   3
    §1.1   Settings in Which Consent Must Be
            Obtained   4
            §1.1.1   Traditional Care Facilities   5
            §1.1.2   Alternate Care Settings   6
    §1.2   The Traditional Approach: Assault and
            Battery   6
    §1.3   The Modern Approach: Negligence Theory   9
            §1.3.1   Policy Justification   11
B. Criteria for a Valid Consent   12
    §1.4   The Issue of Coercion and Undue
            Influence   13
            §1.4.1   Hospital-Based Consent   13
            §1.4.2   Coercion by Hospital Personnel   14
            §1.4.3   Financial Coercion: Medicaid
                      Anti-Dumping Provisions   15

§1.5   Patients' Legal Capacity to Give Consent   17
        §1.5.1   Guardianship or Conservatorship   17
        §1.5.2   Patient Objections Versus Guardian
                 or Conservator Decisions   18
        §1.5.3   Minors' Capacity to Give Consent   19
        §1.5.4   Laws Creating Legal Incapacity   20
§1.6   Patients' Mental Capacity to Give Consent   21
        §1.6.1   Irrational or Delusional Patients   21
        §1.6.2   Mental Incapacity and
                 Authorization of Treatment   22
        §1.6.3   Refusal of Consent Versus Mental
                 Incompetency   23
§1.7   Consent to Specific Procedures   24
        §1.7.1   Ignoring Specific Patient
                 Instructions   24
        §1.7.2   Operating on an Unauthorized Part
                 of a Patient's Body   25
        §1.7.3   Problems with General Consents   26
        §1.7.4   Medical Emergencies and
                 Unanticipated Circumstances   28
§1.8   Use of Understandable Terminology and
        Language   29
§1.9   Answering Patients' Questions   31
§1.10   Valid Forms of Consent   32
        §1.10.1 Expressed or Implied Consent   32
        §1.10.2 Written or Verbal Consent   34
§1.11   Patients' Right to Refuse or Withdraw
        Consent   35
        §1.11.1 Use of Release Forms   37
        §1.11.2 Informed Refusal of Treatment   39
        §1.11.3 Specialists' Duty to Disclose Risk of
                 Refusing Care   41
C. The Need for Adequate Disclosure   42
    §1.12   Patients' Right to Basic Information   44
            §1.12.1 Disclosure of Risk-Benefit
                     Information   45
            §1.12.2 Disclosure of Reasonable
                     Alternative Procedures   50
            §1.12.3 Disclosure of Diagnostic Test
                     Results   55

§1.13   Information That Need Not Be
        Disclosed   59
        §1.13.1   The Medical Community Standard   59
        §1.13.2   The Patient Need Standard   60
        §1.13.3   Legislative Standards Governing
                  Disclosure   62
        §1.13.4   The Effect of the JCAHO
                  Standards on Consent   63
§1.14   Who Should Obtain Consent?   64
        §1.14.1   The Duty to Disclose Rests with the
                  Caregiver   65
        §1.14.2   The Danger of Delegating the
                  Disclosure Responsibility   67
        §1.14.3   Drug Manufacturers: The Limited
                  Duty to Warn   68
        §1.14.4   The Duty of the Health Facility   69
        §1.14.5   The Duty of the Dispensing
                  Pharmacist   70
D. Elements of Negligent Consent Litigation   73
    §1.15   Basic Elements of a Negligent Consent
            Lawsuit   74
            §1.15.1   Patient-Provider Relationship   75
            §1.15.2   Provider's Duty to Provide Risk
                      Information   76
            §1.15.3   Inexcusable Failure of Provider to
                      Disclose Risk Information   78
            §1.15.4   Causation in Negligent Consent   78
            §1.15.5   Nondisclosure as Proximate Cause 81
    §1.16   Defenses to Negligent Consent Litigation   82
            §1.16.1   Remote and Commonly Known
                      Risks   82
            §1.16.2   Patient Acceptance of Treatment
                      Regardless of Risk   84
            §1.16.3   Medical Emergencies   85
            §1.16.4   Justifiable Withholding of
                      Information   86
            §1.16.5   Signed Consent Forms   87
            §1.16.6   Other Available Defenses   89
    §1.17   Statutes of Limitation in Consent
            Actions   89

§1.18   Expert Testimony in Consent Litigation   91
     §1.18.1   Where Expert Testimony Is
              Required   92
     §1.18.2   Where Expert Testimony Is Not
              Required   93
§1.19   Burden of Proof in Consent Actions   94
§1.20   Litigation Checklist for Consent Actions   97

TWO

Exceptions to the Rules

    §2.0   Overview   100
A. When Consent Is Not Necessary   100
    §2.1   A "Process" Approach to Consent   100
         §2.1.1   Flow Chart of General Consent
                  Elements   101
         §2.1.2   Flow Charts of Consent When
                  Exceptions Apply   103
         §2.1.3   Communication and History in
                  Exceptional Cases   105
    §2.2   Medical Emergencies   106
         §2.2.1   Definition of a Medical Emergency   106
         §2.2.2   Declaration of Situations as
                  Emergencies   108
         §2.2.3   Scope of Authorized Emergency
                  Care   109
         §2.2.4   Policy Considerations and
                  Emergency Care   110
    §2.3   Treatment When Consent Is Not Possible   112
    §2.4   Use of Therapeutic Privilege   114
         §2.4.1   Justifiable Use of Therapeutic
                  Privilege   115
                 a.   The use of the privilege must take
                    into account the circumstances
                    of the patient   115
                 b.   The physician must believe that
                    a full disclosure of information will
                    have a significantly adverse impact
                    on the patient   116

		c.	Reasonable discretion must be used in the manner and extent of the disclosure	116
	§2.4.2		Unjustifiable Use of Therapeutic Privilege	117
	§2.4.3		Documentation and Therapeutic Privilege	118
§2.5			Compulsory Treatment and the Need for Consent	118
§2.6			Duty of Third-Party Disclosure	121
	§2.6.1		Duty to Warn Others of Potential Harm	121
	§2.6.2		Duty to Provide Notification of Treatment	122
	§2.6.3		Times When Disclosure Is Not Permissible	123
B. Problem Cases				124
§2.7			Patients' Requests Not to Be Informed	124
	§2.7.1		Implications of Uninformed Consent	125
	§2.7.2		Documentation of the Request	126
§2.8			Patients Undergoing Repetitive or Continuous Treatment	127
§2.9			Placebo, Deception, and Consent	129
	§2.9.1		Placebo, Deception, and Clinical Treatment	129
	§2.9.2		Placebo, Deception, and Human Research	131
		a.	Federal research requirements	131
		b.	State research requirements	132
	§2.9.3		Policy Considerations	134

THREE

Women and Reproductive Matters

§3.0		Introduction	136
A. Birth Control and Consent			137
§3.1		Disclosure with the Pill and IUDs	137
	§3.1.1	The Manufacturer's Duty to Warn	139

		§3.1.2	Packet Inserts Directed at Physicians	143
		§3.1.3	Legal Effect of FDA's "Dear Doctor" Letters	144
		§3.1.4	Patient Packet Inserts and Doctors' Duty to Warn	144
		§3.1.5	Minimizing Litigation and Consent Requirements	146
B.	Sterilization and Consent			148
	§3.2	Criteria for Consent		148
		§3.2.1	Consequences of Invalid Consents	148
		§3.2.2	Amount of Necessary Disclosure	151
			a. Examples of inadequate disclosure	151
			b. A case example of adequate disclosure	153
		§3.2.3	Practical Points	153
	§3.3	Spousal Consent		156
		§3.3.1	The General Rule	156
		§3.3.2	Right of Privacy	157
		§3.3.3	Statutory Law	157
		§3.3.4	Practical Considerations	157
C.	Abortion and Consent			158
	§3.4	Supreme Court Precedent		158
	§3.5	General State Consent Requirements		159
		§3.5.1	Informational Content of Consent	160
			a. Fetal pain	161
			b. Neutral and objective disclosures	162
		§3.5.2	"Consent" Waiting Periods	166
		§3.5.3	Restrictions on Who May Obtain Consent	168
		§3.5.4	Counselling Patients Regarding Abortion	169
	§3.6	Biological Father's Consent to Abortion		170
D.	Conception, Pregnancy, and Consent			172
	§3.7	Artificial Insemination		173
		§3.7.1	Basic Disclosure Requirements	173
		§3.7.2	Need for Spousal Consent	174
		§3.7.3	Status of the Donor	175
		§3.7.4	Unmarried Recipients	176
		§3.7.5	Consent as a Defense to Adultery	176

§3.8 Prenatal Venereal Disease Screening 177
§3.9 Duty to Disclose Risks of Birth Defects and
Delivery Problems 178
§3.9.1 Inadequate Disclosure of Birth
Defect Risk Information 179
a. Tay-Sachs disease cases 180
b. Other wrongful life actions 182
§3.9.2 Necessary Disclosures to
Prospective Parents 183
§3.9.3 Maternal Rubella 184
§3.9.4 Necessary Disclosures to
Prospective Mothers 186
§3.9.5 Delivery Risks 187
§3.9.6 Practical Considerations 190
E. Consent to Medical and Surgical Treatment:
Special Issues of Concern to Women 190
§3.10 Hysterectomy Surgery 191
§3.10.1 Unauthorized Hysterectomies 191
§3.10.2 Failure to Disclose Reasonable
Alternatives 195
§3.10.3 Inadequate Disclosure of Risk
Information 196
§3.10.4 Choosing Risk Information for
Disclosure 197
§3.11 Radiation Treatment and Radium Implants 199
§3.12 Mastectomy Surgery 201
§3.12.1 Statutory Requirements 202
§3.12.2 Physician's Duty to Warn 203
§3.12.3 Breast Biopsy Beyond a Patient's
Authorization 204
§3.12.4 Disclosing Risk of Frozen Section
Biopsies 205
§3.13 Risk Disclosure in Urogenital Surgery and
Diagnostic Procedures on Women 206
§3.13.1 Disclosure of Varying Theories of
Cell Growth 207
§3.13.2 Disclosure of Risks of Foregoing
Pap Smears 208
§3.13.3 Practical Considerations 209
§3.14 Screening for Women's Diseases 210

§3.14.1 Pap Smear Legislation 211
§3.14.2 Pap Smears and Disclosure
Requirements 211
§3.14.3 DES Screening 212
§3.15 Treatment for Rape Victims 212

FOUR

Prisoners and Detainees

A. Voluntary Consent 216
§4.0 Can Consent Be Voluntary? 216
§4.1 Factors Influencing Voluntariness 216
§4.1.1 Survival: The Model Prisoner
Syndrome 217
§4.1.2 Fear: The Coercive Institutional
Setting 217
§4.1.3 Lack of Adequate Explanation 218
§4.2 Good Communication 219
B. Incapacity to Consent 219
§4.3 State Legislation on Inmate Welfare 219
§4.4 Emergency Treatment and Implied Consent 220
§4.5 Intoxication: The Parens Patriae Rule 221
C. Right to Refuse Treatment 223
§4.6 When Can Prisoners Say No? 223
§4.6.1 Legislative Limits 223
§4.6.2 Case Law 225
§4.6.3 Treating Hunger Strikers 231
§4.6.4 Religious Refusals 232
§4.6.5 Probation and Experimental Drug
Therapy 232
D. Compulsory Examination and Treatment 234
§4.7 Venereal Disease 234
§4.7.1 Who Must Submit? 234
§4.7.2 Gaining Cooperation of Prisoners 235
§4.8 Drug Addiction 238
E. Obtaining Evidence: Physical and Surgical "Searches" 239
§4.9 Informed Consent of Suspects 239
§4.10 Implied Consent of Unconscious or
Incapacitated Persons 241

§4.11   Implied Consent of Drunk Driving Suspects   243
§4.12   Invasive Searches of Prisoners' Bodies   247
        §4.12.1   Nonsurgical Invasions   247
        §4.12.2   Surgical Invasions   250

FIVE

Minors

A.   Traditional View of Minors' Consent to Treatment   256
     §5.0   Introduction   256
     §5.1   Minors' Incapacity to Consent   257
     §5.2   Modifications of the Common Law   259
            §5.2.1   Emergency Treatment   259
            §5.2.2   Mature Minors   260
            §5.2.3   Emancipated Minors   266
B.   Legislative Standards for Minors' Consent   267
     §5.3   General Statutory Laws   267
            §5.3.1   Emancipated Minor Legislation   268
            §5.3.2   Age of Consent Legislation   269
            §5.3.3   Immunity and Disaffirmance
                     Legislation   270
            §5.3.4   Parental Notification Requirements   271
            §5.3.5   Third-Party Consent Laws   273
            §5.3.6   Consent from a Minor Parent   274
            §5.3.7   Judicial Interpretation of Consent
                     Legislation   274
C.   Minors and Reproductive Matters   275
     §5.4   Sexually Transmitted Diseases   275
            §5.4.1   General Legislation   275
            §5.4.2   Confidentiality of Treatment   277
     §5.5   Minors and Contraceptives   279
            §5.5.1   Minors' Right to Contraceptives   279
            §5.5.2   Parental Consent and Notification   280
            §5.5.3   Contraceptive Legislation for
                     Minors   284
     §5.6   Minors and Abortion   286
            §5.6.1   Parental Consent to Abortion   286
            §5.6.2   Parental Notification   294

		§5.6.3	Married Minors: Spousal Consent and Notification	298
		§5.6.4	Practical Considerations Regarding Minors and Abortion	299
D.	Drug and Alcohol Abuse Treatment for Minors			301
	§5.7	Statutory Requirements		301
E.	Mentally Ill and Retarded Minors			304
	§5.8	Authorization for Treatment		304
		§5.8.1	Parental Consent	305
		§5.8.2	Authorization by the Minor	305
		§5.8.3	Judicial Limitations on Parental Consent	308
		§5.8.4	Medication for Minors	312
		§5.8.5	Consent to Release of Committed Minors	313
	§5.9	Sterilization of Mentally Incompetent Minors		314
		§5.9.1	Statutory Law	315
		§5.9.2	Judicial Limitations	316
F.	Immunization and Screening of Children			321
	§5.10	Immunization		321
		§5.10.1	Legislative Standards	321
		§5.10.2	Case Decisions	324
	§5.11	Screening of Children for Health Risks		325
		§5.11.1	Newborns	325
		§5.11.2	School-Age Children	327
		§5.11.3	Obtaining Consent	327
G.	Treatment of Minors in Crisis Situations			328
	§5.12	Emergency Treatment		328
		§5.12.1	Sexually Assaulted Minors	330
	§5.13	Child Abuse		331
	§5.14	Delinquent and Deprived Children		332
H.	Drug and Medical Care in Schools			334
	§5.15	Legislation Authorizing Treatment		334
I.	Refusal of Consent to Treatment			335
	§5.16	Parental Refusal		335
		§5.16.1	Statutory Limits	335
		§5.16.2	Judicial Limits	337
		§5.16.3	Treatment Decisions for Disabled Children	344
	§5.17	Refusal of Care for Terminally Ill Children		350

§5.17.1   Court Orders Not to Resuscitate
          for Minors   356
§5.18   Children's Refusal of Treatment   357

SIX

Mental Illness, Mental Retardation, and Consent

§6.0   Introduction   362
A. Commitment for Treatment and Consent   362
    §6.1   Voluntary Commitment and Consent   363
            §6.1.1   Release of Voluntary Patients or
                     Residents   364
    §6.2   Involuntary Commitment and Consent   365
            §6.2.1   Criteria for Involuntary
                     Commitment   366
            §6.2.2   Rights of Institutionalized Patients   369
B. Scope of Permissible Mental Health Treatment   370
    §6.3   Consent to Electroshock Treatment   371
            §6.3.1   State Legislation Regulating the
                     Use of ECT   372
            §6.3.2   Consent Requirements in the
                     Absence of Specific ECT
                     Legislation   375
            §6.3.3   Emergency Use of ECT   376
            §6.3.4   Case Law on Consent to ECT   377
            §6.3.5   Avoiding Consent Actions
                     Involving ECT   381
    §6.4   Consent and the Use of Medication   382
            §6.4.1   Legislative Controls on Medication:
                     Precommitment Therapy   382
            §6.4.2   Legislative Controls of Psychoactive
                     Drugs and Other Medications   384
                     a. Right to refuse medication   385
                     b. Informed consent requirements
                         for medication therapy   386
            §6.4.3   Consent Requirements for Use of
                     Medication Therapy   387
            §6.4.4   Case Law on the Use of Medication   389

§6.4.5   Policy Considerations in the
Forcible Administration of
Medication   401

§6.5   Psychosurgery and the Law of Consent   402

§6.5.1   What Is Psychosurgery?   403

§6.5.2   State Legislation Regulating
Psychosurgery   404

§6.5.3   Factors Influencing Decisions for
Psychosurgery   406

§6.5.4   Case Law   407

    a.   The *Kaimowitz* case and consent
to psychosurgery   407

    b.   The effect of the *Kaimowitz* decision   411

§6.6   Behavioral Modification, Physical Restraint,
and Isolation as Treatment   412

§6.6.1   Aversive Stimuli and Behavioral
Modification   412

§6.6.2   Restraints   414

    a.   Legislative control of restraints   414

    b.   Case law on the use of restraints   415

§6.6.3   Isolation and Seclusion   417

C.   Sterilization of the Mentally Disabled   419

§6.7   State Legislation   420

§6.8   Case Law on Sterilization of Mentally
Incompetent Persons   423

§6.8.1   The Traditional Approach   423

§6.8.2   Judicial Legislating of Sterilization   424

    a.   The New Jersey experience   424

    b.   The Massachusetts experience   428

§6.8.3   Practical Considerations: What to
Do in the Absence of Enabling
Legislation   429

D.   Nonpsychiatric Treatment of the Mentally Disabled   430

§6.9   Medical and Surgical Treatment   430

SEVEN

The Right to Refuse Treatment

§7.0   Introduction   438

A.   Curable, Life-Threatening Illness   439

§7.1   Religious and Philosophical Objections to
        Treatment   439
        §7.1.1   Treatment Compelled Over
                  Religious Objections   440
        §7.1.2   Treatment Not Compelled Over
                  Religious Objections   450
        §7.1.3   State Statutes and Religious
                  Objections   453
        §7.1.4   Other Types of Litigation Involving
                  Religious Objection to Treatment   453
§7.2   Incompetent or Incapacitated Persons   455
        §7.2.1   Incompetent Persons   455
        §7.2.2   Incapacitated Persons   460
        §7.2.3   State Statutes Authorizing
                  Treatment   461
§7.3   Emergency Life-Saving Treatment   463
        §7.3.1   Authority to Provide Treatment   463
        §7.3.2   Patients' Refusal of Treatment   465
        §7.3.3   Relatives' Refusal of Treatment   466
        §7.3.4   Disputes Among Family Members   467
        §7.3.5   Effects of Patients' Written
                  Directives   468
        §7.3.6   Policy Considerations in Providing
                  Treatment   470
                  a.   The use of release forms   471
                  b.   Securing court orders for treatment   471
                  c.   Treatment without authorization   472
B.   Terminal Illness   473
     §7.4   Right to Refuse Terminal Care   473
             §7.4.1   Competent Persons   473
             §7.4.2   Incompetent Persons   475
                       a.   Overview of the law   475
                       b.   Dealing with family members   477
     §7.5   Right to Withdraw Life-Sustaining
             Treatment   480
             §7.5.1   Competent Persons   480
                       a.   Respiratory and cardiopulmonary
                            function issues   480
                       b.   Artificial nutrition and hydration
                            issues   486
             §7.5.2   Incompetent Persons   487

	a. Respiratory and cardiopulmonary function issues	487
	b. Artificial nutrition and hydration issues	490
§7.5.3	Practical Considerations Regarding Other Treatments	505
§7.6	Orders Not to Resuscitate (DNR's)	507
§7.6.1	Case Law	509
§7.6.2	Rules and Regulations	512
§7.6.3	Practical Considerations	514
§7.7	Orders Not to Hospitalize (DNH's)	515
§7.7.1	What Is a DNH Order?	515
§7.7.2	The Practical Significance of DNH Orders	517
§7.8	Living Wills, Patient Directives and Durable Powers of Attorney	518
§7.8.1	Living Wills	518
	a. Types of living wills	518
	b. Practical effect of living wills	519
§7.8.2	Patient Directives	520
§7.8.3	Directives Generated by Health Facilities	522
§7.8.4	Durable Powers of Attorney	524

EIGHT

Human Research and Experimentation

A.	Scope of Federal Regulation	530
§8.0	Historical Background	530
§8.1	Overview of HHS Regulations	532
§8.1.1	General Administrative Requirements	532
§8.1.2	Role of Institutional Review Boards (IRBs)	533
§8.1.3	Requirements for Consent	534
§8.1.4	Documentation Requirements for Consent	536
§8.1.5	General Applicability of HHS Regulations	537

§8.2	Overview of FDA Regulations	537
	§8.2.1 Requirements for Consent	538
	§8.2.2 Standards for Consent Documentation	539
	§8.2.3 Waiver of Consent: Two Major Exceptions	539
	a. Feasibility	539
	b. Preservation of life	540
§8.3	Requirements of Other Federal Agencies and Departments	540
B.	State Controls Over Human Research	541
§8.4	Overview of State Requirements	541
	§8.4.1 The California Approach	541
	§8.4.2 The New York Approach	542
	§8.4.3 The Virginia Approach	542
	§8.4.4 General Statutory Provisions	543
	§8.4.5 Interplay with Federal Regulations	544
§8.5	Overview of Drug Research Laws	544
	§8.5.1 Consent Requirements	545
C.	Reproductive Research: Special Consent Considerations	547
§8.6	Research Involving Pregnant Women: Federal Consent Requirements	547
	§8.6.1 IRB Responsibilities	547
	§8.6.2 Paternal Consent	548
	§8.6.3 Waiver of Consent Provisions	548
§8.7	Research Involving Pregnant Women: State Legislation	549
	§8.7.1 New Mexico: Strict Consent Requirements for Research	549
	§8.7.2 Dual Impact of State and Federal Laws	550
§8.8	Federal Constraints on Fetal Research	551
	§8.8.1 IRB Responsibilities	551
	§8.8.2 Fetal Research In Utero	552
	§8.8.3 Fetal Research Ex Utero	552
	a. Nonviable fetuses	553
	b. Viable fetuses	553
	c. Parental consent requirements	553
	§8.8.4 Exceptions to Federal Control	553
§8.9	State Laws on Fetal Research	554
	§8.9.1 The Massachusetts Example	555

		a.	Criminal penalties and prior judicial review	556
		b.	Maternal consent to research on a dead fetus	556
	§8.9.2		The New Mexico Approach	557
	§8.9.3		Effect of Federal and State Fetal Research Laws	558
§8.10	Federal Laws Governing In Vitro Fertilization Research			560
	§8.10.1		Lack of Specific Consent Requirements	561
	§8.10.2		Authority of the Secretary and Ethical Advisory Boards	561
§8.11	State Laws Governing In Vitro Fertilization Research			562
§8.12	Impact of Governmental Controls on In Vitro Fertilization Research			564
D.	Minors as Research Subjects			565
§8.13	1983 Federal Requirements			565
	§8.13.1		Relationship to Other HHS Regulations	567
	§8.13.2		Children and Permission for Research	567
	§8.13.3		Children's Assent to Research	569
	§8.13.4		Wards as Research Subjects	570
	§8.13.5		Additional Requirements	571
	§8.13.6		FDA Research and Children	571
§8.14	State Laws			572
	§8.14.1		General Provisions	572
	§8.14.2		Institutionalized and Mentally Handicapped Minors	573
	§8.14.3		Parental Consent as a Safeguard	574
	§8.14.4		Minors' Capability to Give Consent	575
§8.15	Impact of Federal and State Research Requirements			576
E.	Research Involving the Mentally Ill, Handicapped, and Developmentally Disabled			577
§8.16	Federal Laws Governing Research			577
	§8.16.1		General Provisions	577
	§8.16.2		Consent Requirements	578
§8.17	State Laws Governing Research			579

§8.17.1   General Requirements   579
§8.17.2   Consent Provisions   580
§8.17.3   Research Review Committees and Consent   582
§8.17.4   Practical Considerations   583
§8.18   Effect of Federal and State Requirements   584
F.   Prisoners as Research Subjects   585
§8.19   Federal Regulations: HHS Regulations   585
§8.19.1   Permissible Research   586
§8.19.2   Responsibilities of the IRB   587
§8.20   Federal Restrictions: FDA Regulations   588
§8.20.1   Permissible Research   588
§8.20.2   Responsibilities of the IRB   589
§8.21   State Limitations   590
§8.21.1   Legislative Constraints: Some State Examples   590
§8.22   Effect of Federal and State Requirements   591
G.   Elderly Persons as Research Subjects   593
§8.23   Federal Regulatory Standards   593
§8.23.1   Consent and Borderline Incompetent Subjects   594
§8.23.2   Institutionalization and Competent Subjects   594
§8.23.3   Duties of the IRB   595
§8.24   State Legislative Requirements   595
§8.24.1   Consent Process for Elderly Incompetent Persons   596
§8.24.2   Consent Process for Questionably Competent Persons   596
§8.25   Effect of Federal and State Requirements   597
H.   Research With Other Vulnerable Populations   599
§8.26   AIDS and ARC Victims   600
I.   Judicial Precedent in Human Research and Consent   601
§8.27   The Need for Adequate Disclosure   601
§8.27.1   Karp v. Cooley: Consent in Experimental Surgery   601
§8.27.2   Novel Radiation Therapy: The Price of Inadequate Disclosure   603
§8.27.3   Consent to Experimental Use of Drugs   604
§8.27.4   Experimental Surgery Upon a

		Prisoner: Consent Without a Full Explanation	606
	§8.27.5	Documenting Consent to Research	607
J.	Practical Pointers for Consent to Human Research		608
	§8.28	Drug Company Sponsored Doctors' Office Trials: Consent Considerations	608
	§8.29	Commercial Use of Human Tissues Procured in the Research Setting	609
	§8.30	A Checklist of Management Considerations	610

NINE

Organ Donation and Autopsy

	§9.0	Introduction		614
A.	Live Organ Donors and Consent			615
	§9.1	Basic Requirements of Consent		615
	§9.2	Competency of Live Organ Donors		617
		§9.2.1	Substituted Judgment and Incompetent Donors	617
		§9.2.2	Substituted Judgment and Best-Interest Theories Combined	618
		§9.2.3	Little v. Little: The "Best" Interests of Mentally Retarded Minors	621
		§9.2.4	Judicial Denial of Permission to Remove Live Organs from Incompetents	623
		§9.2.5	Judicial Review of Parental Decision-Making	625
		§9.2.6	Minors and Consent to Live Tissue Donation	625
	§9.3	Setting Standards for Donations by Incompetent Persons		626
		§9.3.1	Legislative Inroads: The Texas Example	627
		§9.3.2	Other Legislative Controls	629
	§9.4	The Issue of Forced Donation of Organs and Tissues		631
	§9.5	Commercial Use of Human Tissues		633

	§9.5.1	Moore v. University of California Regents: A Case Example	634
	§9.5.2	Practical Considerations	634
B.	Cadaver Organ Transplants and Consent		635
	§9.6	The Anatomical Gift Act and Consent	635
	§9.6.1	Cadaver Organ Transplants and Consent	636
	§9.6.2	Documentation of Cadaver Donations	637
	§9.6.3	Revoking Consent to Organ Donations	637
	§9.6.4	Other Important Provisions of Anatomical Gift Laws	638
	§9.6.5	Litigation Involving the Uniform Anatomical Gift Laws	639
	§9.7	Donor Designation Drivers' Licenses	641
	§9.7.1	Difficulties Associated with Donor Designation Programs	642
	§9.8	The Moment of Death and Cadaver Organ Transplants	643
	§9.8.1	The Harvard Ad Hoc Criteria	644
	§9.8.2	Judicial and Legislative Criteria for Death	644
	§9.8.3	Removal of Organs and Criminal Investigations	647
	§9.9	Removal of Organs by Medical Examiners, Coroners, and Others	649
	§9.9.1	Corneal and Pituitary Gland Removal	650
	§9.9.2	Eye Enucleation Procedures	652
	§9.10	Disposal and Use of Unclaimed Bodies	652
	§9.11	Organ Procurement Legislation	655
	§9.11.1	Federal and State Requirements for Organ Procurement	655
	§9.11.2	Practical Considerations in Organ Procurement	656
C.	Autopsy and Consent		658
	§9.12	Statutory Authority to Conduct Medicolegal Autopsies	658
	§9.13	Power to Conduct Nonmedicolegal Autopsies	660

§9.14   Judicial Action in Contested and
           Unauthorized Autopsies   662
         §9.14.1   Religious Objections to Autopsies   662
         §9.14.2   Unauthorized Autopsies   665
         §9.14.3   Medical Examiners' Power to Order
                 Autopsies Sustained   665
         §9.14.4   The Need for Complete Disclosure   667
D.   Other Medical Uses for Dead Bodies   669
     §9.15   Dealing with the Newly Dead   670

TEN

The Elderly and Consent

§10.0   Introduction   671
A.   The Misunderstandings of Aging and Consent   673
     §10.1   Aging and Its Effect on Capacity to
             Consent   673
B.   Competency and Consent to Treatment   674
     §10.2   Determinants of Competency for Purposes
             of Consent to Treatment   674
     §10.3   Lane v. Candura: The Inability to Identify
             Incompetency   675
     §10.4   Legislative Standards   677
     §10.5   "Incompetent" Persons in Need of Care
             Without Legal Guardians   678
C.   Elderly in Need of Protection   680
     §10.6   The Duty to Warn   680
     §10.7   The Duty to Protect   681
     §10.8   Refusing Assistance   682
     §10.9   Residents' Bills of Rights Legislation   682
D.   Refusing Treatment, Death, Dying, and the Elderly   683
     §10.10   Refusing Treatment   683
     §10.11   Consent Issues and Death and Dying   684

ELEVEN

AIDS and Consent

A.   AIDS and the Law in Perspective   689
     §11.0   Overview of AIDS as a Legal Issue   690
     §11.1   AIDS and Consent: An Overview   691

B.	Consent to AIDS Testing	692
	§11.2 Legislative Requirements	692
	§11.3 Case Law on AIDS Testing	694
C.	Consent to AIDS Testing with Detainees and Prisoners	695
	§11.4 Testing of Detainees	696
	§11.5 Testing of Prisoners	697
D.	Consent to AIDS Testing in Domestic Relations	698
	§11.6 Testing as Part of Divorce Proceedings	698
	§11.7 Testing and Determination of Visitation Rights	699
E.	Confidentiality and the Duty to Disclose AIDS Test Results	700
	§11.8 Blood Banks and Centers	701
	§11.9 Health Facilities and Personnel	702
	§11.10 Family Members and Significant Others	703
	§11.11 Practical Limitations on the Duty to Disclose	704

TWELVE

Documentation of Consent and Practical Rules for Consent

	§12.0 Introduction	708
A.	Documentation of Consent	709
	§12.1 Importance of Documentation	709
	§12.1.1 Forms of Documentation	710
	§12.1.2 Sample Long-Form Consent Document	711
	§12.1.3 Sample Short-Form Consent Document	714
	§12.1.4 Detailed Note in the Patient's Record	716
	§12.1.5 Consent Checklist Form	718
	§12.1.6 Release Forms	718
	§12.2 Retention of Consent Documentation	720
B.	Practical Rules for Consent	721
	§12.3 The Two-Stage Consent Process	721
	§12.4 Duty of Referral, On-Call, and Substitute Physicians	722
	§12.5 Duty of Health Care Facilities	728
	§12.5.1 Quality Assurance Audits and Preoperative Nursing Routines	728

§12.5.2 The Duty of the Health Agency
When Consent Processes Are
Substandard   729
§12.5.3 Effect of DRG's on Consent
Requirements   730
§12.6 Mass Immunization and Consent   731
§12.7 Nontreatment Situations and Consent   732
§12.8 Telephone Consents   733
§12.9 Videotaped Consents   735
§12.10 The Role of the Family in the Consent
Process   735
§12.11 Consent to Treatment and Risk
Management   737
§12.11.1 The Content of a Consent Policy   738
§12.11.2 Utilizing Risk Management and
Quality Assurance Data   740
§12.11.3 Pre-intervention History and
Follow-up   741
§12.12 Contents of a Consent Policy
and Procedure   742

Appendix A   Long Consent Form   743
Appendix B   Short Consent Form   745
Appendix C   Detailed Note in Medical Record   747
Appendix D   Consent Checklist Form   751
Appendix E   Jehovah's Witness Cards and Release Forms   753
Appendix F   Uniform Brain Death Act   761
Appendix G   Uniform Anatomical Gift Act   763
Appendix H   Proposed Uniform Donation Card   769
Table of Cases   771
Table of Statutes   781
Index   801

Foreword

The doctrine of informed consent has developed in the United States from a simple concept to an extremely complex body of law. It has become an area to be feared by every practicing physician and every medical research investigator.

The simplicity of the doctrine relates to the right of every competent person to participate, to the extent desired, in the decisions about that person's medical care. No person should be made to feel less than human, possessed of no feelings, possessed of no perception of what is happening around him or her. To deprive the human being of the power to consent or to refuse medical procedures that affect or touch the body is to treat that human being as an object, not as a person.

In the early history of the medical profession, little or no attention was given to an obligation — moral, ethical, or legal — to secure the knowing consent of patients. The concept is not mentioned in the Oath of Hippocrates. Plato discussed the practical value of telling patients about the benefit expected in a prolonged treatment regime because such knowledge should encourage the patient to cooperate with the physician and to follow instructions when the physician was not physically present to oversee compliance in the often very unpleasant course of ancient efforts at cure. Plato compared this practice with the preparation of a detailed, descriptive *preamble* to a new law, the "whereas clauses" that set forth the serious problems existing in the society to which this particular remedy of a law was designed as a corrective action. Plato therefore stressed the *informing* part of the patient's consent as well as its freedom from coercion on the part of the physician. The philosopher conceived the clinical interchange as a political encounter, a negotiation and agreement between free minds.

Modern American courts have vigorously followed these precepts of Plato. The value of patient autonomy, patient freedom, is supremely protected at law in the 1980s. In many ways, it often seems a higher value than the protection of the patient's safety and welfare in the reception of, or the delivery of, the medical care itself. Physicians often cannot understand the law's insistence on this hierarchy of values.

To physicians, the most important obligations to patients are first, to do them no harm (the basic tenet of the Hippocratic oath) and second, to offer their best efforts to comfort, care for, and hopefully to cure patients' illnesses. This second large obligation is technical in nature. It requires the application of specialized knowledge and skills. It is also basically contractual in modern society: the physician provides these best efforts and the patient, or a third-party payor, negotiates and pays for that technical service. The quality of the service, its success or failure in alleviating or curing the condition or disease, is the key service element in the relationship. All other issues are seen by physicians as minor components that relate to the pleasantness of the encounter, its esthetics, but not to its essence.

At the present time, the law has the upper hand. Within the clinical medical transaction, it requires both good quality of care and a free and very highly informed consent. There is really no way to compromise these legal demands. Hospitals, physicians, nurses, all health care personnel, must respect the patient's power to consent or to refuse their efforts and at the same time these health care providers must deliver the best services they can within the limits of what they are paid to do.

In this Second Edition, the author presents a broadly comprehensive, deeply detailed, yet very practical guide to practitioners concerning the demands placed upon them by American law in this field. I am greatly impressed by the scope of this work. It has made me realize, even more than I had beforehand, the depth and breadth of the consent obligation.

The Second Edition continues to have the most comprehensive coverage I have ever read in one volume concerning the doctrine of informed consent. It deals with a variety of diverse clinical settings plus offers advice on special issues of minors' consent, consent of mentally incapacitated patients, consent in women's health care matters, and consent in experimental investigations. This new edition also contains two important additional chapters on AIDS and the care of the elderly. The scholarship of the author is shown in the depth of citation to cases, statutes, and regulations at the federal level and in the fifty states.

Ms. Rozovsky makes so many important points in the book I can comment only upon a few. She stresses that informed consent is a process, not a single event in time marked by the patient's signing of a formal document. The process is complex. It involves providing information, offering alternatives, providing time for consideration (except in emergencies), and allowing opportunity to ask questions. The benefits of the procedure or treatment should be fully explained as well as the potential risks. It is quite allowable under the law for the physician to offer advice and even to urge the particular treatment or procedure upon the patient short of improperly coercing the patient's choice.

The author is also insightful in urging health care providers not to over-stress the content or the symbolism of the informed consent document or written form. This document should only be evidence of the process, a part of the transaction, not its entire embodiment. Nevertheless, the documents of consent are an important protection to those obliged by law to provide full disclosure of risks and benefits under the growing strictness of our American courts. Considerable care should be taken with composing informed consent documents. This book offers excellent advice on what should and should not be covered in the consent transaction.

There are many special chapters in this book that have never before appeared in a text covering the law of informed consent in medical matters. The author's expertise and experience in women's medical care issues are displayed brilliantly in the chapter on women and reproduction. The chapter covers such subjects as abortion procedures, sterilization, contraception, venereal disease, birth defects, and other surgical procedures specific to women.

Ms. Rozovsky's broad experience in academic medicine, on the faculties of both a medical school and a public health school, are utilized very well in her chapter on the requirements of consent in experimental procedures. At Harvard, the author was the administrator of the institutional ethical review committee for all clinical and epidemiological research involving human subjects. The current federal regulatory system for approval of research protocols is the most stringent and detailed of all American law concerning informed consent. Ms. Rozovsky takes the reader through this system in step-by-step fashion lending great support to the book's subtitle of *A Practical Guide*.

Specialty attorneys in the field of health law, whether representing providers or patients, will continue to find this book the most useful and practical of all available texts on the subject. Because of the clarity of the writing, clinicians and research investigators will also benefit from having this volume close at hand when dealing with the legal and ethical problems of patient informed consent. The dialogue between patients and health care providers will be greatly improved if the practical advice gathered in this book is followed in the future decision making of the American public concerning quality medical services.

William J. Curran
Professor of Legal Medicine
Harvard University

October 1989

Preface

The Second Edition of *Consent to Treatment: A Practical Guide* has come about far more quickly than was anticipated when the First Edition was published in 1984. Extensive changes in state legislation, the AIDS epidemic, and major developments in the area of death and dying necessitated publication of the Second Edition.

In many ways the Second Edition offers a much more practical hands-on approach to consent to treatment than its predecessor. For example, chapters 1 and 2 provide useful insights into consent as a process and chapter 12 provides the reader with practical guidance on consent documentation and risk management.

The Second Edition also includes two new chapters on AIDS and consent and on the elderly and health law. These chapters reflect the growing body of law affecting such matters as competency to consent to treatment and authorizations for testing.

A work of this type is the product of practical experience, consultative work with health professionals, hospitals, and other health care agencies, and valuable feedback from readers. It is also the result of many hours of diligent research. I am indebted to Tom Leggans, Dolores Hurley, Stacy Ross, and Chris Wells for their very capable and thorough research efforts. They are a tribute to the excellent research and writing program at the University of Southern Illinois School of Law.

It takes considerable effort to turn a manuscript into a practical book. I very much appreciate the work of Tom Lincoln, Senior Editor, and Alistair Nevius at Little, Brown and Company for their assistance in making the second edition a reality. Similarly, I wish to acknowledge the work of Juanita Swinamer and Betty Carmichael of my office, LEFAR Health Associates, Inc., for their excellent assistance.

Finally, I cannot thank my family enough for all their understanding and encouragement. My sons have taught me a great deal about the ability of children to give consent to treatment. My husband, Lorne, has always provided tremendous guidance and professional criticism for this work. It is difficult to imagine a more wonderful husband and colleague!

Consent law continues to evolve with new and sometimes startling decisions reported each month. New inroads are always being made by legislators and regulators. Despite all the law on the topic, consent to treatment continues to demand further refinement and discussion. Regular supplementation will be made available to readers to keep the Second Edition current and useful. It is hoped that this book will provide readers with a practical guide to the many challenging issues in consent to treatment encountered by health care professionals and agencies.

Fay A. Rozovsky, J.D., M.P.H.
Halifax, Nova Scotia

August 1989

Consent to Treatment

ONE

The Rules for Consent to Treatment

A. The Law of Consent in Perspective
   §1.0 What Is Consent to Treatment?
   §1.1 Settings in Which Consent Must Be Obtained
        §1.1.1 Traditional Care Facilities
        §1.1.2 Alternate Care Settings
   §1.2 The Traditional Approach: Assault and Battery
   §1.3 The Modern Approach: Negligence Theory
        §1.3.1 Policy Justification
B. Criteria for a Valid Consent
   §1.4 The Issue of Coercion and Undue Influence·
        §1.4.1 Hospital-Based Consent
        §1.4.2 Coercion by Hospital Personnel
        §1.4.3 Financial Coercion: Medicaid Anti-Dumping Provisions
   §1.5 Patients' Legal Capacity to Give Consent
        §1.5.1 Guardianship or Conservatorship
        §1.5.2 Patient Objections Versus Guardian or Conservator
               Decisions
        §1.5.3 Minors' Capacity to Give Consent
        §1.5.4 Laws Creating Legal Incapacity
   §1.6 Patients' Mental Capacity to Give Consent
        §1.6.1 Irrational or Delusional Patients
        §1.6.2 Mental Incapacity and Authorization of Treatment
        §1.6.3 Refusal of Consent Versus Mental Incompetency
   §1.7 Consent to Specific Procedures
        §1.7.1 Ignoring Specific Patient Instructions
        §1.7.2 Operating on an Unauthorized Part of a Patient's Body
        §1.7.3 Problems with General Consents
        §1.7.4 Medical Emergencies and Unanticipated Circumstances

§1.8 Use of Understandable Terminology and Language
§1.9 Answering Patients' Questions
§1.10 Valid Forms of Consent
  §1.10.1 Expressed or Implied Consent
  §1.10.2 Written or Verbal Consent
§1.11 Patients' Right to Refuse or Withdraw Consent
  §1.11.1 Use of Release Forms
  §1.11.2 Informed Refusal of Treatment
  §1.11.3 Duty to Disclose Risk of Refusing Care by Specialist
C. The Need for Adequate Disclosure
§1.12 Patients' Right to Basic Information
  §1.12.1 Disclosure of Risk-Benefit Information
  §1.12.2 Disclosure of Reasonable Alternative Procedures
  §1.12.3 Disclosure of Diagnostic Test Results
§1.13 Information That Need Not Be Disclosed
  §1.13.1 The Medical Community Standard
  §1.13.2 The Patient Need Standard
  §1.13.3 Legislative Standards Governing Disclosure
  §1.13.4 The Effect of the JCAHO Standards on Consent
§1.14 Who Should Obtain Consent?
  §1.14.1 The Duty to Disclose Rests with the Caregiver
  §1.14.2 The Danger of Delegating the Disclosure Responsibility
  §1.14.3 Drug Manufacturers: The Limited Duty to Warn
  §1.14.4 The Duty of the Health Facility
  §1.14.5 The Duty of the Dispensing Pharmacist
D. Elements of Negligent Consent Litigation
§1.15 Basic Elements of a Negligent Consent Lawsuit
  §1.15.1 Patient-Provider Relationship
  §1.15.2 Provider's Duty to Provide Risk Information
  §1.15.3 Inexcusable Failure of Provider to Disclose Risk Information
  §1.15.4 Causation in Negligent Consent
  §1.15.5 Nondisclosure as Proximate Cause
§1.16 Defenses to Negligent Consent Litigation
  §1.16.1 Remote and Commonly Known Risks
  §1.16.2 Patient Acceptance of Treatment Regardless of Risk
  §1.16.3 Medical Emergencies
  §1.16.4 Justifiable Withholding of Information
  §1.16.5 Signed Consent Forms
  §1.16.6 Other Available Defenses
§1.17 Statutes of Limitations in Consent Actions
§1.18 Expert Testimony in Consent Litigation
  §1.18.1 Where Expert Testimony Is Required
  §1.18.2 Where Expert Testimony Is Not Required

§1.19   Burden of Proof in Consent Actions
§1.20   Litigation Checklist for Consent Actions

A. THE LAW OF CONSENT IN PERSPECTIVE

§1.0   What Is Consent to Treatment?

Many people think of consent to treatment as a form. Consent is equated in their minds with the document through which patients agree to procedures their physician believes are advisable or necessary. Such a definition is incorrect and misleading, and in some instances it can be dangerous.

Consent is a process, not a form. As described throughout this book, consent is the dialogue between the patient and the provider of services in which both parties exchange information and questions culminating in the patient's agreeing to a specific medical or surgical intervention. On the one hand, the patient needs certain basic details in order to decide whether to accept the treatment. On the other, the physician also needs information from the patient in order to tailor the disclosure of risks and benefits to him. This process, if it is to be effective, requires active participation from both parties.

A document called a consent form can never replace the exchange of information between a patient and a health care provider. Medical personnel's reliance on the form alone can lead to charges of uninformed consent or unauthorized medical and surgical procedures. Even more to the point, in some instances serious injury or death can result from a practitioner's failure to question a patient about drug sensitivities or health history.

Thinking of consent as a process rather than as a form places certain responsibilities on the providers of care. Those professionals must be the ones who obtain patients' consents rather than delegating the task to nurses or ward clerks. A certain

3

amount of time must be set aside to communicate with patients to effect valid consents. To some extent, providers must get to know their patients and learn what matters are of importance to them.

The process is not, however, a one-way street: there are other responsibilities that the patient must discharge. She must provide accurate information to the physician and pose questions when details relating to a proposed treatment or surgical procedure are unclear.

Casting consent in the form of a process requires reeducation of both health care personnel and patients. To a large extent this is due to a growing awareness and assertiveness of patients regarding their rights. People are more aware of their individual liberties, thus becoming more likely to question the need for and cost of a specific procedure. Patients are also concerned about the risks, benefits, and reasonable alternatives to recommended procedures. They want to know what impact, if any, a proposed course of medical or surgical treatment will have on their health. They are also concerned about the long-term outcome and any changes that may occur in their lifestyle as a result of medical or surgical interventions.

§1.1 Settings in Which Consent Must Be Obtained

Consent to treatment is a necessity for all types of treatment and investigative procedures. This is true whether the treatment is highly invasive or a diagnostic measure that is considered quite routine. Walk-in clinics, satellite surgi-centers, hospitals, nursing homes, and health maintenance organizations are some of the common health care delivery centers in which consent to treatment is a necessity.

"Consent to treatment" can have different connotations in different settings. In federally funded human research, for example, consent to treatment means adhering to well-delineated regulations, approval by an institutional review board, and very precise documentation. In a walk-in blood pressure clinic, the same is not true. Consent may be inferred from the patient's rolling up a sleeve, thereby signifying an interest in having a blood pressure test.

Therefore, consent to treatment must be tailored to the circumstances. This means looking at the setting in which consent is to be obtained and the nature and purpose of the diagnostic or treatment intervention.

§1.1.1 Traditional Care Facilities

It is well understood that consent is an integral part of the physician-patient relationship. Doctors are duty bound to obtain an authorization for care carried out in their offices or other treatment settings. However, the concept of consent extends beyond the medical doctor and the patient and encompasses interventions by other members of the health care team. Dentists, laboratory technicians, radiological technologists, nurses, physiotherapists, podiatrists, and clinical psychologists all require consent prior to embarking upon tests or treatment. This is true whether care is provided in a private office or in a hospital.

The fact that consent is required prior to tests or treatment by such groups is often overlooked by hospitals, whose preoccupation is with physicians. That hospitals require signed consent forms prior to treatment by physicians but not others reinforces the notion of consent as a form and not as a process applicable to all caregivers.

Consent is a requirement for all caregivers, whether or not traditional care facilities demand signed authorizations from patients receiving care from nonmedical caregivers. Given this fact, nonmedical caregivers would do well to examine closely the requirements for a valid consent and develop a uniform approach to securing an authorization for all types of diagnostic and therapeutic measures.

§1.1.2 Alternate Care Settings

Concern about scarce health care dollars and ever-increasing treatment costs has fueled new initiatives often labelled as "alternate" care settings. Free-standing emergency centers, surgicenters, HMOs and walk-in clinics typify the alternate care setting. Others involve facilities closely associated with hospitals such as day surgery units and satellite treatment centers.

The push to hold the line on costs has also resulted in rather innovative approaches to preinvasive procedures. Patients may find themselves undergoing preoperative workups as outpatients in order to avoid the increased costs of similar services provided on an inpatient basis. Shifting the presurgical workup to the outpatient setting could offer additional administrative advantages, including earlier and better opportunities for the consent process. Patients discussing surgery as outpatients may be less threatened or anxious than those confronted with a wide range of new experiences as inpatients.

The alternate care setting also includes the rapidly growing home care industry. Individuals who might have spent days or weeks in a hospital or rehabilitation setting are now receiving such care at home. Physiotherapy, IV treatments, cancer therapy, and other complex care can be provided in the home rather than in a hospital or outpatient department. The fact that treatment is in the home does not alter the fact that consent is required for such care.

Consent as a process is best viewed as a vital part of patient or client management. Consent is best used as a communications tool that forms the basis for a good working relationship between caregiver and patient.

§1.2 The Traditional Approach: Assault and Battery

The common law has long accepted the rule that the touching of another without his consent constitutes an actionable tort.

Strictly speaking, the touching of another without express consent is a battery, whereas placing someone in fear of being touched is an assault.[1] The field of medical treatment has seen the application of these principles time and again.[2] The protection afforded by the law permits an individual to be free of unwarranted and unwanted intrusion. As Mr. Justice Cardozo wrote, "Every human being of adult years and sound mind has a right to determine what shall be done with his own body. . . ."[3]

The law places considerable importance on the principle of personal autonomy, and this is reinforced in legislation dealing with patients' rights. For example, in a New York criminal case, the trial court refused to dismiss an indictment against a nurse for willfully violating provisions of the state Public Health Law.[4] The nurse allegedly searched an 86-year-old resident of a geriatric center for some missing money. The search was carried out over the man's objection. A short time later the man died. As the court pointed out in this criminal case:

> It may well be that this incident reached the attention of the criminal justice system only because, in the end, a man died. In those instances which are equally violative of resident's rights and equally contrary to standards of common decency but which do not result in visible harm to a patient, the acts are nevertheless illegal and subject to prosecution.[5]

To prove a claim of medical assault or battery, the plaintiff would have to show that she was subjected to an examination or treatment for which there was no expressed or implied consent.[6] Moreover, the treatment provided must constitute a substantially different form of care than that which was agreed to

---

§1.2 [1] W.L. Prosser, Law of Torts §10 (4th ed., 1971).
[2] See, e.g., 56 A.L.R.2d 695 (1957) and cases collected therein.
[3] Schloendorff v. Society of New York Hosp., 211 N.Y. 125, 129-130, 105 N.E. 92, 93 (1914).
[4] People v. Coe, 131 Misc. 2d 807, 501 N.Y.S.2d 997 (1986), referring to McKinney's Public Health Law §12-b.
[5] 501 N.Y.S.2d at 1001.
[6] Prosser, Law of Torts, supra n.1, §9.

by the patient and physician. There must be proof as well that the physician intentionally departed from the agreed-to form of care.[7] However, the substitution of a qualified physician for the attending doctor is not a sufficient basis for a battery action if the patient does not object and has agreed to the intended procedure.[8]

Unlike under the more modern negligence theory of consent, there is no need to prove actual harm, although harm may indeed occur. A California case illustrates the consequences of an unauthorized medical examination.[9]

A woman was in a hospital examining room in labor. When she was examined by a young man whom she took to be a medical student, she demanded to be seen by a doctor. The young man left and returned with an older man who conducted an internal examination without first washing his hands. In the delivery room the woman was examined by 10 or 12 young men who were presumably students. She claimed that when she protested they laughed and told her to shut up. Two months later another physician found that the woman had a tear in her uterus, which was infected and heavily discharging.

As the court noted, once the patient objected, the treatment became an assault or trespass upon her body. A student or physician has no more right to unnecessarily or rudely touch a patient than does a layman.[10]

Consent actions on the basis of assault or battery have also involved less spectacular matters. The extension of surgery beyond what was authorized,[11] as well as an operation on a part of the body other than that consented to by the patient,[12] has generated litigation.

In some states lawsuits based on the assault and battery the-

---

[7] Moser v. Stallings, 387 N.W.2d 599 (Iowa 1986); Ipock for Hill v. Gilmore, 354 S.E.2d 315 (N.C. Ct. App. 1987).

[8] Forlano v. Hughes, 471 N.E.2d 1315 (Mass. 1984).

[9] Inderbitzen v. Lane Hosp., 124 Cal. App. 462, 12 P.2d 744 (1932), dismissed on other grounds, 17 Cal. App. 103, 61 P.2d 514 (1936).

[10] Id.

[11] Perry v. Hodgson, 168 Ga. 678, 148 S.E. 659 (1929).

[12] Mohr v. Williams, 95 Minn. 261, 104 N.W. 12 (1905).

ory of consent are still possible.[13] However, in other jurisdictions the same is not true. The right to bring a consent action based on assault or battery has been removed by legislation as part of reform measures.[14] This changing emphasis is indicative of the growing acceptance of the negligence theory of consent.

Such acceptance is not yet universal, however. For example, in Rubino v. Fretias,[15] the United States District Court ruled that state legislation that abrogated the common law cause of action for battery in consent to treatment cases was unconstitutional under the Arizona state constitution.

§1.3 The Modern Approach: Negligence Theory

Over the years it has become evident that the assault and battery theories of consent are no longer adequate. The wrong done by a physician who carries out an unauthorized diagnostic test is far different from that done by a surgeon who conducts a procedure that the patient consented to on the basis of inadequate information. The assault and battery theories of consent could not serve as a basis for suit in the latter instance since the procedure was authorized. Unless fraud, misrepresentation, or breach of contract can be demonstrated, the injured patient has no recourse.

This point has been made all the more important in Georgia, where legislation makes it very difficult to litigate on the issue of consent. In that state a doctor is not under an affirmative duty to disclose risks. However, when a patient asks about risk information the doctor is obliged to respond accordingly. Thus, in a case involving a perforated uterus stemming from the insertion of an IUD, the Court of Appeals of Georgia held

---

[13]See, e.g., Spikes v. Heath, 332 S.E.2d 889 (Ga. Ct. App. 1985), Pugsley v. Privette, 220 Va. 892, 263 S.E.2d 69 (1980).
[14]See, e.g., Tex. Stat. Ann. art. 4590i (1979).
[15]638 F. Supp. 182 (D. Ariz. 1986).

that the failure of a doctor to respond truthfully to patient inquiries regarding risk factors may form the basis for an action based on assault and battery.[1]

Misrepresentation of material information or fraudulent concealment can invalidate a consent to treatment.[2] To establish such a claim, the litigant must prove that the defendant misrepresented or suppressed material details and possessed any knowledge of falsity. It must be clear that there was an intent to induce reliance on the misrepresented information and that there was in fact actual and justifiable reliance on the information. Finally, there must be proof of resulting damages.

In a rather interesting case, the California Court of Appeal ruled that a former professional football player had satisfied the elements necessary for a case of misrepresentation.[3] Over the course of his professional career, team physicians had failed to disclose to the plaintiff the severity of the risk associated with his continued work as a professional football player. The plaintiff had suffered a knee injury while in college. The knee was reinjured during his professional work. Only after he retired from professional football did the plaintiff learn that he had a degenerative and irreversible condition in the knee.

The trial court had found for the defendants, and on appeal the decision was reversed. In sending the case back for retrial on the issue of damages, the appellate court noted that all the elements of a fraudulent concealment had been proven by the plaintiff.

> As the court suggested, the team in its desire to keep appellant on the playing field, respondent consciously failed to make full, meaningful disclosure to him respecting the magnitude of the risk he took in continuing to play a violent contact sport with a profoundly damaged left knee.[4]

The *Krueger* decision is unique because it makes clear that a doctor cannot escape liability for failing to make an adequate

---

§1.3   [1]Spikes v. Heath, 332 S.E.2d 889 (Ga. Ct. App. 1985).
[2]Krueger v. San Francisco Forty-Niners, 234 Cal. Rptr. 579 (Cal. Ct. App. 1987).
[3]Id.
[4]Id. at 584.

disclosure of information simply by arguing that details were not withheld from a patient.[5] It is also important because it demonstrates *how* a plaintiff can successfully litigate on the basis of fraudulent concealment of medical information. The fact that a doctor claims that a gastric partition procedure is a "simple procedure" similar to an appendectomy is not enough to make a successful case for fraudulent concealment of material information. As demonstrated in the *Krueger* decision, there must be misrepresentation or suppression of material information with an *intent* to do so. That a doctor overstates just how "easy" or "simple" a procedure may be is not enough to make a case of fraudulent consent.[6]

To remedy this situation, many states have recognized, through case decisions[7] and legislation,[8] a negligence theory of consent. Although the standards of disclosure vary from state to state (see §1.13, infra), the basic elements of the action remain the same. There must be a failure by the health care practitioner to meet the applicable standard of disclosure and the patient must have consented to and undergone a procedure based on the doctor's disclosure. It must be shown that as a reasonably foreseeable consequence of the inadequate information the patient was injured. Finally the patient must be able to prove that, had he been given all relevant, significant information, he would not have agreed to the procedure.[9]

§1.3.1 Policy Justifications

To prove a case of negligent consent may be less difficult than to establish lack of consent under either of the principles

[5]Id. at 583.
[6]See Leiva v. Nance, 506 So. 2d 131 (La. Ct. App. 1987).
[7]See, e.g., Canterbury v. Spence, 464 F.2d 772 (D.C. Cir. 1972), cert. denied, 409 U.S. 1064 (1973); Cobbs v. Grant, 8 Cal. 3d 224, 501 P.2d 1, 104 Cal. Rptr. 505 (1972); Wilkinson v. Vesey, 110 R.I. 606, 295 A.2d 676 (1972).
[8]See Alaska Stat. §09.55.556 (1976); Fla. Stat. Ann. §768.46 (West 1975); N.Y. Pub. Health Law §2805-d (McKinney 1975); Tenn. Code Ann. §29-26-118 (1976).
[9]See Wilkinson v. Vesey, supra n.7. For a more detailed discussion of the elements of a negligent informed case action, see §1.15, infra.

of assault or battery. The negligence theory cannot, however, be perceived as an easy way for plaintiffs' lawyers to secure significant judgments. Proving causality or that a patient would have foregone surgery had she been properly informed is difficult to establish to the satisfaction of a judge or jury.

The negligence theory of consent puts the patient and the health practitioner on a more even footing than they were previously, particularly when inadequate disclosure of information is concerned. The standards of proof and evidentiary requirements involved make it difficult to prove or disprove a case. If anything, the existence of the negligence theory reinforces the need for greater diligence on the part of health personnel in providing patients with information relevant to their health care. It stresses the need for an informed consumer and, in turn, serves to make the provider more aware of the individual needs, limitations, and concerns of patients. Seen in this light, more thorough disclosure and discussion can end all litigation on the basis of negligent consent.

B. CRITERIA FOR A VALID CONSENT

Although jurisdictions differ over interpretation of the fine details of disclosure standards, there is general agreement on the basic elements constituting a valid consent. In this part of the chapter, the basic criteria for a valid consent are examined, including the need for a voluntary, informed consent to particular procedures. Also discussed is the requirement that the patient possess both legal and mental capacity to give an authorization for treatment. The distinctions between express and implied consent are explored, along with the need for documentation of consent. The patient's right to refuse or to withdraw consent concludes this part of the chapter.

It should be noted that the basic criteria for a valid consent are the same in terms of both the assault and battery and negligence causes of action. Patients must be capable of giving consent and they must possess sufficient information with which to

12

reach a decision regarding treatment. The failure to meet the requirements of consent due to a departure from recognized standards of care may result in negligent-consent litigation. Performing unauthorized treatment may result in civil actions based on assault and battery. The circumstances of each case are important determining factors, as well as whether a state permits consent actions based on either cause of action. These considerations are developed in greater detail in Part D of this chapter.

One of the key factors in the requirements of consent is the matter of adequate disclosure of information. This matter is discussed in depth in Part C.

§1.4 The Issue of Coercion and Undue Influence

Many health professionals will admit that hospitals are intimidating institutions. Individuals are shocked out of their daily routine and told when and sometimes *what* they may eat. After some diagnostic and surgical procedures they are left dependent upon others for even the most simple of human functions. Rather than incur the anger of overworked nurses, interns, and residents and rather than appear less than grateful, patients remain silent. They withhold questions or expressions of fear. The voluntary nature of any consents they may give to procedures is thus compromised.

General hospitals are not the only health facilities in which psychological and sociological pressures may be exerted that influence the voluntariness of a patient's consent. The same is true of retirement centers, nursing homes, extended care facilities, and outpatient or day-care services for the elderly. If the voluntary nature of consent in these settings is in doubt, one is left to question what can be done to correct the situation.

§1.4.1 Hospital-Based Consent

Not all patients are or will be reluctant to pose questions or complain. Only some patients will be affected to the point that their consents are not voluntary. The nature of their questions, complaints, or consents, however, may be less than straightforward. How can the health institution make consent more voluntary?

One step is to set a policy that emphasizes communication between patients and staff. Patients should be encouraged to ask questions and if none are forthcoming, questions should be asked of the patients. Such a policy will serve to make authorizations more informed. It will also place the hospital in a more flexible and humane posture vis-à-vis its patients.

Subtle pressures on patients who feel that they should not "rock the boat" are very difficult to combat. Some inroads may be made with the assistance of hospital-based patient representatives or by teaching staff who consider patient advocacy part of their responsibilities.

§1.4.2 Coercion by Hospital Personnel

Sometimes a patient is more than gently coaxed into giving consent by an overbearing physician or nurse. The pressures applied may be overt or subtle. The setting may be a doctor's office, an outpatient clinic, or a hospital. The validity of the consent thus obtained may be called into doubt if allegations of coercion, duress, or undue influence are proven.

If a doctor tells a patient that she *must* have a particular procedure or else she must find another physician, her consent may or may not be valid, depending on the circumstances of the case. If the physician were one of several dozen equally qualified practitioners in the community, his ultimatum would be but one factor to consider in a charge of undue influence or coercion. If, however, the doctor were the only available physician in the area, or the patient lacked the resources to seek treatment elsewhere, the "take it or leave it" approach might constitute duress, undue influence, or coercion.

Short of giving patients ultimatums, physicians are entitled to gently urge them to follow a particular recommendation. For doctors to tell patients that under similar circumstances they themselves would have a particular type of surgery should not be considered undue pressure. However, a recommendation for surgery couched in exaggerated "do or die" terms — when other reasonable means of care exist — is a basis for complaint. Dean Prosser has pointed out in his treatise that there is little tort case law on the matter of consent given under duress.[1] However, proof of duress would vitiate the consent so obtained.[2] Proof of coercion would also invalidate a patient's consent.[3]

A judge in a District of Columbia case ruled that the expenditure of federal funds should be enjoined in some sterilization cases due to the use of coercion. The evidence demonstrated that a number of poor people had been coerced into agreeing to sterilization procedures. The patients had been informed that unless they agreed to the procedures, a portion of their welfare benefits would be withdrawn. The court stated that such practices based on family planning could not be tolerated under a federal program.[4]

Health personnel, in their efforts to do what they think best for their patients, must not abuse their positions or authority. Patients need to be informed and give consent to treatment, but not through the imposition of unduly burdensome influences, coercion, or duress. Moreover, health personnel must recognize the involvement of institutional, familial, and internal pressures that affect patients' decisions. Additional pressure from the care provider will only further complicate what is often already a difficult process of reaching a voluntary consent.

§1.4.3 Financial Coercion: Medicare Anti-Dumping Provisions

Financial coercion can have a powerful impact upon treatment choices made by patients who cannot pay for required

§1.4 [1] Prosser, Law of Torts 106 (4th ed., 1971).
[2] Id.
[3] Reif v. Weinberger, 372 F. Supp. 1196 (D.D.C. 1974).
[4] Id.

care. Congress recognized this fact in the so-called COBRA provisions (Consolidated Omnibus Budget Reconciliation Act of 1985) which set forth specific requirements for informed consent.[5]

Under the anti-dumping provisions, a hospital with an emergency department must provide appropriate medical screening to any person for whom a request for examination or treatment of a medical condition is made. The examination is limited to a determination of either an emergency medical condition or that a woman is in active labor.

If the individual has an emergency medical condition, the hospital must investigate further or provide treatment necessary to stabilize the medical ailment. In the case of active labor, the hospital must provide appropriate treatment. In lieu of treatment, the hospital may arrange for transfer of the individual to another facility. These requirements apply whether or not the individual is eligible for benefits under Medicare.[6]

A hospital meets its obligation under the law with respect to treatment if it offers the individual further medical examination or care but the person or a "legally responsible person"[7] acting on behalf of the individual declines it. Similarly, the hospital meets its obligation regarding transfer if it offers to send the person to another facility and the individual or a legally responsible person acting on behalf of the patient declines consent to such a move.[8]

The COBRA provisions are filled with precise rules governing transfer, definitions, and enforcement provisions. The requirements bear careful consideration since the requirements for consent to remain in or be transferred by the hospital are not spelled out in the law. Presumably, consent in this context would follow the generally recognized rules for a valid authorization for treatment. Similarly, health facilities should assess carefully the provisions governing transfer of a patient in an

---

[5]See Pub. L. No. 99-272, §9121 (1986).
[6]Id.
[7]Id.
[8]Id.

unstable emergency medical condition or who is in active labor.[9] The law provides a broad formula to be used in weighing the benefits of transfer against the risks to the patient. The weighing of risks and benefits must be made by a physician or otherwise qualified medical personnel.

With or without the COBRA provisions, care must be taken to avoid undue influence from the costs associated with necessary care. The ability to pay should not be used as a weapon in obtaining consent or coercing a patient to choose one form of treatment over another. However, for patients without health insurance, the cost and benefit of one treatment modality over another should be put in context during the consent process. Like the risk of paraplegia or stroke, the prospect of huge financial outlays should be part of the information imparted to patients. This is true in all treatment settings, not just the emergency department of a hospital.

§1.5 Patients' Legal Capacity to Give Consent

In the absence of a judicial order or an applicable piece of legislation, a person is presumed to be capable of giving informed consent to treatment. An individual's legal competency is not altered automatically by commitment to a mental facility. Some states have enacted legislation to reinforce this principle.[1] The same is not true for legal incompetents from whom the power to consent to treatment has been removed.

§1.5.1 Guardianship or Conservatorship

When individuals are under guardianships or conservatorships, their legal capacity may be in doubt. Under legislation or under the terms of the guardian appointment, the patients'

---

[9] Id.
§1.5 [1] See, e.g., R.I. Gen. Laws §40.1-5-5 (1977).

rights to enter into contracts or to authorize medical care may be removed. The scope of the guardianship or conservatorship is dispositive of the issue: a guardianship of a man's estate or a conservatorship that extends to a woman's property does not render either person legally incapacitated for purposes of consent to treatment. If, however, a man or a woman were placed under a guardianship or conservatorship of the person, the legal capacity to consent to care usually would be taken away. In such circumstances it is the duly authorized legal representative, the guardian or conservator, from whom consent must be obtained.

Health care administrators and providers must determine whether an individual actually has been placed under a guardianship or conservatorship of the person. They have a right to demand proof that a third party has the legal authority to act in behalf of the patient. It is also important to review applicable state laws to determine how much authority is vested in the guardian or conservator for purposes of medical care.

§1.5.2 Patient Objections Versus Guardian or Conservator Decisions

A difficulty may arise if the patient (the ward or conservatee) declines to undergo treatment authorized by the guardian or by the conservator. Should the care be provided over the patient's objection or should it be withheld?

From a practical point of view, the hospital, nursing home, nurse, or physician who is to administer treatment usually may legally rely on the consent of the guardian or conservator of the person. In any litigation on the matter the health facility and health personnel could defend themselves by citing applicable legislation and documentation proving that the guardian or conservator had the power to act in matters of medical treatment. Without evidence that shows that the facility or health care personnel knew or ought to have known that the guardian or conservator was not empowered to act for the patient, authorization by the patient's legal representative is usually sufficient. Similarly, unless it is known or ought to be known that the legal representative is not acting in the patient's best interest, his consent should be accepted.

Patients who are confused, the victims of organic brain disease, or the like may not realize that they are incapable of giving consent. Moreover, they may not realize that someone has been appointed by a court to act for them. To avoid confrontations and to eliminate any doubts when patients object to care, sound policy dictates finding out in advance of treatment who is authorized to speak and act for the patient. Such information should be clearly displayed either in the patient's chart, in the case of a hospital, or in a resident's records, in the case of a long-term care facility or nursing home.

§1.5.3 Minors' Capability for Consent

In some jurisdictions, for purposes of consent to treatment, minors are legally incapable. Their status depends upon the legal requirements in each state: some jurisdictions, for example, recognize the principle of the mature minor[2] while others have accepted the idea of the emancipated minor,[3] thereby allowing certain classes of minors to consent to care. Determining whether a child comes within the mature minor criteria must be decided on a case-by-case basis.

A few states have authorized minors to consent to certain types of care, thereby clearly abandoning the notion of legal incapacity due to minority in those situations. Thus minors can give consent to treatment for sexual assault[4] and venereal disease.[5] Other states have resolved the issue of legal incapacity for minors who are parents.[6] Legislation in many states makes it clear that minor parents are legally capable of giving consent to care on behalf of their children.

[2] See Ark. Stat. Ann. §20-9-602 (1981).
[3] Mont. Rev. Code Ann. §41-1-402 (1977).
[4] Colo. Rev. Stat. §13-22-106 (1973); Md. Ann. Code Art. 43, §135B (1978).
[5] Mont. Rev. Code Ann. §41-1-402 (1977).
[6] Del. Code Ann. tit. 18, §707 (1953).

Physicians, hospital administrators, and other health personnel should determine whether minors in their state are deemed legally capable of giving consent. Moreover, they should determine whether there are any limitations or restrictive circumstances in which a minor may be deemed legally capable for some purposes but not others. Knowing relevant requirements will facilitate the establishment of treatment protocols for children, particularly regarding matters of consent. It will avert otherwise serious legal problems when treatment issues arise (see chapter 5 on minors for further discussion of these and related issues).

§1.5.4 Laws Creating Legal Incapacity

In some situations, state legislation effectively creates categories of legal incapacity. This action may be taken for protection of public health or welfare or for the benefit of the patient herself. In each instance the power of the patient to consent or to refuse consent has been removed and treatment is compelled.

A classic example of this principle is found in compulsory venereal disease legislation.[7] Similar examples may be found in other states with respect to arrestees or prisoners. Prison officials or police may be empowered to transport certain categories of prisoners or detainees to a treatment facility. This power may even extend to individuals believed to be intoxicated from alcohol or under the influence of drugs.

In each instance the law permits care regardless of the patient's capacity to give or to refuse consent. These cases demonstrate, in essence, a limited recognition of legal incapacity or emergency exceptions to the general principles of consent. However categorized, the use of compulsory treatment laws must be narrowly applied and only to the most appropriate cases. To do otherwise would make a mockery of the general concepts of consent and self-determination.

[7] R.I. Gen. Laws §23.11.3 (1956).

§1.6   Patients' Mental Capacity to Give Consent

Another important factor of a valid consent is the ability to understand the nature and consequences of authorizing treatment. A patient lacking this mental capacity cannot give a valid consent. Mental illness is not the only reason for lack of such capacity: shock or trauma, a crippling physical injury or illness, or alcohol or drug abuse can all create the same effect. Thus any number of factors can be responsible for a mental incapacity that temporarily or permanently impedes the patient's ability to consent to treatment.

The law presumes that a person possesses the requisite mental capacity to reach an informed choice. This assumption holds even when a person is undergoing treatment for a mental condition with electroshock.[1] Similarly, patients who have periods of confusion or disorientation may be legally capable. As long as the mental condition does not impede the patient's ability to reach an informed decision, undergoing care for a mental problem or a physical malady does not destroy the presumption of mental competency.

§1.6.1   Irrational or Delusional Patients

A difficult problem arises with consent obtained from patients who go through cycles of lucid and irrational thought as well as delusional behavior. Do such patients possess the requisite mental capacity for reaching an informed choice? Can they legally revoke a consent during an irrational phase?

Consent obtained while such individuals are lucid should be reliable, providing that the patient has the mental ability to understand the nature and consequences of consent. The circumstances of the case are determinative here: seemingly erratic or irrational behavior may be quite reasonable if viewed in the context of the facts surrounding the patient. For example, the decision by a 70-year-old man to refuse the respiratory

§1.6   [1]Wilson v. Lehman, 379 S.W.2d 478 (Ky. 1964).

therapy necessary for keeping him alive may seem, on its face, quite irrational. However, the consideration of other facts can change this evaluation. Perhaps his spouse has recently died, and he is terminally ill with at best one year to live. His refusal to continue therapy under these circumstances is quite understandable.

If consent obtained during a lucid phase is valid, then the withdrawal of consent during a lucid phase should also be respected. It is the logical extension of the law of consent that a person who understands the nature and consequences of a decision may withdraw his consent to care.

Particularly troubling for health practitioners are refusals of consent or withdrawals of consent made during a period when lucidity is absent. Consents as well as refusals and withdrawals of consent made during such phases should not be honored because these decisions are not the product of reasoned and considered thinking. The health care provider, however, must be prepared to prove at a later time that the patient lacked the mental ability to understand the nature and consequences of the decision. Evidence must be obtained to back up the conclusion of incapacity. Psychiatric consultations, nurses' notes, and detailed accounts in the patient's record can be used to explain the reasons for a health care provider's decision. Documentation should be written contemporaneously with the determination of mental incapacity.

§1.6.2   Mental Incapacity and Authorization of Treatment

Once it has been determined that a patient lacks the mental ability to give consent to treatment, a decision must be made how to proceed. If a medical emergency exists, no further authorization need be obtained to provide such reasonable care as is necessary to correct a life-threatening situation. (See §2.2 infra.)

In nonemergency circumstances consent must be obtained from someone authorized to act on behalf of the mentally incapacitated patient. Some states have enacted legislation to cover such situations, authorizing designated relatives or other responsible people to act on behalf of the patient.[2] Thus under legislation in Arkansas[3] a parent may consent to treatment for an adult child who is of unsound mind.

Legislation in at least two states, California and Virginia, sets down rules for nonemergency treatment that does not involve consent from a relative.[4] However, both require judicial review and a finding that the person involved requires treatment and is incapable of giving consent. The California law empowers the court to designate a person to give consent whereas the statute in Virginia vests power in the court to order treatment.[5]

In the absence of legislation specifically dealing with consent, it is necessary to review applicable guardianship or conservatorship laws. In nonemergency situations there may be ample time in which to follow standard procedural practice and through the appointment of a guardian of the person, a committee, or a conservator obtain a legal consent to treatment.

§1.6.3 *Refusal of Consent Versus Mental Incompetency*

Although the courts make the legal declaration of incompetency, their judgment is based in part on medical assessments of the patient. Still, a refusal by a competent person will be respected by the courts even though the decision runs contrary to sound medical advice. Physicians and other health professionals may interpret a patient's decision to forgo treatment as more than irrational behavior; they may see it as evidence of mental incompetency. A neutral observer, such as a judge, may find the decision unfortunate but valid.

However disturbing a decision against treatment may be, the

---

[2] See, e.g., Ark. Stat. Ann. §41-41-3 (1984); Idaho Code §39-4303 (1975); Miss. Code Ann. §41-41-3 (1966).

[3] Ark. Stat. Ann. §41-41-3 (1984).

[4] See Cal. Prob. Code §3200-3211 (West 1981); Va. Code §37.1-134.2 (1982).

[5] Cal. Prob. Code §3208 (West 1981); Va. Code §37.1-134.2 (1982).

competent patient retains that prerogative. In the absence of any proof of mental incapacity that makes it impossible for a person to understand the nature and consequences of a refusal of care, her decision must stand.

§1.7   Consent to Specific Procedures

When a patient gives consent to medical or surgical treatment, such authorization is limited to the procedure specifically discussed with the physician. A generalized admitting consent form does not satisfy this requirement. A consent document does not provide a green light for health practitioners to perform a variety of diagnostic, medical, or surgical interventions. Instead, the consent form should be perceived as an historical account of the consent process that took place between the patient and the provider of services, documenting each party's understanding of the agreement. (For further discussion of the role of the consent form see chapter 12.)

While providing authorization for treatment, patients sometimes provide physicians with discretionary leeway. For example, if a patient agrees to a breast biopsy and nothing more, the surgeon is authorized to remove such tissues for examination by a pathologist. If the surgeon goes further, even with the best of intentions, and performs a radical mastectomy on the basis of the biopsy, the original consent does not authorize that decision. The cases mentioned below demonstrate the legal consequences of performing unauthorized procedures.

§1.7.1   Ignoring Specific Patient Instructions

When a patient has given a physician specific instructions not to carry out certain procedures, disregarding such limits can lead to litigation. A Florida woman told her surgeon not to operate on the tip of her nose or to alter the shape of it during rhinoplasty.[1] The doctor disregarded the woman's instructions and a lawsuit was brought for unauthorized surgery. A signed consent form in which the woman agreed to rhinoplasty for the removal of a protrusion on the bridge of her nose was held inadequate to prevent litigation.[2]

A similar conclusion was reached in a case involving specific instructions regarding the use of an anesthetic.[3] A jury's verdict for the plaintiff was affirmed in a case in which the plaintiff experienced partial leg paralysis following an appendectomy. The court ruled that there was sufficient evidence for the jury to find that the patient had told the doctor not to use a spinal anesthetic and that the doctor had agreed. During the operation the physician used a spinal and the patient recovered from surgery with leg paralysis. The court held that absent expressed or implied consent, the surgeon was required to obtain the patient's consent to the anesthetic before using it.[4]

§1.7.2 Operating on an Unauthorized Part of a Patient's Body

It is an actionable matter to perform surgery on a part of a person's body different from that previously authorized by the patient. Whether the surgeon operates by mistake or with good intentions is irrelevant.

This point is illustrated in a case in which a woman underwent surgery involving, as she understood it, an exploratory operation on her left knee.[5] One possible diagnosis was a Baker's cyst. In error, the surgeon operated on her right leg, and the court held in a subsequent lawsuit that this substitution constituted a technical assault for which the plaintiff should be permitted to recover damages.[6]

§1.7 [1]Meretsky v. Ellenby, 370 So. 2d 1222 (Fla. Dist. Ct. App. 1979) (per curiam).
[2]Id.
[3]Chambers v. Nottebaum, 96 So. 2d 716 (Fla. Dist. Ct. App. 1957).
[4]Id.
[5]Lane v. United States, 225 F. Supp. 850 (E.D. Va. 1964).
[6]Id.

A physician cannot decide to operate on a different part of the patient's body once surgery has begun and the patient is anesthetized.[7] This principle was supported by a Minnesota court in a case in which a woman agreed to surgery on her right ear and awoke to find that she had undergone an operation on her left ear. The surgeon claimed that once the patient had received the anesthetic and he had examined her left ear, he found it in a far more serious condition than the right. Therefore he carried out the agreed-to form of surgery on that ear, a practice the court found to be actionable. The surgeon's conduct, because it did not fall within the exceptions permitting treatment without a patient's consent,[8] could not be condoned.

§1.7.3   Problems with General Consents

General consent forms, unlike the blanket admission consent documents patients are often asked to sign, may provide some degree of protection. Their efficacy depends, however, on the circumstances and facts of the individual cases. One court may find the general consent form dispositive of a suit based upon unauthorized treatment, whereas another tribunal may treat the document as less than controlling. Two cases illustrate the difficulty in relying upon general consents.

In one matter, a woman signed an authorization for an exploratory operation, apparently not realizing the extensive scope of her consent.[9] The document authorized procedures

---

[7]Mohr v. Williams, 95 Minn. 26, 104 N.W. 12 (1905). But see Buzzell v. Libi, 340 N.W.2d 36 (N.D. 1983), a malpractice action in which the surgeon carried out an unauthorized operation on the patient's left ear immediately following an authorized procedure on her right ear. Despite the lack of consent for the extension of the surgery, the trial court found that the patient would have agreed to the operation if she had been informed of the material risks associated with the procedure. The court ruled that the necessary element of causation was missing in plaintiff's case.

[8]Mohr v. Williams, 95 Minn. 26, 104 N.W. 12 (1905).

[9]Winfrey v. Citizens Southern Natl. Bank, 149 Ga. App. 488, 254 S.E.2d 725 (1979).

her surgeon might deem advisable besides the exploratory procedure. Based on this document, the surgeon performed a complete hysterectomy.

In a subsequent lawsuit against the doctor, the physician prevailed. The court noted that the plaintiff was bound by the document she had signed, despite the fact that she had not read it. The wording of the document was found to be broad enough to encompass the surgical procedure that the doctor had believed was necessary. In the absence of any proof of fraudulent misrepresentation, the consent was valid.[10]

A different result was reached in a New York case in which the father of a young child signed a document authorizing "routine brain tests" and a "workup."[11] The defendant, a neurosurgeon, conducted a ventriculogram on the child without first obtaining the parents' consent. The court held that the authorization signed by the father offered little proof of consent to a ventriculogram, particularly since the procedure was not even contemplated at the time of admission. Whether the required specific permission for the test was not sought was a jury question.[12]

The use of general surgical consent forms may also run afoul of statutory consent requirements. For example, in a Louisiana case, a woman underwent an exploratory laparotomy and cholecystectomy.[13] The plaintiff had signed a consent form authorizing the gall-bladder operation. The form described the operation and indicated that there were some general risks. However, the form did not delineate specific risks as required under state legislation. As a result, the court suggested that the form alone did not address the question of whether the plaintiff had given informed consent. This meant that under state law further inquiry was necessary to determine if in fact a valid consent had been obtained. In the end, the court determined

---

[10]Id.

[11]Darrah v. Kite, 32 A.D.2d 208, 301 N.Y.S.2d 286 (1969).

[12]Id.

[13]Seals v. Pittman, 499 So. 2d 114 (La. Ct. App. 1986).

that the plaintiff had not proven her case. Nonetheless, the case is illustrative of the point that *general* consent forms offer little in the way of legal protection.

§1.7.4 Medical Emergencies and Unanticipated Circumstances

The law recognizes that, in limited circumstances, a physician may be justified in carrying out a different procedure from that which the patient authorized. The exceptional circumstances in which unauthorized treatment may be provided are medical emergencies and unanticipated events that necessitate action. The physician is justified in proceeding only if it would be impractical or impossible to obtain the consent of the patient or one authorized to act in his behalf. In either instance, the life or health of the patient must be endangered. The application of this "unanticipated events" exception to the rule of consent may arise as a result of surgery or it may be due to an unexpected complication discovered during surgery. The following two cases illustrate this exception.

A woman gave her consent to a tracheotomy and an oophorectomy and during the performance of these procedures the surgeon also removed a mole from the patient's left leg.[14] The plaintiff brought an action alleging assault and battery and the court found in her favor. As the court explained, the plaintiff had signed a consent for two procedures considered necessary by the surgeon. There was no evidence that the mole required immediate surgical removal. Therefore, the doctor erred in proceeding without the patient's consent.[15]

A similar conclusion was reached in a case in which a surgeon performed an ileostomy modification upon a patient in the course of an authorized hernia repair.[16] The defendant found

---

[14]Lloyd v. Kull, 329 F.2d 168 (7th Cir. 1964).
[15]Id.
[16]Demers v. Gerety, 85 N.M. 641, 515 P.2d 645 (1973), remanded on other grounds, 86 N.M. 141, 520 P.2d 869 (1974).

that in order to repair the hernia he would have to revise the patient's ileostomy. This determination was reached after the patient was anesthetized. He did both procedures and, subsequently, was sued by the patient. In finding against the doctor the court held that because the originally agreed-to procedure could not be carried out without performing the unauthorized procedure, neither operation was permissible.[17]

Performing what may seem to be beneficial surgical repairs or medical interventions is not always the most prudent policy for health care professionals. Unless an unanticipated condition is found that necessitates immediate repair or an emergency arises requiring quick action, it is better to stay within the stated grounds of a patient's consent. In either instance the life or health of the patient must be endangered, otherwise additional surgery or medical care can be provided at a later time.[18]

§1.8 Use of Understandable Terminology and Language

Common sense dictates that in order for patients to appreciate the nature and consequences of procedures, the explanations proffered to them must be in terms and language they can understand. The importance of this criterion cannot be overlooked, however, and is deserving of discussion.

A physician or any other health care provider must gear the level of discussion to meet the needs of individual patients. A doctor can use medical terminology and present a more sophisticated explanation to a physician or nurse who is a patient than would be possible with an individual without a medical education. By the same token, the details of an explanation may vary not so much with the level of a patient's education as with her ability to converse in English or the native language of the physician.

[17]Id.
[18]Lipscomb v. Memorial Hosp., 733 F.2d 332 (4th Cir. 1984).

In gearing explanations to and discussions with patients, medical personnel must not talk "down" to them. Conversations must take place on a level at which *both* parties are comfortable. In the clinical setting an appropriate balance can be determined by the exchange of pleasantries as well as by the level of response demonstrated in the patients' replies to requests for personal information and medical history.

Talking down to patients is also damaging to the consent process. Patients may not communicate well or be so affronted that they do not ask important questions that could affect their consent decisions. Explanations and conversations put on too high a level for some patients may intimidate or embarrass them to the point that they are reluctant to say they do not understand.

A health care practitioner can avoid these difficulties by getting to know the patients. The degree of time that can be spent in this process will vary with the setting and the urgency of a treatment decision. However, a few minutes of assessment, if available, should help to put the discussion on the appropriate level.

Language barriers can be overcome easily with the aid of an interpreter. In large metropolitan areas, health facilities can maintain a list of interpreters among the ranks of their employees or in the community at large. In rural settings this option may not be available; however, alternate arrangements can be made, such as using interpreters who can be contacted by telephone.

When faced with a language difference, health care providers should be cautioned not to assume too high a degree of comprehension. A patient may speak English well but lack an equal ability to understand the spoken word. A few brief questions formulated to gauge the level of comprehension may be necessary.

Without care in matching the explanation to the patient and in breaking through language barriers, an otherwise valid consent may be brought into question. This often overlooked factor in the consent process is a criterion just as important as any other in gaining permission to examine or treat a patient.

§1.9 Answering Patients' Questions

In order for patients to give physicians effective consents to treatment, they must have the opportunity to pose questions regarding the information provided. These questions should be answered in as frank a manner as possible while taking the needs and health of the patients into account.

In some circumstances a physician may be permitted to withhold certain information if in her medical judgment its disclosure might endanger a patient's health. This so-called therapeutic privilege is applicable in only limited circumstances. If subsequently challenged, the physician must prove that the decision was reasonable in the circumstances. Paternal notions of "doctor knows best" cannot be the basis of the decision. A physician is not justified in withholding information or in not replying frankly to a patient's question because the disclosure might result in the patient deciding not to have treatment. The patient is the one who must decide, based on relevant information, whether he wishes to have the medical or surgical treatment. (For further discussion of therapeutic privilege, see chapter 2, §2.4.)

The person who will be conducting the operation or doing the medical procedure should answer the patient's questions. This duty should not be delegated to another member of the health care team who is not as well versed in the treatment or procedure. Misleading information, if imparted, could confuse the patient or result in a less than truly informed decision.

In many health care settings a patient has doubts or questions that arise the night before a procedure is to be carried out. At that time the physician who is to perform the intervention may be off-call or unavailable. Quite often this is also the time when a ward clerk or a nurse arrives in the patient's room with an authorization for the procedure. These personnel will ask the patient if she has any questions. A common response to the question "What is this document for?" is that it is a matter of hospital routine.

An authorization for treatment is more than a matter of hospital routine. It is an integral part of a patient's health care.

If a patient should raise questions regarding the document or its content or tell a clerk or nurse about his doubts, the consent process is not complete. Steps should be taken to resolve these concerns or to answer any questions the patient may have before a consent document is signed. To do otherwise is to leave the door open for litigation based upon defective consent.

§1.10   Valid Forms of Consent

Authorizations for treatment may be in one of several forms. They may be clearly spelled out in a written document or else the patient may give a verbal authorization that is quite detailed. These forms are referred to as expressed consent. Consent to treatment may also be given by way of implication, taking into account the surrounding facts and circumstances. Such implied consent may also arise from common law and legislative fictions that imply consent to treatment, as in the case of medical emergencies. (See §2.2, infra.)

In many cases the way in which consent is conveyed is not important. What is of prime consideration is that a valid authorization is obtained. Nonetheless, some state legislation insists upon written consent.[1]

§1.10.1   Expressed or Implied Consent

Expressed consent occurs when a patient in verbal or written form agrees to undergo a specific procedure. The limits of the patient's authorization are usually clearly and understandably voiced. Problems may arise if the patient's consent is based on an inadequate disclosure of risk and benefit information, but the expression of consent itself would not be cause for litigation.

---

§1.10   [1]Some state laws create a rebuttable but conclusive presumption of valid consent if evidenced in writing. See Fla. Stat. Ann. §768.46 (West 1975); Ohio Rev. Code Ann. §2317.54 (Baldwin 1977).

Implied consent arises either from the surrounding facts and circumstances of a particular case or from the legal fiction of implied consent to emergency treatment. An example of the former possibility is when an individual, by going to a community immunization center, rolling up a sleeve, and saying "go ahead," implies consent to treatment. The reasonable expectation is that a consent has been given to an immunization.

If a patient is wheeled into an emergency department unconscious with severe, life-threatening internal bleeding and head wounds, hospital personnel are authorized to provide emergency treatment. The law permits this otherwise unauthorized care due to a legal fiction. If conscious, the patient would presumably give consent to such care. Since the patient is unable to do so, the law implies permission for treatment. However, the treatment can be provided only if the patient is unable to consent and the situation is one that is life- or health-threatening. Even then, the treatment provided must be reasonable for the circumstances of the case. (For further discussion of the emergency exception to the rules of consent, see §2.2, infra.)

There is some case law on the subject of implied consent to treatment.[2] In one case, a man claimed that he had undergone surgery without his consent. The court rejected his claim, noting that he was awake throughout the procedure and could have objected to it at any time.[3] Moreover, he knew that the surgery was to remove a mass from his left breast and his lack of objection implied that he had agreed to it.[4]

In other cases, the implication of consent has involved the extent of a doctor's mandate to correct a particular condition.[5] Whether the doctor's intervention is within the limits of the patient's implied consent will turn upon the facts in a given case and whether the scope of the procedure was reasonably within the limits of the implied consent. Thus in one case a patient agreed to an operation that he knew would involve an incision

[2] See 56 A.L.R.2d 686 (1957) and cases collected therein.
[3] Hernandez v. United States, 465 F. Supp. 1071 (D. Kan. 1979).
[4] Id.
[5] Dicenzo v. Berg, 340 Pa. 305, 16 A.2d 15 (1940); McClees v. Cohen, 158 Md. 60, 148 A. 124 (1930).

in his neck.[6] However, he requested that the doctor not cut too far up his neck. In a lawsuit following the operation a court held that the doctor was authorized to make as high an incision as was reasonably necessary in the case.[7] Even though the patient's consent is not a license for the surgeon to do what she pleases,[8] a surgeon must be given a sufficient degree of latitude in which to operate.

Emergency situations can give rise to litigation involving the scope of implied consent. By using the notion of implied consent to justify emergency treatment, the law has created a legal fiction. In essence the assumption is that if a person were capable of giving consent to care, he would do so in these circumstances. Because the individual is incapacitated and it is impractical or impossible to obtain the consent of anyone who could act for the patient, authorization for care is considered to be implied. The scope of this authorization is not without limit, however: the physician or surgeon may only perform such procedures or surgery as is reasonably necessary in the circumstances. (For further discussion of emergency treatment and consent, see §2.2 infra.)

§1.10.2 Written or Verbal Consent

Unless otherwise required by law in a particular state, authorization of treatment by a patient may be in verbal form. Some state statutes even formally recognize this option.[9] Consent obtained verbally is just as valid as consent gained in writing, providing that all the criteria for a valid consent have been met.

Consent is a process, not a document. Authorization for treatment is the culmination of a discussion between a patient

[6]Dicenzo v. Berg, 340 Pa. 305, 16 A.2d 15 (1940).
[7]Id.
[8]Nolan v. Kechijian, 75 R.I. 165, 64 A.2d 866 (1949).
[9]See, e.g., Idaho Code §39-4305 (1975), which states that it is not essential for the validity of a consent that it be in writing or any other form of expression.

and a health care provider, the disclosure of risk and benefit information, the disclosure of reasonable alternative forms of care, and the posing of questions and answers by both the patient and the provider. Once the patient has agreed to a specific course of treatment, the process is over.

For purposes of treatment and legal defense, some form of documentation is necessary to record this process. For treatment purposes, documentation of consent defines the scope of permissible diagnostic, medical, and surgical procedures, since most health facilities will not allow such interventions to proceed without some demonstrative proof of consent. From a defense point of view, documentation of the patient's authorization may thwart a lawsuit based on negligent consent or a claim of unauthorized treatment. Nevertheless, the documentation, the so-called consent form, is not the consent, for that lies instead in the conclusion of the discussion between the patient and the physician. Bearing in mind the need for documentation or written consent forms in some states, therefore, verbal authorizations for treatment are quite valid.

§1.11 Patients' Right to Refuse or Withdraw Consent

Generally speaking, patients have the right to refuse recommended or alternative forms of treatment. They also have the right to forgo all treatment. This right may be curtailed in certain circumstances, as in communicable disease outbreaks that necessitate treatment or quarantine. Furthermore, patients have the right to withdraw consent to treatment. Such a reversal may be articulated at virtually any stage in the treatment process, assuming that the provider of services can reasonably cease giving care at that time.

Both the right to refuse treatment and the right to withdraw consent are premised on the notion that the patient is capable of making either decision. She must be legally and mentally capable of reaching such a determination. A patient who has received large amounts of medication may not be able to understand the nature and consequences of a decision to withdraw consent. By the same token, a patient who is in extreme pain or in shock may be unable to appreciate the significance of a decision to refuse care.

Whether a patient is or is not capable of refusing treatment or withdrawing consent to care will depend upon the facts and circumstances in the particular case. A refusal of consent necessitates neither a court order declaring that a patient is competent to reach either determination nor an order declaring the patient has a right to make either decision. If a patient is competent to give consent, then he is also competent to refuse or withdraw it.

A determination of capacity to consent can be made by assessing a patient's ability to comprehend information and to respond to questions based on it. If a person is thinking clearly, is not confused or disoriented, and is acting in a rational manner given the condition involved, she should be able to refuse treatment or withdraw consent. That patients are receiving medication or suffering from underlying mental conditions is not a sufficient basis upon which to decide that they are incapable of either giving or refusing consent. Instead, patients must be assessed in the context of their social environment, familial pressures, and their relationships with health care personnel, which together may demonstrate that the individual has the requisite ability to reach a decision.

Once again, whether a physician or nurse regrets a patient's decision to decline treatment or withdraw consent to further care, the patient retains that prerogative. If the patient meets the criteria for capacity to consent, then likewise he meets the standard for refusing or withdrawing authorization for care. A health care provider cannot substitute personal judgment for that of a competent individual nor justifiably twist the criteria for capacity to consent in order to declare a patient incapable. Just as the competency of the patient is reviewable by a court, so too are such conclusions of incapacity. A judge removed from this situation may disagree with the practitioner's conclusion and find that the patient is capable of refusing treatment or withdrawing from further care.

§1.11.1 Use of Release Forms

It is sometimes a good policy for health institutions to ask patients to sign release forms, exculpating them and their employees and staff from liability for any consequences flowing from a decision to refuse care. A similar document can be used when a patient withdraws consent to treatment; on it should be noted the fact that the patient has been apprised of the consequences of his decision. Such a form should be signed and duly witnessed. In addition, an entry in the patient's medical record should indicate the refusal or withdrawal of consent and the execution of a release form. If a patient refuses to sign a release, a note should still be added to the medical record that includes the information that the patient declined to sign the release document.

The duly executed release form can be valuable in any litigation that should arise from the patient's refusal of care or withdrawal of consent. If the patient should suffer adverse consequences or die, a claim could be made that the refusal or withdrawal of consent was invalid and negligently accepted. An argument could be made that the patient was incapable of refusing care or withstanding authorization for treatment.

Evidence that the patient was capable of refusing or withdrawing consent and that the release was executed properly would be a valid defense. Notes in a patient's medical record, including evidence of mental capacity to refuse or withdraw consent, will also assist the defense. In those instances in which a refusal or withdrawal of consent could lead to serious injury or death, psychiatric consultations to establish mental capacity might prove valuable and should be noted in the patient's record. Whether the patient was under the influence of any mind-altering drugs or alcohol that would impair the decision-making process should also be recorded. With sufficient documentation based on sound criteria for the assessment of mental capacity, the practitioner and health facility should have a sound defense.

The failure to document the discussion leading to the patient's decision to refuse diagnostic tests or treatment may prove troublesome for the defense. For example, in a Georgia case, a physician was sued for the wrongful death of a nursing home resident allegedly resulting from the doctor's failure to diagnose and treat the man for renal failure and prostate cancer. The physician claimed that the patient refused to be referred to a urologist and also declined to undergo diagnostic tests for cancer. The doctor claimed that he decided to respect the man's decision because he was lucid and capable of refusing treatment. Moreover, the patient had no immediate family and to the doctor's knowledge, other relatives had not visited him. Given the man's advanced age, it was also unlikely that he would be a candidate for renal dialysis.[1]

Unfortunately, the doctor did not write a note in the patient's record indicating that the patient refused recommended treatment. This led to a genuine issue of material fact in the case since the lack of corroborative evidence raised a question about the credibility of the doctor's testimony. Despite the lack of corroborative evidence, the granting of summary judgment was sustained when the plaintiffs could not support their allegation that the doctor's alleged negligence was the proximate cause of the patient's death.[2]

One final word of caution is in order. The right to refuse treatment is not absolute: there are instances when it is curtailed by legislation or by a court order. Patients may not, for example, refuse compulsory treatment for a venereal disease or other forms of treatment mandated by state law.

Difficulties may arise with respect to the exercise of this right by patients who are terminally ill or who, because of religious beliefs, refuse treatment. In some limited instances a court may order treatment despite a patient's objection. There is often a

§1.11 [1] Kirby v. Spivey, 167 Ga. App. 751 (1983).
[2] Id.

fine line between personal privacy, religious practices, religious guarantees, and state interests — the chief concerns often raised when treatment is refused in such cases. This area of health law is heavily intertwined with medical ethics. As discussed in chapter 7, it has also proven to be an area ripe for judicial intervention.

§1.11.2 Informed Refusal of Treatment

Just as a patient's decision to have treatment must be informed, so must be those decisions involving either a refusal of or withdrawal from treatment. This need for "informed refusal" was highlighted in a California case.[3] The patient was under the care of a general practitioner for approximately six years, during which time she saw him on a fairly regular basis. He gave her pelvic examinations and told her she needed a Pap smear; he did not, however, indicate the risks of declining the test. On at least two occasions she refused to have the test on the basis of its cost. Eventually she was seen by a gynecologist, who then found that she had an advanced cancer of the cervix. Although she underwent treatment, the woman died at the age of 30.

The decedent's two children filed a lawsuit against the general practitioner for their mother's wrongful death. The case went to the jury, which found that the physician had not been negligent. The case went to the Supreme Court of California, which reversed a finding by the state court of appeals upholding the trial court determination. The California Supreme Court found that the jury should have been instructed that the physician was under a duty to inform the patient of the risks of refusing the Pap smear. Without this information, the patient's refusal of the test was not informed and hence invalid.[4]

There has been some suggestion that the California decision

---

[3]Truman v. Thomas, 27 Cal. 3d 285, 611 P.2d 902, 165 Cal. Rptr. 308 (1980).
[4]Id.

has added a new responsibility to the burden of physicians in the area of consent.[5] But has it? Is a patient not entitled to know the probable consequences of refusing a particular course of treatment? Is consent not required prior to performing a diagnostic test? Is it greatly burdensome to require a physician to tell a patient that by not having a Pap smear she may run the risk of letting a cervical cancer go undetected?

Categorizing the principle of informed refusal as a new extension of the law of consent is difficult. It is best seen as an integral part of the consent process. Whether or not a patient decides to have a test or to undergo surgery, her decision must be informed.

Perhaps a different line of argument should be taken by health professionals. How far must they go in providing adequate information to their patients? When may a physician assume that certain information, such as the value of a Pap smear and the consequences of forgoing it, are understood by a patient? What is the impact of health organization or of state-sponsored well-women health education programs that emphasize the importance of regular Pap smear tests? What degree of knowledge can it be assumed that a patient gleans from reading articles in so-called women's magazines on the value of Pap smear screening?

Short of informing the patient individually, it is difficult to ascribe knowledge to patients about the risks of refusing care or diagnostic tests. A practitioner cannot safely rely upon health education programs that promote diagnostic screening. Patients are bombarded by all types of promotional media, from those advocating buying a new laundry detergent or shaving cream to those touting weight control programs. Some, not all, of the information will register. Before practitioners provide treatment or conduct tests, they must obtain patients' consents. This includes informing patients of the risks of forgoing diagnostic studies and treatment.

---

[5] Fagel, The Duty of Informed Refusal, 9 Legal Aspects of Medical Practice 1 (1981).

§1.11.3 Duty to Disclose Risk of Refusing Care by Specialist

As the field of consent develops, courts continue to add new responsibilities to the duty to disclose. A California court recently added the responsibility to disclose the risk of not being examined by a specialist.[6]

The plaintiff was an actor and a real estate salesman. During an examination by an internist at the defendant medical group, the plaintiff pointed out a mole he had noticed on his ear lobe. When asked if it was anything to be worried about, the doctor strongly recommended that the plaintiff see a specialist. Moreover, he told the plaintiff that all moles are deemed suspicious in nature until removed or examined microscopically.

The plaintiff waited more than four months before he acted upon the doctor's advice. In the course of a visit to a dermatologist regarding a leg rash, the plaintiff mentioned the mole on his ear lobe. The dermatologist told him it should be removed immediately for biopsy. This was done a few days later. Pathological examination revealed a malignant melanoma. The plaintiff subsequently underwent extensive surgery to remove part of his left ear and glands in front of the ear and in his neck. The plaintiff was left with some disfigurement and numbness.

Litigation was brought against the physician group and the internist, Dr. Mason, for failure to warn the plaintiff of dangers associated with the mole and the repercussions if he did not have it diagnosed properly. An out-of-court settlement was reached with the physician. However, with regard to the group, a verdict was returned in favor of the plaintiff.

In affirming the trial decision, the appellate court ruled that earlier precedent dealing with "informed refusal" was applicable. Building on the case of Truman v. Thomas,[7] the court pointed out that the plaintiff was entitled to all material infor-

---

[6]Moore v. Preventive Medicine Medical Group, Inc., 178 Cal. App. 3d 728, 223 Cal. Rptr. 859 (Cal. Ct. App. 1986).
[7]27 Cal. 3d 285, 611 P.2d 902, 165 Cal. Rptr. 308 (1980).

mation that would enable him to make an informed choice about whether to see a specialist.[8] Writing about Dr. Mason, the internist, the court noted that he knew he would not have another chance to talk with his patient about the risk of failing to have the mole examined properly. In view of this, it was up to the doctor to impart the information to the patient so he could make an informed choice.

Does this case extend the logic of the *Truman* case too far? Will other states adopt such a precedent? It is difficult to answer either question. However, it is clear that at least in California, the courts are not at all reluctant to extend the scope of the duty to disclose so patients can make an informed refusal of care.

From a practical point of view and from the perspective of preventive law, it would be prudent for clinicians to document in the patient record that the patient has been advised to seek additional diagnostic and treatment services from a specialist. Such documentation should briefly summarize what the patient was told. If a *Moore*-like challenge should arise, such documentation could prove quite valuable for purposes of legal defense.

C. THE NEED FOR ADEQUATE DISCLOSURE

A key element in the criteria for a valid consent is that the patient be adequately informed. The patient must have sufficient details about a proposed procedure, including risk-benefit information. If an authorization for treatment is obtained without the benefit of such information, the consent thus obtained is invalid. Meeting all the other criteria for a valid consent is not sufficient to overcome this deficiency, unless one of the recognized exceptions to disclosure of information is applicable to the situation. (See chapter 2, infra.)

[8] Moore v. Preventive Medicine Medical Group, Inc., supra n.6, at 738, 223 Cal. Rptr. at 863.

C. *The Need for Adequate Disclosure*

The degree of disclosure required for a valid consent varies from state to state. As discussed in this portion of the chapter, there are various trends developing in the United States on how much information must be supplied to a patient. These trends have developed as the result of litigation as well as legislation.

The traditional standard for disclosure is measured by what it is customary practice in the medical community for physicians to disclose to patients. The amount of disclosure based on this physician standard is highly dependent upon the perceptions of the individual physician in each case. Although this "medical community" rule of disclosure has been used for many years, it has been rejected in many states that have embraced the "patient need" standard of disclosure.

The patient need standard is based on what a reasonable person in the patient's position would want to know in the same or similar circumstances. The perceptions of health professionals are *not* used as a yardstick for assessing how much information should be conveyed to patients.

The two rules on disclosure are often cast in terms of subjective and objective standards. This perspective on the standard for disclosure is not very useful, particularly since the courts have taken divergent viewpoints on the standard for causality, which does involve distinctions based on objective and subjective criteria. The terms *subjective* and *objective* must be used with caution to avoid confusion.

The proponents of the medical community rule argue that basing disclosure on medical judgment is quite sound. A physician cannot possibly determine what a reasonable person would want to know. The doctor's job is to do what is best for his patient, and the disclosure of information necessary for consent should be cast in light of what the professional regards as important for the patient. In this way, the physician can delete what he perceives as extraneous or unnecessary details.

The proponents of the patient need rule of disclosure argue that the standard based on medical judgment is outdated. Based as it is on a paternalistic attitude of "doctor knows best," it does not take into account the increase in patients' desire to take an active role in their health care. Patients are not as inclined as in previous years to accept without question a recommendation for treatment. Since treatment constitutes an invasion of their bodily integrity, they want to understand in some detail why proposed care is necessary. They want to know what benefits they may derive from one procedure over another, the relative risks of each option, the effect each option will have on their lives. They are also concerned about the financial costs involved. The patient need standard insists on greater disclosure of information. It is one of the better examples of the consumer movement in the health care industry.

In this portion of the chapter, the rules on disclosure of information are discussed in great detail. Included are examinations of the types of information that should be disclosed and information that a health care provider is not obliged to reveal.

§1.12 Patients' Right to Basic Information

As noted above, there is a general consensus among the states regarding the types of information that should be disclosed to patients. This agreement has been achieved in some states through the vehicle of legislation enacted over the past decade and in others through case decisions. The statutes that set forth basic informational requirements differ in structure. Some declare that if certain information has been disclosed to a patient, by definition, she has been given the information required for consent.[1] In some jurisdictions, failure to meet the informational requirements set forth in the statute constitutes a lack of informed consent, providing other criteria are met.[2]

The case law dealing with informed consent is quite consistent with the legislation. The decisions follow a pattern, includ-

§1.12 [1]See, e.g., Idaho Code §39-4304 (1975); Neb. Rev. Stat. §44-2816 (1976); Pa. Stat. Ann. tit. 40, §1301.103 (Purdon 1976).
[2]Alaska Stat. §09.55.556 (1976); Del. Code Ann. tit. 18, §6852 (1976); Fla. Stat. Ann. §768.46 (West 1975); Utah Code Ann. §78-14-5 (1976); Vt. Stat. Ann. tit. 12, §1909 (1976).

ing such details as the risks and benefits associated with a particular procedure and reasonable alternatives to it.[3]

§1.12.1 Disclosure of Risk-Benefit Information

For patients to reach informed decisions regarding treatment, they must be given certain details. They should be told about the probable benefits to be derived from a procedure, whether it be diagnostic, medical, or surgical. Statutes and legislation in various states, however, have modified this general requirement. For example, in Delaware a statutory definition of consent includes that a patient be told "of the nature of the proposed procedure or treatment."[4] In Washington State, under legislation that creates a cause of action for negligent consent, significant information regarding the nature, character, and anticipated results of treatment must be disclosed.[5]

Risk information must also be revealed to a patient — a requirement indicated by both case decisions[6] and statutes.[7] The amount of required disclosure varies from state to state, dependent in large measure upon the disclosure standards recognized in each jurisdiction.

If a state follows the medical community rule,[8] arguably less

---

[3]See, e.g., Cross v. Trapp, 294 S.E.2d 446 (W. Va. 1982); McPherson v. Ellis, 305 N.C. 266, 287 S.E.2d 892 (1982); Troy v. Long Island Jewish-Hillside Med. Center, 86 A.D.2d 631, 446 N.Y.S.2d 347 (1982); Sard v. Hardy, 281 Md. 432, 379 A.2d 1014 (1977); Wilkinson v. Vesey, 110 R.I. 606, 295 A.2d 676 (1972).

[4]Del. Code Ann. tit. 18, §6801 (1981).

[5]Wash. Rev. Code Ann. §7.70.050 (1975-1976).

[6]Haley v. United States, 739 F.2d 1502 (10th Cir. 1984). See, e.g., McPherson v. Ellis, 305 N.C. 266, 287 S.E.2d 892 (1982); Cross v. Trapp, 294 S.E.2d 446 (W. Va. 1982); Sard v. Hardy, 281 Md. 432, 379 A.2d 1014 (1977); Wilkinson v. Vesey, 110 R.I. 606, 295 A.2d 676 (1972).

[7]Alaska Stat. §09.55.556 (1976); Fla. Stat. Ann. §768.46 (West 1975); N.Y. Pub. Health Law §2805-d (McKinney 1975); Utah Code Ann. §78-14-5 (1976); Wash. Rev. Code Ann. §7.70.050 (1975-1976).

[8]See, e.g., Del. Code Ann. tit. 18, §6852 (1981); Fla. Stat. Ann. §768.46 (West 1975); Neb. Rev. Stat. §44-2816 (1976); and Tenn. Code Ann. §29-26-118 (1976). See also Bloskas v. Murray, 646 P.2d 907 (Colo. 1982); Troy v.

information has to be made available than if the patient need rule were followed. Under the patient need doctrine,[9] disclosure is measured by what a reasonable patient would want or need to know in the same or similar circumstances.

The differences between the rules of disclosure are not totally controlling. A health care provider cannot be charged with knowledge of a probable risk or alternative form of care if it was not recognized as a risk or reasonable option at the time the patient's consent was obtained. The provider is only accountable for risk and optional treatment information that was reasonably foreseeable at the time of consent. Moreover, information about remote risks need not be disclosed. The only time this rule does not apply is when an otherwise remote risk was material or significant to a specific patient in his decision whether to authorize treatment.[10]

The following list identifies the type of information that should be revealed:

1. the likely outcome of diagnostic tests;
2. the likely benefits of diagnostic workups in determining a patient's illness or the extent of his or her injury;
3. the probable outcome of medical and/or surgical interventions;
4. the likely benefits from medical and/or surgical procedures;
5. an explanation of what a diagnostic, medical, or surgical procedure will involve, including any probable complications and any temporary discomfort, disability, or disfigurement;
6. an explanation of any permanent results of a medical or

Long Island Jewish-Hillside Med. Center, 86 A.D.2d 631, 446 N.Y.S.2d 347 (1982); Riedisser v. Nelson, 111 Ariz. 542, 534 P.2d 1052 (1975).

[9]See, e.g., Pa. Stat. Ann. tit. 40, §1301.103 (Purdon 1976). See also McPherson v. Ellis, 305 N.C. 266, 287 S.E.2d 892 (1982); Harnish v. Children's Hosp. Med. Center, 387 Mass. 152, 439 N.E.2d 240 (1982); Cobbs v. Grant, 8 Cal. 3d 229, 502 P.2d 1, 104 Cal. Rptr. 505 (1972); Nickell v. Gonzales, 17 Ohio St. 3d 136, 477 N.E.2d 1145 (1985).

[10]Wilkinson v. Vesey, 110 R.I. 606, 295 A.2d 676 (1972).

surgical procedure (for example, the likelihood of a permanent scar or the creation of a stoma for a permanent ileostomy or colostomy and the care it would require); and
7. a disclosure of risks that are reasonably foreseeable at the time that consent is obtained.
8. Remote risks need not be disclosed. Risks that are probable for particular patients, however, merit disclosure. For example, the remote risk of an allergic reaction to contrast dye used in diagnostic studies need not be disclosed. However, for patients with long-standing histories of severe allergic reactions to foods and medicine, disclosure of allergy to the dye would be necessary.[11]

The criteria for disclosure, established by legislation, differ among the states. For example, in Georgia legislation requires only that a disclosure be cast in general terms.[12] Case law construing the statute holds that a physician is not obliged to disclose risk-of-treatment information.[13] Iowa legislation takes the opposite standpoint, requiring disclosure of such known risks as "death, brain damage, quadriplegia, paraplegia, or loss of function of any organ, limb, or disfiguring scars, . . ."[14] A novel approach has been taken in Hawaii[15] and Texas,[16] where boards have been granted the authority to set standards for the disclosure of information to patients. The Hawaii law is not as detailed as the Texas provision; however, both vest a significant amount of authority in administrative bodies for deciding what benefit and risk information should be provided to a patient.

---

[11]But see Hook v. Rothstein, 316 S.E.2d 690 (S.C. Ct. App. 1984), in which the court ruled that the radiologist's duty to disclose material risks of contrast dye in an intravenous pyelogram is measured by what a reasonable radiologist would disclose in the same or similar circumstances. Liability attaches only if a causal connection exists between the failure to disclose pertinent information and the patient's injury. Causality is established if a reasonable person in the position of the patient would have refused treatment had he been informed of the risk that came to fruition.
[12]Ga. Code §88-2906 (1971).
[13]Butler v. Brown, 162 Ga. App. 376, 290 S.E.2d 293 (1982).
[14]Iowa Code Ann. §147.137 (West 1975).
[15]Haw. Rcv. Stat. §671-3 (1983).
[16]Tex. Stat. Ann. art. 4590i (Vernon 1976).

People desire increasing information about everything from food prices to various aspects of their health care. Health care personnel are being taught the importance of establishing a good rapport and communication with those they treat. Bearing this in mind, the present distinctions between what must be disclosed under the patient need standard and what must be revealed under the medical community standard should come to an end. As a matter of good practice health care practitioners should give their patients ample information about the nature, risks, and benefits of proposed care. This will allow the informed patient to actively participate in her treatment and difficulties can be averted that might arise from undisclosed risks. In order to provide a patient with sufficient information health care providers must obtain an adequate patient history. This is dictated by common sense, and it is a factor recognized in some case law.[17]

What constitutes a sufficient disclosure of risk information has also received judicial review. For example, in a New York case a patient underwent a proctocoloctomy, resulting in organic impotency.[18] In the lawsuit that followed the patient claimed that the mere identification of a risk associated with a procedure — impotency — and the probability of its occurrence does not allow a reasonably prudent patient to make a reasonable choice regarding treatment. Furthermore, the patient claimed that in some instances the doctor must do more, such as disclose the means by which risks are likely to occur.

The court agreed with the plaintiff. Not only does such an elaboration assist a patient in understanding the recommended procedure and its attendant risks, it also enables the individual to know the degree of control the doctor has over these hazards of treatment. As the court pointed out, in some instances knowing the "mechanics" by which injury may occur is important information for the patient to consider in reaching an informed choice.[19]

[17] Brown v. Dahl, 41 Wash. App. 565, 705 P.2d 781 (1985).
[18] Nisenholtz v. Mt. Sinai Hosp., 126 Misc. 2d 658, 483 N.Y.S.2d 568 (Sup. Ct. 1984).
[19] Id.

Clinicians should not be timid in discussing potential risks that may result in permanent and devastating disability. This includes the potential of stroke. When the patient's history indicates that a stroke is a probable risk that may result from a therapeutic or diagnostic[20] intervention, the clinician should impart this information.

A good example of this principle can be found in a case involving a Veteran's Administration hospital.[21] The patient had a documented history of coronary artery disease. Indeed, he had undergone bypass surgery to provide some relief from his condition. A stress test had been administered a little over three weeks earlier, but the physician attending him at the hospital was unable to secure a report. According to the court, the doctor did not seek the information from the appropriate source. Medical record information from the plaintiff's former private physician was never obtained. Furthermore, the doctor did not advise the plaintiff of the difficulties he had encountered in obtaining the report.[22] Although the plaintiff was advised that there were some risks involved in the stress test, he was never apprised of the risk of stroke. The plaintiff suffered a stroke and was left permanently blind. This led to successful litigation based on the theory of malpractice and lack of informed consent.[23]

Physicians dislike discussing risk information that may involve death or crippling disabilities. For their part, patients do not relish hearing such information or weighing it in their decisions regarding treatment. Nevertheless, this type of information should be disclosed by the caregiver but imparted in a way that does not immobilize the patient with fear. It should be presented in the context of each patient's case, bearing in mind the medical history that may make such a risk a significant probability. There is little doubt that some types of risk information cause anxiety. Little can be done to make such informa-

[20] Hedgecorth v. United States, 618 F. Supp. 627 (E.D. Mo. 1985).
[21] Id.
[22] Id.
[23] Id.

tion more palatable. Indeed, it may "frighten away" many would-be patients. This is a fact of life that caregivers must accept and handle within the limits of their professional experience and judgment.

§1.12.2   *Disclosure of Reasonable Alternative Procedures*

In addition to risk and benefit information, a patient should be told of the availability of *reasonable* alternative procedures. The emphasis here is on what is a reasonable substitute. A health care practitioner need not disclose information regarding an alternative diagnostic procedure or medical or surgical intervention unless it can be seen as a reasonable option. This principle has been recognized in some states in legislation[24] and in others by case law.[25]

What is reasonable will depend upon the circumstances of a patient's case. Other influencing factors include the health practitioner's judgment and personal considerations of the patient. For example, a practitioner may believe that cardiac surgery is not a reasonable alternative to medical management for a patient because the need for surgical intervention has not been clearly established. An internist may likewise conclude that surgery is not a reasonable alternative to medical treatment for a patient who is a very poor anesthetic risk.

Patients must decide whether they consent to the proposed course of treatment rather than to a reasonable alternative. Patients may be influenced by a variety of considerations, including the cost of the various procedures, the length of the recuperation, the likely success of each option, the likely risk of the various alternatives, and the impact each option is likely to have on their lifestyles. This is particularly true when patients

---

[24] Fla. Stat. Ann. §768.46 (West 1975); Pa. Stat. Ann. tit. 40, §1301.103 (Purdon 1976); Wash. Rev. Code Ann. §7.70.050 (1975-1976).

[25] Keogh v. Holy Family Hosp., 95 Wash. 2d 306, 622 P.2d 1246 (1980); Sard v. Hardy, 281 Md. 432, 379 A.2d 1014 (1977); McGrady v. Wright, 151 Ariz. 538, 729 P.2d 338 (Ct. App. 1986).

have the option of hormonal therapy as opposed to a hysterectomy.[26]

In most instances, reasonable alternative forms of care seem to involve the same or a similar level of risks and benefits as those found in the proposed form of care, but a Connecticut case casts considerable doubt on this assumption.[27]

A patient with systemic lupus erythematosus was advised to undergo a kidney biopsy to determine the degree of the disease in her kidneys. The attending internist recommended a closed kidney biopsy that would be carried out under a local anesthetic. The patient was never advised of an open biopsy which would be performed under a general anesthetic. Moreover, the patient was not told that the closed biopsy involved the risk of puncturing the gall bladder, an event that did occur during the biopsy, necessitating surgical removal of the gall bladder.

In his charge to the jury in this case, the judge noted that the duty to warn patients of reasonable alternatives did not include options that were more hazardous than the one proposed. The Supreme Court of Connecticut ruled that this constituted reversible error and ordered a retrial on the issue.

The court pointed out that the instruction to the jury that it was not necessary to warn patients of a more hazardous alternative had the damaging effect of limiting the duty of disclosure to the safest procedure. It would relieve physicians of the duty to discuss reasonable options with their patients, a position incompatible with providing sufficient information to patients to permit them to reach intelligent decisions.[28]

The Connecticut decision is troublesome since it provides little direction to physicians in deciding what information should or should not be disclosed to patients. Physicians must shape the scope of their disclosure to meet the needs and condition of the patient. For some individuals, a more hazardous

---

[26]See Smith v. Reisig, 686 P.2d 285 (Okla. 1984), in which the Supreme Court of Oklahoma reversed a demurrer and remanded for trial a claim based on inadequate disclosure of hormonal therapy as an alternative to surgery.

[27]Logan v. Greenwich Hosp. Assn., 465 A.2d 294 (Conn. 1983).

[28]Id.

diagnostic or treatment option may not be viable. Should a physician be obliged to discuss this with the patient?

There is often a fine line between a paternalistic attitude of "doctor knows best" and a determination to disclose treatment options based on a thorough understanding of the needs and condition of the patient. The Connecticut decision only serves to cloud this distinction. Further elaboration from the courts may be necessary to fully understand the extent of required disclosure of hazardous treatment options.

At least one court has made it clear, however, that disclosure of a "reasonable" treatment option does not include the alternative of withholding life-saving surgery and permitting a neonate to die.[29] Renee Iafelice was born four weeks prematurely and was subsequently found to have experienced an intraventricular hemorrhage and secondary hydrocephalus. Prior to surgery to install a ventriculoperitoneal shunt, the neonatologist informed the parents that the situation was serious and that the child would never be normal. They were also advised that without the operation the child would probably die. However, the parents were never advised of the option of no treatment.

The court disagreed with the parents' claim that the doctors had not abided by their duty to disclose reasonable alternative treatment information. Looking at the law as it stood in 1980, when the matter arose, and the circumstances of the case, it could not be said that the doctors were under a legal obligation to disclose the option of withholding life-saving care. Death was not a legally sanctioned alternative.[30]

Although death may not be a legally sanctioned, reasonable alternative, physicians are obliged to discuss the limited options available when patients refuse necessary blood transfusions. This principle was espoused by a United States District Court in a medical malpractice case involving a VA hospital.[31] In that case the patient was a practicing Jehovah's Witness. He was

---

[29] Iafelice v. Zarafu, 501 A.2d 1040 (1985), aff'd, 534 A.2d 417 (N.J. Super. Ct. App. Div. 1987).
[30] Id.
[31] Davis v. United States, 629 F. Supp. 1 (E.D. Ark. 1986).

diagnosed as having a bleeding ulcer that required surgical repair. Because of his beliefs, the patient refused to have the operation if it involved the use of blood transfusions. Physicians at the VA hospital declined to carry out the surgery without the use of blood. Less than 36 hours after his arrival at the hospital, the patient left, against medical advice, and had successful corrective surgery in Houston without the aid of blood transfusions. However, the man sued claiming that his subsequent condition, spondylolitesis, was the result of the VA medical staff negligently failing to inform him of his condition and the limitations upon the scope of care available at the hospital. He claimed that this delayed the decision to send him to Houston for treatment and caused his present condition.

In the end, the court dismissed the complaint. The court pointed out that the doctors did in fact meet their obligation to keep the man informed of his condition and the limited treatment options available to him at the hospital without blood transfusions in surgery.[32]

Cases like this often come down to a question of credibility between the plaintiff and defendant. In this matter, the court believed the testimony on the part of the defendants and the available evidence militated toward dismissing the complaint. Not every case may go the same way. Physicians should take care to document their conversations with patients and their families, including information on the limited options available when religious beliefs circumscribe the list of reasonable alternatives. Moreover, care should be taken to assess the patient's ability to contemplate important information. If, for example, blood volume drops to a point that the patient's ability to think is compromised or the patient goes into shock, how can the patient give consent? These are issues that should be addressed *before* such cases occur. This can be accomplished in an effective policy and procedure manual on consent.

An improper failure to disclose reasonable alternatives cannot be excused. For example, if physicians knowingly withheld information for fear that patients would refuse consent to rec-

---

[32] Id. at 6-8.

ommended procedures if they knew the alternatives available, the consents thus obtained would be invalid. Consent litigation in these circumstances could be based on inadequate disclosure of information, fraudulently obtained authorizations, or misrepresentation.

The only justifiable grounds for not revealing information about alternative procedures are either that the options are not reasonable or that disclosure could be expected to affect the patient adversely.[33] The soundness of such a decision is subject to judicial review. Whether or not nondisclosure was in fact reasonable will be determined in the context of the facts and circumstances of the patient's case. The case will be assessed in terms of what was known at the time the patient gave consent to treatment, not at the time of litigation.

The reasonable alternative-disclosure criterion imposes a duty upon a practitioner to get to know her patients. This process involves learning what factors are important to the patient in deciding whether to undergo surgery or to continue with medical management. Furthermore, the patient must be assessed not only medically but also, to a degree, from a social or personal perspective. To some extent family medicine practitioners, through their increased number of opportunities to get to know the needs and concerns of their patients, have an advantage over specialists in fulfilling these requirements. Specialists, on the other hand, can partially correct that imbalance through effort and pertinent questions.

The patient need standard for disclosure clearly requires a physician to divulge information on reasonable options to proposed treatment. The necessity for such information under the medical community rule is not as clear-cut. However, if it is customary practice for physicians to disclose such information, it is necessary to supply relevant details. Indeed, as a means of avoiding any misunderstandings or litigation, sound policy arguably dictates that practitioners in states following the medical community rule disclose such information as a matter of routine. The better informed a patient is, the less likely the

---

[33] See, e.g., N.Y. Pub. Health Law §2805-d (McKinney 1975).

chance of litigation based on inadequate disclosure or lack of consent.

§1.12.3 Disclosure of Diagnostic Test Results

If the results of a diagnostic procedure will affect a patient's consent to medical or surgical treatment, the information should be provided to the patient. The data fall within the category of information that a reasonable patient would want to consider in deciding whether to have the proposed form of treatment. Diagnostic test results arguably also fall within the scope of information that should be communicated to the patient under the medical community rule of disclosure.

The need to disclose test results is not limitless: it is not incumbent upon a health practitioner, in other words, to disclose *all* diagnostic results, but only those that are significant to a patient's consent to treatment. This is necessary in those states following the patient need rule on disclosure. It would also probably constitute information that it is customary practice to reveal in states taking the medical community perspective on disclosure.

The circumstances of an individual patient's case are also partially determinative. A routine blood test such as a CBC may merit a report to the patient only if he inquires about the results. The practitioner would be obliged, however, to contact the patient and discuss further diagnostic or treatment options if the test revealed a serious health problem.

The duty to disclose the results of tests is not totally based on the law of consent: it also rests upon principles of good medical practice. The failure to disclose or act upon test results, with reasonably foreseeable harm resulting, can give rise to malpractice litigation, as the two following cases illustrate.

In a Washington State case, an ophthalmologist detected an abnormal finding during the course of a routine examination.[34]

[34]Gates v. Jensen, 595 P.2d 919 (Wash. 1979), reversing 579 P.2d 374.

Not only did he not disclose this fact to the patient, he failed to inform her of diagnostic tests that were available that could have identified the significance of the abnormal finding. As the court pointed out, the doctor must disclose those facts and findings that the physician knows or should know the patient requires in order to make an informed choice.[35]

A Louisiana court found that a jury committed manifest error when it failed to find that a practitioner had not met his disclosure duty regarding test results.[36] The patient had had a cervical cancer in situ that was removed by cold conization. She underwent periodic Pap smears thereafter that showed no evidence of cancer. Once when she could not contact her own gynecologist for her periodic Pap smear, she saw another gynecologist who recommended that she have a total hysterectomy. He indicated that it would substantially reduce the risk of cancer. What he did not tell the patient was that a Pap smear he had taken prior to the operation showed no evidence of cancer. In its ruling the court reasoned that this information would have been material to the woman's decision whether to have the hysterectomy.[37] Additional case law supports the duty of a doctor to disclose diagnostic test results, even when those findings indicate a terminal illness.[38]

The burden to disclose test results does not rest entirely upon the physician. Sometimes the patient may be obliged to make inquiries, thus sharing the responsibility with the doctor. This joint duty was demonstrated in a Minnesota case in which a patient sued a physician for medical malpractice.[39]

The patient had selected a physician out of the telephone directory in order to obtain a contraceptive device. During his examination of the patient, the doctor did a Pap smear, the

---

[35] Id.

[36] Steele v. St. Paul Fire & Marine Ins. Co., 371 So. 2d 843 (La. Ct. App. 1979).

[37] Id.

[38] See Blackmon v. Langley, 737 S.W.2d 455 (Ark. 1987).

[39] Ray v. Wagner, 286 Minn. 354, 175 N.W.2d 101 (1970).

results of which came back positive for a possible malignancy. The physician was unable to contact the woman for five months until she paid her bill. She had furnished misleading and incomplete information regarding her employment and had no telephone where she lived. Moreover, she did not try to contact the doctor to inquire about the Pap smear results.

A repeat Pap smear showed cancer. After cobalt and radium therapy the woman became sterile and experienced menopause. In the subsequent malpractice litigation, the Supreme Court of Minnesota held that the physician was under a duty to take whatever reasonable measures necessary to supply the patient with the test results. However, the patient's actions constituted contributory negligence.[40]

The extent of the requirement to disclose test results depends upon the relevant facts and circumstances of an individual case. It also hinges on the standard of disclosure applicable in a particular state. However, taking these factors into account, it is a matter of sound practice and common sense to reveal those test results that suggest further medical or surgical intervention. The law does not require physicians to make extraordinary efforts to contact patients. At the same time, they should make whatever effort is reasonable under the circumstances to notify the patient.

Some case law suggests that health facilities are not duty bound to notify patients of test results, although there is contrary opinion on the matter.[41] This lack of duty is particularly true if the tests are performed at the request of an attending physician who is not employed by the health facility. Unless the hospital is aware of factors that require the institution to intervene, it does not have a duty to intrude upon the physician-patient relationship. Absent unusual concerns, it is best that the test results be sent directly to the physician so that a professional judgment can be made as to their significance.

[40] Id.
[41] Washington Healthcare Corp. v. Barrow, 531 A.2d 226 (D.C. 1987). Cf. Alexander v. Gosner, 711 P.2d 347 (Wash. Ct. App. 1985).

The courts do not take lightly the suggestion that there is a duty to communicate directly to the patient information regarding abnormal test findings. This point was made clear in a Washington, D.C. case.[42] During the course of routine preoperative chest X-rays, the defendant radiologist noticed an increased density in the right lung of the plaintiff. The defendant interpreted this finding as a possible localized infiltration and recommended a follow-up investigation. The next day, the plaintiff cancelled her outpatient surgery and neither she nor her surgeon was made aware of the defendant's X-ray report. Less than a year later, the plaintiff underwent surgery at another hospital for cancer in the lung in which the density had been noticed by the defendant.

The D.C. Court of Appeals reversed and remanded a jury verdict in favor of the defendant. The decision makes it clear that where experts disagree about the proper mechanism for reporting abnormal test results, it is improper to charge the physician with a duty to communicate such information *directly* to the patient or attending surgeon.[43] In the absence of expert testimony to the contrary, however, if in the course of a workup or postoperative investigation an anomaly is detected, the physician discovering the problem should contact the doctor who ordered the test or pathology examination.[44]

Health facilities should learn from this decision. From a defense point of view, it is important to reassess health facility policies and procedures regarding the communication of test results. Do such documents specify to whom the reports should be sent? Do they include provision for reporting despite cancellation of planned outpatient surgery or invasive diagnostic tests? Do they include how and when such information should be recorded? Questions such as these should be addressed as part of a risk prevention program for the health facility. It is an important step in averting litigation based on inadequate disclosure of test results.

---

[42]Stager v. Schneider, 494 A.2d 1307 (D.C. 1985).
[43]Id. at 1312-1313, n.5.
[44]See Mahannah v. Hirsch, 237 Cal. Rptr. 140 (Ct. App. 1987).

§1.13 Information That Need Not Be Disclosed

Since the medical community disclosure standard does not provide any clear-cut guidelines on the type of information that need not be disclosed, the burden is placed upon individual practitioners. Important considerations include the facts of each case as well as the health and prior medical history of individual patients.

For some patients a candid disclosure of risk information may jeopardize their health, whereas for others knowing the probable consequences of a particular procedure will be a welcome relief. Withholding certain details on the basis of therapeutic privilege must be done with caution. That judgment should be based on the total patient.

In other cases, a decision to withhold or provide risk information is not based on the patient's fragile physical or psychological health. Instead the determination must be made in the light of such factors as allergies, chronic or acute illness, age, and family history. For many people a risk may be remote, but the same risk for patients with one of these conditions may be probable. Without the benefit of clear-cut direction on the subject, physicians in states following the medical community rule of disclosure must decide for themselves whether the information is the type that is customarily disclosed. However, what is "customary" is gauged in the light of the surrounding facts of each case.

§1.13.1 *The Medical Community Standard*

There is no hard and fast rule regarding what type of information should or should not be disclosed under the medical community standard. Whether cast in terms of what is customary practice (what a reasonable practitioner would do under the same or similar circumstances) or what is required by medical standards, a case will be decided on its own facts and circumstances. Expert testimony will be necessary to establish the standard that is applicable or to prove that nondisclosure of information was acceptable. The amount of disclosure is largely a matter of medical judgment.

The law comes into play when the physician's lack of disclosure is alleged to constitute a departure from the accepted norm. Courts have found on this basis that it is not necessary for practitioners to reveal information regarding remote risks[1] or those risks that are not recognized as being applicable to a given procedure.[2] This finding may mean, for example, that a surgical procedure that carries a risk of between ½ of 1 percent and 3 percent does not merit discussion with the patient.[3] It may also mean that there is no obligation to disclose the risk of severe reaction that may be encountered in the course of an IVP.[4] Indeed, as one court has suggested, it does not appear to be customary to inform a patient, prior to obtaining the patient's informed consent, that the attending physician may not be present during an operation.[5]

Since the medical community rule rests largely on the circumstances of a particular case as well as on recognized norms, decisions must be made on an individual patient basis. Practitioners must familiarize themselves with the minimum acceptable amount of information that must be disclosed to a patient. They should determine the individual needs of the patient and whether a detailed disclosure is warranted or advisable.

§1.13.2   The Patient Need Standard

There are various formulations of the patient need standard of disclosure. One phrasing is in terms of what a reasonable person in the patient's position would want to know or what a patient would need to know in order to reach an informed choice. However phrased, the standard does not require disclosure of all possible information — only of that information that

§1.13   [1] Tatro v. Lueken, 212 Kan. 606, 512 P.2d 529 (1973).
[2] Collins v. Itoh, 160 Mont. 461, 503 P.2d 36 (1972).
[3] Id.
[4] Pardy v. United States, 783 F.2d 710 (7th Cir. 1986).
[5] Young v. United States, 648 F. Supp. 146 (E.D. Va. 1986).

is material or significant to a patient's decision regarding treatment.[6] Unfortunately, the courts and state legislatures have not been clear on what is or is not "material" or "significant." These words have usually been defined as including risk information that a physician knows or ought to know would be important to a person in the patient's position in deciding whether to have a particular form of treatment.[7] At least one court has said that the "materiality" of information is a function of both the severity of the injury and the likelihood of its occurrence.[8]

In some instances, courts following the patient need standard of disclosure have suggested the types of information that need *not* be revealed. These categories include:

1. risks that are known to the patient;
2. risks that are so obvious that it may be presumed that the patient has knowledge of them;
3. relatively remote risks inherent in a procedure, when it is commonly known that such risks are present but are of very low incidence; and
4. risks that a physician did not know about at the time or in the exercise of ordinary care could not ascertain.[9]

There are also certain instances in which a health provider need not make a disclosure of risk information. These include medical emergencies, therapeutic privilege, and when a patient is legally incapable of understanding the information or lacks the mental capability to give consent.[10]

Nondisclosure of risk information has been the basis for considerable judicial review under the patient need standard of disclosure. Litigation has involved such diverse matters as the

[6]Largey v. Rothman, 540 A.2d 504 (N.J. 1988); Pauscher v. Iowa Methodist Med. Center, 408 N.W.2d 355 (Iowa 1987); Sard v. Hardy, 281 Md. 432, 379 A.2d 1014 (1977); Cobbs v. Grant, 8 Cal. 3d 224, 502 P.2d 1, 104 Cal. Rptr. 505 (1972).

[7]See, e.g., Sard v. Hardy, 281 Md. 432, 379 A.2d 1014 (1977); Wilkinson v. Vesey, 110 R.I. 606, 295 A.2d 676 (1972).

[8]Precourt v. Frederick, 481 N.E.2d 1144 (Mass. 1985).

[9]Id.; Sard v. Hardy, 281 Md. 432, 379 A.2d 1014 (1977).

[10]Sard v. Hardy, 281 Md. 432, 379 A.2d 1014 (1977).

risk that a tubal ligation is not absolute,[11] inadequate disclosure of information prior to the use of radiation treatment,[12] and the failure to disclose risks associated with duodenal ulcer surgery.[13] Litigation will continue on the matter of nondisclosure despite the guidelines on the matter. Plaintiffs will press on with claims that their cases fall outside the scope of what is arguably a matter for nondisclosure.[14]

Perhaps the key difference between the medical community and patient need standards regarding disclosure and nondisclosure is one of perspective. Practitioners are asked, in the case of the patient need rule, to put themselves in the place of the patients or the reasonable patients. They are in essence asked, What would I as a reasonable patient want to know regarding the risks, benefits, and alternatives? Practitioners faced with the medical community rule are asked, What would I as a reasonable practitioner or as a member of the medical community disclose to this patient? Practitioners must be cognizant of the law in the state in which they practice to make certain that the information they decide not to disclose can legally be withheld from a patient.

§1.13.3 Legislative Standards Governing Disclosure

The common law is not the only source of standards for nondisclosure: several statutory provisions provide for it as well. The circumstances in which these exceptions apply, however, are limited. One set of laws permits health care practitioners to withhold certain details if they believe that the disclosure is likely to adversely affect their patients.[15] It is in essence the

---

[11]Id.

[12]Wilkinson v. Vesey, 110 R.I. 606, 295 A.2d 676 (1972).

[13]Cobbs v. Grant, 8 Cal. 3d 224, 502 P.2d, 104 Cal. Rptr. 505 (1972).

[14]See, e.g., Shin v. St. James Mercy Hosp., 675 F. Supp. 94 (W.D.N.Y. 1987), in which a patient unsuccessfully argued that the remote chance of Stevens-Johnson Syndrome from Dilantin and Phenobarbitol required disclosure. As the court pointed out, the likelihood of developing the syndrome was statistically remote.

[15]Alaska Stat. §09.55.556 (1976); Del. Code Ann. tit. 18, §6852 (1981); N.Y. Pub. Health Law §2805-d (McKinney 1975); Pa. Stat. Ann. tit. 40, §1301.103 (Purdon 1976); Utah Code Ann. §78-14-5 (1976).

codification of the common law exception of therapeutic privilege.

Other laws permit nondisclosure in the case of a medical emergency.[16] To some extent, this allowance is also a codification of common law principles in that case law has long recognized the idea of implied consent to emergency treatment when a patient is unable to authorize care.

Some statutes recognize the right of a provider to withhold information about risks that are considered either commonly known[17] or very remote[18] — similar nondisclosure provisions to those recognized in consent case law. Yet another permissible basis for nondisclosure involves patients who ask not to be informed. Although this situation is an exception to the general rule (see §2.7 infra) of practice in consent, it has been given legislative recognition in some states.[19]

The statutory grounds for nondisclosure of information generally have been placed in laws that deal with the elements of consent litigation. The nondisclosure provisions are often cast in the form of valid defenses for health care providers. Along with other defenses provided in such legislation, a health care provider may be well insulated from successful litigation — providing she meets the required criteria for a valid consent.

§1.13.4 The Effect of the JCAHO Standards on Consent

Aside from case law and legislation governing the extent of information to be disclosed, health care facilities and professionals should also take into account provisions set forth by

---

[16] Ga. Code §88-2905 (1971); Ky. Rev. Stat. §304.40-320 (1976); Miss. Code Ann. §41-41-7 (1966); Pa. Stat. Ann. tit. 40, §1301.103 (Purdon 1976); Wash. Rev. Code Ann. §7.70.050 (1975-1976).

[17] Alaska Stat. §09.55.556 (1976); N.Y. Pub. Health Law §2805-d (McKinney 1975); Utah Code Ann. §78-14-5 (1976); Vt. Stat. Ann. tit. 12, §1909 (1976).

[18] See, e.g., Alaska Stat. §09.55.556 (1976).

[19] Alaska Stat. §09.55.556 (1976); Del. Code Ann. tit. 18, §6852 (1982); N.Y. Pub. Health Law §2805-d (McKinney 1975); Utah Code Ann. §78-14-5 (1976); Vt. Stat. Ann. tit. 12, §1909 (1976).

established professional bodies. The most prominent in this respect is the Joint Commission on Accreditation of Healthcare Organizations.

Through its standards, the Joint Commission is often seen as setting a benchmark for health facility performance. The provisions found in the Joint Commission's standards contain information on consent to treatment. This is found in the introductory material to the standards on patients' rights[20] and in various sections throughout the standards book.[21]

In the past, the Joint Commission's standards have been used to establish a legal duty of care.[22] The question remains whether the accreditation standards could be used to set a legal duty of care for consent. Attempts to do this have been made,[23] and there is nothing to prevent a litigant from using the standards in this manner in the future.

The possibility exists that the Joint Commission's pronouncements may be treated as more than moral platitudes; the provisions on consent may in fact be treated as a legal standard. Therefore, health facilities and professionals should be guided by the Joint Commission's stand in determining what information should be disclosed to a patient for purposes of informed consent.

§1.14 Who Should Obtain Consent?

The question is often asked: whose responsibility is it to secure consent from the patient? Does the task belong to the doctor?

---

[20] See Joint Commission on Accreditation of Healthcare Organizations, Accreditation Manual for Hospitals, 1989, xiii.

[21] See, e.g., id. pp. 66, 97, and 99.

[22] Darling v. Charleston Community Memorial Hosp., 211 N.E.2d 253 (Ill. 1965), cert. denied, 383 U.S. 946 (1966).

[23] See, e.g., Pauscher v. Iowa Methodist Med. Center, 408 N.W.2d 355 (Iowa 1987), in which the court affirmed the lower court ruling to refuse admission of the standards into evidence since it did add to or modify its ruling on consent.

The nurse? The ward clerk? If the task belongs to the doctor, can the function be delegated to another caregiver?

The answers to these questions are not always clear-cut. Indeed, as is seen in the following subsections, the response turns upon an understanding of consent as a *process* and documentation of an authorization for care.

§1.14.1 The Duty to Disclose Rests with the Caregiver

The basic rule of thumb is that the duty to disclose pertinent information rests with the caregiver who is to perform diagnostic tests, medical care, or surgery.[1] The responsibility to document consent, while an important part of consent, is not an essential duty of the "hands-on" caregiver. Indeed, in some quarters, getting the so-called signed consent is no more than a clerical function that reduces to paper the fact that the patient has agreed to certain procedures.

It is essential that caregivers get to know the needs and wants of the patient. The same can be said of caregivers providing services to residents in a long-term care setting or home care program clients. Medical and surgical history; medication allergies, intolerances, and sensitivities; ability to pay for care; prognosis; treatment options and the risks of forgoing care all form an integral part of the backdrop for framing a proper disclosure of material or significant information to the patient. By the same token such background information is essential to the caregiver in those jurisdictions in which the medical community standard of disclosure is employed.

The caregiver must have good communication with the patient. This is the bedrock of the caregiver-patient relationship.

---

§1.14 [1]See, e.g., 243 CMR §3.10:1(c) (1988) which states that, "It shall be a physician's responsibility to obtain the informed consent of the patient and to discuss sufficient medical information to enable the patient to decide whether to undergo the proposed treatment. Although the physician is responsible for informing the patient, health care facility personnel may assist in the completion of documentation."

There must be a level of trust and understanding that comes with gaining confidence in and respect for one another.

"Caregiver" is an ambiguous term that does not always mean that a physician will be responsible for disclosing information to a patient. This is a task best carried out by the person to carry out the diagnostic, medical, or surgical intervention. The same can be said of other caregivers who provide medical radiological services, physiotherapy, psychotherapy, social services, and other services. Only those who have the necessary relationship to the patient should be obliged to disclose pertinent information.

A few examples help to illustrate the distinctions. A family practitioner may refer a patient for physiotherapy. The family doctor secures the patient's authorization for the referral. However, the attending physiotherapist must obtain the patient's consent to the therapeutic regimen to be employed. This means that the physiotherapist must get to know the needs and wants of the patient, secure pertinent history information, make appropriate disclosure of consent information, and then obtain the patient's agreement to the proposed therapy. That a ward clerk may get the patient's "signed consent" is anticlimactic, since in most jurisdictions this is nothing more than an historical record of the individual's agreement to undergo the intended physiotherapy.

In a diagnostic setting, the person carrying out the invasive diagnostic test is obliged to obtain consent. A general practitioner may refer a patient to an ambulatory care center for a mammogram, but the radiological technician must secure the patient's consent to the actual procedure. Indeed, in many cases it may be dangerous for the technician to assume that the general practitioner has explained to the patient what is involved in the test. In many if not most instances, all the GP has done is obtained an authorization for referral for the diagnostic test.

Viewing the consent process in this way could prove disturbing. It upsets many of the false assumptions that underpin the idea of passing on responsibility for obtaining consent. However, in the long run, such a rethinking of the consent process should be reassuring. It reinforces the idea of a consent process based on trust, respect, and communication. Moreover, it avoids many of the problems associated with consent, including distrust, inordinate expectations, and anxiety, which flow from poor communication and inadequate relationships. On the whole, it should strengthen the bond between the patient and caregiver and reduce the risk of consent litigation.

§1.14.2   The Danger of Delegating the Disclosure Responsibility

To many busy practitioners the prospect of taking time to get to know patients, their needs, and wants is nothing more than a money-losing proposition. Such attitudes may obscure a deep-seated arrogance or entrenched paternalistic attitude. It may also be a defense mechanism for those caregivers who possess poor communication skills and see themselves purely as technicians.

Whether it is a matter of being strapped for time or feeling discomfort in communicating with patients, many caregivers opt to delegate the consent process to another individual. In a large teaching hospital, the intern, resident, or nurse practitioner may be assigned to fulfill the consent requirement. In a physician's office, the task may be left in the hands of a nurse or patient assistant. In a research project, consent may be obtained by a junior staff person.

Delegating consent is tantamount to playing a deadly game of "chicken." The delegated party may do a fine job in discharging the task of securing consent. However, there is an equal risk that the delegated party may perform the task badly, setting the stage for an invalid consent.

In practical terms, the risks are readily apparent. The person to whom the task is delegated may be able to outline broadly the procedure or test but may not know very much about the patient. Without adequate information regarding history, medications, desires, or needs, the substitute caregiver may not be able to provide accurate information regarding probable risks and benefits or reasonable treatment options. A boilerplate consent in this context will not suffice under either the patient need or medical community standards of disclosure.

Health care is an industry based on communication. In a consumer-oriented society, caregivers cannot afford to be without the fundamentals of good communication. The risks associated with delegating the task of speaking with the patient are so apparent that it is best for the caregiver to retain the function and to personally complete the consent process.

§1.14.3   Drug Manufacturers: The Limited Duty to Warn

The general rule of thumb is that the drug manufacturer has a duty to disclose risk information to the attending physician who, in turn, will use it to properly inform the patient.[2] In this sense, the doctor is viewed as a "learned intermediary" who can use the information from the drug company to decide on an appropriate course of treatment and secure thereby a valid consent.[3]

In recent years, the learned intermediary principle has begun to erode in the area of contraceptive medications. With the FDA insisting upon patient packet inserts from drug manufacturers, some courts have carved out an exception, ruling that the learned intermediary principle does not apply.[4]

The practical wisdom of this new line of legal thinking is open to considerable attack. Patients may not be able to comprehend pertinent information found in the patient packet insert. Placing the onus on the drug manufacturer detracts from the caregiver-patient relationship, diminishing the importance of, and possibly the opportunity for, discussion of probable

---

[2]See, e.g., Swayze v. McNeil Laboratories, Inc., 807 F.2d 464 (5th Cir. 1987); Felix v. Hoffman-LaRoche, Inc., 513 So. 2d 1319 (Fla. Dist. Ct. App. 1987).

[3]See references in note 2.

[4]See Wells v. Ortho Pharmaceutical Corp., 788 F.2d 741 (11th Cir. 1986); MacDonald v. Ortho Pharmaceutical Corp., 394 Mass. 131 (1985).

risks and benefits of contraceptive therapy. It remains to be seen whether the learned intermediary concept will be eroded beyond the contraceptive area. In the interim, caregivers would do well to continue their diligent efforts in securing accurate patient history information and disclosing pertinent drug therapy information. (For further discussion of these points regarding contraceptives, see §3.1.1 infra.)

§1.14.4   The Duty of the Health Facility

The great weight of case law in the field of consent holds that hospitals cannot be held responsible for obtaining patients' authorization for treatment.[5] Moreover, hospitals do not have an independent duty to advise patients of test results conducted at the order of the attending physician.[6] This principle follows from the traditional viewpoint that although the hospital owes an independent duty to its patients, this does not extend into the physician-patient relationship. The responsibility for obtaining consent rests with the attending physician: it is a matter within the realm of his responsibilities to the patient.

Only when a hospital knew or should have known that a doctor had not obtained a patient's consent,[7] or when a doctor acting as an agent of the hospital negligently secured a patient's consent,[8] will a hospital be held liable for inadequate consent procedures. When a hospital follows the policy of having a

[5] See, e.g., Pauscher v. Iowa Methodist Med. Center, 408 N.W.2d 355 (Iowa 1987); Krane v. Saint Anthony Hosp. Sys., 738 P.2d 75 (Colo. Ct. App. 1987); Baltzell v. Baptist Med. Center, 718 S.W.2d 140 (Mo. Ct. App. 1986); Wilson v. Lockwood, 711 S.W.2d 545 (Mo. Ct. App. 1986); Roberson v. Menorah Med. Center, 588 S.W.2d 134 (Mo. Ct. App. 1979); Cooper v. Curry, 92 N.M. 417, 589 P.2d 201 (1978); Garzione v. Vassar Bros. Hosp., 36 A.D.2d 390, 320 N.Y.S.2d 830 (1971).
[6] Alexander v. Gosner, 711 P.2d 347 (Wash. Ct. App. 1985). But see Campbell v. Pitt County Memorial Hosp., Inc., 352 S.E.2d 902 (N.C. Ct. App. 1987), finding hospital responsible under corporate liability for negligent consent.
[7] Fiorentio v. Wenger, 19 N.Y.2d 407, 280 N.Y.S.2d 373, 227 N.E.2d 296 (1967).
[8] See Shenefield v. Greenwich Hosp. Assn., 522 A.2d 829 (Conn. App. Ct. 1987).

nurse or ward clerk obtain patients' signatures on consent forms, it is quite probable that the institution would be put on notice of any deficiencies in the consent process. This would happen if it were standard practice to ask patients if they understand what is involved in procedures or if they have any questions. When patients indicate uncertainty or lack of understanding, or when they have questions, the consent document should not be signed. When an employee allows a patient to execute the form despite deficiencies in the disclosure of information, the hospital as the employer of the nurse or clerk may be held accountable in subsequent litigation. Of course, the patient involved would have to prove all the requisite elements of a consent action in order to prevail. It is possible, however, that in this instance the hospital could be held accountable.

The hospital may also be held responsible when a court takes the view that the institution's direct duty to its patients included making certain that an effective consent was obtained prior to initiating treatment. Whether the hospital's independent duty of care to patients will be extended to include matters of consent remains to be seen.

§1.14.5   *The Duty of the Dispensing Pharmacist*

As with other health care professionals, pharmacists have started taking a greater role in the treatment of patients. This is occurring within health facilities as well as in drug stores and pharmacies. The day is fast approaching when pharmacists will no longer simply dispense medication.

Part of this active role in patient care involves effective communication. For example, making certain that patients know when to take their medication, whether it should be taken with milk or other dairy products, or that the medication may cause a gastrointestinal upset.

It is commendable that pharmacists want to make certain that patients or customers are knowledgeable about the medications they use. However, does this enhanced role mean greater liability for pharmacists? More particularly, does it incur a duty to disclose risk-benefit information? If it does, and the pharmacist fails to meet applicable disclosure standards, will consent litigation follow?

Several cases have dealt with the pharmacist's duty to warn in the law of consent.[9] The general rule is that pharmacists do not owe such a duty to customers. Nonetheless, some of the cases on the topic are instructive and demonstrate the possibilities of consent liability for pharmacists in the future.

In one case the plaintiff claimed that the pharmacist knew the patient was prescribed and received massive doses of the drug placidyl.[10] The patient argued that the pharmacist knew that she was being overmedicated and that in combination with the other drugs she was taking this could cause an adverse reaction.

In rejecting the claim that the pharmacist is under a duty to warn, the court ruled that a druggist cannot be held accountable for correctly filling a prescription. Moreover, the druggist is under no obligation to warn the customer that she is being prescribed dangerous amounts of a drug. Similarly, the pharmacist is not obligated to warn the physician. As the court stated:

> It is the duty of the prescribing physician to know the characteristics of the drug he is prescribing, to know how much of the drug he can give the patient, to elicit from the patient what other drugs the patient is taking, to properly prescribe various combinations of drugs, to warn the patient of any dangers associated with taking the drug, to monitor the patient's dependence on the drug, and to tell the patient when and how to take the drug.[11]

[9]Jones v. Irvin, 602 F. Supp. 399 (S.D. Ill. 1985); Leesley v. West, 518 N.E.2d 758 (Ill. App. Ct. 1988); Maskripodis v. Merrell-Dow Pharmaceuticals, 523 A.2d 374 (Pa. Super. Ct. 1987); Raynor v. Richardson-Merrell, Inc., 643 F. Supp. 238 (D.D.C. 1986); Ramirez v. Richardson-Merrell, Inc., 628 F. Supp. 85 (E.D. Pa. 1986); Ingram v. Hook's Drugs, Inc., 476 N.E.2d 881 (Ind. Ct. App. 1985).
[10]Jones v. Irvin, supra note 9.
[11]Id. at 402.

The court reasoned that to transfer these duties to the pharmacist would make every druggist second guess every prescription in order to avoid liability.[12] Pharmacists were cautioned, however, that the court's decision was a narrow one and that it did not relieve pharmacists of their duty to act with prudence, thoughtfulness, and diligence in filling prescription drugs.[13]

In another case involving an injury to a man who had taken Valium, the court ruled that the pharmacist was not obliged to warn him of the possible side effects of the drug.[14] The plaintiffs attempted to use an Indiana State Board of Pharmacy regulation to establish a duty to warn. The regulation indicated that pharmacists were required to provide customers with directions for the use of dangerous or narcotic drugs, "as contained in the prescription."[15] Here, however, the doctor had not included any warnings.

The court rejected the defense claim that the regulation precluded pharmacists from providing their own warnings. However, the court did make it clear that there was no *statutory* duty for pharmacists to warn customers of all the possible hazards associated with prescription medication. Such an obligation was best reserved for physicians, who know the condition and history of their patients.[16]

Is it possible that a pharmacist could ever be held accountable? A New York court has suggested such liability could attach when the pharmacist knew the customer personally, knew that he was an alcoholic, and knew that the customer took prescribed drugs that the druggist knew were contraindicated in the presence of alcohol.[17] Given the specific facts in such a case, however, a duty to warn of possible side effects is understandable. Moreover, a strong case could be made for a duty to warn

---

[12] Id.
[13] Id. at 403, referring to Jones v. Walgreen, 265 Ill. App. 308 (1932).
[14] Ingram v. Hook's Drugs, Inc., supra note 9.
[15] Id. at 884, citing 865 I.A.C. 1-23-1, sec. 1(f).
[16] Id. at 885-887.
[17] Hand v. Krakowski, 89 A.D. 650, 453 N.Y.S.2d 121 (1982).

the patient *and the prescribing physician* when a pharmacist realizes that a customer is "double-doctoring" in order to obtain copious amounts of dangerous or narcotic drugs. The same could be true if the pharmacist failed to warn the patient or physician of inadequacies in the prescription.[18] The well-being of the community and the customer should override the tendency to remain silent.

The law is far from settled in this area. In part this is attributable to the changing role of the pharmacist from a mere dispenser of drugs to a valuable and informative member of the health care team. As pharmacists become more assertive and establish as customary practice the duty to inform, it is quite possible that the courts will be more receptive to recognizing a legal duty to warn. Future case law will tell the future on this as yet ill-defined legal duty.

D. ELEMENTS OF NEGLIGENT CONSENT LITIGATION

Although most states now recognize the concept of negligent consent, there is a lack of consistency regarding the standards to be employed for determining proper disclosure of information and causality. Some jurisdictions use a combination of a medical community standard of disclosure, which is based on what information physicians customarily reveal to patients, and a subjective standard of causality, based on what the patient would have wanted to know at the time consent was given for a procedure. Other states rely upon the patient need standard of disclosure and an objective standard of causality. In such circumstances the disclosure requirement is based on what a reasonable person in the patient's position would consider material

---

[18]See Riff v. Morgan Pharmacy, 508 A.2d 1247 (Pa. Super. Ct. 1986), in which the court entered judgment on a jury verdict involving a pharmacy's failure to warn the patient or to notify the doctor of inadequacies in the prescription involving the proper use of suppositories.

or significant in reaching an informed consent. The test of causality would be measured by what a reasonable person in the patient's position would have decided had the requisite information been disclosed. Other states have developed different combinations and variations of the disclosure and causality standards.

Neatly categorizing each of these combinations is difficult. Indeed, the use of "subjective" and "objective" labels for the different causality standards may prove dangerous. It is quite easy to lose sight of the original meaning of the terms when they are applied to a particular case. A better method is to think in terms of *how* the causality standard is measured. Is it from the standpoint of the individual patient or is it from the perspective of the reasonable person in the patient's position? This is the key factor.

This segment of the chapter examines the various criteria for negligent consent litigation. Various defenses are explained, along with the burden of proof and other evidentiary elements. As a preliminary consideration the impact of statutes of limitations is discussed.

§1.15   Basic Elements of a Negligent Consent Lawsuit

In some states the grounds for negligent consent actions are provided in legislation along with recognized defenses.[1] In other jurisdictions the criteria for consent actions and defense have been developed through case law.[2]

---

§1.15 [1]See, e.g., Alaska Stat. §09.55.556 (1976); Ark. Stat. Ann. §34-2614 (1979); Del. Code Ann. tit. 18, §6852 (1982); N.H. Rev. Stat. Ann. §507-C:2 (1977); Utah Code Ann. §78-14-5 (1976).

[2]See, e.g., Canterbury v. Spence, 464 F.2d 772 (D.C. Cir. 1972), cert. denied, 409 U.S. 1064 (1973); Cross v. Trapp, 294 S.E.2d 446 (W. Va. 1982); McPherson v. Ellis, 305 N.C. 266, 287 S.E.2d 892 (1982); Cobbs v. Grant, 8 Cal. 3d 229, 502 P.2d 1, 104 Cal. Rptr. 505 (1972); Wilkinson v. Vesey, 110 R.I. 606, 295 A.2d 676 (1972).

The idea of negligent consent follows the general principles of negligence law; however, the states differ over the proper standard or duty of disclosure that must be followed. They also differ on how causation should be assessed. To clarify this situation as much as possible, the following sections lay out the elements of a negligent consent lawsuit in a general way and then look at the effect of the various standards of disclosure and causation.

In order to establish negligent consent a plaintiff generally must prove the following:

1. That there existed a patient-physician relationship;
2. That the provider had a duty to disclose certain risk information;
3. That there was a failure to provide this information and that his or her failure to do so cannot be excused;
4. That, had the provider furnished the patient with the undisclosed information, the patient would not have consented to treatment; and
5. That the provider's failure to disclose this information was the proximate cause of the plaintiff's injury and damages claimed.[3]

Each of these elements must be proven in order to establish a case against a provider. The usual standard of proof for these matters is a preponderance of the evidence.[4]

§1.15.1 *Patient-Provider Relationship*

One method of interpreting the negligent consent requirements suggests that it is the fiduciary relationship between the patient and the health care provider that gives rise to the duty

---

[3] See generally Sard v. Hardy, 281 Md. 432, 379 A.2d 1014 (1977).
[4] Id. See also Alaska Stat. §09.55.556 (1976); Del. Code Ann. tit. 18, §6852 (1982).

to disclose adequate information.[5] A treatment relationship between the patient and the provider of services must exist before the duty to disclose arises. Only the attending physician or surgeon or the technician who is to carry out a procedure is responsible for obtaining the patient's consent. Being directly responsible for treatment or diagnostic testing is what creates accountability for the duty to disclose relevant information to the patient.

§1.15.2 Provider's Duty to Provide Risk Information

The duty to disclose certain information regarding risks arises either from what is customary practice or from what a reasonable person in the patient's position would want to know. Its extent depends upon the standard of disclosure that is applicable in a given state.

According to the medical community standard, physicians are obliged to disclose information that reasonable practitioners would divulge under like circumstances. This standard is sometimes referred to as information that is customarily given by other practitioners in the same or similar locality.[6] Additions or deletions to this customary practice standard may include the requirement that the customary practice involve practitioners with similar training.[7]

A different orientation is taken by the patient need standard. Those jurisdictions measure the duty of disclosure by what a reasonable patient would want to know or by the patient's

---

[5]Miller v. Kennedy, 11 Wash. App. 272, 522 P.2d 852 (1974), aff'd per curiam, 85 Wash. 2d 151, 530 P.2d 334 (1975). The relational test is sometimes cast in terms of a "sufficiently close" doctor-patient relationship. See, e.g., Kissinger v. Lofgren, 836 F.2d 678 (1st Cir. 1988), applying Massachusetts law.

[6]Troy v. Long Island Jewish-Hillside Med. Center, 86 A.D.2d 631, 446 N.Y.S.2d 347 (1982); Riedisser v. Nelson, 111 Ariz. 542, 534 P.2d 1952 (1975); Collins v. Itah, 160 Mont. 461, 503 P.2d 36 (1972). See also Neb. Rev. Stat. §44-2816 (1976); Tenn. Code Ann. §29-26-118 (1976); Vt. Stat. Ann. tit. 12, §1909 (1976).

[7]Ark. Stat. Ann. §34-2614 (1979); Del. Code Ann. tit. 18, §6852 (1982).

need.[8] There is no recourse to what other professionals do in similar circumstances. The patient need standard is based more on the model of the reasonable person found in traditional negligence theory.

Where states have opted for a standardized list of disclosure, problems can arise if specific risk information is not charted for discussion. For example, in Texas, the Medical Disclosure Panel had not made a determination whether risks associated with administration of Premarin warranted disclosure.[9] The plaintiff had been given the drug for a variety of problems. She had not been advised of the risk of drug-induced thrombophlebitis associated with the preparation. When she developed this complication, the plaintiff sued the defendant for, among other things, failing to inform her of the side effects linked to Premarin.

The Texas law in question indicates that absent a determination by the Medical Disclosure Panel, the doctor is obliged to reveal risks or hazards that could influence a reasonable person in giving consent to treatment.[10] This must be accomplished by expert testimony. In this case, the court determined that the risk of thrombophlebitis was a known side effect of the drug Premarin. Moreover, it concluded, this was the type of material risk that merited disclosure.

Caregivers must be careful not to gloss over administratively created categories of risks slated for disclosure. As seen in this Texas case, the fact that a risk had not yet been placed on the list of disclosure did not obviate the duty to reveal such information. Legislation such as this does not remove the need to exercise common sense and sound medical judgment.

A split of opinion divides the states regarding the need for expert testimony to establish the appropriate degree of disclo-

---

[8]McPherson v. Ellis, 305 N.C. 266, 287 S.E.2d 892 (1982); Scaria v. St. Paul Fire & Marine Ins. Co., 68 Wis. 2d 1, 227 N.W.2d 647 (1975); Cobbs v. Grant, 8 Cal. 3d 229, 502 P.2d, 104 Cal. Rptr. 505 (1972); Wilkinson v. Vesey, 110 R.I. 606, 295 A.2d 676 (1972).

[9]See Beal v. Hamilton, 712 S.W.2d 873 (Tex. Ct. App.-Houston 1986).

[10]Tex. Stat. Ann. art. 4590i, §6.07(b) (Vernon Supp. 1986), referred to in Beal v. Hamilton, supra note 9.

sure. However, it is generally believed that expert evidence is necessary where the medical community standard is used. (See discussion at §1.18, infra.)

§1.15.3   Inexcusable Failure of Provider to Disclose Risk Information

Facts must be set forth that prove the practitioner failed to give the patient risk information that should have been disclosed. Under the medical community standard this requires reference to what other providers generally reveal to patients, while the patient need standard focuses on material or significant information that the practitioner knew or should have known would be significant to a patient's decision. Furthermore, the failure of the practitioner to disclose this risk information cannot be excusable. If a recognized exception or defense is applicable, or the situation involves an emergency or a commonly known or remote risk, negligent consent cannot be established. An application of therapeutic privilege would also prevent such an establishment. Negligent consent must involve a circumstance in which the practitioner failed to meet the appropriate standard of disclosure *and* her failure to do so is not justifiable.

§1.15.4   Causation in Negligent Consent

The patient must be able to prove that had he been informed properly, consent to the procedure or treatment would not have been given. As with the standards for disclosure, there are different approaches to the criterion for causality. One point of view emphasizes the unfairness to practitioners involved in gauging what might have happened by what patients say they would have done had the risk information been disclosed. The patient-plaintiffs are thus placed in a unique position and allowed to state in court that, after all is said and done, in retrospect they would not have agreed to treatment. Patients cannot divorce their recreated decision process from hindsight. The same difficulty will trouble triers of fact. No one can be really certain that a patient would have withheld consent at the time if she had known the undisclosed facts. Moreover, if the patient should die as a result of the procedure, reliance upon such a test of causality as this would probably preclude recovery altogether.[11] Some courts, including the Supreme Court of Oregon,[12] nonetheless recognize such a causality standard.

The great preponderance of jurisdictions follows the reasonable person standard of causality,[13] which is perceived by many observers as a much more fair standard to both plaintiffs and defendants. This standard is based on what a reasonable person in the patient's position would have done had risk information been disclosed. What a reasonable person would agree to depends in large measure on the facts and surrounding circumstances of an individual case. The standard reflects the view that obtaining consent must be accomplished on a case-by-case basis, taking into account the peculiar needs and concerns of each patient. In a negligent consent case it is difficult to determine whether applying such a standard of causality is harder than using the test based on what individual patients claim would have been their decision regarding consent to treatment.

Not all would agree that the reasonable person causality standard strikes a fair balance between plaintiff and defendant. Indeed, it could be argued that such a standard affords too much protection to the defense. The standard suggests that

[11]Bowers v. Garfield, 382 F. Supp. 503, 506 (E.D. Pa. 1973), aff'd mem., 503 F.2d 1398 (3d Cir. 1974).
[12]Shelter v. Rochelle, 2 Ariz. App. 358, 409 P.2d 74 (1965); Arena v. Gingrich, 748 P.2d 547 (Or. 1988).
[13]See, e.g., Neb. Rev. Stat. §44-2820 (1976); N.Y. Pub. Health Law §2805-d (McKinney 1975); Utah Code Ann. §78-14-5 (1976); Wash. Rev. Code Ann. §7.70.050 (1975-1976); see also Pardy v. United States, 783 F.2d 710 (1986); Largey v. Rothman, 540 A.2d 504 (N.J. 1988); Phillips By and Through Phillips v. Hull, 516 So. 2d 488 (Miss. 1987); Latham v. Hayes, 495 So. 2d 453 (Miss. 1986); Leonard v. New Orleans East Orthopedic Clinic, 485 So. 2d 1008 (La. Ct. App. 1986) (citing this section of Consent to Treatment: A Practical Guide, 1st ed.); Adams v. El-Bash, 338 S.E.2d 381 (W. Va. 1985); Fain v. Smith, 479 So. 2d 1150 (Ala. 1985) (quoting a portion of this section of Consent to Treatment: A Practical Guide, 1st ed.).

juries cannot be trusted to see through a plaintiff's claim that is based on "twenty-twenty" hindsight. It fails to take into consideration that the triers of fact can look beyond the plaintiff's testimony to discern the truth of the matter.[14]

There is little doubt that the reasonable person standard of causality places a considerable burden on the plaintiff. Indeed, one can argue that it is an unfair judicial creation that takes away much of what was gained with the move toward the negligence theory of consent. It is impossible to predict if other courts will follow the lead of Oregon and adopt an "actual patient" standard. The best policy may be for health care professionals to set their sights on getting to know their patients and deciding from that perspective what the reasonable person *standing in that patient's shoes* would want to know in the same or similar circumstances.

Proving that a properly informed reasonable patient or plaintiff would not have agreed to treatment is a crucial element in a negligent consent case. State legislatures have recognized its significance and have passed legislation that creates a sound defense for the practitioner. If it can be shown that an injured patient assured the practitioner that he wanted the treatment regardless of the risk involved[15] or preferred not to be informed at the time,[16] the plaintiff's case would be destroyed. Similarly, if it can be demonstrated that a reasonable person would have consented to treatment, the plaintiff would not prevail.[17]

By enacting this form of legislation the states have provided practitioners with an added degree of protection on the matter of consent. However, the value of this legislative protection is lost if practitioners do not maintain documentation to support their defense on either theory of causality.

---

[14]See Arena v. Gingrich, 748 P.2d 547, 550 (Or. 1988).

[15]Alaska Stat. §09.55.556 (1976); Del. Code Ann. tit. 18, §6852 (1982); N.Y. Pub. Health Law §2805-d (McKinney 1975); Utah Code Ann. §78-14-5 (1976); Vt. Stat. Ann. tit. 12, §1909 (1976).

[16]See references in note 15.

[17]Fla. Stat. Ann. §768.46 (West 1975).

§1.15.5 Nondisclosure as Proximate Cause

Plaintiffs must establish a causal connection between the failure to disclose information and the injuries they suffer. A mere breach in the duty to reveal risk information is insufficient — unless actual harm followed from it.[18] Moreover, if disclosure of the information would not have altered the patient's decision to have treatment, no causal link is established.

It is here that the split among the states over the standard for proving causation is important. In the majority of states where causality rests on what a reasonable person in the patient's position would have done,[19] if such a person would have had the treatment even if informed, the plaintiff will fail. However, even in those states that follow the reasonable patient standard, evidence of what the individual patient would have done had she known the undisclosed facts may be important.[20]

In the few states where causation rests on what the actual plaintiff would have done had the practitioner disclosed the information, whether the trier of fact accepts the plaintiff's claim made from hindsight is an open question.[21] Jurors and judges are capable of discerning the truth in many matters. Based on the evidence, facts, and circumstances of a given case, it may be found that in fact a patient would *not* have altered the decision if he had known the undisclosed risk factors.

Instructing juries on the application of legal principles such as the "but for" test and proximate cause in a consent action must be done carefully. In some states this may be a matter of applying standardized jury instructions. In other states, the instructions are developed by the court. In a New York case[22] this point was made quite clear on appeal.

In that situation, the jury was asked to decide whether the lack of informed consent proximately caused the retrolental

---

[18] Martin v. Lowney, 517 N.E.2d 162 (Mass. 1988).
[19] Supra, n.13.
[20] See, e.g., Holt v. Nelson, 11 Wash. App. 230, 532 P.2d 211 (1974).
[21] Id.
[22] Flores v. Flushing Hosp. & Med. Center, 109 A.D.2d 198, 490 N.Y.S.2d 770 (1985).

fibroplasia (RLF) suffered by the plaintiff. In reversing the jury's verdict and remanding for a new trial, the court pointed out that lack of informed consent cannot cause physical harm. Rather, it is provision of the treatment based on inadequate disclosure that causes injury. However, for a group of jurors to attempt to apply the instruction in a literal fashion would be an impossible task. Therefore, the issue needed to be retried in the context of a proper understanding of proximate cause.[23]

§1.16   Defenses to Negligent Consent Litigation

In addition to those defenses that are recognized in negligence lawsuits, there are a number of specific defenses that have been created for consent cases. These defenses are largely the creation of legislation, although some have arisen from case law.

§1.16.1   Remote and Commonly Known Risks

According to many statutes and case law,[1] one defense to a negligent consent action centers on risks that are either commonly known or so remote that they did not warrant disclosure. The protection this defense offers, however, is limited by the difficulty in defining either of these characteristics. A commonly known risk is one of which most people with average experience are aware or associate with certain forms of treatment. The risk of serious harm or death that accompanies any surgery or the general dangers associated with anesthesia are

---

[23] Id.

§1.16 [1] See, e.g., Alaska Stat. §09.55.556 (1976); N.Y. Pub. Health Law §2805-d (McKinney 1975); Utah Code Ann. §78-14-5 (1976); Vt. Stat. Ann. tit. 12, §1909 (1976). See also Canterbury v. Spence, 464 F.2d 772 (D.C. Cir. 1972); Mroczkowski v. Straub Clinic & Hosp., Inc., 732 P.2d 1255 (Haw. Ct. App. 1987); Sard v. Hardy, 281 Md. 432, 379 A.2d 1014 (1977); Holt v. Nelson, 11 Wash. App. 230, 523 P.2d 211 (1974).

but two examples. Others could be established through evidence in court.

Another type of commonly known risk is one that, by virtue of her past experience,[2] a particular person appreciates. For example, patients who undergo hemodialysis three times a week do not need to be informed of the risks each and every time they report for treatment. Their previous experience with hemodialysis obviates the need to review this information during each visit. However, should the format for the dialysis change or a new procedure be introduced that changes the pattern of risks, patients must be told.

A defense relying on the definition of remote risks is more tenuous than one dependent on commonly known risks. A physician will not prevail if a so-called remote risk is proven significant in the case of a particular patient. The low risk of anesthetic injury in the general population, for example, may not pertain to a person with drug sensitivity. Physicians must satisfy themselves that their patients, on the basis of individual health, are faced with only remote risks[3] known to exist at the time that consent is obtained.[4] Whether or not a risk is remote should not be measured in hindsight. Rather, it must be assessed in the context of what was known to the patient and caregiver prior to the intended intervention. Such decisions rest on thorough examinations and histories and not on assumptions that any given patient is faced with the same degree of risk as another person.

Evidence plays an important role in the use of either the commonly known or remote risk defense. Both the plaintiff and the defendant must be prepared to produce testimony and other evidence. Plaintiffs are primarily concerned with rebuttal evidence disproving defendants' claims of applicability of either defense. Defendants, on the other hand, require ample proof to establish these defenses.

---

[2] Wilkinson v. Vesey, 110 R.I. 606, 295 A.2d 676, 689 (1972).
[3] Cobbs v. Grant, 8 Cal. 3d 224, 502 P.2d 1, 104 Cal. Rptr. 505 (1972).
[4] See Latham v. Hayes, 495 So. 2d 453 (Miss. 1986), dissenting opinion.

§1.16.2 Patient Acceptance of Treatment Regardless of Risk

If a patient agrees to treatment regardless of the risks or specifically tells the practitioner that he does not wish to be informed, a subsequent consent action will not prevail. The soundness of such a defense has been recognized in case law and legislation.[5]

When a patient accepts treatment in either of the above circumstances, some type of documentation is necessary, particularly for defensive purposes. The documentation may be a detailed note in the patient's health record that indicates that the patient decided to have treatment regardless of the risks and that she was both legally and mentally capable of making such a choice. A similar policy could be followed if the patient decides not to be informed of the risks.

The documentation can also take the form of a consent document that specifically indicates that:

1. The patient is capable of giving consent;
2. That he or she has been told of the existence of risks associated with the proposed diagnostic test or medical or surgical care; and
3. That he or she has either specifically agreed to it regardless of the risks involved or has specifically asked not to be informed of these risks.

In addition to such documentation, it may be advisable in certain situations to require, as a matter of policy, that patients be informed of risk information. If a patient then refuses to be informed, the procedure should not be carried out. This plan of action is particularly advisable for medical or surgical interventions that carry a significant likelihood of injury or death. It affords protection from subsequent claims that no reasonable

[5]See, e.g., Sard v. Hardy, 281 Md. 432, 379 A.2d 1014 (1977); Holt v. Nelson, 11 Wash. App. 230, 523 P.2d 211 (1974). See also Alaska Stat. §09.55.556 (1976); Del. Code Ann. tit. 18, §6852 (1982); N.Y. Pub. Health Law §2805-d (McKinney 1975); Utah Code Ann. §78-14-5 (1976).

person would have agreed to treatment accompanied by such serious risks. New or innovative procedures should also be handled in this fashion.

Another defensive tactic involves the use of witnesses to patients' consents. These individuals would not verify the execution of a consent form but rather the patients' consent process in which they state that they do not wish to be informed or that they agree to the proposed test or treatment regardless of the risks.

Regardless of the defensive measures selected by a health facility or a practitioner, it is important to make certain that adequate proof of the patient's consent is available. Relying on a patient's verbal agreement or signature on a general or standardized consent form may be insufficient; the documentation should be thorough enough to stand alone as proof to persuade the trier of fact.

§1.16.3 Medical Emergencies

An exception to the general rules of consent, a medical emergency may also serve as a valid defense (see chapter 2 for greater detail). Its reliability has been recognized in some legislation and to a greater extent in case law.[6] In order to invoke the defense, a practitioner must be able to establish (a) that the patient was incapable of giving consent, and (b) that he was suffering from a life- or health-threatening event that required prompt attention.[7] Some states go further and add as a requirement the impossibility or impracticality of obtaining the consent of someone who could act on behalf of the patient.[8]

---

[6]Ky. Rev. Stat. §304.40-320 (1976) (no requirement to obtain consent); Pa. Stat. Ann. tit. 40, §1301.103 (Purdon 1976) (no liability attaches in an emergency when consent cannot be obtained). See also Sard v. Hardy, 281 Md. 432, 379 A.2d 1014 (1977); Holt v. Nelson, 11 Wash. App. 231, 523 P.2d 211 (1974).

[7]See, e.g., Chambers v. Nottebaum, 96 So. 2d 716 (Fla. Dist. Ct. App. 1957); Mohr v. Williams, 95 Minn. 261, 104 N.W. 12, 15 (1905).

[8]See, e.g., Ga. Code §88-2905 (1971).

It is important to keep in mind that *all* the criteria must be present to invoke the emergency exception. It is not enough that a patient is suffering from a life-threatening illness; she must also be unable to understand or appreciate the nature and consequences of a decision regarding care. The emergency exception is unavailable as a defense to treatment in the face of a valid refusal of care by the patient.

§1.16.4 Justifiable Withholding of Information

A practitioner may rely upon yet another exception to the general rules for consent: the exception that permits a practitioner to withhold certain details if such a disclosure would likely have an adverse effect on the patient's health or well-being. This principle is recognized in both case law[9] and in some legislation.[10] In order to use this defense, the practitioner must document that the information, if revealed, would have had a substantially adverse impact on the patient's condition[11] or physical or mental well-being.[12] This exception is often referred to as a "therapeutic privilege."

Substantiation of the use of therapeutic privilege, if challenged in court, cannot be achieved entirely by the practitioner's testimony. Documentation written at the time is necessary to support the decision to withhold information. This evidence, in the form of a detailed note in the patient's health record, should indicate:

1. The practitioner's observations of the patient;
2. The reasons why he or she believes certain details should be withheld;

[9]Woolley v. Henderson, 418 A.2d 1123 (Me. 1980); Sard v. Hardy, 281 Md. 432, 379 A.2d 1014 (1977); Canterbury v. Spence, 464 F.2d 772 (D.C. Cir. 1972).
[10]Del. Code Ann. tit. 18, §6852 (1982); N.Y. Pub. Health Law §2508-d (McKinney 1975); Pa. Stat. Ann. tit. 40, §1301.103 (Purdon 1976); Utah Code Ann. §78-14-5 (1976).
[11]Alaska Stat. §09.55.546 (1976).
[12]Sard v. Hardy, 281 Md. 432, 379 A.2d 1014 (1977).

3. The information that was not disclosed;
4. A summary of the medical findings that the practitioner has used to justify the use of therapeutic privilege; and
5. The details that were disclosed to the patient.

In cases in which a practitioner believes the use of therapeutic privilege may be questionable or is uncertain about its use, sound policy dictates obtaining a consultation. This second opinion may come from another physician or a concerned family member of the patient who has demonstrated an interest in the patient's well-being. Relatives of the patient cannot authorize the use of the privilege, but discussion with them may help to determine the value of withholding certain details from the patient. If the consultation results in concurrence, this fact should be added to the detailed note: it may become an important factor in any subsequent consent litigation based on the patient's authorization for treatment.

Therapeutic privilege cannot be used as a defense for wrongfully withholding important information from a patient. A practitioner cannot provide selective information in order to secure a patient's consent to treatment. The disclosure of information must include, depending upon the applicable standard, pertinent information that the patient needs to know or that it is customary to reveal.

§1.16.5 Signed Consent Forms

In some states the weight given to a signed consent form is substantial. If all the criteria for consent are met, the signed document creates a conclusive presumption that the consent thus obtained is valid.[13] A number of these states have enacted legislation that recognizes this principle. Even if a state does not

[13]Tex. Civil Stat. Ann. art. 4590i (Purdon 1979); Utah Code Ann. §78-14-5 (1976); Wash. Rev. Code Ann. §7.70.060 (1975-1976); Hondroulis v. Schuhmacher, 531 So. 2d 450 (La. 1988); Hutton v. Craighead, 530 So. 2d 101 (La. Ct. App. 1988).

recognize a consent document as creating a conclusive presumption of validity, it may serve as part of the defense in a consent action.[14]

The value of a consent document, however, should not be overestimated. Even where the document carries conclusive weight it is but one piece of evidence in a lawsuit. Its value may be diminished by the provision for rebuttal and presentation of other documentary and verbal evidence. The defense may be overcome by proof of misrepresentation, omission of a material fact in obtaining the patient's consent,[15] a lack of good faith,[16] malice[17] on the part of the person obtaining the patient's consent, or an inability on the part of the patient to communicate in the language in which the consent was written.[18]

The plaintiff has the responsibility to present evidence to overcome the presumption of validity. This proof usually takes the form of a preponderance of the evidence,[19] though establishing a misrepresentation of a material fact is a difficult task, as is demonstrating malice or a lack of good faith. A failure to communicate in a language understandable to the patient is a much easier issue on which to base a case.

In the absence of specific legislation on consent forms, the rules of procedure and evidence in a particular jurisdiction will be dispositive of the significance attached to these forms. The rules and bylaws of a particular hospital may also come into play. For example, in an Illinois case the bylaws of a hospital required the medical staff to adopt specific written consent forms for surgery. This was never done. In a negligent consent lawsuit the plaintiff argued that the doctor's failure to abide by the bylaw concerning written consent constituted negligence.

[14]Ohio Rev. Code Ann. §2317.54 (Baldwin 1977); Wash. Rev. Code Ann. §7.70.060 (1975-1976).
[15]Utah Code Ann. §78-14-5 (1976).
[16]Ohio Rev. Code Ann. §2317.54 (Baldwin 1977).
[17]Idaho Code §39-4305 (1975).
[18]Ohio Rev. Code Ann. §2317.54 (Baldwin 1977).
[19]Ohio Rev. Code Ann. §2317.54 (Baldwin 1977); Wash. Rev. Code Ann. §7.70.060 (1975-1976). Cf. Idaho Code §39-4305 (1975) (requires convincing proof); Utah Code Ann. §78-14-5 (1976) (clear and convincing proof is required).

The appeal court disagreed, suggesting that the doctor was not negligent because the medical staff had failed to adopt specific consent forms as mandated by the bylaws.[20]

It should also be pointed out that the documentation of consent in other formats may be quite valuable in litigation. Detailed notes in a patient's health record are a good choice, particularly ones that outline the nature, risks, and benefits of the proposed treatment, the reasonable alternatives to it, and the consequences of foregoing all care. In addition, notations should be made of any questions the patient had on the matter and the answers given. Combined with evidence of a patient's capacity to give consent, the detailed note may prove very useful for the defense.

§1.16.6   Other Available Defenses

In addition to the defenses outlined above, there are a number of other defenses that can be interposed on behalf of the defendant. These include the traditional defenses available in a negligence action: proof of compliance with appropriate standards of disclosure, proof that the harm to the patient was not reasonably foreseeable, proof of a supervening tortfeasor, and the absence of harm are just a few examples. Recognized defenses vary among the states, and proper preparation for counsel of either party in a consent case involves detailed knowledge of negligence law for that jurisdiction.

§1.17   Statutes of Limitation in Consent Actions

Another important consideration in consent litigation is statutes of limitation. Neither the defense nor the plaintiff can afford to ignore this issue: by it a case can be made or broken.

[20]Sheahan v. Dexter, 136 Ill. App. 3d 241, 91 Ill. Dec. 120, 483 N.E.2d 402 (1985).

The period in which litigation may be brought for consent matters is generally covered under the heading of malpractice actions in state legislation.[1] However, some state statutes specifically refer to consent actions in laws relating to limitation periods.[2] Plaintiff's counsel should not fail to find out the exact time frame in which litigation may be filed.

A decision to litigate on the basis of battery as opposed to negligent consent may have serious ramifications if state law has a separate statute of limitations for each theory of consent.[3] Legislative enactments vary from state to state, with some jurisdictions following a modified discovery rule period.[4] In some situations the tolling of statutes is permitted when the plaintiff is under a disability.[5] Moreover, some limitation periods may be extended when there has been knowing concealment[6] or a patient has a foreign object left in his body as the result of medical treatment.[7] These extension periods may be quite helpful for the clients, particularly minors, on whom the degree of harm inflicted may not be well known for a period of time.

Defendants find limitation periods important for two reasons. First, they are a factor in determining retention periods for patient health records. Included in these records is documentation of a patient's authorization to treatment. Health record administrators or other personnel who dispose of health

§1.17   [1]See, e.g., Calif. Civ. Proc. Code §340.5 (West 1975); Ga. Code §3-1101 (1976); Iowa Code Ann. §614.1 (West 1986); Miss. Code Ann. §15-1-36 (1983). See also Lambert v. Stovell, 529 A.2d 710 (Conn. 1987).

[2]Colo. Rev. Stat. §13-80-105 (1977); Haw. Rev. Stat. §657-7.3 (1977); Mont. Rev. Code Ann. §27-2-205 (1973).

[3]Lipscomb v. Memorial Hosp., 733 F.2d 332 (4th Cir. 1984).

[4]See, e.g., Ala. Code §6-5-482 (1975), which is typical of legislation in many states. It places a limit on the time of discovery of injury permitted under the law.

[5]See, e.g., Mo. Ann. Stat. §516.105 (Vernon 1976); Ohio Rev. Code Ann. §2305.11 (Baldwin 1987); Okla. Stat. Ann. tit. 76, §18 (West 1976); R.I. Gen. Laws §9-1-14.1 (1988).

[6]Calif. Civ. Proc. Code §340.5 (West 1975); Colo. Rev. Stat. §13-80-105 (1977); Idaho Code §5-219 (1971); Mont. Code Ann. §27-2-205 (1973); Wis. Stat. Ann. §893.55 (West 1980).

[7]Idaho Code §5-219 (1971); Iowa Code Ann. §614.1 (West 1986); Mo. Ann. Stat. §516.105 (Vernon 1976); N.Y. Civ. Prac. Law §214-a (McKinney 1986); S.C. Code §15-3-545 (1977).

record information and consent documentation before a limitation period has elapsed could severely damage or frustrate their case. Another possible result is the inducing of an otherwise unnecessary settlement. The limitations period should obviously serve as a guide in setting a policy for the destruction of such information.

Second, if a patient launches an action after the period for suit has expired, the physician or health facility may raise the matter as a defense. This tactic serves as a sound defensive move — unless one of the exceptions applies that allow the period of actions to be extended.

The limitations issue should be raised at an initial stage of proceedings to limit the time and expense involved in preparing for a full trial. Where there is a question of application regarding a statute of limitation, a separate proceeding or motion could perhaps be argued. Thus an allegation of fraudulent concealment or of disability of the plaintiff tolling the statute could be overcome if the court finds that the exceptions are inapplicable and the period of actions has expired.

California has recognized the utility of disposing of these matters separately.[8] State law provides for a separate trial on matters relating to the statute of limitations. If these are resolved in favor of the plaintiff, trial then proceeds on the remaining issues.[9] The wisdom of such a procedure lies in the curtailing of costs and the reduction of otherwise extensive preparation time.

§1.18 Expert Testimony in Consent Litigation

Another source of distinction among the states is the need for expert testimony in consent litigation, which has become the subject of statutory law and case decisions.[1] Regardless of these

[8] Cal. Civ. Proc. Code §597.5 (West 1979).
[9] Id.
§1.18 [1] See, e.g., N.H. Rev. Stat. Ann. §507-C:3 (1977); Tenn. Code Ann. §29-26-115 (1980). See also Folger v. Corbett, 118 N.H. 737, 394 A.2d 63 (1978); Luna v. Nering, 426 F.2d 95 (5th Cir. 1970) (applying Texas law).

differences, even those states that do not require experts allow room for these witnesses to provide evidence on risk factors.[2] In other jurisdictions, expert testimony may be necessary to establish the existence of risks.[3]

§1.18.1 Where Expert Testimony Is Required

In consent litigation in most jurisdictions, it is incumbent upon the plaintiff to produce expert testimony on the appropriate standard of disclosure. That standard, in many states, is measured by what it is customary to disclose or what reasonable physicians would reveal to their patients.[4] The theory behind this rule assumes that only a qualified physician can inform the court concerning the usual degree of information given to a patient in the same or similar circumstances. Relying solely on what a patient believes the physician disclosed is felt to place the defendant in an unfair position.

This principle would exclude testimony from a nurse regarding what her employer usually explained about the nature of proposed surgery and the attendant risks. Permitting a nurse to testify about the doctor's standard procedure could be construed by a jury as an implied opinion that the information conveyed was accurate and adequate. This would be an impermissible practice.[5] By the same token, a nurse who ran a consulting firm and who did not participate in an invasive pro-

---

[2] Wilkinson v. Vesey, 110 R.I. 606, 295 A.2d 676 (1972).

[3] See Jocza v. Hottenstein, 528 A.2d 606 (Pa. Super. Ct. 1987), in which the court suggested that the expert witness must establish the nature of the risk, but it is up to the trier of fact to determine the materiality of the harm and whether a reasonable person would want to consider it in deciding upon medical care.

[4] See, e.g., Weekly v. Solomon, 510 N.E.2d 152 (Ill. App. Ct. 1987); Stallings v. Ratliff, 356 S.E.2d 414 (S.C. Ct. App. 1987).

[5] Rogers v. Lu, 485 A.2d 54 (Pa. Super. Ct. 1984). See also Gaskin v. Booth, 437 So. 2d 580 (Ala. Civ. App. 1983), in which the court excluded testimony of physician's receptionist regarding his routine practice of informing patients of possible complications associated with the proposed procedure. In this case the defendant failed to meet evidentiary requirements for admissibility of testimony on habit or routine practice.

cedure was precluded from testifying as an expert witness in the area of consent. As the court put it, the nurse was not an expert on the disclosure of risks.[6]

Failure to produce expert testimony when it is necessary to establish the appropriate standard of disclosure can preclude a plaintiff from winning a case.[7] In jurisdictions that subscribe to the medical community rule of disclosure, therefore, plaintiff's counsel must make every effort to secure qualified and respected experts to testify.

In some states, legislation limits who may appear as an expert witness.[8] For example, in Delaware no one may appear as an expert witness unless he is familiar with the degree of ordinary skill used in the community or locality where the alleged incident occurred.[9] In addition, other conditions may pertain to the calling of a physician as an expert witness.[10]

Beyond such legislative requirements there are other considerations. The strength of the physician as an "expert" is assessed not only by credentials but also by such trial tactics as appearance in court, ability to withstand cross-examination, and credibility as an expert. These considerations cannot be ignored by counsel.

§1.18.2   Where Expert Testimony Is Not Required

The patient need standard measures disclosure by what a reasonable person in the patient's position would want to know. It obviates the necessity of expert testimony. What a patient would like to be told in a given situation thus has greater import in states that apply this standard than in the majority of states.[11]

---

[6]See Wilson v. Lockwood, 711 S.W.2d 545 (Mo. Ct. App. 1986).
[7]See German v. Nichopoulos, 577 S.W.2d 197 (Tenn. Ct. App. 1978); Niccoli v. Thompson, 713 S.W.2d 579 (Mo. Ct. App. 1986); Conrod v. Imatani, 724 P.2d 89 (Colo. Ct. App. 1986).
[8]Del. Code Ann. tit. 18, §6854 (1982).
[9]Id.
[10]Years of actual practice and location of practice may be conditions imposed by legislation. See Del. Code Ann. tit. 18, §6854 (1982).
[11]Sard v. Hardy, 281 Md. 432, 379 A.2d 1014 (1977); Wilkinson v. Vesey, 110 R.I. 606, 295 A.2d 676 (1972).

It is still the responsibility of plaintiffs, though, to prove that undisclosed information was material to their decision to undergo treatment. Juries will hear their evidence along with that of defendants; the issue then becomes a matter of credibility and belief. A jury may find, for example, that what the plaintiff thinks was said is different from what the evidence actually revealed. The standard thus places considerable responsibility upon the trier of fact.

As noted earlier, the fact that the patient need standard does not require expert testimony does not preclude it. Experts may be called by the defendant to establish the community standard of disclosure, if one exists in a particular instance.[12] Expert testimony may also be necessary to provide information regarding known risk factors in the procedure in issue.[13] Another way of stating it is that expert testimony is necessary to prove the materiality of specific factual matters.[14] However, once materiality is established, the value of expert testimony takes on secondary importance.[15]

A jury may be able to reach a decision about the disclosure of information without recourse to an external standard of medical practice. However, if a physician, as defendant, provides testimony on the standard of disclosure common among her colleagues, the plaintiff must be prepared to counter such evidence. A great deal of credibility could be attached to such professional medical testimony.

§1.19 Burden of Proof in Consent Actions

As in other actions based on negligence, plaintiffs carry the burden of proving that defendants did not discharge their duty of disclosure in accordance with acceptable standards. They

[12] Wilkinson v. Vesey, supra n.11.
[13] Id. See also Sagala v. Tavares, 533 A.2d 165 (Pa. Super. Ct. 1987); Jocza v. Hottenstein, 528 A.2d 606 (Pa. Super. Ct. 1987).
[14] Brown v. Dahl, 41 Wash. App. 565, 705 P.2d 1781 (1985).
[15] Id.

must also prove that their consent to treatment was uninformed and that, had they been informed, they would not have agreed to treatment.[1]

A plaintiff's responsibility in establishing a claim based on negligent consent does not end with proof of a departure from the appropriate standard of disclosure. The plaintiff must make out a prima facie case of negligence, including such considerations as proof of a legal relationship with the defendant, the duty that is applicable in the situation, a departure from it, proximate cause, and resulting injury.[2] These responsibilities have been set forth in legislation and case law.[3] Sometimes additional criteria are added to the burden of proof, most notably proof that treatment was provided in the absence of an emergency.[4]

A plaintiff must establish his case in light of the prevailing standard of proof. Most states follow the practice of proving a case by the preponderance of evidence.[5] There are some exceptions, as when a consent document is challenged on the grounds of fraud or misrepresentation of a material fact.[6] In these instances it may be necessary to establish clear and convincing evidence of an allegation.

A defendant also bears responsibility in terms of the burden of proof. Once the plaintiff establishes his prima facie case and demonstrates a departure from the applicable standard of disclosure, the defendant must counter this evidence. The burden of the defendant involves coming forward with evidence that justifies her failure to disclose information.[7] Phrased differ-

---

§1.19 [1]See, e.g., Garst v. Cullum, 726 S.W.2d 271 (Ark. 1987); Harrigan v. United States, 408 F. Supp. 177 (E.D. Pa. 1976); Funke v. Fieldman, 212 Kan. 606, 512 P.2d 539 (1973).
[2]Utah Code Ann. §78-14-5 (1976).
[3]Ark. Stat. Ann. §34-2614 (1979), N.H. Rev. Stat. Ann. §507-C:2 (1977); Tenn. Code Ann. §29-26-118 (1976); Vt. Stat. Ann. tit. 12, §§1908 to 1909 (1976). See also People v. Sargent, 77 Wis. 2d 612, 253 N.W.2d 459 (1977); Short v. Downs, 537 P.2d 754 (Colo. Ct. App. 1975).
[4]Ark. Stat. Ann. §34-2614 (1979); N.H. Rev. Stat. Ann. §507-C:2 (1977).
[5]Alaska Stat. §09.55.556 (1976).
[6]§1.16.5 supra. See also Rook v. Trout, 747 P.2d 61 (Idaho 1987).
[7]People v. Sargent, 77 Wis. 2d 612, 253 N.W.2d 459 (1977); Short v. Downs, 36 Colo. App. 109, 537 P.2d 754 (1975).

ently, the plaintiff carries the burden of establishing nondisclosure, as well as other elements of a negligence action. The defendant must then be able to prove that her failure to disclose information was in conformity with applicable standards.

Part of the process of justifying nondisclosure or proving that failure to reveal information was consistent with applicable standards is reviewing acceptable defenses. These generally include:

1. The risks involved were either remote or commonly known and therefore did not require disclosure;
2. Evidence that the patient authorized treatment regardless of the risks or that he or she did not wish to know such information;
3. A judgment on the part of the defendant that the disclosure of the information would have had an adverse effect on the patient's condition;[8]
4. Proof that the patient knew of the risks inherent in the procedure;
5. Proof (in some jurisdictions) that a reasonable person in the patient's position would have undergone treatment had he or she been properly informed;[9]
6. Proof that the patient was in an emergency situation that obviated the need for consent;[10]
7. Proof (in many states) that it is not customary practice among physicians in the same or similar circumstances to reveal the undisclosed information;[11] and
8. Alternatively, that the undisclosed information was not significant or material to the patient's decision.

The specific defenses available for consent actions vary from state to state. Counsel must review the situation in the specific jurisdiction to determine which defenses are recognized. It is

[8] Alaska Stat. §09.55.556 (1976); Utah Code Ann. §78-14-5 (1976).
[9] Vt. Stat. Ann. tit. 12, §1909 (1976).
[10] Pa. Stat. Ann. tit. 40, §1301.103 (Purdon 1976).
[11] Fla. Stat. Ann. §768.46 (West 1975).

also important to review trial and evidentiary requirements to ascertain exactly on which matters each party carries the burden of proof.

§1.20 Litigation Checklist for Consent Actions

There are many considerations that must be addressed in any lawsuit, but a case in the consent field involves particular concerns that must be taken into account. Plaintiffs, defense counsel, would-be defendants such as physicians and health facilities — all interested parties are affected by these factors. The following is a checklist of some of the more important considerations for all concerned.

1. A cause of action:
   a. Are all the elements for litigation present?
   b. What are the available defenses?
   c. Can the actions of the defendant be justified?
2. Application of the statute of limitations:
   a. Is the incident within the limitations period?
   b. Can it be tolled for any recognized reason?
3. Filing a cause of action:
   a. Do the pleadings meet procedural requirements?
   b. Are all the relevant parties specified in the complaint? Should others be joined in the case?
   c. Is there a basis for arguing that the complaint fails to state a cause of action? For arguing for summary judgment?
4. The discovery period:
   a. Has all relevant documentation been obtained?
   b. Is there anything in the medical record on the consent process other than the consent form?
   c. Have you been sure to request the entire medical record, not a summary discharge sheet?
5. The trial stage:
   a. In medical community standard jurisdictions, does the

plaintiff have authoritative testimony on the standard of disclosure? Does the defendant?

b. In patient need standard states, can the plaintiff prove that the information that was not disclosed was significant or material to his or her consent?

c. Can the failure of the defendant to disclose information be justified — for example, by the need for emergency treatment, a plaintiff's asking not to be informed, or the involvement of remote or commonly known risks?

d. In those states that do not require expert testimony, should the defendant nonetheless introduce expert evidence? Would it be of help to the jury to know what is the customary practice of disclosure in such circumstances?

e. In those states that base causality on what the patient would have done had he or she been informed, is the patient's testimony credible? Can defense counsel successfully attack the plaintiff's testimony?

f. Is there sufficient proof of causality?

g. Are the court's instructions to the jury consistent with consent requirements in the state?

h. If the court refuses to instruct the jury as requested, has an objection been raised and has it been noted in the record for appeal purposes?

6. The appeal process:

a. Was the jury instructed properly?[1] If not, are there grounds for an appeal?

b. Was evidence admitted that should not have been presented to the jury? If so, is it a basis for appeal?

c. Did the trial court follow applicable standards for disclosure and causality? If not, are there sufficient grounds for appeal?

---

§1.20 [1]Madsen v. Park Nicollet Med. Center, 419 N.W.2d 511 (Minn. Ct. App. 1988).

TWO

Exceptions to the Rules

§2.0 Overview
A. When Consent Is Not Necessary
  §2.1 A "Process" Approach to Consent
    §2.1.1 Flow Chart of General Consent Elements
    §2.1.2 Flow Charts of Consent When Exceptions Apply
    §2.1.3 Communication and History in Exceptional Cases
  §2.2 Medical Emergencies
    §2.2.1 Definition of a Medical Emergency
    §2.2.2 Declaration of Situations as Emergencies
    §2.2.3 Scope of Authorized Emergency Care
    §2.2.4 Policy Considerations and Emergency Care
  §2.3 Treatment When Consent Is Not Possible
  §2.4 Use of Therapeutic Privilege
    §2.4.1 Justifiable Use of Therapeutic Privilege
    §2.4.2 Unjustifiable Use of Therapeutic Privilege
    §2.4.3 Documentation and Therapeutic Privilege
  §2.5 Compulsory Treatment and the Need for Consent
  §2.6 Duty of Third-Party Disclosure
    §2.6.1 Duty to Warn Others of Potential Harm
    §2.6.2 Duty to Provide Notification of Treatment
    §2.6.3 Times When Disclosure Is Not Permissible
B. Problem Cases
  §2.7 Patients' Requests Not to Be Informed
    §2.7.1 Implications of Uninformed Consent
    §2.7.2 Documentation of the Request
  §2.8 Patients Undergoing Repetitive or Continuous Treatment
  §2.9 Placebo, Deception, and Consent
    §2.9.1 Placebo, Deception, and Clinical Treatment
    §2.9.2 Placebo, Deception, and Human Research
    §2.9.3 Policy Considerations

§2.0   Overview

There are certain instances in which the rules for consent do not apply, situations in which treatment may be given without a patient's consent. The authority for these exceptional circumstances rests on case law and legislation. Their scope is quite limited, obliging practitioners to consider carefully before giving treatment without authorization.

In health services there are also a number of problem situations that obviate the need for disclosure of information to the patient. Examples include the disabling and incapacitating of patients as well as patients' decisions not to be informed. The use of therapeutic privilege, the requirement to administer compulsory treatment, and the duty to disclose information to third parties are areas of concern in which general consent rules do not apply. Each of these topics is addressed in this chapter, along with a discussion of such matters as consent in the context of repetitive procedures and the use of placebo and deception.

A.   WHEN CONSENT IS NOT NECESSARY

§2.1   A "Process" Approach to Consent

Consent can be viewed as a process (figure 1) that contains a number of important elements, including: (1) illness or injury; (2) development of a treatment relationship; (3) history taking and examination; (4) treatment or test recommendation; (5) disclosure of pertinent information; (6) exchange of questions and answers; and (7) agreement on what is to be done.

As seen in this section, the cut-and-dried steps of the consent process are often disregarded in medicolegal emergencies, when it is impossible to complete the process; when therapeutic privilege is invoked; and in compulsory treatment situations. However, even in these circumstances, some aspects of the consent process remain vital to quality patient care.

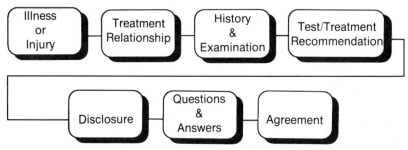

Figure One. The Consent Process for Routine Care

§2.1.1 Flow Chart of General Consent Elements

The consent process entails a number of elements. First, the patient must be sufficiently ill or injured to seek out treatment. In routine situations, this leads to a caregiver-patient relationship. While this second step does not always go smoothly, it is an important aspect of consent.

The consent process continues with the caregiver obtaining a detailed history from the patient of such matters as previous illnesses or surgeries and current medications. A thorough history will involve a series of questions about the onset of symptoms or cause of injury. The caregiver should inquire about current medical conditions as well as drug allergies, sensitivities, and intolerances.

The patient history is not enough. Proper treatment will involve a careful examination of the patient, too. A good physical is essential when the patient is injured. It may be just as valuable when the patient has palpable lumps suggestive of cancerous tumors.

Based on the information provided by the patient and the physical examination, the caregiver should be able to recommend either tests or treatment. This fourth step is important since it serves as the springboard for the most difficult aspect of the consent process: disclosure of pertinent information.

As seen in chapter 1, the standards for disclosure vary from the medical community standard of information imparted to patients to the patient need standard, which is based on what a reasonable person would want to know. Disclosure under the patient need standard turns upon what is deemed material or significant information.

Caregivers must know which disclosure standard is followed in the state. Never assume that the standard followed in Illinois will "cover" the actions of the doctor who subsequently sets up practice in Texas or Alaska.

Disclosure assumes that the caregiver will use terminology that the patient can understand. It also assumes that the delivery of information will not be in a vacuum, but will be sensitive to the needs of the patient and that the disclosure will be couched in terms of the patient's situation. For example:

1. In recommending a lumpectomy for a 74-year-old woman with suspected breast cancer, the surgeon should be sensitive to the needs of the patient. Must the surgery be performed immediately or could it be delayed three days to permit the patient to attend her grandson's wedding?

2. A Mexican immigrant requires a CT Scan to determine if his left-side weakness is attributable to a brain tumor. The man speaks English with a very heavy accent. The doctor who wants the diagnostic test does not speak Spanish. Although she gives the patient the usual information, she is concerned about the man's ability to understand the test and to convey information about his previous medical history. Would it not be better to defer the test until a translator can be located to assist the caregiver and the patient?

3. A 24-year-old single woman requires extensive surgery and orthodontic work for TMJ and a severe overbite. She is without any health care plan and is not eligible for Medicaid. The woman is the sole support for three minor children and she works as a waitress. What information should be given to the patient? Should she not be told that the surgery could be performed at a university hospital teaching clinic at a much reduced price?

The answers in each example are self-evident: stock disclosure is inadequate. A good consent process is marked by information presented in the context of the patient's needs, desires, and overall circumstances.

The next step in the normal consent process involves an exchange of questions and answers. This important step should not be glossed over by caregivers. Questions posed by patients may signal a lack of understanding of the proposed intervention or reveal a high level of anxiety or confusion. In either instance, questions suggest that the consent process is incomplete and that it may be necessary to retrace certain steps in the process to secure a valid authorization for treatment.

Answers must be clear and frank. Except in those situations noted later in the chapter dealing with therapeutic privilege, caregivers should never hold back information. The fact that answers may provoke tears, anger, or embarrassment should not be used as an excuse for refraining from candid responses.

Once the steps of the routine consent are complete, the caregiver and patient reach an agreement on what is to be done. This is the real culmination of the successful consent process, not the form or document used to record the transaction.

§2.1.2 Flow Charts of Consent When Exceptions Apply

Health care is marked by many exceptions. Emergencies, compulsory treatment, and therapeutic privilege cases are but a few broad categories in which caregivers often find themselves working with consent issues.

As the accompanying illustrations suggest (figures 2 and 3), consent in exceptional cases collapses or even eliminates many of the steps found in routine circumstances.

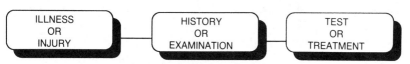

Figure Two.   Consent Process for Medicolegal Emergency

Figure Three.   Consent Process for Care when Consent Is Impossible to Obtain; Therapeutic Privilege; and Compulsory Treatment

In a medicolegal emergency, it is virtually impossible to establish a treatment relationship or to discuss the pros and cons of recommended tests or treatments. As seen later in this chapter, emergencies are situations in which patients have life- or health-threatening injury or illness requiring immediate attention, and due to the illness or injury or some underlying disorder the patients are incapable of participating in the consent process. Moreover, there is no time to secure consent from someone else. The consent process is distilled into three broad steps of presenting illness or injury; history and examination; and provision of appropriate tests or treatment. After the acute problem is over, caregivers then document why the situation was deemed an emergency and the type of treatment provided.

In some exceptional circumstances, the consent process involves the addition of one other step: dialogue. Patients with heart attacks in progress, strokes, asthma attacks, or bee sting reactions may be fully capable of participating in the consent process. However, there is no time for the type of consent process found in routine care situations. Such situations require prompt action involving a history (if possible), examination, and appropriate tests or treatment.

Dialogue with patients in these exceptional circumstances is required. Prostitutes may be under a compulsory treatment order. Nonetheless, it is imperative for caregivers to determine if such patients have had similar treatment in the past and if adverse reactions occurred. If follow-up is required, this too should be explained. By the same token, to lessen anxiety caregivers should describe to bee sting reaction or asthma patients what is being done for them. It is also prudent to ask them if they have taken any medication en route to the health facility and what has happened in the past during similar attacks.

By viewing dialogue as an integral part of the consent process in these exceptional cases, caregivers avoid falling victim to the trap of viewing patients as inanimate objects who are only recipients of care. Those who are the objects of well-intentioned care may have valuable information to contribute to their own well-being. Moreover, those objects of attention have feelings and anxiety during acute illness that need to be addressed as treatment is provided.

§2.1.3 Communication and History in Exceptional Cases

If consent is truly a "communications" process, then it is imperative that this fact be borne in mind whether the care is routine or exceptional. Communication takes on particular significance in those situations in which patients face life- or health-threatening episodes and yet are able to converse with caregivers. It also has particular meaning in those cases in which it is deemed important to refrain from providing a full disclosure for fear of causing harm to patients.

Many caregivers are adept at conversing with patients. Others find it an awkward task and go to almost any length to avoid speaking with patients. Somewhere in between the two extremes are those who recognize the importance of dialogue but engage in it in a mediocre fashion.

Whether caregivers are physicians, nurses, dentists, technicians, or therapists, it is essential that they possess the requisite ability to communicate effectively with patients. They must understand their role in the consent process and what information should be conveyed to patients.

Patient history is another important element — even in many exceptional cases when the full consent process is side-stepped in favor of a condensed approach. Caregivers should not ignore protests from patients or their families that particular drugs have provoked nasty reactions in the past or that loved ones think patients took some drugs prior to coming to the health facility.

Patient history provides clues about prior treatment and helps caregivers gain a perspective on the needs of patients. Determining "where patients are coming from" can facilitate a situation-specific consent that assures quality care and minimizes the risk of litigation. As such, patient history and communication should not be ignored even in those exceptional cases in which the full consent process is abandoned in favor of an appropriate condensed approach.

§2.2 Medical Emergencies

The law has long recognized the right to provide treatment in an emergency situation without a patient's consent.[1] In some states this principle has been codified in legislation, to the point of even specifying who may administer the emergency care.[2] Difficulties remain, however, in applying this principle to specific instances — in other words, in defining what is and is not an emergency that legally falls under this exception to the general rules for consent.

§2.2.1 Definition of a Medical Emergency

Generally speaking, two factors must be present for a situation to be defined as a medical emergency. First, the patient is incapacitated and cannot exercise his mental ability to reach an informed choice. This limitation may be attributable to an injury or sudden illness, to alcohol or drug intoxication, to shock

---

§2.2 [1] See, e.g., Luka v. Lowrie, 171 Mich. 122, 136 N.W. 1106 (1912). See also Pratt v. Davis, 224 Ill. 300, 79 N.E. 562 (1906), which also supports the proposition of emergency care without authorization in some instances.

[2] See, e.g., Ala. Code §22-8-1 (1971); Ga. Code §88-2905 (1971); Idaho Code §39-4303 (1975); Miss. Code Ann. §41-41-7 (1966); Pa. Stat. Ann. tit. 35, §10104 (Purdon 1970) (emergency treatment for minors). Some legislation specifically authorizes treatment by emergency medical care personnel, some of whom are referred to as EMTs. See, e.g., Idaho Code §39-136 (1980) (removes liability for providing treatment without consent).

or trauma, or to an underlying mental or physical disease or handicap that precludes a reasoned choice regarding treatment. It does not follow, however, that a person who has consumed a moderate amount of alcohol or drugs or who has a history of psychiatric problems is automatically incapable of giving consent: the facts and circumstances of individual cases are essential to such determinations.

Second, a life- or health-threatening disease or injury that requires immediate treatment is present. The nature of the illness or injury must be serious enough to preclude any attempts to garner consent from one authorized to act on behalf of the patient. Any delay in such a situation would mean certain death or serious permanent impairment.[3]

It is common to find legislation that authorizes certain people to act for the patient.[4] If they are unavailable or if attempting to contact them, in light of the urgency of the situation, is impractical, treatment may proceed.[5]

Case law holds that the facts of a particular instance determine whether a patient experienced a medical emergency. Reviewing the facts of a case in hindsight, courts are reluctant to overrule the finding of a medical emergency in the absence of evidence that suggests an authorization for treatment should have been obtained.

For example, in a Louisiana case, a diabetic woman admitted for diagnostic cancer tests developed ketoacidosis and a severe thrombophlebitis in her left leg. Although the woman responded well to treatment of the ketoacidosis, medical management of the thrombophlebitis was unsuccessful. Gangrene developed in the left leg and during the evening of her third hospital day the condition worsened to the point that immediate amputation of the leg above the knee was required. When attempts to obtain a telephone consent from the son proved unsuccessful, doctors went ahead with the surgery. The woman subsequently died of acute heart failure.[6]

[3] See Ga. Code §88-2905 (1971).
[4] Ark. Stat. Ann. §20-9-602 (1981); Ga. Code §88-2904 (1972); Idaho Code §39-4303 (1975).
[5] Ga. Code §88-2905 (1971).
[6] Stafford v. Louisiana State Univ., 448 So. 2d 852 (La. Ct. App. 1984).

In the malpractice action that followed, the court pointed out that two days before the operation doctors had anticipated the need to amputate the leg. Conservative treatment had been instituted in the hope of saving as much of the leg as possible. However, when the patient's condition became life-threatening and good-faith efforts to reach the appropriate next of kin failed, the physicians were well within the statutory limits of Louisiana law in proceeding on the basis of a medical emergency.[7]

What constitutes a medical emergency is a matter of medical judgment. Judicial opinions and legislative requirements of an emergency delineate the legal limits of this legitimate exception to the requirements of consent. Physicians must be guided by their experience and the needs of their patients in determining whether a medical emergency exists.

§2.2.2 *Declaration of Situations as Emergencies*

The law can only set rules or criteria for authorization of treatment in emergency situations; the task of meeting these criteria in specific situations is left to medical personnel. For a legal authorization they must find that both an incapacity to consent and a need for immediate treatment are present. When patients are incapacitated but do not require life- or health-saving treatment, practitioners cannot proceed. Conversely, patients who are capable of giving consent cannot be treated without authorization just because they are suffering from a disease or injury that requires life-saving treatment. In most instances it is their right to refuse even life-saving treatment. (See §7.3.2 infra.)

When there is time to secure consent for a patient who is incapacitated and suffering from a severe but not life-threatening illness, the law requires legally effective consent. Permission to treat patients may come from a duly authorized legal representative, a relative designated by statute in some

[7]Id., referring to La. Rev. Stat. Ann. §40:1299.54 (West 1982).

states,[8] or court orders compelling treatment or appointing someone to act for the patient.

In actions following unauthorized treatment, practitioners must be able to prove that an emergency existed that justified their intervention. The court will then examine whether the criteria for emergency treatment were present and applied correctly. Supplying the necessary proof is a lot easier for health facilities and practitioners if they set treatment protocols for emergency situations. Only those patients who meet the assessment criteria should be given care without their consent. Applied properly, these guidelines should preclude successful suits based upon unauthorized treatment.

A note of caution must be added about the application of criteria for emergency care. When a patient is capable and refuses treatment, her decision should be respected. Health personnel are not justified in forging ahead with care if the patient should become unconscious or otherwise incapable. In the absence of legislation or case law to the contrary, the patient's initial decision prevails.

Moreover, the meaning of the term *capacity to consent* cannot be twisted or applied in such a way as to conclude that an otherwise capable patient does not possess the ability to reach an informed choice. However much health personnel may disagree with a patient, in the absence of genuine factors pointing to incapacity, his decision must be respected.

§2.2.3 Scope of Authorized Emergency Care

Treatment permitted under the emergency exception is limited to what is reasonable under the circumstances. The patient's condition is the measure of what is a reasonable, even if unauthorized, response. Extensive thoracic surgery, for example, may be warranted for a patient with a gunshot wound to the chest. An amputation of a finger may be reasonable if it is badly mangled and there is no known means of restoring it.

[8] Ark. Stat. Ann. §20-9-602 (1981); Ga. Code §88-2904 (1971).

Even hospitalization of a severely inebriated individual may be permissible, despite the fact the person did not voluntarily present himself for care.[9]

However, a procedure that is not necessary or reasonable in the context of emergency treatment is not authorized. Thus the performance of a separate elective procedure during the course of emergency care or the carrying out of extensive, radical surgery when conservative medical treatment would suffice cannot be excused under the emergency exception. The key is that the treatment must be reasonable and it must fit the assumption that the patient, if capable, would give consent to such treatment.

The fiction of implied consent to emergency care may also be applied to a life- or health-threatening incident that occurs during an authorized operation. A patient under the influence of a general anesthetic cannot give consent. Moreover, waiting until the patient regains consciousness or consent of a relative is obtained may be impractical or impossible. Unanticipated occurrences that require life- or health-saving treatment during an operation, therefore, are a proper context for an emergency exception. Such treatment as is reasonable in the circumstances is permissible, including the extension of the original operation or the performance of a different procedure.[10]

§2.2.4 Policy Considerations and Emergency Care

As noted above, the law has created a fiction, more accurately termed a privilege,[11] that implies consent when a patient is incapable of giving it and immediate treatment is necessary. However described, this legal fiction reflects a policy judgment

---

[9]See, e.g., Davis v. Charter-by-the-Sea, Inc., 358 S.E.2d 865 (Ga. Ct. App. 1987), where an intoxicated patient was brought to the treatment facility against her will and kept overnight. The patient lost her claim of false imprisonment.

[10]Wheeler v. Barker, 92 Cal. App. 2d 776, 208 P.2d 68 (1949).

[11]Restatement of Torts §62 (1934), special note accompanying the section.

that a reasonable person would rather be treated than suffer permanent injury or death. It is a narrow exception to the general concept of the patient being the one to decide what shall be done to his body.

Some practitioners believe that the scope of this exception is broader than it appears. They assume that if they act in good faith in providing treatment they will be insulated from litigation. This is not necessarily the case. However well-meaning a physician or surgeon may be, her unauthorized treatment of a patient will not be excused unless it occurs in the context of a well-documented exception to the rules of consent.

Unauthorized treatment that does not fit within the definition of the emergency exception may result in a nominal damages award. A small sum may be awarded if the treatment provided did not involve any physical harm to the patient, but did include an unauthorized or unwarranted invasion of the patient's person. Unauthorized treatment, if litigated under the negligence theory of consent, requires proof of actual harm. If the plaintiff did not experience any injury his only recourse would be to sue under the battery theory of consent in those states that still recognize such a cause of action. If such is the case, the plaintiff must meet the requirements of a battery action, including that the unauthorized care or touching was intentional and that it was in fact done without any valid consent.

Larger damages awards may arise from unauthorized treatment when, as a result of the care provided, patients suffer significant injuries. Procedures that are performed on the basis of an "emergency" when the patient is fully capable of reaching an informed decision against treatment fall in this category. Medical or surgical interventions that render a person permanently disabled or remove reproductive capacity are likely to cause courts and juries to award substantial damages. The fact that a physician or surgeon adopted an attitude of "doctor knows best" will not prove to be an adequate defense. Any physician who decides to risk a procedure on the assumption that the worst eventuality will be a nominal judgment should be aware of the possibility of substanti ¹ damages awards.

§2.3   Treatment When Consent Is Not Possible

There is an ill-defined exception to the general rule that permits treatment when consent is not possible. Logically extending from the exception pertaining to emergencies, this exception allows treatment in those instances in which a true emergency does not exist but the situation is exigent. The exception has been recognized in legislation. For example, in Alaska a defense to an action based on failure to obtain informed consent lies in the fact that "under the circumstances, consent by or on behalf of the patient was not possible."[1] Similar provisions can be found in other states.[2]

Possibly, this vague style of drafting actually encompasses the emergency exception. (If so, then the standards for defining an emergency have been relaxed greatly.) It is also possible that the exception constitutes a new basis for permitting care without consent — in other words, even in circumstances when a patient is capable of giving consent or the patient's legal representative is available. The rationale for the extension lies in the serious jeopardy of life or health that the delay involved in going through the entire consent process may cause. As the Alaska statute suggests, circumstances are the determining factor in taking a treatment situation out of the general consent requirements.[3]

Because the exception is so broad and untried, practitioners should be cautious in its use. It is possible that this "impossibility of consent" situation is just another way of stating the emergency rule. If this is the case, then the requirements for applying this exception to the rules of consent must be followed. However, it is more probable that the impossibility standard is a practical extension of the principles underlying the emergency rule that does not require a patient to be incapable of consent but does require the patient to be in such an exigent situation that treatment should be applied without taking time

§2.3   [1] Alaska Stat. §09.55.556 (1976).
[2] See, e.g., N.Y. Pub. Health Law §2805-d (McKinney 1975); Vt. Stat. Ann. tit. 12, §1909 (1976).
[3] Alaska Stat. §09.55.556 (1976).

to engage the patient in a lengthy dialogue. This perspective of the impossibility exception is based on the facts and circumstances of each individual case, and it is on this basis that the health care provider must decide whether treatment should be undertaken without obtaining the consent of the patient or a duly authorized legal representative.

Serious insect or snake bites and severe allergic reactions are examples of the type of situation in which immediate attention is required. While the patient may be able to communicate, delaying treatment until the fine points of the consent process have been met would be medically unsound. A New Mexico case involving the use of Antivenin falls in this category.[4] The plaintiff, an amateur snake handler, was bitten by a snake on two fingers of his left hand. The defendant treated the plaintiff at a hospital, injecting Antivenin into the base of the two fingers and into the patient's arm. A lawsuit followed when the patient lost both fingers.

On the issue of consent, the Supreme Court of New Mexico held that it was not necessary to go through the entire process of consent. As the court noted:

> It would indeed be most unusual for a doctor, with his patient who had just been bitten by a venomous snake, to calmly sit down and first fully discuss the various available methods of treating snakebite and the possible consequences, while the venom was being pumped through the patient's body.[5]

The New Mexico court characterized the case as an emergency, but it did not meet all the criteria for that exception. Rather, what existed was an unusual circumstance that made a full consent impossible or impractical.

Patients who enter an emergency department with severe allergic reactions, asthma, or a heart attack in progress may also be treated under the category of impossibility or impracticality of full consent. They may be quite capable of understanding

[4]Crouch v. Most, 78 N.M. 406, 432 P.2d 250 (1967).
[5]Id. at 410, 432 P.2d at 254.

the nature and consequences of a proposed treatment and any reasonable alternatives, but the need for quick action prevents any discussion. By arriving for treatment they are implying consent to care.

In supplying treatment under this exception physicians must keep two important considerations in mind. First, although the full consent process need not be undertaken, it is important to put patients at ease and inform them, at least to some degree, as to what is going to be done. Good practice dictates such action as much as does the law. If the patient should object or indicate that certain medication should not be administered, the warning should be heeded. Any other useful information that the patient provides should be considered carefully. Reasons that support abandoning a lengthy consent process do not imply the right to cut off all communication with the patient.

Second, physicians should be aware of the permissible scope of treatment under this exception. Since the impossibility of consent exception is so closely related in theory to the emergency exception, the application of the latter rule can reasonably suggest the scope of the former. In other words, a patient can be given such medical or surgical care as is *reasonably* necessary in the circumstances. If in the circumstances it is reasonable to perform open heart massage or insert an airway in a patient's throat, the law will permit that treatment. As always, however, the practitioner must be able to prove at a later point that the factor essential for relying on the exception was present: here, a lack of time to complete the consent process. The more threatening the incident to the health or life of the patient, the more likely the application of the exception.

§2.4   Use of Therapeutic Privilege

On some occasions a candid and thorough disclosure of information will have an adverse effect on the patient's condition or health. By recognizing this situation the law allows a physician, in her discretion, to withhold such information or to phrase it in a manner that will not upset the patient. This therapeutic privilege may serve as a valid defense in negligent consent litigation.[1] It also constitutes a recognized exception to the general rules for consent.

§2.4.1 *Justifiable Use of Therapeutic Privilege*

Both legislation and case law have set forth the general circumstances in which information may be withheld from a patient. The decision to withhold such information is based on a practitioner's medical judgment and must be substantiated in order to stand up in a court of law. If this can be done, then a claim of damages for nondisclosure of information cannot succeed. The proper use of therapeutic privilege involves proof that a physician has considered three basic criteria. Each should be taken into account in reaching the conclusion that information will be withheld or phrased in such a way as not to upset the patient.

a. *The use of the privilege must take into account the circumstances of the patient.* The physician must survey the context and circumstances of a patient's case.[2] Is the patient very tense, emotionally upset, or nervous? Can the patient assimilate candid information or should it be presented in a general way with few specifics? These are just a few of the questions that a practitioner should consider in assessing the situation. If a decision is made against a full explanation, then the disclosure must be tailored to meet the needs of the patient. The following case illustrates this point.

In a diversity action in Alabama, the court held that — given the circumstances of the case — the physician was justified in giving a less than candid disclosure regarding the risks of the

§2.4 [1]See, e.g., Alaska Stat. §09.55.556 (1976); Del. Code Ann. tit. 18, §6852 (1981); N.Y. Pub. Health Law §2805-d (McKinney 1975); Pa. Stat. Ann. tit. 40, §1301.103 (Purdon 1976); Utah Code Ann. §78-14-5 (1976).

[2]See, e.g., Alaska Stat. §09.55.556 (1976), which requires that a health care provider consider "all the attendant facts and circumstances. . . ."

operation.[3] The patient underwent a thyroidectomy that resulted in her vocal cord being paralyzed. Before surgery she had been worried about the thyroidectomy as well as another procedure that was to be performed at the same time. Among other facts, she was told that the operation would be similar to the first thyroidectomy she had undergone in 1954. The court found that this disclosure was adequate under the circumstances because the risks involved were of a technical nature beyond the patient's understanding. The defendant, having properly advised her of the seriousness of the operation,[4] had fulfilled his duty.

b. The physician must believe that a full disclosure of information will have a significantly adverse impact on the patient. This element is variously formulated as "a substantially adverse effect,"[5] "to adversely and substantially affect,"[6] to result in a "seriously adverse effect,"[7] and "a substantial and adverse effect."[8] Each of these phrases defines the impact of the disclosure as more than a projected mild upset. The patient must be in danger of significant detriment and impairment of his condition[9] or treatment.

This medical judgment can be made only on a patient-by-patient basis and is based on the rapport or relationship a physician has with a patient. Although consultation with others, including the patient's family, may be taken into account, the decision whether the disclosure of certain information would have adverse consequences must be made by the practitioner.

c. Reasonable discretion must be used in the manner and extent of the disclosure. Under the therapeutic privilege exception, the amount of information that is revealed to patients depends

[3] Roberts v. Woods, 206 F. Supp. 579 (S.D. Ala. 1962).
[4] Id. at 583.
[5] Alaska Stat. §09.55.556 (1976).
[6] N.Y. Pub. Health Law §2805-d (McKinney 1975).
[7] Pa. Stat. Ann. tit. 40, §1301.103 (Purdon 1976).
[8] Utah Code Ann. §78-14-5 (1976).
[9] Alaska Stat. §09.55.556 (1976); N.Y. Pub. Health Law §2805-d (McKinney 1975).

upon the judgment of the practitioners. Through the exercise of their discretion they select what information is reasonable to provide in the circumstances. The disclosure of that information should then be handled in a reasonable manner — i.e., geared to avoid an adverse impact on the patient's well-being.

Underlying circumstances may transform a seemingly wrongful withholding of information into a reasonable course of action. Using that same perspective to interpret the way in which information is transmitted can also be the basis of a successful defense. It is essential to this purpose that a physician can prove that the amount and method of disclosure were chosen on an individual case basis.

§2.4.2 Unjustifiable Use of Therapeutic Privilege

Without the substantiation of all three criteria listed above, reliance on the therapeutic privilege is unjustifiable. Certainly the exception cannot be invoked to warrant withholding important information that a practitioner feels will cause a patient to refuse recommended treatment. In other words, the manner or extent of disclosure cannot be molded to assure the conclusion desired by the physician. Knowing misrepresentation of significant facts, willful deception, and fraud are not protected by the therapeutic exception. The well-intentioned practitioner can avoid such accusations by withholding information to which the patient is entitled only when the situation fits squarely within the therapeutic privilege.

As discussed previously (§1.16.4, supra), when a plaintiff proves that there was a failure to disclose relevant information, it is incumbent upon the practitioner to show that the departure from the standard was excusable. Therapeutic privilege provides such a defense; however, reliance on testimony that a physician believed he was doing what was right will be insufficient to establish that exception. Additional evidence must indicate that at the time consent was obtained, the disclosure of information would probably have had an adverse impact upon the patient.

§2.4.3   Documentation and Therapeutic Privilege

The documentation should be written as close as possible to the decision to use therapeutic privilege. A detailed note in the patient's records is usually sufficient (see §1.16.4, supra). However, health facilities may also require additional documentation. If health institutions rely upon detailed documentation in the patient's health record, it should contain a discussion of why the privilege is being used, the nature and circumstances surrounding the patient's case, why it is believed that a full disclosure would have an adverse impact, and a summary of what information was provided to the patient.

The context of the case, the detailed note, and any other relevant evidence will substantiate the use of the privilege. Additional notations may also be of assistance, an example being an indication that the practitioner consulted with the patient's next-of-kin and they agreed that a full and frank disclosure would be detrimental. Such evidence may not be controlling but it will certainly have weight in any proceedings for failure to obtain a fully informed consent.

§2.5   Compulsory Treatment and the Need for Consent

In those situations in which the law removes the need for consent and authorizes compulsory treatment, a policy judgment allows individuals to be treated for their own well-being or that of the community. In effect, these patients are deemed legally incapable of consent within the limitations of this rule. Even compulsory treatment, however, has limitations.

One of the most common forms of compulsory treatment arises from legislative authority regarding venereal disease.[1]

§2.5   [1]See, e.g., Ga. Code §88-1604 (1964); N.M. Stat. Ann. §30-9-5 (1963); N.J. Stat. Ann. §26:4-49.7 (West 1953), §26:4-49.8 (West 1945); Okla. Stat. Ann. tit. 63, §1-524 (West 1963); S.C. Code §44-29-100 (1963).

These cases often involve prisoners.[2] Courts can order examinations of individuals and issue orders for treatment.[3] In some states designated officials may have the same authority.[4]

Examination and treatment for other forms of disease can be compelled among the general population[5] — even though in some instances the subject may not be suffering from communicable disease at all. Thus treatment in Minnesota may be compelled for habitual users of narcotics[6] and in Colorado a person may be committed involuntarily for alcohol treatment.[7]

Some laws make it necessary to undergo certain forms of diagnostic work: those designed for pregnant women are a good example. One that is required is serologic testing for venereal disease,[8] while other disease factors may also be identified. Such legislation attempts to identify potential risk factors for the fetus that may be prevented or reduced in severity.

Other legislative enactments require individuals to be immunized. Children typically undergo a range of immunizations before beginning school,[9] and such treatment may be required of others for contagious or infectious diseases.[10]

Because these requirements encroach upon the individual's liberty and privacy, the laws must be strictly applied. Furthermore, due process concerns control the application of the laws; they can be found formalized in the requirements for hearings, notice, and other considerations of constitutional and state law.[11] The action taken or care provided must be expressly

---

[2]Conn. Gen. Stat. §53a-90 (1981); N.J. Stat. Ann. §26:4-49.7 (West 1953); Ohio Rev. Code Ann. §2907.27 (Baldwin 1974).

[3]Conn. Gen. Stat. §53a-90 (1981); N.M. Stat. Ann. §30-9-5 (1963); N.J. Stat. Ann. §26:4-49.7 (West 1953).

[4]Ga. Code §88-1604 (1964); Okla. Stat. Ann. tit. 63, §1-524 (West 1963).

[5]Me. Rev. Stat. Ann. tit. 22, §1021 (1977).

[6]Minn. Stat. Ann. §254.09 (West 1923).

[7]Colo. Rev. Stat. §25-1-311 (1977).

[8]See, e.g., Ga. Code §88-1606 (1964); S.C. Code §44-29-120 (1962).

[9]Conn. Gen. Stat. §10-204a (1981); Ohio Rev. Code Ann. §3313.671 (Baldwin 1984); Vt. Stat. Ann. tit. 18, §1121 (1981).

[10]Ga. Code §88-1203 (1964).

[11]See, e.g., Colo. Rev. Stat. §25-1-311 (1977); Me. Rev. Stat. Ann. tit. 22, §1021 (1981).

permitted by law[12] and reasonably related to the health interest that the state seeks to promote.[13] Furthermore, the treatment must be carried out in a reasonable manner.[14]

Another type of legislation recognizes exceptions to treatments otherwise required by law. Thus immunization may be refused if there is a recognized religious objection[15] or if the immunization is not medically advisable.[16] Alternative measures short of actual treatment are sometimes instituted, such as isolation or quarantine.[17]

Statutes that require such screening as a precondition to obtaining a marriage license in effect make certain blood tests compulsory.[18] The screening is usually performed to detect venereal disease or a venereal disease at a communicable stage,[19] although other diseases or genetic traits that affect offspring may also be detected.[20] Some exceptions to these tests are recognized in legislation.[21]

All these laws have one factor in common: a legal recognition that, in the situations covered by the laws, consent on the part of the patient is not necessary. Concomitantly, of course, these laws impose on practitioners the responsibility to know the bounds of authorized treatment and to stay within them. Additional issues also require consideration from practitioners. For example, although they may be authorized to treat a patient

[12]Ex parte Arata, 52 Cal. App. 380, 198 P. 814 (1921).
[13]Huffman v. D.C., 29 A.2d 558 (D.C. 1944).
[14]People ex rel. Baker v. Strautz, 386 Ill. 360, 54 N.E.2d 441 (1944).
[15]See, e.g., Conn. Gen. Stat. §10-204a (1981); Ill. Ann. Stat. ch. 111 1/2, §22.12 (Smith-Hurd 1975); Ohio Rev. Code Ann. §3313.671 (Baldwin 1978); Vt. Stat. Ann. tit. 18, §1122 (1981).
[16]See references in previous footnote.
[17]Ga. Code §88-1204 (1964); S.C. Code §44-29-90 (1962).
[18]Conn. Gen. Stat. §46b-26 (1979); Tenn. Code Ann. §36-502 (1950); Vt. Stat. Ann. tit. 18, §5134 (1951); W. Va. Code §48-1-6 (1978).
[19]Ga. Code §53-215 (1977); N.H. Rev. Stat. Ann. §457: 23 (1988); N.J. Stat. Ann. §37:1-20 (West 1953); W. Va. Code §48-1-6 (1978).
[20]Ga. Code §53-216 (1972) (sickle cell anemia) and §53-217.1 (1978) (female partner rubella immunity); Idaho Code §32-412 (1980) (female partner rubella immunity); R.I. Gen. Laws §15-2-3 (1975) (female partner rubella immunity).
[21]Idaho Code §32-414 (1979); Ind. Code Ann. §31-1-1-7 (Burns 1981); Tenn. Code Ann. §36-508 (1950).

without her consent, they should still obtain sufficient history and conduct an appropriate examination. Penicillin may be the drug of choice for treating venereal disease, but its use may be contraindicated for a patient with known or suspected allergies. Blood studies may be warranted for most individuals — except those with a bleeding disorder. Thus, as a matter of good practice, sufficient information should be obtained from a patient before treatment is administered.

§2.6 Duty of Third-Party Disclosure

At times the confidentiality of the treatment may be legally broken by a practitioner. In these instances the welfare of others or the needs of the state are judged as taking precedence over the privacy of the patient. This is more an issue in the laws of confidentiality than it is a matter of consent. Nonetheless, to the degree that a physician is permitted to make an unauthorized disclosure, the consent law is involved.

§2.6.1 Duty to Warn Others of Potential Harm

Some of the laws that require disclosure focus on the need of the patient to be protected from harm, or on the need of certain other individuals who might be injured by the patient. Thus mandatory reporting laws for known or suspected cases of child abuse[1] and venereal disease[2] come within this category. The failure to carry out these requirements may be an actionable matter.[3]

Some case law has also developed on the duty to warn third

§2.6 [1]Fla. Stat. Ann. §827.07 (West Supp. 1981); Ill. Ann. Stat. ch. 23, §2054 (Smith-Hurd 1982).
[2]Conn. Gen. Stat. 19-89 (1981); N.Y. Pub. Health Law §2306 (McKinney 1980).
[3]See Landeros v. Flood, 17 Cal. App. 3d 399, 551 P.2d 389, 131 Cal. Rptr. 69 (1976); People v. Stockton Pregnancy Control Med. Clinic, 249 Cal. Rptr. 762 (Cal. Ct. App. 1988).

parties of potential harm. Common subjects are mental health patients or individuals under psychiatric care who pose a threat to an identified third party.[4] The failure to warn has proven grounds for legal action.[5] Some courts reject the concept of a duty to warn in the absence of an identifiable victim,[6] but other courts are less stringent and do not require an identifiable subject of harm.[7] The scope of the "duty" must be defined more precisely, particularly as attempts are made to expand the concept to include victims of mutated drugs administered to others[8] and to define the legal relationships underpinning the obligation to warn.[9]

§2.6.2 Duty to Provide Notification of Treatment

In a few states legislation permits a practitioner to alert a child's parents to the fact that treatment is to be provided.[10]

---

[4]Tarasoff v. Regents of the Univ. of Cal., 17 Cal. 3d 425, 551 P. 2d 334, 131 Cal. Rptr. 14 (1976); Peck v. Counseling Serv. of Addison County, Inc., 499 A.2d 422 (Vt. 1985).

[5]Williams v. United States, 450 F. Supp. 1040 (D.S.C. 1978); McIntosh v. Milano, 168 N.J. Super. 466, 403 A.2d 500 (1979).

[6]Schuster v. Altenberg, 424 N.W.2d 159 (Wis. 1988); Kirk v. M. Reese Hosp. & Med. Center, 513 N.E.2d 387 (Ill. 1987), revg. 483 N.E.2d 906 (Ill. App. Ct. 1985).

[7]See Perreira v. State, — P.2d — (Colo. 1989), in which the court expanded the concept of foreseeability to include a police officer as a foreseeable victim despite the fact that the assailant had not made specific threats against the policeman.

[8]See Crawford v. Wojnas, 754 P.2d 1302 (Wash. Ct. App. 1988), where the court declined to expand the duty to warn to include the mother of a patient given live oral polio vaccine. In this case the drug mutated and the mother developed polio.

[9]See Hinkelman v. Borgess Med. Center, 403 N.W.2d 547 (Mich. Ct. App. 1987).

[10]Colo. Rev. Stat. §13-22-106 (1973) (physician must make a reasonable attempt to notify the parent of a minor patient seeking treatment for sexual assault); Del. Code Ann. tit. 13, §708 (1974) (physician may use discretion in providing or withholding from a minor's parents information regarding treatment for communicable disease); Md. Pub. Health Code Ann. art. 43, §135A (1971) (physician may inform minor's parent of treatment needed or given for mental or emotional disorder).

This practice reflects the belief that the parents, if notified, can assist the child in his health care. It also suggests that the minor's right of confidentiality in seeking such treatment is not as encompassing as that of an adult — a conclusion open to debate.

In a few instances the duty to warn involves notifying state agencies or officials. Certain types of injuries, such as stab or gunshot wounds, may be the subject of mandatory reporting.[11] The possibility that criminal activity was the cause of such injuries forms the basis for the duty to report.

§2.6.3 Times When Disclosure Is Not Permissible

Generally, a health facility or practitioner must maintain the confidentiality of patient information. Confidentiality may be breached, as noted above, only in authorized situations. Thus disclosures may be made for purposes other than child abuse or communicable disease. This would include provisions under federal regulations governing Medicaid[12] and human research.[13] In the absence of authority, the only other time health information may be revealed is at the request of patients or their legal representatives.

Insurance companies or prospective employers commonly request health information; however, the physician or health facility to which such a request is directed should request a signed authorization from the patient. That form should specify what documentary data may be released, as well as the scope of the practitioner's authority to discuss the patient's health with a representative of the insurance company or prospective employer. The authorization should also be time limited. Under no circumstances should the health facility or the physician — without the patient's explicit consent — respond to requests for information over the phone or by letter. By acting

[11] See, e.g., N.Y. Penal Law §265.25 (McKinney 1965).
[12] 42 C.F.R. §431.107 (1979).
[13] See 45 C.F.R. §46.101 (1981).

without authority, a practitioner or a health facility becomes subject to litigation for any subsequent injury. A breach of confidentiality can be the basis for litigation.[14] Should the criteria for a consent action be present, a lawsuit could be brought on that basis also.

Setting guidelines for disclosure of information is a wise measure for both health facilities and practitioners. They should apprise themselves of those state and federal laws that permit or require disclosure and should develop a policy for documentation of consent by patients who request information be released to third parties.

B. PROBLEM CASES

Situations occur from time to time that do not necessarily merit a total adherence to the requirements for informed consent. Only a modest amount of statutory and case law covers these instances, and many answers must be derived by analogy to other areas of law.

§2.7   Patients' Requests Not to Be Informed

As noted previously (§1.13.3 and §1.16.2, supra), when patients agree to procedures regardless of the risks or tell practitioners that they do not wish to be informed, treatment may proceed. These patients' statements constitute both an exception to the general requirements for consent and a defense to any action

---

[14]See Tower v. Hirschorn, 397 Mass. 581, 492 N.E.2d 728 (1986), in which the court ruled that plaintiff was entitled to recover damages for invasion of privacy where the defendant neurologist disclosed confidential medical information without the plaintiff's consent.

based on failure to provide adequate information. Both case law[1] and statutes[2] have recognized this principle.

Difficulty in this area stems from two concerns. First, does the patient really understand the implications of her consent to treatment without being informed? Second, what measures should practitioners take to protect themselves in the event of litigation?

§2.7.1 Implications of Uninformed Consent

There is no sure method to determine whether a patient understands what will follow from consenting to unknown treatment; there is no certainty about how well-informed *any* patient's consent is — regardless of the amount of information disclosed. However, patients who receive material information are more likely to understand the nature of a proposed medical treatment or surgery. For those who decline to be informed but who agree to treatment, the remaining course of action is to disclose at least a minimum amount of information. Following are some of the issues that could be raised:

1. That the procedure involves certain known risks, some of which may or may not be serious. Whether this is true for the specific patient must be decided by the practitioner. If it is, then it should be disclosed.
2. That there are some benefits that may be reasonably anticipated. These should be outlined for the patient.
3. That following the procedure the patient may experience some discomfort or pain.
4. That the patient may have to remain in bed or in the hospital for ____ number of days and cannot expect to resume a usual schedule for ____ days or weeks (include numbers relevant to procedure).

§2.7 [1] Holt v. Nelson, 11 Wash. App. 230, 523 P.2d 211 (1974).
[2] Alaska Stat. §09.55.556(1976); Del. Code Ann. tit. 18, §6852 (1976); N.Y. Pub. Health Law §2805-d (McKinney 1975); Utah Code Ann. §78-14-5 (1976); Vt. Stat. Ann. tit. 12, §1909 (1976).

This limited disclosure may whet the patient's curiosity and prompt him to ask questions. These inquiries should be answered in as candid and thorough a manner as is reasonable in the circumstances. If the patient persists in agreeing to the procedure without the benefit of a full consent process, treatment may proceed. Whether a practitioner initiates care, or whether a health facility permits treatment under such circumstances, is a matter of individual judgment. Fear of litigation, however, may prevent treatment.

§2.7.2 Documentation of the Request

Documentation of the exchange with patients is essential for purposes of legal defense in any action that might arise out of treatment. That purpose is served by notes in a patient's chart, outlining what was disclosed and, additionally, indicating that the patient was capable of giving consent but decided to undergo the procedure regardless of the risks involved or did not wish to be informed. The note should be written immediately or shortly after the discussion with the patient, and it should be dated and signed.

Another possible avenue is to require the patient's signature on a consent document. One version of that follows:

> I, (name), hereby agree to the performance of a (name of procedure). I have agreed to this procedure (list how: regardless of the risk involved, without being told information to which I am entitled, etc.). The nondisclosure of this information is being done at my request and I accept the consequences of agreeing to treatment without being so informed.

Alternatively, the patient could sign a document indicating that she is aware that some known risks exist, that some benefits may be reasonably anticipated, and that some discomfort may follow. This document would also contain information regarding the projected recovery period, including the amount of time before the patient can resume normal activities. None of these avenues is dispositive in consent litigation: they are tools of persuasion, not final determination.

A practitioner has yet another recourse: to refrain from carrying out the proposed treatment. Such a decision, based on sound medical judgment not to proceed without the patient's fully informed consent, could withstand challenge. This conclusion is particularly valid for tests or treatments that require the participation of the patient. Patients' rights do not preclude the exercise of a practitioner's right to insist upon certain practice standards. After a decision to refuse medical or surgical care without informed consent, the physician should make every effort to refer the patient to another physician.

§2.8 Patients Undergoing Repetitive or Continuous Treatment

Effort would be unnecessarily wasted and the consent process partially compromised if a fully informed authorization to repetitive forms of care were required. Procedures such as allergy desensitization, renal dialysis, chemotherapy, and cobalt treatment fall into this category. However, some degree of communication and exchange with the patient is necessary.

Keeping the performance of the procedure the same obviates the need for going through with the entire consent process every time. This is not the case if any changes are introduced that alter the risks, benefits, or discomfort involved or introduce new side effects that may hamper the patient's ability to carry out daily activities. Then a new consent is necessary.

At any point in a continuous treatment process the patient may pose questions relating to treatment. These inquiries should be encouraged and answered before treatment is provided: the responses may cause the patient to withhold his consent to further care. Any such decision to withdraw consent should be an informed one, and it is the duty of the provider of services to alert the patient to the consequences of the decision.

A patient's persistence in refraining from further care should be documented, either in his chart or in a form that recounts the facts leading to the decision and the information disclosed.

The fact that consent need not be obtained each visit does not excuse providers from soliciting feedback of information from patients. Patients should be asked if they have experienced any difficulties or symptoms since the last treatment and, if so, to describe the symptoms. Positive responses should be taken as warning signals not to initiate further treatment until these problems have been resolved. Because continued treatment could be contraindicated or dangerous, it should be part of the treatment protocol to question patients at the outset of each session. A complication may require a change in the treatment process and thus a reassessment of the patient's condition and needs. A new fully informed consent would also be necessary.

Otherwise, the only time a full consent would be necessary for each treatment is when a state requires a written authorization. That policy then takes precedence over the simpler approach described above. Even in these states, however, a short-form document might be used (see chapter 12 infra).

Either way, documentation of the treatment provided to patients must be maintained. This is necessary for treatment, billing, and utilization review, and is also used for purposes such as legal defense. Patients' health records should note whether the patient had any questions or, in response to staff inquiries, voiced any complaints or symptoms. Details should be included of the answers to these questions and any responses from the patients, as well as of whatever action was taken concerning the complaints.

Much of the concern in continuous or repetitive treatment is more a matter of effective communication with patients and good medical practice than it is of the law of consent. Particularly with patients who require continuous or repetitive treatment it is unwise to take their understanding and acceptance for granted. Instead, running dialogues with patients help foster the understanding essential to the consent process and to participation in their own health care.

§2.9 Placebo, Deception, and Consent

Some occasions call for the administration of a placebo, perhaps as the final "therapy" in an attempt to differentiate a psychosomatic disease from one of physical origin. Consent issues are raised when a practitioner believes that a full disclosure of information will be harmful to a highly suggestible patient — in other words, disclosing a risk of paralysis would result in the patient developing those symptoms. What can be done in these circumstances in order to meet the requirements of consent but at the same time provide the most reasonable care?

§2.9.1 *Placebo, Deception, and Clinical Treatment*

The answer lies in the general principles of consent and in the exception known as therapeutic privilege. Under the medical community rule of disclosure, a practitioner need reveal only that amount of information that a reasonable physician in like or similar circumstances would disclose. Disclosure is also sometimes measured by what is customary practice in such circumstances. A placebo may be administered to patients under the medical community rule of disclosure, providing that it is customary practice to withhold information regarding its use. Whether it is customary practice or whether a reasonable physician would take such a step depends upon the facts and circumstances of each case.

Under the patient need rule the disclosure by a practitioner need only cover significant risks, in other words, considerations that are important to a patient in reaching an informed choice. This standard of disclosure is a measure of what a reasonable patient would want to know in the same or similar circumstances. Implementing this standard raises two important issues. First, is the fact that a placebo will be used or information withheld material to patients' choices? Whether they will be affected by this knowledge — regardless of what the placebo or withheld information actually is — can only be determined on a case by case basis.

Second, how the reasonable patient standard applies to this situation is not entirely clear. Would a *reasonable* patient want to know that she is receiving a placebo because of a suspected psychosomatic illness? Would a *reasonable* patient object to non-disclosure of some information if the physician believed that disclosure might bring on a suggestive illness? These questions must be answered on an individual patient basis. However, in all likelihood, a reasonable person would object to the nondisclosure of a significant risk of death or serious harm.

Apart from these concerns, the law has carved out the therapeutic privilege exception to cover certain nondisclosures of information. Applicable to treatment situations governed by both the medical community and patient need rules of disclosure, the privilege serves as a defense to actions based on lack of consent. Generally speaking, the privilege may be invoked when disclosure of information is likely to have a substantial and adverse impact upon the patient and his condition or treatment. Such a result is certainly possible when placebos or suggestible patients are factors. It is incumbent upon the practitioner in these cases to show that a revelation of the information at issue would cause substantial harm.

A physician's use of this defense relies on the existence of detailed documentation — for example, an explanatory note in the patient's chart recorded contemporaneously with the decision to use the privilege. The note should explain why the information is being withheld or why a placebo is being used. If necessary in questionable cases, the physician should seek a consultation to reinforce her clinical conclusions.

The use of the privilege in this context should not be taken lightly. The courts will not excuse outright deception, which would run counter to the law's policy of allowing patients to decide what shall be done to their bodies. Only when the withholding of information can be justified on sound clinical grounds will the law permit the privilege to be invoked.

§2.9.2 Placebo, Deception, and Human Research

a. Federal research requirements. According to federal research regulations promulgated by the Department of Health
and Human Services, a research subject — unless certain exemptions are met — must give her informed consent to participate in a study.[1] Some categories of research are removed from
the scope of the law, including studies that are commonly accepted in educational settings such as those involving the use of
educational tests and interview or survey work.[2]

In these cases the use of placebo or deception may proceed,
bearing in mind that state law requirements must also be satisfied. However, even these exempted research areas may be
placed under federal regulation if, for example, the research
subjects may be identified[3] or if certain information, if released, could prove damaging to them.[4]

A research project that would normally necessitate obtaining
informed consent can sometimes be made an exception to these
regulatory requirements. Institutional review boards (IRBs),
which make these decisions, impose the following four conditions for less than a full consent:

1. The study must not involve more than minimal risk;[5] that
   is, the risk of harm anticipated in the study should not be
   any greater than that found in daily life or that found in a
   routine physical or psychological examination.
2. By modifying or waiving the requirements of consent, the
   rights and welfare of the patient will not be adversely affected.
3. It would not be practical to conduct the study without the
   waiver or modification of requirements.

---

§2.9   [1]45 C.F.R. §§46.101 et seq. (1981). See also chapter 8, infra.
[2]45 C.F.R. §46.101 (1981).
[3]Id.
[4]Id.
[5]45 C.F.R. §46.102 (1981).

4. When possible, following the study the subjects will be furnished with additional information.[6]

The fact that the use of a placebo or the withholding of information cannot involve more than minimal risk should be emphasized. The federal requirements are not flexible on this point: the welfare and safety of the research subject must come first. One alternative, of course, is to let control and case subjects alike know that placebos will be used in the study. Such a course does not entail indicating at the outset which group will receive the placebo: that information may be disclosed following the study, the time when the federal regulations suggest revealing additional pertinent information.[7]

b. State research requirements. State law takes a different approach to research involving placebos and deception than does the federal Department of Health and Human Services. The difference is particularly noticeable in California,[8] New York,[9] and Virginia,[10] where specific legislation on human research may be found. In California, the definition of "voluntary informed consent" expressly excludes the use of deceit.[11] However, a placebo may be used in a medical experiment, providing that all subjects are told that it will be administered during the study. They need not be informed whether they will be given the placebo.[12]

Under New York law the definition of voluntary informed consent also precludes the use of deceit.[13] Unlike the California provision, no mention is made of the dispensing and use of placebos during a research study.

[6]45 C.F.R. §46.116 (1981).
[7]Id.
[8]Cal. Health & Safety Code §§24170 et seq. (West 1978).
[9]N.Y. Pub. Health Law §§2440-2446 (McKinney 1975).
[10]Va. Code §§37.1-234 to 37.1-238 (1979).
[11]Cal. Health & Safety Code §24172 (West 1978).
[12]Cal. Health & Safety Code §24173 (West 1978).
[13]N.Y. Pub. Health Law §2441 (McKinney 1975).

Virginia's human research legislation prohibits the use of deceit in a voluntary informed consent.[14] However, as in its federal counterpart, certain latitude is vested in a human research review committee. That committee can alter the requirements for consent, providing that evidence is offered to prove that the subjects are not at serious risk, meeting the requirements for consent would invalidate important objectives of the study, and alternatives to meet these objectives would prove less advantageous to the research subjects.[15]

In other states the law of consent relating to research is less well developed. In all likelihood, however, the use of deception in a research setting would be frowned upon. This assumption follows from the fact that in a treatment situation, deception would not be considered appropriate. The use of therapeutic privilege in research that is not beneficial to the subject cannot be supported. The privilege is intended for use in a *treatment* — not research — setting.

It should also be kept in mind that obtaining consent to a research project through outright trickery cannot be defended as a necessary withholding of information that might compromise the study. Revealing the general nature and objective of the research can be done without disclosing the fact, for example, that it is designed to measure suggestibility to illness. Subjects could be told of any known risks as well as other pertinent consent information. Without compromising the objectives of the study, in other words, the disclosure could be designed to meet the standards of human research protocols.

When placebos are involved a similar format could be followed to that established under California law. The validity of the research data is not compromised by the participants' knowledge that certain unidentified participants may receive a placebo. If the individual agrees to participate on these terms consent would be informed providing other consent criteria are met.

[14]Va. Code §37.1-234 (1979).
[15]Va. Code §37.1-235 (1979).

§2.9.3 Policy Considerations

To a large degree the strict requirements for consent found in the clinical or research setting are designed for the protection of the patient/subject. They protect the subject's or patient's right to know the consequences before embarking upon a course of treatment or experimentation. In a sense, they also embody a contract that sets forth the scope of the agreement between patient and physician or researcher and subject.

A sometimes overlooked corollary of this strict adherence to consent requirements is the benefit to the practitioner or researcher. By following the law they gain a measure of protection against any subsequent claims of failure to obtain informed consent. Faced with fulfilled criteria for consent and sufficient documentation, the plaintiff would be hard pressed to establish a case against the practitioner or researcher — a good example of preventive medical law.

THREE

Women and Reproductive Matters

§3.0   Introduction
A. Birth Control and Consent
  §3.1   Disclosure with the Pill and IUDs
    §3.1.1   The Manufacturer's Duty to Warn
    §3.1.2   Packet Inserts Directed at Physicians
    §3.1.3   Legal Effect of FDA's "Dear Doctor" Letters
    §3.1.4   Patient Packet Inserts and Doctors' Duty to Warn
    §3.1.5   Minimizing Litigation and Consent Requirements
B. Sterilization and Consent
  §3.2   Criteria for Consent
    §3.2.1   Consequences of Invalid Consents
    §3.2.2   Amount of Necessary Disclosure
    §3.2.3   Practical Points
  §3.3   Spousal Consent
    §3.3.1   The General Rule
    §3.3.2   Right of Privacy
    §3.3.3   Statutory Law
    §3.3.4   Practical Considerations
C. Abortion and Consent
  §3.4   Supreme Court Precedent
  §3.5   General State Consent Requirements
    §3.5.1   Informational Content of Consent
    §3.5.2   "Consent" Waiting Periods
    §3.5.3   Restrictions on Who May Obtain Consent
    §3.5.4   Counselling Patients Regarding Abortion
  §3.6   Biological Father's Consent to Abortion
D. Conception, Pregnancy, and Consent
  §3.7   Artificial Insemination
    §3.7.1   Basic Disclosure Requirements

§3.7.2   Need for Spousal Consent
§3.7.3   Status of the Donor
§3.7.4   Unmarried Recipients
§3.7.5   Consent as a Defense to Adultery
§3.8   Prenatal Venereal Disease Screening
§3.9   Duty to Disclose Risks of Birth Defects and Delivery Problems
        §3.9.1   Inadequate Disclosure of Birth Defect Risk
                  Information
        §3.9.2   Necessary Disclosures to Prospective Parents
        §3.9.3   Maternal Rubella
        §3.9.4   Necessary Disclosures to Prospective Mothers
        §3.9.5   Delivery Risks
        §3.9.6   Practical Considerations
E. Consent to Medical and Surgical Treatment: Special Issues of Concern
    to Women
    §3.10   Hysterectomy Surgery
            §3.10.1   Unauthorized Hysterectomies
            §3.10.2   Failure to Disclose Reasonable Alternatives
            §3.10.3   Inadequate Disclosure of Risk Information
            §3.10.4   Choosing Risk Information for Disclosure
    §3.11   Radiation Treatment and Radium Implants
    §3.12   Mastectomy Surgery
            §3.12.1   Statutory Requirements
            §3.12.2   Physician's Duty to Warn
            §3.12.3   Breast Biopsy Beyond a Patient's Authorization
            §3.12.4   Disclosing Risk of Frozen Section Biopsies
    §3.13   Risk Disclosure in Urogenital Surgery and Diagnostic
            Procedures on Women
            §3.13.1   Disclosure of Varying Theories of Cell Growth
            §3.13.2   Disclosure of Risks of Foregoing Pap Smears
            §3.13.3   Practical Considerations
    §3.14   Screening for Women's Diseases
            §3.14.1   Pap Smear Legislation
            §3.14.2   Pap Smears and Disclosure Requirements
            §3.14.3   DES Screening
    §3.15   Treatment for Rape Victims

§3.0   Introduction

This chapter examines consent to treatment as it relates to women and reproductive matters. The duty to disclose risk information related to various birth control methods, the risks of conception following tubal ligation and vasectomy, and the need for a spouse's consent prior to sterilization are discussed in the first part of the chapter. Following is an examination of state-mandated premarital and prenatal venereal disease tests, statutory requirements for artificial insemination, and the duty to disclose possible birth defects. Abortion is explored in terms of United States Supreme Court precedent and lower court decisions. The chapter concludes with a look at so-called women's problems: mastectomy, hysterectomy, Pap smears, and DES screening tests.

A. BIRTH CONTROL AND CONSENT

§3.1 Disclosure with the Pill and IUDs

In the United States a considerable amount of litigation involves injuries linked to birth control. Those cases dealing with the duty to disclose risk information are central to this discussion of women and the consent process. Many cases have focused on a physician's alleged failure to warn her patient about risks that subsequently materialized. Plaintiffs usually argue that their consent to using birth control medication, devices, or other hormonal drugs was defective because they were not fully informed of the risks.[1] A discussion of a few of these cases will illustrate the legal contentions on both sides.

In Klink v. G.D. Searle & Co., a married woman sued her

§3.1 [1]See, e.g., Klink v. G.D. Searle & Co., 26 Wash. App. 951, 614 P.2d 701 (1980); Hamilton v. Hardy, 37 Colo. App. 375, 549 P.2d 1099 (1976), both dealing with birth control medication. For cases involving intrauterine devices (IUDs), see Nutting v. Associates in Obstetrics and Gynecology, P.C., 515 N.Y.S.2d 926 (App. Div. 1987); Duffey v. Fear, 505 N.Y.S.2d 136 (App. Div. 1986); Tresemer v. Barke, 86 Cal. App. 3d 656, 150 Cal. Rptr. 384 (1978); 9 A.L.R. 4th 364 (1981). For an interesting case involving Provera, see Lynch v. Bay Ridge Obstetrical and Gynecological Assocs., P.C., 1988 WL 112,515 (N.Y.).

physician for medical negligence. The woman had started taking Ovulen-21, a birth control pill, at the age of 19; seventeeen months later she suffered a bilateral stroke.[2] The trial disclosed that the doctor had not told her that her underlying amenorrhea condition could be a sign of infertility, nor that the contraceptive was not a treatment for her condition. As the plaintiff indicated in her testimony, had she been so informed and had she been given other information relating to her condition, she would not have consented to taking the pill.

On appeal, the Washington Court of Appeals affirmed the lower court's ruling. It rejected the defendant's argument that the trial court had improperly excluded a survey of other physicians regarding the duty to disclose risks associated with birth control pills. That exclusion was deemed proper since it only revealed what other physicians told their patients. The evidence did nothing to establish a defense justifying the defendant's failure to disclose certain facts to the patient.[3]

In another case, the Colorado Court of Appeals reversed a trial court's decision dismissing an action against a physician who had prescribed birth control pills.[4] The patient, who had suffered a stroke, claimed that the doctor never informed her of the risks of abnormal blood clotting associated with birth control pills and that he never gave her any literature or booklets on the subject. The plaintiff claimed that when she went to her doctor with complaints of severe headaches, he could not find any reason to discontinue the birth control medication.

In remanding the case, the appellate court held that the issues relating to informed consent should have been presented to the jury. The plaintiff had made out a prima facie case and it was incumbent upon the defendant to show that his lack of disclosure was consistent with community standards. The court also held that causality would be gauged by what a reasonable person in the patient's position would have decided had she been properly informed.[5]

[2]Klink v. G.D. Searle & Co., 26 Wash. App. 951, 614 P.2d 701 (1980).
[3]Id.
[4]Hamilton v. Hardy, 37 Colo. App. 375, 549 P.2d 1099 (1976).
[5]Id.

Birth control medication has not been the sole basis for litigation involving a failure to disclose risk information. In a California case, a woman sued her physician for failure to disclose information relating to the risks of the Dalkon Shield intrauterine device (IUD).[6] The theory underlying the plaintiff's case was that after the defendant had inserted the IUD, he negligently failed to warn her of hazards of which he was aware, which constituted a breach of the physician's duty to warn. In reversing the trial court's summary judgment in favor of the doctor, the California appellate court ruled that the patient had stated a cause of action based on a failure to warn. It based its ruling on the confidential physician-patient relationship.[7]

§3.1.1 The Manufacturer's Duty to Warn

The great weight of authority limits the manufacturer's duty to warn to the dispensing physician,[8] with the rationale being that it would be impractical for the manufacturer to contact each and every consumer of a given birth control device or preparation. The physician, presumably, is in a better position than the patient to assess and weigh the risks and benefits of a drug or device for a particular individual.[9] The physician is a "learned intermediary" who can draw upon his professional expertise in deciding whether a patient should receive birth control medication.[10]

That the duty to warn runs from the manufacturer to the physician has been called into question in a Massachusetts case.[11] A woman who had taken birth control pills for three

[6]Tresemer v. Barke, 86 Cal. App. 3d 656, 150 Cal. Rptr. 384 (1978).
[7]Id.
[8]See, e.g., Chambers v. G.D. Searle & Co., 567 F.2d (4th Cir. 1977), affd., 441 F. Supp. 377 (Md. 1975); Vaughn v. G.D. Searle & Co., 272 Or. 367, 536 P.2d 1247 (1975); McEwen v. Ortho Pharmaceutical Corp., 270 Or. 375, 528 P.2d 522 (1974); Carmichael v. Reitz, 17 Cal. App. 3d 958, 95 Cal. Rptr. 381 (1971); Eiser v. Feldman, 507 N.Y.S.2d 386 (App. Div. 1986).
[9]M. Dixon, Drug Product Liability §902[2] (1981).
[10]Pierluisi v. Squibb, 44 F. Supp. 691 (D.P.R. 1977).
[11]MacDonald v. Ortho Pharmaceutical Corp., 394 Mass. 131 (1985).

years suffered a stroke that left her permanently disabled. She sued the manufacturer of the contraceptives, Ortho Pharmaceutical Corporation, claiming that Ortho had been negligent in failing to give her an adequate warning of the risks associated with the birth control pills. The jury returned a verdict in favor of the plaintiff. However, the trial court entered judgment in favor of the defendant indicating that the manufacturer had no duty to warn the plaintiff.

In overturning the trial court determination the Massachusetts Supreme Court held that the manufacturer *does have* a duty to directly warn the consumer of the inherent dangers of using birth control pills. In taking this position, the court drew a distinction between oral contraceptives and other medication. According to the court it is feasible for manufacturers of birth control medication to warn consumers directly of the dangers associated with the use of the pills. Unlike other situations in which physicians have frequent contact with their patients who are taking prescribed medication, doctors who prescribe birth control pills see their patients on an annual basis when they review the prescription for the drugs. As the court pointed out, these encounters between physicians and patients may be inadequate "to apprise consumers of the product's dangers at the time the initial selection of a contraceptive method is made as well as at subsequent points when alternative methods may be considered."[12] Furthermore, to augment its ruling that the manufacturer had a direct duty to warn patients, the court noted that consumers took an increased role in deciding whether to use birth control pills, compared to patients receiving prescriptions for treatment of illnesses.[13]

The defendant argued that if in fact it had the duty to warn the plaintiff, the warning conveyed in its consumer booklet, which met the requirements of the Food and Drug Administration, was adequate. Moreover, the defendant argued that compliance with FDA requirements preempted or delineated the bounds of the common law duty to warn. The Massachusetts

[12] Id. at 138.
[13] Id.

court disagreed, noting that "in instances where a trier of fact could reasonably conclude that a manufacturer's compliance with FDA labeling requirements or guidelines did not adequately apprise oral contraceptive users of inherent risks, the manufacturer should not be shielded from liability by such compliance."[14] In this case the jury could have determined that despite the manufacturer's compliance with FDA labelling requirements, the failure to mention "stroke" as a risk breached the duty to warn.[15]

The court went further, indicating that the adequacy of a warning must be judged not only by what is stated but by how it is conveyed. According to the court, the jury may well have decided, based on their common experience and the evidence given by the plaintiff, that the failure to mention stroke as a risk undercut the warning's impact or did not make the risk reasonably understandable to the average consumer.[16]

The Massachusetts Supreme Court decision should be read as an exception to the prevailing rule of law on the drug manufacturer's duty to warn the consumer. As evinced in the lone dissenting opinion in the case, the decision is subject to criticism.[17]

If as the court indicated the would-be oral contraceptive user is more actively involved in deciding whether to use the pill, does it not follow that she is better informed and need not rely upon a patient packet insert as her chief source of risk information? Does not the decision threaten the physician-patient relationship by shifting the duty to disclose risk information to someone unfamiliar with the unique characteristics of the patient's case? If the jury were entitled to draw upon its own common experience, then should not some consideration be given to the constant coverage in the media and women's journals over the last decade about the risks associated with use of birth control pills?

The manufacturer's duty to warn the patient may not be

[14] Id. at 139.
[15] Id. at 140.
[16] Id. at 141.
[17] Id. at 142-148.

restricted to the "pill." Indeed, it may extend to other forms of contraception, including spermicide.[18] For example, in a federal court case applying Georgia law, the court ruled that if the manufacturer has either actual or constructive knowledge of the potential harm associated with its product, it must warn the consumer at the time of sale and delivery.[19] In that case, a child was born with multiple deformities allegedly caused by the mother using the spermicide for about one month following conception. Studies introduced into evidence by the plaintiff relating spermicide absorption to birth defects were deemed sufficient to establish causation.

It is noteworthy that the FDA had determined it was unnecessary to put a birth defects warning on nonionic surfactant spermicides such as the one used in this case. This was not a sufficient defense for purposes of Georgia tort law.[20] The fact that the manufacturer had actual or constructive knowledge of the risk of birth defects from its product placed it under a duty to warn potential consumers of this information.

Notwithstanding these decisions, the role of the physician as a learned intermediary cannot be underestimated. (See §3.1.5 infra.) The attending physician is responsible for taking an adequate history of the patient and using this information in conjunction with details from the manufacturer, learned treatises, and journals in framing the risks and benefits of all types of contraceptives for that individual. Standardized warnings mandated by the FDA can never replace the consent process between a provider and patient. Physicians would do well to monitor patients on birth control medication on a more frequent basis than the annual renewal of prescriptions. This is particularly important for patients whose previous personal or family history puts them at risk for serious side effects. Frequent office visits can be effected by limiting the renewal of prescriptions to every three to six months. It can also be

---

[18]See Wells v. Ortho Pharmaceutical Corp., 788 F.2d 741 (11th Cir. 1986), applying Georgia law.
[19]Id.
[20]Id. at 746.

achieved by establishing the proper relationship between doctor and patient during the consent process.

The role of the physician cannot be underestimated in other ways. Many patients look to their physicians for detailed advice in family planning. Care should be taken to discuss the importance of discontinuing the use of preparations that have or are believed to have the potential for causing birth defects. Moreover, physicians should take care to obtain an accurate history from the patient once pregnancy is suspected or established. The *Wells* case is a good example of the need for such careful screening.

It is often difficult for health professionals to understand the difference in approach between health sciences and law. The Georgia case only adds fuel to this concern. Whereas physicians and researchers are concerned with epidemiological precision and statistical significance, the courts may settle for less exactness. There is a difference between legal sufficiency and scientific certainty.[21] The realities of the situation make accurate history taking and discussion of risk an important part of the treatment process.

The manufacturer, however, in conveying warnings to a physician must meet a certain standard in order to escape liability. The information the company provides, for example, must be shown to be consistent with the manufacturer's actual knowledge, whether obtained through research or reports of adverse reaction. Additionally, the warnings must measure up to the manufacturer's constructive knowledge available from scientific literature and other forms of communication.[22]

§3.1.2 Packet Inserts Directed at Physicians

Packet inserts accompanying a drug that describe risk information about birth control medication are not sufficient to dis-

[21] Wells v. Ortho, supra n.18, citing Ferebee v. Chevron Chemical Co., 736 F.2d 1529, 1536 (D.C. Cir.), cert. denied, 469 U.S. 1062 (1984).
[22] Dixon, Drug Product Liability, supra n.9, at §9.03 (supp.), quoting Dulke v. Upjohn, 555 F.2d 245, 248 (9th Cir. 1977).

charge the manufacturer's duty to warn. This point was made clear in a Massachusetts case dealing with the drug manufacturer's duty to warn the ultimate consumer of birth control preparations.[23] As that case pointed out, compliance with FDA packet insert regulations did not preclude the need for an adequate warning of risks. Moreover, adherence to FDA guidelines could not insulate the manufacturer from liability.[24] Whether risk information is disseminated for the benefit of physicians or patients, the key issue for the manufacturer is the adequacy of the details provided in packet inserts. Failure to provide significant, material information could render such documents ineffective as evidence of compliance with the duty to warn.

§3.1.3   Legal Effect of FDA's "Dear Doctor" Letters

Similarly, manufacturers would be ill advised to rely on the information provided by government agencies for protection. From time to time the FDA publishes so-called Dear Doctor letters, which alert physicians to certain risks associated with medications. The fact that the FDA issues such a letter regarding oral contraceptives does not relieve the manufacturer of the obligation to provide adequate warnings of known or possible danger. These letters may, however, have some bearing on the issue of a physician's independent knowledge of dangers associated with drugs she prescribes.[25]

§3.1.4   Patient Packet Inserts and Doctors' Duty to Warn

One possible method of dealing with these issues, as yet not fully tested, is the government-backed idea of manufacturers

---

[23] MacDonald v. Ortho Pharmaceutical Corp., 394 Mass. 131 (1985).
[24] Id.
[25] Id.

conveying warnings directly to consumers by means of a "patient packet insert." Such a policy, it is argued, would make all options available to a patient, including the gathering of risk information about birth control medication and devices. According to this theory, the patient would then be able to give a fully informed consent.[26]

The FDA has already issued regulations requiring patient packet inserts for birth control medication and IUDs.[27] Its action was followed by the filing of a major lawsuit by the Pharmaceutical Manufacturers' Association challenging the requirement for oral contraceptives. That suit was unsuccessful, however: both the trial and appellate courts found that the FDA had the authority to initiate a warning system for consumers of oral contraceptives.[28]

Doctors should not view patient packet inserts as relieving them of the obligation to inform their patients fully prior to prescribing birth control medication or devices. First of all, the packet insert is only available to consumers when they pick up the prescription — in other words, after the choice of birth control has been made and *after* the doctor has supposedly obtained a fully informed consent. The availability of the packets cannot supersede the need for a physician's initially obtaining a thorough history of the patient and explaining the risks and benefits of a suggested birth control medication along with those of alternative methods. It is at that point — not when a prescription and packet insert are in hand — that the patient must decide to give her informed consent.

Second, many consumers will not read the inserts accompanying oral contraceptives and IUDs, and among those that do, a proportion will not understand the information. A standardized form cannot replace the doctor-patient exchange that should occur before medication is prescribed.

The patient packet inserts may be an indication that the FDA

[26]Dixon, Drug Product Liability, supra n.9, at §6.10(4) (6), ref. 18, quoting a speech by the commissioner of the FDA on the subject.
[27]21 C.F.R. §5.11 (1982).
[28]Pharmaceutical Mfrs. Assn. v. FDA, 484 F. Supp. 1179 (D. Del. 1980), affd., 634 F.2d 106 (3d Cir. 1981) (per curiam).

is not satisfied with the amount of information patients are receiving before a course of contraceptive therapy is initiated. The insert information is a stopgap measure to make certain that patients fully understand the risks and benefits associated with their choice. Some patients may even act on the information provided and call and discuss it with their physicians.

Lawsuits are bound to continue over the failure to warn women about the risks of IUDs and oral contraceptives. Whether the risk information contained in packet inserts will be imputed to a patient, however, remains to be seen. Similarly, it is debatable whether risk information gained from articles in the popular press will be imputed to patients. Such articles could result in the imparting of constructive knowledge to patients.

§3.1.5   Minimizing Litigation and Consent Requirements

The care with which physicians handle the prescription and consent processes determines their vulnerability to litigation on these issues. Doctors should, for instance, keep themselves up to date on developments involving oral contraceptives and IUDs. The should *thoroughly* explain risk information, including side effects and possible health implications, to their patients who desire birth control pills. Merely recounting what is considered routine precaution is not sufficient. Patients should be informed of *specific dangers* associated with the use of birth control medication or IUDs.[29]

The choice of a prescription should be preceded by a careful history, which is aimed at identifying those for whom birth control pills or IUDs are medically contraindicated, and followed by an admonition to contact the doctor immediately if a

---

[29]See Marshall v. Clinic for Women, P.A., 490 So. 2d 861 (Miss. 1986) (dissenting opinion), in which the judge argues that patients are entitled to information regarding the specific dangers associated with the use of a particular type of IUD in order to make intelligent choices regarding treatment.

problem arises. Prescriptions should be limited so that patients must come back for checkups and a reassessment of continued use. Reasonable efforts should be made to contact those who fail to return for these follow-up visits. An instruction sheet describing possible side effects, their significance, and the suggested patient response should be given to each person for whom birth control pills or IUDs are prescribed. Physicians should make careful notations in patients' records describing the information conveyed to them and the medication or device prescribed. The notes should also be dated and signed. Such efforts will not prevent all litigation for failure to disclose risks, but they will equip physicians with sound defense material and, perhaps, even prevent patient injury.

Failure to take a cautious, informative attitude with patients can prove detrimental to physicians. For example, in a Georgia case the court ruled that a patient could sue her physician for willfully misrepresenting to her the risks associated with insertion of an IUD.[30] The action was brought under rather restrictive state legislation, which does not obligate physicians to inform patients of the risks associated with procedures. Under the legislation, all that need be done is to inform patients of the general terms of care to be provided.[31] However, as the court suggested, when a patient asks about the risks of the proposed treatment, the doctor is obligated to provide a truthful response.[32]

In this case the plaintiff claimed that she asked the doctor about the risks associated with inserting the IUD. He purportedly informed the patient that unless she was pregnant she faced no risks and the prospect of only minor side effects. In fact, the woman experienced persistent pain and bleeding over several days. She subsequently underwent extensive surgery to correct a perforated uterus.[33]

In reversing the lower court's judgment in favor of the doc-

---

[30]Spikes v. Heath, 175 Ga. App. 187, 332 S.E.2d 889 (1985).
[31]Id.
[32]Id.
[33]Id.

tor, the court ruled that if it were determined that the representations and assurances provided by the doctor were false and all the elements of fraud were met, the plaintiff would be entitled to recover damages. Such a finding would be based on assault and battery due to the failure to obtain a valid consent.[34]

Whether a physician practices in Georgia or in a state that follows the doctrine of informed consent, practical, preventive measures should be taken to minimize litigation. The better informed a patient is, and the greater the level of communication between the doctor and the patient, the less chance of litigation. All litigation involving consent and contraceptives cannot be eliminated. Nonetheless, preventive measures can be put in place to reduce its likelihood.

B. STERILIZATION AND CONSENT

§3.2 Criteria for Consent

As with the prescribing of oral birth control medication and IUDs, physicians must meet consent standards prior to sterilizing a man or woman. The requirements are recognized in common law precedent[1] as well as in statutory[2] and regulatory law;[3] they apply whether the sterilization is incident to some other authorized procedure or stands as the sole objective.

§3.2.1 Consequences of Invalid Consents

Failure to obtain valid authorization for a sterilization procedure has resulted in litigation focusing on informed consent.

---

[34]Id.

§3.2 [1]See Thimatariga v. Chambers, 46 Md. 213, 416 A.2d 1326 (1980).
[2]Calif. Welf. & Inst. Code §14191 (West 1975).
[3]45 C.F.R. §205.35 (1981). See also 42 C.F.R. §441.253 (1981), involving hysterectomies funded under Medicaid.

One Maryland case involved a 25-year-old unmarried mother of two boys who sued her surgeon for unauthorized removal of her reproductive organs.[4] During surgery for removal of the woman's ovarian cyst, the doctor contended, he found that her left fallopian tube had been ruptured by an apparent tubal pregnancy. In addition, the ovarian cyst on the patient's left ovary was found to be quite large. The doctor claimed, furthermore, that his examination of the woman's right ovary and right fallopian tube indicated that neither was in a functional condition. He proceeded to remove both ovaries and both tubes as well as her uterus, rendering the woman sterile. Later, a pathologist's report disputed the defendant's findings, followed by the plaintiff's expert witness claiming that, had the uterus and right fallopian tube and ovary been left intact, the woman would have been able to bear more children. In finding for the plaintiff, the Maryland court applied that state's consent rule as developed in an earlier case.[5] In so doing it held that had she been properly informed, a reasonable person in the patient's position would not have authorized the surgery.[6]

A similar result was reached in a Louisiana case concerning a woman who had had a tubal ligation following a caesarean section.[7] On several occasions prior to the delivery of the plaintiff's last child, the doctor had broached the question of a tubal ligation, to which the plaintiff claimed that she never agreed. On the consent form presented prior to delivery, the plaintiff or a nurse at her insistence struck out language relating to sterilization. During the caesarean section, when he realized that the patient had not executed a hospital tubal ligation form, the doctor sent a nurse out of the operating room to secure the signed consent of the patient's husband.

In reversing the lower court's determination in favor of the defendant, the Louisiana Court of Appeal held that, absent an emergency, a physician must secure the consent of a patient

[4]Thimatariga v. Chambers, supra n.1.
[5]Sard v. Hardy, 281 Md. 432, 379 A.2d 1014 (1977).
[6]Thimatariga v. Chambers, supra n.1.
[7]Beck v. Lovell, 361 So. 2d 245 (La. Ct. App. 1978).

prior to a surgical procedure. A physician who operates in the absence of that consent is liable for damages — even if the unauthorized operation is skillfully performed. The consent of the husband in this case, the court held, did not satisfy that obligation. In other than emergent circumstances the husband-wife relationship does not vest one spouse with power to consent to surgery upon the other.[8]

In some states battery actions for unauthorized sterilization procedures remain a valid cause of action. For example, in a California case, the court of appeal ruled that there was a genuine issue of fact whether the plaintiff had authorized a tubal ligation. When the plaintiff was pregnant she discussed with the defendant doctor the idea of having the sterilization procedure after the delivery of her child. The patient informed the doctor, however, that she did not want the operation if the child was born with any abnormalities. Following the delivery of the child, the patient underwent a tubal ligation. After the operation the patient learned that her child was afflicted with Trisomy 18 and the infant died two months later. In vacating the defendant's demurrer to the claim of battery, the court pointed out that the plaintiff's claim was sufficient for a cause of action based on this theory.[9]

The striking feature of this California case is that it occurred in a state in which a major court decision[10] largely eroded battery actions. However, as the California Court of Appeal pointed out, the decision of Cobbs v. Grant still reserved the right to bring an action on this basis when an operation is performed without the patient's consent.

Providing patients with adequate information is not enough; clinicians must be certain that patients understand the nature and lasting consequences of sterilization procedures. Moreover, there must be clear and specific consent to such operations.

---

[8] Id. at 250.

[9] Grieves v. Superior Court, 157 Cal. App. 3d 129, 203 Cal. Rptr. 556 (1984).

[10] Cobbs v. Grant, 8 Cal. 3d 229, 104 Cal. Rptr. 505, 502 P.2d 1 (1972).

§3.2.2 Amount of Necessary Disclosure

Another consent issue involving sterilization procedures focuses on the standard of disclosure. As some cases have revealed, tubal ligations and vasectomies are not always successful; additional children have been born after the wife or husband has been "sterilized."[11] Negligence actions are then sometimes brought over children born after one of the parents has undergone a sterilization procedure. For physicians, warning patients of the risks of this eventuality and reasonable alternative means of sterilization is essential. A few cases illustrate this point.

a. Examples of inadequate disclosure. A Minnesota couple decided not to have any more children following the birth of their seventh child.[12] Several weeks after the husband underwent a vasectomy, he brought a sperm sample in for analysis. He was later told by his physician that the results were negative. The doctor did not, however, inform the man of the need for further sperm analysis nor did he advise continuing the use of contraceptives (which he had done immediately following the procedure). As it turned out, the test results were positive, and without contraceptives, the wife became pregnant. In a decision in which a judgment for the plaintiff was reversed on other grounds, the Supreme Court of Minnesota held that the jury had before it sufficient evidence to warrant a finding of negligence. As the court noted, the physician was negligent in that he failed to properly inform the patient and as a direct result of his negligence, the patient's wife became pregnant and bore another child.[13]

In a Maryland case, a woman and her husband sued her physician following an unsuccessful tubal ligation and birth of

---

[11]Sherlock v. Stillwater Clinic, 260 N.W.2d 169 (Minn. 1977); Sard v. Hardy, 281 Md. 432, 379 A.2d 1014 (1977).
[12]Sherlock v. Stillwater Clinic, supra n.11.
[13]Id.

her fourth child.[14] The woman claimed that the defendant had told her that women about to undergo their third caesarean section usually did not have any more children. She informed the doctor that given the complications she had experienced in an earlier pregnancy and the inability to afford any more children, she wished to take steps to prevent having more children. The doctor never mentioned to either the woman or her husband the various methods of tubal ligation that were available. Moreover, he did not disclose the rates of failure associated with the available procedures or that the likelihood of such a procedure's failure dropped appreciably when performed at a time other than at a caesarean birth. The patient claimed that the doctor never warned her of the risk of future pregnancies. Indeed, the woman claimed that he had assured her prior to the operation that she would not have any more children.

In its ruling, the Maryland Court of Appeals held that the duty to disclose was to be measured by materiality — that is, risk information that is significant to a reasonable person in the patient's position in determining whether to undergo a surgical or medical procedure.[15] As applied to this case, given the woman's concern for her health and her financial ability to handle more children, a jury could find that a reasonable person in the woman's position would term significant any information about the failure of tubal ligations and the risk of continued fertility.[16]

On the issue of causality the Maryland court ruled that if it could be shown that a reasonable person in the patient's position would have withheld authorization for surgery had all material risk information been revealed, there would be a causal relationship between failure to disclose and the harm suffered. In this case, based on the evidence supporting the inference of materiality relating to the standard of disclosure, there

[14]Sard v. Hardy, 281 Md. 432, 379 A.2d 1014 (1977). The woman's first child was dead at birth. Including the child born following her failed tubal ligation, she had three live births.
[15]Id. at 437, 379 A.2d at 1022.
[16]Id. at 439, 379 A.2d at 1023.

were sufficient facts to support a determination of proximate cause.[17]

b. A case example of adequate disclosure. Not all cases based on an allegation of failure to disclose fertility information following sterilization have resulted in judgments against physicians. For example, in Bennett v. Graves, the Kentucky Court of Appeals affirmed a judgment in favor of a physician who had allegedly improperly informed his patient about the efficacy of a tubal ligation.[18] After the woman's eighth child, the doctor performed a tubal ligation using a technique considered to have a low failure rate. Subsequently, she bore her ninth child. The patient had signed a consent form with her husband that stated in part:

> The risks involved and the possibility of complications have been explained to me. Even though good results are expected I acknowledge that no guarantee or assurance has been given to me as to the results that may be obtained.[19]

In view of the signed consent form and considering the fact that the woman had already borne eight children, the court found it inconceivable that the patient would not have discussed the risk of failure associated with tubal ligation.[20]

§3.2.3 Practical Points

Physicians engaged in sterilization procedures must be diligent in informing patients of the risk of failure as well as of the improbability of reversal. Care must be taken to avoid promising or warranting to patients a successful sterilization procedure.[21]

---

[17]Id. at 440, 370 A.2d at 1025.
[18]557 S.W.2d 893 (Ky. Ct. App. 1977).
[19]Id. at 894.
[20]Id.
[21]See Murray v. University of Pa. Hosp., 490 A.2d 839 (Pa. Super. Ct. 1985).

Physicians must be certain to have the patient's consent prior to performing a sterilization procedure. If sterilizations are performed in a hospital, doctors must make sure that they meet the facility's consent policy. In addition, doctors should be aware of any applicable federal, state, or local laws that set forth consent requirements. This is particularly true in Georgia, where state legislation has been interpreted to require only disclosure of the intended results of a sterilization operation and *not* the possible risks and complications associated with it.[22]

For the lawyer advising physician clients or defending negligent consent claims involving sterilization, there are some important practical tips. For example, it is probably prudent to advise physician clients to obtain consent themselves rather than to delegate this task to a nurse. It is not that a nurse is any less competent or articulate than the physician. Rather, discussion of risks, benefits, and reasonable alternatives is better addressed by the *treating physician* than by a nurse who is not as well versed in the particular needs and traits of a patient. Moreover, the treating physician may put more emphasis on certain risk factors and the need for poststerilization contraception than another health care provider. Information provided by the attending physician may be given greater weight by the patient than details imparted by another caregiver. Patients identify more strongly with the attending physician than with a nurse or even another medical practitioner. This is an area ripe for flaws in the consent process. It is also an area quite amenable to preventive law or risk control by advising clients to secure consent themselves rather than delegating the task to someone else.[23]

---

[22]Robinson v. Parrish, 720 F.2d 1548 (11th Cir. 1983). The question of statutory interpretation in this case was certified to the Georgia Supreme Court (Robinson v. Parrish, 251 Ga. 496, 306 S.E.2d 922 (1983)) regarding Ga. Code Ann. 24-4536 (Harrison 1981) upon which the Seventh Circuit decision is based.

[23]See Phillips v. Hull, Supreme Court of Mississippi, No. 55989, December 17, 1986, in which the "delegated consent process" was touched upon by the court in a failed sterilization case. The court determined that a genuine issue of material fact existed regarding the adequacy of the patient's consent, thus precluding summary judgment.

Documentation is also an important, practical matter. That a physician discussed the likelihood of a failed sterilization and, in the case of vasectomy, that it is important to use some form of contraceptive until it is determined the operation was effective, should be documented in the patient record. The lack of evidence of such documentation could be the measure of success for the plaintiff.

For the defense and plaintiff's bar, it is important to distinguish between the need for expert testimony to establish the likelihood of risks associated with recommended procedures, the availability of reasonable treatment alternatives, and the need for such evidence in proving *materiality* of such risks. This point was made clear in a failed tubal ligation case in Pennsylvania.[24] Moreover, care should be taken in determining which rule is followed regarding the use of expert witnesses in such cases. The facts and circumstances of the matter may make a solid case for the plaintiff. However, if the practical niceties of expert testimony are overlooked, it could spell victory for the defendant.

Finally, the difficult issue of causation in failed sterilization cases deserves attention. Plaintiffs may be able to prove that physicians failed to discuss the fact that a vasectomy may not be a permanent form of sterilization. Nonetheless, the defendant-physicians may prevail if the plaintiffs cannot establish their cases on the issue of causation. Such was the case in a claim filed under the Federal Tort Claims Act in Massachusetts.[25] In this situation, applying Massachusetts precedent, the court ruled that a reasonable person, upon learning of the small risk of failure associated with vasectomy, would have chosen this form of sterilization over other methods with a greater risk of failure and complications.[26]

The application of the reasonable person standard for causality in failed sterilization cases, such as this case from Massachusetts, may illustrate the unfairness of such a legal principle.

[24]Festa v. Greenberg, 511 A.2d 1371 (Pa. Super. Ct. 1986).
[25]Ostergard v. United States, 677 F. Supp. 1259 (D. Mass. 1987).
[26]Id. at 1264.

It does not take into account the personal interests or traits of
the *actual* patient. On the other hand, it is important to guard
against plaintiffs with "twenty-twenty" hindsight who experience a poststerilization pregnancy.[27]

In some instances laws based on coverage of health care costs
may be involved.[28] Being cognizant of the requirements for
informed consent and applying the provisions of the law in an
appropriate fashion could be instrumental in avoiding litigation for lack of proper authorization in sterilization operations.

§3.3   Spousal Consent

An issue of some concern to those engaged in sterilization procedures is spousal consent. A belief common among many
health professionals and health administrators is that both
spouses' consent must be obtained before the woman undergoes a tubal ligation. A smaller number of people believe the
same type of dual consent requirement applies to vasectomies.
Neither is correct.

§3.3.1   The General Rule

The law is clear that in the absence of statutory or regulatory
law to the contrary, a competent adult may consent to undergoing sterilization without the additional consent of his or her
spouse. Married adult women are no longer deemed a chattel
or property interest of their husbands. Thus, if they are competent, their consent is sufficient whether the surgery involves
tubal ligation or removal of veins.[1] At old common law, the

[27]Marshall v. University of Chicago Hosps. and Clinics, — N.E.2d —
(Ill. App. Ct. 1987).
[28]See, e.g., 45 C.F.R. §205.35 (1981).
§3.3 [1]See Jeffcoat v. Phillips, 417 S.W.2d 903 (Tex. Civ. App. 1967),
wherein a woman underwent surgery for removal of leg veins without her
husband's consent. The court held his approval was not necessary.

property interest analysis did not apply in reverse: women did not have the same basis of claim vis-à-vis their husbands. Therefore, men could consent to medical procedures or surgery without the approval of their wives. The same rule applies today regardless of sex: spousal consent is unnecessary.

§3.3.2 Right of Privacy

Under modern law, the legal basis upon which a court might find spousal consent unnecessary is the constitutional right of privacy. Such was the finding in a New Jersey case in which a court declared that a woman had the right to undergo a sterilization operation without her husband's consent.[2] The court noted that the sterilization issue is closely related to the matter of abortion. Since the courts now hold that a woman has a constitutional right to control her reproductive functions, the same constitutional provisions extend to unilateral decisions relating to sterilization.

§3.3.3 Statutory Law

There is little if any statutory law that expressly states that a patient need not obtain spousal consent prior to undergoing sterilization. There is, however, an Oregon statute that insulates a hospital or surgeon from liability for conducting a sterilization without first receiving the consent of the patient's spouse.[3]

§3.3.4 Practical Considerations

From a practical perspective, despite what the law requires, it may be a wise idea to involve the patient's spouse in a discussion

[2] Ponter v. Ponter, 132 N.J. Super. 50, 342 A.2d 574 (1975). See also Murray v. Vandervander, 522 P.2d 302 (Okla. Ct. App. 1974).
[3] Or. Rev. Stat. §435.305 (1975).

of the proposed procedure. A decision to do so must be based on the circumstances of each case and be preceded by the patient's permission. Involving both spouses in a dialogue is not so much a means of securing their collective consent as it is a way to make certain that both parties understand completely the nature and consequences of sterilization. Discussing risk information and the probable irreversibility of the procedure with both spouses recognizes the lasting nature of sterilization and its great impact on a marital relationship. Although ultimately the decision to undergo sterilization must be left to the patient, there is nothing in law to prevent a physician from making certain that those most concerned understand the meaning of sterilization.

C. ABORTION AND CONSENT

§3.4 Supreme Court Precedent

Since January 1973 when the United States Supreme Court decided Roe v. Wade[1] and Doe v. Bolton,[2] the decision to undergo an abortion has legally belonged to the patient in consultation with her physician.[3] As the Court pointed out in *Roe,* the abortion decision is based on the woman's constitutional right of privacy. That right, however, is not absolute, as is shown by the decision in Webster v. Reproductive Health Services.[4]

In *Webster,* the Court abandoned the trimester analysis used since *Roe.* Instead, the Court suggested that a state's interest in the potentiality of life need not come into existence only at the time of viability. By extending the state's interest throughout pregnancy, the Court opened the door for greater regulation

§3.4 [1] 410 U.S. 113 (1973).
[2] 410 U.S. 179 (1973).
[3] Roe v. Wade, supra n.1, at 164.
[4] — U.S. —, 1989 WL 70,950.

of abortion practices. This includes the right to restrict the use of public facilities and funding for abortions, as well as the right to permit viability testing after the twentieth gestational week.

Webster did not reverse Roe v. Wade. Indeed, the Court was careful to distinguish the situation of criminalized abortion, which was the subject of *Roe,* from the challenged Missouri provisions in *Webster.*

The *Webster* decision by no means settles the abortion decision once and for all. The Court was badly split, and the 1990 term promises other abortion decisions. Significant legislative activity can also be anticipated as legislators across the country reconsider the need for revised state legislation on the topic.

In the years following Roe v. Wade, a number of states passed legislation relating to abortion. Many have statutory consent requirements detailing the type of information a physician must disclose to a patient[5] and 24- or 48-hour[6] waiting periods between the time the information is provided and the giving of consent or performance of abortion. From this volume of legislative activity has come additional judicial interpretation of the law of abortion.

§3.5 General State Consent Requirements

Since the 1973 Supreme Court abortion decisions, a number of states have enacted laws governing consent requirements for the termination of a pregnancy. It is fair to say that no other medical procedure has been singled out for such attention. Laws outlining the informational content of the consent pro-

---

[5]See, e.g., Conn. Gen. Stat. §19-66g (1979); Ill. Ann. Stat. ch. 38, §81-23.2 (Smith-Hurd 1979); Me. Rev. Stat. Ann. tit. 22, §1598 (1979); Mo. Stat. Ann. §188.039 (Vernon 1979); R.I. Gen. Laws §§23-4.7-1 and 23-4.7-2 (1980); Tenn. Code Ann. §39-302 (1979).

[6]Concerning the 24-hour period, see, e.g., Ill. Ann. Stat. ch. 38, §81-23.2 (Smith-Hurd 1979); Ind. Code Ann. §35-1-58.5-2 (Burns 1978); Ky. Rev. Stat. §436.023 (1978).

Concerning the 48-hour period, see, e.g., Me. Rev. Stat. Ann. tit. 22, §1598 (1979); N.D. Cent. Code §14-02.1-03 (1979); Tenn. Code Ann. §39-302 (1979).

cess, requiring waiting periods between disclosure and authorization, and designating the health professional who must obtain the patient's authorization have been enacted. As discussed in this section, these state attempts to curtail abortion practices have resulted in a significant amount of litigation and further interpretation of the rights delineated by the United States Supreme Court.

§3.5.1 Informational Content of Consent

One area of debate for courts reviewing state abortion laws is how far states can go in setting informational standards for abortion. From the growing body of case law on the subject, it is clear that as early as the first trimester a state may require that women execute consent forms prior to undergoing abortions.[1] The United States Supreme Court, in Planned Parenthood of Central Missouri v. Danforth, ruled on the constitutionality of such a state abortion consent provision.[2] That statute provided that for an abortion in the first 12 weeks of pregnancy, a woman would have to indicate in writing that her consent was informed and given freely. The Court pointed out that the decision to undergo an abortion is stressful and important. Whatever decision is made should be based on a woman's full knowledge of the nature and consequences of the procedure. The state, through its statute, may constitutionally provide for her written consent prior to the abortion.[3]

In a footnote the Court dealt with the appellants' argument of vagueness, here in reference to the word "informed." The Court accepted the district court's interpretation of the term as the providing of information regarding what is to be done and its consequences. As the Court cautioned: "To ascribe more meaning than this might well confine the attending physician in

§3.5 [1]Planned Parenthood of Central Missouri v. Danforth, 428 U.S. 52 (1976). See also Wolfe v. Schroering, 541 F.2d 523 (6th Cir. 1976); Doe v. Deschamps, 461 F. Supp. 682 (D. Mont. 1976).
[2]428 U.S. 52 (1976).
[3]Id. at 67.

an undersized and uncomfortable straitjacket in the practice of his profession."[4]

Following the *Danforth* opinion other courts were faced with statutes that arguably imposed consent straitjackets on physicians and patients alike.[5] In some of these cases the courts reviewed statutory language that was far more precise. One resulting argument has been that the information these laws require to be conveyed has little if any relevance to the abortion decision, and the requirement itself is an unwarranted invasion of the physician-patient relationship. A few cases will illustrate the point.

a. Fetal pain. In Charles v. Carey, the Seventh Circuit Court of Appeals reviewed provisions of Illinois law relating to abortion.[6] According to the law, women had to receive the information enumerated by statute before giving their informed and voluntary consent. This data comprised the name of the physician who would conduct the abortion and the medical risks linked to the type of procedure to be employed. In addition, each woman was to be informed of the gestational age of the fetus, its anatomical characteristics, and the possibility of organic pain to the fetus from the abortion as well as the means available to control the pain. The court found that these and other parts of the consent provisions of the abortion law were an unconstitutional straitjacket on doctors' consultations with their patients' best medical interests in mind. The court specifically noted that the disclosure requirements concerning fetal pain and its control were meaningless from a medical perspective. Moreover, it typified those requirements as confusing,

---

[4]Id. at 68, n.8.

[5]See Planned Parenthood League of Massachusetts v. Bellotti, 641 F.2d 1008 (1st Cir. 1981); Charles v. Carey, 627 F.2d 772 (7th Cir. 1980); Frieman v. Ashcroft, 584 F.2d 247 (8th Cir. 1978); Wolfe v. Schroering, 541 F.2d 523 (6th Cir. 1976); Charles v. Carey, 579 F. Supp. 464 (N.D. Ill. 1983); Planned Parenthood of Kansas City, Missouri, Inc. v. Ashcroft, 483 F. Supp. 679 (W.D. Mo. 1980); Women's Services, P.C. v. Thone, 483 F. Supp. 1022 (D. Neb. 1979).

[6]627 F.2d 772 (7th Cir. 1980).

unjustified, and likely to cause cruel and harmful stress to the women involved.[7]

Subsequent to the Seventh Circuit's decision in Charles v. Carey, yet another action was filed challenging the constitutionality of the Illinois abortion law. In that case the defendants submitted affidavits that they thought would overcome the constitutional deficiencies found in the "fetal pain" provision in the Illinois law. As the U.S. District Court pointed out, at most the new evidence demonstrated a difference of opinion in the medical community on the issue of fetal pain during an abortion. This evidence, however, did not alter the finding that the disclosure requirement cast an unwarranted burden on the exercise of discretion by the pregnant woman's physician. The provision was declared unconstitutional and was permanently enjoined from being enforced.[8]

b. Neutral and objective disclosures. In a decision involving the Massachusetts abortion law, the First Court of Appeals reviewed a consent provision requiring that the woman receive a description of the fetal stage of development.[9] As the court pointed out, this was a far less graphic description requirement than that interpreted by the courts in Charles v. Carey. Nonetheless, the court found this provision impermissible because the information that the state required was not neutral and objective. The imposition of any specific values or ethical assessments, according to the court, runs afoul of First and Fourteenth Amendment principles.[10]

Decisions such as these do not prevent states from imposing informational requirements on the abortion decision. However, as one court has warned, the information to be imparted must be reasonably related to the purpose of informed consent.[11] The state may not unnecessarily intrude into the

[7]Id. at 784.
[8]Charles v. Carey, 579 F. Supp. 464, 470-471 (N.D. Ill. 1983).
[9]Planned Parenthood League of Massachusetts v. Bellotti, 641 F.2d 1008 (1st Cir. 1981).
[10]Id. at 1022.
[11]Frieman v. Ashcroft, 584 F.2d 247 (8th Cir. 1978).

physician-patient relationship by requiring the disclosure of ir-relevant, extraneous, or stressful details. Doing otherwise vio-lates due process requirements relating to the woman's right to consult her doctor without undue state interference.[12]

In the informed consent cases relating to abortion, disclosure requirements that have come under attack have gone beyond descriptions of fetal growth and development. Thus in Frie-man v. Ashcroft, the court held that a requirement that the doctor disclose information relating to custody of a child born alive during an abortion constituted a denial of procedural due process.[13] Once again the court considered this type of revela-tion an unwarranted intrusion into the physician-patient rela-tionship. As in all of the foregoing cases, the court is not denying the state's right to set requirements for informed con-sent in abortion procedures; what it is refusing is the state's imposition of moral or ethical judgments on the women in-volved by requiring the disclosure of information not reason-ably related to their medical interests.

Perhaps the most telling judicial pronouncement on state involvement in the consent process for abortion is found in Thornburgh v. American College of Obstetricians and Gy-necologists.[14] The decision represents a detailed view of so-called informed consent provisions of Pennsylvania's abortion legislation. In the end the United States Supreme Court re-affirmed its stance, first enunciated in Roe v. Wade, regarding the right of a woman, with the guidance of her physician, to make an abortion decision.

The Pennsylvania law in question required that the woman give her free and voluntary consent to an abortion.[15] The fail-ure of the physician to abide by these terms could have led to disciplinary action. Moreover, for other individuals obliged to disclose information for purposes of informed consent, the fail-ure to do so carried criminal penalties.[16]

[12]Id.
[13]Id. at 251.
[14]476 U.S. 747 (1986).
[15]18 Pa. Cons. Stat. §3205(a) (1983).
[16]Id. at §3205(c).

The law specified seven kinds of information that must be conveyed to the woman at least 24 hours prior to her giving consent for an abortion. These included the following, which must be disclosed by the attending doctor:

1. the name of the doctor who is to carry out the procedure;
2. the information that there may be detrimental physical or psychological results that are not accurately foreseeable;
3. the medical risks attendant upon the type of abortion method to be used;
4. the probable gestational age of the fetus;
5. the medical risks attendant upon carrying the child to term;
6. the information that there may be medical assistance benefits for prenatal care, childbirth and neonatal care; and
7. the fact that the father is responsible for child support even if he has offered to pay for the abortion.[17]

In addition, the woman was to be informed that materials prepared by the Commonwealth of Pennsylvania are available for her to review. She had to be told that these materials describe the fetus and list agencies offering options other than abortion.[18] The description of the fetus delineated anatomical and physiological characteristics of the fetus at two-week gestational increments.[19]

Writing for the majority in this 5-4 decision, Mr. Justice Harry Blackmun noted that the Pennsylvania statute exceeded permissible state involvement in the consent process for two reasons. First, the information that was to be disclosed under the Pennsylvania law was not really designed to ensure the woman's informed consent. Rather, it was intended to discourage her from authorizing the abortion.[20]

The second reason was that the mandatory disclosure re-

[17] Id. at §3205.
[18] Id.
[19] Id. at §3208(a)(2).
[20] 476 U.S. at 762.

quirements removed the discretion of the pregnant woman's doctor to determine what is appropriate information to be conveyed under the circumstances.[21] Indeed, the Court described the printed material provided by the state as:

> nothing less than an outright attempt to wedge the Commonwealth's message discouraging abortion into the privacy of the informed-consent dialogue between the woman and her physician.[22]

The Court continued:

> Forcing the physician or counselor to present the materials and the list to the woman makes him or her in effect an agent of the State in treating the woman and places his or her imprimatur upon both the materials and the list.[23]

Justice Blackmun warned that this type of state intrusion in the consent process was the "antithesis of informed consent."[24] As such the Court struck down the consent provisions as being facially unconstitutional.[25]

It is worthwhile to note that despite the sharp division among the members of the Court, the judges did reaffirm the holding in Roe v. Wade. As the majority opinion concluded:

> Our cases long have recognized that the Constitution embodies a promise that a certain private sphere of individual liberty will be kept largely beyond the reach of government. That promise extends to women as well as to men. Few decisions are more personal and intimate, more properly private, or more basic to individual dignity and autonomy, than a woman's decision — with the guidance of her physician and within the limits specified in *Roe* — whether to end her pregnancy. A woman's right to make that choice freely is fundamental. Any other re-

[21] Id. at 763.
[22] Id. at 762.
[23] Id. at 763.
[24] Id. at 764.
[25] Id.

sult, in our view, would protect inadequately a central part of the sphere of liberty that our law guarantees equally to all.[26]

Recurrent attempts to circumscribe the availability of abortion in the name of "informed consent" are bound to fail unless they can be shown to promote the state's interest in protecting the health of the pregnant woman. This is true even with respect to mandatory disclosure of a patient's pregnancy status. As one court pointed out, such a provision presents an impermissible intrusion into the private physician-patient relationship. It denies the woman an opportunity to consult with her doctor and to rely upon his professional advice.[27]

§3.5.2 *"Consent" Waiting Periods*

As well as mandating the revelation of certain information, some states have set a mandatory waiting period — either between the time the patient is informed and she consents or between the time of consent and the abortion procedure. Several courts have reviewed these laws;[28] for example, the First Circuit Court of Appeals, in Planned Parenthood League of Massachusetts v. Bellotti, held that a 24-hour waiting period before executing an abortion consent form was an impermissible provision.[29] In its decision, the court determined that the waiting period was a state-created burden on the women's fundamental right to an abortion that could not be justified by a compelling state interest. The state characterized its interest as the need to provide women with an opportunity to reflect freely upon their decision and resolve the issue in a truly informed manner. In rejecting this argument, the court pointed

[26] Id. at 772.

[27] See Reproductive Health Servs. v. Webster, 655 F. Supp. 1300 (W.D. Mo. 1987). But see Webster v. Reproductive Health Servs., — U.S. — , 1989 WL 70,950.

[28] Planned Parenthood League of Massachusetts v. Bellotti, supra n.9; Charles v. Carey, 627 F.2d 772 (7th Cir. 1980); Wolfe v. Schroering, 541 F.2d 523 (6th Cir. 1976); Women's Services, P.C. v. Thone, 483 F. Supp. 1022 (D. Neb. 1979).

[29] Supra n.9.

out that there was no proof that the delay imposed by the law actually promoted the state's interest. As the evidence from the lower court suggested, most women give considerable thought to a decision to abort long before they actually have an abortion. Moreover, it was noted that the time surrounding an abortion decision and procedure was a stressful one and a mandatory delay would not therefore facilitate calm thought. In addition, there was no proof that absent a waiting period, a truly informed consent was impossible.[30]

Other courts have handed down similar rulings. In Charles v. Carey, the Seventh Circuit Court of Appeals found an Illinois 24-hour waiting period unconstitutional.[31] The court held that the delay amounted to an impermissible burden upon the woman's right to decide whether she wanted to bear a child. The state interest in making certain that abortion decisions were not coerced was not found to be served by the statute. It was not written in a manner that would further the state's interest in patients' making informed decisions.[32] A 48-hour waiting period provision in the Nebraska abortion law was also found impermissible in Women's Services, P.C. v. Thone.[33] That time delay was viewed as an undue burden upon the woman's freedom to seek an abortion, and as a result, the provision was permanently enjoined.[34]

Not all courts, however, have found waiting provisions in state abortion laws unconstitutional. For example, in a Sixth Circuit Court of Appeals decision, a 24-hour delay in the Kentucky abortion law was held permissible.[35] There the provision was characterized as an insignificant burden on the woman's rights in the abortion process. At the same time, though, unlike the provisions of other state statutes, emergency abortions undertaken to save the life of a woman are exempted from the Kentucky waiting period requirement.[36]

[30]Supra n.9 at 1015-1016.
[31]Supra n.6.
[32]Supra n.6 at 785-786.
[33]483 F. Supp. 1022 (D. Neb. 1979).
[34]Id. at 1050.
[35]Wolfe v. Schroering, 541 F.2d 523 (6th Cir. 1976).
[36]Id. at 528.

The courts' split on the waiting period requirement has kept the issue from being resolved. A partial conclusion could be drawn, however, that for the state to prevail, it must present a sound, compelling interest in order to overcome the fundamental rights involved. Statutory waiting periods must also be narrowly drawn to promote the state's asserted interest with exceptions built in for exigent situations.

§3.5.3   Restrictions on Who May Obtain Consent

A third type of statutory provision that has come under attack is the requirement that the physician who is to perform the abortion also conduct the consent consultation with the patient. Several courts have found the so-called same doctor rule to be an impermissible burden on the right to obtain an abortion.[37] As one court has explained:

> If a woman consulted her personal physician prior to reaching her decision and was then referred to another doctor for an abortion, she would have to undergo the expense and inconvenience of another pregnancy test and informed consent procedure. Since the defendants provided no justification for this requirement it could not stand.[38]

A different result was reached by a United States District Court in Missouri.[39] Missouri law provided that the attending doctor must personally provide information to the woman as part of the consent process. The court found that this arrangement furthered legitimate state concerns in making certain that a woman based' her decision on full knowledge of the nature and consequences of abortion.[40]

It is common in other medical treatment situations — indeed

---

[37] See City of Akron v. Akron Center for Reproductive Health, Inc., 462 U.S. 416 (1983); Margaret S. v. Edwards, 794 F.2d 994 (5th Cir. 1986); Reproductive Health Servs. v. Webster, 655 F. Supp. 1300 (W.D. Mo. 1987); Charles v. Carey, 627 F.2d 772 (7th Cir. 1980).

[38] Charles v. Carey, supra n.37, at 784.

[39] Planned Parenthood of Kansas City, Missouri, Inc. v. Ashcroft, 483 F. Supp. 679 (W.D. Mo. 1980).

[40] Id. at 689.

preferable — for the physician who is to treat a patient to also be responsible for informing that patient. In that light, the same-doctor rule in abortion cases does not seem to be an unusual burden. Unlike provisions that require the revealing of graphic details about a fetus or impose waiting periods, this requisite seems to have both legal and medical merit. It is not difficult, for example, to imagine a situation in which a woman sues a physician for negligent failure to obtain a fully informed consent for an abortion. If the patient were "informed" by a nurse or an abortion counsellor who did not disclose risks that would have dissuaded her from undergoing the procedure and the doctor relied upon this "consent," significant legal problems could develop. In those cases in which the physician employs the nurse or counsellor, the doctor could be held to be responsible, on the basis of vicarious liability, for a negligent consent process. Even in the absence of an employment relationship, the doctor could be found negligent for failure to discharge her own consent duties.

Regardless of a state's requirements, the better policy is for the attending physician to complete the consent process in abortion cases. The doctor should ask whether the patient understands what is involved and whether she still wishes to proceed. He should be satisfied that the patient has no underlying medical condition (allergy to drugs and anesthetics, high blood pressure, a blood disorder, etc.) that would make the proposed procedure inadvisable. Defined in these terms, the same-doctor rule should not fall under the same censure as the morality-laden state law provisions that demand graphic disclosure of fetal development.

§3.5.4 Counselling Patients Regarding Abortion

A federal attempt to restrict family planning counsellor's advising clients about abortions has met with resistance. The federal initiative arose from Title X regulations under the Public Health Services Act.[41] The regulations banned the expenditure

---

[41] See 42 U.S.C. §300a-6 (1982).

of federal funds in programs in which abortion was counselled as a form of family planning.[42]

At least two U.S. District Courts have enjoined implementation of the regulations.[43] In doing so, both courts pointed out that the regulation violated First Amendment rights of free speech and ran contrary to Congressional intent under the Public Health Services Act.

§3.6 Biological Father's Consent to Abortion

The issue of abortion also raises the question of the rights of the spouse of the women involved or the natural father of the fetus in the decision to abort. More specifically, the issue is whether the consent of the spouse or natural father is necessary as a prerequisite to the woman undergoing an abortion. That point has been addressed by a number of courts since the Roe v. Wade decision of the United States Supreme Court in 1973.[1] The cases discussed here illustrate the legal reasoning behind the rule holding that a spouse's or natural father's consent is not necessary.

In Planned Parenthood of Central Missouri v. Danforth, the United States Supreme Court held unconstitutional a Missouri law that required prior written consent of a woman's spouse for an abortion during the first 12 weeks of pregnancy.[2] (Doctor-certified emergency abortions to preserve the life of the mother were an acceptable exception to this requirement.) Missouri

---

[42] See 42 C.F.R. §59.8(a)(1) (1988).

[43] See Commonwealth of Mass. v. Bowen, 679 F. Supp. 137 (D. Mass. 1988); Planned Parenthood Fedn. of America v. Bowen, 680 F. Supp. 1465 (D. Colo. 1988).

§3.6 [1] Planned Parenthood of Central Missouri v. Danforth, 428 U.S. 52 (1976); Coe v. Gerstein, 376 F. Supp. 695 (S.D. Dis. 1973), appeal dismissed, 417 U.S. 279 (1974), and affd., 417 U.S. 281 (1974); Coleman v. Coleman, 57 Md. App. 755, 471 A.2d 1115 (1984); Rothenberger v. Doe, 149 N.J. Super. 478, 374 A.2d 57 (1977); Doe v. Doe, 365 Mass. 556, 314 N.E.2d 128 (1974); Jones v. Smith, 278 So. 2d 339 (Fla. 1973).

[2] Supra n.1.

contended that the law was based on the state legislature's view of marriage as an institution. The state argued that mutual consent is generally required to start a family; therefore, the state legislature determined that the same general requirement should apply to terminating a pregnancy. In response the law's opponents noted that the law gave the husband veto power whether or not he was in fact the father of the fetus. They contended that this provision ran afoul of Roe v. Wade, Doe v. Bolton, and a number of lower court opinions.

In holding the law unconstitutional, the Supreme Court ruled that the state cannot delegate authority to a spouse that the state itself is banned from exercising during the first trimester of pregnancy. Although it took cognizance of the state's concerns about the effect of an abortion decision on the marital relationship, this consideration was not sufficient to vest a woman's spouse with a unilateral veto power over a decision to undergo an abortion.[3]

A New Jersey case dealt with the additional complication of an illegitimate fetus.[4] In March 1977 the parties had intercourse that resulted in the woman becoming pregnant. The couple were not married, nor were they married to other persons. When he learned that the woman was going to have an abortion, the plaintiff objected. The court rejected the plaintiff's argument, noting that the decision to abort is one exclusively within the woman's prerogative and is based on her constitutional right of privacy. That decision is not conditioned upon the consent of her husband or that of the natural father. The court also pointed out that courts in other jurisdictions had rejected the argument that a unilateral decision to abort by the woman interfered with the man's right to procreate. In each instance, the right of the woman prevailed.[5]

The woman's right of choice is also legally supported when she decides to continue the pregnancy. For example, in an Alabama case the father of an illegitimate child was ordered to

[3]Id. at 68-70.
[4]Rothenberger v. Doe, supra n.1.
[5]Id.

pay child support.[6] He had asked his girlfriend to consent to an abortion, which she refused even though he had agreed to pay for the procedure. As the court noted in the child support proceeding, the decision to abort belonged to the unmarried mother; her refusal was not a legal justification for the father to shirk his statutory support obligations.[7]

The case law on spousal consent or authorization by the father clearly indicates that the decision to abort belongs solely to the woman. In the weeks after the first trimester, the state's right to impose regulations reasonably related to maternal health cannot justify requiring consent from a woman's spouse or the father of the fetus. The laws imposed by a state at this point in the pregnancy must be narrowly drawn to meet state objectives related to maternal considerations. Consent of another does not fall within this category. In the second and third trimesters, when the state can regulate certain aspects of abortion, the same principle holds true even if the state could delegate its authority to the spouse or father. At the point when the state interest attaches to the potentiality of life, it is true that abortion may be restricted or prohibited except when it is necessary to preserve the life or health of the mother. However, the state could not grant a husband or the father a veto that would override an exception created to preserve maternal life or health.

D. CONCEPTION, PREGNANCY, AND CONSENT

The law of consent also extends to matters of conception. Some states have enacted legislation regulating artificial insemination, whereas others have passed laws requiring prenatal venereal disease checks. Furthermore, as medical science has become better equipped to diagnose possible birth defects in utero, a new type of consent case has arisen. Issues involved in

[6] Harris v. State, 356 So. 2d 623 (Ala. 1978).
[7] Id.

these cases include the failure of a physician to disclose the probability of birth defects that she knew or ought to have known about beforehand.

§3.7 Artificial Insemination

There are two basic types of artificial insemination. The first uses the sperm of the husband and is referred to as A.I.H.; the second uses the sperm of a donor and is referred to as A.I.D.[1] No real legal difficulties arise in the former case. Quite a different situation is created, however, when a woman is inseminated with the sperm of a donor: here adultery and the legitimacy of the child become concerns. In the states in which legislation has been passed on the subject, yet a third issue has been recognized: the need for consent. Unfortunately, these issues have often been lumped together, creating confusion about the need for consent and from whom it should be obtained.

§3.7.1 Basic Disclosure Requirements

A.I.D. is a medical procedure; it is incumbent upon the attending physician to secure the consent of his patient. This process would include a reasonable explanation of the procedure, any known probable risks, and such other information as is deemed necessary in the circumstances. Any questions the patient has should be answered in as candid a manner as possible. For example, if a woman wants to know whether the donor was matched as closely as possible to her husband in terms of height, hair coloring, and ethnic origin or whether the donor was screened for possible genetic defects, she would be entitled to a response. Information about any reasonable alternative methods of achieving conception should be discussed. The fact that A.I.D. is a medical intervention or intrusion into another person's body cannot be overlooked: it triggers the need for a fully informed consent.

§3.7 [1] H. H. Clark, Jr., Law of Domestic Relations, §5.1, n.21 (1968).

§3.7.2   Need for Spousal Consent

What has confused and concerned medical authorities is the need for the husband's consent if a donor is involved. The argument has been made that if the procedure is performed using donor sperm, the child born as a result is illegitimate. The result at common law would not necessarily change even if the procedure was carried out with the husband's consent. As Clark suggests in his treatise on family law, this has resulted in case decisions that are by no means consistent.[2] To overcome this difficulty, some parents resort to adoption proceedings.[3] A more satisfactory method for many people has been the intervention of state legislatures in passing essentially "legitimizing" statues.

Several states have laws relating to the practice of artificial insemination by donors.[4] California's law is illustrative of many of these statutes. It provides in part:

> If, under the supervision of a licensed physician *and with the consent of her husband,* a wife is inseminated artificially with semen donated by a man not her husband, the husband is treated in law as if he were the natural father of a child thereby conceived.[5] (Emphasis added.)

The statutes usually require that the husband's consent be in writing along with that of his wife.[6] If the couple consent to the use of donor sperm, then the child born as a result is given the status of legitimate offspring. As the Connecticut statute suggests:

[2]Id. at 157.
[3]Id. at n.28.
[4]See, e.g., Cal. Civ. Code §7005 (West 1979); Ga. Code §74-101.1 (1964); N.Y. Dom. Rel. Law §73 (McKinney 1974); Okla. Stat. Ann. tit. 10, §551 (West 1967); Wash. Rev. Code Ann. §26.20.050 (1976); Wis. Stat. Ann. §891.40 (West 1984).
[5]Cal. Civ. Code §7005 (West 1979).
[6]See Cal. Civ. Code §7005 (West 1979); Conn. Gen. Stat. §45-69.g (1980); Kan. Stat. Ann. §23-128 (1968); N.Y. Dom. Rel. Law §73 (McKinney 1974); Or. Rev. Stat. §677.365 (1977).

Any child or children born as a result of A.I.D. shall be deemed to acquire, in all respects, the status of a naturally conceived legitimate child of the husband and wife who consented to and requested the use of A.I.D.[7]

In those states with legislation on artificial insemination, it is unlikely that a woman could undergo the procedure in the absence of her husband's consent. The laws may specifically prevent her doing so, as in Connecticut,[8] or the physician may decline to inseminate the woman out of a concern for his professional well-being or the child's legal status. An opposing argument based on privacy would claim that, since the woman's body alone is involved, the consent of her husband is irrelevant. A strong rebuttal to this argument can be made, however: the state interests in family integrity, preserving marital relationships, and protecting children from illegitimacy override any privacy interest that attaches to artificial insemination without spousal consent.

§3.7.3 Status of the Donor

The status of the donor is set out in many of the state laws, which usually rule out the possibility of the donor being treated at law as the father of the child.[9] Some statutes take an even harder line by blocking any person claiming through or by the donor to have an interest or right in the child.[10] By the same token, the donor is not liable for the support of the child.[11] Exceptions to these conditions do exist: under the Washington law, the woman and the donor may agree in writing that the latter shall be the child's father.[12] As a result, under general

---

[7] Conn. Gen. Stat. §45-69.i (1980).
[8] Id. at §45-69.g (1980).
[9] See Cal. Civ. Code §7005 (West 1979); Wash. Rev. Code Ann. §26.26.50 (1976); Wis. Stat. Ann. §891.40 (West 1984).
[10] Conn. Gen. Stat. §45-69.j (1980).
[11] Wis. Stat. Ann. §891.40 (West 1984).
[12] Wash. Rev. Code Ann. §26.26.50 (1976).

principles of family law, the donor would then arguably have a responsibility for support of his offspring.

§3.7.4   Unmarried Recipients

Related questions are raised when unmarried women seek artificial insemination. Most relevant statutes assume the woman involved is married, though there is at least one exception. The Oregon statute reads in part: "Artificial insemination shall not be performed upon a woman without her prior request and consent *and, if she is married,* the prior written request and consent of her husband."[13] Presumably, unmarried women in Oregon have the right to request insemination.

Elsewhere it is an open issue. A doctor may be reluctant to aid and abet the conception of an illegitimate child. She may experience societal condemnation for such an act and perhaps even disciplinary proceedings for violating a professional licensure or registration law. The woman herself may have difficulty finding a doctor willing to inseminate an unmarried female. As long as society and the law stigmatize a child born out of wedlock, this situation will not change.

§3.7.5   Consent as a Defense to Adultery

Artificial insemination raises the issue of adultery. The leading case on the subject is from Canada. In Orford v. Orford, the husband argued that the wife had committed an act of adultery by undergoing artificial insemination without his consent.[14] The court ruled in the husband's favor, finding that the wife's conception through the surrendering of her reproductive powers to another supported the accusation of adultery. Artificial insemination admittedly seems far removed from the usual activity that results in divorce on the ground of adultery.

[13] Or. Rev. Stat. §677.365 (1977).
[14] [1921] 58 D.L.R. 251 (Ont.).

If the procedure is carried out with the informed consent of both the husband and wife, however, it is difficult to see how a case could be made subsequently on this basis.[15]

In those jurisdictions without legislation on artificial insemination, fertility specialists must be conversant with the legal requirements in their respective states. They should not only fulfill the usual medical consent requirements but also adequately address the special concerns relating to the husband and wife or family relationship.

§3.8 Prenatal Venereal Disease Screening

The deep concern about exposure to sexually transmitted diseases has resulted in states passing a variety of laws requiring examination and treatment of those suspected of having venereal disease. Venereal disease during pregnancy is of special concern. Most states have laws on prenatal detection of sexually transmitted diseases,[1] with testing generally focusing on syphilis. Many make such tests mandatory;[2] elsewhere an individual's consent is required.[3] Some jurisdictions have provided for exemptions for religious beliefs and/or practices.[4]

[15] See H. H. Clark, Jr., Law of Domestic Relations, §12.2 (1968).

§3.8 [1] See, e.g., Fla. Stat. Ann. §383.08 (West 1945); Idaho Code §39-1001 (1974); Iowa Code Ann. §140.12 (West 1969); Kan. Stat. Ann. §65-153f (1974); Me. Rev. Stat. Ann. tit. 22, §1231 (1954); Mont. Code Ann. §50-19-103 (1973); Nev. Rev. Stat. §442.010 (1981); N.M. Stat. Ann. §24-1-10 (1973); Okla. Stat. Ann. tit. 63, §1-515 (West 1961); Or. Rev. Stat. §434.200 (1973); Pa. Stat. Ann. tit. 35, §521.13 (Purdon 1955); S.C. Code Ann. §44-29-120 (1972); S.D. Codified Laws Ann. §34-23-10 (1960); Vt. Stat. Ann. tit. 18, §1102 (1961); Va. Code §32.1-60 (1984); Wash. Rev. Code Ann. §70.24.090 (1939); Wyo. Stat. §35-4-502 (1957).

[2] See, e.g., Fla. Stat. Ann. §383.08 (West 1945); Ill. Ann. Stat. ch. 111 1/2, §4801 (Smith-Hurd 1979); Md. Pub. Health Code Ann. 43 §31B (1974); Mont. Code Ann. §50-19-103 (1973); Neb. Rev. Stat. §71-1116 (1967); Okla. Stat. Ann. tit. 63, §1-515 (West 1963); Vt. Stat. Ann. tit. 18, §1102 (1961).

[3] See Me. Rev. Stat. Ann. tit. 22, §1189 (1954); Mo. Ann. Stat. §210.030 (1986); N.D. Cent. Code §23-07-07.1 (1957); Or. Rev. Stat. §434.200 (1973).

[4] Ill. Ann. Stat. ch. 111 1/2, §4801 (Smith-Hurd 1979); Ind. Code Ann. §16-1-11-20 (Burns 1988); Md. Pub. Health Code Ann. 43 §31B (1974); Nev. Rev. Stat. §442.010 (1981); Okla. Stat. Ann. tit. 63, §1-516.1 (West 1963).

The general rule in the prenatal venereal disease legislation is to keep positive test results confidential.[5] Limited disclosure is permitted in Montana and then at the patient's request.[6] The concern for confidentiality also extends to a child's birth certificate or to a stillborn child. In many jurisdictions whether the test has or has not been conducted on the mother may be indicated on the certificate, but the test results may not be disclosed.[7]

Pennsylvania has a rather interesting provision regarding consent to prenatal testing for venereal disease.[8] A blood sample cannot be taken from the woman if she dissents. However, if she rejects the test the doctor has the statutory duty to explain to the woman why the test is desirable.

§3.9   Duty to Disclose Risks of Birth Defects and Delivery Problems

Application of the law of consent has been expanded through technological advancements in medicine in the area of prenatal diagnosis of probable birth defects. Amniocentesis has enabled physicians to alert potential parents to the probability of Down's syndrome and other anomalies.[1] Parents, once advised

[5]See, e.g., Idaho Code §39-1004 (1974); Iowa Code Ann. §140.12 (West 1969); Neb. Rev. Stat. §71-1116 (1967); N.D. Cent. Code §23-07-07.3 (1957); Okla. Stat. Ann. tit. 63, §1-516 (West 1963); S.D. Codified Laws Ann. §34-23-12 (1960); W. Va. Code §16-4A-4 (1945).
[6]Mont. Code Ann. §50-19-107 (1973) (test results are to be exhibited by the physician to the patient; at the patient's request, the results may be shown to her spouse).
[7]Idaho Code §39-1005 (1943), Ill. Ann. Stat. ch. 111 1/2, §4802 (Smith-Hurd 1939); Iowa Code Ann. §140.12 (West 1969); Neb. Rev. Stat. §71-1116 (1967); N.D. Cent. Code §23-07-07.3 (1957); Okla. Stat. Ann. tit. 63, §1-516 (West 1963); S.D. Codified Laws Ann. §34-23-12 (1960); W. Va. Code §16-4A-4 (1945).
[8]Pa. Stat. Ann. tit. 35, §521.13 (Purdon 1955).
§3.9 [1]See C. Stern, Principles of Human Genetics 808-810 (1973); P. Reilly, Genetics, Law and Social Policy 23-26 (1977). See also Wilson v. Kuenzi, 751 S.W.2d 741 (Mo. 1988) (en banc), in which the court held that a

of the prospects, can decide whether to abort or to allow the pregnancy to go to term.

Legal implications include the questions of whether a doctor has a duty to disclose the availability of such testing and what risk disclosure must be made about possible birth defects in individual pregnancies.[2] A number of cases have been decided on the matter of inborn birth defects. In addition, courts have ruled on cases in which the disclosure of risk information was considered inadequate due to maternal exposure to rubella. The judiciary has also been called upon to rule on disclosure requirements relating to delivery methods that carry particular risks. In this section risk disclosure is examined in the context of birth defects and the duty to warn.

§3.9.1 Inadequate Disclosure of Birth Defect Risk Information

In two New York Court of Appeals decisions, a cause of action was recognized for pecuniary damages suffered by parents as a consequence of their children being born with birth defects.[3] In one case, a 37-year-old woman claimed that she had not been informed by her obstetrician of the increased risk of Down's syndrome in children born to women over 35 years of age. In addition, the woman was not advised of the availability

---

woman could not maintain either a wrongful birth or wrongful life action in connection with a doctor's failure to advise her of the availability of amniocentesis for Down's syndrome; Haymon v. Wilkerson, 535 A.2d 880 (D.C. 1987), in which the court stated that a woman could maintain a wrongful birth action against a doctor who failed to advise her of the availability of amniocentesis.

[2] See, e.g., Spencer by and Through Spencer v. Seikel, 742 P.2d 1126 (Okla. 1987), where the court held that a physician did not have to advise a patient about the option of abortion when it was discovered that her 23- or 24-week-old fetus was suffering from hydrocephalus; Pratt v. University of Minn. Affiliated Hosps., 414 N.W.2d 399 (Minn. 1987), where the court stated that the diagnosis of a condition, when all proper tests have been carried out, does not give rise to a requirement to disclose risks inherent in undiagnosed condition.

[3] Becker v. Schwartz, 46 N.Y.2d 401, 386 N.E.2d 807, 413 N.Y.S.2d 895 (1978).

of amniocentesis to determine the presence of this anomaly. A lawsuit followed the birth of her child, who suffered from Down's syndrome. In the second case, a woman had given birth to a child with polycystic kidney disease and the child died five hours later. Concerned that future offspring would be at risk for the disease, the woman and her husband consulted with the obstetrician who had attended her during her earlier pregnancy. The couple was advised that the disease was not hereditary and that the chances of having a second child afflicted with the disorder were negligible. Based on this information, the couple conceived again. Their second child, also born with the disease, lived for 2½ years.

In both instances, the New York court said the parents could maintain actions based upon the physicians' alleged negligence in failing to provide them with accurate risk information. Pecuniary damages were available to each set of parents if they proved their case. However, public policy precluded damages for psychic or emotional injuries resulting from the birth of impaired children.[4]

a. Tay-Sachs disease cases. Litigation has involved children born with Tay-Sachs disease,[5] but the courts have not been in agreement on the outcome or the theory upon which the cases were decided. Nevertheless, they illustrate the need for accurate disclosure of genetic risk information.

In Howard v. Leecher, the New York Court of Appeals held that the parents of a child born with Tay-Sachs could not recover for their mental distress.[6] The parents claimed that the attending doctor was aware that both parties were of Eastern European Jewish extraction and that he should have known of the high risk of Tay-Sachs for their child. They also claimed that had they known of the danger involved and the availability

---

[4]Id.

[5]Curlender v. Bio-Science Laboratories, Inc., 106 Cal. App. 3d 811, 165 Cal. Rptr. 477 (1980); Gildiner v. Thomas Jefferson Union Hosp., 451 F. Supp. 692 (E.D. Pa. 1978); Howard v. Leecher, 42 N.Y.2d 109, 366 N.E.2d 64, 397 N.Y.S.2d 363 (1977).

[6]Howard v. Leecher, supra n.5.

of tests to determine the presence of the disease, they would have undergone the tests. If the results were positive for Tay-Sachs, they claimed that they would have sought an abortion. Instead, the child was born with the disease and ultimately succumbed. Although sympathetic to the stressful consequences endured by the parents, the court rejected their suit for damages based on emotional trauma. The New York court felt this went far beyond traditional tort concepts and refused to overstep those bounds.[7]

In the Pennsylvania case of Gildiner v. Thomas Jefferson University Hospital, the court reached the opposite conclusion.[8] In this case the parents were aware of the risk of Tay-Sachs disease in their offspring and they agreed to amniocentesis. The test was conducted in a negligent manner and as a result, the pregnancy went to term and the child was born with the disease. In allowing the parents to recover, the court pointed out:

> Tay-Sachs disease can be prevented only by accurate genetic testing combined with the right of parents to abort afflicted fetuses within the appropriate time limitations.
>
> Society has an interest in insuring that genetic testing is properly performed and interpreted.[9]

Perhaps the most interesting Tay-Sachs detection case arose in California. Unlike the other cases in which the parents sued on their own behalf, Curlender v. Bio-Science Laboratories, Inc. involved a claim by the child for "wrongful life."[10] A case of first impression in California, the question was what remedy, if any, was available to a person born genetically defective due to the negligence of those who conducted genetic tests upon the child's parents. It was asserted that, had the tests been performed correctly, both parents would have been recognized as carriers of Tay-Sachs disease. In giving credence to the action

---

[7]Id. at 110, 366 N.E.2d at 65.
[8]451 F. Supp. 692 (E.D. Pa. 1978).
[9]Id. at 696.
[10]106 Cal. App. 3d 811, 165 Cal. Rptr. 477 (1980).

for "wrongful life," the court pointed out that the defendants owed a duty of ordinary care to parents who seek genetic testing and to their unborn children. Under those circumstances the child could recover for pain, suffering, and pecuniary damages that accrued only during his actual life span.[11]

b. Other wrongful life actions. The Court of Appeals of North Carolina has also recognized an action based on wrongful life in a case in which the attending obstetrician and his nurse practitioner failed to give adequate information about amniocentesis to a pregnant 36-year-old woman.[12] The woman claimed that she specifically asked both the nurse and the doctor about the advisability of having the test done. The nurse responded by telling the woman of her personal and religious prejudices against the procedure. The doctor apparently told her that she did not need the test or that it was not advisable since only women 37 years of age and older were in the risk category. The woman relied upon the defendant's advice and subsequently gave birth to a male child afflicted with Down's syndrome.

In the malpractice litigation that followed, the North Carolina Court of Appeals ruled that the defendants had a duty to inform the parents of "material information" regarding genetic abnormalities. The alleged failure to advise the parents of the need for amniocentesis constituted a breach of this duty. The parents claimed that had they been properly advised, the woman would have undergone the test. If they had been informed that the child was afflicted with Down's syndrome, she would have undergone a legal abortion. Moreover, the duty to advise extended to the child vicariously through his parents. Based on this determination, the court reversed the lower court's dismissal of the child's claim for wrongful life.[13]

The concept of wrongful life does not enjoy widespread sup-

---

[11] Id. at 831, 165 Cal. Rptr. at 489.
[12] Azzolino v. Dingfelder, 322 S.E.2d 567 (N.C. Ct. App. 1984).
[13] Id.

port.[14] Many courts are uneasy saying life is not worth living. On a more practical level, there is great concern about assessing damages for wrongful life. Nonetheless, there are members of the judiciary who are prepared to change the law to accept wrongful life actions. These judges ignore the philosophical problems of life versus nonlife and they have little difficulty in assessing damages. This is all the more so where the litigation is based on a known genetic disorder confined to a specific ethnic group and a physician fails to inform parents of the risk of their offspring being born with such a disease.[15]

§3.9.2 Necessary Disclosures to Prospective Parents

Curlender v. Bio-Science Laboratories, Inc. (§3.9.1 supra) is not a decision resting squarely on principles of consent to treatment; moreover, the Supreme Court of California has not spoken on the matter. However, like the *Gildiner* case, it points out the need for accurate genetic testing and proper disclosure of risk information. Physicians engaged in obstetrics or genetic counselling must obtain sufficient family histories and background information in order to advise their patients correctly about genetic screening. Patients and their husbands should be informed — when appropriate — of the availability of screening measures, the risks and benefits of the tests, the reasonable alternatives, if any, the likelihood of false-positive and false-negative findings, as well as of the recourse available after positive genetic disease determinations.

Many states are reluctant to allow defective children a remedy for wrongful life. Some states may even bar wrongful birth actions.[16] Nonetheless, the opportunity does exist for litigation

---

[14]See, e.g., Lininger v. Eisenbaum, 764 P.2d 1202 (Colo. 1988), and Proffitt v. Bartolo, 412 N.W.2d 232 (Mich. Ct. App. 1987), in which the courts rejected claims for wrongful life but did permit actions based on wrongful birth. See also Goldberg v. Ruskin, 113 Ill. 2d 482, 101 Ill. Dec. 818, 499 N.E.2d 406 (1986).

[15]Goldberg v. Ruskin, 499 N.E.2d at 410-413, Clark, C.J., dissenting.

[16]See Hickman v. Group Health Plan, Inc., 396 N.W.2d 10 (Minn. 1986), holding constitutional state legislation barring wrongful birth actions.

based on inadequate disclosure or negligent disclosure of risk information. The task remains for plaintiffs to prove, however, that had they been properly informed they would have opted for termination of the affected pregnancies. Such questions are issues of fact that must be resolved in individual cases by the trier of fact.

§3.9.3 Maternal Rubella

Another group of cases involves children born with various anomalies to women who were exposed to rubella during pregnancy. Like the litigation dealing with Down's syndrome and Tay-Sachs, plaintiffs' arguments usually include an assertion based on failure to disclose risk information.

In a Texas case, a woman contracted rubella during her first trimester of pregnancy and later gave birth to a child with defects of several major organs.[17] In a lawsuit by the parents against the attending physician, it was argued that he had been negligent in failing to diagnose rubella and to advise the couple of the risks to the fetus. Plaintiffs claimed that, had they been properly informed about the risks associated with rubella during gestation, they would have terminated the pregnancy. In reversing an order of summary judgment in favor of the doctor, the Supreme Court of Texas held that the doctor was not excused from providing the patient with a proper diagnosis by reason of the state's criminal abortion law at the time. Nor was he excused from presenting risk information about the effects of rubella upon a developing fetus. The doctor was under a duty to make such a disclosure as would be expected of any reasonable practitioner in the circumstances.[18]

A similar case arose in Wisconsin.[19] During the first trimester of pregnancy, a woman went to the emergency department of a hospital for treatment of a rash on the upper part of her body.

---

[17]Jacobs v. Theimer, 519 S.W.2d 846 (Tex. 1975).
[18]Id.
[19]Dumer v. St. Michael's Hosp., 69 Wis. 2d 766, 233 N.W.2d 372 (1975).

She informed the nurses and doctor treating her that she thought she had rubella. The doctor diagnosed the rash as an allergic reaction and discharged her. When their daughter was subsequently born with defects attributable to "rubella syndrome," the parents instituted a medical malpractice action. In reversing in part a dismissal of the case, the Supreme Court of Wisconsin held that the plaintiffs had stated a cause of action based on negligent diagnosis and failure to warn of the possible effects of rubella on a developing fetus. If the plaintiffs could prove at trial that the doctor was negligent in not diagnosing rubella and in not inquiring as to whether the woman was pregnant, he would then have had a duty to warn of the effects of maternal rubella. The plaintiff would then have to convince the trier of fact that she would have submitted to an abortion, and, moreover, that one was legally available to her at the time.

The maternal rubella cases may not be neatly categorized as negligent disclosure matters. Sometimes the cause of action may be wrongful birth. In a New Hampshire case[20] the plaintiff alleged that early in her pregnancy she contracted rubella. The defendants, who specialized in obstetrics and gynecology, prescribed Keflex when plaintiff had nausea, abdominal pain, and a late menstrual period. It was also recommended that the plaintiff have a pregnancy test if her menstrual period did not begin. Two days later, the plaintiff contacted the defendants about an itchy rash and a fever. This was diagnosed as an allergic reaction to the antibiotic Keflex. Subsequently, the plaintiff learned that she was pregnant. It was not until she was in her second trimester of pregnancy that the plaintiff learned that she had been exposed to rubella. A baby girl was born in early 1980 to the plaintiff with deficits consistent with maternal rubella exposure.[21]

The Supreme Court of New Hampshire, ruling on questions transferred to it by the trial court, held that a cause of action could rest on the basis of wrongful birth. However, the court declined to recognize a wrongful life action on the part of the

[20]Smith v. Cote, 513 A.2d 341 (N.H. 1986).
[21]Id.

child.[22] Nevertheless, wrongful birth litigation, based on inadequate diagnosis and warning of maternal rubella syndrome, is an important issue for clinicians to be aware of in obstetrics.

In causes of action for failure to diagnose and warn about the risks of maternal rubella arising since 1973, the legality of abortions is no longer an issue.[23] The only possible exception would be for abortions performed after viability, roughly during the third trimester. Under Roe v. Wade, supra, abortion during this stage could be limited by the state except when the mother's life or health is threatened.

§3.9.4   Necessary Disclosures to Prospective Mothers

Whether done on the basis of common sense or as the result of a legislative mandate,[24] caregivers should discuss with prospective mothers the significance of nonimmunity to rubella. The same is true of caregivers dealing with pregnant patients who either have rubella or who are suspected of having the disease. The implications of maternal rubella exposure for the fetus must be explained to patients.

Should a woman not know whether she has had rubella in the past, the physician should alert her to the need for prompt diagnosis if she develops rubella-like symptoms. An alternative would be to order blood tests to determine if the woman has rubella antigens in her body. A carefully informed patient, if exposed to rubella during pregnancy, can then make a decision whether to abort or carry the pregnancy to term. To avoid difficulties with subsequent allegations of failure to inform patients of the risks of maternal rubella, a physician should write a detailed entry into the patient's chart. The note should point

[22] Id.

[23] A New Jersey court, in Gleitman v. Cosgrove, 49 N.J. 122, 227 A.2d 689 (1967), had rejected a damages action stemming from a maternal rubella case, in part on the termination of pregnancy aspect of the case. The precedent set in this case was overruled in part in the subsequent matter of Berman v. Allen, 80 N.J. 421, 404 A.2d 8 (1979).

[24] See, e.g., Idaho Code §32-412 (1985).

out what information was provided to the patient, as well as a summary of any questions posed by her and the physician's responses.

§3.9.5 Delivery Risks

Also at issue is negligent disclosure of delivery information. Sometimes a child is born with injuries due to the type of method used in delivery. These cases are far different than those involving children born with genetically linked anomalies or defects attributable to maternal rubella. The two cases following illustrate the consent aspect of delivery defects.

In a New York case, a woman and her 22-year-old son sued her obstetrician for medical malpractice.[25] Plaintiffs claimed that as a result of the defendant's negligent care during pregnancy and at the time of birth and because of a lack of informed consent, the boy was born maimed and deformed. The court held that the young man stated a good cause of action against the defendant for lack of informed consent. It ruled that, although the defendant's duty to disclose was to the boy's mother, the then unborn child was within the scope of individuals to be protected. Failure to obtain informed consent of the mother would have an impact upon the unborn child. Any conduct that threatened harm to the mother would, in turn, pose a risk of danger to the unborn child. The situation was one of derivative liability.[26]

Quite a different result was reached in an Illinois case in which it was alleged that the attending physician had been negligent in the course of delivering the plaintiff's baby.[27] A general practitioner with delivery privileges performed an amniotomy (rupturing the membranes artificially) to increase the speed of delivery for a woman in labor. After the procedure was performed the doctor, for the first time, became aware that

---

[25] Shack v. Holland, 89 Misc. 2d 78, 389 N.Y.S.2d 988 (1976).
[26] Id. at 85, 389 N.Y.S.2d at 993.
[27] Carman v. Dippold, 63 Ill. App. 3d 419, 379 N.E.2d 1365 (1978).

the baby was in a breech position. He did not inform the patient of this development. As a result of the baby's position, the doctor had difficulty in delivering the baby's head. About four hours after birth the baby died from what one expert indicated was a lack of oxygen during delivery.

Plaintiff argued that the doctor was negligent as a matter of law. The contention was based on the defendant's failure to advise of the birth position and the failure to obtain consent for delivery through the birth canal in view of the breech position. The court rejected the argument, pointing out that the patient had signed a consent document, agreeing "to all treatments and operations . . . which in the judgment of the attending physician may be considered necessary or advisable."[28] The court found the language of the signed consent was broad enough to include birth canal delivery despite the breech presentation. Furthermore, the court held, to try to obtain the woman's additional consent to the delivery method used might have been unwise in the situation. The woman was tense and her blood pressure had risen.[29]

A more recent case of negligent disclosure of delivery risk information arose in Minnesota.[30] A woman in her forty-third week of gestation entered the hospital and agreed to a caesarean section. An attempt to induce labor a week beforehand had failed. Hospital policy required that the patient be given a second opinion on the need for a caesarean section. The doctor who carried out this consultation performed a nitrazine test, which demonstrated leakage of amniotic fluid. The patient was not apprised of the fact that her membranes had begun to rupture. The doctor was concerned about the risk of infection and she ordered an injection of Pitocin to accelerate the natural labor that had already commenced. When the woman's attending physician could not be reached, his associate was contacted who agreed with the use of Pitocin.

Although the patient indicated that she did not want a vagi-

[28] Id. at 423, 379 N.E.2d at 1370.
[29] Id. at 422, 379 N.E.2d at 1369-1370.
[30] Kohoutek v. Hafner, 366 N.W.2d 633 (Minn. 1985).

nal delivery and that she opposed the intravenous injection of Pitocin, she did not refuse its use. At no time did the consulting physician disclose to the patient the risks of a vaginal delivery. In the consultant's opinion, the risks associated with vaginal delivery were far less than those of infection.[31]

The intravenous Pitocin was continued for several hours. The attending physician was unable to deliver the baby's shoulders due to shoulder dystocia. A considerable amount of time passed until the shoulders were delivered. By this time the baby had suffered permanent brain damage.[32]

In the lawsuit that followed the plaintiffs alleged battery, negligent nondisclosure of information, and negligent treatment. The case ultimately came before the Minnesota Court of Appeals for review.[33]

In remanding the case for further proceedings the court pointed out that the trial court had erred in not letting the case go to the jury on the issue of battery. As the court suggested, there was testimony to suggest that the patient was either opposed to or confused about the switch in the form of delivery and that she objected to the use of Pitocin. Moreover, the hospital had a so-called Pregnant Patient's Bill of Rights, which provided in part that prior to the use of any medication or procedure the patient was to be informed of the effects, risks, or hazards that it posed to her or the unborn child.[34] Given the facts in the case, there was sufficient question of fact to permit a jury to consider the claim of battery.

The court also indicated that there was sufficient evidence to raise a question about negligent nondisclosure of risk information regarding shoulder dystocia.[35] As the court suggested, taking into account the postterm status of the patient and the size of the baby, the risk of shoulder dystocia was so great that it should have been disclosed to the patient.[36]

[31] Id.
[32] Id.
[33] Id.
[34] Id. at 637.
[35] Id. at 639.
[36] Id.

§3.9.6   Practical Considerations

Delivery methods, the reasonable alternatives, if any, the risks and consequences, and the reasons why it is sometimes necessary to adopt a different birth method than that planned are matters that should be discussed with every pregnant patient.[37] This is an obligation that runs to the mother as well as the unborn child.[38]

In addition, the doctor should seek out patient history information relating to medication sensitivities; at that point any drugs known to cause reactions should be recorded on the patient's record. This information should also be transmitted to the anesthesiology department of the hospital where the birth is expected to occur. In addition, when a planned delivery involves possible or known risk factors, the patient and her husband should be informed accordingly. Breech presentations, RH factor problems, premature deliveries, and complications registered on fetal monitors are but a few examples in this category. A patient who is properly informed is less likely to launch subsequent litigation over undisclosed risks that have become manifest. Still, risk information must be presented in a manner that does not unduly alarm or threaten the prospective parents.

E.   CONSENT TO MEDICAL AND SURGICAL TREATMENT: SPECIAL ISSUES OF CONCERN TO WOMEN

In a number of cases resolved by the courts the issue of consent has arisen relating to hysterectomy. Consent to mastectomy procedures has also been before the courts, as have other surgical interventions for women. Much of the opinion writing has focused on risk disclosure when, subsequent to an operation,

[37] See id.
[38] Roberts v. Patel, 620 F. Supp. 323 (N.D. Ill. 1985).

an undisclosed complication becomes manifest. Consent has also become an issue in diagnostic procedures such as Pap smears. Finally, in some states the legislatures have become involved in urogenital screening and breast examinations for women. These matters are discussed here with particular emphasis on the matter of consent.

§3.10 Hysterectomy Surgery

The section dealing with sterilization emphasized the importance of obtaining the fully informed consent of patients prior to commencing that type of surgery. Hysterectomies performed for medical reasons require a similar standard of consent. Patients should be advised of the effects of a hysterectomy, probable length of disability following surgery, possible permanent scarring, risks and benefits, reasonable alternative procedures, if any, and such other information as the patient requests. If a hysterectomy is contemplated as part of an exploratory operation, this option should also be discussed with the patient. The duty to obtain full consent rests with the attending surgeon, not the hospital.[1] Although many reported cases have been decided in favor of physician-defendants, it is nonetheless important for doctors to observe the requirements for informed consent. Doing so not only avoids possible adverse judgments but also helps avert litigation. A patient who is aware of such risks as permanent scarring and ureterovaginal fistulas is less likely to sue for lack of informed consent. The following case examples illustrate the types of situations in which allegations of incomplete consent have arisen.

§3.10.1 Unauthorized Hysterectomies

One type of litigation stemming from hysterectomies results from allegedly unauthorized surgery. For example, in a Geor-

§3.10 [1] Roberson v. Menorah Med. Center, 588 S.W.2d 134 (Mo. Ct. App. 1979).

gia case, it was claimed that the patient executed a consent form for exploratory surgery without reading it.[2] The form contained language that authorized the surgeon to perform those procedures the surgeon considered necessary or advisable in the operation. In affirming the trial court's grant of summary judgment in favor of the defendant, the appellate court held that the plaintiff could not complain that her hysterectomy was unauthorized. Under Georgia law and according to the facts in the case, the plaintiff's consent was conclusively presumed to have been given voluntarily. Moreover, in view of the plaintiff's testimony that the doctor discussed the course of treatment in general terms, it could not be said that the disclosure aspect of the consent was inadequate.[3]

Claims of unauthorized hysterectomies have also arisen following emergency surgery to stop postpartum hemorrhaging. For example, in a Louisiana case, a woman alleged that her physician was negligent.[4] The woman had delivered without complication following an amniotomy (puncturing the amniotic sac to speed up delivery). When the plaintiff experienced postpartum hemorrhaging, external and internal massage of the uterus was performed and drugs were administered to stop the bleeding. An emergency hysterectomy was performed after these efforts failed. The patient claimed that she had not been given sufficient information in order to give an informed consent to the amniotomy. Her position was rejected by the court. It held that the doctor had not breached his duty since postpartum hemorrhaging is not an additional danger relevant only to an amniotomy. Rather, it is a risk that can be encountered in delivery under any circumstances.[5]

Some claims of unauthorized hysterectomies have gone against the defendants. In a Louisiana case, a woman with a confirmed history of endometriosis and pelvic inflammatory

[2]Winfrey v. Citizens Southern Natl. Bank, 149 Ga. App. 488, 254 S.E.2d 725 (1979).
[3]Id.
[4]Parker v. St. Paul Fire & Marine Ins. Co., 335 So. 2d 725 (La. Ct. App. 1976.)
[5]Id. See also Davidson v. Shirley, 616 F.2d 224 (5th Cir. 1980).

disease agreed to a laparotomy. During the procedure the defendant found the disease was more extensive than he had anticipated and he performed a total hysterectomy and bilateral salpingo-oophorectomy. Action followed against the surgeon for unauthorized removal of the plaintiff's reproductive organs.[6]

In reversing both the trial court and appellate court decisions, the Supreme Court of Louisiana ruled the doctor had committed a battery on the plaintiff. There was no evidence in the case to suggest that the plaintiff was suffering from a life- or health-threatening emergency necessitating the unauthorized removal of the woman's reproductive organs. Moreover, the patient neither expressly nor implicitly agreed to the action taken by the doctor during surgery. That the patient signed a blanket authorization for treatment at the time of her admission to the hospital did not cover the extension of the agreed-to operation. As the court pointed out, the form was so ambiguous as to be virtually worthless.[7]

Physicians should proceed cautiously in performing unauthorized hysterectomies. Unless the situation fits within a recognized exception to the rules for consent, or an authorization for the procedure can be obtained from someone who has the legal right to act for the patient, physicians should refrain from such surgery. Good intentions and trying to save patients under anesthetic from yet another operation will not block successful litigation based on unauthorized surgery.

Physicians must be careful in extending agreed-upon surgery to include hysterectomy and bilateral salpingo-oophorectomy. As one opinion suggests, spousal authorization for additional surgery will be scrutinized closely. Moreover, the court will look closely at language in the consent form that seemingly permits the scope of the authorized surgery to be enlarged.[8] The following case illustrates these points.

The patient signed a consent form authorizing the doctor to

[6]Pizzalotto v. Wilson, 437 So. 2d 859 (La. 1983).
[7]Id.
[8]Ipock v. Gilmore, 326 S.E.2d 271 (N.C. Ct. App. 1985).

perform a laparoscopy with fulguration of the tubes or the use of Hulka clips. The form also indicated that:

> The operation is to include whatever procedures are required in attempting to accomplish such purpose. If any conditions are revealed at the time of the operation that were not recognized before and which call for procedures in addition to those originally contemplated, I authorize the performance of such procedures.[9]

Once the laparoscopy was underway, the doctor determined that the patient had widespread adhesions that completely obscured the pelvic organs. This made it impossible to carry out the sterilization. He decided to proceed instead with a bilateral partial salpingectomy. After making an incision to carry out this procedure, the doctor found further adhesions that were binding down the tubes and ovaries. A cystic mass on the left was also detected, as was a considerable amount of chronic infection. This finding made it clear that the bilateral partial salpingectomy could not be carried out safely and that a total abdominal hysterectomy and bilateral salpingo-oophorectomy were in order.

The doctor discussed the matter with the patient's spouse who, in turn, gave his consent to the extensive operation. The surgery was carried out, but either during the surgery or in the immediate postoperative period the patient suffered extensive hypoxic brain damage.[10] A medical malpractice action followed.

In its ruling on the lower court's summary judgment order in favor of the defendant, the appellate court indicated that the language of the consent form did not authorize the hysterectomy. The court suggested that the language that permitted the doctor to carry out additional procedures referred to measures designed to accomplish the original purpose, namely the laparoscopy. It did not authorize a total hysterectomy. Thus, un-

[9]Id. at 277-278.
[10]Id. at 278.

less the doctor secured the husband's valid consent, the hysterectomy was unauthorized.[11]

As the court stated, the husband does not become the wife's agent by virtue of their marital relationship. Nonetheless, in an emergency the husband may have the power to authorize life-saving care. In this case, because there was no emergency, there was a material issue of fact whether the husband had the power to act for his wife.[12]

§3.10.2 Failure to Disclose Reasonable Alternatives

Another type of litigation has occurred over a physician's alleged failure to tell a patient that she had alternatives to hysterectomy.[13] In one particular case the woman had given birth to a child. During a subsequent office visit to her gynecologist, she had a Pap smear that was indicative of dysplasia (precancerous change in the cells) or cancer in situ. She underwent a D & C as well as a cold conization. Test results revealed that she had cancer — which the doctor believed he had completely removed. Subsequently, the woman was placed on a program of repeat Pap smears. Over a period of several months two came back normal. When she could not contact her doctor for another Pap smear she saw another physician, the defendant. He convinced her to have a total abdominal hysterectomy as he did not agree with the treatment she had received. Prior to the operation the plaintiff had another Pap smear that was normal, but the defendant did not convey these results to her. The pathology tests following the surgery indicated that the plaintiff did not have cancer.

In their action, the woman and her husband claimed that the doctor had performed an unnecessary operation. It was alleged

[11] Id. at 279.
[12] Id. at 280.
[13] Smith v. Reisig, M.D., Inc., 686 P.2d 285 (Okla. 1984), (cause of action dealing with failure to disclose hormonal therapy as an alternative to hysterectomy); Steele v. St. Paul Fire & Marine Ins. Co., 371 So. 2d 843 (La. Ct. App. 1979), cert. denied, 374 So. 2d 658 (La. 1980).

that he had not obtained the woman's informed consent: she was not told of a reasonable alternative procedure that would have allowed her to have retained her childbearing capacity. In reversing a jury verdict in favor of the defendant, the court held that the doctor had breached his duty to disclose material information. He did not tell the woman that many physicians believed the course of treatment she had been receiving was effective. He had also breached his duty of disclosure by failing to tell the patient of the negative Pap smear prior to surgery.[14]

§3.10.3 Inadequate Disclosure of Risk Information

Other hysterectomy cases have involved allegations of inadequate disclosure of risk information. For example, in a Tennessee case, a woman sued her surgeon after she developed a ureterovaginal fistula following a hysterectomy.[15] She claimed that her consent to the surgery was not informed since the defendant did not disclose the risk of the fistula. The court disagreed. It was pointed out that the development of the fistula in an area disassociated from that of the surgery was not the sort of potential harm about which the surgeon had a duty to disclose. Moreover, it was not of such a material nature that the failure to reveal information about it would vitiate the patient's consent.[16]

A similar conclusion was reached in a Kansas decision.[17] Prior to performing a hysterectomy, the defendant explained the nature of the operation, the techniques to be used, and the organs involved. He did so verbally and with the aid of diagrams. Following the operation, the plaintiff developed a vesicovaginal fistula and she sued the surgeon. In affirming a judgment in favor of the defendant, the Supreme Court of Kansas noted limitations on the doctor's duty of disclosure. The court pointed out that the extent of the duty is to be measured

[14]Steele v. St. Paul Fire & Marine Ins. Co., supra n.13.
[15]Longmire v. Hoey, 512 S.W.2d 307 (Tenn. Ct. App. 1974).
[16]Id.
[17]Tatro v. Lueken, 212 Kan. 606, 512 P.2d 529 (1973).

by what a reasonable physician would have revealed under the same or similar circumstances. Whether the failure to disclose the chance of a postoperative fistula prior to the surgery amounted to negligence was a question for the jury. In this case the Supreme Court of Kansas held that the evidence supported the jury's decision in favor of the doctor.[18]

Not all jurisdictions follow the principle that a physician's standard of disclosure is measured by what a reasonable practitioner would have revealed in the same or similar circumstances (see chapter 1 about rules for consent). However, Kansas is not alone in applying the standard to a hysterectomy-fistula case.[19] The rule is of questionable application, particularly where risks of postsurgical complications are far from remote possibilities. Physicians in those jurisdictions that follow the reasonable practitioner or medical community standard of disclosure should not totally rely on that rule safeguarding them from litigation, however. Expert testimony may be readily available to dispute the claim that withholding of postsurgical risk information is acceptable. A sensible approach in such jurisdictions is to judge the need for disclosure according to the increasing probability of the risk. Following this principle, however, does not preclude a doctor from withholding information in emergency situations or from emotionally unstable persons (see chapter 2, Exceptions to the Rules). As practitioners are finding in those states that follow the alternative standard of what a reasonable person in the patient's position would want to know, information patients are likely to consider significant merits disclosure. Risks of fistulas following hysterectomies falls into this category.

§3.10.4 Choosing Risk Information for Disclosure

Other complications or risks stemming from hysterectomies may also merit disclosure. For example, the likelihood of ab-

---

[18]Id.
[19]See Riedisser v. Nelson, 111 Ariz. 542, 534 P.2d 1052 (1975).

dominal scars may be of significance to some women. Those whose livelihoods involve exposure of the abdomen — e.g., dancers or models — may deem it material to know that scarring will occur with abdominal hysterectomies and that an alternative may be to undergo a vaginal hysterectomy. Even women whose careers would not be affected by the scarring may consider its probability as significant information. The following case demonstrates this kind of response to scarring.[20]

Following a hysterectomy, a Louisiana woman and her husband sued the surgeon for an abdominal scar. The patient had agreed to a vaginal hysterectomy, but during the operation complications developed that dictated an abdominal incision. The additional surgery was a life-saving necessity. In reversing a judgment in favor of the plaintiffs, the court held that the claim that a scarless abdomen was of paramount concern had not been proven. For liability to attach, it would have been necessary for the plaintiff to have advised the defendant that she wanted a vaginal hysterectomy to avoid scarring. At that point it would have been the surgeon's duty to advise the patient of the remote possibility of complications requiring an abdominal incision. As the court noted, a physician withholding such information and option from the patient would breach her duty to inform and would be liable for the ensuing damage. However, such was not the situation in the case before the court.[21]

The wisdom of the Louisiana court's ruling is open to question: it places a burden upon the patient to advise the physician of factors that would then trigger the latter's duty to disclose. The minimal level of disclosure required of a surgeon in such circumstances is quite low. Many patients may not realize that they have more than one surgical option. Patients awakening following surgery — as in the case above — may be quite alarmed or disturbed to find that the operation extended beyond what was authorized.

---

[20] Bourgeois v. Davis, 337 So. 2d 575 (La. Ct. App. 1976).
[21] Id.

A frank discussion of risk factors prior to surgery could avert such unwelcome outcomes. True, the law enforces disclosure of only those risks that are material or probable as opposed to those that are remote. A physician would do well, however, to go beyond minimum requirements by ascertaining the needs and desires of his patient and discussing possible as well as probable risk information relevant to that individual. A woman 60 years of age may not be bothered by the prospect of scarring, whereas a woman 35 years her junior could be greatly disturbed by it. Taking the extra time to learn what a patient expects and wants means less likelihood of unanticipated surgical outcomes — and less chance of litigation.

§3.11 Radiation Treatment and Radium Implants

A somewhat novel technique sometimes used in treating uterine cancer is the implanting of radium. As with other forms of invasive treatment, the risks associated with the procedure merit disclosure to patients. A similar policy should be followed with any radiation therapy that may affect the reproductive organs. Cases have already arisen involving consent and the use of radiation affecting the urogenital area, one of which is discussed below.

In a U.S. District Court matter, a physician recommended that his patient undergo a radium implant following a cervical conization.[1] The doctor made an appointment for her with the defendant surgeon. The woman was admitted to the hospital and prepared by nurses for the implant without meeting with the defendant or the doctor who had made the appointment. The defendant saw her thereafter on a few occasions. The woman claimed that she learned of the radium implant in her uterus when a nurse told her that she was being moved to

§3.11   [1] Pegram v. Sisco, 406 F. Supp. 776, affd., 547 F.2d 117 (8th Cir. 1976).

surgery for the defendant to remove it. Following her discharge from hospital, the plaintiff experienced a burning sensation, diarrhea, and fatigue. She telephoned the doctor, who told her such symptoms were quite normal. Another doctor subsequently saw the patient after she began to pass fecal material vaginally. He diagnosed the problem as a large fistula between the uterus and colon. To rectify her condition, the woman underwent a radical hysterectomy and bowel surgery.

The plaintiff's expert testimony established that it was standard medical practice in the area to notify patients of the side effects and risk of fistulas and burns stemming from a radium implant. Moreover, the experts established that it was also standard practice to convey information about reasonable alternatives to radium implants. The plaintiff claimed that neither had been done.

In his defense, the surgeon raised two arguments. First, he was only a consultant; it was the duty of the treating/referring physician to obtain the patient's informed consent. This approach was rejected by the court. It was pointed out that a surgeon has a special responsibility to inform his patient about the proposed procedure. In this case this duty was breached.

Second, the surgeon claimed that the plaintiff could not say that she had not consented since she had signed a consent form. In rejecting this contention the court noted that the document was a standard consent form that bore insufficient information to make it viable. The signed document was ineffectual because the patient had not been told of known dangers associated with the specific procedure at issue. Nor had she been informed of material risk information that might have had an impact on her decision. For these reasons the court rendered judgment in the plaintiff's favor.[2]

As manifested in this case, physicians administering radiation treatment should consider the duty to obtain a patient's consent imperative. It is unwise, at the very least, to rely upon a referral physician to discharge this responsibility. The duty to disclose risk and alternative treatment information, as well as

[2]Id.

an explanation of the proposed procedure, rests with the physician who is to carry it out.

The use of radiation should be preceded by the disclosure of information about probable short-term and long-term side effects. If the area to be irradiated includes the reproductive organs, the physician should discuss with the patient the probable impact the treatment will have on reproductive capacity.

The discussion with the patient should be noted in the chart with an account of what was discussed. The names of witnesses to the discussion should also be recorded. This record should be dated and signed. Should risks subsequently materialize and litigation ensue, the detailed note — and a signed consent document in those hospitals that use forms — will be vital to the establishment of the doctor's argument.

§3.12 Mastectomy Surgery

Mastectomy is a procedure undertaken predominantly in women. Patients sometimes complain — without taking action — that they went into the operating room for a breast biopsy, only to awake in the recovery room with a modified or radical mastectomy. Failure of physicians to disclose reasonable alternatives to the procedure that may be applicable in given instances has also been the basis of complaint. Books for lay women have been written on the subject[1] and state legislatures have also enacted laws on the matter.[2]

---

§3.12 [1]See, e.g., O. Cope, The Breast (1978).
[2]Cal. Health & Safety Code §1704.5 (West 1980) and Cal. Bus. & Prof. Code §2257 (West 1980) (making a violation of Health & Safety Code §1704.5 an act of unprofessional conduct); Fla. Stat. Ann. §458.324 (West 1986) and §459.0125 (West 1984); Kan. Stat. Ann. §65-2836 (1987) (permitting revocation, suspension, or limitation of licenses for failure to disclose treatment alternatives for breast cancer); Ky. Rev. Stat. §311.935 (1984); Md. Ann. Code §20-113 (1986); Mass. Gen. Laws Ann. ch. 111, §70E (West 1979); Minn. Stat. Ann. §144.651 (West 1986); N.J. Stat. Ann. §45:9-22.2 (West 1984); N.Y. Pub. Health Law §2404 (McKinney 1985); Pa. Stat. Ann. tit. 35, §5641 (Purdon 1986) and §5642 (Purdon 1984); Va. Code §54.1-2971 (1988).

§3.12.1 Statutory Requirements

Statutory law is instructive to those engaged in such surgery. California provides that a physician or surgeon is guilty of unprofessional conduct if he or she fails:

> to inform a patient by means of a standardized written summary, as developed by the department on the recommendation of the Cancer Advisory Council, in layman's language and in a language understood by the patient of alternative efficacious methods of treatment which may be medically viable, including surgical, radiological, or chemotherapeutic treatments or combinations thereof, when the patient is being treated for any form of breast cancer. . . .[3]

That law also characterizes the provision to a patient of the standardized written summary mentioned above as constituting compliance with the statute. In addition to the information about alternative means of care, the law requires that the summary inform patients of the "advantages, disadvantages, risks and descriptions of the procedures. . . ."[4]

The Massachusetts provision is not as sweeping in its coverage. The state's patients' rights law provides that a patient suffering from breast cancer has the right "to complete information on all alternative treatments which are medically viable."[5] The law goes further, stating that a person whose rights have been violated may file a civil action under the state's applicable legislation.

Not all jurisdictions have gone the route of California and Massachusetts, which have passed specialized consent legislation applicable to breast cancer. The California and Massachusetts laws do not differ markedly from case law and other state statutes covering the basic requirements for informed consent. The statutes reflect a concern on the part of state legislators (at least in two states) that physicians must be certain to inform

---

[3]Cal. Health & Safety Code §1704.5 (West 1980).
[4]Id.
[5]Mass. Gen. Laws Ann. ch. 111, §70E (West 1979).

their patients of treatment alternatives when breast cancer has been diagnosed. It remains to be seen whether other states will follow suit in enacting specialized consent laws relating to breast cancer treatment.

§3.12.2 Physicians' Duty to Warn

Not only must physicians disclose information relating to the risks and benefits of treatment alternatives, they must also alert their patients to the possibility that certain symptoms may be indicative of breast cancer. This issue is noted in the following 1979 Tennessee case.[6]

In 1974, the plaintiff noticed a change in the size and firmness of her left breast, as well as some discoloration of the nipples. Pain followed the application of pressure. During treatment for another disorder, she brought this condition to the attention of the defendant, her family physician. He did not make an examination at that time. She returned approximately a month and a half later with further complaints of numbness and a sharp pain in the breast. This time the doctor examined her and told her to return a month later. During this time the patient was to observe the breast for any change in symptoms. The doctor never mentioned the possibility of cancer. When no changes in her symptoms were evident after one month, the plaintiff telephoned the doctor's office to see if she should keep her appointment. Having not heard from the doctor, she assumed she need not return. However, a few weeks later her condition worsened and she was seen by a specialist. The subsequent diagnosis was metastatic breast cancer. Despite a radical mastectomy, chemotherapy, and other treatment, the woman died of cancer within weeks of the conclusion of the negligence action against the physician.

The Supreme Court of Tennessee affirmed the trial court's judgment against the defendant. The court ruled that the jury could have reasonably found the doctor negligent for not in-

[6]Truan v. Smith, 578 S.W.2d 73 (Tenn. 1979).

forming the patient of the possibility of cancer as a cause for her complaint. This finding was particularly important because the physician had concluded after first examining the woman that her condition was probably serious.[7]

§3.12.3   Breast Biopsy Beyond a Patient's Authorization

Consideration of a mastectomy should be accompanied by fully informing the patient. Included in a proper disclosure are descriptions of those procedures during which a patient undergoes a biopsy and a frozen section analysis if made while the patient is still under anesthesia. If the biopsy report were to come back showing cancer, the physician must have the patient's permission to extend the operation to a mastectomy. Otherwise, a two-stage procedure is indicated, with the biopsy on one occasion and the mastectomy on another. As demonstrated in the California case that follows, the surgeon should never extend the scope of an operative procedure beyond that authorized by the patient.[8]

In this case a woman agreed to undergo a biopsy of a gland in her right armpit, and the excised tissue was sent to the hospital's laboratory for examination. Five or ten minutes later the report came back: cancer of the breast. The defendants then prepared to remove the woman's right breast. One preparatory incision had been made when a second report was received from the laboratory stating that the first report had been erroneous: the correct diagnosis was lymphoma or possibly Hodgkin's disease. Despite the later report, the surgeons continued, eventually removing the patient's breast.

The appellate court reversed and remanded a nonsuit judgment against the two operating surgeons. Viewing the facts in a light most favorable to the plaintiff, it stated that it could not understand how the consent document signed by the woman

[7]Id.
[8]Valdez v. Percy, 35 Cal. App. 2d 485, 96 P.2d 142 (1939).

and her husband authorized the additional operation unless under necessity. The law in the state clearly made unauthorized operations a technical assault and battery. It held that the trial court should have submitted the matter to the jury.[9]

§3.12.4 Disclosing Risk of Frozen Section Biopsies

As discussed above, performing a biopsy with the possibility of a subsequent mastectomy during the same operation requires thoroughly informing the patient. How far the physician has to go in disclosing risk information, however, is limited too, at least according to the following decision of a Louisiana court.[10]

In 1974, the plaintiff agreed to the removal of a lesion of her left breast. She understood that while she was under general anesthetic, the tissue would be examined by a pathologist. If he found that the lesion was cancerous the breast would be removed. Otherwise, the incision would be closed and she would be discharged the next day. The excision of the lesion went as planned. The pathologist made a quick freeze diagnosis of the lesion and determined that it was cancerous. He informed the surgeon of the results and the patient's left breast was removed. However, the next day a permanent section study was performed that reversed the previous diagnosis.

The woman filed an action for damages claiming, among other things, that the surgeon had failed to comply with the Louisiana law of informed consent. She asserted that he should have told her of the availability of the two pathology studies so that she could decide whether she wanted to have both done before any surgery was performed. That failure, she claimed, constituted a lack of informed consent. In affirming a judgment favorable to the defendants, the court found that the doctor had not breached his duty of disclosure. The patient indeed did have the requisite information for making an intelli-

[9]Id.
[10]Hanks v. Rawson Swan & Burch Ltd., 359 So. 2d 1089 (La. Ct. App. 1978), cert. denied, 360 So. 2d 1178 (La. 1979).

gent judgment. Testimony in the case revealed that the risk of an erroneous diagnosis attributable to the frozen section study was so rare or remote that the surgeon could not have reasonably anticipated it.[11]

It is unclear whether other courts faced with a similar situation would reach the same conclusion. The risk of an incorrect diagnosis due to one method of analysis as opposed to another is perhaps something a patient should consider. In the case of mastectomy the value of using the two different methods of diagnosis must be weighed against the prospect of two separate operations. If general anesthesia is to be used in both procedures, this is a risk factor for a patient to ponder. A doctor's judgment must be fully exercised in discussing these options with a patient. If, for example, a physician knows that her patient is extremely concerned about losing her breast, the risk of false-positive results from frozen studies should be disclosed. The physician may then propose a two-stage procedure instead, if medical conditions warrant. The patient could also consider other nonsurgical options. If, however, the patient accepts the risk of false findings from the one-stage operation, she cannot successfully take action on the basis of lack of sufficient information. Deciding what to disclose depends on the circumstances of *each* case; the physician must take into account the needs and sensibilities of the individual patient.

§3.13   Risk Disclosure in Urogenital Surgery and Diagnostic Procedures on Women

Two California cases illustrate the difficulties faced by physicians in deciding what they should tell their patients about probable risks with urogenital surgery. One matter arose in the context of pathology results following surgery.[1] The other oc-

---

[11]Id. at 1093.

§3.13 [1]Jamison v. Lindsay, 108 Cal. App. 3d 223, 166 Cal. Rptr. 443 (1980).

curred when a patient declined a recommended diagnostic procedure.[2]

§3.13.1 Disclosure of Varying Theories of Cell Growth

In the first case, a 16-year-old girl underwent surgery in which her right ovary and a large cystic mass were removed.[3] The tissue was sent to the hospital's pathology department, where the chief pathologist determined that it was a benign teratoma. In his written pathology report he did not disclose that the specimen contained some immature tissues that some pathologists believe are malignant or potentially so. Weeks later the plaintiff was seen by a physician who had assisted in her surgery. The examination and X-rays revealed a nine-centimeter tumor to the right of the plaintiff's spinal column, as well as lesions in the lung. She underwent additional surgery and radiation and chemotherapy were prescribed. Even so, a portion of the tumor could not be removed.

During the trial in which the first surgeon and the pathologist were sued for malpractice, the defense contended that the ovarian teratoma had not spread. Rather, it was argued, the plaintiff had two unrelated tumors. A pediatric oncologist, testifying on behalf of the plaintiff, claimed that the use of chemotherapy right after the first operation would probably have prevented the development of the later tumor.

Among the plaintiff's contentions was a lack of informed consent. She claimed that she should have been told that pathologists are of differing opinions concerning the actual or potential malignancy of immature tissue. Her position was rejected by the court. It was noted that the jury instruction requested by the plaintiff on the lack of informed consent was inapplicable to evidence before the trial court and that the trial

---

[2]Truman v. Thomas, 27 Cal. 3d 285, 611 P.2d 902, 165 Cal. Rptr. 308 (1980).

[3]Jamison v. Lindsay, supra n.1.

judge had no duty to make the proposed instruction conform to the evidence presented.[4]

§3.13.2 *Disclosure of Risks of Foregoing Pap Smears*

In the second California case, a wrongful death action was launched by the surviving children of a woman who died of cancer.[5] The patient had been seen often during a six-year period by the defendant, who was her primary physician. During this time he requested permission to perform Pap smears on the decedent, who refused. On at least two occasions the defendant claimed that the decedent said she did not feel like having the test or that she could not afford the cost. He offered to defer payment, but this avenue was rejected by the decedent. At no time did the physician tell her of the purpose of a Pap smear. Around the same time the woman saw a urologist for treatment of a urinary tract infection. He discovered that her cervix was quite rough and that she had a heavy vaginal discharge. When she did not make an appointment with a gynecologist as she had been advised to, he made one for her. The gynecologist found a large cervical tumor that was too advanced for surgery. Her condition was treated unsuccessfully by other means and she died several months later.

At trial, expert testimony established that, had the woman undergone a Pap smear during the five- or six-year period in which she was under the defendant's care, the tumor would have probably been discovered in time to save her life. The key issue in the case was whether the defendant breached his duty of care to the decedent when he did not tell her of the potentially fatal consequences of foregoing a Pap smear. The defendant claimed that the duty of disclosure set by earlier California precedent applied only to situations in which a patient agrees to the recommended procedure. Furthermore, he argued that the patient who rejects a doctor's advice must bear the responsibil-

---

[4]Id. at 231, 166 Cal. Rptr. at 447.
[5]Truman v. Thomas, supra n.2.

ity to ask about the possible consequences of her decision. This stance was rejected by the Supreme Court of California. As the court pointed out, the duty to disclose does not end with the recommended procedure. The physician must explain the consequences of a decision that rejects the proposed care or diagnostic intervention.

The defendant also argued that he did not have a duty to disclose because the risk involved in failing to have a Pap smear was commonly known to be remote. The Supreme Court responded to this contention by noting it was a jury question whether the risk was material to the patient. Even if the disclosure was not generally required, the court pointed out that the circumstances of the case might establish that the defendant did have an obligation to reveal the risks of foregoing a Pap smear. Given the reasons voiced by the decedent in rejecting Pap smears, a jury could conclude that the defendant had a duty to warn because it was not reasonable for him to assume that she understood the potentially lethal results of her decision.[6]

§3.13.3   *Practical Considerations*

Although a physician need not disclose to a patient the split of professional opinion about a pathology specimen, still the doctor should discuss possible postsurgical options available to a patient. The first case turned in part on a technical point involving jury instructions, but it is advisable for a physician to warn the attending surgeon and patient of questionable pathology findings. Patients must have the benefit of the full spectrum of possible interpretation, including information available for proper follow-up care. To do otherwise could lead to a false sense of well-being. Physicians should look at the disclosure of such information as part of good patient care and as a means of avoiding litigation. The next plaintiff in a similar situation is not likely to falter on a poorly worded jury instruction.

[6]Id.

Negative criticism has been voiced concerning the second of these California cases.[7] One possible interpretation is as a precedent that opens a medicolegal Pandora's box: just how far does a physician have to go in securing a fully informed *negative* consent? However, the facts of the case itself do not invite such speculation. For some time the rule in California has dictated that a physician must disclose the risk and benefits of a proposed procedure as well as the consequences of a decision not to proceed.[8] A thoughtful and diligent practitioner, faced with a rejection of the recommended procedure, would probably ask for reasons. At a minimum, he should explain the hazards of such conduct. This issue is what the California court seems to be emphasizing.

Where critics may have cause for concern is when a patient refuses to listen to the risks that attend foregoing treatment. If a patient declines the proposed procedure without knowing these risks and the alternative procedures available, her decision cannot be interpreted as truly informed. When litigation subsequently arises, what defenses are available to the doctor? This problem is discussed in detail in §2.7 supra.

§3.14 Screening for Women's Diseases

As discussed in this section, a few states have enacted laws that provide for the detection of diseases affecting women. Legislative attention has focused on Pap smears and public education programs associated with DES screening. The fact that many states have not taken similar legislative initiative does not relieve the attending physician from responsibility for adequate

---

[7] See, e.g., Fagel, The Duty of Informed Refusal, 9 Legal Aspects of Medical Practice 1-2, 6 (September 1981).

[8] Cobbs v. Grant, 8 Cal. 3d 229, 502 P.2d 1, 104 Cal. Rptr. 505 (1972). It should be noted, however, that the facts of the *Truman* case precede the *Cobbs* decision. However, even under case precedent, it is arguable that the duty to disclose existed in the instant case. See Salgo v. Leland Stanford Jr. Univ. Bd. of Trustees, 154 Cal. App. 2d 560, 317 P.2d 170 (1957).

disclosure of information regarding screening and detection of women's illnesses.

§3.14.1 Pap Smear Legislation

In some jurisdictions, legislation has been enacted creating screening programs for certain maladies experienced by women. For example, in Illinois,[1] Maryland,[2] and Ohio,[3] hospitals must offer Pap smears to women who are inpatients. The tests must be offered to women 20 years of age and over in Illinois[4] and to those 18 years or older in Maryland and Ohio.[5] The state laws provide that the Pap smears should not be given if the woman has undergone the same procedure within the preceding year or if the doctor considers it contraindicated. The patient also has the right to refuse the Pap smear.[6]

§3.14.2 Pap Smears and Disclosure Requirements

Even in the absence of such legislation, it is important for physicians to discuss with patients the purpose, need, desirability, and accuracy of Pap smear tests. Risks and benefits must be explained, as should the risks of foregoing the test. In those jurisdictions with laws governing Pap smears, medical personnel should make an effort to determine the relevant consent requirements — including not only the amount of disclosure and procedure for dealing with uninformed refusal (see §3.13.2 supra), but also the need to warn patients of positive test results. Absent specific statutes or regulations in this re-

---

§3.14 [1] Ill. Ann. Stat. ch. 111 1/2, §53.31 (Smith-Hurd 1973).
[2] Md. Pub. Health Code Ann. 43 §556F (1978).
[3] Ohio Rev. Code Ann. §3701.60 (Baldwin 1976).
[4] Ill. Ann. Stat., supra n.1.
[5] Md. Pub. Health Code Ann., supra n.2; Ohio Rev. Code Ann., supra n.3.
[6] Ill. Ann. Stat., supra n.1; Md. Pub. Health Code Ann., supra n.2; Ohio Rev. Code Ann., supra n.3.

gard, general consent laws should be reviewed, as well as case precedent.

§3.14.3   DES Screening

Another type of screening program that has been implemented in some states is for the identification of persons exposed to diethylstilbestrol (DES).[7] From the late 1940s until the early 1970s, DES was given to pregnant women who were experiencing problem pregnancies. In 1971 a statistical association was made between maternal ingestion of DES and vaginal and cervical lesions in female offspring. DES has also been charged as the cause of adenocarcinoma among these young women.[8] Illinois is one state with DES screening legislation.[9]

Those engaged in DES screening programs should recognize the legal requirements of consent applicable to the situation. Some DES screening laws and regulations may have specific consent provisions. If not, one should look to the state's general consent provisions or case precedent. From a practical standpoint, the information provided should include details on the purpose and nature of DES screening, the risks and benefits associated in both having and not having the screening, and any reasonable alternatives. The information provided should also take into account disclosure of test results and any follow-up care instructions.

§3.15   Treatment for Rape Victims

From a practical perspective, treating victims of rape can be quite complex. The caregiver must be cognizant of the victim's

[7] See, e.g., Ill. Ann. Stat. ch. 111 1/2, §§4503 et seq. (Smith-Hurd 1981).

[8] Herbst et al., Adenocarcinoma of the Vagina: Association of Maternal Stilbestrol Therapy with Tumor Appearance in Young Women, 298 New Eng. J. Med. 763 (1971).

[9] Ill. Ann. Stat., supra n.1.

physical as well as emotional needs. Moreover, for purposes of criminal prosecution of the assailant, care must be taken in gathering evidence.

Securing consent to treatment from a rape victim triggers concern about the mental capacity of the patient to authorize care. Has the trauma of the assault incapacitated the patient? Can the patient understand the nature and consequences of intended treatment? If treatment protocols include prophylaxis with penicillin, does standard policy also include history screening for allergy to such medication? Questions such as these face caregivers in emergency departments everywhere. The ability of patients to consent and to give an accurate medication allergy history will vary from case to case. One factor remains constant, however: the vulnerability of the victim. A Maryland case[1] illustrates this point.

A woman was kidnapped at gunpoint and raped. Immediately after the assault, the woman was taken to the Rape Crisis Center at a Baltimore health center. The treating physician administered medication to prevent venereal disease and he also prescribed a drug called Estrace to prevent pregnancy. The plaintiff filled the prescription and took it according to instructions. Subsequently, the plaintiff learned that she was pregnant with the child of her assailant. Strong religious beliefs on the part of the plaintiff precluded an abortion.

There were several grounds to the litigation that followed against the treating physician and the health facility. Of particular interest is the issue of informed consent. The court held that the plaintiff did not properly plead the issue of informed consent in her case. Moreover, even if it had been properly drawn, the jury instruction requested by plaintiff was in error as it amounted to a directed verdict.[2]

What the plaintiff tried to establish in this case was that the drug Estrace was untested or experimental and that the physician did not disclose to her the true nature of the preparation.

§3.15 [1] Zeller v. Greater Baltimore Med. Center, 67 Md. App. 75, 506 A.2d 646 (1986).
[2] Id.

Although it is a matter of speculation, had the issue of informed consent been pleaded correctly and the instruction correctly worded, the plaintiff might have prevailed.

What lessons should be drawn from this case? Physicians should take care to explain to rape victims what courses of treatment are available to them, including details on the likelihood of success, side effects, and reasonable alternative forms of care. The pros and cons of postcoital preparations should be discussed. The risk of pregnancy should be disclosed as well. Moreover, the physician should take the time to document what was discussed with the rape victim. Such a notation should also include the clinician's professional impression of the patient's ability to understand and appreciate the information provided.

No one can prevent litigation based on allegations of negligent disclosure. It is quite another matter, however, to prevail in such a case. Careful history taking, good communication with the patient, and adequate disclosure of information are essential to a solid defense. Courts may be impressed with the emotional state of the patient at the time of rape treatment. In this context, a boilerplate form with spaces to complete may not be viewed as very credible evidence of the consent process. However, a detailed note in the patient record in which the emotional status of the patient was discussed along with a brief account of the consent process may be the cornerstone for the physician's defense.

FOUR

Prisoners and Detainees

A. Voluntary Consent
  §4.0   Can Consent Be Voluntary?
  §4.1   Factors Influencing Voluntariness
         §4.1.1   Survival: The Model Prisoner Syndrome
         §4.1.2   Fear: The Coercive Institutional Setting
         §4.1.3   Lack of Adequate Explanation
  §4.2   Good Communication
B. Incapacity to Consent
  §4.3   State Legislation on Inmate Welfare
  §4.4   Emergency Treatment and Implied Consent
  §4.5   Intoxication: The Parens Patriae Rule
C. Right to Refuse Treatment
  §4.6   When Can Prisoners Say No?
         §4.6.1   Legislative Limits
         §4.6.2   Case Law
         §4.6.3   Treating Hunger Strikers
         §4.6.4   Religious Refusals
         §4.6.5   Probation and Experimental Drug Therapy
D. Compulsory Examination and Treatment
  §4.7   Venereal Disease
         §4.7.1   Who Must Submit?
         §4.7.2   Gaining Cooperation of Prisoners
  §4.8   Drug Addiction
E. Obtaining Evidence: Physical and Surgical "Searches"
  §4.9   Informed Consent of Suspects
  §4.10 Implied Consent of Unconscious or Incapacitated Persons
  §4.11 Implied Consent of Drunk Driving Suspects
  §4.12 Invasive Searchers of Prisoners' Bodies
         §4.12.1   Nonsurgical Invasions
         §4.12.2   Surgical Invasions

A. VOLUNTARY CONSENT

§4.0   Can Consent Be Voluntary?

It is generally accepted that incarceration or detention for a criminal act does not remove an individual's right to consent to treatment. As in other settings, the extent to which a prisoner may exercise that right is not absolute. Despite the laws governing medical consent, including the right to refuse care, various states have enacted laws requiring prisoners and detainees to undergo compulsory examinations and treatment. These largely focus on such communicable illnesses as venereal disease and AIDS. Statutes have also created a type of "implied" consent authorizing breath or urine samples from persons suspected of being intoxicated while operating a motor vehicle. Some laws go still further and imply the consent of drivers or pedestrians who are incapable of authorizing the removal of blood or urine specimens.

In this chapter these matters are discussed from the perspective of medical consent. (The discussion of AIDS and prisoners is found in chapter 11 on AIDS, infra.) To some degree this perspective includes a discussion of criminal procedure, though a detailed analysis of federal and state requirements is left to treatises on criminal law. Another topic considered here is the matter of emergency treatment of criminal detainees and prisoners. The removal of incriminating evidence at surgery and the physician's duty to report stab and gunshot wounds come within this category. The use of prisoners as research subjects is developed in chapter 8 infra.

§4.1   Factors Influencing Voluntariness

Many people believe obtaining informed consent to treatment from criminal detainees or prisoners is impossible. They argue that truly informed consent that meets the usual legal requirements, including voluntariness (see chapter 1, supra), cannot take place in a correctional facility.

216

§4.1.1   Survival: The Model Prisoner Syndrome

One recognized assumption about prisoner behavior is that those aspiring to parole will conduct themselves as model prisoners. That means they are loath to do *anything* that will rock the boat. If a volunteer blood donation program is announced, they will gladly give a pint of blood. If a prison physician or nurse says they must take a particular medication or submit to an immunization, they do so without question. Their willingness in these situations, however, is not informed; it is motivated by the fear of retaliation by the system for noncompliance. The question is, how accurate is this impression about America's correctional facilities?

A quick review of the growing body of case law in the United States involving prisoners and medical treatment suggests that the model of the unquestioning prisoner is fast disappearing. Prisoners have sued on the basis of civil rights violations when medical treatment has not been provided or it has allegedly been inadequate.[1] If prisoners are prepared to assert their rights in terms of an acceptable standard of medical care it follows that they will also demand to make informed and non-coerced decisions about that care. Otherwise, litigation will follow. Prisoners may be prepared to go along with the system to some extent. Matters involving health care and integrity of the person mark the outer limits of this attitude of cooperativeness. The case law developing in the United States is a clear indicator that prisoners will not quietly submit to medical care over which they do not have informed control.

§4.1.2   Fear: The Coercive Institutional Setting

The giving of consent — even informed consent — does not necessarily imply that the decision is voluntary. Prisoners may be quick to assert their rights after bodily injury, but how voluntary can their consent be before a procedure? Like any institutional setting, though to a greater degree, a correctional

§4.1   [1]See generally 28 A.L.R. Fed. 279 (1976).

facility or a detention center is a coercive setting. Unlike routine patients, who often actively seek information, prisoners and detainees may fear that challenging a doctor or nurse could result in reprisals.

Retaliation would not even necessarily come from the medical staff. More likely it would come from a prison guard who feels he will teach the inmate a lesson about questioning the doctor or nurse. Retaliation may take the form of a recorded remark in the prisoner's files that could be interpreted as evidence against granting parole. How realistic these fears of coercive responses are depends on the particular institution involved. Regardless, health professionals should deal with the fear itself, even if unsupported by facts, since it can result in prisoners' or detainees' feeling coerced into agreeing to medical treatments.

§4.1.3 Lack of Adequate Explanation

The basic requirements for informed consent apply to prisoners and detainees as well as to the average citizen. When the procedure to be performed is irreversible or has an impact upon reproductive capacity, the implications must be explained in adequate detail. A prisoner must not feel that agreeing to sterilization guarantees her parole. In that situation consent cannot be considered voluntary. Since the fundamental right of procreation is involved, the courts are bound to give particular consideration to the issue of consent. Health professionals must explain the nature and purpose of the procedure or drug, the foreseeable benefits and risks, any reasonable alternatives, and the consequences of foregoing any care at all. The prisoner must be legally and mentally capable of agreeing to the care to be provided.

There is little that a health professional can do to relieve the coerciveness of the institutional setting. Nonetheless, if a physician establishes a good, trusting rapport with the prisoner/patient, it is more likely that the latter will ask questions of material significance. Although such a practice takes time, by establishing a reputation for fairness and by maintaining a physician-patient relationship to the extent permitted by the setting, health professionals can overcome some of the handicaps imposed by the correctional atmosphere.

§4.2 Good Communication

Good communication with a patient is necessary for quality care. Informed patients who can consult openly with the doctor or nurse can more effectively participate in their own care. From a legal perspective, a well-informed patient who communicates well with health care providers is less likely to sue for lack of consent or negligence when treatment is less than successful. Those treating prisoners and detainees are as susceptible as their colleagues in a general hospital setting to lawsuits based on inadequate consent or negligence. Since those they are treating are not as free to exercise their rights as routine patients, prison physicians and nurses should make an extra effort to secure informed consent to treatment.

B. INCAPACITY TO CONSENT

§4.3 State Legislation on Inmate Welfare

Legislation has been enacted to cover prisoners who are incapable of giving consent to medical treatment. For example, in Illinois the chief executive officer of a correctional facility under certain conditions is authorized to consent to medical or surgical treatment on behalf of a prisoner. The prisoner must be unable to consent; the care required must be of an immediate nature to correct a life-threatening, impairing, or disfiguring condition; and the administrative officer must obtain the advice of one or more licensed physicians on the matter.[1]

In Missouri, the administrative officer of a correctional institution is authorized to order medical, dental, surgical, or psychiatric care of a standard variety as is considered necessary "for the welfare of an inmate."[2] However, if the inmate is capable of giving a written informed consent for any nonemergency surgical or other procedure considered advisable or necessary, the administrative officer may rely upon the inmate's consent. However, if the competent inmate withholds his consent, the procedure cannot take place.[3] Other states have similar laws authorizing chief administrative officers to consent to various forms of health care for inmates.[4]

§4.4 Emergency Treatment and Implied Consent

Without statutes and regulations authorizing emergency treatment, state common law principles prevail. In many, if not most, jurisdictions a health professional may render emergency treatment to someone incapable of consent. Some jurisdictions label this justification for treatment as implied consent. Two conditions must be present:

1. The individual must be in need of life-saving care; and
2. The individual must be incapable of giving consent as a result of injuries or health condition.

The health professional must not exceed what is reasonable in the circumstances and may only provide treatment for the life-threatening condition or injuries. Providing care when an

§4.3 [1] Ill. Ann. Stat. ch. 38, §1003-6-2 (Smith-Hurd 1987).
[2] Mo. Ann. Stat. §105.700 (Vernon 1980).
[3] Id.
[4] See, e.g., N.J. Stat. Ann. §30:4-72 (West 1969), in which the administrative officer is authorized to consent to various categories of care for inmates who are incompetent or who are of "non-age."

emergency does not exist or exceeding the bounds of medically reasonable care could result in litigation. (For further discussion, see §1.7.4 and §2.2 supra.)

In a correctional setting the emergency treatment rule applies as it would in a hospital's emergency department. If an inmate is seriously stabbed and left unconscious by fellow prisoners and requires immediate attention, there is no need to await approval of the superintendent for medical care. Even in Illinois, where the chief executive officer of a correctional facility must obtain the advice of one or more licensed physicians, a reasonable person is not going to await the consultation of a doctor miles away while an inmate bleeds internally from a punctured lung. Reasonable measures must be taken to prevent a prisoner's death.

Correction officials must understandably be empowered to maintain prison security and to protect the welfare of inmates. Laws that authorize officials to consent to medical care of a nonemergency type, however, are troublesome: they run counter to the premise that prisoners do not give up their right to consent to treatment. How can the need for prison security overcome the right of privacy and personal integrity when nonemergency care is concerned? Given the growing emphasis on the constitutional right of privacy, this question may not remain unanswered for long.[1]

§4.5   Intoxication: The Parens Patriae Rule

A different type of incapacity arises from intoxication. Problems of consent in this area arise when individuals are placed in protective custody or are assisted to a treatment facility by

§4.4   [1]See, e.g., Runnels v. Rosendale, 499 F.2d 733 (9th Cir. 1974), in which the court recognized the constitutional right of privacy possessed by the prisoner in matters involving medical care. The court noted that the right of privacy may be overcome on a showing of compelling state interest. See also Commissioner of Corrections v. Myers, 379 Mass. 255, 399 N.E.2d 452 (1979).

police officers. Michigan, for example, has a law that allows a person believed to be incapacitated in a public place to be placed in protective custody.[1] At a treatment facility the individual must be examined by a physician or her representative. A chemical test to determine the alcohol content in the person's bloodstream may be conducted; the test may also, according to the statute, be requested by the individual who must be informed of his right in this regard. If found to be incapacitated, the person is to receive treatment.[2]

With the growing emphasis on privacy and personal integrity, how can this law and ones similar to it be justified? How can an individual be examined without her consent on the ground of suspected incapacitation?

The legitimacy of some of these laws, and the state's resultant power, rests on the principle of parens patriae. In other words, the state may step in to protect those who cannot protect themselves, including those who are incapacitated due to intoxication. This authority is limited and should be honored by health professionals and law enforcement personnel. Examinations and treatment must deal with the source of the incapacitation and not extend to treatment of other anomalies. Still, as seen time and again in the medical treatment context, the right of privacy is not absolute. The state's interest in protecting those who cannot look after themselves is perceived as taking precedence over an individual's interest in bodily integrity.

Statutory authority also exists for examinations of those arrested for misdemeanors who appear to be incapacitated.[3] Provision is often made for examinations and treatment to be conducted by health personnel.

Regardless of the wrong committed, health personnel are committed to conducting themselves in accordance with statutory requirements. Any requests by police to "go beyond" treatment authorized by these statues should not be heeded: police

---

§4.5   [1] Mich. Comp. Laws, §§333.6501 to 333.6502 (1980).
[2] Id.
[3] Mich. Comp. Laws, §333.6501 (1980).

and officials of the health facility must adhere to the proper procedure.

C. RIGHT TO REFUSE TREATMENT

§4.6 When Can Prisoners Say No?

Just as prisoners or detainees have the right to consent to treatment, so do they have the right — within limits — to decline care. Case law, however, is not totally supportive of a prisoner's prerogative to exercise this right. At times courts have upheld the state's right to compel treatment based on interests perceived as being paramount to those of the prisoner.[1]

§4.6.1 Legislative Limits

Some state legislatures have been sympathetic, within limits, to those prisoners who wish to refuse care. For example, in Louisiana any sane inmate of the state penitentiary may decline care or treatment offered to him by the state. Prisoners cannot, however, refuse care required by state laws and regulations relating to infectious or contagious disease.[2]

Another interesting provision is found in North Carolina's laws. When a prisoner refuses consent to treatment for a self-inflicted wound, the chief medical officer of the prison hospital or institution may give or withhold consent on behalf of the prisoner.[3] This decision is made after the Secretary of Corrections determines that the wounds were in fact willfully and intentionally self-inflicted and that treatment is necessary for

§4.6 [1]Commissioner of Corrections v. Myers, 379 Mass. 255, 399 N.E.2d 452 (1979).
[2]La. Rev. Stat. Ann. §15.860 (West 1948).
[3]N.C. Gen. Stat. §148-46.2 (1981).

the restoration or preservation of the prisoner's health. The secretary must also find that the patient is competent and that efforts to obtain consent have resulted in failure.[4]

The interesting feature of the law lies in the medical officer's option not to override the patient's refusal of consent. He may find that medical or surgical intervention is unreasonable in the circumstances. Another consideration is the impact of withholding treatment upon prison security and decorum, in the event that without care the prisoner dies. The North Carolina legislation thus grants considerable authority to the prison medical officer. His discretion must be exercised thoughtfully, after a complete consideration of the important factors in the case.

Simply because legislative safeguards have been put in place to permit prisoners to refuse treatment does not necessarily mean that these rights are respected. Judicial intervention may be necessary to enforce these provisions or to interpret the applicability of these laws in specific circumstances. A California case exemplifies this point.[5]

Two taxpayers brought suit claiming that prisoners were receiving involuntary treatment with psychotropic drugs at the California Medical Facility at Vacaville. Based on the decision of the chairman of an institutional review board, prisoners were administered psychotropic drugs on a long-term basis. Prisoners were referred by a prison psychiatrist who would make an oral presentation on the matter. The board would evaluate and discuss the prisoner's file and he would also be interviewed. The chairman, a psychiatrist, would then make his determination. The prisoner was not afforded the right to counsel at the board meetings. Furthermore, prisoners were not accorded a right to judicial review of the board's determination.[6]

The court ruled that state prisoners and nonprisoners alike are entitled to a judicial interpretation of their competency to

[4] Id.
[5] Keyhea v. Rushen, 178 Cal. App. 3d 526, 223 Cal. Rptr. 746 (1986).
[6] Id. 178 Cal. App. 3d at 531.

decline treatment before being compelled to submit to long-term psychotropic drug therapy. The court pointed out that the basis for this conclusion was found in the Lanterman-Petris-Short Act.[7] Although the requirement of a judicial interpretation of competency to refuse consent to treatment was seen in some quarters as being cumbersome, the court noted that "this is a price of life in a free society. Forced drugging is one of the earmarks of the gulag. It should be permitted in state institutions only after adherence to stringent substantive and procedure safeguards."[8]

§4.6.2 Case Law

In the absence of specific legislation, how will the rights of the inmate be asserted in the face of state insistence upon treatment? Should a prisoner be allowed to prevail, and, if so, on what grounds? The following case examples illustrate how the courts have resolved these and related issues.

In a Massachusetts case, a 24-year-old inmate refused to continue hemodialysis for his kidney condition.[9] The man was single, without dependents, and competent. He was in a medium-level correctional facility and was serving a number of concurrent sentences. Although to a large extent the matter was rendered factually moot, the Massachusetts Supreme Judicial Court found that there was sufficient basis upon which it could render a decision.[10]

For one year the inmate had submitted to hemodialysis treatment three times a week and to regular administration of medication. At an evidentiary hearing involving the state's authority to compel treatment, it was found that the reasons for the in-

[7]Cal. Welf. & Inst. Code §§5000 et seq.
[8]Keyhea v. Rushen, supra n.5, 178 Cal. App. 3d at 542.
[9]Commissioner of Corrections v. Myers, 379 Mass. 255, 399 N.E.2d 452 (1979).
[10]The prisoner had obtained a kidney transplant, which would probably obviate the need for dialysis. However, the prospect of his body's rejecting the organ and thereby again necessitating dialysis was enough, taken with other considerations, to cause the court to find that the case was not moot.

mate's refusal were not related to his disease or the dialysis. Rather, he was protesting against his placement in a medium as opposed to a minimum security facility. The defendant believed that the dialysis weakened him and compromised his ability to defend himself against other prisoners.

In affirming the lower court's order declaring that the state could force a competent prisoner to undergo dialysis, the Supreme Judicial Court balanced identified state interests against those of the defendant. It found the state's concern for the preservation of life to be closely matched to the individual's interest in avoiding the significant, nonconsensual invasion of his body by dialysis. Essential to the court's finding that the state could compel treatment was its interest in orderly prison administration.[11] The court noted that the state interest covered such matters as the threat to prison administration and security posed by the prisoner's actions. Failing to prevent the death of an inmate who sought to manipulate his status in the corrections system by refusing life-saving care would further undermine prison order.[12] The court pointed out that the United States Supreme Court has ruled that the "purpose" underlying the exercise of a constitutional right is an element that prison officials may legitimately take into consideration,[13] However, the state interests must be balanced against those of the individual in each case, with due consideration of the relevant facts.

In other court actions treatment instituted in spite of prisoner refusal has not necessarily been life saving in nature. For example, in a United States District Court case from Kansas,[14] a prisoner claimed that he had been forcibly medicated against his will. He brought a civil rights action claiming that this coercion had violated his First Amendment rights. The court granted the motion of summary judgment that had been filed by the defendants. It was determined that the defendants, a

[11]Commissioner of Corrections v. Myers, supra n.9 at 261, 399 N.E.2d at 457.
[12]Id. at 261, 399 N.E.2d at 458.
[13]Id. at 261 n.4, 399 N.E.2d at 458 n.4, citing Jones v. North Carolina Prisoners' Labor Union, 433 U.S. 119, 126 (1977).
[14]Sconiers v. Jarvis, 458 F. Supp. 37 (D.C. Kan. 1978).

prison physician and a psychiatrist, possessed the authority to medicate the plaintiff against his will. Where, as here, forcible administration of drugs was believed to be necessary to protect the prisoner as well as others from harm posed by the prisoner's psychotic behavior, medical personnel acted reasonably. Their actions could not be considered arbitrary or capricious, given the substantial threat to safety and prison security due to the prisoner's behavior.[15]

The judiciary is not necessarily as inclined to sustain a prison physician's actions when the inmate's condition is neither life threatening nor a threat to prison security. In one case brought by a state prisoner under the Civil Rights Act, it was alleged that prison medical personnel had performed a hemorrhoidectomy upon him without his consent.[16] In reversing an order of summary judgment in favor of the defendant, the United States Ninth Circuit Court of Appeals pointed out that the right of security and bodily privacy could be violated by prison officials in the course of medical care — but only after a showing of a compelling state interest. Considering the dependence of prisoners upon the institution for medical treatment and their vulnerability while incarcerated, the prisoner's privacy interest could be violated by a substantial threat to physical integrity posed by major surgery that is neither consented to nor required for state interests.[17]

At least one court has addressed the issue of forcible administration of antipsychotic drugs to pretrial detainees.[18] The case involved a civil rights claim stemming from the forcible use of thorazine. It is interesting to note that the detainee initially requested the drug and threatened to kill himself if he did not get it. However, when he began experiencing side effects of the drug, he refused to take it. After receiving forcible injection of the drug, the detainee agreed to take it orally because of the threat of further involuntary administration of thorazine.[19]

[15] Id.
[16] Runnels v. Rosendale, 499 F.2d 733 (9th Cir. 1974).
[17] Id.
[18] Bee v. Greaves, 744 F.2d 1387 (10th Cir. 1984).
[19] Id. at 1389-1390.

According to the Tenth Circuit Court of Appeals, the pretrial detainee's privacy interests create a constitutionally protected right to decide whether to accept potentially dangerous drugs.[20] Moreover, the court indicated that the First Amendment guarantee of the free communication of ideas includes protection of the capacity to formulate ideas. That antipsychotic drugs may hamper the ability to think and communicate implicates these First Amendment rights.[21]

Although the individual has these constitutional guarantees, these interests are not absolute. The pretrial detainee's interests must be balanced against those of the state to determine which should prevail. In this case, the state named three specific interests:

1. the right and obligation to treat a mentally ill detainee;
2. the jail's interest in keeping the detainee in a competent state to stand trial; and
3. the obligation of the jail to safeguard security and to prevent injury inflicted by a violent prisoner on himself or others.[22]

Although the court acknowledged that the jail is under a constitutional duty to satisfy the medical needs of pretrial detainees, it cannot provide such care when it is not desired by a competent individual. The underlying purpose of the constitutional duty is to prohibit the deliberate failure to provide necessary care. It does not, however, include the right to involuntary medication of a pretrial detainee. Indeed, the court suggested that treatment under such circumstances may amount to unconstitutional punishment.[23]

The court also held that the second interest was without foundation. In this case the detainee had been determined by a state court not to be mentally ill and to be competent to stand trial. With such a finding the state could not claim that forcible

---

[20] Id. at 1392-1393.
[21] Id. at 1393-1394.
[22] Id. at 1394.
[23] Id. at 1395.

administration of antipsychotic medication was necessary to keep the detainee competent to stand trial.[24]

The third and final point — the duty to protect staff and other persons from violence — was the most serious concern the court addressed. The court readily agreed that in an emergency forcible use of antipsychotic drugs may be reasonably related to the legitimate interests of safety and security. Whether a genuine emergency exists necessitating the use of antipsychotic drugs is a matter of professional judgment. The decision should be based on appropriate medical standards, taking into account the interests of the individual, the safety of others, and the availability of less restrictive methods of overcoming the emergency.[25]

The court reversed and remanded the lower court's summary judgment in favor of the defendants. In so doing, the court pointed out that there was a disputed issue of material fact in the case that precluded the granting of summary judgment.[26]

A health professional asserting a need for a convict to be medicated with psychoactive drugs is not sufficient to overcome the person's objection to such treatment. This point was made clear in an Arizona case in which that state's supreme court relied upon the Arizona constitution in finding a violation of due process guarantees.[27]

The convict in question had been transferred from a penal institution to a mental health facility operated by the Arizona Department of Corrections. Forcible and indefinite treatment with Navane followed an altercation between the convict and another patient. Other drugs were also administered to overcome the side effects of the psychoactive drugs.

The court found that forcible administration of medication to control behavior was a form of bodily restraint. It also said that an individual has a due process right or liberty interest to be free of arbitrary and involuntary administration of medica-

---

[24] Id.
[25] Id. at 1395-1396.
[26] Id. at 1396-1397.
[27] Large v. Superior Court, 714 P.2d 399 (Ariz. 1986).

tion at the hands of the government. This liberty interest likewise applies to convicted criminals. However, the right of a prisoner to refuse psychoactive care is not absolute and must give way when the government's action is "both substantially related to the purpose it is to serve and not excessive in response to the problem addressed."[28]

The state argued that forcible administration of the drug was necessary for purposes of security. The court rejected this claim, indicating that in the absence of an emergency forcible use of dangerous medication is not "reasonably" necessary for security.[29] Forcible use of dangerous psychoactive drugs must be limited to specific emergency conditions, and this must be under procedural safeguards.[30]

The state also claimed that in this case the drug was needed for "treatment" of the prisoner. The court rejected that claim indicating that dangerous psychoactive drugs may only be used for treatment when authorized by appropriate procedural regulations. Moreover, the drug must be administered after approval by a "qualified" medical determination and for valid "medical" reasons.[31]

As the court warned:

Valid reasons include cure or control of the diagnosed mental disorder; they do not include chemicals to keep prisoners docile and manageable regardless of potential serious physical and emotional consequences. The legislature has the authority and power to provide for punishment and incarceration of criminals. It does not have and cannot give to the Department of Corrections the power to immobilize and warehouse prisoners by using chemicals with known adverse consequences, only to release them — possibly severely impaired — at the end of their sentence. Such an Orwellian result is not permitted by our state constitution.[32]

[28] Id. at 407.
[29] Id. at 407-408.
[30] Id. at 408.
[31] Id. at 409.
[32] Id.

Although this case is based on a state constitutional interpretation, it is likely that a similar tack may be taken under precedent set by the United States Supreme Court. The courts will not give state mental health or penal officials carte blanche to use dangerous drugs. To ensure the proper use of psychoactive drugs there should be clearly delineated standards and procedural safeguards. Moreover, there should be proof of adherence to these standards and procedures, buttressed by valid medical reasons for the use of such medication. Follow-up of the impact of the drugs and adequate documentation are also important considerations.

§4.6.3 Treating Hunger Strikers

Inmates who have been on hunger strikes and who have refused care pose yet another problem in terms of consent. In response, the U.S. government has promulgated regulations dealing with judicial administration and the Bureau of Prisons.[33] Under the procedure set forth in the regulations, a medical officer may consider using forced treatment upon an inmate whose life or health is threatened if care is not provided immediately. Reasonable efforts must be made by the staff to persuade the prisoner to accept treatment voluntarily. She must be informed of the medical risks involved if care is refused. If the inmate persists in her refusal or if an emergency arises requiring immediate attention, the medical officer can order treatment without the inmate's consent. The medical staff must document their treatment efforts in the prisoner's medical record.[34]

On a state level, requirements or procedures may be found that have policy guidelines similar to those of the Federal Bureau of Prisons. If not, prison officials could probably resort to judicial remedies to compel prisoners to undergo treatment during a hunger strike. State interests in the preservation of life

[33] 28 C.F.R. §549.65 (1980).
[34] Id.

and orderly prison administration, as discussed earlier, may persuade a court to compel care when a life-threatening illness exists — regardless of the prisoner's right of privacy.

§4.6.4   Religious Refusals

When an inmate refuses care on a religious ground, how will his argument be received by the courts? Would they require treatment in all circumstances, or would they engage in the type of analysis now being used frequently in Jehovah's Witness cases? (See chapter 7 on the right to refuse care on religious grounds.)

In part, a court's analysis will assess the purpose underlying the prisoner's refusal.[35] A refusal that is a protest against prison conditions or matters unrelated to the prisoner's medical condition may be overridden on a showing of compelling state interests. Should the prisoner's refusal of consent be founded on a religious belief, however, the court may not necessarily order treatment. For example, when a prisoner is suffering from a terminal illness or has an injury that makes recovery unlikely, the court may decline to compel treatment. Should an inmate with a curable injury or illness be unmarried and without dependents the court may take a similar position. However, quite the opposite stance may be taken when the prisoner is the parent of minor children and the degree of proposed medical intrusion is not significant. Only a case-by-case analysis by the courts, with a careful balancing of state and individual interests, can resolve these conflicting claims.

§4.6.5   Probation and Experimental Drug Therapy

Although judges have significant latitude in setting the terms and conditions for a criminal defendant's probation, there are

---

[35]See Jones v. North Carolina Prisoners' Labor Union, 433 U.S. 119, 126 n.4 (1977).

definite limits. Requiring a convicted sex offender to submit to treatment with an experimental drug to control his sexual drive was beyond the authority of the sentencing court.[36]

The defendant pleaded nolo contendere to a criminal charge of sexual misconduct with his 14-year-old stepdaughter. He was sentenced to a five-year probationary period with the first year to be served in the county jail. In addition, as a condition to his probation, the defendant was to submit to chemical castration during his five-year period, using the drug Depo-Provera.

The defendant raised a number of constitutional arguments in opposition to the use of the drug. The Michigan Court of Appeals never addressed these contentions, instead deciding the challenge on the basis that the drug requirement was an unlawful condition of probation.

As the court pointed out, the Food and Drug Administration granted limited approval to the experimental use of Depo-Provera for reducing male sexual drive. However, it had not been recognized or given full approval as a drug for chemical castration.[37]

The use of the drug as a condition of probation was improper because it violated Michigan law. State statutes limited prescribed drugs for inmates to those deemed necessary for the health of the prisoner.[38] Given the experimental nature of the drug in containing male sexual drive, the limited experience with the drug in male sex offenders, the logistics of administering the drug during the year the defendant was to spend in the county jail, and the requirements of informed consent, the use of the drug as a condition of sentencing violated the state probation statute.[39]

In other situations, experimental use of drugs in the care and rehabilitation of prisoners may be permissible. However, a key ingredient is that prisoners *voluntarily* agree to take part in such

[36] People v. Gauntlett, 134 Mich. App. 737, 352 N.W.2d 310 (1984).
[37] Id.
[38] Mich. Comp. Laws §800.282 (1982).
[39] Mich. Comp. Laws §771.3(4) (1982), referred to in People v. Gauntlett, supra n.36.

research. Both state and federal laws on human research should be closely examined to make certain of compliance with applicable consent requirements. (See chapter 8.) In the absence of legislation that permits it, use of experimental drugs should not be used as a condition to probation or release from prison. To permit such sentencing ignores an important requirement of consent: that treatment given or experiments performed be based on the voluntary authorization of the patient, free of undue influence and coercion.

D. COMPULSORY EXAMINATION AND TREATMENT

§4.7 Venereal Disease

Substantial legislative inroads have been made on the right of prisoners and detainees to refuse certain types of physical examinations and treatment. Included in this category are venereal disease testing and determinations for drug abuse.

In some instances court action has ensued when prisoners or detainees have believed that there was insufficient basis for examination or care. In this section, the authority incident to compulsory examination and treatment of prisoners and detainees is examined in the context of the law of consent to treatment.

§4.7.1 Who Must Submit?

Throughout the United States legislation authorizes the examination and treatment of prisoners for venereal disease.[1] Even the format of the laws is similar. Authorities are em-

§4.7 [1]Fla. Stat. Ann. §384.32 (West 1986); Idaho Code §39-604 (1974); N.D. Cent. Code §23-07-08 (1943); Or. Rev. Stat. §434.170 (1973); S.C. Code §44-29-100 (1962); Utah Code Ann. §26-6-19 (1981); Va. Code §32.1-59 (1979); Wyo. Stat. §35-4-134 (1957).

powered to have prisoners known or suspected to have venereal disease examined. A few states do recognize that a prisoner may refuse this examination or treatment, though such refusal is sometimes not without consequences. For example, in New Jersey a prisoner who refuses to permit an examination or the taking of specimens for venereal disease may be isolated within the institution.[2] The person in charge of the prison may notify the local health officer of the anticipated date of the prisoner's release and the facts of the case.[3] Presumably this action could trigger compulsory examination and treatment under other state laws.[4]

Another body of state law permits the examination of certain suspects or convicts for venereal disease. Included in this category are persons who have been arrested and charged with prostitution,[5] lewd behavior,[6] as well as those who have been convicted of prostitution or of patronizing prostitutes.[7] Individuals who have been arrested for sex crimes[8] or any crime[9] may be compelled to submit to an examination for venereal disease.

§4.7.2 Gaining Cooperation of Prisoners

There must be reasonable grounds to believe that a prisoner or detainee has an infectious venereal disease before an exami-

---

[2]N.J. Stat. Ann. §26:4-49.8 (West 1945). Oklahoma has a similar law. See Okla. Stat. Ann. tit. 63, §1-524 (West 1963).

[3]Id.

[4]See N.J. Stat. Ann. §§26:4-27 (West 1945), et seq. Note that another statutory provision also considers religious objection for *treatment* but not for examination for venereal disease. N.J. Stat. Ann. §26:4-48.1 (West 1945).

[5]N.J. Stat. Ann. §26:4-32 (West 1924); N.Y. Pub. Health Law §2302 (McKinney 1967); Ohio Rev. Code Ann. §2907.27 (Baldwin 1974); W. Va. Code §§16-4-4 to 16-4-5 (1923).

[6]N.J. Stat. Ann. §26:4-32 (West 1924); Pa. Stat. Ann. tit. 35, §521.8 (Purdon 1959).

[7]N.M. Stat. Ann. §30-9-5 (1963).

[8]Pa. Stat. Ann. tit. 35, §521.8 (Purdon 1959); W. Va. Code §§16-4-4 to 16-4-5 (1923).

[9]N.J. Stat. Ann. 26:4-49.7 (West 1953).

nation or treatment may be conducted.[10] Notwithstanding this fact, litigation has arisen involving the permissibility of such examination and treatment, as illustrated by the following cases.

In Kansas, two sisters filed petitions for habeas corpus following their arrest and incarceration for vagrancy and drunkenness.[11] Pursuant to a city ordinance, they were referred and reported to the local health officer by means of a "request for internment." Suspected by police of having venereal disease, the women were similarly judged by the health officer, on the basis of their frequenting places with a poor reputation, associating with people of low moral character, and other considerations. The women were held for 22 days without being formally charged with any offense, without being offered a trial, and without being released on bond.

In granting the petitions for habeas corpus, the court made it clear that the language of the ordinance and the rules of the board of health required examinations of the detainees. To hold them under the conditions used in this instance, as a means of forcing the women to submit to the examinations, was improper. The officials should have followed the lawful provisions at hand that provided for forcible examinations.[12]

In a Colorado case, the United States Court of Appeals for the Tenth Circuit took a different position in a case involving allegedly unlawful behavior on the part of police and city officials.[13] In this case the plaintiff was a self-confessed model and prostitute. Over a two-year span she had been arrested for soliciting and prostitution. On other occasions she received walk-in orders requiring her to report to the Department of Health and Hospitals for examination and possible treatment of venereal disease. In May 1972 she refused the examination. The next month she was arrested in a hotel room for soliciting and prostitution. She was given the choice of being detained in

---

[10] Id.
[11] Welch v. Shephard, 165 Kan. 394, 196 P.2d 235 (1948).
[12] Id.
[13] Reynolds v. McNichols, 488 F.2d 1378 (10th Cir. 1973).

jail for 48 hours, during which period she would be examined and treated for venereal disease if necessary, or simply taking penicillin without benefit of an examination and thereby becoming eligible for immediate release. She chose the latter alternative and was released. She also filed a civil rights action under 42 U.S.C. §§1983 and 1985.

In its ruling the court held that detention for purposes of examination and treatment of venereal disease is a valid constitutional exercise of police powers. As applied to the plaintiff, the ordinance was constitutional. Of particular interest regarding the matter of consent is the court's statement: "There was no particular risk involved in taking the penicillin shot nor was there any injurious effect from the injection of one who did not in fact have gonorrhea."[14] The court also determined that, on the facts presented, there had been no unconstitutional coercion of the plaintiff.[15]

Although in this case there was no evident risk to the plaintiff from taking the penicillin, what about the next man or woman who is faced with this alternative? Would he or she not opt for immediate release from incarceration? Were there sufficient safeguards to ensure that the plaintiff's "consent" was voluntary?

Health professionals should be cautious about obtaining the consent of prisoners and detainees in these circumstances. They must still explain to patients the purpose of the medication, its attendant risks and consequences, as well as any reasonable alternative means of care. Only after obtaining a sufficient medical history from the prisoner-patient can the treating health professional determine whether or not the drug of choice should be administered. Not only must the patient be properly informed but the health professional is required to maintain an acceptable level of care. Her failure to obtain adequate background information, which then results in unacceptable treatment or substandard disclosure of information, may be grounds for negligence litigation.

[14] Id. at 1383.
[15] Id.

There is little the health professional can do to ensure a voluntary consent by prisoners particularly when the treatment to be provided is mandated by statute or local law. The health professional should, however, remain well within the letter of the law. No measures should be undertaken that are not authorized specifically by statute, ordinance, or regulation. Guidance on the law in a particular jurisdiction should come from local counsel, such as a district attorney, attorney general, or city solicitor.

§4.8 Drug Addiction

Some states have enacted legislation allowing examination and treatment for drug problems of criminal defendants or prisoners. For example, in Maryland, when a state prisoner is medically determined to be a drug addict, he can be put on a supervised methadone treatment program.[1] However, the prescribed treatment cannot be initiated without the written consent of the prisoner.[2] In Delaware, those convicted of the use or possession of controlled substances must undergo a medical examination to determine if they are substance dependent.[3] The examination may take place prior to conviction with the defendant's consent. The court may order treatment, including outpatient care or hospitalization.[4]

Absent specific state statutes on the subject, state penal regulations, as well as judicial powers, may be relevant. For example, judges may have the authority to order care for a criminal defendant who is known or believed to be a substance abuser. The superintendent of a state prison or correctional facility may also be empowered to provide a prisoner with an examination and treatment for drug therapy.

Should a detainee or a prisoner refuse examination or care

§4.8 [1]Md. Code Ann. art. 27, §700F (1971).
[2]Id.
[3]Del. Code Ann. tit. 16, §4765 (1975).
[4]Id.

for substance abuse, her refusal may be overruled by court order. Moreover, as seen earlier in the chapter, some prison officials are authorized to consent to treatment for prisoners,[5] either competent or incompetent.

A considerable difficulty arises from prisoners' refusing participation in supervised detoxification programs. Withdrawal from certain drugs without following a carefully designed program could prove harmful to a prisoner and disruptive of prison discipline. Given these concerns, prison officials may have sufficient grounds for court intervention that overrules the refusal of care.

E. OBTAINING EVIDENCE: PHYSICAL AND SURGICAL "SEARCHES"

§4.9 Informed Consent of Suspects

A sizable collection of case law has developed regarding the authority of physicians and others to conduct intrusive searches or examinations of prisoners and detainees. These intrusions are often conducted for criminal investigations as well as medical reasons.

Often state law authorizes physical examination of prisoners. For example, in Tennessee, county sheriffs are empowered to have complete physical examinations performed upon persons placed in their custody.[1] The stated purpose of the examinations is to prevent the spread of communicable disease. Women prisoners are to be examined by a female registered nurse; men are to be examined by a male registered nurse. The law specifically indicates that the examination may include blood tests and Pap smears, as well as any other tests approved and

---

[5]See, e.g., Mo. Ann. Stat. §105.700 (Vernon 1980); N.J. Stat. Ann. §30:4-7.2 (West 1969).

§4.9 [1]Tenn. Code Ann. §41-4-138 (1980).

recommended by the county health officer.[2] Some of these authorized tests seemingly exceed the purpose of the law: Pap smears have little, if anything, to do with the spread of communicable disease.

Difficulties generally arise from police requesting physical examinations of prisoners and detainees. Should physicians and other health personnel simply accede to such requests or should they wait for some type of court order? What should they do if a prisoner refuses the examination? How intrusive should the examination be? Should it involve the use of stomach pumps or emetics?

The answers to some of these questions may be found in state statutes and regulations regarding the physical search of prisoners and detainees. In addition, case law on the subject is highly instructive.[3] Some of these useful cases are discussed below. It should be noted, however, that while this area of law is often fraught with claims of compulsory self-incrimination, unreasonable search and seizure, denial of due process, and the like, the following discussion is limited to the issue of consent.

A health professional who has been requested to assist law enforcement officials by collecting evidence from a suspect should consider a number of factors. First, is he authorized to take part in the evidence-gathering? Second, is there a court order requiring the health professional to conduct the test? Third, what legal liability could he incur for performing a test that is authorized neither by law nor court order? Last, what must the patient be told, if anything, about the test?

A physician must determine whether, in the absence of a court order, the relevant state laws permit her to assist in the gathering of criminal or potentially criminal evidence. At a minimum, a doctor should not rely upon verbal assurances by police that drawing a blood specimen or performing a similar procedure is perfectly legal. The doctor's duty is to the patient — not to the police — unless state law requires the doctor's assistance in the evidence gathering.

[2] Id.
[3] See generally 25 A.L.R.2d 1407 (1952).

Performing tests that are not medically necessary or not required by law or court order can result in legal action against the physician. The same holds true of tests performed on the pretext of medical care. The extent of legal responsibility runs from unauthorized medical care and tests to more serious litigation under civil rights legislation. The severity of the suit depends on a number of factors including the degree of intrusion upon the individual's right of privacy.

Physicians are often placed in a difficult position in regard to what they should tell patients under suspicion. Individuals are entitled to know the purpose of any proposed tests, as well as related details, to determine whether they will give their consent. Doctors should not engage in a charade about the underlying reason for the test or examination. Their responsibility to their patients remains after the police have gone; to do something that misrepresents the true nature of the care patients are receiving could destroy the physician-patient relationship. Litigation, as noted above, could be another unwanted result.

Perhaps the safest course in these situations is to have an established hospital or clinic policy long before problems occur. Meetings between hospital and police officials are possible forums for developing a workable policy. Officers may be disgruntled about having to obtain court orders, but the hospital and its doctors must safeguard their own position. Patients, whether they be victim or assailant, are still *patients* and must be treated accordingly.

§4.10 Implied Consent of Unconscious or Incapacitated Persons

Individuals brought to the hospital unconscious or totally incoherent can neither consent to nor refuse the taking of bodily fluid specimens. Likewise, having received general anesthesia, a person undergoing surgery cannot respond to a police request for samples or other specimens. From a legal perspective, may a physician or other health professional conduct such tests under these conditions?

In some jurisdictions provisions setting forth an implied consent to blood or urine tests for intoxicated drivers also provide for an implied consent from an unconscious person or one otherwise incapable of giving consent.[1] These laws make it clear that the individual's implied consent to the tests is not removed by his incapacity. Some criminal case law supports the principle that withdrawing samples of bodily fluids from unconscious or incapable persons is permissible in situations involving intoxicated drivers.[2]

If a statute or regulation authorizes health personnel to take blood or other samples from an unconscious person, they may do so — but only in accordance with the law. The same rule applies to situations involving persons who are incapable of consent. Health personnel also may be authorized to act upon a properly issued court order.

In the absence of legislative, regulatory, or judicial authority, it would be unwise to comply with requests from police to draw blood samples from an unconscious or incapacitated patient. This policy does not apply however, when a blood sample is needed for emergency medical treatment. In those situations the common law rules (or statutes, in some states) allowing emergency care govern. A blood sample drawn for medical purposes should not be turned over to police, nor should test results. The rules permitting emergency care do not encompass such a release; the police or prosecution must obtain a judicial ruling to obtain the sample or test results. Once again, failure to follow the course of action outlined above could result in litigation.

§4.10 [1] Iowa Code Ann. §321B.5 (West 1963); Miss. Code Ann. §63-11-7 (1972); Neb. Rev. Stat. §39-669.10 (1959); N.H. Rev. Stat. Ann. §262-A:69-d (1965); N.M. Stat. Ann. §66-8-108 (1978); N.D. Cent. Code §39-20-03 (1969).
[2] State v. Bryant, 5 N.C. App. 21, 167 S.E.2d 841 (1969); State v. Wood, 576 P.2d 1181 (Okla. Crim. App. 1978).

§4.11 Implied Consent of Drunk Driving Suspects

According to one expert, drunk driving is the most common criminal offense in the United States.[1] Many state laws refer only to driving while intoxicated from alcohol,[2] although in some, driving under the influence of drugs or other substances is also a punishable offense.[3]

In many states an implied consent on the part of drivers allows tests to determine alcohol or drug blood levels. The tests may include blood, breath, or urine analysis. Provision is also made in many of these laws to obtain blood, breath, or urine samples from a person who is unconscious or incapable of refusing consent. The laws usually state that individuals in such a condition are deemed not to have withdrawn their agreement to these tests.[4]

The procedural requirements in the implied consent laws are quite detailed. The operator must be told why she is being stopped, and, if arrested, informed of her rights. A driver generally must be told that refusal of the tests set out in the statute may result in the suspension or revocation of her license. As in any other criminal matter, the officer involved must have reasonable grounds to make the arrest.[5]

---

§4.11 [1]L.E. Taylor, Drunk Driving Defense (2d ed. 1986). See also R.E. Erwin & M. Minzer, Defense of Drunk Driving Cases: Criminal-Civil (3d ed. 1977).

[2]See, e.g., Ala. Code §32-5-192 (1983); Haw. Rev. Stat. §286-151 (1987); La. Rev. Stat. Ann. §661 (West 1985); Miss. Code Ann. §63-11-5 (1988); Neb. Rev. Stat. §39-669.08 (1987); S.C. Code §56-2950 (1969); Wash. Rev. Code Ann. §46.20.308 (1987).

[3]See Ga. Code Ann. §68A-902.1 (1977); Nev. Rev. Stat. §484.383 (1987); N.H. Rev. Stat. Ann. §262-A:69-a (1971); N.M. Stat. Ann. §66-8-107 (1985); Okla. Stat. Ann. tit. 47, §751 (West 1982); R.I. Gen. Laws §31-27-2.1 (1980); Tenn. Code Ann. §55-10-406 (1987); Wis. Stat. Ann. §343.305 (West 1988).

[4]Ala. Code §32-5-192 (1983); Iowa Code Ann. §321B.5 (West 1963); Nev. Rev. Stat. §484.383 (1986).

[5]See, e.g., Ala. Code §32-5-192 (1983); Minn. Stat. Ann. §169.123 (West 1988); Nev. Rev. Stat. §484.383 (1987).

Notwithstanding the exception for unconscious or incapacitated individuals, it is clear that the tests may not be conducted on anyone who has made a competent refusal. The emphasis in much of the legislation is on what procedures police and state officials must follow upon a refusal. In some states, unless the individual has a valid medical or other reason for refusal, machinery will be set in motion to suspend or revoke the driver's operating privilege.[6] In addition, the refusal may have a damaging impact at trial, where the inference can be drawn that the defendant declined the test because of consciousness of guilt. Whether a court will permit a jury to consider this evidence depends upon the evidentiary laws in a particular state.[7]

When a person agrees to alcohol or drug blood-level testing, the scope of the permissible intrusion is limited. For example, blood samples may not be drawn from persons known to have hemophilia[8] or any illness requiring anticoagulants. Alternate means of testing must be employed in these situations. Testing must be performed in a manner consistent with established standards and the actual taking of blood samples must be conducted by specified individuals.[9] The same limitation does not apply to breath or urine samples, which can be taken by a physician, nurse, or technician of the patient's own choosing.[10]

---

[6]See, e.g., N.H. Rev. Stat. Ann. §262-A:69-a (1971), which exempts from blood samples individuals who have hemophilia, diabetes, or any condition involving the use of anticoagulants under medical supervision. His license will not be revoked if the director of motor vehicles is convinced after notice and hearing that the individual has such a condition.

[7]See L.E. Taylor, Drunk Driving Defense, supra n.1, at §2.4.3.

[8]See, e.g., Mass. Gen. Laws Ann. ch. 90, §24 (West 1980); N.H. Rev. Stat. Ann. §262-A:69-a (1971); Nev. Rev. Stat. §484.383 (1986) (hemophilia or heart condition requiring anticoagulant therapy). See also, N.D. Cent. Code §39-20-14 (1985), in which a person need not submit to a breath screening test at a hospital if the attending doctor is not first informed of the test or if he or she objects on the ground that it is contraindicated to the proper care of the patient.

[9]Ga. Code Ann. §68A-902.1 (1977); Haw. Rev. Stat. §286-152 (1986); Kan. Stat. Ann. §8-1001 (1986); Minn. Stat. Ann. §169.123 (West 1980); Miss. Code Ann. §63-11-9 (1972); Nev. Rev. Stat. §484.383 (1987); S.D. Codified Laws Ann. §32-23-14 (1975).

[10]N.C. Gen. Stat. §20-139.1 (1981); S.D. Codified Laws Ann. §32-23-15 (1975).

Taking urine samples, as a Mississippi statute provides, must be done in a specific fashion:

> [T]he person tested shall be given such privacy in the taking of the urine specimens as will insure the accuracy of the specimen and, at the same time, maintain the dignity of the individual involved.[11]

Health professionals involved in gathering blood, breath, or urine samples must recognize the importance of securing the individual's consent prior to taking the specimens. This acceptance is significant not only for legal defense but also diagnostic purposes. This consent is independent of that obtained by police under the implied consent laws. The individual should be informed of the nature of the sampling and testing as well as of any attendant risks. By securing vital health information, the physician can ascertain, among other things, whether the person has any known bleeding disorders or respiratory anomalies that would make blood or breath sampling contraindicated. Information should also be collected on whether the individual is on a prescribed drug regimen, and, if so, the type of drug(s) and dosage level(s). Being on a prescription drug will not excuse a reckless driving charge,[12] but it may help to explain the presence of certain amounts of medication in the individual's bloodstream.

At no time should health personnel compel a patient to submit to tests required by police for a drunk driving offense. When a person refuses to undergo testing, his decision should be respected. As noted earlier, many state laws deem an unconscious or incapacitated person to have consented to whatever testing is allowed by statute. In these circumstances, health professionals are permitted to take necessary samples. They should be cautious, however, in applying the implied consent exception: the applicable definitions of incapacity vary from state to state. In any subsequent action, the onus is on the health pro-

---

[11] Miss. Code Ann. §63-11-11 (1972).
[12] Taylor, Drunk Driving Defense, supra n.1, §1.7.

fessionals to show that the individual, at the time of testing, was incapable of giving her consent.

The health care specialist who is conducting the tests or specimen collection should not extend the scope of his work beyond that authorized by legislation. If further tests are required or if the specimens collected are to be used for treatment purposes, this situation should be explained to the patient. This requirement would not apply in medical emergencies, when tests and treatment could be performed without the express consent of the patient. Determining whether this exception applies is possible through a review of applicable state law. Some jurisdictions have emergency treatment laws, whereas others have accepted the common law permitting emergency care.

Health professionals are concerned about liability for drawing specimens or conducting tests under implied consent laws.[13] Some state legislation grants immunity from civil liability for performing these tasks — though only when the tests are performed properly.[14] Taking blood samples while ignoring a warning about hemophilia could result in harm that might constitute improper conduct. This action could take the health professional outside the grant of immunity. Withdrawing blood samples without a prior request by law enforcement personnel may also prevent immunity protection.[15]

---

[13] See Brown v. Sisters of Mercy, — N.E.2d — (Ohio Ct. App. 1988), in which a former patient sued the hospital, the attending physician, and others in connection with release of blood alcohol test results to police. The plaintiff, having suffered serious injuries, had been admitted to the facility following an automobile accident, and a number of tests were performed. In affirming the trial court's grant of summary judgment, the appellate court found that there had not been any battery and that the hospital had not violated the plaintiff's right of privacy. Moreover, the court held that he had not been defamed. Despite the favorable disposition for the hospital and caregivers, the case illustrates the concerns of caregivers in this area and the need for compliance with applicable state law.

[14] Neb. Rev. Stat. §39-669.12 (1975) (does not excuse gross negligence); S.D. Codified Laws Ann. §32-23-13 (1983).

[15] S.D. Codified Laws Ann. §32-23-13 (1983).

§4.12 Invasive Searches of Prisoners' Bodies

Physicians are sometimes involved by law enforcement officers in the search and seizure of contraband hidden within a person's body. Requests are also made to secure bullets lodged in a prisoner's or suspect's body — evidence that may prove quite persuasive in a criminal trial.

Both noninvasive and invasive searches require some type of authorization, whether it be from the prisoner or by court order. In this section, these matters are discussed, along with a review of applicable case law on the subject.

§4.12.1 Nonsurgical Invasions

On some occasions law enforcement officials seek the assistance of health personnel in searching a person for illegal substances. Possible methods include rectal examination, fluoroscopy, stomach pumping, or the use of emetics. Health professionals' chief concern in this area revolves around two related questions: should they participate in these examinations? and, if so, under what circumstances?

Some case law can be found on the subject, but so far it has involved criminal procedure and arguments against unreasonable search and seizure.[1] Nevertheless, the facts of some of these cases are both interesting and instructive.

In one case, a man was taken to hospital after police witnessed him swallowing some balloons.[2] At their request, personnel at the hospital administered an emetic that forced the defendant to regurgitate the balloons, which were found to contain heroin. At no time did the defendant consent to the procedure. In granting a defense motion to suppress the evidence, the court held that the method of obtaining it amounted

---

§4.12 [1] Huguez v. United States, 406 F.2d 366 (9th Cir. 1969); People v. Rodriguez, 71 Cal. App. 3d 547, 139 Cal. Rptr. 509 (1977); People v. Jones, 20 Cal. App. 3d 201, 97 Cal. Rptr. 492 (1971).
[2] People v. Rodriguez, supra n.1.

to an unconstitutional search and seizure. The court based its decision on the lack of consent to the examination, as well as the lack of any indication that heroin had entered the defendant's digestive tract. The police could not justify their behavior as a way of preserving evidence, nor could they argue that the procedure was life preserving. Had they waited, the balloons would have safely passed through the defendant's digestive system, and recovery of the evidence could have then taken place.[3]

The use of emetics may be constitutional in some circumstances. For example, in one case some people were stopped at a border crossing and searched.[4] The border agents had been warned to be on the lookout for the defendant, who was believed to be smuggling narcotics from Mexico through the United States and into Canada. It was believed that he would be transporting the heroin in his stomach, having swallowed packets of the drug. At the border the defendant and his companion were stopped and searched. With consent from each man, a physician performed a rectal examination, which proved negative. Eventually, tubes were passed through each man's nose into the stomach and an emetic was introduced, causing each of them to regurgitate the heroin packets. Evidence showed that force was used in the procedure, but only the degree necessary to permit the introduction of the emetic. The court held that on the facts there had not been a violation of either man's constitutional rights. The discomfort involved was found to be no greater than a rectal probe and the manner in which it was conducted was free of brutality. Furthermore, the search was based on sufficient information for the border agents to believe that the suspects had heroin packets in their stomachs.[5]

Health professionals called upon to administer an emetic or to pump a person's stomach must obtain the individual's consent. Should the person refuse, the procedure should not be initiated despite protestations from law enforcement officials. There are, however, exceptional circumstances. For example, a

[3] Id.
[4] Blefare v. United States, 362 F.2d 870 (9th Cir. 1966).
[5] Id.

duly issued court order may authorize the procedure when the individual's condition constitutes a medicolegal emergency. In the latter case, common law permits treatment without an authorization based on an inability to consent due to physical or mental state, combined with a medical judgment that stomach pumping or the use of emetics is a necessary life-saving procedure. In some states emergency treatment statutes also authorize care when a patient-defendant's life or health is at stake (see chapter 1 supra). The fact that health personnel recover narcotics does not mean that they must turn them over to police. Depending on state law, however, they may have to report their findings to specified officials.

On some occasions health professionals feel obliged to assist police, whether or not they have been called upon to do so. Their assistance may involve nothing more than an intrusive body search. One relevant case involved the seizure of a quantity of narcotics.[6] In a border search, without any background information from agents, a physician conducted a rectal examination upon a man. Three customs agents held the man down against a table during the examination. The man was handcuffed at the time and the force with which he was restrained by the agents caused the handcuffs to dig into his wrists. A quantity of narcotics was recovered. In reversing a conviction on the basis of an illegal search and seizure, the court pointed out that the so-called medical examination was nothing more than a "forced process" that could not be justified as a constitutional border search. According to the court, the bodily search could not be condoned without a warrant or without clear indication that the man had concealed narcotics in his rectal cavity. The defendant had been subjected to an unwarranted invasion of his privacy.[7]

Quite a different result occurred in another case.[8] The defendant had taken an unknown number of tablets that were apparently barbiturates. A physician treating the defendant at

[6]Huguez v. United States, supra n.1.
[7]Id.
[8]People v. Jones, supra n.1.

a medical center was of the opinion that the man could have taken a lethal dose of drug. Rather than waiting to find out if problems developed, the doctor performed a gastric lavage upon the defendant. Throughout the treatment the defendant was described as being very cooperative. The court held that on the facts of the situation, the gastric lavage could not be held an unreasonable search and seizure. The procedure had not been done at the request of police, but on the doctor's own initiative out of concern for the life of his patient.[9]

As these cases suggest, physicians and other health professionals need not feel obligated to assist law enforcement officials without a court order or other process authorizing them to do so. However, a physician may justifiably proceed with what she believes is life- or health-saving care for a criminal defendant-patient. If this treatment results in evidence that police could then use in a criminal prosecution, the defendant may try to suppress it. If the circumstances justified the doctor's actions, a court would be hard pressed to rule the evidence illegally obtained. Aiding police in gathering evidence during the course of a forced medical examination cannot be equated legally with finding evidence during a life-saving medical procedure.

§4.12.2 Surgical Invasions

Sometimes police ask health professionals to turn over bullets or other objects found during surgery upon a criminal defendant or suspect. On other occasions they insist upon a surgeon performing an operation to remove what is considered to be important evidence. In the first situation the police should obtain some sort of court order or otherwise have statutory authority requiring the hospital to turn over the evidence found at surgery. This evidence may include pathology reports or tissue committee findings related to the surgical procedure.

Compelling a defendant to undergo surgery for the removal

[9]Id.

of evidence is quite another matter. In some instances, courts have held that compelling surgery in these circumstances constitutes an unreasonable search that violates the defendant's Fourth Amendment guarantee.[10] Other courts do not always follow this reasoning or reach the same conclusion.

For example, a Florida court held that surgery could be performed on a defendant's leg to remove a bullet lodged in it.[11] The court had initially ruled that the surgery was unreasonable because due to the length of time the bullet was in the leg its identifying characteristics had probably disappeared. However, on rehearing the court determined that the bullet could be removed. It was found that the surgery was a reasonable intrusion: the evidence to be obtained was relevant to the prosecution's case and the caliber of the bullet could be positively identified. The court pointed out that the surgery would involve only a negligible risk of harm to the defendant and did not violate his right of privacy.[12]

As one law review commentator has pointed out,[13] many of the nonconsensual surgery cases have invoked Schmerber v. California[14] as authority for ordering or sustaining such intervention. *Schmerber* involved a nonconsensual blood test performed in a hospital setting with careful attention to medical safeguards. The U.S. Supreme Court held that the Constitution did not preclude state intrusion of a minor nature into a person's body under strictly limited conditions. It is difficult to see how precedents authorizing the taking of a blood sample could serve as a justification for even minor invasive surgery, but, as noted, such has been the trend in this area.

If some courts are willing to authorize nonconsensual surgery that is perceived as minor with negligible risk to the

[10]Lee v. Winston, 717 F.2d 888 (4th Cir. 1983). See, e.g., State v. Haynie, 240 Ga. 866, 242 S.E.2d 713 (1978); State v. Overstreet, 551 S.W.2d 621 (Mo. 1977).
[11]Doe (McCaskill) v. State, 409 So.2d 25 (Fla. Dist. Ct. App. 1982).
[12]Id.
[13]Note, Nonconsensual Surgery: The Unkindest Cut of All, 53 Notre Dame L. Rev., 291, 293 (1977).
[14]384 U.S. 757 (1966).

defendant, what about more intrusive or dangerous procedures? At least two courts have rejected requests permitting major surgery. In one case, a man involved in a robbery and murder was shot while leaving the scene of the crime.[15] The bullet became lodged in the man's spinal cord. According to expert testimony, efforts to remove it would aggravate his condition and the operation would involve major surgery. The request for a search warrant was turned down on the ground that it exceeded the permissible bounds set by U.S. Supreme Court precedent.[16]

The other case involved a murder suspect who police believed had a bullet located in his chest wall.[17] A doctor who examined the accused said the operation to remove it would be major surgery. Medical tests suggested that leaving the bullet in place would not jeopardize the man's life. This factor weighed against the seriousness of the operation was enough for the court to turn down the requested operation as a violation of the accused's constitutional rights.[18]

A decision by the United States Supreme Court has confirmed the need for decision-making on a case-by-case basis regarding surgical removal of criminal evidence from the body of a suspect.[19] Moreover, the decision requires application of the *Schmerber* balancing test and full consideration of the suspect's right to bodily privacy.

In Winston v. Lee, a robbery suspect had a bullet lodged under his left collarbone. There was considerable dispute among medical experts as to the degree of risk posed by the intended operation. This involved not only the length of time required to carry out the procedure but also the use of a general anesthetic.[20]

The Supreme Court pointed out that performing the in-

[15] Bowden v. State, 256 Ark. 820, 510 S.W.2d 879 (1974).
[16] Id.
[17] People v. Smith, 80 Misc. 2d 210, 362 N.Y.S.2d 909 (Sup. Ct., Queens County 1974).
[18] Id.
[19] Winston v. Lee, 470 U.S. 753 (1985).
[20] Id. at 764.

tended operation over the objection of the suspect involved a virtual "total divestment of the respondent's ordinary control over surgical probing beneath the skin."[21] This would be a severe intrusion upon the suspect's privacy interests and sense of bodily integrity.

Balanced against the disputed surgical risks and unwanted bodily intrusion was the fact that the prosecution had ample evidence to link the suspect with the robbery. The state therefore was unable to demonstrate a compelling need for the operation and it amounted to an "unreasonable" search under the Fourth Amendment.[22]

The Court provided a good rule of thumb for future cases, which police and prosecutors should consider carefully:

> [T]he Fourth Amendment's command that searches be "reasonable" requires that when the State seeks to intrude upon an area in which our society recognizes a significantly heightened privacy interest, a more substantial justification is required to make the search "reasonable."[23]

Invasive procedures such as surgery with demonstrable risks will henceforth require careful thought, particularly when prisoners object to such operations and additional evidence is at the disposal of the prosecution.

It is important for physicians and surgeons in these cases to obtain adequate medical history and background information from a defendant in determining whether surgery is warranted. A so-called minor procedure may not be so routine if the accused has an underlying medical condition that makes surgery contraindicated. Under no circumstances should a physician perform surgery in these cases unless the patient has consented or a court has given authorization. To do otherwise could lead to liability. Of course, this rule does not pertain to emergency surgical procedures to which the patient is unable to

[21] Id. at 765.
[22] Id. at 766.
[23] Id.

consent and that are believed to be necessary to save the life or health of the patient. The same principle holds true with respect to procedures authorized under emergency treatment laws. (See §2.2, supra.)

For lawyers in these matters, whether they represent the accused or the prosecution, it is essential to obtain sound medical expert testimony to present to the court. In addition, they should familiarize themselves with the case law on the topic and develop strong constitutional and practical arguments to put before the court. Judges in the future may not be inclined to divide surgical removal of evidence cases into sharply defined categories of minor and major operations. Even if they do, it is important to bring out any unique health factors that — depending on the side one represents — turn a minor procedure into a major one and vice-versa.

FIVE

Minors

A. Traditional View of Minors' Consent to Treatment
    §5.0   Introduction
    §5.1   Minors' Incapacity to Consent
    §5.2   Modifications of the Common Law
        §5.2.1   Emergency Treatment
        §5.2.2   Mature Minors
        §5.2.3   Emancipated Minors
B. Legislative Standards for Minors' Consent
    §5.3   General Statutory Laws
        §5.3.1   Emancipated Minor Legislation
        §5.3.2   Age of Consent Legislation
        §5.3.3   Immunity and Disaffirmance Legislation
        §5.3.4   Parental Notification Requirements
        §5.3.5   Third-Party Consent Laws
        §5.3.6   Consent from a Minor Parent
        §5.3.7   Judicial Interpretation of Consent Legislation
C. Minors and Reproductive Matters
    §5.4   Sexually Transmitted Diseases
        §5.4.1   General Legislation
        §5.4.2   Confidentiality of Treatment
    §5.5   Minors and Contraceptives
        §5.5.1   Minors' Right to Contraceptives
        §5.5.2   Parental Consent and Notification
        §5.5.3   Contraceptive Legislation for Minors
    §5.6   Minors and Abortion
        §5.6.1   Parental Consent to Abortion
        §5.6.2   Parental Notification
        §5.6.3   Married Minors: Spousal Consent and Notification
        §5.6.4   Practical Considerations Regarding Minors and Abortion
D. Drug and Alcohol Abuse Treatment for Minors
    §5.7   Statutory Requirements

E. Mentally Ill and Retarded Minors
    §5.8   Authorization for Treatment
            §5.8.1   Parental Consent
            §5.8.2   Authorization by the Minor
            §5.8.3   Judicial Limitations on Parental Consent
            §5.8.4   Medication for Minors
            §5.8.5   Consent to Release of Committed Minors
    §5.9   Sterilization of Mentally Incompetent Minors
            §5.9.1   Statutory Law
            §5.9.2   Judicial Limitations
F. Immunization and Screening of Children
    §5.10   Immunization
            §5.10.1   Legislative Standards
            §5.10.2   Case Decisions
    §5.11   Screening of Children for Health Risks
            §5.11.1   Newborns
            §5.11.2   School-Age Children
            §5.11.3   Obtaining Consent
G. Treatment of Minors in Crisis Situations
    §5.12   Emergency Treatment
            §5.12.1   Sexually Assaulted Minors
    §5.13   Child Abuse
    §5.14   Delinquent and Deprived Children
H. Drug and Medical Care in Schools
    §5.15   Legislation Authorizing Treatment
I. Refusal of Consent to Treatment
    §5.16   Parental Refusal
            §5.16.1   Statutory Limits
            §5.16.2   Judicial Limits
            §5.16.3   Treatment Decisions for Disabled Children
    §5.17   Refusal of Care for Terminally Ill Children
            §5.17.1   Court Orders Not to Resuscitate for Minors
    §5.18   Children's Refusal of Treatment

A. TRADITIONAL VIEW OF MINORS' CONSENT TO TREATMENT

§5.0 Introduction

With few exceptions, no area of the law has received more attention from legislators and judges than minors and consent

256

to treatment. Issues such as abortion and contraception have often been the focus of these legislative and judicial initiatives. However, other aspects of medical treatment of minors have also received attention, including child abuse care, mental health, and physical screening for hearing and visual impairments.

In this chapter the subject of minors and consent to treatment begins with an examination of basic common law principles. Legislation either codifying or modifying the authority of parents to refuse treatment on behalf of their children is examined. Specific topics of concern are also addressed, including abortion, treatment of sexually transmitted diseases, drug abuse, and childhood immunizations.

§5.1 Minors' Incapacity to Consent

The traditional common law view was that a minor could not consent to medical or surgical treatment.[1] A physician was obliged to obtain the consent of the child's parent or of someone standing in loco parentis to the minor.[2] The only acceptable exception was an emergency, when it was either impractical to obtain parental consent,[3] or any delay would unduly endanger the patient's life.[4] For purposes of the traditional rule, a minor was usually defined as below the age of majority.

These restrictions on minors under traditional common law principles reflect the opinion that they were deemed incapable of exercising sufficient judgment.[5] Similarly, the law has traditionally viewed minors as being incapable of executing contracts, except those for necessaries.[6] Since the physician-patient relationship is often viewed as being contractual in nature, the

---

§5.1   [1] In re Hudson, 13 Wash. 2d 673, 126 P.2d 765 (1942).
[2] Id.
[3] Tabor v. Scobee, 254 S.W.2d 474 (Ky. 1952).
[4] Jackovach v. Yocum, 212 Iowa 914, 237 N.W. 444 (1931).
[5] Wilkins, Children's Rights: Removing the Parental Consent Barrier to Medical Treatment of Minors, 1975 Ariz. St. L.J. 31, 40.
[6] Id.

inability of a minor to execute binding contracts strengthened the traditional argument that a minor was incapable of giving a valid consent. The logical conclusion was that authority to consent to medical treatment on his behalf must be vested in someone else. That power has devolved to the natural guardians of the minor — his parents.

As the law has developed, parents can sue physicians for any unauthorized nonemergency medical treatment of their child. Traditionally, these actions were based in battery, for an intentional touching (medical care) without parental consent. Battery actions have been successfully brought against physicians for providing treatment to a child with permission from an adult other than the child's parents. The two following cases illustrate the legal reasoning in such circumstances.

In Moss v. Rishworth,[7] an 11-year-old girl was taken by one of her adult sisters for medical treatment. The physician who examined the child determined that she had badly infected tonsils that should be surgically removed. On a subsequent visit, the child was accompanied by her two adult sisters, who consented to the operation. At no time was an effort made to obtain the consent of the child's father. The child did not survive the operation.

In a lawsuit brought by the father, the doctor was held liable for unauthorized surgery. The child's interest in her bodily integrity had been violated by the doctor, which formed the basis for liability. A key feature in the case was that at no time did the sisters represent themselves to the doctor as being capable of giving a valid consent to the operation. As temporary guardians of their younger sister, they had no authority to permit the surgery.[8]

A similar conclusion was reached in Zoslei v. Gaines.[9] In that case a 9-year-old boy was taken to a city physician by a visiting nurse. She suspected that the youngster had tonsillitis. He was later transferred to a private doctor, who removed the boy's

[7]222 S.W. 225 (Tex. Commn. App. 1920).
[8]Id.
[9]271 Mich. 1, 260 N.W. 99 (1935).

tonsils at the request of the city physician. At no time were the child's parents contacted. They filed suit against the private doctor and they won a battery judgment. The court, following the traditional common law rule, held that a physician cannot operate on a child without the permission of either his parents or guardian.[10]

§5.2 Modifications of the Common Law

The traditional common law approach to minors and consent to treatment has undergone a number of modifications. Medical emergencies have provided an inroad, permitting treatment without parental consent in certain situations. The "mature minor" and "emancipated minor" rules, in which certain children are considered capable of giving consent, have also gained recognition. Many of these changes have come through case law, but to a certain degree legislative action is accountable for the more enlightened attitude toward the minor and her ability to authorize treatment.

§5.2.1 Emergency Treatment

The strict common law approach does recognize some exceptions. The most clear-cut deals with medical emergencies, when the child requires immediate care in order to save his life or to prevent serious jeopardy to health. Case law on the subject strongly supports this exception:[1] courts hearing these cases often broadly define medical emergencies. Thus parental consent was not necessary for the setting of a child's broken forearm while using chloroform as the anesthetic,[2] using ether

---

[10] Id.

§5.2 [1] See, e.g., Tabor v. Scobee, 254 S.W.2d 474 (Ky. 1952); Jackovach v. Yocum, 212 Iowa 914, 237 N.W. 444 (1931); Luka v. Lowrie, 171 Mich. 122, 136 N.W. 1106 (1912).

[2] Wells v. McGehee, 39 So. 2d 196 (La. 1949).

to set a young man's broken ankle,[3] or surgical removal of a young woman's swollen and pus-laden fallopian tubes in the course of an appendectomy.[4] In each case, the court viewed the minor's condition as requiring *immediate treatment* or as presenting an *immediate danger* to the child's health. In the *Sullivan* case,[5] the court went one step further and emphasized the continued pain and suffering the young man would have experienced had the physician waited for permission to proceed with surgical repair of the broken ankle.

In medical emergency cases, the courts have discussed an implied consent to treatment. Permission by the parents or guardian for medical or surgical care is implied by the law, assuming that had the parents known of the situation, they would have authorized treatment.[6] The more urgent the circumstances, the more likely that the courts will find a basis for implied consent. It was and is today in many jurisdictions a matter of case-by-case decision-making. The exception was not and is not, however, a license for a health provider to forge ahead with all treatment of a minor without parental consent. The concepts of medical emergencies and implied consent apply only to certain types of medical situations. In any litigation challenging the application of the medical emergency implied consent rule, the burden is on the health provider to demonstrate that an emergency existed.[7]

§5.2.2   Mature Minors

Another group covered by an exception to the rule requiring parental consent are mature minors. Judicially recognized as possessing sufficient understanding and appreciation of the nature and consequences of treatment despite their chronological age, these minors can give an informed consent of their own.

---

[3]Sullivan v. Montgomery, 155 Misc. 448, 279 N.Y.S. 575 (1935).
[4]Tabor v. Scobee, supra n.1.
[5]Sullivan v. Montgomery, supra n.3.
[6]See Jackovach v. Yocum, supra n.1, and Luka v. Lowrie, supra n.1.
[7]Roger v. Sells, 178 Okla. 103, 61 P.2d 1018 (1936).

Determining which minors come within the mature category is necessarily a case-by-case judgment. The following cases illustrate this point.

In one of the earliest statements of the mature minor rule, a 17-year-old male underwent surgery for removal of a tumor from his ear.[8] The young man had previously been treated for the condition and he had always been accompanied by his aunts and sisters. His father was aware of his condition, but he did not know about the operation. Prior to surgery, chloroform was administered; just as the surgeon was about to start the operation, the young man's heart stopped beating. Attempts to revive him were unsuccessful. In a lawsuit by the father for wrongful death and unauthorized surgery, the Michigan Supreme Court sustained a directed verdict in favor of the defendants. The court assessed all the facts in the case, including the young man's independence of action regarding his illness and his proximity to adulthood. It was pointed out as well that adult members of the young man's family were kept informed over the course of his treatment. According to one commentator, however, a main feature in the case was the decedent's apparent ability to decide for himself whether treatment was necessary.[9]

A minor was also held capable of consenting to a vaccination that was a requirement of his employment.[10] The 17-year-old was found to be capable of understanding the nature and consequences of a simple procedure such as a vaccination and thus, parental consent was not required.

The consent of a minor to a "pinch-graft," a relatively simple procedure utilizing skin from the wrist to repair a severed fingertip, was also held sufficient to overcome a claim of unauthorized surgical treatment.[11] The young woman in question was 17 years old. She was injured when her finger was caught in

[8]Bakker v. Welsh, 144 Mich. 632, 108 N.W. 94 (1906).
[9]See Wilkins, Children's Rights: Removing the Parental Consent Barrier to Medical Treatment of Minors, 1975 Ariz. St. L.J. 31.
[10]Gulf & Ship Island R.R. Co. v. Sullivan, 155 Miss. 1, 119 So. 501 (1928).
[11]Younts v. St. Francis Hosp. & School of Nursing, 469 P.2d 330 (Kan. 1970).

the hinge of a door while the young woman was visiting her mother in the hospital. At that time she was taken to the emergency room where the grafting was performed. The mother was still unconscious as a result of her operation. The minor's father was 200 miles away and his exact location was unknown. The family doctor was consulted and he gave his permission for the procedure. As the court pointed out, the young woman possessed the ability to appreciate the nature of the operation, its attendant risks, and the likelihood of achieving the desired outcome. The consent of one of her parents therefore was not necessary.

At least one court has held that a 19-year-old youth could object to and overrule his mother's approval of the type of anesthetic to be used in his tonsillectomy. The mother had stipulated that ether, not cocaine, was to be employed as the anesthetic. However, when the youth was brought to the operating room, he requested a local anesthetic and cocaine was used. He died. In a lawsuit against the physician, the court held he was not liable. Since the young man could enter into a contract for necessaries, the court reasoned that he could also modify a contract executed on his behalf.[12]

In a well-documented and detailed discussion, the Supreme Court of Tennessee has also adopted the mature minor principle. The court did so in a case in which a young woman, 17 years, 7 months of age, went on her own to seek help from an osteopathic physician.[13]

The young woman had a long-standing history of back pain for which she had been given conservative treatment by medical doctors. It was suspected that she had a herniated disc. Both the young woman and her parents had declined the suggestion that she undergo a myelogram.

Her father had seen the defendant on numerous occasions for treatment of a back ailment. Having seen her family physician for a sore throat, the young woman spontaneously decided to see the defendant. She gave him the details of her previous

---

[12]Bishop v. Shurley, 237 Mich. 76, 211 N.W. 75 (1926).
[13]Cardwell v. Bechtol, 724 S.W.2d 739 (Tenn. 1987).

treatment and indicated that her father had been the defendant's patient. The defendant examined the young woman and determined that her problem was not a herniated disc but subluxation of the spine and a bilateral sacroiliac slip.[14] He then performed a number of manipulations and asked her to return for several further sessions of treatment. She paid the defendant $25.00 with one of her father's blank, signed checks that the young woman had been authorized to use when she required money.

Over the next several hours the young woman found it increasingly difficult to walk, she developed urinary retention, and was hospitalized. Diagnostic testing revealed a herniated disc and a laminectomy was performed. Postoperatively, the young woman experienced difficulty in walking as well as bowel and bladder retention. Although she experienced some improvement in her condition, at the time of trial she had not regained bowel control or complete sensation in her buttocks and one of her legs.[15]

An appeal followed from the lower court's directed verdict to one cause of action and the jury's finding in favor of the defendant on the theories of battery and informed consent. The state court of appeals reversed on the theory of battery, indicating that Tennessee had not adopted the principle of the mature minor.[16]

As the Supreme Court of Tennessee pointed out, the common law has for some time recognized that minors achieve varying degrees of maturity and capacity. This has been well delineated in the so-called Rule of Sevens, that is:

1. under seven years of age there is no capacity;
2. between 7 and 14 years of age there is a rebuttable presumption of *no* capacity; and
3. between 14 and 21 years of age there is a rebuttable presumption *of* capacity.[17]

---

[14] Id. at 741-742.
[15] Id. at 742.
[16] Id.
[17] Id. at 747.

The Rule of Sevens has had its impact in a variety of areas, including tort law, criminal law, and the ability of minors to give testimony.[18] According to the court, the Rule of Sevens has had an influence on Tennessee legislation.[19]

In holding that Tennessee common law recognizes the "mature minor" rule, the court cautioned that it was not abandoning the "general rule" requiring parental consent for medical treatment of minors. As the court stated:

> it would rarely, if ever, be reasonable, absent an applicable statutory exception, for a physician to treat a minor under seven years, and that between the ages of seven and fourteen, the rebuttable presumption is that a minor would not have the capacity to consent; moreover, while between the ages of fourteen and eighteen, a presumption of capacity does arise, that presumption may be rebutted by evidence of incapacity, thereby exposing a physician or care provider to an action for battery.[20]

For the Tennessee Supreme Court, the proper application of the mature minor rule was a question of fact to be decided by the jury. If the trier of fact determined that in a particular case the minor could appreciate the nature, risks, and consequences of medical care and had the capacity to consent, an authorization for treatment would be deemed valid. Factors that should influence such a determination include the age, ability, experience, education, and exhibited degree of maturity and demeanor of the minor.[21]

From a practical perspective, the Tennessee ruling provides little comfort to caregivers. They can always find themselves in a "Monday-morning quarterback" situation, in which the critical eye of hindsight can judge them wrong on the maturity of the minor. In times of "defensive" medicine, few caregivers are going to put themselves in this position.

The Rule of Sevens does not fit as neatly into health care as

[18] Id.
[19] Id. at 748.
[20] Id. at 749.
[21] Id.

the court seems to suggest. Children today are more "street-wise" and knowledgeable than children were even a few decades ago. Some children of very tender years exposed to continuous types of care are able to give or refuse consent. They may be far more skilled at discussing the pros and cons, the risks and benefits of bone marrow transplants or chemotherapy than a first-year medical student. However, there are also teenagers and young adults who lack the maturity to understand the risks of pregnancy from casual sex and the importance of contraception.

Perhaps it is this uncertainty that has driven many states to enact statutory ages of consent. An arbitrary rule seems to be much easier to apply than one that requires the caregiver to assess the minor and to make a professional judgment regarding maturity. The inflexibility of an arbitrary age of consent, however, can handcuff the caregiver, too. A happy and more practical medium should be found. Perhaps the answer will be found in statutory laws of consent that incorporate an element of the mature minor rule. Such laws should go one step further, immunizing caregivers from liability for battery when they have made a good-faith assessment of maturity. Liability would only be considered for assessments of maturity that appear to be grossly negligent. This would allow flexibility in the treatment of minors, giving caregivers and young people alike an opportunity to work together effectively. Parental involvement would not be precluded, but held in reserve for appropriate cases. It is an idea worthy of consideration in view of the timidity with which many caregivers approach the mature minor rule.

As the foregoing cases suggest, the common law has carved out a definite exception for consent by minors to treatment. Although the scope of the exception is not well defined, it appears that a minor must demonstrate maturity of understanding and intelligence along with chronological age. The degrees of risk and complexity associated with a particular procedure also seem to be factors considered by the courts. The more routine the procedure and the more minimal the risk of harm, the more likely that a minor will fall within the exception. Without statutory law this determination must be made on a case-by-case basis (discussed infra).

§5.2.3 Emancipated Minors

Another common law principle that has created an exception in the area of minors and consent to health care is that of emancipation. With emancipation a minor obtains the legal capacity of an adult. Over the years, American courts have recognized degrees of emancipation, thus leaving minors with some disabilities of childhood.[22] Professor Clark suggests in his treatise on domestic relations that to determine whether a child is emancipated from or relieved of a disability of childhood requires an examination of relevant circumstances.[23] Thus, when a minor is living on her own,[24] self-supporting,[25] in the armed forces,[26] or any combination of factors such as these, courts may recognize her as emancipated.

Whether a minor falls within the emancipation exception is a question of fact to be determined in each case. In the area of consent to health care, emancipation is important: it may affect the parents' obligation to pay for services provided to their child. A decision could be made that a minor is sufficiently emancipated for purposes of consent, although his parents remain financially obligated to pay the medical expenses. Such a determination may be based on common law principles[27] or on a court order.[28]

The following case illustrates the emancipation exception in consent to a surgical procedure.[29] An 18-year-old man, married and the father of one child, wanted a vasectomy. He had myasthenia gravis, a progressive, incurable disease of the mus-

[22] 24 H.H. Clark, Jr., Law of Domestic Relations §8.3 (1968).
[23] Id.
[24] Id.
[25] Blue v. Blue, 152 Nev. 82, 40 N.W.2d 268 (1949).
[26] Swenson v. Swenson, 241 Mo. App. 21, 227 S.W.2d 103 (1950).
[27] See, e.g., Porter v. Powell, 79 Iowa 151, 44 N.W. 295 (1890).
[28] See 32 A.L.R.3d 1055 (1970) and annotations collected therein.
[29] Smith v. Seibly, 72 Wash. 2d 16, 431 P.2d 719 (1967).

cle tissue. He and his wife decided that he should be sterilized since his progressive disease could affect his ability to support himself and his family. The patient's family physician declined to perform the operation due to the man's young age. Another physician agreed to perform the vasectomy, and he did so after explaining the nature and consequences of the surgery. Prior to the surgery, both the patient and his wife signed a consent form. Subsequently, when the youth reached the age of majority, an action was brought alleging that the doctor wrongfully performed a vasectomy on a minor and that it was done without valid consent. The Washington Supreme Court affirmed a jury verdict in favor of the defendant physician. In doing so, the court pointed out that the young man was sufficiently educated, intelligent, and knowledgeable to give his consent. The fact that he was married, the head of his own household, and earning his own living was sufficient proof that he was emancipated. The court said that his consent to the vasectomy was valid and informed: he had been provided with a full disclosure of the ramifications, implications, and probable consequences of the surgery.[30]

The emancipated minor exception to the law of consent has received considerable legislative attention in the United States.[31] This is discussed in some detail in the section dealing with statutory laws of consent for minors, infra.

B. LEGISLATIVE STANDARDS FOR MINORS' CONSENT

§5.3 General Statutory Laws

Over the years a majority of the states have enacted legislation changing the common law approach to minors and consent to

---

[30] Id.

[31] See Alaska Stat. §09.65.100 (1975); Ariz. Rev. Stat. Ann. §44-132 (1962); Cal. Civ. Code §62 (West 1979); Mont. Code Ann. §41-1-402 (1977); N.M. Stat. Ann. §24-10-1 (1972); Wyo. Stat. §14-1-101 (1981).

health care. Much of this legislation was enacted in the 1970s, although some took effect at an earlier date. Definite patterns are discernible in this legislative maze, suggesting that a number of model bills have been enacted into law. The statutes described in this part of the chapter are of a general nature. In subsequent sections, laws are discussed relating to consent of minors and mental health treatment, care for drug and alcohol abuse, childhood immunizations, screening for health impairments, venereal disease treatment, rape and sexual assault treatment, contraceptives, and abortion.

§5.3.1 Emancipated Minor Legislation

A number of state statutes recognize that a minor who is emancipated may consent to her own health care. The Alaska statute is typical of this sort of legislative recognition. It states that a minor who is living apart from parents or legal guardian and who is managing his own financial affairs — regardless of the source or extent of income — may give consent for medical and dental services.[1] A number of other states have taken a similar approach, including Alabama,[2] Colorado,[3] Massachusetts,[4] Montana,[5] and Nevada.[6] These states characterize a minor as being emancipated for purposes of consent when one or more of the criteria set out in the statute is met.

Many states also recognize emancipated minors on the basis of their either being married or having borne a child. In this group are such states as Illinois,[7] Louisiana,[8] Maryland,[9] Mis-

---

§5.3 [1] Alaska Stat. §09.65.100 (1975).
[2] Ala. Code §22-8-4 (1971).
[3] Colo. Rev. Stat. §13-22-103 (1979).
[4] Mass. Gen. Laws Ann. ch. 112, §12F (West 1975).
[5] Mont. Code Ann. §41-1-402 (1977). The statute refers specifically to emancipation.
[6] Nev. Rev. Stat. §129.030 (1981).
[7] Ill. Ann. Stat. ch. 111, §4501 (Smith-Hurd 1972).
[8] La. Rev. Stat. Ann. §40:1299.53 (West 1975).
[9] Md. Pub. Health Code Ann. art. 43, §135 (1978).

souri,[10] New York,[11] Oklahoma,[12] Pennsylvania,[13] and Utah.[14] Others have added additional alternate criteria, including the minor's being on active service in the armed forces.[15]

A few states have taken the approach of specifically stating that an emancipated minor may consent to treatment. Included in this group of jurisdictions are Arizona,[16] Kentucky,[17] New Mexico,[18] West Virginia,[19] and Wyoming.[20]

Another type of statutory device is also used to list alternative criteria for determining whether a minor can consent to her own health care. These statutes set out an emancipated minor rule as well as a mature minor provision. Arkansas[21] and Mississippi[22] have such legislation. When minors meet either standard they can consent to their own health care.

§5.3.2 Age of Consent Legislation

Some states, notably Kansas,[23] Rhode Island,[24] and South Carolina,[25] have adopted a different approach. Rather than relying upon the application of mature minor or emancipation assessment criteria, these statutes set a statutory age of consent. Unlike the emancipation legislation, these statutes limit the authority or situations in which a minor can consent to treatment. The Rhode Island law restricts consent to "routine emergency

---

[10] Mo. Ann. Stat. §431.061 (Vernon 1977).
[11] N.Y. Pub. Health Law §2504 (McKinney 1972).
[12] Okla. Stat. Ann. tit. 63, §2602 (West 1976).
[13] Pa. Cons. Stat. Ann. tit. 35, §10102 (Purdon 1972).
[14] Utah Code Ann. §78-14-5 (1976).
[15] See, e.g., Wyo. Stat. §14-1-101 (1981).
[16] Ariz. Rev. Stat. Ann. §44-132 (1962).
[17] Ky. Rev. Stat. §214.185 (2) (1974).
[18] N.M. Stat. Ann. §24-10-1 (1972).
[19] W. Va. Code §49-7-27 (1977).
[20] Wyo. Stat. §14-1-101 (1981).
[21] Ark. Stat. Ann. §20-9-602 (1981).
[22] Miss. Code Ann. §41-41-3 (1984).
[23] Kan. Stat. Ann. §38-123b (1969).
[24] R.I. Gen. Laws §23-4.6-1 (1979).
[25] S.C. Code §20-7-280 (1981).

medical or surgical care"[26] to individuals 16 years of age or over or married. South Carolina's provision requires no parental consent for health services provided to minors 16 years of age or older, unless a surgical procedure is involved. Emergency surgery can be performed without parental consent if it is "essential to the health or life" of the child.[27] Kansas has a far less restrictive statute, authorizing a minor 16 years of age or older to consent to medical, hospital, or surgical care "where no parent or guardian is immediately available."[28]

Other states have developed an emancipated minor law that also incorporates age as a criterion; for example, the Colorado statute states in part:

> [A] minor fifteen years of age or older who is living separate and apart from his parent, parents, or legal guardian, with or without the consent of his parent, parents or legal guardian, and is managing his own financial affairs, regardless of the source of his income . . . may give consent. . . .[29]

§5.3.3 Immunity and Disaffirmance Legislation

Within their minor treatment laws many states have included provisions that insulate the health care provider from liability for unauthorized care of a minor. These statutes typically protect those who acted in good faith in the reasonable belief that a minor met statutory criteria enabling consent.[30] However, it is sometimes specifically stated in these laws that the good-faith immunity does not extend to acts of negligence.[31]

Another common piece of legislative drafting in the statutes

[26] R.I. Gen. Laws §23-4.6-1 (1979).
[27] S.C. Code §20-7-280 (1981).
[28] Kan. Stat. Ann. §38-123b (1969).
[29] Colo. Rev. Stat. §13-22-103 (1979).
[30] Statutes with the good faith provision include Alaska Stat. §09.65.100 (1975); Ala. Code §22-8-7 (1971); Ky. Rev. Stat. 214.185 (1974); Mass. Gen. Laws Ann. ch. 112, §12F (West 1975); Mo. Ann. Stat. §431.061 (Vernon 1977); N.Y. Pub. Health Law §2504 (McKinney 1972).
[31] See, e.g., Alaska Stat. §09.65.100 (1975); Mont. Code Ann. §41-1-407 (1974); Okla. Stat. Ann. tit. 63, §2602 (West 1976).

relating to care of minors is a statement on disaffirmance. The laws usually state that the consent of a minor is not subject to disaffirmance due to his minority.[32] Other provisions indicate that consent by a minor cannot be disaffirmed if the minor is divorced or her marriage annulled.[33] Implications of this consent legislation extend to who will pay for the health care provided to a minor.

§5.3.4 Parental Notification Requirements

Although a minor may be authorized by statute to consent to his own medical care, whether the parents should be notified remains an issue. Arguably, when minors are to be treated as if they were adults for purposes of consent, there should be no disclosure to parents or guardians. Confidentiality of care is a basic component of the physician-patient relationship; in the absence of statutory disclosure requirements, it should not be abridged.

The policy argument favoring parental notification is based on a concern that minors receive appropriate follow-up care. This continuity of care could be provided by their parents, but a prerequisite is informing them of the nature of the treatment provided. However, in some treatment situations — such as care for sexually transmitted diseases or the side effects of birth control pills — familial ties may be strained or broken following disclosure.

A number of states have reached a compromise on the issue of parental notification. Disclosure to a minor's parents may be made in certain circumstances and not in others. Missouri has such a law, which provides in part:

A physician or surgeon may, with or without the consent of the minor patient, advise the parent, parents, or conservator of

[32]See Ariz. Rev. Stat. Ann. §44-132 (1962); Cal. Civ. Code §25.6 (West 1970); Colo. Rev. Stat. §13-22-103 (1979); Kan. Stat. Ann. §38-123b (1969); Mont. Code Ann. §41-1-407 (1974).
[33]See Ariz. Rev. Stat. Ann. §44-132 (1962); Cal. Civ. Code §25.6 (West 1970); Ky. Rev. Stat. §214.185 (1974); N.M. Stat. Ann. §24-10-1 (1972).

the examination, treatment, hospitalization, medical and surgical care given or needed if the physician or surgeon has reason to know the whereabouts of the parent, parents, or conservator. Such notification or disclosure shall not constitute libel or slander, a violation of the right of privacy or a violation of the rule of privileged communication. In the event that the *minor is found not to be pregnant or not afflicted with a venereal disease or not suffering from drug or substance abuse, then no information* with respect to any appointment, examination, test or other medical procedure *shall be given to the parent, parents, conservator or any other person.*[34] (Emphasis added.)

Other jurisdictions have enacted parental disclosure laws, including Louisiana,[35] Minnesota,[36] Montana,[37] and Oklahoma.[38]

North Carolina's statute forbids a physician from making a disclosure to a minor's parent, legal guardian, or a person standing in loco parentis without the patient's consent — except in two instances. Notification is permitted if, in the physician's opinion, it is essential to the minor's life or health. Authorization also follows when the parent, guardian, or person standing in loco parentis contacts the physician.[39]

In the absence of laws authorizing parental disclosure or notification, it is *not* advisable to provide them with information without permission from the minor patient. Under applicable law, such disclosures could amount to actionable breaches of privacy or confidentiality. A state may even have laws prohibiting disclosures to parents.[40] Physicians are put in a difficult situation when parents telephone to find out if their child has received medical care and for what purpose. They may be alerted by a notice from their health insurer. The better policy in these circumstances is to let minors decide whether they want to discuss their medical care with their parents. The best legal protection available to health care providers — absent statutory

---

[34] Mo. Ann. Stat. §431.062 (Vernon 1987).
[35] La. Rev. Stat. Ann. §1095 (West 1972).
[36] Minn. Stat. Ann. §144.346 (West 1971).
[37] Mont. Code Ann. §41-1-403 (1974).
[38] Okla. Stat. Ann. tit. 63, §2602 (West 1976).
[39] N.C. Gen. Stat. §90-21.4 (1985).
[40] See, e.g., Mass. Gen. Laws Ann. ch. 112, §12F (West 1975).

directives, court orders, or written authorization by the minor — is to refuse disclosure to a child's parents.

§5.3.5 Third-Party Consent Laws

In addition to laws enabling minors to consent to their own health care, many states have statutes authorizing others to consent to treatment on behalf of a child. Some of these provisions are incorporated in statutes listing various family members who can give consent when a child is not emancipated or does not meet mature minor criteria. For example, a Georgia law recognizes that the following persons can give consent to medical or surgical care for a minor:

(2) Any parent, whether an adult or a minor, for his minor child;
(3) Any married person, whether an adult or a minor, for himself, and for his spouse;
(4) Any person temporarily standing in loco parentis whether formally serving or not, for the minor under his care and any guardian for his ward; . . .
(6) In the absence of a parent, any adult, for his minor brother or sister;
(7) In the absence of a parent, any grandparent for his minor grandchild.[41]

Several other states have similar provisions.[42] In addition, some jurisdictions have codified the common law, authorizing either parent or a parent or legal guardian to consent to medical care for a minor child. California,[43] Illinois,[44] and Oklahoma[45] have such legislation.

[41]Ga. Code §88-2904 (1975).
[42]See, e.g., Ark. Stat. Ann. §82-363 (1981); La. Rev. Stat. Ann. §1299.53 (West 1975); Miss. Code Ann. §41-41-3 (1984); Utah Code Ann. §78-14-5 (1976).
[43]Cal. Civ. Code §25.8 (West 1981).
[44]Ill. Ann. Stat. ch. 111, §4502 (Smith-Hurd 1972).
[45]Okla. Stat. Ann. tit. 10, §170.1 (West 1984).

§5.3.6 Consent from a Minor Parent

Some health care providers and institutions have been reluctant to accept consent to treatment for a child from a minor parent. The argument raised is that a minor parent is under a legal disability that bars her from giving an effective consent. Although the law of consent imposes no prohibition on consent by a minor parent, several state legislatures have enacted statutes on the subject. All of these laws authorize a parent who is a minor to give legally valid consent to treatment on behalf of his child.[46] Even in the absence of such legislation, it would seem legally incorrect to require consent from a minor parent's father or mother or from the youthful parent's adult sister or brother. Treatment provided without the authority of the minor parent could lead to a suit for battery. The better approach in the absence of legislation is to obtain consent to treatment from the minor parent. Such a policy is in keeping with the long-standing common law rule that a parent must consent to care for her unemancipated child. The only exception to consent from a minor parent is when he is incapable of giving a knowing and informed authorization to treatment. Such an exception applies in all consent situations and is therefore not an unusual principle applied only to minor parents.

§5.3.7 Judicial Interpretation of Consent Legislation

Due to the latitude incorporated in the minor consent laws, it is likely that challenges will be brought testing the applicability of statutes in particular instances. One challenge has already occurred in California.[47] The parents of a 17-year-old girl living away from home sued a physician for infliction of

[46]See Alaska Stat. §09.65.100 (1975); Ala. Code §22-8-5 (1971); Ark. Stat. Ann. §82-363 (1983); Fla. Stat. Ann. §743.065 (West 1979); Ga. Code §88-2904 (1975); Kan. Stat. Ann. §38-122 (1967); Mass. Gen. Laws Ann. ch. 112, §12F (West 1975); Mo. Ann. Stat. §431.061 (Vernon 1977); N.Y. Pub. Health Law §2504 (McKinney 1972); Okla. Stat. Ann. tit. 63, §2602 (West 1976).
[47]Carter v. Cangello, 105 Cal. App. 3d 348, 164 Cal. Rptr. 361 (1980).

emotional distress to them in connection with procedures performed on their daughter. The patient was living in the home of another woman, who gave her free room and board in exchange for her performing household chores. The minor also made her own financial decisions. The California Court of Appeals held that the facts of the situation fit within the meaning of California Civil Code §34.6, which authorizes such a minor to consent to his own health care.[48] Further litigation of this variety can be expected in jurisdictions whose statutory language is broadly written regarding mature and emancipated minors.

The mature or emancipated minor as recognized in state legislation varies from jurisdiction to jurisdiction. With the tremendous volume of statutory law affecting this segment of the population has come legislative refinement from time to time. Keeping abreast of statutory developments in one's own state is therefore important.

C. MINORS AND REPRODUCTIVE MATTERS

§5.4 Sexually Transmitted Diseases

Many states have enacted laws authorizing the treatment of minors for venereal diseases or, as now more appropriately phrased, sexually transmitted diseases (STD). The statutory format and scope of these laws varies from jurisdiction to jurisdiction.

§5.4.1 General Legislation

A common element running through many of these statutes is a grant of immunity to physicians treating a minor for ve-

---

[48] Id.

nereal disease. The immunity granted, however, only excludes assault and battery in treatment of a minor without parental consent or permission of the child's guardian.[1] It does not exculpate a physician for negligence.

Many of the state laws authorize a minor to undergo examination, diagnosis, and treatment for venereal disease in a hospital or clinic.[2] The laws usually state that the minor may consent to such care[3] or that, for purposes of the statute, the minor is to be treated as if she had reached majority.[4] A few indicate that it is not necessary to obtain consent from a minor's parent or legal guardian.[5]

In some states there are statutory ages of consent for examination and treatment of venereal disease — some set at 12,[6] others at 14.[7] Whether or not a jurisdiction has adopted an age for consent to venereal disease treatment, it is usually noted in the statute that the child's authorization for care is not subject to disaffirmance due to minority.[8]

A number of states have enacted unique features in their

§5.4 [1]See Ky. Rev. Stat. §214.185 (1974); Mass. Gen. Laws Ann. ch. 111, §117 (West 1974); Md. Pub. Health Code Ann. §135 (1978); Tenn. Code Ann. §68-10-104 (1980); Wyo. Stat. §35-4-131 (1973).

[2]Ariz. Rev. Stat. Ann. §44-132.01 (1971); Fla. Stat. Ann. §384.061 (West 1981); Ga. Code §74-104.3 (1971); Idaho Code §39-3801 (1971); Iowa Code Ann. §140.9 (West 1974); Nev. Rev. Stat. §129.060 (1971).

[3]See, e.g., Iowa Code Ann. §140.9 (West 1974); Kan. Stat. Ann. §65-2892 (1972); Mont. Code Ann. §41-1-402 (1977); Ohio Rev. Code Ann. §3709.241 (Baldwin 1971); Okla. Stat. Ann. tit. 63, §2602 (West 1976); W. Va. Code §16-4-10 (1971).

[4]See Fla. Stat. Ann. §384.061 (West 1981); Ga. Code §74-104.3 (1971); La. Rev. Stat. Ann. §40:1065.1 (West 1970).

[5]See, e.g., Ala. Code §22-16-9 (1971); Ga. Code §74-104.3 (1971); Idaho Code §39-3801 (1971); Ill. Ann. Stat. ch. 111, §4504 (Smith-Hurd 1980); Ohio Rev. Code Ann. §3709.241 (Baldwin 1971); Vt. Stat. Ann. tit. 18, §422b (1975).

[6]Ill. Ann. Stat. ch. 111, §4504 (Smith-Hurd 1980); Vt. Stat. Ann tit. 18, §4226 (1975).

[7]Idaho Code §39-3801 (1971); N.H. Rev. Stat. Ann. §141.11-a (1972); N.D. Cent. Code §14-10-17 (1977); Wash. Rev. Code Ann. §70.24.110 (1969).

[8]See, e.g., Ark. Stat. Ann. §82-629 (1970); Idaho Code §39-3801 (1971); S.D. Codified Laws Ann. §34-23-16 (1971); Wash. Rev. Code Ann. §70-24-110 (1969).

minor-venereal disease treatment laws. For example, the statutes in Kansas,[9] Nebraska,[10] and South Dakota[11] specify that care includes prophylactic treatment of venereal disease. Nebraska also has a provision that removes civil or criminal liability from a physician resulting from an adverse reaction to medication. A prerequisite to the applicability of this provision, however, is that reasonable care was taken to elicit from any such person under 20 years of age any history of sensitivity or previous reaction to medication.[12]

§5.4.2 Confidentiality of Treatment

Perhaps the most interesting legal aspect of these venereal disease treatment laws is the matter of confidentiality. Many of the statutes do permit disclosure. For example, Colorado's law requires any physician, intern, or other individual who diagnoses or treats a person for venereal disease to notify health authorities.[13] States that permit disclosure often include a provision protecting physicians from legal action for releasing information to a child's parents, guardian, or anyone else specified in the statute.[14]

Several jurisdictions have also tackled the issue of whether the parents or guardian of a minor should be notified when the child has received treatment for venereal disease. Many have taken the position that the minor's parents should not be informed;[15] others have vested the health care provider with dis-

[9] Kan. Stat. Ann. §65-2892 (1972).
[10] Neb. Rev. Stat. §71-1121 (1972).
[11] S.D. Codified Laws Ann. §34-23-16 (1971).
[12] Neb. Rev. Stat. §71-1121 (1972).
[13] Colo. Rev. Stat. §25-4-402 (1978).
[14] See Kan. Stat. Ann. §65-2892 (1971); Mont. Code Ann. §41-1-403 (1974). See also Or. Rev. Stat. §109.650 (1977).
[15] Neb. Rev. Stat. §71-1121 (1972); Okla. Stat. Ann. tit. 63, §2602 (West 1976) (as long as the minor is found not to have a communicable disease, no information is to be revealed to the minor's spouse, parent, or legal guardian without his or her consent).

cretion, stating that he may inform the minor's spouse, parent, or guardian but is not obligated to do so.[16]

The better policy in these situations is to refrain from such disclosure without the patient's permission. The only exception is when a reporting or notification provision is incorporated in the public health statute for contact tracing. When the facts of the situation fit the statutory exception, then the health provider is probably protected from liability. Making this determination is possible by reviewing individual state law.

In those states that have in place the so-called contact tracing system for venereal disease, at least this amount of disclosure is authorized. The information revealed extends only to the name or names of persons with whom the patient has had sexual contact — who are then located if possible and warned of the need for examination or treatment. This type of disclosure for public health purposes does not fall into the same category as notification of a minor's parents or guardian to alert them of their child's sexual activity.

Those states that have enacted laws permitting minors to consent to examination and treatment of venereal disease have taken the position that these individuals possess sufficient intellectual ability and understanding to authorize care. The fact that many of these jurisdictions also vest a physician with discretion to notify the minor's parents, spouse, or guardian presumably indicates a concern for the health and well-being of the youth and her family. Exercising that option, however, could have a less than positive effect: division of a family, marital separations, or divorce are all possible consequences, as well as parental abuse of the minor. Disclosure should be made only after thorough consideration of each individual case and any probable consequences.

[16]Ga. Code §74-104.3 (1971) (even over express refusal of the minor to divulge this information); Ill. Ann. Stat. ch. 111, §4505 (Smith-Hurd 1984); La. Rev. Stat. Ann. §1065.1 (West 1970); Me. Rev. Stat. Ann. tit. 32, §2595 (1979); Or. Rev. Stat. §109.650 (1977); Vt. Stat. Ann. tit. 18, §4226 (1975) (parents or legal guardian to be notified if the minor requires hospitalization for treatment of a venereal disease).

§5.5   Minors and Contraceptives

A number of states have enacted legislation that authorizes the dissemination of information about and distribution of contraceptives to minors.[1] Restrictions are, however, sometimes placed on the class of minors who can receive the information or the contraceptives. In other jurisdictions a nonlegislative route has been taken: several court decisions have been handed down involving minors and contraceptives.[2]

In this section, case law is discussed first with emphasis on the issues of access, privacy, state restrictions, and parental notification. The legislation on minors and contraceptives is then examined.

§5.5.1   *Minors' Right to Contraceptives*

Although a number of decisions on minors and contraceptives have been handed down, a key decision was Carey v. Population Serv. Intl.[3] This case involved a New York statute that prohibited the distribution of contraceptives to persons under 16 years of age.[4] In holding the law invalid, the U.S. Supreme Court found that New York had failed to show a sufficient state interest to justify restrictions on a minor's right to prevent pregnancy. It also pointed out, however, that an individual's right of privacy did not preclude all state limitations. The Court decided to treat minors differently from adults. Unlike adult legislation, which must pass a test of *compelling* state interest, laws restricting a minor's right of privacy must demonstrate only a significant state interest. The Court justified the lesser standard for minors by noting the state's right to regulate matters pertaining to minors more closely than those affecting

§5.5   [1]Colo. Rev. Stat. §§13-22-105, 25-6-102 (1973); Me. Rev. Stat. Ann. tit. 22, §1908 (1973); Miss. Code Ann. §41-42-7 (1972).
[2]See, e.g., Carey v. Population Serv. Intl., 431 U.S. 678 (1977); Doe v. Irwin, 615 F.2d 1162 (6th Cir. 1980), cert. denied, 449 U.S. 829 (1980).
[3]431 U.S. 678 (1977).
[4]Id.

adults. Its reasoning was based on the minor's independence in making decisions, including those regarding procreation, and the traditional view that minors are less capable than adults to make important decisions.[5]

The Court dealt with a number of other matters in the *Carey* case, which, however, are not as significant to a discussion of consent by minors. Because of the Court's justification outlined above, states can impose different consent standards on minors than on adults. The state's burden in showing reason for this distinction is also less stringent. Indeed, a state statute need only use the Court's own three-part rationale to meet a constitutional challenge.

§5.5.2 *Parental Consent and Notification*

An area of state initiatives involves the matter of parental consent or notification. Attempts have been made to impose such a requirement as a condition for minors' receiving contraceptives. In 1983, the Department of Health and Human Services promulgated a regulation requiring parental notification for minors seeking contraceptives from federally financed family planning clinics.[6] This regulation was later declared unconstitutional on the ground that the authorizing legislation did not authorize mandatory notification of parents.[7] Additional court action has followed other attempts to require parental consent or notification in the case of minors seeking contraceptives.

A Utah regulation that required parental consent prior to a minor's receiving family planning assistance was held invalid.[8] Some federal funding was used to support the program. In holding that the state-imposed restrictions were unconstitu-

---

[5]Id.
[6]State of New York v. Heckler, 719 F.2d 1191 (2d Cir. 1983).
[7]Id.
[8]T. — H. — v. Jones, 425 F. Supp. 873 (D. Utah 1975), affd., 425 U.S. 986 (1976).

tional, the court pointed out that the requirement of parental consent was an unjustifiable burden upon the minor's right of privacy. The state's argument, which centered on the need to protect minor women from the harmful effects of illicit sexual activity and to enforce parental authority in families, was not enough to overcome the minor's right of privacy in obtaining family planning assistance.

In yet another Utah case, a federal district court ruling limited the right of the state to impose a requirement of parental notification prior to a minor's receiving contraceptives.[9] As the court pointed out, legislation like that found in Utah, which imposes a blanket parental notification requirement on minors seeking contraceptives intrudes upon the constitutionally protected right to decide whether to have children. Relying upon pronouncements of the Supreme Court of the United States regarding parental notification in the area of abortions,[10] the district court indicated that the Utah law failed because it did not provide a mechanism for mature minors, nor one for immature minors for whom parental notification was not in their best interests, to obtain contraceptives confidentially.[11]

The issue of parental consent continues to be an interesting source of litigation. For example, the Tenth Circuit Court of Appeals sustained a lower court order enjoining enforcement of a Utah Health Department requirement of parental consent for unmarried minors seeking family planning services.[12] The funding for the program came from federal grants under Title X of the Public Health Services Act.[13]

The regulations governing these federally funded services make it clear that the services are to be provided without regard to age.[14] Attempts by the Department of Health and Human

---

[9]Planned Parenthood Assn. of Utah v. Matheson, 582 F. Supp. 1001 (D. Utah 1983).
[10]See H.L. v. Matheson, 450 U.S. 398 (1981); City of Akron v. Akron Center for Reproductive Health, 462 U.S. 416 (1983).
[11]Planned Parenthood Assn. v. Matheson, supra n.9.
[12]Jane Does v. State of Utah Dept. of Health, 776 F.2d 253 (10th Cir. 1985).
[13]42 U.S.C. §300.
[14]42 C.F.R. §59.5(a)(4).

Services — the federal agency charged with administering Title X grants — to impose a parental consent requirement had already been ruled invalid by other courts.[15] In this case, the parental consent provision was imposed by the grantee of the federal funding — the Utah Health Department.

The Department of Health and Human Services was aware of the fact that the state was in violation of the federal law prohibiting a parental consent requirement. As both the lower court and court of appeals suggested, this acquiescence on the part of the federal agency was an attempt "to perpetuate its proposed regulation as to consent heretofore held invalid as a violation of Title X."[16]

The court also pointed out that a referral system for minors who are denied services without prior parental consent does not cure the violation of Title X. The plaintiffs, who would in fact be the principal providers of such alternate services in urban settings, refused to do so. Their position was that such a policy would be in violation of Title X.[17] The court agreed noting that the referral system "is nothing more than what should be done after a refusal of services based on impermissible standards."[18]

That the issues of parental consent and parental notification continue to be the source of litigation indicates that this area of the law is not well settled.[19] Those opposed to unmarried minors receiving contraceptive advice, medication, or devices will continue in their attempts to devise some legislative or regulatory means of circumscribing such activities.

In a subsequent decision, another court ruled that for unemancipated minors parental notification was legally un-

[15]State of New York v. Heckler, 719 F.2d 1191 (2d Cir. 1983); Planned Parenthood Fedn. of America v. Heckler, 712 F.2d 650 (D.C. Cir. 1983).
[16]Jane Does v. State of Utah Dept. of Health, supra n.12, at 255.
[17]Id. at 256.
[18]Id.
[19]See also Attorney General Opinion, State of Oklahoma, Opinion No. 85-73, January 24, 1986, in which state legislation requiring state entities receiving Title X funds to obtain parental consent was construed to be in violation of the federal Health Services Act, 42 U.S.C. §§300, et seq.

sound.[20] This case involved a Michigan voluntary birth control clinic. The court recognized that parents of unemancipated minors still retain their traditional right of care, custody, and control over their children. Nothing in constitutional law, however, required parental notification before a child received contraceptive medication and devices.[21]

Whether the result in this case is still good law has been called into question by a U.S. Supreme Court decision involving parental notification and abortions. In H.L. v. Matheson,[22] the Court held constitutional a Utah statute that required a physician, if possible, to notify the parents of an unemancipated or immature minor who was seeking an abortion. Chief Justice Burger, writing for the majority, held that the statute served significant state interests that included family integrity and protection of immature and dependent minors.[23] The notification also gave parents the opportunity to provide essential medical and other information to a physician. Since the statute was narrowly drawn to protect only the interests of those of the class to whom it was applied, it did not violate any constitutional guarantees.

In the matter of contraception, the state interests to be served by requiring parental notification are not as strong as in the abortion issue. When, as in *Carey*, the significant state interest test is applied, parental notification may pass judicial review. To do so it must be narrowly drawn, as noted in *Matheson*, supra, and any burden it places on the minor's right of privacy must be supported by plausible, constitutional arguments. A challenge would be sustained if the law applied to emancipated and mature minors, as well as to unemancipated and dependent minors.

Perhaps the most interesting medicolegal argument that would have significant weight is the opportunity for parents to

---

[20] Doe v. Irwin, 615 F.2d 1162 (6th Cir. 1980), cert. denied, 449 U.S. 829 (1980).
[21] Id.
[22] 450 U.S. 398 (1981).
[23] Id.

provide the minor's physician with essential medical and related information. A minor may not be fully aware of a familial history that makes certain contraceptive medication contraindicated and dangerous. The minor also may have emotional difficulties about which the physician is not aware. Without these types of information the physician may treat a patient without the information necessary to recommend a specific form of contraception. This dilemma underlines the tension between the minor's right of privacy and the physician's need for sufficient information. If a minor subsequently suffered an injury due to prescribed contraceptive medication, the physician might be sued for negligent treatment. Such a lawsuit could be successful if the physician had failed to obtain sufficient information on which to base treatment.

The fact that the physician respected the minor's right of privacy and did not contact her parents for further information would not be an adequate defense. The right of privacy has nothing to do with an appropriate medical standard of care in the circumstances. When physicians are faced with minor patients about whom they do not have sufficient information, they should refrain from dispensing contraceptives known to have dangerous side effects or risks. If a minor is unable to provide the necessary background information, a physician should obtain it from the patient's guardian or parents. Absent statutory law to the contrary, a doctor should first seek a minor's consent to consult with her parents. Should the minor refuse permission, the doctor should withhold prescribing any medication, turning instead to other contraceptive methods. The minor's reluctance to involve her parents and the physician's respect for the patient's constitutional right of privacy do not justify a departure from accepted standards of practice.

§5.5.3   Contraceptive Legislation for Minors

Some state legislatures have jumped into the controversy involving minors and contraception. At least five states have passed legislation[24] that, in part, places restrictions on which minors can receive contraceptive information and services. For example, the legislation in Colorado,[25] Florida,[26] Maine,[27] Mississippi,[28] and Tennessee[29] states that birth control information and services can be provided to any minor who is married, is a parent, or has the consent of a parent or legal guardian. Some of the states have additional provisions: the laws in Colorado,[30] Mississippi,[31] and Tennessee[32] authorize physicians to provide contraceptive care for and information to minors who are referred by a family planning clinic, a clergyman, a school or institution of higher learning, or any agency or instrumentality of the state. Florida[33] and Maine[34] authorize the provision of contraceptive information and services to minors who, in the physician's opinion, would otherwise probably experience health hazards. Additional statutory law in Colorado prohibits an unmarried minor less than 18 years of age from consenting to sterilization without parental consent.[35] Tennessee has a law that allows sterilization of a person less than 18 if he or she is legally married and the patient's request is in writing.[36]

In some states, state agencies or departments have promulgated regulations relating to minors' obtaining contraceptive counselling or treatment. Legal advice on individual state statutory or case law on birth control for minors is important, given the speed with which this area of the law is changing.

[24] Colo. Rev. Stat. §13-22-105 (1973); Fla. Stat. Ann. §381.382 (West 1972); Me. Rev. Stat. Ann. tit. 22, §1908 (1973); Miss. Code Ann. §41-42-7 (1972); Tenn. Code Ann. §68-34-104 (1980).
[25] Colo. Rev. Stat. §13-22-105 (1973).
[26] Fla. Stat. Ann. §381.382 (West 1972).
[27] Me. Rev. Stat. Ann. tit. 22, §1908 (1973).
[28] Miss. Code Ann. §41-42-7 (1972).
[29] Tenn. Code Ann. §§53-4604 and 53-4607 (1971).
[30] Colo. Rev. Stat. §13-22-105 (1973).
[31] Miss. Code Ann. §41-42-7 (1972).
[32] Tenn. Code Ann. §53-4607 (1971).
[33] Fla. Stat. Ann. §381.382 (West 1972).
[34] Me. Rev. Stat. Ann. tit. 22, §1908 (1973).
[35] Colo. Rev. Stat. §25-6-102 (1973).
[36] Tenn. Code Ann. §53-4608 (1971).

§5.6   Minors and Abortion

Since the landmark abortion decisions of Roe v. Wade[1] and
Doe v. Bolton,[2] legislation and case law have made many inroads on the right of a minor to terminate a pregnancy. It is fair
to say, however, that in the United States today, an emancipated minor can consent to an abortion within the framework
required in *Roe* and *Doe*.

For unemancipated minors, however, two major areas of
concern remain unresolved: parental consent and parental
notification. Additionally, the matters of spousal consent and
notice for married minors has received some attention. In this
portion of the chapter these issues are addressed with attention
to the judicial opinions that have set legal guidelines on consent.

§5.6.1   Parental Consent to Abortion

In the landmark case of Planned Parenthood of Central Missouri v. Danforth,[3] the U.S. Supreme Court held that a state
could not condition a minor's abortion on the consent of her
parents. The Court was emphatic: a third party could not be
given an absolute and possibly arbitrary blanket veto over a
decision to abort reached by a minor and her physician.

No state interest could be found that compelled a requirement of parental consent. The Court rejected the suggestion
that giving parents an absolute veto power would strengthen
the family unit. Furthermore, the Court ruled that this veto
authority was not likely to enhance the interest of parental
authority where the parents and child were at odds over an
abortion.[4]

The *Danforth* case did not end the debate over parental con-

---

§5.6   [1] Roe v. Wade, 410 U.S. 113 (1973).
[2] Doe v. Bolton, 410 U.S. 1979 (1973).
[3] Planned Parenthood of Central Missouri v. Danforth, 428 U.S. 52 (1976).
[4] Id.

sent to abortions. The Two Massachusetts cases[5] (referred to herein as *Bellotti I* and *Bellotti II*) followed, testing statutory language that carved out certain parental powers in the termination of pregnancy. The *Bellotti* opinions reflect an attitude of persistent judicial decision-making, given the long case histories.[6]

In *Bellotti II*, the Court reviewed a Massachusetts statute that provided that in the case of an unmarried minor less than 18 years of age, consent of both the minor and her parents was required for an abortion.[7] It also stated that, in the event of one or both of the minor's parents refusing consent, a judge of the state superior court could issue an order authorizing the abortion. The standard the court was to employ was "for good cause shown" following a hearing.[8]

The Court noted that a state must act cautiously when it tries, through legislation, to encourage parental involvement in minors' abortions. A minor's right of privacy and the uniqueness of each abortion decision requires such circumspection. As noted in *Danforth,* supra, the nature and consequences of a determination to undergo an abortion make it constitutionally unsound to place total veto authority in the hands of a minor's parents. A state can, however, allow parental consent if an alternative method is instituted when the parents refuse to give their consent. This second method need not necessarily

---

[5] Bellotti v. Baird, 428 U.S. 132 (1976) (*Bellotti I*); Bellotti v. Baird, 443 U.S. 622 (1979) (*Bellotti II*).

[6] *Bellotti I* was brought to the Supreme Court after probable jurisdiction was noted. The case involved review of a decision by the U.S. District Court for the District of Massachusetts, which invalidated ch. 112, §12S of the Massachusetts General Laws (1974). The Supreme Court, after receiving briefs and oral arguments, noted that the statute was susceptible to an interpretation that would render it constitutional. It then vacated the district court's decision and remanded it, indicating that the lower court should have abstained and certified questions to the Massachusetts Supreme Judicial Court to interpret the statute. The district court complied, and the questions were answered in Baird v. Attorney General, 371 Mass. 741, 360 N.E.2d 288 (1977). The district court again held the statute unconstitutional and enjoined its enforcement. For a second time, the Supreme Court noted probable jurisdiction, 439 U.S. 925 (1978), and hence, the decision in *Bellotti II*.

[7] Consent of a guardian or another person with similar duties is necessary when a child has been deserted by her parents or when they are dead.

[8] Mass. Gen. Laws Ann. ch. 112, §12S (West 1977).

involve a court; an administrative agency or officer, properly constituted, would suffice.[9] According to the Court, in such a proceeding the minor is entitled to demonstrate that she is sufficiently mature and well informed to consent to an abortion independent of her parents' desires or that she is capable of independent decision. In such an alternative procedure, the minor's anonymity must be secured and a decision must be reached expeditiously.[10]

Measured against this standard, the Massachusetts statute was held unconstitutional for two reasons. First, as construed by the Massachusetts Supreme Judicial Court, the statute required that the minor consult with her parents prior to going to court for an independent judicial interpretation of her ability to consent. Thus, an attempt to obtain parental consent was required first. If it was refused, then opportunity for judicial review was provided. Seen in this light, the law imposed an undue burden upon the right of a minor to seek an abortion. The court noted that while all parents would not do so, the possibility remains that some parents might prevent a minor from obtaining an abortion or block her access to court.[11]

Second, the statute failed because it allowed a judge of the superior court to withhold authorization for an abortion from a minor found to be mature and competent enough to make her own decision. The Supreme Court agreed with the lower court, which held that once a minor had been found mature and competent to give an independent informed consent, the state no longer had a basis upon which to impose legal restrictions on her determination.[12]

The Court also discussed the extent of parental involvement that was constitutionally permissible under statutes like that in Massachusetts. The context of the discussion was an enumeration of the steps a court should follow if a minor is deemed incapable of making an informed choice regarding an abortion.

[9]Bellotti v. Baird, 443 U.S. 622, 625, n.2 (1981).
[10]Id. at 645.
[11]Id. at 648.
[12]Id. at 648.

An abortion request can be denied in the absence of a consultation between the minor and her parents that is deemed to be in the child's best interest.[13] Alternatively, the court can defer making a decision on the abortion until after a parental consultation in which the court participates.[14]

Even before the *Danforth* and *Bellotti* decisions, the constitutionality of parental consent provisions was contested.[15] The trend among the lower courts was to strike down such legislation as being unconstitutional.[16] After *Bellotti*, many states — Massachusetts in particular — carried on the debate through legislative amendments, standing judicial orders, and litigation.

In 1980, the Massachusetts state legislature amended the abortion law that had been interpreted by the U.S. Supreme Court in *Bellotti II*. As amended, the law applies only to unmarried minors and insists upon either parental consent or judicial authorization prior to an abortion. Parental consent must be given by (a) both parents having custody, (b) the only parent available within a reasonable period of time, or (c) authorization of a guardian. Judicial approval follows a judge's either finding that a minor is mature and capable of informed consent or deciding that the abortion is in the child's best interest.[17]

In 1981, the United States First Circuit Court of Appeals had occasion to consider the parental consent provision along with other aspects of the law. The court held that making it a prerequisite for a minor to obtain parental consent or judicial approval for an abortion did not offend the constitutional standards of due process or equal protection. It explained that there had not been a sufficient showing of undue burden upon the rights of the unmarried minors. From an equal protection standpoint, the court found that the test of strict scrutiny was

[13] Id. at 649.
[14] Id.
[15] State v. Koome, 84 Wash. 2d 901, 530 P.2d 260 (1975).
[16] See, e.g., Wynn v. Carey, 582 F.2d 1375 (7th Cir. 1978) (Ill. Abortion Parental Consent Act); Hoe v. Brown, 446 F. Supp. 329 (N.D. Ohio 1976); Abortion Coalition of Michigan v. Michigan Dept. of Health, 426 F. Supp. 471 (E.D. Mich. 1977).
[17] Mass. Gen. Laws ch. 112, §12S, as amended by 1980 Mass. Acts 240.

inapplicable and that on the basis of the rational basis standard, the statute was reasonably related to legitimate state interests.[18]

Prior to the flurry of action in the federal courts, the Massachusetts Superior Court issued a standing order for procedures to be followed in motions or petitions for abortions.[19] The First Circuit Court of Appeals considered this order in reaching its decision noted above. Subsequently, the Massachusetts Supreme Judicial Court issued an opinion in which it set "guidelines" to clear up any confusion in implementing the law.[20] Despite these developments, uncertainty remained as to the authority vested in a judge in ordering an abortion for a minor. The following judicial opinion, issued by the Massachusetts Appeals Court, seems to have lessened the uncertainty.[21]

A 14-year-old unmarried and pregnant minor sought judicial authorization for a first trimester abortion. Her petition was filed under the amended Massachusetts statute. Following a hearing, the trial court judge determined that the minor was not sufficiently mature to give an informed consent to an abortion. He then considered whether an abortion was in her best interests. The judge decided that it was not, at least without first consulting one of the minor's parents. The petition was denied, with leave to resubmit the matter once one of the parents was contacted. An appeal followed.

In reversing the trial court's decision, the Massachusetts Appeals Court did not disturb the determination of immaturity. Instead, it focused on conditioning a "best interests" authorization on prior parental consultation. As the court suggested,

[18] Planned Parenthood League of Massachusetts v. Bellotti, 641 F.2d 1008, 1111-1113 (1st Cir. 1981), affd. in part, vacated in part, and remanded, 499 F. Supp. 215 (D. Mass. 1980). It should be noted that the case came before the First Circuit after the U.S. District Court for Massachusetts had denied a preliminary injunction. This aspect of the case was consolidated with a motion to stay before the appellate court. The court pointed out that in view of the posture of the case, its conclusions as to merits of the issues presented were to be interpreted as statements of likely outcome.

[19] Superior Court, Standing Order No. 12-80, Sept. 3, 1980.

[20] Planned Parenthood League of Massachusetts v. Bellotti, 9 M.L.W. 1063 (June 22, 1981).

[21] Matter of Mary Moe, 12 Mass. App. Ct. 298, 423 N.E.2d 1038 (1981).

once the trial judge determined that the minor was not equipped to handle the responsibility of a child and that the situation required immediate action, it was an error of law to condition judicial approval on parental consultation. As interpreted by the appeals court, the statute was designed to provide a judicial alternative when the minor decides not to seek parental consent.[22]

The court suggested that when a judge is put in the position of making a "best interest" analysis, certain factors should be included in his decision-making, including the following determinations:

1. Any ambivalence on the part of the minor about her decision;
2. Any evidence of pressure on the minor to undergo the abortion;
3. Any previous professional counselling for the minor;
4. Whether the minor understood the nature and risks of the procedure; and
5. The existence of any arrangements made by the minor with a reputable facility to perform the abortion.

When this type of evidence is lacking, then a minor living in Massachusetts must seek parental consent. If this is refused, then the court must allow the minor to present additional evidence on the issue of the abortion being in her best interest.[23]

Although a state may or may not have a statute relating to parental permission for abortions, a primary consideration is the issue of informed consent. The debate and court battles over abortions for unmarried minors have often ignored this crux of the problem in favor of a preoccupation with the intricacies of constitutional law. On a practical day-to-day level, the informed consent issue probably deserves more consideration than the nuances of privacy and significant state interests. Proper authorization for terminating an adolescent's pregnancy is essential.

[22] Id.
[23] Id.

If, however, the court determines that the minor is sufficiently mature to decide for herself whether she wants an abortion, the judge cannot base her finding on the young woman's meeting certain conditions that the judge deems advisable.[24] In yet another case entitled In the Matter of Mary Moe, the Massachusetts Appeals Court ruled that the trial judge could neither specify the type of abortion the minor was to undergo nor the facility in which it was to take place as a condition to his finding the young woman capable of giving informed consent to the procedure. To permit such judicial action would exceed the bounds set forth in applicable state legislation.[25]

The progeny of *Bellotti II* and other landmark cases have begun to appear in court.[26] In two decisions, the Supreme Court of the United States made it clear that state laws *must* provide an option to parental consent in the case of minors who cannot authorize an abortion.[27] Thus an Akron city ordinance that denied abortions to unmarried minors under 15 years of age unless they had parental consent or a court order for the performance of the procedure was declared unconstitutional.[28] The age prohibition was in the nature of a blanket prohibition and state law did not make it clear whether the juvenile court had the authority to conduct case-by-case evaluations of the maturity of pregnant minors.

While court actions may exhaust the possible options for interpreting the requirements for parental consent, there are bound to be legislative initiatives to tighten up the procedural aspects of minors and access to abortion. Indeed, a Pennsylvania case demonstrates that these associated issues may focus on rules dealing with parents in the courtroom during judicial

[24] In the Matter of Mary Moe, 12 Mass. App. Ct. 727 (1984).
[25] Id.
[26] See, e.g., Jacksonville Clergy Consultation Serv. v. Martinez, 696 F. Supp. 1445 (M.D. Fla. 1988); In re Emergency Amend. to R. Civ. P., 532 So. 2d 1058 (Fla. 1988).
[27] See City of Akron v. Akron Center for Reproductive Health, 462 U.S. 416 (1983); Planned Parenthood Assn. of Kansas City, Missouri v. Ashcroft, 462 U.S. 476 (1983).
[28] City of Akron v. Akron Center for Reproductive Health, supra n.27.

proceedings as well as the speed with which courts must render judgments.[29]

What should be made clear is that parental consent to abortion need not be an issue of constitutional law. Indeed, violation of state legislation on the subject may give rise to successful litigation based on battery. Such was the situation in a Louisiana case.[30]

When the defendant confirmed that the young woman was pregnant, she supplied him with a document purportedly containing her mother's authorization for an abortion. The young woman was 16 years of age at the time and Louisiana law required an authorization from a parent, legal guardian, or tutor. When the young woman's mother found out that her daughter had undergone an abortion, litigation ensued.

After trial, the court dismissed the plaintiffs' claims for failure to prove either negligence or battery on the part of the defendant. However, this determination was reversed in part by the Court of Appeals of Louisiana.[31]

In this situation, the "authorization" had been falsified by the young woman's cousin. Moreover, the consent did not measure up to state law, which required that the authorization be notarized. As such, the abortion procedure was not properly authorized and there had been a battery. The court awarded the young woman $3,400 in damages. The court rejected a further claim on the part of the young woman's parents that as a result of his actions, the defendant had denied them a right to grandparenthood. In this instance there was nothing in law to support such a claim for recovery.[32]

From a practical perspective, care must be taken to meet the state-specific requirements for consent to treatment. This is as true for a diagnostic test as it is for an abortion. That states have set forth such criteria to assist minors by making certain that they have the benefit of an adult's advice and by requiring an

[29]American College of Obstetricians and Gynecologists, Pa. Section, v. Thornburgh, 656 F. Supp. 879 (E.D. Pa. 1987).
[30]Cage v. Wood, 484 So. 2d 850 (La. Ct. App. 1986).
[31]Id. at 851.
[32]Id. at 853.

authenticated consent document should not be overlooked. As seen in this case, the failure to do so may result in successful litigation.

§5.6.2 Parental Notification

Another type of state statute relating to adolescent abortions centers on the notification, rather than the consent, of parents.[33] As with other legislative mechanisms dealing with abortions for minors, parental notification has received judicial review. In H.L. v. Matheson, the U.S. Supreme Court held that the Utah parental notification provision *was* constitutional.[34] In its decision, the Supreme Court addressed itself to the narrow issue of facial constitutionality.

The situation involved a 15-year-old unmarried minor who was dependent upon and living with her parents. She challenged the constitutionality of the state statute in a class action proceeding. The statute required, when possible, notification of a minor's parents prior to performing an abortion. The court identified at least three state interests in holding the law constitutional: protecting adolescents, preserving family integrity, and providing parents with an opportunity to give medical and emotional information to their daughter's physician.[35] It rejected the suggestion that the statute was unconstitutional because it may inhibit some minors from seeking abortions.

While parental notification for abortions on unmarried, dependent minors may be constitutional, still unresolved is the application of the same practice to mature minors. The Court noted that it could not assume that the statute, when applied to mature minors, would be constitutionally sound.[36]

Parental notice requirements are not seen by the Court in the

----

[33] Mont. Code Ann. §50-20-107 (1974); Tenn. Code Ann. §39-302 (1979); Utah Code Ann. §76-7-304 (1974).
[34] 450 U.S. 398 (1981).
[35] Id.
[36] Id. at 407.

same light as parental consent provisions. It is arguable that if significant state interests can be demonstrated to support a parental notice requirement for mature minors, such a requirement *may* pass muster. However, this remains an unanswered question.

That the courts will continue to closely scrutinize state laws that impose restrictions upon the right of a minor to secure an abortion is illustrated by a case challenging Nevada legislation.[37] The legislation at issue required a doctor either to notify the parents of an unemancipated minor prior to performing an abortion or have a court order permitting the procedure. The unemancipated minor could seek an order authorizing the doctor to carry out the abortion. If the court denied the request, the minor could seek a court decree waiving the notification requirement. The court could fulfill such a request if it determined either that the minor was mature enough to make the abortion decision or that she was too immature to do so, but that the waiver of notification was in her best interests.[38]

As the court pointed out, the standard by which the Nevada law should be evaluated was set out by the United States Supreme Court. For a so-called consent bypass to pass constitutional muster, "the State must provide an alternative procedure whereby a pregnant minor may demonstrate that she is sufficiently mature to make the abortion decision herself or that, despite her immaturity, an abortion would be in her best interests."[39]

In this case, the Nevada two-tier judicial process was found not to meet this standard. In the first tier the minor was interviewed by the court and the court would issue an order either permitting or denying the abortion. If the court did not issue an order, then authorization was deemed to have been given for the procedure.[40]

---

[37]Glick v. McKay, 616 F. Supp. 322 (D. Nev. 1985).
[38]Nev. Rev. Stat. §442.255 (1985).
[39]City of Akron v. Akron Center for Reproductive Health, 462 U.S. 416, 439-440 (1983), quoted in Glick v. McKay, supra n.37, at 325.
[40]Nev. Rev. Stat. §442.255 (1985), discussed in Glick v. McKay, supra n.37, at 325.

As the court pointed out, this placed the doctor in a very difficult position, because the physician was subject to liability if the abortion was carried out without proper authorization. When the court neither granted nor denied approval for the abortion, no record was made of the authorization, and hence the doctor had no tangible guide.

The statute was also deemed to be flawed in that it did not ensure confidentiality. This too failed to meet the standards of United States Supreme Court case law, which requires "specific assurances" of confidentiality in the consent bypass mechanism.[41]

If an abortion was not approved, under the two-tier system the minor could seek a waiver of the notification requirement. However, the law did not incorporate a time frame in which the court was required to render its decision. Without such statutory guidance it was unclear how the plaintiff could pursue an expeditious appeal of an adverse decision. This could have resulted in serious hardship for the plaintiff and impede an effective opportunity to secure an abortion. As such, the court indicated that until the Supreme Court of Nevada promulgated rules or regulations to correct the problem, the law was fundamentally defective and enjoined the enforcement of this aspect of the Nevada law.[42]

It is worthwhile to note that despite the fundamental defect in the Nevada law, the court went on to hold another provision of the legislation constitutional. Specifically, the court found that a requirement that the physician explain the physical and emotional impact of undergoing an abortion was permissible under existing United States Supreme Court precedent. In this case, the court determined that this requirement was consistent with the state interest in making certain that the abortion decision was based on a full knowledge of its nature and consequences.[43]

Legislation in Ohio and Minnesota dealing with minors and

[41]Glick v. McKay, supra n.37, at 325-326.
[42]Id. at 327.
[43]Id. at 327-328.

abortion has also come under close scrutiny. The Ohio law was successfully challenged in the United States District Court because of flaws dealing with parental notification of a minor's abortion.[44] The court found several flaws with the state law. In particular, the court ruled that it was a violation of due process to require "clear and convincing" evidence that the minor was mature enough and properly informed to opt for an abortion without parental notification. Similarly, the court ruled that employing the same standard of proof to demonstrate that parental notification was not in the young woman's best interest violated due process considerations.[45] The court found other deficiencies, including requirements regarding the pleadings in a case[46] and confidentiality of personal identity if the minor decides to utilize the "waiver" provision of the law regarding parental notification.[47] The District Court's ruling was subsequently affirmed by the Sixth Circuit Court of Appeals.[48]

The Minnesota law was also deemed flawed in part by the court. The court dealt with what is fast becoming a commonplace issue in such cases, the so-called judicial bypass option to parental notification or consent.[49] Of specific interest, however, is the ruling on the Minnesota requirement that both parents be notified that the young woman is pregnant. Although the lower court had found the two-parent notification requirement too burdensome,[50] the Eighth Circuit Court of Appeals disagreed and found that portion of the Minnesota statute constitutional.[51]

---

[44] Akron Center for Reproductive Health v. Rosen, 633 F. Supp. 1123 (N.D. Ohio 1986).

[45] Id. at 1135-1137.

[46] Id. at 1137-1138.

[47] Id. at 1143-1144.

[48] See Akron Center for Reproductive Health v. Slaby, 854 F.2d 852 (6th Cir. 1988).

[49] Hodgson v. State of Minnesota, 853 F.2d 1452 (8th Cir. 1988), reversing Hodgson v. State of Minnesota, 648 F. Supp. 756 (D. Minn. 1986).

[50] See Hodgson v. State of Minnesota, 648 F. Supp. 756, 777 (D. Minn. 1986).

[51] See Hodgson v. State of Minnesota, 853 F.2d 1452, 1465 (8th Cir. 1988).

§5.6.3   Married Minors: Spousal Consent and Notification

The issue of spousal consent for adult women seeking abortions has been addressed by the Supreme Court. In Planned Parenthood of Central Missouri v. Danforth, the Court held that a spousal consent requirement for abortions in the first 12 weeks of pregnancy was unconstitutional. It was noted that states cannot delegate a veto power for a decision over which the state itself has no authority to legislate. (See §3.6, supra, for further discussion of spousal consent for abortions performed on adult women.) Since *Danforth*, legislation has been enacted in some states on the matter of spousal consent or notification for abortions to be performed on married minors.[52] The states provide some exceptions, as when the husband and wife are living separately or when an abortion must be performed on an emergency basis.[53]

In view of the decision in *Danforth*, supra, it is questionable whether spousal consent requirements for married minors meet constitutional requirements. As the Supreme Court indicated in Roe v. Wade, the decision whether to abort during the first trimester is to be made by the attending doctor in consultation with his patient.[54] The state may not intrude upon this decision. Only during the second trimester does the state begin to have the right to regulate — and then for matters related to maternal health. Even during the third trimester, when the state may prohibit abortions, it cannot ban those deemed necessary to preserve the life or health of the woman.[55]

Since the state is limited in what burdens it may directly place on the abortion decision, delegating any authority to impede an abortion requires careful review. Laws granting the husband of a married minor authority to consent, particularly as to first trimester abortions, would probably run afoul of the Court's

---

[52]See, e.g., Fla. Stat. Ann. §390.001 (West 1980) (notification of husband).
[53]Id.
[54]410 U.S. 113, 166-167 (1973).
[55]Id.

analysis in Roe v. Wade, supra. It is difficult to imagine how a state could successfully argue that spousal consent serves maternal health needs in the second trimester. In the third trimester, a determination that termination of a pregnancy is necessary to sustain a woman's life or health is a medical judgment far removed from the issue of a husband's approval. Whether a pregnant woman is a minor is an insufficient basis upon which to impose special consent — particularly when in many states, by common and statutory law, marriage places the woman in the category of adulthood.

Spousal notification is a more uncertain issue. The Supreme Court has left unanswered the constitutionality of statutes requiring parental notification for emancipated and mature minors.[56] The legality of laws requiring spousal notification will turn on many of the considerations reviewed in the abortion cases following Roe v. Wade. At a minimum, the state will have to demonstrate significant interests to overcome the married minor's right of privacy.

§5.6.4 Practical Considerations Regarding Minors and Abortion

There is little doubt that judges are placed under considerable strain by state laws dealing with the maturity of minors to consent to abortion. A decision regarding maturity to consent to an abortion has broad implications, particularly with respect to the requirement of parental notification. (See §5.6.2 supra.) What is the yardstick by which judges assess maturity or immaturity? This is an important consideration for those representing minors who argue maturity or, in the alternative, hope to forestall parental notification. A Utah case illustrates the types of factors considered by the courts in such matters.[57]

The United States Supreme Court has not defined "maturity" in explicit detail in terms of parental consent to, or notifi-

[56] H.L. v. Matheson, 450 U.S. 398 (1981).
[57] H.B. v. Wilkinson, 639 F. Supp. 952 (D. Utah 1986).

cation of, an abortion on a minor. Maturity is not merely a matter of social and verbal skills or level of intelligence.[58] As the District Court pointed out, maturity involves experience, perspective, and judgment.[59]

What is meant by "experience," "perspective," and "judgment"? The court describes each category as follows:

Experience: prior work experience, living away from home, handling of personal finances.

Perspective: ability to appreciate and understand "the relative gravity and possible detrimental impact"[60] of each alternative, realistic evaluation and perception of short- and long-term outcomes of each alternative, including the abortion option.

Judgment: being fully informed in order to assess each option in a realistic and independent manner. For the court, judgment was of great relevance to the matter of maturity. Indeed, it suggested that a minor's conduct was "a measure of good judgment."[61]

Applying these criteria to the case before it, the court determined that the minor was not mature. The court reached its conclusion by making certain findings of facts. For example, the minor was unmarried and an unemancipated minor. She was 17 years of age and totally dependent upon her parents for financial resources. She had never been regularly employed, and she had never lived away from home. The home environment was one that was loving, supportive, and concerned with her best interests. When she became sexually active with her 17-year-old boyfriend, she decided not to use contraceptives because she thought she could easily obtain an abortion without her parents finding out about it. Indeed, she thought that should complications arise incident to the abortion, she could hide the true facts from her parents. Rather than seeking the advice of an adult outside the health center — as recommended by them — the minor sought the advice of teenagers. Although

[58] Id. at 954.
[59] Id.
[60] Id.
[61] Id. citing In re T.P., 475 N.E.2d 312 (Ind. 1975).

the minor feared physical and emotional discipline from her
father if he was told that she was pregnant, she did not have the
same concerns about her mother. However, the youngster felt
if she did inform her mother, she would, in turn, disclose the
minor's pregnancy to her father.[62]

Based on these findings the court ruled that the minor lacked
the experience, perspective, and judgment to be considered
mature. The demeanor of the young woman as well as the
evidence adduced suggested that she lacked the ability to appreciate and avoid options that could be adverse to her interests. As a result, the court suggested parental notification "in a
discreet way"[63] was in order at least as to the minor's mother.

Would other judges agree? Would the outcome be the same
in similar cases? It is difficult to predict. One thing is clear,
however: the matter of deciding who is and who is not a mature
minor for purposes of state abortion laws is a difficult task.
Perhaps it is one reason why so many abortion cases continue to
come before the courts, testing what is considered cumbersome
and unconstitutional legislation.

D. DRUG AND ALCOHOL ABUSE
TREATMENT FOR MINORS

§5.7 Statutory Requirements

Many states have enacted statutes that authorize minors to consent to treatment for alcoholism[1] and drug or substance abuse.[2]

---

[62] H.B. v. Wilkinson, 639 F. Supp. at 955-958.

[63] Id. at 958.

§5.7 [1] Cal. Civ. Code §34.10 (West 1977); Fla. Stat. Ann. §396.082 (West
1976); Ga. Code §88-403.1 (1979); Ind. Code Ann. §16-13-6.1-23 (Burns
1976); Ky. Rev. Stat. §222.440 (1972); Minn. Stat. Ann. §144.343 (West
1980).

[2] Colo. Rev. Stat. §13-22-102 (1963); Ga. Code §88-403.1 (1979); Idaho
Code §37-3102 (1972); Ind. Code Ann. §16-13-6.1-23 (Burns 1976); Wis.
Stat. Ann. §51.47 (West 1986).

Some state statutes authorize treatment of minors without parental consent when a child has reached a certain age. Most of these laws have set 12 years of age[3] as the standard, although other ages have been used as well.[4]

Although most of the laws allowing treatment of minors for drug or alcohol abuse do not require parental consent, many do permit notification of parents.[5] The decision whether to contact a minor's parents is usually left to the discretion of the attending physician. In Maryland, contact can be made with the parents even over the express objection of the minor.[6]

Like some of the minor treatment statutes for venereal disease, some of the alcohol and drug abuse legislation immunizes a physician from liability for providing treatment without parental consent. The immunity granted, however, does not extend to negligent acts or omissions.[7] Many of the statutes also prevent lawsuits for unauthorized treatment by stating that the consent of the minor is not subject to later disclaimer or disaffirmance.[8]

A few states have taken a different approach with alcohol and drug abuse treatment for minors. For example, in at least two states parental consent *is required* prior to placing a minor on a methadone treatment program.[9] Some legislation also in-

[3]Cal. Civ. Code §34.10 (West 1977); Ga. Code §§88-403.1 (1979); Mass. Gen. Laws Ann. ch. 112, §12E (West 1973); Wis. Stat. Ann. §51.47 (West 1986).

[4]Fla. Stat. Ann. §396.082 (West 1976) (minor under 18 years of age may consent to alcoholism treatment); N.D. Cent. Code §14-10-17 (1973) (any minor 14 years of age or older may contract for treatment of alcoholism or drug abuse); Wash. Rev. Code Ann. §69.54.060 (1971) (any person 14 years of age or older may consent to care for drug or alcohol abuse).

[5]Ind. Code Ann. §16-13-6.1-23 (Burns 1976); La. Rev. Stat. Ann. §1096 (West 1972) (includes notification of a minor's spouse); Me. Rev. Stat. Ann. tit. 32, §§3817, 6221, 7004 (1979); Tenn. Code Ann. §63-6-220 (1980).

[6]Md. Pub. Health Code Ann. §135 (1978).

[7]Colo. Rev. Stat. §13-22-102 (1963); Ind. Code Ann. §16-13-6.1-23 (Burns 1976); Neb. Rev. Stat. §71-5041 (1980); Ohio Rev. Code Ann. §3719.012 (Baldwin 1982); W. Va. Code §60-6-23 (1977) (alcoholism); Wis. Stat. Ann. §51.47 (1979).

[8]Cal. Civ. Code §34.10 (West 1977); Fla. Stat. Ann. §396.082 (West 1976); Mass. Gen. Laws Ann. ch. 112, §12E (West 1973); Ohio Rev. Code Ann. §3719.012 (Baldwin 1982).

[9]Cal. Civ. Code §34.10 (West 1977); S.C. Code Ann. §44-53-760 (1980).

cludes a parental consent requirement for institutionalization associated with drug and alcohol abuse treatment.[10]

Care should be taken in construing the meaning of statutory provisions regarding drug and alcohol abuse treatment for minors. Legislation may seem to require consent of a minor to such care but the courts may rule that this is not necessarily the case. A Florida decision[11] illustrates this point.

Straight, Inc., a nonprofit company, provided drug treatment and rehabilitation. Licensed by the Florida Department of Health and Rehabilitation Services, the corporation asked the court to declare that applicable state law[12] did not preclude a parent from placing a minor in a drug treatment program without first obtaining the consent of the child or judicial review of his involuntary commitment. The regulatory agency took quite the opposite point of view. The lower court granted declaratory judgment for Straight, Inc. and the state appealed.

As the Florida District Court of Appeals noted, even though there may be state legislation designed to facilitate drug treatment for minors who recognize that they have a problem, this does not mean such care may be provided only with their authorization. The legislation does not restrict parents from exercising their rights and responsibilities to educate, train, and control their children. Only where parental authority is exercised in an unreasonable manner or is otherwise abused will the state intervene between parents and their offspring. In ruling in favor of the position taken by the nonprofit corporation, the court noted:

> The fact that the decision of the parent is not agreeable to the child or involves risks does not automatically transfer power to make the decision from the parents to some agency or officer of the state.[13]

[10] Ga. Code §88-403.1 (1979); Wash. Rev. Code Ann. §69.54.060 (1982); Wis. Stat. Ann. §51.47 (West 1986).
[11] See Department of Health and Rehabilitation Servs. v. Straight, Inc., 497 So. 2d 692 (Fla. App. 1986).
[12] Fla. Stat. Ann. §397.052.
[13] Department of Health and Rehabilitation Servs. v. Straight, Inc., supra n.11, at 694.

That a child may be unable to make sound decisions regarding medical care tipped the scales in favor of a parental role in authorizing treatment. For the court, this was all the more appropriate when the issue was therapy for minors who were drug dependent or abusers.

In the absence of state legislation specifically authorizing alcohol or drug abuse care for minors, it is important to review applicable case law and general minor consent statutes. In either body of law, language may be found that is sufficiently broad to authorize treatment. Even in those states with an established age of consent, some flexibility exists. New Hampshire has included such latitude in its statute permitting minors to receive drug abuse treatment without parental permission. Although the law indicates that a person 12 years of age or older may consent to treatment, it also provides:

> Nothing contained herein shall be construed to mean that any minor of sound mind is legally incapable of consenting to medical treatment provided that such minor is of sufficient maturity to understand the nature of such treatment and the consequences thereof.[14]

E. MENTALLY ILL AND RETARDED MINORS

§5.8 Authorization for Treatment

Many states have passed legislation covering the rights of minors who receive treatment for mental or emotional illness.[1] Additional legislation can be found setting forth requirements

---

[14]N.H. Rev. Stat. Ann. §318-B:12a (1971).

§5.8 [1]Alaska Stat. §47.30.690 (1984); Cal. Civ. Code §25.9 (West 1983); Colo. Rev. Stat. §27-10-103 (1987); Conn. Gen. Stat. §17-205f (1986); Ill. Ann. Stat. ch. 91 1/2 §§3-501 to 3-503 (Smith-Hurd 1979) and §3-504 (Smith-Hurd 1984); N.M. Stat. Ann. §43-1-17 (1978); N.Y. Mental Hyg. Law §9.13 (McKinney 1977). See P.F. v. Walsh, 648 P.2d 1067 (Colo. 1982).

for mentally retarded minors.[2] The courts have also had opportunities to interpret the application of these laws.[3] In this section, these matters are discussed in terms of consent to treatment and from whom authorization must be obtained.

§5.8.1 Parental Consent

The extent of parental authority to place a child in either an inpatient or outpatient mental health treatment setting varies from state to state. Some laws focus on commitment, whereas others emphasize consent requirements for medical or invasive procedures.

Legislation in Missouri[4] and Oregon[5] is illustrative of those laws requiring parental consent for commitment of a minor to a mental health facility. Under the Missouri statute, a private or public mental health facility may accept a minor for evaluation when voluntary admission has been requested for him by her parents or legal custodian. When the minor is diagnosed as having a mental disorder suitable for treatment by the facility, she may be admitted for inpatient treatment.[6] The Oregon law requires the parent, legal guardian, or next of kin of a person under 18 years of age to execute an application seeking admission of the minor to a state hospital for treatment. The law also sets forth requirements for discharge and parental notification when a minor is admitted or released from a hospital.[7]

§5.8.2 Authorization by the Minor

Another common statutory construction allows minors of a certain age to consent to mental health services. Some of these

[2]N.Y. Mental Hyg. Law §15.13 (McKinney 1986); La. Rev. Stat. Ann. §28:390 (West 1979).
[3]See, e.g., Secretary of Public Welfare of Pennsylvania v. Institutionalized Juveniles, 442 U.S. 640 (1979), on remand, 81 F.R.D. 463 (1980).
[4]Mo. Ann. Stat. §632.110 (Vernon 1980).
[5]Or. Rev. Stat. §426.220 (1975).
[6]Mo. Ann. Stat. §632.110 (Vernon 1980).
[7]Or. Rev. Stat. §426.220 (1975).

extend only to outpatient services,[8] although others include
voluntary admissions for treatment.[9] A few allow a minor as
young as 12 years of age to make this decision without parental
involvement,[10] although other jurisdictions have set higher age
thresholds.[11]

As with other types of minor consent statutes, those providing for treatment in the absence of parental permission may
allow notification of a child's parents. Laws in at least six states
authorize mental health professionals, at their discretion, to
notify parents.[12]

Statutes that permit minors to consent to mental health or
emotional illness treatment often include limitations beyond
the matter of age. California, for example, permits a person 12
years of age or older to give consent to outpatient care when, in
the opinion of the mental health professional, the minor is
considered: "Mature enough to participate intelligently in mental health treatment or counseling on an outpatient basis and
(1) would present a danger of serious physical or mental harm
to himself or others without such mental health treatment or
counseling, or (2) has been the alleged victim of incest or child
abuse. . . ."[13] Montana has a similar law, allowing a minor to
consent if it is believed that without these services the patient
(a) may self-inflict harm or be a danger to others and (b) his

[8]Cal. Civ. Code §25.9 (West 1983); Ill. Ann. Stat. ch. 91 1/2, §3-501 (Smith-
Hurd 1979); Mont. Code Ann. §41-1-406 (1983).
[9]Conn. Gen. Stat. §17-205f (1986); Ill. Ann. Stat. ch. 91 1/2, §3-502 (Smith-
Hurd 1979); N.M. Stat. Ann. §43-1-16 (1978); N.Y. Mental Hyg. Law §9.13
(McKinney 1986); Vt. Stat. Ann. tit. 18, §7503 (1977).
[10]Cal. Civ. Code §25.9 (West 1983); N.M. Stat. Ann. §43-1-16 (1978).
[11]Conn. Gen. Stat. §17-205f (1979) (14 years of age or over); Ill. Ann. Stat.
ch. 91 1/2, §3-501 (14 years of age or over for outpatient services) and §3-502
(16 years of age or over for voluntary self-admission) (Smith-Hurd 1979); Pa.
Stat. Ann. tit. 50, §720 (Purdon 1978) (14 years of age or over); Vt. Stat. Ann.
tit. 18, §7503 (1977) (14 years of age or older). See P.F. v. Walsh, 648 P.2d
1067 (Colo. 1982).
[12]Cal. Civ. Code §25.9 (West 1983); Conn. Gen. Stat. §17-205f (1986) (parents of voluntarily admitted children 14 years of age or over are to be notified
within five days of admission); Ill. Stat. Ann. ch. 91 1/2, §§3-501, 3-502
(Smith-Hurd 1979); Pa. Stat. Ann. tit. 50, §7204 (Purdon 1976).
[13]Cal. Civ. Code §25.9 (West 1983).

parent, guardian, or spouse is not available to authorize treatment.[14]

In several states the laws authorizing treatment of minors for mental disorders include restrictions on certain types of therapy. Most of the laws deal with electroconvulsive shock treatment,[15] psychosurgery,[16] or medication.[17] Requirements vary from state to state, with judicial approval or parental authorization generally set as a prerequisite.[18] A few states have enacted procedurally technical laws to safeguard the rights of minors; notable in this category are Missouri, New Mexico, and Tennessee.[19] There are also some exceptions provided within the legislation. In at least five states mental health treatment may proceed without parental or guardian approval when the minor's condition presents a danger of self-inflicted harm or harm to others.[20] In other states medical or surgical care can be provided without parental or guardian consent on an emergency basis[21] or with the approval of the superintendent of a

[14]Mont. Code Ann. §41-1-406 (1977).
[15]Cal. Civ. Code §25.9 (West 1983); Kan. Stat. Ann. §59-2929 (1986); Mo. Ann. Stat. §630.130 (Vernon 1980); N.M. Stat. Ann. §43-1-16 (1978); Tenn. Code Ann. §33-320 (1978).
[16]Cal. Civ. Code §25.9 (West 1983); Conn. Gen. Stat. §17-205h (1979); Kan. Stat. Ann. §59-2929 (1986); Mo. Ann. Stat. §630.133 (Vernon 1980); N.M. Stat. Ann. §43-1-17 (1978); Tenn. Code Ann. §33-320 (1978).
[17]Cal. Civ. Code §25.9 (West 1983); N.M. Stat. Ann. §43-1-17 (1978).
[18]Cal. Civ. Code §25.9 (West 1983) (consent of parents or guardian); Colo. Rev. Stat. §13-20-403 (1979) (no electroconvulsive therapy under 16 years of age; between 16 and 18 years of age parental approval required); N.M. Stat. Ann. §43-1-17 (1978) (no psychosurgery or electroconvulsive therapy without court approval; except in emergency, no psychotropic drug medication without parental, guardian, or court approval); N.D. Cent. Code §25-01.2-11 (1981) (court approval for psychosurgery); Tenn. Code Ann. §33-320 (1978) (electroconvulsive therapy requires court approval; no lobotomies allowed on minors).
[19]Mo. Ann. Stat. §§630.130, 630.133 (Vernon 1980); N.M. Stat. Ann. §43-1-17 (1978); Tenn. Code Ann. §33-320 (1978).
[20]Cal. Civ. Code §25.9 (West 1983); Conn. Gen. Stat. §17-205h (1979); Mont. Code Ann. §41-1-406 (1977); N.M. Stat. Ann. §43-1-17 (1978) (psychotropic drug treatment may be administered on an emergency basis to a minor); Tenn. Code Ann. §33-320 (1978) (provision included for emergency electroconvulsive therapy on minor).
[21]See, e.g., Nev. Rev. Stat. §433.484 (1985).

facility.[22] The silence of many state statutes on the matter does not prevent emergency treatment of a minor under applicable common law principles (see §5.2.1, supra).

In some jurisdictions the right of the minor and/or her parent or guardian to be informed of treatment is spelled out specifically in legislation. Often this requirement is included in so-called patient bills of rights.[23]

An important component of many state laws dealing with mentally ill and mentally retarded minors is the matter of refusing treatment. In those states that recognize the right to refuse treatment, the right may be exercised by minors or by their parent or guardian on their behalf.[24] A refusal may be overruled, as when it is necessary to prevent a patient from causing serious injury to himself or others.[25]

With the vast inroads in the law of informed consent relating to treatment of mental illness and retardation have come a number of significant court decisions. These are discussed below.

§5.8.3 Judicial Limitations on Parental Consent

In 1979, the U.S. Supreme Court considered two cases dealing with commitment of children for mental health treatment. Both cases are instructive on the scope of parental authority in the institutionalization of minors. In the first case, Parham v. J.R., the Supreme Court reviewed the judgment of a three-judge district court that had held certain Georgia statutes unconstitutional.[26] The lower court had held that the legislation did not adequately safeguard the due process rights of minors.

---

[22] Conn. Gen. Stat. §17-205h (1979); La. Rev. Stat. Ann. §40:1299.58 (West 1978) (applicable to mentally retarded residents of state schools).

[23] See, e.g., Kan. Stat. Ann. §59-2929 (1986); La. Rev. Stat. Ann. §28:390 (West 1979) (mentally retarded persons' bill of rights); Me. Rev. Stat. Ann. tit. 34-B §5605 (1984) (rights of mentally retarded); Mo. Ann. Stat. §630.115 (Vernon 1980); Wis. Stat. Ann. §51.61 (1986).

[24] Neb. Rev. Stat. §83-1066 (1976); N.D. Cent. Code §25-01.2-15 (1981).

[25] Id.

[26] 442 U.S. 584 (1979).

The specific issue before the court was whether an adversary proceeding was necessary prior to or after institutionalization of minors.

The Georgia law in question provided for voluntary admission to a state hospital of children for whom an application had been filed by parent or guardian. The state mental health director never published a statewide set of regulations outlining the procedures to be followed in admitting a person less than 18 years of age. Each state hospital superintendent set the procedures to be employed in his institution, leading to considerable variation within the state.[27]

The district court had held that the commitment of a child constituted a severe deprivation of liberty. Liberty was defined in terms of freedom from physical restraint and freedom from emotional and psychic harm. It then held that, given the liberty interest involved, due process required the right to be heard by an impartial tribunal.[28]

The Supreme Court in its opinion applied a three-part balancing test in determining whether the Georgia law met due process standards. It considered:

1. Privacy interest affected by commitment.
2. Government interest.
3. Risk of erroneous deprivation of privacy interest through procedure employed.[29]

Concerning the privacy interest involved in commitment, the Court noted that it involved a combination of the concerns of the child and her parents. A child does have a liberty interest, which is protectible in terms of the child's being free of unwarranted bodily restraints and in not being labelled due to an erroneous decision on the part of a state hospital superintendent.[30] Parents, too, the Court noted, have a discernible inter-

---

[27] Id. at 592.
[28] J.L. v. Parham, 412 F. Supp. 112, 137 (14 D. Ga. 1976), discussed in Parham v. J.R., 442 U.S. 584 (1979).
[29] Parham v. J.R., supra n.28 at 600.
[30] Id. at 602.

est. Parents have traditionally been presumed to act in the best interests of their child. Although some may make decisions adverse to these interests, the Court was prepared to reject this presumption. Absent a determination of abuse or neglect, the parents are to retain their traditional role in the decision-making regarding commitment. However, the authority vested in parents is not absolute in view of the rights possessed by the child.[31]

The Court identified the state's interest in terms of restricting use of costly mental health facilities. It also pointed out that the state had a significant interest in not setting unwarranted procedural hurdles that might dissuade those seeking mental health services. Chief Justice Burger pointed out the likely consequences of adopting the appellee's argument for greater procedural safeguards. By emphasizing procedural considerations, involving the time and expense of staff diverted to hearings, the system would ultimately detract from its main purpose of offering care.[32]

In terms of the third part of the balancing test outlined above the Court concluded:

> [T]he risk of error inherent in the parental decision to have a child institutionalized for mental health care is sufficiently great that some kind of inquiry should be made by a "neutral fact-finder" to determine whether the statutory requirements for admission are satisfied.[33]

The inquiry, the Court noted, must include an interview with the child, as well as a probe into his background using available sources of information. The decision maker must have the authority to decline to admit a child who does not meet the medical criteria for institutionalized care. Furthermore, the child must be assessed from time to time in an independent procedure to determine whether his commitment should be con-

---

[31] Id. at 605.
[32] Id. at 606.
[33] Id. at 607.

tinued. The Court declined to set out what procedures were to be followed in these review assessments, pointing out that since the district court had not decided on the issue, it had no reason to consider it in the opinion.[34]

Of particular interest in the opinion is the Court's refusal to require a judicial inquiry for commitment of minors. Rather, a determination could be made by a staff physician, provided she were given the latitude to evaluate the mental and emotional state of the child and the need for care. Furthermore, the Court indicated that the hearing need not be formal — or even quasi-formal.

To support this type of approach, the Court suggested that the decision to be made was medical rather than judicial in origin. Requiring formalized proceedings also had the potential of jeopardizing the parent-child relationship, given the adversarial nature of such inquiries. Although some parents may successfully mislead the physician into erroneously diagnosing their child as being in need of committal, the Court concluded that this possibility was not a sufficient basis for nullifying the legislative framework followed in more than 30 states.[35]

In the balance of its opinion, the Court held the Georgia law constitutional. The case was, however, remanded to the district court for further proceedings. Included in the inquiry on remand was the procedural soundness of the periodic review procedures utilized at various Georgia hospitals.

Although minors who are wards of the state are in a different position from those with parents, the Court declined to require separate admission standards for each group. The lack of a concerned adult to care for a child who might otherwise be lost in the system, though, might justify different review procedures for minors who are state wards. This issue was also left to the district court on remand.[36]

In the companion class action case of Secretary of Public Welfare of Pennsylvania v. Institutionalized Juveniles, the Su-

[34] Id.
[35] Id. at 613, n.20.
[36] Id. at 621.

preme Court assessed the procedures outlined for voluntary commitment of children in that state.[37] Unlike the statutory scheme in Georgia, which was cast in general terms with admission procedures set on a hospital-by-hospital basis, the Pennsylvania statute and regulations were quite specific. They set forth certain time frames for evaluation and reassessment. The law also provided for a child to voice his objection to a plan of treatment, as well as three different ways for securing the release of a child less than 14 years of age. In addition, certain safeguards were included for the protection of mentally retarded minors. In view of the due process requirements set forth by the court in Parham v. J.R., it was held that the Pennsylvania laws were constitutional. As in *Parham*, the case was remanded to a U.S. district court for further proceedings. In the Pennsylvania case on remand, individual claims within the class as well as the matter of postadmission assessment procedures were to be reviewed.[38]

Although the Supreme Court has helped to clarify the law regarding admission of minors to mental health facilities, it has not addressed related issues. Some of the lower courts have had an opportunity to discuss these matters, including the use of medication and discharge of minor patients.

§5.8.4 Medication for Minors

In Johnson v. Solomon, a class action suit from Maryland, a U.S. district court held that ample precedent was available for developing guidelines regarding medication administered to minor patients.[39] The court held that in administering drugs to civilly committed juveniles, a notation must be made in the patient's record indicating, among other things, the therapeutic

[37] 442 U.S. 640 (1979).
[38] Id.
[39] 484 F. Supp. 278 (D. Md. 1979), referring to Nelson v. Hayne, 491 F.2d 352 (7th Cir. 1978), cert. denied, 417 U.S. 976 (1974); Pena v. New York State Div. of Youth, 419 F. Supp. 203 (S.D.N.Y. 1976).

reason for prescribing the medication. Furthermore, the court ruled that drugs cannot be used routinely except in an emergency.[40] As discussed in chapter 6, infra, a new body of case law is developing on the forcible administration of medication to mental health patients, which is bound to have some application to minors. Keeping abreast of these case law developments is therefore helpful in the discussion of the rights of minors.

§5.8.5 Consent to Release of Committed Minors

Another area of concern is the release from hospital of committed minor patients. At least one state statute addresses this issue squarely and provides for parental consent.[41] Some, however, are not clear on the matter. In a New Jersey case, a state law was challenged that did not specifically require parental consent or notice for the discharge of a minor patient.[42] A 15-year-old youth, who had been admitted to a mental hospital with his parent's signature, sought his own release. The court held that to require parental consent for the boy to leave the hospital would convert the child's status from that of a voluntary to an involuntary patient. This could not be done under applicable law. A minor or an adult has the right to be released after giving 72 hours' notice. Hospital authorities, believing a person to pose a serious danger to life or property if released, could apply to a court for involuntary commitment proceedings. However, absent such a belief, a minor does not require parental approval to secure her release.[43]

The decisions of the Supreme Court involving voluntary commitment of minors could be criticized on the ground that the opinions do not provide adequate protection to minors. What is often missed in the decisions of the various courts is the matter of consent. To be sure, constitutional rights are impor-

[40] Id. at 308-309, 315-316.
[41] Wyo. Stat. §25-3-109 (1981), in which release of a minor patient may be conditioned upon parental consent.
[42] In re Williams, 140 N.J. Super. 495, 356 A.2d 468 (1976).
[43] Id.

tant; however, in assessing whether a minor should be institutionalized for care, medical standards are not the only criteria. The decision should also take into account whether the person who is turning the child over for treatment understands the nature and risks of commitment, the various therapies to be used, and the availability — where applicable — of other modes of treatment. In those situations in which a minor seeks mental health or emotional treatment, the health care provider must make certain that the child understands the nature and consequences of psychiatric or psychological therapy. The rules for obtaining consent apply whether the minor is an outpatient or an inpatient. Constitutional safeguards may protect certain interests, but the law of consent applies to the day-to-day practical concerns of treatment.

Parental consent aside, there is a practical need to consider *notification* when a young person leaves a facility. Although it may be difficult to demonstrate a causal relationship between lack of notification and subsequent injury of a young person,[44] basic risk-management principles and common sense suggest it is best to avoid undue liability exposure by making it a policy to notify parents when their children are released.

§5.9   Sterilization of Mentally Incompetent Minors

Sterilization of minors has been the subject of a considerable number of legislative initiatives and judicial decisions. Deeply rooted in the issue of sterilization — whether it be for minors or adults — is the matter of consent. In this section, the contents of legislation on the subject are briefly discussed. Greater emphasis is placed on the case law found on sterilization of minors. It is this area of law that is the most provocative, for as pointed out below, judges are beginning to authorize the sterilization of

[44]See Hefty v. Comprehensive Care Corp., 752 P.2d 1231 (Or. Ct. App. 1988).

314

minors in the absence of a clear-cut legislative mandate to do so.

§5.9.1 Statutory Law

Over the years a number of states have enacted legislation setting forth procedural requirements for sterilization of mentally retarded minors. Although state sterilization laws sometimes specifically refer to minors, most legislation refers to individuals in terms of the mental handicap. Caution must be exercised in applying these laws in the absence of a clear-cut indication that the sterilization provisions apply to minors. Notwithstanding this concern, a few statutory examples are discussed in this section. The sterilization laws include a variety of legislative provisions. Most of the laws, however, require notice, an opportunity for a hearing, standards for decision-making, and appeal procedures.[1] Most of the laws apply to institutionalized individuals for whom an order for sterilization is requested by a parent[2] or the director of the health institution in which the patient resides.[3] Some of these laws do require that the patient voluntarily submit to the sterilization procedure.[4] Montana's law requires that, when possible, the consent of the patient be obtained.[5] If this is not possible, then the individual must be given an explanation of the proposed procedure. Standards of proof are also found in some of the laws. In two states the hearing body must be satisfied by a showing of clear and convincing evidence that the sterilization is necessary.[6] In West Virginia there must be proof that other forms of birth control

§5.9 [1] Idaho Code §§39-3901 et seq. (1971).

[2] Idaho Code §39-3903 (1971) (the director of the state department of health and welfare may also file the petition).

[3] N.C. Gen. Stat. §35-36 (1981). North Carolina also has a provision relating to sterilization of mentally retarded persons who are not institutionalized, N.C. Gen. Stat. §35-37 (1981).

[4] Mont. Code Ann. §53-23-104 (1974); Vt. Stat. Ann. tit. 18, §8702 (1968).

[5] Mont. Code Ann. §53-23-104 (1969).

[6] N.D. Cent. Code §25-01.2-11 (1981); Va. Code §54.325.9 (1981).

are not feasible.[7] Utah has enacted a sterilization law that delineates in very clear terms the requirements for informed consent.[8] The legislation deals with minors[9] and the factors to be considered in deciding on sterilization for a person incapable of giving informed consent.[10]

Despite this kind of specific legislation, a large portion of jurisdictions are without statutory law on sterilization of mentally retarded minors. Consequently, a body of case law has developed on the authority of courts to authorize sterilization of minors without enabling legislation.[11] Even in those jurisdictions with statutory law, a considerable number of decisions have been handed down on the subject.

§5.9.2 Judicial Limitations

In the United States, a split is evident among those courts that recognize the judiciary's authority to order sterilization in the absence of legislation[12] and those that do not.[13] In those states in which the courts have held that sterilizations may not proceed without enabling laws, the basis for decision has turned on lack of jurisdiction.[14] Many judges believe that authority to order sterilizations has to come from a specific grant of power from the legislature. In recent years, however, two state supreme courts have taken the position that additional specific power is not necessary to enable a court to order the sterilization of mentally retarded persons.[15] In each decision,

---

[7] W. Va. Code §27-16-1 (1974).

[8] Utah Code §§62A-6-101 through 62A-6-116 (1988).

[9] See Utah Code §62A-6-103 (1988).

[10] Utah Code §62A-6-108 (1988).

[11] See 74 A.L.R.3d 1210 (1976) and cases collected therein dealing with minors.

[12] See, e.g., In re Grady, 85 N.J. 235, 426 A.2d 467 (1981); Guardianship of Hayes, 93 Wash. 2d 228, 608 P.2d 635 (1980).

[13] In the Matter of D.D., 64 A.D.2d 898, 408 N.Y.S.2d 104 (1978); In re MKR, 515 S.W.2d 467 (Mo. 1974). See also 74 A.L.R.3d 1210 (1976).

[14] 74 A.L.R.3d 1210 (1976), and cases collected therein.

[15] In re Grady, 85 N.J. 235, 426 A.2d 467 (1981); Guardianship of Hayes, 93 Wash. 2d 228, 608 P.2d 635 (1980).

the court set forth specific guidelines for the trial court to follow in considering such matters. Of the two cases, the following addresses the issue of mentally retarded minors.

In the Matter of Guardianship of Hayes, the mother of a 16-year-old mentally retarded girl sought a court order appointing her as guardian of the child's person with authority to consent to a sterilization procedure.[16] The child functioned at the level of a 4- or 5-year-old. She was believed to be sexually active and it was considered quite likely that she might become pregnant. Both her parents and the physicians attending her believed that the long-term effects of traditional birth control were potentially harmful. They concluded that sterilization was the most desirable means of preventing her from having an unwanted pregnancy.

The Supreme Court of Washington reversed and remanded the lower court's decision dismissing the petition for lack of authority. In its opinion, the Washington Supreme Court held that the state constitution granted the trial court sufficient authority to consider and rule upon the petition.[17] It then proceeded to set forth some guiding principles in weighing the individual's right of privacy and fundamental right of procreation against those interests that favored sterilization. The guidelines set down are not too dissimilar from those included in a decision of the New Jersey Supreme Court dealing with a mentally retarded adult.[18] Nor is it the first time a court has put forth a procedure for assessing whether a retarded person should be sterilized.[19] The Washington court's principles are instructive and may be useful to those involved in similar proceedings. These include the following:

1. A disinterested guardian ad litem must be appointed to represent the incompetent.
2. The court is to obtain independent advice, including a

[16] 93 Wash. 2d 228, 608 P.2d 635 (Wash. 1980).
[17] Id.
[18] See In re Grady, 85 N.J. 235, 426 A.2d 467 (1981).
[19] See Wyatt v. Alderholt, 368 F. Supp. 1382 (Ala. 1973) (per curiam).

medical, social, and psychological assessment of the individual.

3. The court should seek and take into account the view of the individual.

The following determinations must be made on the basis of clear, convincing, and cogent evidence:

4. The individual is not capable of making a decision about sterilization.
5. The individual is unlikely in the foreseeable future to develop the facility for making an informed consent regarding sterilization.
6. The person is capable of bearing or fathering children.
7. The individual is or will in the near future engage in sexual activity that will likely result in conception.
8. Based on empirical evidence and not merely on standardized test criteria, the individual's disability leaves him or her permanently unable to care for a child, even with assistance.
9. All less drastic means of contraception have been attempted and have been found unworkable or inapplicable.
10. The proposed sterilization method is the least invasive of the individual's body.
11. The current state of medical science does not offer the prospect in the near future of a reversible sterilization procedure or other less drastic contraceptive.
12. Science is not on the verge of breakthrough in the treatment of the individual's disability.[20]

The court went one step further with minors. It noted that there is a "heavy presumption" against sterilization of a person who is not capable of giving an informed consent.[21] This presumption must be overcome by the individual seeking the

---

[20]Guardianship of Hayes, supra n.15, at 641.
[21]Id.

sterilization for the minor. The court added that with minors, due to their youth, this task would be more difficult or impossible to establish, requiring:

> Clear, cogent, and convincing evidence that he or she will never be capable of making an informed judgment about sterilization or of caring for a child.[22]

Should other courts adopt these judicial criteria for authorizing sterilizations in the absence of enabling legislation, meeting the test for minors would be impossible. The standard of proof, taken together with the Washington court's statement on minors, may effectively block sterilization of minors in those jurisdictions that follow the lead of Washington's high court.

In other states where statutory authority sets forth provisions governing sterilizations, the rights of some mentally retarded persons have been decided in cases involving minors. One notable case is Ruby v. Massey.[23] In that case three sets of parents sought an injunction to compel the University of Connecticut Health Center to end its refusal to perform sterilization operations on their three retarded daughters. All three were severely mentally retarded, blind, and deaf. They were residents of a special school during the week and they lived with their parents on weekends. Given their condition, it was inevitable that the children would require custodial care. One of the girls had begun menstruating and she could not look after her own personal hygiene. It was believed that the other two girls would follow a similar pattern. None of them could use standard forms of contraception. Their parents felt that their becoming pregnant could pose a serious threat to their health and lives: none of them could communicate with their physicians. In its ruling, the court held that, in the absence of statutory authority, the parents could not give consent to the sterilization of their children. The court also went one step further, noting that Connecticut law denied the parents equal protection of the

[22] Id.
[23] 452 F. Supp. 361 (D. Conn. 1978).

law in that statutory authority was available for the sterilization of some people confined to state institutions. The court issued an injunction barring the defendants from refusing to perform the sterilizations that would otherwise be available to inmates of state schools. As with the category of retarded persons confined to state facilities, consent or permission for the operations to be performed on noninstitutionalized persons is to be obtained from a probate court.[24] Not all courts, however, agree with the U.S. district court's analysis in *Ruby*.[25]

State laws specifically authorizing sterilization have also been the subject of judicial review. In the case of In re Moore's Sterilization, the Supreme Court of North Carolina was faced with a challenge to a state law allowing the sterilization of mentally ill or retarded persons.[26] Both the patient, a minor, and his mother consented to the performance of a vasectomy. The young man had a Full Scale IQ of below 40, and a Test Age Score of 8. In reversing the lower court's ruling that the laws were unconstitutional, the North Carolina Supreme Court held that the statutes did not offend due process or equal protection principles. The laws did provide an adequate judicial standard by which to assess each case. As applied to the case before it, the laws did not amount to cruel and unusual punishment. The court noted that in order for a sterilization order to issue, the evidence must be strong, convincing, and clear. While it could not give much weight to the patient's consent, his mother was certainly in a position to know what was in her son's best interests.[27]

Other courts have reviewed cases involving the application of state sterilization laws. However, these cases have principally involved adults.[28] Generally speaking, the courts have looked

[24] Id.
[25] Guardianship of Kemp, 43 Cal. App. 3d 758, 118 Cal. Rptr. 64 (1974).
[26] 221 S.E.2d 307 (N.C. 1976).
[27] Id.
[28] See, e.g., Matter of Johnson, 45 N.C. App. 649, 263 S.E.2d 805 (1980); North Carolina Assn. for Retarded Children v. State, 420 F. Supp. 451 (M.D.N.D. 1976); In re Cavitt, 174 Neb. 249, 157 N.W.2d 566 (1968), revd. and remanded, Neb. 157, N.W.2d 171 (1968).

for proper application of statutory requirements as well as constitutional considerations.[29] Procedural as well as substantive issues have been major considerations.

Sterilization being a virtually permanent form of contraception has caused the courts to move very cautiously, particularly with mentally incompetent individuals. Although a few courts are now prepared to recognize the authority of the judiciary to act upon sterilization petitions in the absence of specific legislation, the standards the petitioner must meet are very strict. In many cases, the petitioner will be unsuccessful in his bid.

F. IMMUNIZATION AND SCREENING OF CHILDREN

§5.10   Immunization

A topic of considerable importance to public health officials is the matter of immunization of children. As discussed below, state legislation typically outlines when children must be immunized, as well as those exceptional circumstances in which the requirement may be waived. The immunization of children goes beyond state legislative standards and includes the issue of consent to treatment. Some older case law suggests that consent may not be necessary. In this section, the legislative and judicial requirements for childhood immunization are discussed along with practical consent considerations.

§5.10.1   Legislative Standards

The vast majority of states have laws that govern childhood immunizations. Most prohibit school-age children from entering public or private educational facilities without a certificate

[29] 53 A.L.R.3d 960 (1973).

stating that they have the required immunizing vaccinations.[1] Some laws establish a provisional status that allows children to attend school while in the process of undergoing an immunization program.[2] Other laws extend beyond schools to include Head Start and day care programs.[3] Many of the laws set forth the specific series of shots a minor must receive.[4] Exemptions can be found that permit students to attend school without being immunized. The bases for these exemptions include religious beliefs and practices,[5] possibility of a danger to life or health from the immunizations,[6] and personal beliefs against immunizations.[7] In many jurisdictions, in the event of an epidemic, an unimmunized child may be temporarily suspended or excluded from school until the outbreak is over. Alternatively, she may be quarantined. Exclusion, suspension,

§5.10 [1] Ga. Code §32-911 (1979); Haw. Rev. Stat. §298-42 (1985); Iowa Code Ann. §139.9 (West 1985); Minn. Stat. Ann. §123.70 (1989); Miss. Code Ann. §41-23-37 (1978); Nev. Rev. Stat. §392.435 (1987); N.D. Cent. Code §23-07-17.1 (1979); Ohio Rev. Code Ann. §3313.671 (Baldwin 1984).

[2] Minn. Stat. Ann. §123.70 (West 1989); Miss. Code §41-23-37 (1983); Nev. Rev. Stat. §392.435 (1987); Ohio Rev. Code Ann. §3313.671 (Baldwin 1984); S.D. Codified Laws Ann. §13-28-7.1 (1978); Utah Code Ann. §55-22a-2 (1975).

[3] Ga. Code §99-223 (1977) (day care centers); Iowa Code Ann. §139.9 (West 1985) (child care center); N.D. Cent. Code §23-07-17.1 (1979) (day care center, child care facility, and Head Start program); Tenn. Code Ann. §49-6-5001 (1984) (day care).

[4] Fla. Stat. Ann. §232.032 (West 1986); Haw. Rev. Stat. §325-32 (1974); Minn. Stat. Ann. §123.70 (West 1989); Nev. Rev. Stat. §392.435 (1987); Texas Educ. Code Ann. §2.09 (Vernon 1981); W. Va. Code §16-3-4 (1987).

[5] Colo. Rev. Stat. §25-4-903 (1978); Conn. Gen. Stat. §10-204a (1984); Del. Code Ann. tit. 14, §131 (1980); Fla. Stat. Ann. §232.032 (West 1986); Ga. Code §32-911 (1979) and §99-223 (1977); Nev. Rev. Stat. §392.437 (1971); S.D. Codified Laws Ann. §13-28-7.1 (1978); Va. Code §32.1-46 (1981).

[6] Colo. Rev. Stat. §25-4-903 (1978); Conn. Gen. Stat. §10-204a (1978); Haw. Rev. Stat. §325-34 (1974); Minn. Stat. Ann. §123.70 (1989); Miss. Code Ann. §41-23-37 (1978).

[7] Colo. Rev. Stat. §25-4-903 (1978); Minn. Stat. Ann. §123.70 (1980) (conscientiously held beliefs); Mo. Ann. Stat. §167.181 (Vernon 1973) (written objection by parent or guardian); Ohio Rev. Code Ann. §3313.671 (Baldwin 1984) (parent or guardian objects to immunization for good cause); Okla. Stat. Ann. tit. 70, §1210.192 (West 1970) (written parental or guardian objection) and tit. 10, §413 (West 1979) (other reasons given by parent or guardian opposed to immunization); Wash. Rev. Code Ann. §28A.31.106 (1984).

or quarantine, however, can only be imposed for the diseases for which the child is not immunized.[8] In other states in the event of an epidemic, children may have to undergo immunization despite religious objections.[9]

A most interesting feature of Delaware's statute is the inclusion of a standardized affidavit that must be completed by a child's parents or guardian when claiming an exemption for religious belief.[10] In other states, the agencies charged with enforcing the immunization law are given the responsibility for promulgating rules and regulations.[11] Presumably, under this authority, methods are available for giving effect to claimed exemptions.

With specific vaccinations a condition to school attendance, little is set forth in state laws regarding informed consent or information to be provided to parents. There are exceptions. For example, Maine's statute requires that prior to vaccinating a female child of childbearing age against rubella, she is to be provided, as well as an individual in a parental role, with:

> . . . a description of the risks and benefits of receiving rubella vaccine, and the risks related to becoming pregnant within 3 months of receiving rubella vaccine.[12]

In New York the law requests that the "consent" of the person in a parental relation to the child be obtained.[13] Proper consent would probably entail some explanation of the risks and benefits and purpose of the prescribed vaccinations.

Even when a state law or regulation is silent on the issue, the

---

[8]Colo. Rev. Stat. §25-4-908 (1978) (quarantine legal alternative to immunization) (repeal effective July 1, 1983); Del. Code Ann. tit. 14, §131 (1980); Me. Rev. Stat. Ann. tit. 20, §1194 (1977); Mont. Code Ann. §20-5-405 (1983); Nev. Rev. Stat. §392.446 (1979); Wyo. Stat. §24-1-309 (1979).

[9]Ga. Code §32-911 (1979) and §99-223 (1977); Ky. Rev. Stat. §214.036 (1980).

[10]Del. Code Ann. tit. 14, §131 (1980).

[11]Cal. Health & Safety Code §303.5 (West 1979); N.C. Gen. Stat. §130-87 (1979).

[12]Me. Rev. Stat. Ann. tit. 20-A §6351 (1983).

[13]N.Y. Pub. Health Law §2164 (McKinney 1979).

health care provider must obtain consent prior to vaccinating a minor. His parents or guardian should be told the purpose of the vaccination as well as the risks and benefits. In addition, they should be forewarned about any reactions to expect or look for following the vaccination. Many state laws imply that a physician must discuss with and inform parents of immunizations. A dialogue with parents is necessary for the effective use of exemptions based on medical reasons. To determine if there is an appropriate basis for exempting a child from immunization, a physician must obtain an adequate medical history. Furthermore, failing to fully inform and to obtain the consent of the parents or legal guardian of the child could result in civil action. From a policy standpoint, parents or guardians reluctant to have a child immunized may change their minds if fully informed. Immunization should not be treated differently from any other medical procedure in terms of consent. Obtaining consent for this procedure is an important consideration that should not be overlooked by health professionals.

§5.10.2   *Case Decisions*

An important constitutional decision of the U.S. Supreme Court involved immunization.[14] A law review argues that, unlike the older cases based on religious beliefs and practices, the expanding right of privacy may form the basis for new decision-making in the area of immunization.[15] Whether such change would be readily accepted remains to be seen. The right of privacy is not absolute: it may be overcome by such compelling state interests as public welfare and prevention of epidemics.

In cases decided by state courts, one principal issue has been

---

[14]Jacobson v. Commonwealth of Massachusetts, 197 U.S. 11 (1905).
[15]Note, An Evaluation of Immunization Regulations in Light of Religious Objections and the Developing Right of Privacy. 4 U. Dayton L. Rev. 401-424 (1979).

the exemption from immunization based on religious beliefs,[16] although there have been other bases for challenge.[17] One opinion also included a consideration of whether a parent or guardian must be an actual member of a recognized religious sect or whether it was sufficient that she followed the religion's practices and beliefs.[18] The cases have not, however, focused on consent issues.

§5.11 Screening of Children for Health Risks

Several states have enacted laws designed to detect and prevent disabling illnesses in children. Some of the laws cover newborns, whereas others focus on school-age children. As with state laws for the immunization of school children, many jurisdictions grant religious exemptions to screening programs. Unlike vaccination, however, the potential for harm from testing is much reduced. Nonetheless, consent is still part of these procedures.

§5.11.1 Newborns

Two types of state laws discuss newborns and screening. Many states authorize the testing of newborns for metabolic disorders that can lead to serious consequences, including mental retardation. Among the diseases for which screening of newborns is performed are hypothyroidism,[1] phenylketonuria

---

[16]See, e.g., Sherr v. Northport-East Northport Univ. Free School Dist., 672 F. Supp. 81 (E.D.N.Y. 1987); Wright v. DeWitt School Dist., 238 Ark. 906, 385 S.W.2d 644 (1965); In re Gregory S., 85 Misc. 2d 846, 380 N.Y.S.2d 620 (1976).

[17]See, e.g., Hartman v. May, 168 Miss. 477, 151 So. 737 (1934) (immunization laws held not to be in conflict with compulsory education laws).

[18]Maier v. Bessler, 73 Misc. 2d 241, 341 N.Y.S.2d 411 (1972).

§5.11 [1]See, e.g., Ala. Code §22-20-3 (1979); Conn. Gen. Stat. §19-216 (1978); Kan. Stat. Ann. §65-180 (1980); Miss. Code Ann. §§41-21-201 and 41-21-203 (1988); Neb. Rev. Stat. §71-604.03 (1979); Tenn. Code Ann. §§68-5-301 and 68-5-302 (1980).

(PKU),[2] galactosemia,[3] sickle cell anemia or sickle cell trait,[4] maple syrup urine disease,[5] homocystinuria,[6] and other diseases.[7] In a few states, parents who object to this type of testing on religious grounds may have their child exempted from the screening procedures.[8]

The other type of medical procedure related to newborns involves prevention of blindness from ophthalmia neonatorum. The disease is defined as gonococcal conjunctivitis in the newborn.[9] Most states have laws that direct or authorize a health professional attending a birth to administer a prophylactic solution into a newborn's eyes.[10] Unlike those for the screening process for inborn metabolic disorders, the laws providing for prevention of infant blindness include few exceptions based on religious or other beliefs.[11] At least one state's law requires informing parents of the nature, risks, and consequences of not using the prophylactic solution in the child's eyes at birth.[12]

[2]See, e.g., Haw. Rev. Stat. §321-52.5 (1985); Ill. Ann. Stat. ch. 111 1/2, §4903 (Smith-Hurd 1983) and §4904 (Smith-Hurd 1982); N.J. Stat. Ann. 26:2-111 (1981); Pa. Stat. Ann. tit. 35, §621 (Purdon 1965).

[3]See, e.g., Conn. Gen. Stat. §19-216 (1978); La. Rev. Stat. Ann. §§40:1299, 40:1299.1 (West 1987); Ohio Rev. Code Ann. §3701.501 (Baldwin 1981); Wis. Stat. Ann. §146.02 (West 1986).

[4]See, e.g., Ga. Code §88-1201.1 (1972); N.Y. Pub. Health Law §2500-a (McKinney 1977).

[5]See, e.g., Wis. Stat. Ann. §146.02 (West 1986).

[6]See, e.g., N.Y. Pub. Health Law §2500-a (McKinney 1977); Ohio Rev. Code Ann. §3701.501 (Baldwin 1981).

[7]N.Y. Pub. Health Law §2500-a (McKinney 1977) (branched-chain ketonuria, histidinemia).

[8]See, e.g., Ala. Code §22-20-3 (1979); Conn. Gen. Stat. §19-216 (1978); Haw. Rev. Stat. §321-52.5 (1985); Ill. Ann. Stat. ch. 111 1/2, §4905 (Smith-Hurd 1965).

[9]Stedman's Medical Dictionary 986 (4th lawyers ed. 1976).

[10]See, e.g., Conn. Gen. Stat. §19-92 (1977); Fla. Stat. Ann. §383.04 (West 1987); Iowa Code Ann. §140.13 (West 1969); Kan. Stat. Ann. §65-153b (1974); Nev. Rev. Stat. §442.050 (1921); R.I. Gen. Laws §23-13-4 (1979); Wyo. Stat. §35-4-138 (1957).

[11]See, e.g., Fla. Stat. Ann. §383.04 (West 1987); Iowa Code Ann. §140.13 (West 1969); Kan. Stat. Ann. §65-153b (1974).

[12]S.D. Codified Laws Ann. §34-24-6 (1980).

§5.11.2   School-Age Children

Many jurisdictions have enacted laws directed at school-age children who may be at risk for certain types of health problems. Along with immunizations administered prior to or after entering school, many states require physical examinations and health assessments.[13] This may include tuberculosis testing and chest X-rays.[14] Once the children are enrolled, many states require school authorities to provide certain screening programs for them. These tests are usually designed to detect hearing[15] and visual[16] problems and sickle cell anemia,[17] as well as physicial defects such as scoliosis.[18] Provision is made in many of these laws for parents to object to examination of their children.[19]

§5.11.3   Obtaining Consent

Throughout the statutory laws setting forth screening programs for children, the matter of parental or guardian consent is given little attention. Those charged with administering these programs should consult with their legal advisors ·regarding

[13]See, e.g., Ill. Ann. Stat. ch. 122, §27-8.1 (Smith-Hurd 1988); Neb. Rev. Stat. §79-444 (1986); Va. Code §22.1-270 (1985).

[14]See, e.g., W. Va. Code §16-3-4a (1983) (tuberculosis testing and X-rays for those with positive tests).

[15]See, e.g., Ill. Ann. Stat. ch. 23, §233 (Smith-Hurd 1979); Me. Rev. Stat. Ann. tit. 20, §6451 (1983); Md. Educ. Code Ann. §7-403 (1978); Nev. Rev. Stat. §392.420 (1981); N.J. Stat. Ann. §18A:40-4 (West 1980).

[16]Ill. Ann. Stat. ch. 23, §2229 (Smith-Hurd 1979); Kan. Stat. Ann. §72-5205 (1959); Md. Educ. Code Ann. §7-403 (1978); Nev. Rev. Stat. §392.420 (1981); N.J. Stat. Ann. §18A:40-4 (West 1980).

[17]See, e.g., Mass. Gen. Laws. Ann. ch. 76, §15A (West 1971) (children may be tested prior to entering school); Miss. Code Ann. §41-24-1 (1983); N.M. Stat. Ann. §24-3-1 (1973).

[18]See, e.g., Nev. Rev. Stat. §392.420 (1981); Wash. Rev. Code Ann. §28A.31.134 (1985).

[19]See, e.g., Ill. Ann. Stat. ch. 23, §2336 (Smith-Hurd 1979); Nev. Rev. Stat. §392.420 (1981); N.J. Stat. Ann. §18A:40-4 (West 1980); Wash. Rev. Code Ann. §28A.31.140 (1985).

requirements for obtaining authorization for these tests. At a minimum, parents should be notified of the tests' availability, the purpose for the examinations, probable risks and benefits, as well as other relevant follow-up information. Notice about the tests should not be transmitted to parents by letters taken home by students, unless there is a requirement that the parents in some way indicate their desire for the child to have the tests. This could take the form of a written authorization taken back to the school by the student or a telephone call to the school offices. Parental or guardian permission is necessary: the tests do involve medical interventions. So-called negative consent, in which the burden is on parents to voice their objection before testing proceeds, does not really constitute a valid consent. A sound procedure to inform parents and to gain their cooperation is the most satisfactory means of dealing with school-based screening programs.

G. TREATMENT OF MINORS IN CRISIS SITUATIONS

§5.12   Emergency Treatment

As noted earlier in the chapter (§5.2.1), the courts in some states have recognized in the common law an exception allowing for emergency treatment of minors. In other states a different approach has been taken: legislation has been enacted authorizing such care without parental or guardian permission.[1] The format of the emergency treatment laws vary; some

§5.12 [1]See, e.g., Ill. Ann. Stat. ch. 111, §4503 (Smith-Hurd 1984); Fla. Stat. Ann. §743.064 (West 1986); La. Rev. Stat. Ann. §40:1299.54 (West 1975); Miss. Code Ann. §41-41-7 (1966); Okla. Stat. Ann. tit. 10, §170.2 (West 1974).

include definitions of the type of emergency that will excuse consent.[2] For example, in Missouri, an emergency is defined as:

> a situation wherein, in competent medical judgment, the proposed surgical or medical treatment or procedures are immediately or imminently necessary and any delay occasioned by an attempt to obtain a consent would reasonably jeopardize the life, health or limb of the person affected, or would reasonably result in disfigurement or impairment of faculties.[3]

In a few states minors are specifically singled out for application of emergency treatment laws,[4] whereas in others they are included in legislation also applicable to adults.[5]

Provisions in some of the emergency treatment laws exculpate health professionals from liability for providing treatment without parental consent.[6] It is important to note, however, that these laws will not insulate professionals from liability for acts of negligence.[7]

If legislation is silent on the matter of emergency treatment of minors, health personnel should check applicable common law principles in the state. The common law in many states has long recognized that an emergency will excuse the need for consent from a child's parent or guardian;[8] authorization may

---

[2] See, e.g., La. Rev. Stat. Ann. §40:1299.54 (West 1975); Miss. Code Ann. §41-41-7 (1966).

[3] Mo. Ann. Stat. §431.063 (Vernon 1977).

[4] Ill. Ann. Stat. ch. 111, §4503 (Smith-Hurd 1984); Fla. Stat. Ann. §743.064 (West 1986); Kan. Stat. Ann. §65-2891 (1986); Okla. Stat. Ann. tit. 10, §170.2 (West 1974).

[5] La. Rev. Stat. Ann. §1299.54 (West 1975); Miss. Code Ann. §41-41-7 (1966); Mo. Ann. Stat. §431.063 (Vernon 1977). See also Miss. Code Ann. §41-41-9 (1966). Under this statute courts can order treatment for minors and adults of unsound mind who are in need of immediate surgical or medical care.

[6] Kan. Stat. Ann. §65-2891 (1986).

[7] Id.

[8] See, e.g., Tabor v. Scobee, 254 S.W.2d 474 (Ky. 1952); Wells v. McGehee, 39 So.2d 196 (La. 1949); Sullivan v. Montgomery, 155 Misc. 448, 278 N.Y.S. 575 (1938).

be implied.[9] It is necessary, however, to make certain the situation meets the criteria for an "emergency."

§5.12.1 Sexually Assaulted Minors

Several state legislatures have enacted statutes authorizing the examination and treatment of minors alleged to be the victims of sexual assault.[10] The laws also authorize the collection of evidence during the examination for use against the victim's assailant in subsequent action.[11] Physicians examining and treating minors are usually obliged to notify their parents or guardians,[12] unless there is a suspicion that the assault was perpetrated by one of those individuals.[13] The California statute requires the treating physician to write a specific note in the patient's chart regarding attempts to contact the child's parent or guardian.[14]

The statutes generally require that minors agree to examination and treatment. Parental or guardian permission is not necessary.[15] In some states, minors are also to be informed of the availability of services for venereal disease, pregnancy, medical, and psychiatric care.[16]

Since many states are without statutory law authorizing the care and treatment of minors believed to be sexually assaulted,

[9]See, e.g., Jackovach v. Yocum, 212 Iowa 914, 237 N.W. 444 (1931).
[10]Cal. Civ. Code §34.9 (West 1977); Colo. Rev. Stat. §13-22-106 (1979); Kan. Stat. Ann. §65-448 (1977); Ky. Rev. Stat. §216B.400 (1978); Mo. Ann. Stat. §191.225 (Vernon 1980); Ohio Rev. Code Ann. §2907.29 (Baldwin 1975).
[11]Id.
[12]Cal. Civ. Code §34.9 (West 1977); Colo. Rev. Stat. §13-22-106 (1979); Ky. Rev. Stat. §65-448 (1977); Mo. Ann. Stat. §191.225 (Vernon 1980); Ohio Rev. Code Ann. §2907.29 (Baldwin 1975).
[13]Cal. Civ. Code §34.9 (West 1977).
[14]Id.
[15]Cal. Civ. Code §34.9 (West 1977); Colo. Rev. Stat. §13-22-106 (1979); Kan. Stat. Ann. §65-448 (1977); Ky. Rev. Stat. §216B.400 (1978); Mo. Ann. Stat. §191.225 (Vernon 1980); Ohio Rev. Code Ann. §2907.29 (Baldwin 1975).
[16]Ky. Rev. Stat. §216B.400 (1978); Ohio Rev. Code Ann. §2907.29 (Baldwin 1975).

it is necessary to review other applicable laws. Sexually assaulted minors might fall within the scope of mature minor or emancipated minor legislation or case law. In addition, a given state might provide for treatment in the absence of parental authority under applicable emergency treatment laws and cases or child abuse legislation.

Throughout the United States rape crisis centers and counselling personnel are available whose assistance can be invaluable in working with sexually assaulted minors. Some programs are hospital based. These programs and counselling officers work with health professionals and law enforcement personnel to develop examination and evidence collection techniques, as well as to provide the types of information to be disclosed to the victim regarding available services.

§5.13   Child Abuse

A variety of legislation can be found dealing with child abuse and neglect.[1] Some legislation includes reporting requirements about suspected or known cases of child abuse.[2] There is also some case authority about the duty to warn regarding suspected cases of child abuse.[3]

In addition to the reporting requirements, provision is made for medical examination and treatment of abused or neglected children. In Texas a physician or dentist having reason to believe that a child has been abused or neglected may examine him without the consent of the child or parent.[4] However, no examination can take place when the child is 16 years of age or older and refuses, or when a court has issued an order refusing consent to the examination. The physician or dentist is immune

---

§5.13   [1] For a compilation of statutory law on child abuse and neglect in the United States, see U.S. Dept. of Health and Human Services, Child Abuse and Neglect, 35 (D.H.H.S. Publication No. (OHDS) 80-30265) (1979).
[2] Id. at 3-4.
[3] Landeros v. Flood, 17 Cal. 3d 399, 551 P.2d 389, 131 Cal. Rptr. 69 (1976).
[4] Texas Fam. Code Ann. §35.04 (Vernon 1975).

from liability for examining the child without consent, unless she is negligent.[5]

Courts can order examination and treatment of children suspected of being abused or neglected.[6] Judicial authority often extends to ordering care for children who have been determined after a court hearing to be abused or neglected.[7] In some states other individuals may be authorized to consent to treatment for abused or neglected children.[8]

If state legislation is silent on authorization for medical examination and treatment of children suspected of being abused or neglected, health personnel should review applicable state child welfare or health regulations. Under this body of law, power may be provided to conduct these examinations and to dispense care in the absence of consent from a parent or guardian. In lieu of regulatory authority, another avenue is emergency treatment legislation and case law. A child who, due to abuse or neglect, requires immediate or life-saving treatment may come within this type of law.

§5.14 Delinquent and Deprived Children

Children placed under or committed to the authority of a state agency for delinquent or deprived minors are the subject of various pieces of state legislation. In some instances, courts are empowered to order medical, physical, and psychological examinations, which are taken into account in final adjudication.[1]

---

[5]Id.

[6]See, e.g., N.J. Stat. Ann. §9:6-8.31 (West 1977).

[7]See, e.g., Minn. Stat. Ann. §260.191 (West 1978), wherein a court can order special treatment for a child who has been found neglected, dependent or neglected and in foster care.

[8]N.Y. Soc. Serv. Law §383-b (McKinney 1986), wherein the local commissioner of social services or local commissioner of health is authorized to consent to medical, dental, and other services for abused or neglected children.

§5.14   [1]Colo. Rev. Stat. §23-23-103 (1983); La. Rev. Stat. Ann. §13:1583 (West 1979); Miss. Code Ann. §43-23-21 (1964).

Medical care and surgical treatment can also be initiated whenever it is found necessary for the child's well-being prior to a final disposition.[2] Other governmental bodies or agencies — or individuals in some states — are authorized to consent to needed care for a child in their custody.[3]

Both Kansas and Oregon have interesting statutory provisions dealing with consent to treatment for children who are deprived or delinquent. The Kansas statute indicates the types of procedures to which the person having custody of the child may consent. Provision is made for objection of the child or parent to certain forms of care that are contrary to religious beliefs or tenets.[4] A separate provision immunizes health care providers who, in good faith and according to statutory law, provide treatment to a child without first obtaining parental consent. Health care providers are immune from civil or criminal liability for lack of consent.[5]

The Oregon law also details those situations in which a physician, a dentist, or a hospital may treat a child who is the ward of a court, dependent, or delinquent. The Oregon statute bars assault and battery actions against those who meet the statutory requirements.[6]

Foster care programs often set out requirements for consent in the event that a child is in need of medical attention.[7] For example, in California persons providing residential foster care may not give consent to medical or dental treatment for a foster child except "that consent may be given for ordinary medical treatment . . . including but not limited to immunizations, physicial examinations and x-rays. . . ."[8]

In the absence of statutory law on treatment of delinquent

---

[2]Nev. Rev. Stat. §62.240 (1963); Tenn. Code. Ann. 37-1-128 (1981); Va. Code §16.1-275 (1984).

[3]Kan. Stat. Ann. §38-843 (1979); Ky. Rev. Stat. §208A.230 (eff. July 1982); Me. Rev. Stat. Ann. tit. 22, §3-B (1977).

[4]Kan. Stat. Ann. §38-843 (1979).

[5]Kan. Stat. Ann. §38-845 (1979).

[6]Or. Rev. Stat. §418.307 (1975).

[7]Cal. Health and Safety Code §1530.6 (1977).

[8]Id.

and deprived minors, health personnel should turn to pertinent regulations. These can contain rules and procedures for consent to medical or surgical care for minors in a custodial setting. Additionally, the common law rule relating to emergency treatment or statutory emergency care legislation may provide authority for treatment of those minors requiring either immediate or life-saving attention.

H. DRUG AND MEDICAL CARE IN SCHOOLS

§5.15   Legislation Authorizing Treatment

Some legislation has been passed to deal with the administration of drugs or medical treatment in school. The laws extend from giving students prescribed medication[1] to taking a child, if necessary, to a hospital for evaluation or treatment.[2] The rules vary in whom they authorize to administer care to a student. For example, in Massachusetts a registered nurse or a licensed physician can administer psychotropic medication to a public school student.[3] In Michigan school administrators and teachers can administer medication to a student with the written permission of the child's parent or guardian. Additionally, the drug must be administered in the presence of another adult. As long as the drug is given in good faith and in compliance with the instructions of a physician and the statute, the teacher or administrator cannot be criminally or civilly liable. However, he does remain liable for gross negligence or willful and wanton negligence.[4]

In other states, school administrators have the authority to dispense medication to students. At a minimum, school person-

---

§5.15   [1] Mich. Stat. Ann. §380.1178 (1978).
[2] Mass. Gen. Laws Ann. ch. 71, §55A (West 1985); N.J. Stat. Ann. §18A:40-4.1 (West 1972).
[3] Mass. Gen. Laws Ann. ch. 71, §54B (West 1973).
[4] Mich. Stat. Ann. §380.1178 (1978).

nel should have a written letter from a child's parent or guardian requesting that the teacher or administrator give the child the medication. Prior to giving a drug to a child, the teacher or administrator should understand completely the means of dispensing the medication, as well as the dosage. When possible side effects or reactions to the drug can be anticipated, this information and instructions for follow-up care should be provided to school personnel.

Should a student become ill or be injured while at school, established procedures usually exist for getting the child needed medical attention. These include contacting the school nurse, school physician, and the child's parent or guardian. In a serious situation, either the common law or statutory emergency treatment rule applies.

I. REFUSAL OF CONSENT TO TREATMENT

§5.16 Parental Refusal

Over the years, American courts and legislatures have developed laws relating to parents who refuse medical treatment for their children. Different approaches have developed for life-saving treatment and elective measures refused by parents on behalf of their offspring. Similarly, different steps have been taken with persons who decline medical care in favor of spiritual healing from those taken with individuals who simply do not provide treatment for their children. Yet a more difficult category comprises children with terminal or potentially terminal illnesses. These situations are all addressed below in the context of the right to refuse treatment for children.

§5.16.1 Statutory Limits

Several states have passed laws recognizing the right of patients, including minors, to decline treatment that conflicts with their religious beliefs and practices.[1] The exercise of this right may, however, be limited when there is the threat of communicable disease or possible danger to the health of others.[2]

In other jurisdictions, statutes recognize that parents may treat their children through spiritual means. In Oklahoma, for example, parental rights cannot be terminated solely on the basis that the parents, in good faith, provided spiritual rather than medical treatment for their children. However, a court may assume custody of and order treatment for the child.[3]

Parents refusing life-saving medical care for their children may have their wishes overruled by court order. For example, in Idaho,[4] Maine,[5] and North Carolina,[6] physicians or other health personnel designated in the statutes may petition a court for an order compelling medical treatment. The order is sought when parents fail or refuse to give their consent and professional opinion suggests that without care, the child's life is greatly endangered.[7] The Maine provision requires a summary of the medical diagnosis and treatment alternatives, as well as a request for the court to order a particular type of treatment.[8] In acute circumstances, health personnel may act on a judge's verbal order.[9] Opportunity for a hearing is included, and provided the situation allows for it, a proceeding prior to issuing the order authorizing treatment.[10] The Idaho law specifically states that the court, in issuing an order overriding the parent's refusal of consent,

§5.16 [1]Cal. Welf. & Inst. Code §5006 (West 1969); N.J. Stat. Ann. §26:1A-66 (West 1947); N.J. Stat. Ann. §30:4-7.6 (West 1969), and §9.1-1.1 (West 1950); Pa. Stat. Ann. tit. 24, §14-1419 (Purdon 1957); Utah Code Ann. §26-15-86 (1953).

[2]See, e.g., N.J. Stat. Ann. §26:1A-66 (West 1947), §9:6-1.1 (West 1950); Utah Code Ann. §26-15-86 (1953).

[3]Okla. Stat. Ann. tit. 10, §1130 (West 1987).

[4]Idaho Code §16-1616 (1976).

[5]Me. Rev. Stat. Ann. tit. 22, §4071 (1979).

[6]N.C. Gen. Stat. §7A-732 (1979).

[7]Idaho Code §16-1616 (1976).

[8]Me. Rev. Stat. Ann. tit. 22, §4070 (1979).

[9]Idaho Code §16-1616 (1976); N.C. Gen. Stat. §7A-732 (1979).

[10]Id. See also Me. Rev. Stat. Ann. tit. 22, §4071 (1979).

take into consideration any treatment being given the child by spiritual means alone, if the child or his parent, guardian or legal custodian are adherents of a bona fide religious denomination that relies exclusively on this form of treatment in lieu of medical treatment.[11]

In other jurisdictions, courts may be empowered to order treatment despite parental objection under child welfare or child neglect legislation. Resort to the courts under appropriate legislation to compel medical care for minors has been done frequently with the Jehovah's Witnesses, who decline blood transfusions as being contrary to their religious beliefs.[12] However, as seen in the discussion below, this group is not alone as the subject of litigation for refusing medical treatment for children.

§5.16.2   Judicial Limits

In the United States, the courts have usually drawn a distinction between children requiring immediate attention and those for whom remedial or elective care is required. Cases have reached the courts when parents have declined treatment on the basis of religious[13] or philosophical belief[14] or of selection of a type of treatment different from that recommended by physicians.[15] Courts will not permit parents to withhold treatment when the only option is death.[16]

The courts have generally authorized medical care for children requiring immediate, life-saving treatment. Many cases

[11]Idaho Code §16-1616 (1976).
[12]See, e.g., Bates v. Jensen, 20 Wash. App. 81, 579 P.2d 374 (1978); Jehovah's Witnesses in the State of Washington v. King County Hosp., 278 F. Supp. 488 (W.D. Wash. 1967); In re Vasko, 238 A.D. 128, 263 N.Y.S. 552 (1933).
[13]See references in n.12.
[14]In Heinemann's Appeal, 96 Pa. 112 (1880).
[15]Matter of Hofbauer, 65 A.D.2d 108, 411 N.Y.S.2d 416 (1979).
[16]See Joswick by Joswick v. Lenox Hill Hosp., 510 N.Y.S.2d 803 (Sup. Ct. 1986).

have arisen when parents have declined to permit treatment on the ground that it conflicts with religious beliefs and practices.[17] Actions are then instituted under applicable child welfare and neglect legislation or other statutes to have the child removed — at least temporarily — from the custody of the parents. The agency or person in whom custody is vested is then authorized to consent to such medical care as is deemed necessary.[18]

The basis for court intervention is rooted firmly in both constitutional and common law. Over 100 years ago, the U.S. Supreme Court drew a distinction between religious belief and religious practice.[19] The court held that the First Amendment protects religious belief, but the state may impose restrictions on practice. Thus a religious practice that jeopardizes the health, safety, or welfare of the people can be limited.[20]

The other basis for court intervention is the state's parens patriae power. Parents are presumed at law to provide for the necessities of life required by their children. If a parent fails in this regard, by refusing to provide the child with necessary medical care, the state may step in to protect the child and get the required care.[21]

Both the constitutional and common law have come together in cases in which parents have refused consent to medical care for their children.[22] In other cases the matter of religious freedom was not squarely at issue and instead the courts were faced with a challenge to the state's asserted parens patriae power. For example, in a Missouri case an action was filed under child neglect statutes in order to enable doctors to provide blood transfusions to a 12-day-old infant suffering from erythroblastic anemia.[23] The child was made a ward of the court, which

---

[17] See, e.g., In re Vasko, 238 A.D. 128, 263 N.Y.S. 552 (1933); In re Willmann, 24 Ohio App. 3d 191, 493 N.E.2d 1380 (1986).
[18] See, e.g., Mitchell v. Davis, 205 S.W.2d 812 (Tex. Civ. App. 1947).
[19] Reynolds v. United States, 98 U.S. 145 (1887).
[20] Hill v. State, 38 Ala. App. 404, 88 So. 2d 880, cert. denied, 264 Ala. 697, 88 So. 2d 887 (1956) (state ban on snake-handling ritual sustained).
[21] In re Vasko, 238 A.D. 128, 263 N.Y.S. 552 (1933).
[22] See, e.g., Gates v. Jensen, 20 Wash. App. 81, 579 P.2d 374 (1978).
[23] Morrison v. State, 252 S.W.2d 97 (Mo. Ct. App. 1952).

ordered that the treatment be given. In an appeal of the decision, the child's father, a Jehovah's Witness, asserted that he had refused consent because blood transfusions were contrary to his religion. It was argued that a child could not be "neglected" within the meaning of the legislation simply because the parents refused medical care. The court held that, under its parens patriae authority, the state could act to safeguard and protect the child. As the court pointed out:

> The fact that the subject is an infant child of a parent who, arbitrarily, puts his own theological belief higher than his duty to preserve the life of his child cannot prevail over the considered judgment of an entire people, in a case such as this.[24]

There have been many more cases involving Jehovah's Witnesses who have refused blood transfusions for their children. The courts have followed the same approach as described above: when a child is in need of immediate care, it is to be provided even over parental objection. Children, in the eyes of the courts, cannot be made to suffer as a result of religious principles held by their parents.[25]

Parents who insist upon treating their children through spiritual healing have also been the subject of litigation. In an Oregon case, a 15-month-old child was put in state custody for surgical treatment of hydrocephaly.[26] Her parents were opposed to surgery on the ground that they believed in treatment of illness through prayer. The Oregon Court of Appeals affirmed the juvenile court's ruling. Although the child was not in immediate danger, the court noted that without corrective surgery the infant would be mentally retarded and suffer severe physical difficulties. Among the arguments raised on appeal, the parents contended that the order placing the child in state custody and compelling treatment violated their constitu-

[24] Id. at 101.
[25] See, e.g., State v. Perricone, 37 N.J. Super. 517, 171 A.2d 140 (Juv. Ct. 1961); Application of Brooklyn Hosp., 45 Misc. 2d 914, 258 N.Y.S.2d 621 (Sup. Ct. 1965); In re Clark, 21 Ohio Op. 2d 86, 185 N.E.2d 128 (1962).
[26] Gates v. Jensen, 20 Wash. App. 81, 579 P.2d 374 (1978).

tionally protected rights to family integrity, privacy, and freedom of religion. The court rejected these assertions, stating that the parental right to provide a child with religious training did not extend to a denial of treatment necessary for the child's health and well-being.[27]

In Mitchell v. Davis, a 12-year-old boy was declared neglected and placed in state custody when his mother refused to provide him with necessary medical attention.[28] The youngster had an arthritic condition that had deteriorated over time. His mother believed in healing through prayer and was opposed to traditional medical treatment. In its ruling on the matter, the Texas Court of Civil Appeals stated:

> Medicines, medical treatment and attention are in a category with food, clothing, lodging and education as necessaries from parent to child, for which the former is held legally responsible.
> . . . An omission to do this is a public wrong which the state, under its police power may prevent.[29]

Generalized religious or philosophical beliefs against medical care stated as the basis for denying a child life-saving treatment can also be overcome in a proper challenge. This power was demonstrated in a New York decision involving a 2-year-old girl who had a tumor behind her left eye that doctors believed was malignant.[30] Left untouched, it would probably spread to the brain and cause death. A 50 percent chance of cure was estimated if the permanently blinded eye and the tumor were removed. The child's parents opposed surgery. Her mother preferred to have the child as she was without the operation. She believed that God had given her the child; it was up to God to do what He wanted with her. The appellate court affirmed the lower court's ruling that the child fell within the scope of child neglect legislation. It pointed out that laws had been

---

[27]Id.
[28]205 S.W.2d 812 (Tex. Civ. App. 1947).
[29]Id. at 813.
[30]In re Vasko, 238 A.D. 128, 263 N.Y.S. 552 (1933).

enacted for the protection of children and the child in this case was entitled to benefit from the legislation.[31]

In situations in which a child is not afflicted with a life-threatening disease or illness, the courts have been more reluctant to step in and require treatment. For example, in a Pennsylvania case the supreme court of that state reversed a lower court finding that declared a 16-year-old boy a neglected child.[32] The youngster had suffered two bouts of polio that left him with a severe curvature of the spine, impeding his ability to walk or stand. There was some suggestion that without an operation to correct the spinal curvature, the boy would become bedridden and ultimately experience a shortened life span. However, no evidence pointed to the youngster's life being in immediate danger without surgery. His mother, a Jehovah's Witness, consented to the recommended spinal surgery on the condition that it be performed without blood transfusions. Proceedings were then commenced to have the child declared neglected and to have a guardian appointed who would consent to the surgery without such a limitation.

In revising the lower court's ruling, the Supreme Court of Pennsylvania noted that this case was distinguishable from others in which parental religious objections were overriden by a state interest in protecting a child whose life was imminently endangered. Since the boy in this case was not in immediate danger, no sufficient basis existed to overrule the mother's religious principles. The court went one step further and remanded the case to the family division of the court of common pleas for a determination of any religious conflicts between the youth and his mother.[33]

In a New York case, a similar conclusion was reached involving a 14-year-old boy with a cleft palate and harelip.[34] The boy's father objected to corrective surgery, preferring that his son undergo self-healing in accordance with the father's per-

---

[31] Id.

[32] In re Green, 448 Pa. 338, 292 A.2d 387 (1972), revg., 220 Pa. Super. 191, 286 A.2d 681 (1971).

[33] Id.

[34] In re Seiforth, 309 N.Y. 80, 127 N.E.2d 820 (1955).

sonal philosophy. A judge of the children's court denied a petition by local health department officials for a court order authorizing surgery. Evidence revealed that no emergency was involved. The boy followed his father's philosophy and wanted to continue trying to heal himself through natural means. In addition, it was revealed that even with the corrective surgery, the boy would never speak normally without total cooperation in a concentrated program of speech therapy. The trial court doubted that the youngster would be cooperative, given the philosophy he shared with his father and the latter's influence.

In affirming the children's court ruling, the New York Court of Appeals noted that this was not a situation in which the child's life was endangered. Given the lower court's findings, the initial decision had been proper not to compel surgery.[35]

Not all courts agree, however, that lack of interference is proper in nonemergency situations. A New York court ordered that a rather risky operation be performed on a 15-year-old boy who suffered from a disfiguring, incurable disease.[36] Although not fatal, the illness had badly distorted the boy's facial features and neck. Due to his appearance the youth had been exempted from school, and as a result he was behind educationally and psychologically.[37] The court found that the boy came within the category of neglected children. Despite the religious objections of the child's mother to the use of any blood transfusions, the court order stated that whole blood could be administered. It was noted by the court that the judiciary may order surgery even when the child's underlying condition poses no risk to his life or health, particularly in situations where an operation "was required."[38] The lower court ruling was sustained per curiam by the New York Court of Appeals.[39]

Intervention may also occur when posttreatment monitoring

[35] Id.
[36] In re Sampson, 29 N.Y.2d 900, 328 N.Y.S.2d 686, 278 N.E.2d 918 (1972) (per curiam).
[37] In re Sampson, 65 Misc. 2d 658, 317 N.Y.S.2d 641, affd., 37 A.D.2d 668, 323 N.Y.S.2d 253 (1970).
[38] Id.
[39] Supra n.36.

is at issue. For example, in a California case,[40] a child had undergone surgical removal of one eye for retinal blastoma. After the operation, the physicians treating the youngster expressed concern that the malignancy had not been removed completely and recommended chemotherapy and radiation, which his parents refused. The parents were Christian Scientists who preferred that the child see an accredited Christian Science practitioner. In January 1984 the youngster was declared a dependent child. The boy was placed in the custody of his parents and they had to facilitate the youngster's receiving a series of regularly specified tests and treatments. This included spinal taps, radiation, and chemotherapy.

The county social services agency overseeing the child's case was advised by the attending physician that court-ordered treatment would conclude in March 1985. However, the doctor recommended a two-year "observation phase"[41] that would require similar testing and procedures but on a less frequent basis. A periodic review hearing was held before a juvenile court referee. The idea of an observational phase was the subject of much testimony. The referee ordered that the child be kept in dependent child status. When the juvenile court refused to reconsider the referee's order an appeal followed.[42]

The parents claimed that the juvenile court was without jurisdiction to continue the child's dependency status. The court quickly dispatched this contention. As the court indicated, the state need not wait until there is a need for immediate treatment in order to take action. "Reasonable apprehension stands as an accepted basis for the exercise of State power."[43] Although in this case there was no evidence of cancer, there was no reason in law why the state should forestall the exercise of its protective powers until the threatened harm became an actuality. Therefore, the court ruled that the court had jurisdiction to continue the child's dependency status.

[40] In re Eric B. v. Ted B., 189 Cal. App. 3d 996, 235 Cal. Rptr. 22 (1987).
[41] Id. at 1000, 235 Cal. Rptr. at 23.
[42] Id. at 1001, 235 Cal. Rptr. at 24.
[43] Id. at 1003, 235 Cal. Rptr. at 25.

The finding of the referee that continued dependency was in the child's best interests was substantiated by the evidence. As medical testimony indicated, there was a 25 percent chance of recurrence of the cancer and perhaps a 40 percent chance of death without follow-up testing and corrective action. The child's father made it clear that unless ordered by the court to do so, he would not have his son's condition monitored. This was sufficient evidence to suggest that it was in the child's best interests to continue his dependency status.

The *Sampson* ruling is perhaps an exception that proves the generally accepted rule concerning court compulsion of medical care for minors. The case involved a relatively risky surgical procedure that could not cure the child's underlying disease. The decision was based on what the court labelled "required" surgery, yet there was no explanation of what distinction could be drawn between required and life-threatening surgery. Moreover, the court did not fully develop its authority for the proposition that a court could overrule parental religious objections when a child's life or health was not endangered, though it did rely heavily on a U.S. district court decision.[44] Whether other courts will depart from the general rule as well and adopt the *Sampson* court's broad construction of a judge's mandate remains to be seen.

§5.16.3   Treatment Decisions for Disabled Children

Children born with severe physical defects requiring medical or surgical intervention may be refused treatment when their parents decline to authorize care. This situation was publicized in an article that appeared in the New England Journal of Medicine in 1973.[45] Withdrawing or withholding medical treat-

---

[44]Jehovah's Witnesses in the State of Washington v. King County Hosp., 278 F. Supp. 488 (W.D. Wash. 1967), affd., 390 U.S. 598 (1968), rehg. denied, 391 U.S. 961 (1968).

[45]Duff & Campbell, Moral and Ethical Dilemmas in the Special-Care Nursery, 289 New Eng. J. Med. 890 (1973).

ment from disabled children has been hotly debated by ethicists and clergy;[46] the matter has also received judicial attention.[47]

In a California case, a 12-year-old boy with Down's syndrome had a ventricular septal defect of the heart that his physicians believed necessitated surgery. Left untouched, the heart problem could result in death.[48] His parents decided against the surgery and refused their consent. Evidence in the case revealed that the child, due to the Down's syndrome, ran a greater than average risk of postsurgical complications. In fact his congenital heart defect had already caused some vascular changes. There was also a risk that surgery could damage the nerves controlling the child's hearbeat, resulting in the need for a pacemaker.

The appellate court affirmed the lower court's ruling dismissing a petition to have the boy declared a dependent child. In its opinion the court noted that parental autonomy over children is not absolute. The state may step in when parents fail to discharge their responsibilities toward their children. The court made it clear that the state's request to intervene must take into account several factors, including the seriousness of harm to the child, an assessment by physicians for care, risks of providing treatment, and the child's preferences, if any.[49] Throughout its evaluation, the paramount considerations for the state are the child's welfare and whether surgery would be in his best interest. In reviewing the evidence presented, the appellate court found that there was sufficient evidence to support the lower tribunal's ruling against declaring the child dependent for purposes of authorizing surgery.[50]

In a New York decision involving a minor born with menin-

---

[46]Fletcher, Abortion, Euthanasia and Care of Defective Newborns, 292 New Eng. J. Med. 75-78 (1975); McCormick, To Save or Let Die: The Dilemma of Modern Medicine, 229 JAMA 172-176 (1974).

[47]In re Phillip B., 92 Cal. App. 3d 796, 156 Cal. Rptr. 48 (1979), cert. denied, Bothman v. Warren B., 445 U.S. 949 (1980); Application of Cicero, 101 Misc. 2d 699, 421 N.Y.S.2d 965 (N.Y. Sup. Ct. 1979).

[48]In re Phillip B., 92 Cal. App. 3d 796, 156 Cal. Rptr. 48 (1979), cert. denied, Bothman v. Warren B., 445 U.S. 949 (1980).

[49]Id.

[50]Id.

gomyelocele, a spinal disorder, treatment was ordered over parental objection.[51] Doctors notified the parents that the spinal lesion should be surgically repaired within 48 hours of birth to avoid infection and possibly death. Initially, the father gave his consent to the operation but withdrew it upon learning of the full range of difficulties that could be involved. The infant would probably lack sphincter control of her anus and bladder, which could be compensated for medically and surgically. She would also require short leg braces in order to walk. Children with this disorder run a risk of hydrocephalus, a condition that can be controlled by surgically implanting a shunt to drain excess fluid from the cranium. The newborn girl did not, however, have this condition at birth.[52]

In ruling that a guardian be appointed with authority to consent to the spinal surgery — and shunt surgery if needed — the court pointed out that under its general equity powers it could act as parens patriae to safeguard the interests of the infant. This was a situation, the court noted, where the child's welfare demanded judicial intervention. Citing earlier New York and California cases, the court cautioned that judicial intervention may not be warranted in each case in which the parents reject a course of treatment recommended by physicians,[53] "but where, as here, a child has a reasonable chance to live a useful, fulfilled life, the court will not permit parental inaction to deny that chance."[54]

The California and New York cases are not the only ones that deal with children with health defects. In an unreported decision in Maine, a court authorized the guardian ad litem of a newborn baby to consent to surgical repair of a tracheal esophageal fistula.[55] The infant was born with multiple problems

[51] Application of Cicero, 101 Misc. 2d 699, 421 N.Y.S.2d 965 (N.Y. Sup. Ct. 1979).
[52] Id.
[53] Id. at 704, 421 N.Y.S.2d at 968, citing Matter of Seiforth, 309 N.Y. 80, 127 N.E.2d 820 (1955); Matter of Hofbauer, 65 A.D.2d 108, 411 N.Y.S.2d 416 (1979); In re Phillip B., 92 Cal. App. 3d 796, 156 Cal. Rptr. 48 (1979).
[54] Supra n.51 at 705, 421 N.Y.S.2d at 968.
[55] Maine Med. Center v. Houle, No. 74-145 (Superior Ct., filed February 14, 1974).

besides the fistula, which prevented him from normal feeding and respiration. The child's father had directed that no surgical repair be made of the fistula and intravenous feedings be ceased. As the child's condition worsened, his attending physician recommended that all life-support measures be withdrawn due to probable brain damage. In a sharp rebuke of the doctor, the court said:

> Were it his opinion that life itself could not be preserved, heroic measures ought not to be required. However, the doctor's qualitative evaluation of the value of the life to be preserved is not legally within the scope of his expertise.[56]

The court went on to hold that the actions of the parents in refusing treatment for their child amounted to legal neglect. Therefore it ordered steps to be taken by the guardian ad litem.[57]

The case of "Baby Doe" and federal attempts to regulate in the area of disabled newborns are well known in medical, nursing, and health-law circles. Regulations promulgated by the Department of Health and Human Services under Section 504 of the Rehabilitation Act of 1973 were successfully challenged.[58] Congress has made a fresh attempt to regulate care of disabled newborns under the Child Abuse Amendments of 1984.[59] Notwithstanding this new approach, the United States Supreme Court has rendered its decision in Bowen v. American Hospital Association,[60] dealing with regulations promulgated pursuant to Section 504 of the Rehabilitation Act of 1973. In so doing, the Court ruled that the regulations were not authorized by the enabling legislation. The ruling deserves careful analysis and in the end should not be read to obviate the need for *informed* decision-making in treatment decisions for handicapped newborns.

[56] Id. at 4.
[57] Id.
[58] American Hosp. Assn. v. Heckler, 794 F.2d 676 (2d Cir. 1984), invalidating 45 C.F.R. Part 84.55 (1984), affd., 472 U.S. 610 (1985).
[59] Pub. L. No. 98-457.
[60] American Hosp. Assn. v. Bowen, 476 U.S. 610 (1985).

Section 504 states:

> No otherwise *qualified handicapped individual* . . . shall, solely by
> reason of his handicap, be excluded from the participation in, be
> denied the benefits of, or be subjected to discrimination under
> any program or activity receiving Federal financial assistance.
> (Emphasis added.)[61]

In its ruling, the Supreme Court focused on the four mandatory provisions of the Final Rules promulgated by the Department of Health and Human Services (hereinafter DHHS) pursuant to Section 504. These included:

1. Posting of an informational notice in health facilities receiving federal assistance in one of two approved forms. In essence, the message conveyed in either notice is that Section 504 of the Rehabilitation Act prohibited discrimination on the basis of handicap. In view of this fact, nourishment and medically beneficial treatment should not be denied to handicapped infants solely on the ground of their known or anticipated mental or physical disability.
2. The responsibilities of state child protective service agencies, including a requirement that health care providers report known or suspected cases of unlawful medical neglect of handicapped infants.
3. Expedited record access on a 24-hour basis when deemed necessary to "protect the life or health of a handicapped individual."[62]
4. An expedited compliance provision to allow the government to seek a temporary restraining order in order to sustain the life of a handicapped infant who is in imminent danger of death.[63]

The Supreme Court pointed out that before DHHS embarked upon its rule-making activity, state law was well settled

[61] 29 U.S.C. §794 (1973).
[62] 45 C.F.R. §84.55(d) (1985).
[63] 45 C.F.R. §84.55(e) (1985).

that decision-making responsibility was vested in parents. The state reserved the right to review such determinations only in exceptional instances under parens patriae authority.[64]

What DHHS overlooked in this regard was what could legitimately trigger the application of Section 504 of the Rehabilitation Act. The Court made it clear that an infant born with a congenital anomaly was a "handicapped individual" for purposes of Section 504.[65] However, to avail herself of the provisions of Section 504 the infant must be "otherwise qualified" for benefits in a federally assisted program or activity.[66]

That the parents of a handicapped newborn rather than the hospital made the decision to withhold treatment did not trigger Section 504. The hospital and not the parents of the child are the recipients of federal financial assistance. As such, the parental decision does not amount to discriminatory denial of care by hospitals.[67]

The last part of the Court's ruling puts the issue in sharper focus:

> Nothing in the statute authorizes the Secretary to dispense with the law's focus on discrimination and instead to employ federal resources to save the lives of handicapped newborns, without regard to whether they are victims of discrimination by recipients of federal funds or not. Section 504 does not authorize the Secretary to give unsolicited advice either to parents, to hospitals, or to state officials who are faced with difficult treatment decisions concerning handicapped children.[68]

The Court concluded that the Secretary of the Department of Health and Human Services had overstepped his statutory powers. The handicapped infant rules were declared invalid.[69]

That the federal government cannot use Section 504 of the

---

[64] American Hosp. Assn. v. Bowen, supra n.60, at 628-629 n.13.
[65] Id. at 624.
[66] Id.
[67] Id. at 630.
[68] Id. at 647.
[69] Id.

Rehabilitation Act as a ploy to stop nontreatment decisions for handicapped newborns does not end the matter. As the Supreme Court pointed out, there is still the need to make "difficult" treatment determinations.[70] This will require the development of practical guidelines for health professionals, institutions, and parents to follow. If this is not done, the burden of decision-making may fall upon legislators to develop statutory requirements or it may devolve upon state courts to decide such matters, which may in fact make the situation worse. It is far better for those who are most intimately involved in such situations to develop a workable set of guidelines that incorporate the fundamental principles of consent.

In the future, courts will probably be presented with more cases in which a decision must be made regarding authorization for treatment that is opposed by the parents. Decisions favoring treatment will likely result in those cases in which the recommended surgical or medical treatment is of a life-saving nature and the benefits far outweigh the attendant risks. As the discussion in the next section suggests, measures that hope to, or are intended to, prolong a terminally ill child's life may not be compelled over parental objection.

§5.17 Refusal of Care for Terminally Ill Children

As opposed to the many decisions concerning life-threatening but curable conditions, the courts have not had occasion to deliver many reported decisions involving the right to withhold treatment from a child with a potentially fatal disease. At least three courts have, however, rendered opinions on the subject.[1]

---

[70] Id.

§5.17 [1] Custody of a Minor, 375 Mass. 733, 379 N.E.2d 1053 (1978); Custody of a Minor, 378 Mass. 732, 393 N.E.2d 836 (1979); Matter of Hofbauer, 47 N.Y.2d 648, 419 N.Y.S.2d 936, 393 N.E.2d 1009 (1979). See also In re Guardianship of Barry, 445 So. 2d 365 (Fla. Dist. Ct. App. 1984), in which the court affirmed a ruling that the natural parents as legal guardians of a ten-month-old boy could assert the child's privacy interest and order life-support

In a Massachusetts case, a 2-year-old boy was found to be in need of care and protection after his parents refused to continue medical treatment for his leukemia.[2] For a time the child had received standard chemotherapy treatment and was in a state of remission. Without telling the doctor, the parents stopped giving the boy his oral medication: three months later the leukemia reoccurred. The child's mother admitted that she and her husband had stopped giving the boy his oral cancer medication but persisted in the refusal to resume treatment. The present action was commenced and a temporary guardian was appointed with authority to consent to treatment. Treatment was resumed and, once again, the leukemia was brought under remission.[3]

In their challenge to the lower court's ruling, the parents presented arguments contesting the decision on procedural grounds. The Massachusetts Supreme Judicial Court held that the parents' contention provided no basis for reversing the lower court's ruling as to procedural matters.[4] As to the substantive issues involved, the court held that the judge's ruling below had given proper consideration to the constitutional rights asserted by the parents. Furthermore, his findings were supported by the evidence, with a decision made in the best interests of the child and in light of applicable state interests.[5]

The court weighed three compelling interests in reaching a decision favoring medical treatment for the child over the objection of his parents: the rights of the parents, the duty of the state, and the needs of the child.[6] As to the parents' natural rights, the court said that the rights of parents to control and nurture their children is in the nature of a trust. When they fail

---

therapy discontinued. The child was lacking cognitive brain function and experts indicated that without the life support he would die in a matter of hours. The state's interest in preserving life was far outweighed by the terminally ill child's privacy interest in removal of the life-support equipment.

[2] Custody of a Minor, 375 Mass. 733, 379 N.E.2d 1053 (1978).
[3] Id. at 741, 379 N.E.2d at 1057.
[4] Id. at 742, 379 N.E.2d at 1056.
[5] Id. at 753, 379 N.E.2d at 1062.
[6] Id. at 754-758, 379 N.E.2d at 1061-1062.

to discharge their responsibilities properly and the welfare of the child is threatened, the state may intervene. Under applicable child care and protection legislation in Massachusetts, that course had been taken in this instance. The trial judge made four findings that supported the conclusion that the boy was without necessary and appropriate care and that his parents would not provide it for him. The lower court enumerated the following: (a) without treatment the type of leukemia the youngster had is fatal in children; (b) chemotherapy is the only known means available that offers a cure; (c) the risks of treatment were far outweighed by the consequences of not treating the child; and (d) the parents were unwilling to continue chemotherapy despite the probable consequences to the boy.[7] The parents refused treatment because they were concerned about the discomfort caused by the chemotherapy and were pessimistic about the likelihood of a cure. They were content to offer him a program of dietary manipulation and prayer. Given the overwhelming evidence that these efforts could not effect a cure — whereas there was proof that chemotherapy was successful in treating the leukemia experienced by the boy, whose life was at stake — the lower court was held to be justified in removing the child from the custody of his parents.[8]

As to the interests of the child, the court noted that the judge below had applied the doctrine of substituted judgment. This was found to be consistent with the "best interests" test for children of tender years, since the basis for analysis is the same. Evidence that there was a substantial chance of cure, that chemotherapy was most effective in treating children in this age group, that no other effective treatment was available, and that the adverse effects of chemotherapy were minimal was sufficient to warrant a finding that treatment was in the best interests of the boy.[9]

The court found that the judge had correctly identified three state interests warranting an order for medical treatment over

[7] Id. at 755-756, 379 N.E.2d at 1063-1064.
[8] Id. at 756, 379 N.E.2d at 1064.
[9] Id. at 756, 379 N.E.2d at 1065-1066.

the objection of the child's parents. The first was the state's long-standing interest in safeguarding the welfare of children. Ample precedent existed for the state to intervene when parents refused medical care for their child. The second state interest involved the preservation of life. It was pointed out that this interest applied with full force when, as here, chemotherapy was the only real hope the child had for cure. The last state interest involved the ethical integrity of the medical profession and hospitals. The court noted that both physicians and health facilities required the opportunity to care for those under their control.[10]

In concluding its decision, the court said that, under applicable Massachusetts legislation, the parents could ask for a review and redetermination every six months. Should they wish to present further evidence regarding the child's situation, the parents could do so under this legislation.[11] The parents did follow this suggestion the following year.[12] After hearing, the trial judge ordered that the chemotherapy treatments continue. Furthermore, the custody of the parents was restricted to the point required to ensure medical care mandated by the court order. On appeal, the Massachusetts Supreme Judicial Court affirmed.[13]

In its review of the case, the Supreme Judicial Court noted that for the first time the boy's parents had accepted the need for having the child receive chemotherapy. However, they also wanted legal permission to supplement the medical program with their own schedule of "metabolic therapy," including large doses of vitamins, laetrile, and enzyme enemas.[14] The parents had begun this metabolic program without informing the boy's doctor. Once he learned of the therapy schedule from the press, he ordered tests to see if the boy were being adversely affected by the parents' regimen. Results showed that the youngster had low-grade chronic cyanide poisoning that the

[10]Id. at 756, 379 N.E.2d at 1066.
[11]Id. at 756, 379 N.E.2d at 1067.
[12]Custody of a Minor, 378 Mass. 732, 393 N.E.2d 836 (1979).
[13]Id.
[14]Id.

trial court attributed to his exposure to laetrile. He had hyper-
vitaminosis due to large doses of Vitamin A, a condition that
could eventually destroy the liver. The trial court found, based
on the evidence presented, that the metabolic therapy program
was of no value in treating cancer and that the program was
potentially harmful to the boy.[15]

After reiterating the reasons for the earlier decision in the
case, the court found that state intervention with the parents'
rights in this case was justified. However well intentioned the
parents might be, their actions ran contrary to the overwhelming medical evidence in the case.[16]

In contrast to the Massachusetts decisions, the New York
Court of Appeals in 1979 upheld a family court decision denying a request to declare a 9-year-old boy with Hodgkin's disease
a neglected child.[17] The boy had been diagnosed as having the
ailment in 1977 and his attending physician recommended that
he be cared for by an oncologist or hemotologist who would
institute a program of radiation treatment and possibly chemotherapy. The boy's parents rejected this advice and took their
son to a Jamaican clinic, where he received metabolic therapy
and laetrile injections. Upon his return to New York, a neglect
proceeding was instituted. Eventually the boy was placed under
the care of a New York physician, who advocated metabolic
therapy. The court required that at least one other physician
examine the boy periodically and make reports to the court.[18]

In the testimony before the family court sharp and conflicting expert evidence was presented by proponents of conventional medical treatment and supporters of metabolic care. The
boy's father and the attending physician who had prescribed
metabolic therapy both stated that, should his condition

[15] Id. at 754, 393 N.E.2d at 842.

[16] Id. at 751, 393 N.E.2d at 846. It should be noted that prior to the Supreme Judicial Court ruling in the case in 1979, the parents removed the
child to Mexico in violation of a trial court order. The boy later died in
Mexico.

[17] Matter of Hofbauer, 47 N.Y.2d 648, 419 N.Y.S.2d 936, 393 N.E.2d 1009
(1979).

[18] Id. at 652-653, 419 N.Y.S.2d at 938, 393 N.E.2d at 1013.

worsen, they would agree to conventional treatment. The family court, on the evidence presented, found that the youngster was not a neglected child and that, indeed, his parents had made a conscientious attempt to obtain an alternative form of medical care for their son.[19]

In its review of the case, the New York Court of Appeals noted that the most significant fact in deciding whether a child is being denied adequate medical attention (within the meaning of applicable legislation) is:

> . . . whether the parents, once having sought accredited medical assistance and having been made aware of the seriousness of their child's affliction and the possibility of cure if a certain mode of treatment is undertaken, have provided for their child a treatment which is recommended by their physician and which has not been totally rejected by all responsible medical authority.[20]

As measured against this test, the court of appeals found that the state had not proven its allegation of neglect. The state's claim that the boy had received inadequate and ineffective care was not consistent with the evidence presented to the family court.[21]

The decisions of the Massachusetts and New York courts can be distinguished on the facts in each case. It is difficult to predict how other courts would react to similar cases. However, should a child have a life-threatening disease that is curable and should there be no reasonable alternative to the treatment offered by physicians, the court would more likely than not come down in favor of treatment. Such a decision would be made in view of the accepted interest in the preservation of life,[22] as well

---

[19] Id. at 654, 419 N.Y.S.2d at 939, 393 N.E.2d at 1012.

[20] Id. at 656, 419 N.Y.S.2d at 941, 393 N.E.2d at 1014.

[21] Id. at 657, 419 N.Y.S.2d at 941, 393 N.E.2d at 1014. The court of appeals noted that by its decision it was not condoning metabolic therapy or laetrile in the treatment of cancer.

[22] See, e.g., Custody of a Minor, 375 Mass. 733, 379 N.E.2d 1053 (1978); Superintendent of Belchertown State School v. Saikewicz, 373 Mass. 728, 370 N.E.2d 417 (1977).

as the body of case law authorizing life-saving treatment.[23] A different result would likely occur if the child's condition were terminal or if the benefits of medical treatment were largely uncertain.

The desire of parents to block unwanted treatment for a terminally ill child may generate novel arguments. Indeed, such has already occurred in a Pennsylvania case in which the parents of a cystic fibrosis victim claimed that efforts to prolong their daughter's life with aggressive treatment violated §504 of the Rehabilitation Act.[24] Although the plaintiffs lost their claim, the case suggests that physicians should think twice before administering aggressive treatment in the face of hopeless situations. Such treatment might motivate litigation by surviving parents who feel that the right of their child to refuse care was ignored because of the patient's inability to articulate a choice.

§5.17.1 Court Orders Not to Resuscitate for Minors

At least one court has claimed a right to issue an order not to resuscitate a minor.[25] The case involved an infant born in Massachusetts who suffered from an incurable heart defect and whose life expectancy was anywhere from two months to two years. The child was discharged from hospital into the custody of trained foster parents.

When the child was readmitted to hospital for treatment of a bacterial infection, he was placed on a respirator. The attending physicians wanted to issue a no-code order in view of his underlying fatal illness. Because the child was under a care and protection order, the request to issue the no-code declaration had to go before the state agency for social services, as well as the child's guardian ad litem. Both refused to give consent and court action followed.[26]

[23] See §5.16.2 supra.
[24] Gerben v. Holslaw, 692 F. Supp. 557 (E.D. Pa. 1988).
[25] Custody of a Minor, 385 Mass. 697, 434 N.E.2d 601 (1982).
[26] Id.

In affirming the juvenile court's ruling authorizing the no-code order, the Massachusetts Supreme Judicial Court ruled that, in view of the parents' failure to take an active interest in the child's welfare, a decision had to be made by the court. This action was taken on the basis of the substituted judgment test, which purports to judge what the child would want done if he were capable of articulating personal interests and desires. Taking into account the degree of pain and suffering the child would experience if resuscitated and his underlying condition, the ruling of the lower court was appropriate.[27]

Orders not to resuscitate present many difficult moral dilemmas, whether the patient is an adult or an infant. Although the law may have great empathy for a child's family, attending physicians, and other concerned people, its main responsibility is the rights of the child. An order not to resuscitate must be based on sound medical standards with full consent from the patient or from one who is authorized to act for her. The grounds for issuing the order must be well documented in the patient's chart.

Not all courts would require judicial approval for a no-code order for a minor, but it may be necessary. Some employ the best interest test rather than substituted judgments. If the parents or legal guardians are in dispute among themselves, or if the child is a ward of the state, applicable legislation and case precedent may make judicial review a requirement. If this is the case, the mechanisms for invoking judicial action should be set into motion quickly so that a rapid response may be made available. Speed is essential primarily for the well-being of the child, but also for the health facility and all others committed to the child's treatment.

§5.18 Children's Refusal of Treatment

Parents may quite acceptably refuse treatment for their children, but children themselves may reach the same decisions.

[27] Id.

The question is whether the determinations by children are valid. Such a situation is possible when a child grows tired of the sickening side effects of treatment for leukemia or other illnesses. Children may also decline certain types of treatment on the basis of religious convictions.[1] An unmarried pregnant minor may refuse an abortion insisted upon by her parents. Children who have been on a long-term regime of chemotherapy for cancer or of treatment for aplastic anemia become quite knowledgeable about their illnesses. Although they are chronologically still children, their medical conditions have — for many purposes — jolted them into adulthood. If children in these situations refuse further treatment, should their wishes be heeded?

Children in a nonterminal state may also object to medical treatment insisted upon by their parents. For example, an adolescent's parents may insist that a doctor insert an IUD or prescribe birth control pills to prevent a young woman from "getting into trouble." Yet the minor may not be sexually active or be totally averse to such behavior. Should her objection to treatment be recognized and overrule her parents' wishes?

In the category of birth control pills or devices — or even an abortion — medical intervention should not be thrust upon a minor over her objection. She may be of an age to understand and appreciate the consequences of foregoing such care. Should she meet the criteria of a state's common law or statutory requirements for mature or emancipated minors, the situation would be more clear-cut. The decision would then belong to the minor, not her parents.

A refusal of consent by a minor who is not emancipated or not considered a mature minor poses more difficult questions. Realistically, how is the minor to enforce his refusal to undergo care? Unless a child protection agency is involved, no successful way may be available for the child to prevail. However, the physician whom the parents have asked to treat the minor may

§5.18   [1]See, e.g., In the Interest of E.G., 515 N.E.2d 287 (Ill. App. Ct. 1987), in which a 17-year-old female who opposed blood transfusions for treatment of leukemia on the basis of religious belief was deemed mature enough to make such a choice.

be in a position to bring the matter into perspective. Perhaps the parents simply do not appreciate the feelings of their child. A third person not as intimately involved may be able to help them understand the situation. When the parents remain adamant, the doctor has the option of refusing to accommodate them. She is treating the minor *not* the parents, and a reasonable refusal on the minor's part should be heeded.

Still, situations will arise when the minor's refusal or care is unreasonable. In those circumstances, the physician should consult with the patient and explain why the medical or surgical intervention is necessary, as well as provide information about the expected benefits. At whatever point the physician deems advisable, the child's parents should be involved in these discussions.

With the growing body of case law on the subject of treating or withholding care from the terminally ill, there seems to be little justification for compelling treatment in cases involving minors. Children aged 12 or 13 who are veterans of prolonged therapy regimens and who sense or know that further treatment would be futile should have their wishes to withhold additional intervention respected. The difficulty is in finding an appropriate legal mechanism to effectuate this right of children to refuse treatment.

In New Mexico, the Right to Die Act provides for a minor to have executed on the child's behalf a document directing others not to use medical treatment to sustain life when he is terminally ill.[2] The document must be executed by the minor's spouse, if of majority age, or by the parent or guardian. However, a parent or guardian may not execute the document if there is opposition to it by another parent, guardian, or the minor's spouse if of majority age.[3]

In other states, giving effect to a terminally ill minor's decision to refuse treatment may require judicial intervention. Application of the best interest test may result in a finding that further treatment is not in the best interests of the minor. In

---

[2] N.M. Stat. Ann. §24-7-4 (1984).
[3] Id.

other instances the court may be called upon to use its equity powers to enjoin or restrain others from treating the minor without her approval.

Another possibility is the application of common law or legislative enactments dealing with mature minors. It is possible that a court could find a 14- or 15-year-old sufficiently mature and capable to understand the consequences of refusing additional treatments. Expert evidence may be a prerequisite to proving that the minor has the capacity to act in an intelligent and mature fashion and that the decision to refuse care is not motivated by a sense of despair or depression. Evidence that the child is terminally ill and that further treatment will not cure but only prolong his life would also weigh heavily in favor of giving effect to the child's request.

It is difficult to imagine at this point that a health facility would give effect to a minor's decision to refuse treatment, particularly when the parents insist on continued therapy. The use of "prognosis committees" or the like suggested by the New Jersey Supreme Court in the *Quinlan* case (see §7.5.2 infra) for incompetents may not fit smoothly into those situations where minors are concerned. The long-standing right of the state to intervene as parens patriae, particularly for children, would likely require a more structured and detached decision-making body than that available in the facility in which a child is receiving treatment.

The right of minors to refuse life-prolonging care must be carefully examined in the future. Satisfactory means for recognizing the minor's decision will probably come from the legislatures and courts throughout the country.

SIX

Mental Illness, Mental Retardation, and Consent

§6.0   Introduction
A.   Commitment for Treatment and Consent
  §6.1   Voluntary Commitment and Consent
    §6.1.1   Release of Voluntary Patients or Residents
  §6.2   Involuntary Commitment and Consent
    §6.2.1   Criteria for Involuntary Commitment
    §6.2.2   Rights of Institutionalized Patients
B.   Scope of Permissible Mental Health Treatment
  §6.3   Consent to Electroshock Treatment
    §6.3.1   State Legislation Regulating the Use of ECT
    §6.3.2   Consent Requirements in the Absence of Specific ECT Legislation
    §6.3.3   Emergency Use of ECT
    §6.3.4   Case Law on Consent to ECT
    §6.3.5   Avoiding Consent Actions Involving ECT
  §6.4   Consent and the Use of Medication
    §6.4.1   Legislative Controls on Medication: Precommitment Therapy
    §6.4.2   Legislative Controls of Psychoactive Drugs and Other Medications
    §6.4.3   Consent Requirements for Use of Medication Therapy
    §6.4.4   Case Law on the Use of Medication
    §6.4.5   Policy Considerations in the Forcible Administration of Medication
  §6.5   Psychosurgery and the Law of Consent
    §6.5.1   What Is Psychosurgery?
    §6.5.2   State Legislation Regulating Psychosurgery
    §6.5.3   Factors Influencing Decisions for Psychosurgery
    §6.5.4   Case Law

§6.6   Behavioral Modification, Physical Restraint, and Isolation as Treatment
    §6.6.1   Aversive Stimuli and Behavioral Modification
    §6.6.2   Restraints
    §6.6.3   Isolation and Seclusion
C.   Sterilization of the Mentally Disabled
    §6.7   State Legislation
    §6.8   Case Law on Sterilization of Mentally Incompetent Persons
    §6.8.1   The Traditional Approach
    §6.8.2   Judicial Legislating of Sterilization
    §6.8.3   Practical Considerations: What to Do in the Absence of Enabling Legislation
D.   Nonpsychiatric Treatment of the Mentally Disabled
    §6.9   Medical and Surgical Treatment

§6.0   Introduction

Mental illness and retardation are extensive subject areas: the right to treatment has been examined in depth by the courts and has been the subject of much legislation. This chapter focuses on matters of consent relating to the mentally ill and mentally retarded. It covers the scope of permissible mental health treatment, the right to be subjected to certain forms of treatment, sterilization of mentally disabled persons, and the right to medical or surgical care.

A.   COMMITMENT FOR TREATMENT AND CONSENT

The law of commitment for mental illness or mental retardation is heavily oriented to due process considerations. A review of state legislation demonstrates that a key consideration is the recognition of the constitutional rights of the patient. Case law on the subject reinforces this respect for individual liberties, with some courts exercising considerable power to safeguard the rights of the mentally retarded.

Although not emphasized as much as constitutional issues, the right of the patient to consent to commitment for mental health care is a key consideration. In this portion of the chapter both voluntary and involuntary commitment are discussed in relation to the law of consent. Release of voluntary patients is also examined.

§6.1 Voluntary Commitment and Consent

In many ways, voluntary admission or commitment for mental health treatment does not differ greatly in procedure from voluntary hospitalization for a physical illness. Both require that a patient understand the nature and consequences of a decision to undergo care. Both mean that a patient gives up certain liberties. However, voluntary admission for mental illness or mental retardation results in a far greater degree of restriction of liberties, as well as in the imposition of social stigmas.

State legislators have become increasingly concerned about the needs and rights of voluntary patients. Laws have been enacted that recognize the rights of voluntary and involuntary mental health patients,[1] with some states including provisions for redress or remedies.[2] Many of these laws include so-called patients' bills of rights.[3]

In the case of mentally retarded persons seeking admission

§6.1 [1]See, e.g., Cal. Welf. & Inst. Code §5325 (West 1981); Fla. Stat. Ann. §393.13 (West 1979); Ky. Rev. Stat. §202A.180 (1976); Wash. Rev. Code Ann. §71.05.370 (1974); W. Va. Code §27-5-9 (1977).
[2]Fla. Stat. Ann. §393.13 (West 1979); Me. Rev. Stat. Ann. tit. 34, §2144 (1977).
[3]See, e.g., Fla. Stat. Ann. §393.13 (West 1979); Minn. Stat. Ann. §144.651 (West 1982). Other states simply enumerate the rights of the mentally ill or mentally retarded while institutionalized. See N.J. Stat. Ann. §30:4-24.2 (West 1975); Neb. Rev. Stat. §83-1066 (1976); Or. Rev. Stat. §426.385 (1973).

for treatment, statutory thresholds must be overcome. The person must be capable of consenting to institutionalization and the decision must be made free of duress or coercion.[4] When an individual is deemed incapable of making such a decision, then it must be decided whether another person should be appointed to represent his interests in a proceeding for admission, as outlined in state procedures on the subject.

For the mentally ill person seeking voluntary admission for treatment, similar due process requirements must be met. Two initial determinations are whether the person is in need of hospitalization, and, if so, whether she is capable of consenting to admission for treatment. When the individual is deemed incapable, other mechanisms must be examined for institutionalization. One possibility is involuntary commitment.[5]

Mental health legislation in Vermont provides a good example of state law on voluntary admission.[6] Persons 14 years of age or over in Vermont may seek voluntary admission. They must execute a signed consent indicating that they understand that treatment will be on an inpatient basis and that they desire and agree to admission free of coercion or duress.[7]

§6.1.1 Release of Voluntary Patients or Residents

When a person is capable of seeking voluntary admission for mental health care, he should be equally capable of obtaining release from the facility. Many state laws anticipate requests by voluntary patients for their release or discharge from treatment. Although in many circumstances the patient's or resident's request is honored, a number of states provide for the

[4]N.Y. Mental Hyg. Law §15.15 (McKinney 1977). See R.I. Gen. Laws §40.1-5-5 (1977) (the capacity does not have to be of the level to enter into a contract, but a person must be able to understand the nature and consequences of seeking admission).
[5]Haw. Rev. Stat. §334-60 (1985).
[6]Vt. Stat. Ann. tit. 18, §7503 (1977).
[7]Id.

retention of a patient or a change in his status to that of involuntary commitment.[8]

For example, in New York when a voluntary resident of a school for the mentally retarded is in need of involuntary care and treatment, she can be kept in the school for 72 hours.[9] Before the end of that time the resident must either be released or the director of the school must apply for a court order authorizing retention of the resident. If the court finds that the resident is mentally retarded and in need of treatment in a school setting, it may issue an order to make such care possible.[10]

Some state laws specifically provide for temporary absences for voluntary patients.[11] Release must be preceded by permission from a designated official and must not interfere with the patient's treatment.[12] The patient must be capable of a temporary release and he must not pose a threat to himself or others.

§6.2 Involuntary Commitment and Consent

When a person is admitted involuntarily or on an emergency basis, her right to consent is removed temporarily and for a specific purpose. Involuntary commitment to a psychiatric hospital or a psychiatric ward of a general hospital entails a legal presupposition of incapacity. This determination is reached on the basis of medical or psychiatric opinion, or a judicial determination that the person poses a danger to herself or others. It also includes a finding that the person is in need of mental health treatment.

This legal incapacity is not all-encompassing: it relates only to the matter of admission. The legal competency of the patient in

[8]N.Y. Mental Hyg. Law §9.13 (McKinney 1985); W. Va. Code §27-4-3 (1975).
[9]N.Y. Mental Hyg. Law §15.13 (McKinney 1977).
[10]Id.
[11]See, e.g., Or. Rev. Stat. §426.220 (1969).
[12]Id.

other matters, such as the right to vote,[1] remains intact. State legislation[2] has supported this distinction; however, an adjudication of incompetency — an issue separate and distinct from the matter of admission — may result in a deprivation of rights, including the right to vote or the right to dispose of property.[3] The status of someone in this situation depends on the scope of the adjudication of incompetency and whether it relates to matters of property, the person of the individual, or both.

§6.2.1 Criteria for Involuntary Commitment

Because involuntary commitment involves a deprivation of basic rights, a number of constitutional and procedural considerations are involved. Legislation throughout the country sets forth specific criteria for involuntary commitment, as well as procedural safeguards. These criteria are quite similar across the country: (a) the person must be suffering from a mental illness and as a result, pose a danger to himself or others, (b) he must be in need of care or treatment, and (c) there must be no less restrictive or reasonable alternative to institutional care.[4]

In contrast, the procedural aspects of involuntary admission do differ across the country. For example, in Rhode Island a person may be committed involuntarily on an emergency basis or upon civil court certification.[5] Hawaii also has an emergency admissions statute.[6] At some stage in the involuntary commitment of a patient, judicial review occurs either initially, as is the

§6.2 [1]W. Va. Code §27-5-9 (1977).
[2]Fla. Stat. Ann. §393.12 (West 1980); N.J. Stat. Ann. §30:4-24.2 (West 1975); W. Va. Code §27-5-9 (1977); Wyo. Stat. §25-3-125 (1963). Cf. Wis. Stat. Ann. §51.59 (1978), which recognizes that incompetency is not implied by an individual's admission to a facility. However, the provision does not authorize an involuntary patient to refuse treatment during her institutionalization.
[3]Id.
[4]See, e.g., Haw. Rev. Stat. §334-60 (1977) (includes as a possible factor damage to property).
[5]R.I. Gen. Laws §40.1-5-5 (1977).
[6]Haw. Rev. Stat. §334-59 (1977).

case in most nonemergency involuntary admissions, or within a short period of time following an emergency admission.[7] There is also provision for periodic review of a patient's need for continued hospitalization.[8]

The mentally retarded are covered by similar legislative provisions. For example, in Illinois a person 18 years of age or over may be admitted to a facility for the mentally retarded if a court finds that she is mentally retarded and is reasonably expected to cause serious harm to herself or others.[9] Emergency restraint of a person believed to be mentally retarded may be carried out by a law enforcement officer in Maine if it is believed that the individual poses an imminent threat of substantial physical harm to self or others.[10] In addition, emergency admission procedures for the mentally retarded may be found in Maine[11] and in other states.[12]

As with the mentally ill, there are specific procedural due process considerations that must be met in the involuntary commitment of a mentally retarded person. Included are some sort of judicial inquiry as well as a periodic review.[13]

There are also practical considerations in the involuntary commitment of mentally ill persons. For example, what should be done with a person who has AIDS, organic brain damage, schizophrenia, delusions, or hallucinations and whose behavior in a general hospital is controlled by physical and chemical restraints?

Such was the question in a New Jersey case[14] in which a general hospital petitioned for the involuntary commitment of a patient who had a long-standing history of psychiatric hospital admissions. Now afflicted with organic brain damage and

---

[7]See, e.g., Ariz. Rev. Stat. Ann. §36-526 (1983).
[8]Kan. Stat. Ann. §59-2917a (1976).
[9]Ill. Ann. Stat. ch. 91 1/2, §4-500 (Smith-Hurd 1979).
[10]Me. Rev. Stat. Ann. tit. 34B, §5477 (1984).
[11]Id.
[12]See, e.g., Ariz. Rev. Stat. Ann. §36-560 (1981).
[13]Colo. Rev. Stat. Ann. §27-10.5-109 (1975).
[14]Matter of Commitment of B.S., 213 N.J. Super. 243, 517 A.2d 146 (Super. Ct. App. Div. 1986).

AIDS — along with schizophrenia — the patient was combative and had a history of biting and hitting nurses. She would also wander the corridors and get into bed with other patients. She was, in short, a management problem. A male guard, physical restraints, and heavy doses of thorazine were used to control her behavior.[15]

The Chancery Division of the New Jersey Superior Court ruled that B. S. was not shown to be dangerous to herself or others or property. Therefore, she was not a proper subject for commitment to a psychiatric hospital. This decision was reversed on appeal.

As the court noted, the chief psychiatrist of the state Division of Mental Health had expressed a "flawed" opinion regarding the need for commitment. The doctor's view was that unless patients were suicidal or homicidal, they could not be involuntarily hospitalized.[16] Here there was clear and convincing evidence that B. S. posed a danger to others. Moreover, she was unable to care for herself. Although the court tried to sidestep the issue of AIDS, it could not do so completely. Addressing the issue of individual liberties the court noted:

> The focus of judicial concern with commitment of the mentally ill is the protection of their individual liberties against inappropriate intrusion. Realism requires a recognition that B. S.'s future holds little opportunity to exercise individual liberties, whatever our disposition of this matter.[17]

For the reviewing court, it was unfair to consider B. S. as she appeared under heavy amounts of medication. Indeed, as the evidence suggested, commitment offered less restriction on her freedom than what the court termed the "draconian" means of managing her care in a general hospital.[18]

Involuntary commitment can sometimes offer more benefit than harm. Such is the message of this case. Keeping an indi-

[15] Id.
[16] Id.
[17] Id. at 249, 517 A.2d at 149.
[18] Id. at 248, 517 A.2d at 148.

vidual under guard, in physical restraints, and on heavy dosages of medication can be far worse than commitment to a mental health facility. Courts are faced with complex issues in such cases, particularly in balancing individual liberty interests against societal concerns. That a mentally ill, combative patient has AIDS can only complicate matters. Nonetheless, decisions must be made that strike a balance between competing individual and societal interests. Evidence in such cases will be the turning point in deciding the propriety of involuntary commitment.

§6.2.2 Rights of Institutionalized Patients

In addition to their federal constitutional guarantees, involuntary patients, like voluntary patients, have been accorded certain substantive rights by state legislation. These are often found in bills of rights and cover a wide spectrum of matters — including wearing personal clothing, using a telephone, and being informed about treatment.[19] In some instances legislation is more specific, requiring patients' consent to certain forms of care or recognizing the right of patients to refuse certain types of medication or surgery.[20]

From a practical point of view, these legislative enactments create difficulties for professional staff. How exactly is a client's right to privacy or dignity — which is enumerated in some state law[21] — protected? What is meant by these terms? Are they to be interpreted as absolutes, or should their meaning vary according to the context of particular situations?

In order to meet these requirements, however defined, it is important for administrators and health professionals to set a

---

[19] Ark. Stat. Ann. §59-1416 (1981); Me. Rev. Stat. Ann. tit. 34B §5605 (1984); N.J. Stat. Ann. §30:4-24.2 (West 1975).

[20] Cal. Welf. & Inst. Code §5325 (West 1981); Kan. Stat. Ann. §59-2929 (1986); Ky. Rev. Stat. §202A.180 (1976); Mont. Code Ann. §53-21-148 (1979); N.J. Stat. Ann. §30:4-24.2 (West 1975).

[21] See, e.g., Fla. Stat. Ann. §393.13 (West 1979); N.J. Stat. Ann. §30:4-24.2 (West 1975).

high level of discipline and to encourage the proper attitude toward patients among staff personnel. Health professionals should, within reason and to the best of their ability, carry out the requirements set out in these laws.

Patients' bills of rights are more than moral statements on what the law ought to be. A failure to meet the requirements established in these provisions that results in reasonably foreseeable harm may constitute negligence. A patient who is not adequately informed about a particular medication or treatment as required by law and who suffers harm has grounds for a consent action. Some states reinforce this notion by specific consent provisions for mentally ill and retarded persons who are institutionalized for treatment.[22]

Patients' bills of rights and statutory requirements for institutionalization must be taken seriously. Under this umbrella fall the relevant requirements on consent for the mentally ill and mentally retarded. Practitioners and administrators alike should familiarize themselves with these provisions in their respective states. Gaining this knowledge is a simple and practical way to avoid unnecessary litigation.

B. SCOPE OF PERMISSIBLE MENTAL HEALTH TREATMENT

Much legislative attention has been directed toward the use of certain forms of treatment for the mentally ill and the mentally retarded. Electroshock, psychoactive drugs and other medication, psychosurgery, restraints, and isolation have all been covered in depth. Large numbers of cases have also considered the use of drugs and other forms of care. These matters are dealt with here in the context of consent to treatment and in light of both case law and legislation.

[22]Fla. Stat. Ann. §393.13 (West 1979); Kan. Stat. Ann. §59-2929 (1986).

370

§6.3 Consent to Electroshock Treatment

Over the years much controversy has surrounded the practice of electroshock therapy. Law review articles,[1] case law,[2] and legislation[3] have all considered its ramifications.

Despite adverse publicity and the attention paid to it by the law, electroshock therapy (ECT) has gained wide acceptance as the treatment of choice for certain mental illnesses. There have been some encouraging accomplishments using electroshock therapy. The practice, however, is not free of significant risks for the patient, including serious physical injuries as well as memory loss.[4] The treatment is also viewed by some as a significant intrusion upon the individual integrity of the patient. These concerns have been largely responsible for triggering the legal inroads on the use of ECT.

In the past, the risk of harm associated with ECT was greater if precautions were not taken to prevent patients from aspirating substances into the lungs or to prevent serious spinal injuries. Today, however, appropriate preventive measures are followed. Since anesthetics are administered prior to the use of electroshock, the added factor of known and probable risks of anesthesia must be considered in the consent process in addition to those more directly related to the procedure.

The context of consent to treatment implies the consideration of certain factors in the use of ECT. The basic premise is that the patient must be thoroughly informed of the risks, benefits, and reasonable alternative forms of care that are available. The decision to have such treatment must be made by the patient, unless he is incapable legally or mentally of giving an

---

§6.3 [1] See, e.g., R. Plotkin, Limiting the Therapeutic Orgy: Mental Patients' Right to Refuse Treatment, 72 Nw. U.L. Rev. 461-525 (1977).

[2] See, e.g., Gundy v. Pauley, 619 S.W.2d 730 (Ky. Ct. App. 1981); Matter of W.S., 152 N.J. Super. 298, 377 A.2d 969 (Juv. & Dom. Rel. Ct., Essex County 1977).

[3] Colo. Rev. Stat. §13-20-402 (1982); Fla. Stat. Ann. §458.325 (West 1979); Mo. Ann. Stat. §630.130 (Vernon 1980); N.M. Stat. Ann. §43-1-15 (1979).

[4] See 94 A.L.R.3d 317 (1976); Dornbush, Memory and Induced ECT Convulsions, 4 Seminars Psych. 47 (1972).

authorization. The fact that a person is an inpatient in a mental health facility or in a psychiatric ward of a general hospital does not automatically remove his legal capacity to consent to or to refuse consent to ECT.

One difficulty facing administrators and physicians is the matter of consent from legally or mentally incapable people. Who may authorize ECT on their behalf? The answer to this and other questions regarding the procedure may be found in legislation in many states.

§6.3.1   State Legislation Regulating the Use of ECT

In those states with legislation regulating the use of electroshock or convulsive therapy, the legislation makes it quite clear that a patient has a right to refuse consent to such procedures.[5] However, the right to refuse consent is not without limit. In Missouri, for example, involuntary electroconvulsive therapy may be administered under a court order.[6] First the court must make two findings, which are to be based upon clear and convincing evidence:

1. That there is a strong likelihood of cure or improvement for a length of time and that the treatment will not incur any serious functional injury.
2. That there exists no less drastic means of care that could lead to substantial improvement for the patient.[7]

Based upon these criteria, the court may compel the patient to submit to a specified number of treatments.

Apart from the laws regulating involuntary ECT treatment, the emphasis in most state legislation is on due process considerations that ensure the rights of those persons who may be

---

[5] See Cal. Welf. & Inst. Code §5326.85 (West 1981); Mass. Gen. Laws Ann. ch. 123, §23 (West 1981); Mo. Ann. Stat. §630.130 (Vernon 1980).
[6] Mo. Ann. Stat. §630.130 (Vernon 1980).
[7] Id.

subject to such therapy. In the case of persons who are legally incompetent or who are believed incapable of giving effective consent, the laws provide for substitute decision-making. In some states this is done by a legal guardian,[8] whereas in other jurisdictions the decision is made by a court.[9]

Once the competency issue is determined, focus shifts to the matter of consent. Preliminary factors must be documented to establish the need for ECT. In a Montana provision dealing with the developmentally disabled, for example, electroshock devices are considered a research technique. ECT can only be used in those situations where it is believed necessary to prevent self-mutilation leading to permanent harm to the disabled person. In addition, other forms of care must be explored first.[10] Although most states do not follow Montana in classifying electroshock as a research procedure, it is not uncommon to find that concurring opinions must be obtained from physicians not involved in the patient's treatment prior to the administration of ECT.[11]

Many state laws specify the type of information that must be disclosed to the patient or her guardian prior to the administration of ECT. Florida legislation specifies disclosure of the common side effects of convulsive therapy, alternative forms of care, the projected number of treatment sessions, as well as notice to the patient or guardian that consent to the therapy may be revoked prior to or between treatment sessions.[12] In other states such as Colorado, the requirements for consent are less specific, including only an admonition that the patient's written informed consent on a standardized form be obtained prior to the administration of electroconvulsive therapy.[13]

---

[8]Fla. Stat. Ann. §458.325 (West 1979); Mass. Gen. Laws Ann. ch. 123, §22 (West 1980) (consent by the person's legal guardian or nearest living relative); N.M. Stat. Ann. §43-1-15 (1979) (consent of the treatment guardian).

[9]Mo. Ann. Stat. §630.130 (Vernon 1980) (court order required for involuntary ECT for minors and incompetent patients); N.J. Stat. Ann. §30:4-24.2 (West 1975) (for patients adjudicated incompetent).

[10]Mont. Code Ann. §53-20-146 (1979).

[11]Fla. Stat. Ann. §458.325 (West 1979).

[12]Id.

[13]Colo. Rev. Stat. §13-20-402 (1982).

Some state laws specifically refer to the role of relatives in the consent process. California legislation that provided for notice to a "responsible relative" was struck down as an unconstitutional infringement upon the patient's right of privacy. The court concluded that the state interests involved were not sufficiently compelling to permit such an encroachment upon the patient's rights.[14]

Other states outline the role of relatives — particularly that of parents of minor children in need of electroshock — in law. Unlike in the California law, however, the focus here is on minors in need of treatment for whom a decision may be made by their parents. The issue is not one of notification of proposed care, as in the California statute. In some jurisdictions parents may give consent for electroshock when the minor is less than 18 years of age. This practice is followed in Michigan where parental authorization is necessary unless the parents cannot be found. As an alternative, a probate court may consent to ECT.[15] This approach is not uniform across the country: in Missouri parents of minor patients are required to obtain a court order permitting the use of electroconvulsive therapy.[16]

The divergence of approach regarding parental and family consent to ECT reflects a split of opinion among state legislators. In the eyes of some state legislators, parents and other relatives are presumed to act in the best interests of the patient and would therefore not permit any unnecessary medical or surgical procedures. That attitude is not shared by other lawmakers. Although parents and concerned relatives may try to act in the best interests of the patient, they may not be well enough informed to authorize ECT, or there may be less drastic means of care of which they are not aware. The procedure may conflict with the physical, emotional, cultural, or religious needs of the patient. In other cases, parents or relatives may not act in good faith or in the best interests of patients.

---

[14] Aden v. Younger, 57 Cal. App. 3d 662, 129 Cal. Rptr. 535 (1976).
[15] Mich. Comp. Laws Ann. §330.1716 (1974).
[16] Mo. Ann. Stat. §630.130 (1980).

These and similar concerns account for the varying legislative approaches to parental and responsible relative consent to ECT for minors and incompetent patients.

§6.3.2 Consent Requirements in the Absence of Specific ECT Legislation

Not all states have enacted specific legislation governing the use of electroshock or electroconvulsive therapy. Some states may have left the fine points regarding such treatment to regulations or intrainstitutional policy making. Lawyers, physicians, and administrators should familiarize themselves with regulations and facility policies in their states. This is particularly important with respect to determining which patients are eligible for ECT as well as for standards for consent and disclosure of risk-benefit information.

In the absence of specific legislation, regulations, or policies, applicable case law and statutes of a more general nature on the subject of consent to treatment should be reviewed. Standards for disclosure of information, as well as criteria for a valid consent, may be found that are pertinent to the use of ECT.

At a minimum, the generally accepted requirements for an effective consent must be met before ECT is instituted. The patient's authorization must be voluntary and uncoerced. He must be both legally and mentally capable of giving consent. The explanation to the patient must be understandable yet thorough, outlining the risks, benefits, reasonable alternative forms of treatment, likely discomfort if any, the probable number of treatments, and other relevant information. Additional topics for coverage include pretherapeutic measures that must be followed regarding the consumption of food or beverages.

When a patient is not legally or mentally capable of giving consent, authorization must be obtained from someone who can act on behalf of the patient — e.g., a guardian, conservator, or committee. Whether the legal representative may give an authorization depends on the scope of her authority in matters of consent to care. A person appointed solely as the guardian, conservator, or committee of the patient's estate certainly cannot give an effective authorization. In some cases even the legal representative of the person of the patient may not be able to give consent: the extent of her authority depends on the actual letters of appointment and relevant statutory powers.

§6.3.3 Emergency Use of ECT

Certain situations may arise requiring emergency administration of ECT. In order for ECT to be used without prior consent, however, generally the patient must be proved to be incapable of giving consent and to be experiencing a life- or health-threatening illness that requires immediate care. Some state statutes set forth similar as well as additional criteria for medicolegal emergencies; these should be reviewed by practitioners in those states. State mental health statutes may also address the issue.

In some circumstances, emergency use of ECT can be avoided with proper patient management. Clinicians may be able to foresee the need for the use of the therapy well enough in advance to obtain the consent of the patient, his legal representative, or a court. Such foresight limits legal proceedings that question the urgency of the situation and the provision of treatment without consent.

When a situation arises requiring ECT on an emergency basis, documentation should be gathered on the need for the treatment in the absence of consent. This should be done in the patient's chart, outlining (a) why the patient is believed to be incapable of giving consent, (b) why, if a legal representative exists, it is impractical or impossible to obtain her consent, (c) the nature of the life-threatening illness, and (d) the reason why ECT is believed to be the least drastic form of intervention in the circumstances. The clinician who is to administer the therapy should write the entry in the record within a reasonable time of the therapy and he should sign and date it.

A written account in the patient's chart that conforms with state law on treatment in medical emergencies as well as on the use of ECT is important in the event of subsequent litigation. It may thwart the success of attempts by patients or their legal representatives to contest unauthorized care. The key is to demonstrate why it was believed at the time that ECT was administered that an emergency existed that required such care without prior approval of the patient or legal representative.

§6.3.4 Case Law on Consent to ECT

A body of case law has developed on the subject of consent to electroshock therapy. Some of it has focused on the application or interpretation of legislation dealing with ECT.

A Kentucky case makes it clear that electroshock therapy may not be administered simply because it is considered to be in the best interests of the patient.[17] As the court noted, in the absence of a judicial declaration of incompetency or an emergency situation in which the patient posed an imminent danger to himself or others, an involuntarily committed patient could not be subjected to electroshock therapy against his will.[18]

In one case a woman who was institutionalized and who was suffering from chronic schizophrenia declined consent to electroshock therapy. The case involved the application of a New York Mental Hygiene provision. Evidence in the case demonstrated that the woman was prone to acute flare-ups and that she was sufficiently mentally ill to require further retention for treatment. However, independent psychiatric evaluations permitted by the court concluded that she possessed the requisite mental capacity to consent or to withhold consent to ECT. The court denied the application requesting permission to administer the treatment.[19]

An interesting case arose in New Jersey involving the appli-

[17]Gundy v. Pauley, 619 S.W.2d 730 (Ky. Ct. App. 1981).
[18]Id.
[19]New York City Health & Hosps. Corp. v. Stein, 70 Misc. 2d 944, 335 N.Y.S.2d 461 (Sup. Ct., N.Y. County 1972).

cation of both federal and state law.[20] A 34-year-old veteran involuntarily committed for mental health care at a Veterans Administration Hospital was believed to be in need of ECT. Both the Veterans' Omnibus Health Care Act of 1976 and the legislative history supporting it were strongly behind the idea of informed consent of the patient or his representative prior to the administration of treatment.[21] Although it took notice of the federal law, the state court pointed out that New Jersey law was controlling: the care of mentally ill persons is a state function. The court went on to point out that state law was followed in this case. The patient was incapable of giving consent for the purpose of ECT and the hospital had shown that the patient was in need of this treatment on an emergency basis. Moreover, his parents were agreeable to the use of ECT and each was willing to serve as a special guardian for the purpose of giving consent to the treatment. The patient's own psychiatrist also recommended the use of electroshock.[22]

Although state legislation and regulations governing electroshock therapy may be quite detailed, court challenges can be anticipated involving the application of these laws. In one California case, the court ruled that a trial judge exceeded the bounds of his authority in an evidentiary hearing regarding the ability of the patient to consent to ECT.[23] In the course of the hearing the judge heard evidence regarding the need for the treatment and that the proposed therapy was the least drastic means of care available. However, the error was deemed harmless since other evidence demonstrated that the patient was incapable of acting intelligently upon the information provided to her by the treating physician.[24]

In another California case, the court ruled that the appropriate standard of proof required for determining whether a con-

---

[20] Matter of W.S., 152 N.J. Super. 298, 377 A.2d 969 (Juv. & Dom. Rel. Ct., Essex County 1977).
[21] Id.
[22] Id.
[23] In re Fadley, 205 Cal. Rptr. 572 (Cal. Ct. App. 1984).
[24] Id.

servatee had the ability to consent to ECT was that of clear and convincing evidence. The trial court had used a less stringent standard necessitating an order to set aside the lower court's decision.[25]

Yet another California case[26] illustrates that a patient who declines ECT after receiving information mandated by statute is not necessarily incapable of giving informed consent to such an intervention. In that instance, a conservator had been appointed when it was found that the patient was incapable of providing for his essential personal needs. He had a long-standing history of mental illness for which he had been receiving lithium. His condition was relatively stable until the medication was discontinued due to its side effects. He then became severely psychotic and was hospitalized with a diagnosis of "schizo-affective illness, excited phase."[27] Several ECT hearings were held and subsequently ECT was administered. On appeal, the court pointed out that while the patient was extremely psychotic and experienced delusional fears, his psychotic state of mind was intermittent. He appreciated that ECT was proposed to help him. However, having heard the possible effects and side effects of the treatment, the patient believed that it would scramble his brain and kill him. Indeed, he became agitated and psychotic when doctors tried to discuss the treatment with him. At a hearing on his refusal to authorize ECT, the patient was responsive and he followed a logical series of questions and answers. As the appellate court noted, this evidenced a coherent train of rational thought. The man having experienced ECT before, now feared he could die from it and he felt he could get better with medications.[28]

On appeal, the court determined that there was no evidence that the patient could not appreciate and act intelligently upon the information required to be disclosed under California state

[25] Lillian F. v. Superior Court, 206 Cal. Rptr. 603 (Cal. Ct. App. 1984).
[26] Conservatorship of Waltz, 180 Cal. App. 3d 722, 227 Cal. Rptr. 436 (Cal. Ct. App. 1986).
[27] Id. at 727, 227 Cal. Rptr. at 438.
[28] Id. at 730, 227 Cal. Rptr. at 440.

law. He had both a psychotic and rational fear of ECT that caused him to refuse consent to such treatment. The court concluded that the record was absent of any clear and convincing evidence to support the finding of incapacity to give informed consent.[29]

That the trier of fact must be careful to follow state legislation governing ECT and to permit the patient ample time to prepare her case is also demonstrated in a Washington state decision.[30] Although in this case ECT was carried out because the lower court denied a stay pending appeal, it does appear that henceforth in Washington the failure to follow due process and statutory requirements may be sufficient grounds to overturn an order for ECT. According to the Supreme Court of Washington, ECT cannot be ordered for a nonconsenting patient unless there is sufficient evidence:

1. of the patient's desires;
2. of a significant state interest in treatment; and
3. that treatment is both necessary and effective.

The degree of proof necessary is measured in terms of "clear, cogent, and convincing" evidence.[31] Moreover, the patient's attorney must be accorded adequate time to develop his case for the ECT hearing.[32]

Additional case law may be found on the matter of ECT and consent. The case law is fairly consistent in requiring proper application of statutory and regulatory provisions, though there is room for interpretation based on the facts of specific cases. As demonstrated above, a patient may be mentally ill yet retain the ability to refuse consent. The laws governing ECT require diligent assessment of the facts of each case, as well as an evaluation of the patient's mental capacity to give or refuse consent.

[29] Id. at 734, 227 Cal. Rptr. at 441.
[30] In re Schuoler, 106 Wash. 2d 500, 723 P.2d 1103 (1986).
[31] Id. at 510-513; 723 P.2d at 1110-1111.
[32] Id. at 513; 723 P.2d at 1111.

Challenges to state provisions regarding ECT may follow from misapplication of the law. They may also stem from perceived constitutional infirmities in the legislation.[33] The issue of consent may or may not be part of the challenge.

§6.3.5 Avoiding Consent Actions Involving ECT

One of the most significant concerns involving consent to electroshock therapy is the failure of medical personnel to provide sufficient information on which the patient or her legal representative can base a valid authorization. As in other areas of treatment, the information provided must follow state disclosure standards. A failure to do so combined with subsequent injury could lead to litigation. Unless state law has additional requirements, there is no need to disclose *all* known risks associated with ECT. Appropriate disclosure is instead determined by what is customarily revealed by physicians in the same or similar circumstances (medical community standard) or by what a reasonable patient would want to know in similar circumstances (patient need standard). Under the patient need standard, disclosure should focus on those matters that are significant to a patient in his decision-making. Potential benefits and risks are of primary importance, with the probable number of treatments and duration of probable benefits also of interest.

Since the consent process is two-way, the psychiatrist who wishes to administer ECT must have sufficient information with which to assess the advisability of such treatment. Patients with osteoporosis, for example, may be poor candidates for ECT due to the likelihood of injury from the treatment. Patients with known allergies to anesthetics may also prove to be poor candidates unless a safe anesthetic can be identified for them.

Those patients for whom the risks of harm of ECT are above average must be warned of their increased potential for injury. If they are incapable of giving consent, the information should

---

[33] Aden v. Younger, 57 Cal. App. 3d 662, 129 Cal. Rptr. 535 (1976).

be disclosed to the legal representatives who are authorized to act for them or to the judges who will decide whether to permit ECT. Careful consideration and application of the basic requirements for consent will decrease the likelihood of legal problems involving authorization for electroshock therapy.

§6.4 Consent and the Use of Medication

In the last number of years controversy has surrounded the involuntary treatment of patients with medication. Some of these cases have gone before the U.S. Supreme Court — with little resulting case law of precedential value.[1] Also of great concern are the risks associated with such pharmacological therapy. Are patients, whether they voluntarily or involuntarily undergo treatment, being warned of the potential side effects of these types of care? Are there any reasonable alternative forms of therapy? How much information must be disclosed? This section examines both judicial precedent and legislation in these areas.

§6.4.1 Legislative Controls on Medication: Precommitment Therapy

In some states the right to refuse medication is recognized for the limited purpose of precommitment detention.[2] The exercise of this right of refusal may be proscribed when medication is believed necessary as a means of preserving the patient's life[3] or as a way of preventing serious harm to the patient or

§6.4 [1]Mills v. Rogers, 457 U.S. 291 (1982). The Court had also accepted for review a similar case from New Jersey; however, it did not render a decision in the case. Instead, it remanded the case in light of the opinion in Youngberg v. Romeo, 457 U.S. 307 (1982). See Rennie v. Klein, 653 F.2d 836 (3d Cir. 1982), modified and remanded, 458 U.S. 1119 (1982).
[2]Kan. Stat. Ann. §59-2910 (1986); Okla. Stat. Ann. tit. 43A, §5-204 (West 1988); Wis. Stat. Ann. §51.61 (West 1978).
[3]See Kan. Stat. Ann. §§59-2910 and 59-2916a (1986).

others.[4] The decision to administer therapy under these latter circumstances may be made by a physician or by a court.[5] The medication administered should not interfere with the patient's ability to think clearly or take an active part in the preparation of her case at the commitment hearing. In some states medication that does have an interfering effect may be used if it is believed necessary to preserve life or to prevent serious harm to the patient or others.[6]

Practitioners faced with a decision regarding forcible administration of medication prior to a commitment proceeding should document the need for such therapy in the patient's chart. They should detail circumstances giving rise to the required medication and the lack of suitable alternative forms of care. To avoid litigation from drug therapy in these circumstances, applicable state legislation should be reviewed. Time limits in legislation may be in place restricting the period in which medication may be administered.[7] Any additional requirements must be met prior to instituting such care.

Legislation may also provide immunity from suit for administration of medication to a person in these circumstances. For example, Oklahoma legislation provides that a physician who in good faith administers medication to persons during a period of detention is immune from civil suits for damages.[8] This immunity provision seemingly also covers actions based upon consent. The statute authorizes the physician to determine whether such care is necessary to protect the nonconsenting patient, the facility, or others from serious harm. As long as the physician acts with good faith and bases judgment on the statu-

[4]Wis. Stat. Ann. §51.61 (West 1981).
[5]See, e.g., Okla. Stat. Ann. tit. 43A, §5-204 (West 1988), which allows the administration of medication to a nonconsenting individual upon the written order of a physician. See also Wis. Stat. Ann. §51.61 (West 1986), which permits a court to order medication therapy prior to the final commitment hearing if it is necessary to protect the patient or others from serious physical harm.
[6]Kan. Stat. Ann. §59-2910 (1986).
[7]Ark. Stat. Ann. §59-1415 (1983); Okla. Stat. Ann. tit. 43A, §5-204 (West 1988).
[8]Supra n.5.

tory criteria, he should be protected from civil actions for damages.

Other states may not set forth as clear an indication of immunity from suit. Still another danger is the possibility of action based on federal civil rights legislation. Obviously, no one can be completely protected from the prospect of lawsuits. The likelihood of their success, however, is remote when documentation establishes that a practitioner followed applicable law and decided to administer medication to a nonconsenting patient on the basis of sound medical judgment.

§6.4.2 Legislative Controls of Psychoactive Drugs and Other Medications

In a number of states, legislation recognizes the use of psychoactive drugs and other medication as a treatment for mental illness[9] and in the care of the mentally retarded or developmentally disabled.[10] This legislative recognition is not an open license for practitioners to prescribe or dispense such drugs. Rather, it takes the form of strict limitations on the use of medication and sometimes accepts the right of patients to refuse such therapy.

One common form of legislative control applicable to both the mentally ill and retarded or disabled makes it clear that medication cannot be used as a form of punishment,[11] nor can it be used for the convenience of the staff. Many of the laws also provide that drugs cannot replace the patient's individual treat-

[9]Ark. Stat. Ann. §59-1416 (1979); Conn. Gen. Stat. §17-206d (1980); La. Rev. Stat. §28:171 (West 1978); Mont. Code Ann. §53-21-145 (1979); N.C. Gen. Stat. §122-55.6 (1973).

[10]Ariz. Rev. Stat. Ann. §36-551.01 (1981); Colo. Rev. Stat. §27-10.5-114 (1975); Fla. Stat. Ann. §393.13 (West 1979); Ill. Ann. Stat. ch. 91 1/2, §2-107 (Smith-Hurd 1988).

[11]Ariz. Rev. Stat. Ann. §36-551.01 (1981); Ark. Stat. Ann. §59-1416 (1979); Fla. Stat. Ann. §393.13 (West 1979); La. Rev. Stat. §28:171 (West 1978); Mont. Code Ann. §53-21-145 (1979).

ment or program plan and the dosage administered should not interfere with that treatment plan.[12]

A significant burden is placed upon physicians by many of these statutes. When a drug is available only upon a prescription, its use must be authorized by a physician, who must also direct its administration.[13] Still other laws require periodic review of a patient's drug regimen.[14] Other health personnel may also bear burdens with respect to the medication. For example, in Montana a registered nurse or a pharmacist must review each developmentally disabled resident's medication record on a monthly basis. They must check for allergies, interactions, contraindications, and other matters specified in legislation. Any problems must be reported to the physician.[15]

Prescriptions for psychoactive medication and other drugs may also be subject to time limitations. Some laws indicate that the prescription for such medication must have a termination date or that the prescription cannot exceed a set number of days.[16]

    a. Right to refuse medication.   In many states legislation recognizes the right of the patient to refuse excessive or unnecessary medication.[17] The right to refuse drug treatment in these circumstances is often found in so-called patients' bills of rights.[18] This right applies to mentally ill, mentally retarded, and developmentally disabled persons. New Jersey has a provi-

---

[12]Ariz. Rev. Stat. Ann. §36-551.01 (1981); Ark. Stat. Ann. §59-1416 (1979); Fla. Stat. Ann. §393.13 (West 1979); Mont. Code Ann. §53-21-145 (1979); N.J. Stat. Ann. §30:4-24.2 (West 1975).

[13]Ariz. Rev. Stat. Ann. §36-551.01 (1981).

[14]Fla. Stat. Ann. §393.13 (West 1979); Mont. Code Ann. §53-21-145 (1979).

[15]Mont. Code Ann. §53-20-145 (1979).

[16]Fla. Stat. Ann. §393.13 (West 1979); Mont. Code Ann. §53-21-145 (1979).

[17]Ariz. Rev. Stat. Ann. §36-551.01 (1981); Ark. Stat. Ann. §59-1416 (1979); Colo. Rev. Stat. §27-10.5-114 (1975); Mont. Code Ann. §§53-20-145 (1979) and 53-21-145 (1979); N.C. Gen. Stat. §122-55.6 (1981).

[18]See, e.g., Fla. Stat. Ann. §393.13 (West 1979); N.J. Stat. Ann. §30:4-24.2 (West 1975).

sion that specifically acknowledges the right of a voluntary patient to refuse medication.[19] In some states a patient's refusal that is based upon religious beliefs must also be recognized.[20]

The right of a patient to refuse psychoactive drugs or other medication is not absolute. It may be overridden if the treatment is believed necessary to prevent serious harm by the patient to self or others.[21] Medication is sometimes recognized as a matter of chemical restraint.[22]

The burden is upon the prescribing physician to demonstrate a need to overrule the patient's refusal of medication. This need should be documented in the patient's chart in accordance with state legislative criteria for administering medication in these circumstances. It is an important consideration in the event of litigation challenging unauthorized drug therapy.

b. Informed consent requirements for medication therapy. Some state laws include a specific requirement for physicians to obtain, where possible, a patient's informed consent to treatment with medication.[23] The laws may not necessarily outline what information must be disclosed to the patient: this decision is left to the attending physician. Her choice, however, must comport with applicable state guidelines on divulging information.

In other states the need for informed consent may be set out in a patients' bill of rights for the mentally ill or the mentally retarded.[24] It may also be set out in general provisions of mental health legislation. For example, under Wisconsin law a voluntarily admitted inpatient cannot be subjected to any course of care without his written consent.[25] In addition, requirements for informed consent may be found in case law or statutes regarding authorization to treatment. It is incumbent upon

---

[19] Id.
[20] Wis. Stat. Ann. §51.61 (West 1978).
[21] Ill. Ann. Stat. ch. 91 1/2, §2-107 (Smith-Hurd 1988); Wis. Stat. Ann. §51.61 (West 1978).
[22] S.D. Codified Laws Ann. §27A-12-6 (1987).
[23] Conn. Gen. Stat. §17-206d (1980).
[24] Fla. Stat. Ann. §394.459 (West 1985).
[25] Wis. Stat. Ann. §51.61 (West 1985).

practitioners to familiarize themselves with the specific requirements in their states prior to prescribing a course of medication therapy.

In some jurisdictions a patient or resident must be warned of the risks associated with refusing a course of therapy, including medication. For example, under Illinois law an adult recipient of mental health or developmental disability services may refuse such care.[26] The director of the facility in which the patient receives care is charged with the responsibility of informing the person of alternative services that are available. She must also tell the patient of the consequences that could result from refusal of care.[27]

§6.4.3 Consent Requirements for Use of Medication Therapy

In the absence of specific statutory consent requirements, applicable state case law on the use of medication therapy for mentally ill, mentally retarded, or developmentally disabled persons must be followed. The law of consent requires that a person's decision to undergo such treatment must be voluntary and that he must be both mentally and legally capable of giving consent. In addition, the decision to have such treatment must be fully informed.

The standards for disclosure vary from state to state (see chapter 1). In the majority of states required disclosure is based upon what it is customary practice for physicians to reveal in similar circumstances. In other states, which follow the patient need standard for disclosure, a physician must inform a patient of those details that a reasonable person in the patient's position would want to know in the same or similar circumstances. Of particular importance to many patients is risk-benefit information, while others will want to consider the availability of

[26] Ill. Ann. Stat. ch. 91 1/2, §2-107 (Smith-Hurd 1988).
[27] Id.

alternative forms of therapy. The risks associated with refusing drug therapy may also merit disclosure.

Particularly troubling from a medicolegal perspective are the known risks associated with the use of some psychopharmacological agents. The known risks include tardive dyskinesia, a potentially permanent disorder;[28] in some instances, death may result from antipsychotic drugs.[29] If a patient may be "cured" of her mental illness but be left with a permanent physical impairment, should the patient be informed of this risk? Should a person be told that medication that may allow her to function outside of an institution could cause permanent harm?

The answer to these questions lies at the very heart of the law of consent. A person should be informed sufficiently so that he can make a reasoned choice. If the patient is incapable of making that decision, then his legal representative should be informed. It is arguable that under the medical community standard, based as it is on customary medical practice, a permissible disclosure may not include information involving risk of permanent harm.

Some physicians believe that they may withhold risk information regarding permanent harm from drugs under the therapeutic privilege doctrine. This stance may obtain in states following either rule of disclosure. In most psychoactive drug circumstances, relying upon the therapeutic privilege doctrine is incorrect. The rule may only be invoked when the disclosure is believed likely to cause a substantial or adverse impact upon the patient or her health. It cannot be used to justify withholding information that a physician knows or should know may cause a patient to refuse treatment because of the risks involved. Some patients may decline drug therapy in view of the likelihood of tardive dyskinesia and other serious side effects,

---

[28] Byck, Drugs and the Treatment of Psychiatric Disorders, in Goodman & Gilman, The Pharmacological Basis of Therapeutics 169 (1975).

[29] Brooks, The Constitutional Right to Refuse Antipsychotic Medications, 8 Bull. Am. Acad. Psychiatry & L. 179 (1981); Comment, Madness and Medicine: The Forcible Administration of Psychotropic Drugs, 1980 Wis. L. Rev. 487, 530-539.

deciding instead in favor of more traditional and less risky forms of therapy. That decision is one the patient is entitled to make based on an adequate disclosure of information. A failure to provide such information when its disclosure is not likely to cause a substantial or adverse impact upon the patient or her health cannot be justified. Any consent based on less than a sufficient disclosure of information, where the procedure results in harm, could be cause for litigation.[30] The same line of reasoning applies to consent information that must be disclosed to an incapable patient's legal representative.

The best policy is to furnish a patient with sufficient information to make a decision regarding drug therapy. Moreover, the patient's consent or that of his legal representative should be documented — either in a consent form or through a note in the patient's chart, depending on the requirements of state law. Either type of documentation should include the information revealed to the patient or his legal representative — e.g., the details of risk, benefits, and reasonable alternative forms of care. If authorization is obtained from a legal representative, it should be clear that she is authorized to act on behalf of the patient.

§6.4.4 Case Law on the Use of Medication

As noted at the outset of this section, there is at least one U.S. Supreme Court decision involving the forcible use of medication in the mental health setting.[31] The case arose in the U.S. District Court for the District of Massachusetts as a class action proceeding. The class included both voluntarily and involuntarily admitted mental hospital patients who had received treatment at one 'time or another. During their hospitalization all had received antipsychotic medication against their will. The district court ruled that antipsychotic medication could not be administered without the consent of the patient — or his

---

[30]See, e.g., Barclay v. Campbell, 704 S.W.2d 8 (Tex. 1986).
[31]Mills v. Rogers, 457 U.S. 291 (1982).

guardian in the case of an incompetent individual. Only in an emergency may the patient's constitutionally protected liberty interests be overridden by the state.[32] Following a ruling by the First Circuit Court of Appeals in the case, the U.S. Supreme Court granted certiorari. After considering the case, the Court remanded it to the circuit court in light of a Massachusetts Supreme Judicial Court decision that had been handed down, which the Court felt was dispositive of the case.[33]

Although the Court did not squarely address the issue before it, the decision is important as a recognition that in some instances the protection afforded by state law may be greater than that found under federal law. This balance has implications for both substantive and procedural aspects of a person's liberty interests.

The Massachusetts case referred to by the Supreme Court offers a unique approach to the right of a mentally ill patient to refuse psychoactive drug therapy. The court's opinion is not based solely upon constitutional considerations: it specifically mentions that common law principles also form a basis for its ruling. The court ruled that in the absence of an emergency, antipsychotic drugs can only be administered to an incompetent person when ordered by a court of law.[34] Although the decision is specifically limited to noninstitutionalized persons, it may have relevance to institutionalized patients in other states.

In its ruling, the Massachusetts Supreme Judicial Court determined that in the case of incompetent persons, the decision to administer antipsychotic drugs cannot be made by a guardian. The decision is to be made by a court, which will examine the incompetent person's values and preferences. The ruling follows an earlier line of reasoning in Massachusetts regarding medical care for incompetent persons.[35]

The Massachusetts court listed six factors that are to be taken

---

[32]Rogers v. Okin, 478 F. Supp. 1342 (D. Mass. 1979).
[33]Mills v. Rogers, supra n.31, at 306.
[34]Guardianship of Roe, III, 383 Mass. 415, 434, 421 N.E.2d 40, 51 (1981). See also Guardianship of Linda, — N.E.2d — (Mass. 1988).
[35]Guardianship of Roe, III, supra n.34, at 442-443, 421 N.E.2d at 56.

into account in making a decision for the incompetent individual. These considerations, as well as other factors, should help courts reach a decision similar to the one the person would have chosen if she were capable of doing so. These include:

1. the ward's express preferences regarding treatment;
2. the ward's religious beliefs;
3. the impact upon the ward's family;
4. the probability of adverse side effects;
5. the consequences if treatment is refused; and
6. the prognosis with treatment.[36]

If, after considering these and other factors, the judge finds that the incompetent person would authorize the use of antipsychotic drugs, he may authorize such care.

In the event that the judge finds that the person if capable would refuse consent to such therapy, another judicial mechanism must be followed. The Massachusetts Supreme Judicial Court ruled that there must be a compelling state interest present to justify the forcible administration of antipsychotic drugs. Preventing the infliction of harm upon the community by persons suffering from mental illness was identified as such a state interest.[37]

The court equated forcible administration of antipsychotic drugs with involuntary commitment. Both involve deprivation of an important right, the interest in personal liberty. As such the court thought that the standard of proof used in either situation should be the same. In Massachusetts, the standard for commitment of a person without consent is proof of the likelihood of serious harm to self or others established beyond a reasonable doubt.

The court also extended the substituted judgment role of the lower courts. It noted that two means are available to protect the state interest in preventing violence in the community: involuntary commitment and involuntary medication. The least

[36] Id. at 444, 421 N.E.2d at 57.
[37] Id. at 450, 421 N.E.2d at 60.

intrusive means is to be used upon the incompetent person, based on the court's substituted judgment.[38]

A great deal of additional case law has accrued in the aftermath of the United States Supreme Court ruling in Mills v. Rogers.[39] The litigation has been quite diverse, focusing on religious objections to psychotropic drug therapy,[40] the power of a court to order the withdrawal of psychotropic drugs in order to determine the reason for an apparent remission in defendant's mental illness,[41] a claim that a forensic patient had a constitutional right to be informed of the potential risks associated with psychotropic drugs before he voluntarily took the medication,[42] and forcible medication of a defendant who had been determined to be incompetent to stand trial.[43]

Of particular interest, however, are the due process requirements involved in the use of psychotropic drugs.[44] These focus not only on who may determine whether an involuntarily committed mentally ill person is capable of deciding to undergo psychotropic drug therapy but also on who may make the treatment decision in the case of the incompetent.

The United States Court of Appeals for the First Circuit ruled in Rogers v. Okin that Massachusetts requirements of judicial decision-making in determining whether an involuntarily committed, mentally ill person was capable of making a treatment decision afforded more than the minimal procedural

---

[38] Id. at 452, 421 N.E.2d at 60.

[39] See Rogers v. Okin, 738 F.2d 1 (1st Cir. 1984); Rennie v. Klein, 720 F.2d 266 (3d Cir. 1983); R. A. J. v. Miller, 590 F. Supp. 1319 (N.D. Tex. 1984); Weiss v. Missouri Dept. of Mental Health, 587 F. Supp. 1157 (E.D. Mo. 1984); United States v. Leatherman, 580 F. Supp. 977 (D.D.C. 1983); In re Burton, 11 Ohio St. 3d 147, 464 N.E.2d 530 (1984); Kolocontronis v. Ritterbusch, 667 S.W.2d 430 (Mo. Ct. App. 1984); Rogers v. Commissioner of Dept. of Mental Health, 390 Mass. 489, 458 N.E.2d 308 (1983); Barclay v. Campbell, 704 S.W.2d 8 (Tex. 1986); People v. Medina, 146 Ariz. 284, 705 P.2d 961 (1985); Savastano v. Saribeyoglu, 126 Misc. 2d 52, 480 N.Y.S.2d 977 (Sup. Ct., Queens County 1984).

[40] Kolocontronis v. Ritterbusch, supra n.39.

[41] In re Burton, supra n.39.

[42] Weiss v. Missouri Dept. of Mental Health, supra n.39.

[43] United States v. Charters, 829 F.2d 479 (4th Cir. 1987).

[44] See Rogers v. Okin, supra n.39; Rennie v. Klein, supra n.39.

protections required in safeguarding the patient's liberty interests. This was particularly true in view of additional safeguards such as an adversary proceeding and regulations on the use of chemical restraints.[45]

In contrast, in Rennie v. Klein the United States Circuit Court for the Third Circuit found less stringent New Jersey procedural safeguards sufficient for the forcible administration of psychotropic drugs to involuntarily committed mentally ill patients.[46] Unlike the situation in Massachusetts, the New Jersey requirements did not require judicial decision-making in the determination to forcibly medicate.

What is minimally necessary from the standpoint of due process? Differing approaches taken in two states have satisfied due process requirements in the estimation of two United States Circuit Courts of Appeal. Earlier decisions by the United States Supreme Court in Mills v. Rogers,[47] involving Massachusetts law, and in Youngberg v. Romeo,[48] focusing on a "professional judgment" standard in the use of physical restraints on a mentally retarded inmate, provide little guidance on the basic due process requirements for forcible administration of psychotropic drugs. Clarification is bound to emerge from both statutory refinements and further case law.

Indeed, the case law has begun to emerge. Several state courts have now authored decisions[49] that should please those concerned about the degree of protection afforded involuntarily committed patients. What seems to be emerging is a consen-

---

[45] Rogers v. Okin, supra n.39.
[46] Rennie v. Klein, supra n.39.
[47] 457 U.S. 291 (1982).
[48] 457 U.S. 307 (1982).
[49] See, e.g., Jarvis v. Levine, 418 N.W.2d 139 (Minn. 1988); Riese v. St. Mary's Hosp. & Med. Center, 243 Cal. Rptr. 241 (Cal. Ct. App. 1987); Rivers v. Katz, 67 N.Y.2d 485, 495 N.E.2d 337 (1986); In Interest of Gust, 392 N.W.2d 824 (N.D. 1986); Matter of Danielson, 398 N.W.2d 32 (Minn. Ct. App. 1986); In re Mental Commitment of M.P., 510 N.E.2d 645 (Ind. 1987), remanding N.E.2d 216 (Ind. Ct. App. 1986); State ex rel. Jones v. Gerhardstein, 400 N.W.2d 1 (Wis. Ct. App. 1986), affd., 416 N.W.2d 883 (Wis. 1987); Eleanor R. v. South Oaks Hosp., 506 N.Y.S.2d 763 (App. Div. 1986).

sus that involuntary commitment for treatment for mental illness is not an implicit finding of incompetency. Moreover, from an evidentiary and legal point of view, the states will have to go to great lengths to assuage the courts before involuntary use of antipsychotic medication is permitted.

Perhaps the most telling state court decision is that of Rivers v. Katz,[50] from the New York Court of Appeals. Based on state constitutional and common law requirements, the *Rivers* decision provides a blueprint for lower courts to follow in deciding the complex issue of medicating involuntary patients with antipsychotic drugs.

At the outset, the New York Court of Appeals cited a whole line of cases starting with the famous *Schloendorff* decision[51] to reinforce the point that it is the *patient* who should decide what is done to her body. This common law right was seen as being "coextensive" with the patient's liberty interest protected under the New York State Constitution's due process clause.[52]

In the case of involuntarily committed mental health patients, the state argued that they are presumptively incompetent to exercise this right of self-determination. It was argued that by committing persons for treatment, the courts are implicitly determining that they lack the ability to make decisions regarding treatment. This was rejected by the New York court. That individuals are mentally ill or that they have been involuntarily committed for treatment is an adequate basis for saying that they lack the mental capacity to understand the consequences of refusing medication therapy.[53]

The court did recognize, however, that the liberty interest in refusing antipsychotic medications is not absolute. There may be compelling state interests that override the individual's choice. This would be particularly true if the patient poses a danger to himself or others or if the patient is involved in

---

[50] 67 N.Y.2d 485, 495 N.E.2d 337 (1986).
[51] Id. at 341, quoting Schloendorff v. Society of N.Y. Hosp., 211 N.Y. 125, 129, 105 N.E.2d 92 (1914).
[52] Id. at 341.
[53] Id. at 341-342.

dangerous or potentially destructive activities within the institution. In such emergency conditions the state's police powers could be exercised to permit forcible medication. However, this could only be carried out for as long as the emergency exists.

In a footnote, the court added a cautionary note. When speaking of a compelling state interest, the court wrote:

> Any implication that State interests unrelated to the patient's well-being or those around him can outweigh his fundamental autonomy is rejected. Thus, the State's interest in providing a therapeutic environment, in preserving time and resources of the hospital staff, in increasing the process of deinstitutionalization and in maintaining the ethical integrity of the medical profession, while important, cannot outweigh the fundamental individual rights here asserted.[54]

When, however, the state's interest is not based on the exercise of its police power authority but on parens patriae considerations, a different set of requirements comes into play. When patients refuse consent to antipsychotic medication, there must be a judicial inquiry of whether such patients have the capacity to make reasoned choices in this regard. This necessitates a hearing at which the state must prove by clear and convincing evidence that patients lack the capacity to make a treatment decision. If it is found that patients possess the requisite capacity, the state cannot forcibly administer antipsychotic medication.

When, however, patients are considered incapable of giving consent, the following determinations must be made:

1. that the treatment is "narrowly tailored to give substantive effect"[55] to the patients' liberty interest;
2. that it reflects the consideration of the patients' best interests;
3. that it demonstrates the gains to be achieved with treatment; and

[54] Id. at 343.
[55] Id. at 344.

4. that it identifies adverse side effects as well as less invasive, alternative forms of care.[56]

The court noted that the current state administrative review procedures were inadequate in that the due process rights of involuntarily confined patients guaranteed under state constitutional law were not protected. What was needed was better articulation of the standards or criteria to be employed throughout the administrative process.[57]

The *Rivers* decision creates a two-prong method of analysis. Where the basis for seeking forcible administration of antipsychotic medication is the state's police powers, the state may be permitted to compel treatment for a brief time; that is, as long as the emergency continues. However, where the argument is that patients are unable to care for themselves and the state feels medication is needed to treat them, the parens patriae analysis is employed. This must be predicated on a finding of incapacity on the part of patients to make treatment decisions.[58]

What kinds of factors enter into a finding of capacity to refuse or to give consent? In a footnote to its *Rivers* opinion,[59] the New York Court of Appeals pointed out that one commentator has identified eight points for consideration. These include:

1. whether the person knows he has a choice to make;
2. whether the individual has the ability to appreciate treatment options and their relative advantages and disadvantages;
3. whether the patient has the "cognitive" ability to consider pertinent information;[60]
4. whether there were any pathological beliefs, such as delusions, surrounding the choice to be made;

[56] Id.
[57] Id.
[58] Id. at 345.
[59] Id. at 344, citing one article and a law review.
[60] Id.

5. whether there was any emotional state, such as severe manic depression or an emotional disability;
6. whether there was present or absent any pathologic motivational pressure;
7. whether the patient had the perception of a pathologic relationship, such as being helplessly dependent upon another individual; and
8. whether the patient had an appreciation of how other people view the choice, including social attitudes toward the options as well as an understanding of the basis for his decision to depart from the general social viewpoint if he does so.

The *Rivers* decision is an important one. Authored by a respected court, it demonstrates a common law and state constitutional law approach to the issue of forcible administration of psychoactive medication. The court has taken a strong point of view that it is the judiciary, and not doctors, who should decide whether antipsychotic medications should be administered to those incapable of making decisions for themselves. However, the fact remains that the courts, in sifting out capacity from incapacity, will be heavily dependent upon evidence presented by health professionals. If the eight factors identified are any indication, the judiciary may find it quite a challenge to decide who is and who is not capable of making reasoned choices regarding the use of antipsychotic drugs.

Not all courts agree with the Massachusetts/New York models for substituted consent in the case of mentally incapable individuals. Some may find the requirement of judicial or administrative decision-making cumbersome and unnecessary. Carefully chosen guardians could instead authorize treatment, after giving considerable thought and attention to the best interests of their wards. Additional safeguards may also protect patients' rights without the need for judicial or administrative involvement in each and every case where drug therapy is recommended — e.g., periodic review of a patient's progress and an assessment of drug therapy on a monthly basis by both the attending doctor and a physician not involved in the patient's case. Moreover, prescriptions for psychoactive drugs could be time limited, which requires the attending physician to re-evaluate the patient prior to instituting a new course of drug treatment.

To be sure, there are significant constitutional interests involved in the forcible administration of psychoactive drugs. At least one court has recognized a patient's First Amendment rights as being implicated in forcible administration of such medication since the drugs affected his mental processes.[61]

The difficult cases involve patients who are in need of treatment but who express an objection to such treatment. In one New Jersey case, a patient suffering from paranoid schizophrenia refused treatment with Prolixin, a psychotropic medication.[62] He based his refusal on the side effects he had experienced with another psychotropic medication, as well as his own observations of other patients taking such drugs. However, there were other delusional reasons behind the patient's refusal. Taking these factors together with New Jersey legislation that did not recognize the right of involuntarily committed patients to refuse medication, the court held that the state had the authority to treat the patient without his consent.[63]

Not all courts agree with the New Jersey approach. As the Massachusetts court noted, to deny the legally incompetent individual the right to refuse antipsychotic drug therapy is to "degrade those whose disabilities make them wholly reliant on other, more fortunate, individuals."[64] Other courts have restricted the forcible administration of such drugs to legally incompetent people. For example, a court in the District of Columbia remanded a case to a lower court to determine if, in using the substituted judgment approach, an incompetent person would continue to refuse antipsychotic medication. If she

---

[61] Scott v. Plante, 532 F.2d 939 (3d Cir. 1976).

[62] In the Matter of the Hospitalization of B, 156 N.J. Super. 231, 383 A.2d 760 (1977).

[63] Id.

[64] Guardianship of Roe, III, 383 Mass. at 434, 421 N.E.2d at 51.

would and no compelling state interest justified overriding her choice, no medication could be administered.[65]

Legally and mentally incapable patients are not the only ones for whom concern has been raised regarding the use of antipsychotic drugs. The right of competent patients to decline such treatment has also come before the courts. For example, in an Oklahoma case the superintendent of a state mental hospital sought a declaratory judgment regarding the right of mentally capable but mentally ill persons to refuse antipsychotic drugs.[66] The patient involved suffered from schizophrenia, and the trial court authorized the hospital to take such measures as were necessary to provide the proposed treatment. On appeal, the Supreme Court of Oklahoma reversed the decision. The court noted that since the law recognized the autonomy of the individual to make decisions affecting her life, the significance of this right was not diminished by the fact that the individual was mentally ill. Since the patient would be the one to experience the consequences of drug treatment, she must have the power to make the decision regarding such care.[67]

A similar result was reached in a Colorado case involving a patient suffering from a form of schizophrenia.[68] As the Supreme Court of Colorado pointed out, in the absence of proof that the patient was incapable of making decisions regarding his treatment or that his refusal of drug therapy was irrational or unreasonable, both statutory and common law protected his right to decline such care. Testimony in the case revealed that physicians proposed to use the drug Prolixin to change the patient's psychotic thought patterns and to reduce his dangerousness. The patient based his refusal on the fact that when he was treated with it in the past he had experienced some short-term side effects. Expert testimony revealed that serious long-

---

[65] In re Boyd, 403 A.2d 744 (D.C. 1979).
[66] In re Mental Health of K.K.B., 602 P.2d 747 (Okla. 1980).
[67] Id.
[68] Goedecke v. State Dept. of Institutions, 198 Colo. 407, 603 P.2d 123 (1979).

term consequences of the drug could also result. Reasonable alternative forms of care did exist, including milieu therapy and psychotherapy. The court viewed the situation as one in which Colorado law protected the patient's right to refuse a form of treatment that involved significant risks.[69]

Colorado has also examined the right of an incompetent, mentally ill, and nonconsenting patient to refuse antipsychotic medication.[70] The court built upon precedent that a competent mental health patient had a qualified right to refuse antipsychotic drugs.[71] The court ruled that in the absence of an emergency involving an immediate and substantial threat to life or safety of the patient or other persons in the institution, the nonconsenting, mentally ill, incapable patient may be subjected to administration of antipsychotic medication. However, for this to occur, the court must be satisfied on the basis of clear and convincing evidence that:

1. the patient is incompetent to effectively participate in the treatment decision;
2. treatment by antipsychotic medication is necessary to prevent a significant and likely long-term deterioration in the patient's mental condition or to prevent the likelihood of the patient's causing serious harm to himself or herself or others in the institution;
3. a less intrusive treatment alternative is not available; and
4. the patient's need for treatment by antipsychotic medication is sufficiently compelling to override any bona fide and legitimate interest of the patient in refusing treatment.[72]

It does not appear that the issue of forcible use of psychoactive drugs is about to disappear. Many questions remain. The *Rivers* court touched on one, namely, the proper role of medical experts in decisions regarding forcible use of psychoactive drugs. Not all judges are convinced that the "professional judg-

---

[69] Id.
[70] People v. Medina, 705 P.2d 961 (Colo. 1985).
[71] Goedecke v. State Dept. of Institutions, 603 P.2d 123 (Colo. 1979).
[72] People v. Medina, supra n.70, at 963-964.

ment" standard is well suited to the question of compelling treatment with medication.[73] Furthermore, state laws designed to protect those who are subject to compelled treatment will be scrutinized to make certain that there is adequate protection of rights and guarantees.[74] Forcible use of psychoactive drugs will be permitted by some courts[75] and deemed inappropriate by others.[76] This will probably be the scenario for some time until the difficult issues surrounding forcible administration of medications are resolved.

From a practical perspective, mental health facilities and personnel must secure specific legal advice. Legal counsel should alert facilities and professionals to essential state case law and legislation in this area. This should be done frequently to keep abreast of developments from the courts and state legislatures.

§6.4.5 Policy Considerations in the Forcible Administration of Medication

Although many cases can be found involving the right to refuse antipsychotic drugs,[77] the courts have seemingly taken a defensive position regarding the right of the mentally ill to refuse drug treatment. Commitment alone does not remove the right of consent. Even in the case of legally incapable persons, the right to refuse therapy remains intact. The difficulty in this last situation is deciding who may exercise this right on behalf of the patient.

Both constitutional and consent principles are factors in these cases. The patient's rights of privacy and free expression will be protected in the absence of compelling evidence that state interests should prevail or that treatment is in the patient's

---

[73] See In re Mental Commitment of M.P., supra n.49, dissenting opinion.
[74] See State ex rel. Jones v. Gerhardstein, supra n.49, ruling that Wisconsin legislation denied equal protection to involuntary patients.
[75] See, e.g., In Interest of Gust; Eleanor R. v. South Oaks Hosp., supra n.49.
[76] In the Matter of Danielson, supra note 49.
[77] See, e.g., Rennie v. Klein, 653 F.2d 836 (3d Cir. 1981), modified and remanded, 653 F.2d 836 (1982).

best interests. The law of consent requires proof that the proposed treatment is considered in terms of likely risks and benefits. The availability of less intrusive but nonetheless reasonable treatment alternatives must be addressed.

The reasons behind a patient's refusal must be considered. The explanation may be reasonable — based on religious beliefs,[78] previous experience with the same or similar drugs, or the experience of others with medication therapy. If the patient's decision is rational, no exigency exists requiring such treatment, and reasonable alternative forms of treatment are available, forcible use of psychotic medication cannot be allowed.

A patient's signature on a form that documents refusal of treatment has potential legal implications. If the patient's refusal was made at a time of competency and no justification existed for forcible administration of drug therapy, the existence of such a form could create sufficient grounds for litigation in the event that medication was administered. The law of consent could be a factor, but so could constitutional and legislative rights. The decision to overrule a patient's refusal should not be taken lightly. The health facility in which forcible administration of drugs is permitted should consider carefully when and under what circumstances, if any, such practices may be permitted. As noted earlier, legislation and case law in some states recognize certain instances in which there is no other recourse but to administer psychoactive drugs. The important consideration for health care administrators and physicians is to make certain the practice is followed only when it is permissible by law.

§6.5   Psychosurgery and the Law of Consent

Psychosurgery is a matter largely governed in the United States by legislation. It has been at the center of considerable controversy regarding the need for such intrusive measures, as

---

[78] See Guardianship of Roe, III, 383 Mass. 415, 421 N.E.2d 40 (1981). For further consideration of religious beliefs and medication therapy, see Winters v. Miller, 446 F.2d 65 (2d Cir. 1971), cert. denied, 404 U.S. 985 (1971).

seen in a 1977 report from the National Commission for the Protection of Human Subjects of Biomedical and Behavioral Research.[1] It has also been the subject of one highly publicized case in the state of Michigan. See §6.5.4 infra.

Whether psychosurgery is an acceptable therapeutic medium for certain classes of psychiatric patients is beyond the scope of this volume. It is a matter that must be left to medical experts. What is of importance here, however, is the right of the patient to be fully informed of the probable risks and benefits associated with psychosurgery, as well as of any reasonable alternative forms of treatment. The legal and mental capacity of individuals to authorize such treatment in a voluntary manner is another important consent issue associated with the use of psychosurgery. This section addresses these matters and reviews state legislation and case law on the subject.

§6.5.1 What Is Psychosurgery?

The term *psychosurgery* applies to a variety of intrusive measures that are designed to destroy or remove normal brain tissue in order to alter a patient's behavior.[2] The term is often defined as including prefrontal lobotomies,[3] but as the National Commission suggested, it may include the implanting of electrodes, the use of lasers or ultrasound intended to destroy brain tissue, as well as techniques designed to remove the emotional response to pain.[4] Psychosurgery does not, however, include surgical procedures to remove tumors, invasive techniques designed to correct movement disorders, or electric shock treatment.[5]

---

§6.5 [1] Use of Psychosurgery in Practice and Research: Report and Recommendations for Public Comment, 42 Fed. Reg. 26317, May 23, 1977.
[2] Id.
[3] Cf. Comment, Psychosurgery and the Involuntarily Confined, 24 Vill. L. Rev. 949, 951 (1978-1979), wherein the author points out that proponents of psychosurgery take sharp exception to including prefrontal lobotomies in the same category with the more sophisticated psychosurgical operations.
[4] Supra n.1.
[5] Id.

The definition of psychosurgery is important since certain procedures that come within the meaning of the term may be curtailed or highly regulated by state legislation. The definition also has implications for the requirements of informed consent: psychosurgery may be seen more as a last resort than as one of many reasonable alternative forms of care. Due to the irreparable nature of psychosurgery, the requirements of informed consent also take on added significance.

§6.5.2 State Legislation Regulating Psychosurgery

In a number of states, statutory patients' bills of rights clearly state that an individual may refuse psychosurgery.[6] Others make it clear that psychosurgery cannot be performed without the express and informed consent of the patient or her legal representative.[7] California, in its patients' rights provision relating to psychosurgery, also supplies a definition of the term,[8] a practice that is not common throughout the country.

What is more frequently found throughout the United States is legislation specifically governing the practice of psychosurgery. Most state statutes require the consent of the patient if he is capable of giving it.[9] In addition, some states require that the patient consult with legal counsel or another interested party before authorizing a procedure involving psychosurgery.[10] Still others require consultations by physicians not involved in the patient's case to make certain that psychosurgery is necessary.[11]

Another interesting measure found in some state laws is

[6]Ark. Stat. Ann. §59-1416 (1979); Cal. Welf. & Inst. Code §5325 (West 1978); Ky. Rev. Stat. §202A.180 (1976); Mass. Gen. Laws Ann. ch. 123, §23 (West 1978) (refers to the right to refuse lobotomy only).
[7]N.J. Stat. Ann. §30:4-24.2 (West 1975); N.D. Cent. Code §25-03.1-40 (1977); Wis. Stat. Ann. §51.61 (West 1978).
[8]Cal. Welf. & Inst. Code §5325 (West 1978).
[9]Conn. Gen. Stat. §17-206d (1980); Fla. Stat. Ann. §458.325 (West 1979); Ill. Ann. Stat. ch. 91 1/2, §2-110 (Smith-Hurd 1979); Mont. Code Ann. §53-21-148 (1979) (lobotomies); N.M. Stat. Ann. §43-1-15 (1978).
[10]N.J. Stat. Ann. §30:4-24.2 (West 1975).
[11]Fla. Stat. Ann. §458.325 (West 1979).

a requirement for co-consent prior to the performance of psychosurgery. Not only must the consent of the patient be obtained but that of a legal representative or a designated relative as well. Montana has such a law that requires co-consent from the patient's counsel, her legal guardian, a friend of the patient appointed by a court, or any other interested person of the patient's choice.[12]

This type of co-consent legislation is designed to ensure a voluntary and informed consent prior to the performance of psychosurgery. It is a fail-safe measure, designed to protect the rights of the patient in the event that either he is incapable of giving informed consent or consent was not given freely.

In the event that a physician recommends that an incompetent patient undergo psychosurgery, additional safeguards are applied to make certain that the authorization of a third party is fully informed. This often means a hearing with the usual due process considerations of a right to representation by counsel, as well as the right to confront and cross-examine witnesses who assert that psychosurgery is necessary.[13] The burden of proof also rests with the party claiming that psychosurgery is necessary.[14]

The degree of proof necessary to establish the need for psychosurgery may vary. For example, under North Dakota law, a court may order psychosurgery for a developmentally disabled person only upon clear and convincing evidence that the operation is in the individual's best interests and no less drastic treatment is feasible.[15] Other courts, whether by legislation or case decisions, may take a different view. The need must be established, probably in terms of the patient's best interests, but the degree of proof may be by a preponderance of the evidence. Details depend on the requirements of state law in a particular jurisdiction.

[12] Mont. Code Ann. §53-21-148 (1979).
[13] N.J. Stat. Ann. §30:4-24.2 (West 1975). See also N.M. Stat. Ann. §43-1-15 (1979); N.D. Cent. Code §25-01.2-11 (1983); Wash. Rev. Code Ann. §11.92.040 (1985).
[14] N.J. Stat. Ann. §30:4-24.2 (West 1975).
[15] N.D. Cent. Code §25-01.2-11 (1981).

§6.5.3 Factors Influencing Decisions for Psychosurgery

Since psychosurgery is often a drastic and irreversible measure, an authorization for it must be considered carefully. This is all the more important when the authorization comes from a third party on behalf of a legally or mentally incapable person. Some state legislation has specified the types of factors that should be weighed in considering psychosurgery.[16] It is helpful to outline some of these and other factors for the benefit of those who must decide upon a course of psychosurgery.

1. Do the probable benefits of the procedure outweigh the likely risks?
2. Are there any other feasible alternative forms of treatment that are less intrusive?
3. Have other more conventional and less intrusive forms of care been examined and tried? If so, how successful were these forms of treatment? Is it worthwhile to continue with a more conservative course of treatment?
4. What is the likelihood of improvement or recovery for the patient without the operation? What is the likelihood of success with the procedure?
5. Is the patient a good candidate for the operation?
6. What impact will the operation have on the patient's lifestyle and his or her ability to live and work outside of an institutionalized or structured environment?
7. How does the patient feel about the prospect of psychosurgery? Does it violate his or her religious or cultural beliefs?
8. If concerned relatives or friends are available, how do they view the proposed operation in terms of what the patient, if capable, would want to do?
9. Have second opinions been obtained from physicians not associated with the patient's case or with the institution in which he or she is institutionalized?
10. Is the particular type of psychosurgical procedure the best

[16]Fla. Stat. Ann. §458.325 (West 1979); Or. Rev. Stat. §426.715 (1973).

suited for the patient's problem? Are there other types of surgical interventions that would be more appropriate from a medical perspective?

11. Who will pay the costs involved in the patient's hospitalization and the surgery? Who will pay for any costs incurred in the patient's postoperative recovery and disability period?

12. Is the proposed operation part of an experiment or research protocol? If so, has the principal investigator on the study disclosed what part of the procedure is experimental or research? Will it benefit the patient or is it nontherapeutic? Have applicable federal and state laws relating to human research been met, particularly those dealing with consent?

Additional factors could be enumerated for consideration by all parties concerned in a proposed psychosurgery case. It is important, however, to review applicable state laws to determine if specific provisions apply to institutionalized and/or incapable individuals that are not relevant to nonhospitalized or competent patients. Due to the deprivation of liberty involved in institutionalization as well as the need for protection of the individual rights of incompetent people, state law may impose higher standards as threshold considerations for psychosurgery.

§6.5.4 Case Law

There is one highly publicized case involving consent to psychosurgery. A careful examination of the facts and circumstances of this case will be helpful in determining what would be permissible in similar situations. It also points out the legal concerns that make psychosurgery a procedure necessarily subject to careful examination.

a. The Kaimowitz *case and consent to psychosurgery.* In 1955, Louis Smith (referred to as John Doe in the court's written opinion) was committed to the Ionia State Hospital in Michigan as a criminal sexual psychopath.[17] He had been committed without a trial under the terms of then existing legislation following a charge of murder and subsequent rape of a nursing student at a mental health hospital while he was confined there as a patient.[18]

In 1972, two physicians at a Michigan Mental Health Department clinic received funding from the state legislature for a study of treatment of uncontrollable aggression. Louis Smith was transferred to the clinic, where he was determined to be the only appropriate research subject for the study available within the state mental health system.

The study was designed to compare the effectiveness of experimental psychosurgery on the amygdaloid component of the limbic system of the brain with the impact of the drug cyproterone acetate on the secretion of the male hormones. The researchers hoped to determine whether either means could control the aggressive tendencies of institutionalized men. A further aim of the protocol was the permanent ending of aggression in the particular patient under study.[19]

Smith signed a document before he was transferred from the state hospital to the clinic that authorized his participation in the experiment. His parents gave their consent to the operation, although exactly what they authorized was in dispute.[20] In addition, the researchers had two different three-man committees assess the scientific merit of the study as well as the validity of the patient's consent.[21]

In early January 1973, the plaintiff, Mr. Kaimowitz, learned of the impending experiment and brought it to the attention of the media, which resulted in the researchers abandoning their plans to carry out the project.[22] Mr. Kaimowitz also launched a

---

[17] Kaimowitz v. Dept. of Mental Health for State of Michigan, 2 Prison L. Rptr. 433 (1973).
[18] Id.
[19] Id.
[20] Id. at 434.
[21] Id.
[22] Id.

legal action in behalf of Louis Smith and the Medical Committee for Human Rights, seeking a writ of habeas corpus. Upon the request of counsel, the case was heard before a three-judge court.[23]

The court decided that the case was not moot just because the research project was not being pursued. Rather it characterized the case as being ripe for declaratory judgment; nothing prevented the proposal from going forward at a future date. The court viewed the case as exemplifying the question of whether involuntarily confined adults in the mental health system of the state could give legally effective consent to experimental or innovative procedures involving the brain. The court also took on the task of deciding whether the state should allow such human research if it was determined that the patient could give legally effective consent.

The court noted that animal studies and noninvasive human experimentation had not been exhausted in studying the function of the brain. The court said that where an experimentation is to be carried out on the human brain, particularly where it does not involve a life-threatening circumstance but is intrusive and irreparable, it should be undertaken very cautiously. Such experimentation should only be done when knowledge cannot be obtained from animal research and nonintrusive human experimentation.[24]

The court held that psychosurgery should not be performed on an involuntarily committed person where risks are high and benefits are low. The court reasoned that obtaining informed consent from someone in this situation would be impossible: his incarceration lessens the capacity to give a valid authorization. Although patients may be competent to understand their circumstances, their mental conditions make them vulnerable. They would also experience certain deprivations by reason of their involuntary commitment that would affect their capacity to give consent. The court was also concerned about the effects of institutionalization upon a person's ability to give consent:

[23] Id.
[24] Id. at 474.

Institutionalization tends to strip the individual of the support which permits him to maintain his sense of self-worth and the value of his own physical and mental integrity. An involuntarily confined mental patient clearly has diminished capacity for making a decision about irreversible experimental psychosurgery.[25]

The court noted that another critical element necessary for a valid consent was missing in this situation. The lack of factual data surrounding the effect and consequences of the procedure made it impossible for the patient's consent to be knowledgeable. Without adequate knowledge, his authorization for psychosurgery was legally ineffective.[26]

The last factor necessary for effective consent was also missing: it could not be said that in the circumstances, the patient's consent was voluntary. The court noted that an involuntarily committed patient, in making a decision, could not possibly divorce herself from the effects of undisclosed forms of restraint and coercion. Her ability to gain release might rest upon the level of cooperation with officials and a consent to experimental surgery. In this particular case, the patient's pattern of living for the preceding 17 years indicated that virtually every important aspect of his life had been decided for him. Taking into account the inherently coercive atmosphere of the institution, the court found that the patient, like other involuntary patients, could not take part on an equal footing with physicians and administrators in deciding whether he should have pyschosurgery.[27]

The court continued by considering constitutional arguments in its ruling. It held that the First Amendment protected the individual's right to the free development and exchange of ideas and that this guarantee would not permit psychosurgery in the absence of a compelling state interest. In this case, the state failed to show that the use of experimental psychosurgery on involuntary mental patients was a compelling justification to override the patient's First Amendment guarantee.[28]

[25] Id. at 476.
[26] Id. at 477.
[27] Id.
[28] Id. at 478.

The patient's constitutional right of privacy was also considered. Intruding into the intellect of an involuntarily confined patient amounted to an invasion of the individual's right of privacy. The court again ruled that the state had not made a sufficient case for overruling this constitutional right.

The court concluded that when the state of psychosurgery develops to the point that the proposed procedure is no longer experimental and an appropriate means for review has been developed, an involuntarily detained mental patient could give consent to this type of surgery. Until that time, based on the facts of this case, an involuntarily committed mental patient cannot give legally effective consent to innovative or experimental brain surgery.[29]

b. The effect of the Kaimowitz *decision.* The *Kaimowitz* case is illustrative of many important considerations regarding consent and the use of psychosurgery. It emphasizes the difficulty of obtaining a truly voluntary, not unduly influenced or coerced, consent from a person who is institutionalized. It also underlines the advisability of devoting greater care to the consent process when the proposed form of intervention is an experimental rather than a traditional type of treatment.

Since there is a paucity of case law on the subject of psychosurgery and consent, it is difficult to predict how another court would react to a proposal for psychosurgery as treatment rather than as an experimental protocol. *Kaimowitz* involved a man who had been hospitalized as a criminal sexual psychopath, a designation different from that of many other involuntary mental health patients. However, the common experience of involuntary hospitalization would cause many courts to question the voluntariness of patients' consent — for exactly the reasons set forth in the *Kaimowitz* case.

With a growing number of states now enacting legislation on the use of human subjects in medical research, and with increased federal regulations on the subject (see chapter 8 infra), experimental psychosurgery on involuntarily committed patients will become increasingly difficult to institute. The legal

[29] Id.

hurdles involved may be insurmountable or at least sufficient to deter a researcher from going forward with a study.

In the treatment context, failure to obtain the requisite informed consent for psychosurgery could lead to significant litigation. Physicians must disclose to their patients relevant information regarding probable benefits, risks, reasonable alternative medical or surgical care, if any, and such other information as is considered appropriate. As with experimental psychosurgery, it is important that there be adequate documentation of consent — either in a consent form or in a detailed note in the patient's health record. Any suggestion of coercion or undue influence, as found in the *Kaimowitz* case, will invalidate or deter the consent process. Psychosurgery may be a valid and recommended form of care for some mentally ill patients, but the law insists on a truly valid consent before the procedure may be performed.

§6.6 Behavioral Modification, Physical Restraint, and Isolation as Treatment

Both in clinical practice and in legislation other forms of care are recognized for mentally ill and mentally retarded persons. Some of these treatment modalities, however, are subject to statutory restrictions or legislation that specifies that consent must be obtained prior to administration. Procedures limited in this fashion include the use of aversive stimuli, behavioral modification, physical or mechanical restraints, and isolation.

§6.6.1 Aversive Stimuli and Behavioral Modification

In some state laws the use of aversive stimuli or behavioral modification is recognized as a form of permissible treatment.[1]

§6.6 [1]Colo. Rev. Stat. §27-10.5-115 (1975) (developmentally disabled); Mont. Code Ann. §53-20-146 (1979) (developmentally disabled); Ohio Rev. Code Ann. §5123.86 (Baldwin 1981) (mentally retarded).

Before such treatment can be administered, however, full and express consent must be obtained from the patient or his legal representative. For example, in Montana behavioral modification programs involving aversive stimuli for developmentally disabled persons must be reviewed and approved by a mental disabilities board.[2] The express and informed consent of the patient must be obtained, as well as that of his parents or guardian, or a responsible person appointed by a court. Furthermore, the consent process must allow for an opportunity to consult independent specialists and legal counsel.[3] Similar laws may be found in other states.[4]

Whether or not state legislation specifies the need for informed consent, it is important to review applicable case law. Prior to the use of behavioral modifications or aversive stimuli, consent requirements must be met as with any other form of care. However, there are specific issues that must be addressed in the consent process for such treatment. These include the following:

1. Is the patient legally and mentally capable of giving consent?
2. If not, does he or she have a legal representative who is authorized to act in matters of treatment?
3. If not, what legal procedures must be invoked to have a legal guardian appointed for purposes of treatment?
4. Once the matter of who may consent is resolved, has the authorization for treatment been obtained voluntarily, without any coercion or undue influence?
5. How much information will be disclosed must also be considered — e.g., how much will be said about the probable risks and benefits of treatment, any reasonable alternative forms of .care, the risks of foregoing all treatment, the probable consequences the treatment will have on the

[2]Mont. Code Ann. §53-20-146 (1979).
[3]Id.
[4]Colo. Rev. Stat. §27-10.5-115 (1975); Ohio Rev. Code Ann. §5123.86 (Baldwin 1981).

patient's lifestyle, the probable length and number of treatments, the probability of achieving a temporary or permanent cure, and the impact the treatment will have on the individual's continued institutionalization. A further decision is whether the proposed treatment is the least intrusive form of care available and whether other less invasive measures have been exhausted.

6. The exact nature of the behavioral modification or aversive stimuli treatment should be described to the patient or legal representative; any questions about the steps involved or the risk, benefits, and other information disclosed should be answered.

From the institutional point of view, adequate documentation of consent can take the form of either a detailed note in the patient's chart or a consent form. State law may dictate what type of documentation may be used.

When the aversive therapy involves the use of noxious substances, only a thorough medical history of the patient can prevent the untoward consequences due to sensitivity reactions. When a patient is unable to provide this information, medical personnel should turn to the patient's parents, legal guardian, or personal physician.

§6.6.2   Restraints

A significant body of legislation governs the use of restraints in mental health care.[5] Some case law can also be found on the subject.[6] Both sources of law clearly indicate that physical and mechanical restraints can be used in some circumstances.

a. Legislative control of restraints. The use of restraints is closely controlled by state law. Some statutes require that the

[5]Colo. Rev. Stat. §27-10.5-115 (1975); D.C. Code Ann. §6-1690 (1979); Fla. Stat. Ann. §393.13 (West 1979); 1980 Haw. Sess. Laws 272 (1980); Idaho Code §66-345 (1981).

[6]Youngberg v. Romeo, 455 U.S. 915 (1982).

head of an institution or a physician determine that mechanical restraints are medically necessary for the patient.[7] Other laws indicate that restraints should not be used unless alternative techniques have failed and then only if the restraint employed involves the least possible restriction for the purpose.[8]

State legislation prohibits the use of restraints as a form of punishment, for the convenience of staff, or as a substitute for a patient's treatment program.[9] The amount of time restraints may be used is also restricted by legislation in some jurisdictions. For example, in Colorado restraint cannot be used for more than six continuous hours.[10] In the District of Columbia the patient must be given at least 10 minutes of exercise during every two-hour period in which restraint is used.[11]

Patients placed in restraints must be monitored closely at stated intervals, in many jurisdictions,[12] whereas others require checking of patients at reasonable intervals.[13] Another common requirement is documentation of the reasons for the use of restraints.[14]

b.   Case law on the use of restraints.   In 1982 the U.S. Supreme Court issued a decision involving the constitutional permissibility of the use of restraints.[15] The case involved a civil rights action under 42 U.S.C. §1983, brought by the mother of an involuntarily committed, mentally retarded man who had been injured while in the institution.

In its ruling, the Court held that the man had protected

---

[7]Colo. Rev. Stat. §27-10.5-115 (1975); Or. Rev. Stat. §426.385 (1981); S.C. Code §44-23-1020 (1974).
[8]Colo. Rev. Stat. §27-10.5-115 (1975); D.C. Code Ann. §6-1690 (1979); Mont. Code Ann. §53-20-146 (1979).
[9]Colo. Rev. Stat. §27-10.5-115 (1975); D.C. Code Ann. §6-1690 (1979); Fla. Stat. Ann. §393.13 (West 1979); Me. Rev. Stat. Ann. tit. 34B §5605 (1984); Mont. Code Ann. §53-20-146 (1979).
[10]Colo. Rev. Stat. §27-10.5-155 (1975).
[11]D.C. Code Ann. §6-1690 (1979).
[12]Colo. Rev. Stat. §27-10.5-115 (1975); D.C. Code Ann. §6-1690 (1979).
[13]S.D. Codified Laws Ann. §27A-12-6 (1987).
[14]Ind. Code Ann. §16-14-1.6-6 (Burns 1979); Nev. Rev. Stat. §433.484 (1981); Or. Rev. Stat. §426.385 (1983).
[15]Youngberg v. Romeo, supra n.6.

liberty interests under the due process clause of the Fourteenth Amendment, which gave him the right to be free of unreasonable bodily restraints. As the Court noted in quoting an earlier concurring opinion by Justice Powell,

> [l]iberty from bodily restraint always has been recognized as the core of the liberty protected by the Due Process Clause from arbitrary governmental action.[16]

Having recognized the liberty interest in freedom from bodily restraint, the Court pointed out that the interest was not absolute and could be limited for the protection of the individual as well as of others and while the person participated in training programs. Whether the use of restraints was unreasonable required a balancing of the individual's liberty interest against relevant state interests.[17] For this purpose the Court chose the exercise of professional judgment as the proper standard for judging whether a state had provided adequate protection of the rights of the involuntarily committed mentally retarded person. The lower courts were instructed to consider the judgment exercised by a professional to be presumptively valid. The only time liability may be imposed for a physician's unreasonable use of restraints is if the actions of the professional constitute:

> such a substantial departure from accepted professional judgment, practice or standards as to demonstrate that the person responsible actually did not base the decision on such a judgment.[18]

This decision of the U.S. Supreme Court does not involve the matter of consent to treatment. However, the right to be free from unreasonable bodily restraints does go to the root of the law of consent: the right of the individual to decide what shall be done to her own body. For this reason along with a recognition of the potential for abuse in the use of restraints, both case

---

[16]Id. at 316.
[17]Id. at 321.
[18]Id. at 323.

law and legislation set strict standards for this form of treatment.

Health professionals and mental health facilities, while taking into consideration the requirements of state law, should set clear-cut guidelines on the use of restraints. At a minimum the following matters should be reviewed in setting a policy:

1. Under what circumstances will restraints be employed?
2. Have other less restrictive methods been used? If so, have these methods failed?
3. For what periods of time will restraints be permitted? Will written orders be required that are time limited?
4. What type of restraints may be used?
5. Who will have authority to order the use of restraints?
6. What staff personnel will be permitted to attach the restraints?
7. At what time intervals will the restraints be removed so that a person may exercise?
8. What arrangements have been made for toilet privileges and eating during the use of restraints?
9. At what intervals will the physical condition of the individual be checked while he or she is under restraint?
10. What documentation will be necessary for the use of restraints?
11. What mechanism will be put in place to allow for the discontinuance of restraints once the basis for such treatment has ended?

§6.6.3   Isolation and Seclusion

Certain types of isolation are prohibited in many jurisdictions. One example is leaving a person in a closed room as a form of punishment and is usually labelled seclusion. Colorado,[19] Montana,[20] and the District of Columbia[21] all have

---

[19]Colo. Rev. Stat. §27-10.5-115 (1975).
[20]Mont. Code Ann. §53-20-146 (1979).
[21]D.C. Code Ann. §6-1690 (1979).

outlawed this type of isolation. These laws do permit a so-called time-out procedure, which involves the separation of an individual from other persons and group activities[22] — providing the isolation occurs under close supervision and in appropriate circumstances.

Other states are not as restrictive in their use of seclusion or isolation. In Hawaii seclusion can be used to prevent injury to the individual or to others, as part of a patient's treatment plan, and as a means of protecting the rights of other patients and staff.[23] Use of seclusion or isolation as a means of ensuring the safety of the patient or of others is sometimes acceptable in other states as well.[24]

As in the case of restraints, some states place other conditions on the use of isolation or seclusion. Their statutes mention documentation of the need for such measures,[25] as well as periodic recorded observations of the patient while in seclusion.[26] Close supervision by professionals may also be a factor in the acceptability of seclusion.[27]

The particular statutory requirements in states should be reviewed carefully in setting a policy on the use of isolation and seclusion. With respect to consent, patients should be told at the outset of their treatment that isolation, seclusion, and restraints may be used in those instances when permitted by law. Although a patient may not be in a position at a subsequent time to refuse consent to the use of these procedures, he is entitled to know the potential forms of treatment that may be encountered. The information may also have a deterrent effect upon otherwise abhorrent behavior.

A mental health facility policy or set of guidelines on the use of seclusion and isolation should outline specifically when and under what circumstances these steps may be taken. It should also indicate who may order such treatment and that the order

---

[22] Colo. Rev. Stat. §27-10.5-115 (1975).
[23] 1980 Haw. Sess. Laws 272 (1980).
[24] Idaho Code §66-345 (1982).
[25] Ind. Code Ann. §16-14-1.6-6 (Burns 1979).
[26] Id.
[27] Mont. Code Ann. §53-20-146 (1979).

should be in writing and time limited. Periodic evaluations of the application of these measures should be incorporated to determine whether other treatment modalities might be more appropriate.

Failure to abide by legislative and internal documents on the use of these and other measures can lead to significant litigation. One possibility is civil rights actions. The ruling by the U.S. Supreme Court in the case of Youngberg v. Romeo,[28] however, suggests that the failure to exercise "professional judgment" in the use of restraints will be the measure employed in these cases. Although the decision includes a presumption of validity with respect to the decisions of a qualified professional, the presumption is not absolute. A showing of sufficient proof will overcome it. Therefore specific guidelines as suggested above must be set.

C. STERILIZATION OF THE MENTALLY DISABLED

Throughout this century eugenic sterilization — the practice of preventing procreation by persons possessing "undesirable" hereditary traits — has been at the forefront of legal and ethical debate. To many opponents of involuntary sterilization of mentally deficient individuals, the famous case of Buck v. Bell[1] is the high-water mark in the denial of civil rights and of the fundamental freedom to procreate.

Because of the growing awareness of the constitutional right of privacy, and the protection afforded by it, legal debate has again emerged regarding eugenic sterilization. In many instances, state legislatures have enacted highly detailed laws allowing procedural protection to candidates for eugenic sterilization. There is also a growing body of case law on the

[28]Supra n.6.
§6.7 [1]274 U.S. 200 (1927).

authority of state courts to order such sterilizations in the absence of legislative authority.

Sterilization of mentally disabled people is a subject that could fill volumes of learned treatises. Here, however, the discussion is limited to the consent issues involved. In this portion of the chapter the matter of consent is examined in the context of the involuntary sterilization of incompetent adults. The right to perform similar surgery upon minors is discussed in chapter 5 supra.

§6.7   State Legislation

In 1927 the U.S. Supreme Court upheld the sterilization of a "feeble-minded" Virginia woman, stating that a law permitting the superintendent of a state mental institution to order the procedure did not offend the Fourteenth Amendment due process clause.[2] The court apparently accepted the prevailing eugenic distaste for one generation of mentally deficient individuals begetting another. As Justice Holmes wrote, "Three generations of imbeciles are enough."[3]

Even today legislation can be found in the United States that reflects the same attitude.[4] These laws, however, have built-in procedural safeguards for the protection of the rights of patients. These typically include the right to notice, the right to a hearing, and the right of appeal.

More recent legislation is cast in terms of "voluntary" consent by mentally disabled persons to sterilization procedures. For example, in Colorado a mentally retarded person 18 years old or older may consent to her sterilization. Co-consent, however, must come from a parent or legal guardian; in addition, consent must be obtained from a psychiatric or psychological consultant and from someone in the field of mental retardation.[5]

[2] Id.
[3] Id. at 207.
[4] Miss. Code Ann. §41-45-1 (1984).
[5] Colo. Rev. Stat. §27-10.5-128 (1975).

When a retarded individual is incompetent for purposes of giving consent to a sterilization procedure, the operation cannot be performed.[6] Other states have also enacted "voluntary" sterilization laws that balance the needs of the patient against those of society. Many require a careful assessment of whether the operation is in the patient's best interests.[7]

To a large extent, the modern sterilization statutes focus on consent considerations.[8] The sterilization statute in Virginia requires a full explanation of the nature and consequences of the operation, as well as of other forms of contraception that are available. When a person is incapable of understanding this explanation and a petition has been filed by a designated party requesting the sterilization, the court, in reaching its decision, must consider a number of factors including:

1. a demonstration of the need for some form of contraception;
2. the failure to find a reasonable alternative to sterilization as a form of contraception; and
3. the assurance that the method to be employed adheres to medical practice standards and does not pose an unreasonable risk to the life or health of the patient.[9]

Whether mentally disabled individuals are capable of a knowing and intelligent consent is open to question. There is also reason to doubt that an institutionalized person is in a position to give consent that is truly voluntary and free of undue influence or coercion to *any* procedure. (See §6.5.4 supra.) Perhaps due to these concerns, a number of states sometimes require co-consent prior to the performance of sterilization

---

[6] Colo. Rev. Stat. §27-10.5-130 (1975).

[7] Conn. Gen. Stat. §§45-78q (1982), 45-78w (1982), and 45-78y (1982); N.D. Cent. Code §25-01.2-11 (1981).

[8] Colo. Rev. Stat. §27-10.5-128 (1975); §27-10.5-130 (1975); Conn. Gen. Stat. §§45-78q through 45-78y (1982); N.J. Stat. Ann. §§30:6D-5 (West 1977) and 30:4-24.2 (1975); Ohio Rev. Code Ann. §5122.271 (Baldwin 1981); Va. Code §§54-325.9 through 54-325.12 (1981).

[9] Va. Code §54-325.12 (1981).

procedures on mentally disabled people.[10] Others outline a judicial review,[11] while still others prohibit eugenic sterilization when a patient cannot consent to the procedure.[12]

When a court review is required, the standard of necessary proof is often set forth by statute. It is sometimes set at the threshold of clear and convincing evidence,[13] reflecting legislative concern for the degree of intrusion involved in sterilization procedures.

Modern judicial thinking is averse to the eugenics argument as the basis for sterilization decisions. Indeed, at least two courts have made it clear that the state has no compelling justification for the sterilization of its citizens.[14] The more modern approach is to abandon the practice of compulsory or eugenic sterilization and to give mentally disabled persons the opportunity to exercise the right to be sterilized when they are incapable of giving consent.[15] Difficult procedural issues are involved with who should make this decision on behalf of the patient and what safeguards should be employed to protect the rights of the mentally disabled.

Even in those states with legislation the courts have been exacting in terms of the evidence needed to satisfy statutory requirements.[16] The Supreme Court of California has taken a very critical view of state legislation prohibiting the sterilization of persons under a conservatorship. Indeed, the law was deemed an impermissible denial of the privacy and liberty interests protected under both the United States and California constitutions.[17]

---

[10]Colo. Rev. Stat. §27-10.5-128 (1975).

[11]Conn. Gen. Stat. §§45-78q et seq. (1982); Ohio Rev. Code Ann. §5123.86 (Baldwin 1981).

[12]Colo. Rev. Stat. §27-10.5-130 (1975).

[13]Conn. Gen. Stat. §45-78y (1982); Ga. Code §84-933 (1986); Idaho Code §39-3903 (1974); N.D. Cent. Code §25-01.2-11 (1983); Utah Code Ann. §62A-6-112 (1988); Va. Code §54-325.12 (1981); Vt. Stat. Ann. tit. 18, §8711 (1981).

[14]In the Matter of Mary Moe, 385 Mass. 555, 432 N.E.2d 712 (1982); In the Matter of A.W., 637 P.2d 366 (Colo. 1981).

[15]Id.

[16]See, e.g., Matter of Truesdell, 313 N.C. 421, 329 S.E.2d 630 (1985); Matter of Welfare of Hillstrom, 363 N.W.2d 871 (Minn. 1985).

[17]See Conservatorship of Valerie N., 40 Cal. 3d 143, 219 Cal. Rptr. 387, 707 P.2d 760 (1985).

Some courts, in the process of interpreting statutory material on sterilization, have borrowed judicially created criteria from states without such legislation.[18] Indeed, the Supreme Court of North Carolina has indicated that the trial judge may consider these factors in making specific findings of fact relating to what would be in the individual's best interest.[19]

If a trend can be discerned, it is toward the necessity of a greater degree of proof based on specific factual information. That the right to procreate is implicated in the decision to sterilize an incompetent person is resulting in careful analysis and determinations.

§6.8 Case Law on Sterilization of Mentally Incompetent Persons

A large body of case law interprets the validity of legislation authorizing the sterilization of mentally incapable people.[1] Since the case law is specific to the statutory requirements in individual states, it is not useful to include it in this discussion. What is of interest, however, is the case law dealing with sterilization in the absence of enabling legislation.

§6.8.1 The Traditional Approach

The prevailing view among many state courts is that in the absence of legislation authorizing the sterilization of mentally defective individuals, no orders can be issued for such procedures.[2] The rationale for this approach has been traditionally

---

[18] See, e.g., Matter of Truesdell, supra n.16.
[19] Id.
§6.8 [1] See 53 A.L.R.3d 960 (1972) and cases cited therein. See also Avila v. New York City Health and Hosps. Corp., 518 N.Y.S.2d 574 (Sup. Ct. 1987), in which the court discussed the issue of voluntariness on the part of a mildly retarded woman to consent to sterilization. In denying a motion to dismiss, the court ruled that the facility could not prevent the mentally competent person from freely submitting to the procedure.
[2] See 74 A.L.R.3d 1210 (1974).

expressed as a lack of jurisdiction and a preference for these questions to be resolved by legislation.[3]

In recent years, this judicial reluctance to act without legislation has come under fire from other courts faced with similar cases.[4] These cases suggest that a court, given the authority of general jurisdiction, has the power to decide sterilization cases involving the mentally disabled. As one court has noted, the judicial restraint approach has produced inconclusive results as well as the "abdication of the judicial function."[5]

Because the two schools of thought are so different, it is unlikely that a compromise will be struck to accommodate both. The traditional rule reflects judicial restraint or deference to legislative authority, whereas the recent trend is an example of judicial activism. Because the courts following this latter perspective have fashioned rules and criteria for the sterilization of the mentally incompetent in the absence of state legislation, it is useful to look at a few examples of their work.

§6.8.2 *Judicial Legislating of Sterilization*

As noted above, a number of courts have held that the courts do possess the authority to rule in cases involving the sterilization of the mentally incompetent, despite the lack of enabling legislation.[6] In particular, cases from New Jersey and Massachusetts exemplify this approach.

    a. The New Jersey experience. In a New Jersey case, a 19-year-old woman afflicted with Down's syndrome was the subject of litigation before the Chancery Division of the Superior

[3]Guardianship of Kemp, 43 Cal. App. 3d 758, 118 Cal. Rptr. 64 (1974); Frazier v. Levi, 440 S.W.2d 393 (Tex. Civ. App. 1969); Holmes v. Powers, 439 S.W.2d 579 (Ky. 1968).
[4]In the Matter of Mary Moe, 385 Mass. 555, 432 N.E.2d 712 (1982); In re Grady, 85 N.J. 235, 426 A.2d 467 (1981); Guardianship of Hayes, 93 Wash. 2d 228, 608 P.2d 635 (1980); In re Sallmaier, 85 Misc. 2d 295, 378 N.Y.S.2d 989 (Sup. Ct. 1976).
[5]Guardianship of Hayes, supra n.4, at 231, 608 P.2d at 637.
[6]In the Matter of Mary Moe, supra n.4; In re Grady, supra n.4; Guardianship of Hayes, supra n.4; In re Sallmaier, supra n.4.

Court.[7] The woman had been taking contraceptive pills for the previous four years as a precautionary measure. She did not comprehend the significance of sexual relationships and, if she became pregnant, would not understand her condition or be able to care for any children on her own. The parents wished to place their daughter in a sheltered work group and then a group home for retarded adults. In addition, they felt that a continuous form of contraception was imperative. On the advice of their doctor they sought to have the young woman sterilized. When a hospital refused their request to perform the sterilization procedure without judicial authorization, legal proceedings were initiated.[8]

The trial court ruled that its inherent parens patriae jurisdiction empowered it to authorize substitute consent for the sterilization. Because the Supreme Court of New Jersey differed with the lower court on the standards to be applied in this and similar cases, the case was vacated and remanded for further proceedings.[9]

The court noted that the individual's right of privacy included the right to undergo voluntary sterilization. The difficulty that the court faced was deciding who could exercise this right on behalf of an incompetent individual.[10] The court noted that the parents of the young woman were in a position to assert this right on behalf of their daughter. The court pointed out, however, that only a judicial body and not the parents could decide whether consent would be given for the sterilization procedure. In noting the divergence of this decision from that in the case of Karen Ann Quinlan,[11] the court asserted that the prospect of sterilization was far different from the withdrawal of life-support equipment in terms of the number of factors that must be considered in deciding what is in the best interests of the incompetent. Moreover, the *Quinlan* court

---

[7] In re Grady, supra n.4.
[8] Id. at 241, 426 A.2d at 470.
[9] Id. at 243, 426 A.2d at 471.
[10] Id. at 246, 426 A.2d at 474.
[11] In re Quinlan, 70 N.J. 10, 355 A.2d 647 (1979), cert. denied, 429 U.S. 922 (1976).

believed the best course lay in permitting the parents to make the decision, providing adequate safeguards were met.[12]

The court noted that the history of sterilization of incompetent persons was marked by instances of abuse. It felt that this could not continue:

> Since the sterilization decision involves a variety of factors well suited to rational development in judicial proceedings, a court can take cognizance of these factors and reach a fair decision of what is the incompetent's best interest.[13]

In its ruling the court indicated that a number of procedural requirements must be followed and preliminary findings assessed if a court is to rule on the request for sterilization of a mentally incompetent individual. An independent guardian ad litem must be appointed to represent the person, and he should be given a full opportunity to meet with the incompetent individual, to present evidence, and to cross-examine witnesses at a hearing. Independent psychological and medical evaluations should be performed on incompetent persons by qualified professionals. Although the patient need not be physically present at the hearing if the court determines that it would not be helpful in protecting her rights, the trial judge must personally meet with the individual. This meeting then serves as the basis of the judge's opinion of the competency of the patient. The trial court must also find that the person lacks the ability to make a decision about sterilization and that this incapacity is unlikely to change in the foreseeable future.[14] In seeking such a decision, the party desiring the sterilization must prove by clear and convincing evidence that the person is incapable of giving or withholding her consent.[15]

The court, in determining by clear and convincing proof that a sterilization is in the best interests of the incompetent person, should assess at least the following factors:

[12] In re Grady, supra n.4, at 246, 426 A.2d at 475.
[13] Id.
[14] Id. at 258, 426 A.2d at 482.
[15] Id. at 259, 426 A.2d at 483.

1. The possibility that the incompetent person can become pregnant.
2. The possibility that the incompetent person will suffer trauma or psychological harm if
   a. she becomes pregnant,
   b. gives birth,
   c. has a sterilization procedure.
3. The possibility that the incompetent person will take part in sexual activity or be placed in circumstances in which it is imposed.
4. The inability of the incompetent individual to appreciate reproduction and contraception as well as the likelihood that this lack of comprehension is permanent.
5. Whether it is feasible and medically advisable to use less drastic means of contraception at the present time and in the foreseeable future.
6. Whether sterilization is advisable at the present time — as opposed to the future.
7. The capability of the patient to look after a child and the likelihood that at a subsequent time she may be able to get married and, with the assistance of her spouse, care for a child.
8. A demonstration that within the foreseeable future, scientific or medical developments may take place that will either improve the person's condition or make available less drastic means of dealing with the problem than sterilization.
9. Evidence that those seeking the sterilization are acting in good faith and that their chief consideration is the best interests of the incompetent person — not their own or society's convenience.[16]

In a footnote, the court pointed out that a similar analysis should be used in considering the sterilization of incompetent males. Sex is unimportant: the chief concern must be the best interests of the incompetent person involved.[17] The case was

[16] Id. at 259, 426 A.2d at 483.
[17] Id. at 259, n.10; 426 A.2d at 483, n.10.

remanded for further proceedings in light of the Supreme Court of New Jersey's decision.[18]

b. The Massachusetts experience. In the Massachusetts case mentioned at the beginning of this section, a mother as guardian of a mentally retarded woman sought a court order permitting a tubal ligation to be performed on her ward.[19] The case ultimately was ruled on by the Massachusetts Supreme Judicial Court, which held that in the absence of enabling legislation, the probate court as a court of general jurisdiction has the power in some cases to act upon a request for the sterilization of an incompetent person.[20]

In view of the effect sterilization would have on the ward's fundamental right of procreation, the court held that neither a parent nor a guardian could consent to such a procedure without a judicial order. The court, in turn, must apply the substituted judgment test in deciding whether to issue such an order.[21]

The Massachusetts court followed a pattern similar to that of the New Jersey Supreme Court. It set down requirements for notice, the appointment of a guardian ad litem, and the right to a hearing. It also provided for a right of appeal and the appointment of independent medical and psychological experts.[22]

The Supreme Judicial Court indicated that as a threshold consideration, the court must decide whether the patient is capable of making an informed choice about the proposed sterilization — despite her mental retardation. It must also determine whether her condition is likely to change in the near future.[23] The court indicated that other facts should enter into the decision-making process, including:

1. The ability of the incompetent to procreate.
2. A finding that all other less drastic means of contraception

---

[18] Id. at 264, 426 A.2d at 486.
[19] In the Matter of Mary Moe, supra n.4.
[20] Id. at 560, 432 N.E.2d at 715.
[21] Id. at 566, 432 N.E.2d at 720.
[22] Id. at 566, 432 N.E.2d at 721.
[23] Id.

are not feasible. Moreover, the sterilization procedure chosen must be the least intrusive available.

3. The medical need for the procedure.
4. The type and degree of the person's disability, taking into account (a) the capacity of the individual to care for a child with reasonable assistance and (b) the possibility that the incompetent could marry in the future and look after a child with the aid of her spouse.
5. The probability that the incompetent will take part in sexual activity that is likely to result in pregnancy.
6. The likelihood of health risks as well as of trauma and psychological harm from sterilization, pregnancy, or childbirth.[24]

The court pointed out that the religious beliefs, if any, of the ward must be taken into account in reaching a decision. Other "special circumstances" must also be addressed by the court.[25]

The court specifically rejected using "beyond a reasonable doubt" as the required standard of proof. Establishing such a high degree of proof would possibly impede the incompetent from deciding whether or not to exercise her right to procreate. Instead, the court cautioned judges hearing such cases "to exercise the utmost care in reviewing all the evidence presented and in determining whether the ward would consent to sterilization if competent to make such a decision."[26]

§6.8.3 Practical Considerations: What to Do in the Absence of Enabling Legislation

Although some courts are now taking a more assertive stand when state legislation is silent on the right of incompetents to undergo sterilization, not all courts have as yet followed suit. A considerable degree of reluctance remains on the part of many courts to adopt the posture of judicial activism. A number have not yet been presented with a case on the subject: predicting how they would rule would only be speculation.

[24] Id. at 567, 432 N.E.2d at 721-722.
[25] Id. at 567, 432 N.E.2d at 722.
[26] Id. at 569, 432 N.E.2d at 724.

Medical practitioners who are faced with good-faith requests by parents or legal guardians to have a mentally retarded adult sterilized should do nothing in the absence of case law or legislation that permits such surgery. Health facilities in which sterilization procedures may be performed should be equally reluctant to act without specific legal authorization. To forge ahead with sterilization procedures without meeting legal requirements certainly could form the basis of significant litigation. Reaching a decision that is in the best interests of the incompetent person involved is no easy task.

One way to resolve this question is through litigation, but the expense and time involved in having a court determine that the person is legally incapable of giving or withholding consent to a sterilization procedure must be considered carefully. The court may authorize the operation, empower a guardian to make the decision, or block the sterilization. For health facilities, practitioners, and concerned citizen groups faced with these cases repeatedly, the best path may lie in seeking legislative redress in the form of laws that specify by whom, and under what circumstances, a sterilization procedure can be performed on an incompetent individual. The right to have a sterilization procedure is one possessed by competent and incompetent persons alike. The difficulty is in determining who should decide for those who cannot give consent themselves.

D.　NONPSYCHIATRIC TREATMENT OF THE MENTALLY DISABLED

§6.9　Medical and Surgical Treatment

In a number of states legislation has been enacted that governs medical and surgical care of the mentally disabled.[1] The legislation applies to routine treatment[2] and to emergency care.[3]

---

§6.9 [1]Colo. Rev. Stat. §27-10.5-114 (1975) (developmentally disabled); Fla. Stat. Ann. §393.13 (West 1979) (mentally retarded); Fla. Stat. Ann.

The identity of the individual who can consent to medical, dental, or surgical treatment for a mentally ill or mentally retarded person is often set forth in state statutes. The medical director of a facility[4] or the administrator or superintendent of the facility may be empowered to give consent.[5] In some instances, state legislation may be silent on the subject, but case law will often indicate who is authorized to act for the mentally incapable patient.[6] However, when a mentally ill or mentally retarded person is capable of understanding the proposed treatment, authorization for care should be sought from her.[7]

In several instances, state legislatures have codified the common law emergency treatment rule, which permits care in the absence of a specific authorization from the patient or his legal representative.[8] This rule is not absolute: in some jurisdictions, the head of the health facility in which the person is a patient has to give authorization for emergency care.[9] The laws often

---

§394.459 (West 1985) (mentally ill); Ind. Code Ann. §16-8-3-1 (Burns 1987); La. Rev. Stat. Ann. §28:171 (West 1978); Minn. Stat. Ann. §253A.17 (West 1968); Mo. Ann. Stat. §630.183 (Vernon 1983).

[2] Ark. Stat. Ann. §59-1416 (1979) (mentally ill and retarded persons); Colo. Rev. Stat. §27-10.5-114 (1975); N.D. Cent. Code §25-03.1-40 (1977) (mentally ill).

[3] Ga. Code §88-502.6 (1978); La. Rev. Stat. Ann. §28:171 (West 1978); Minn. Stat. Ann. §253A.17 (West 1968); Okla. Stat. Ann. tit. 43A, §4-104 (West 1986); R.I. Gen. Laws §40.1-22-23 (1978) (mentally retarded); S.D. Codified Laws Ann. §27A-12-19 (1975).

[4] Ariz. Rev. Stat. Ann. §36-512 (1979).

[5] Fla. Stat. Ann. §394.459 (West 1984) (mentally ill); Minn. Stat. Ann. §253A.17 (West 1968); Mo. Ann. Stat. §630.183 (Vernon 1983); R.I. Gen. Laws §40.1-22-23 (1978) (mentally retarded).

[6] See Ritz v. Florida Patient's Compensation Fund, 436 So. 2d 987 (Fla. Dist. Ct. App. 1983), in which the court ruled that in the absence of a duly appointed legal guardian, the parent of a mentally retarded adult had the power to consent to necessary treatment.

[7] See Cal. Welf. & Inst. Code §7518 (West 1981) (developmentally disabled); R.I. Gen. Laws §40.1-22-23 (1978) (mentally retarded).

[8] Fla. Stat. Ann. §393.13 (West 1984) (mentally retarded); Fla. Stat. Ann. §394.459 (West 1985) (mentally ill); Ga. Code §88-502.6 (1978); Okla. Stat. Ann. tit. 43A, §4104 (West 1986); S.D. Codified Laws Ann. §27A-12-19 (1975). See also Va. Code §54-325.2:1 (1979), in which circumstances are set forth for permissible treatment in lieu of consent for the mentally ill and mentally retarded.

[9] Ariz. Rev. Stat. Ann. §36-512 (1979); La. Rev. Stat. Ann. §28:171 (West 1978); Minn. Stat. Ann. §253A.17 (West 1968).

require documentation or an opinion from a physician that a medical emergency exists that necessitates treatment.[10]

Even with statutory provisions governing medical or surgical care of mentally disabled persons, there is still ample opportunity for judicial involvement. This is particularly so when the application of both the federal and a state constitution or state legislation is called into question. An Ohio case provides a good example of this point as well as the limits of religious belief as a ground for refusing care.[11]

The patient had been hospitalized for several years at the Central Ohio Psychiatric Hospital. She had been experiencing a fixed delusion that she was married to evangelist Leroy Jenkins. In late 1985 it was determined that she had a malignant tumor in her uterus. The following month proceedings were instituted to secure an authorization for treatment.[12]

The patient refused to authorize treatment because she was convinced that the evangelist would soon remove her from the hospital and cure her cancerous condition. Two psychiatrists testified that the patient was working from a fixed delusion. Following a probate court order authorizing treatment, an appeal was taken to the Ohio Court of Appeals.[13]

Ohio legislation permits the requirements of consent to be circumvented when a patient is "unable to receive" details required for surgery.[14] As the court found, there was clear and convincing evidence to demonstrate that the patient's mental condition precluded her from receiving the required information for surgery.

As to the issue of the patient's religious beliefs as a ground for refusing care, the court stated that:

> A pure delusion, even though it involves the concept of God, should not be the basis for thwarting the statutory scheme which

[10] Ariz. Rev. Stat. Ann. §36-512 (1979); Ga. Code §88-502.6 (1978); La. Rev. Stat. Ann. §28:171 (West 1978).
[11] In re Milton, 25 Ohio St. 3d 20, 505 N.E.2d 255 (1987), cert. denied, — U.S. —, 108 S. Ct. 79, 98 L. Ed. 2d 41 (1987), reversing In re Milton, Court of Appeals of Ohio, Slip Opinion No. 86AP-630, July 18, 1986.
[12] Court of Appeals decision at 2.
[13] Id.
[14] Id. at 3, referring to Ohio Rev. Code Ann. §5122.271 (Baldwin 1981).

does make allowances for alternatives where an individual is pursuing a pattern of treatment in accordance with honestly held religious beliefs.[15]

As a result, the appellate court affirmed the ruling authorizing surgery. This determination was reversed on appeal by the Supreme Court of Ohio.[16]

The reason for the higher court's ruling was quite important: at no time was the patient ever found incompetent under state law. Moreover, the fact that she had a delusion about the Reverend Jenkins and thought that he could heal her did not remove the patient's constitutional guarantee to choose and to practice the religion of her choice.

What particularly impressed the court was that the health facility's own witness, a psychiatrist, felt that the patient's belief in spiritual healing stood on its own without regard to her fixed delusion. Bearing this in mind, the court noted that only when the state can demonstrate danger to paramount interests may it intervene to provide protection. It was erroneous for the appellate court to have examined the content of the appellant's religious beliefs and to determine that it constituted a delusion. In holding that a legally competent adult can decline treatment that, while life extending, violates individual religious beliefs, the Supreme Court of Ohio concluded:

> We cannot evalute the "correctness" or propriety of appellant's beliefs. Absent the most exigent circumstances, courts should never be a party to branding a citizen's religious views as baseless on the grounds that they are non-traditional, unorthodox or at war with what the state or others perceive as reality.[17]

This Ohio case demonstrates the difficulty in distinguishing religious belief and mental illness. When should a caregiver accept a refusal of treatment from someone who has a readily identified mental illness? In the Ohio case, the professional staff attending the patient were quite ready and indeed did

---

[15] Id. at 4.
[16] In re Milton, 25 Ohio St. 3d 20, 505 N.E.2d 261 (1987).
[17] Id. at 26, 505 N.E.2d at 260.

accept her consent to testing, including a biopsy that led to the diagnosis of cancer. If the staff were successful in securing the patient's informed consent to testing, why, when she refused invasive treatment, did they not accept her decision? That was the issue that troubled Ohio's highest court. That the patient was under a delusion throughout did not seem to bother caregivers when obtaining consent to testing. It only became an issue when the patient refused treatment.

Competency is an illusive topic. In the real world of treating the mentally ill and mentally disabled it is not all black and white. Legislation and case law have yet to come to grips with this fact. Until they do, care must be taken not to abridge the rights of mentally ill and mentally disabled persons. In particular, caregivers should be careful not to seek compulsory treatment for patients who, while mentally ill, are still considered legally competent.

When a state does not have specific legislation relating to emergency treatment of mentally disabled persons, health facilities and professionals should not hesitate to provide necessary care. The right to treat in these circumstances may be dealt with under state common law, in a general emergency consent law, or in a statute on consent to treatment. This authorization or legal authority to provide treatment can be determined with the assistance of legal counsel. Refraining from providing necessary life- or health-saving treatment for fear of litigation is an inappropriate response — particularly when a state or private institution has undertaken to provide necessary medical or surgical care to its residents, clients, or patients. The legal and monetary consequences could be far more serious if a patient dies or suffers a crippling disability as the result of personnel's not providing emergency treatment than if they chose to give care without specific authorization.

The key factor in providing treatment for mentally ill or mentally retarded persons is to stay within the limits of authorized care. These guidelines may be set out in statute[18] or in a patient's overall treatment plan.

[18]Colo. Rev. Stat. §27-10.5-114 (1975).

Some health professionals are reluctant to perform operative procedures that may as a result leave an individual infertile. This response has been anticipated in the legislation of many states.[19] The laws permit medical or surgical procedures that are necessary for sound therapeutic reasons — which may incidentally destroy a mentally incompetent person's reproductive functions or leave her sterilized.[20] Similarly, a state agency acting in good faith and in the best interests of an incompetent, mentally retarded person may be authorized to consent to an abortion for that person. According to one court, this is particularly appropriate when the pregnancy is the result of a sexual assault and the victim suffers from a seizure disorder and cerebral palsy.[21]

Mentally ill or mentally retarded persons should not be denied necessary medical or surgical treatment for fear that it may leave them sterile. As long as the physician or surgeon meets the requirements of state law in this regard, no concern need be generated regarding consent for unauthorized sterilization. Where state law is silent on the subject, health facilities and professionals should be guided by what is therapeutically required in the circumstances. A careful medical assessment will determine if the proposed form of treatment is necessary and whether any less intrusive means are available that would not alter the individual's reproductive capacity. The courts will scrutinize requests for radical or disfiguring surgery to determine if a less aggressive means of care is available.[22] However, it is doubtful that the courts will insist upon judicial involvement when what is at issue is a purported need for antibiotic therapy.[23]

[19]Conn. Gen. Stat. §45-78z (1979); Ga. Code §84-935.1 (1970); Idaho Code §39-3908 (1971); Miss. Code Ann. §41-45-19 (1928); Okla. Stat. Ann. tit. 43A, §346 (West 1931); Va. Code §54-325.15 (1981).
[20]Id.
[21]See In re Doe, 533 A.2d 523 (R.I. 1987).
[22]See, e.g., Matter of Shirley C., 519 N.Y.S.2d 328 (Sup. Ct. 1987).
[23]See Matter of Salisbury, 524 N.Y.S.2d 352 (Sup. Ct. 1988), in which the court ruled that a psychiatric center need not apply to the court for an order authorizing antibiotic treatment for a patient at risk of developing complications from diabetes, poor circulation, and leg and ankle fractures.

Documentation of the consent process should be included in the individual's health record. Authorization for treatment should be obtained from the mentally disabled person if he is able to give consent — otherwise, from someone permitted to act in his behalf.

Difficulties involving consent to medical, dental, and surgical treatment for the mentally ill and mentally retarded can be avoided by developing a set of guidelines or a policy.[24] Health institutions and health professionals, with the assistance of legal counsel, should review the requirements of state law as well as the needs of the health facility. They should anticipate the types of difficulties that are likely to occur and the guidelines or policy should be written in a responsive way. State requirements for consent and documentation of treatment authorizations should be incorporated into these policies. In this way, health institutions can avoid delaying necessary treatment of mentally disabled persons in their care.

[24]Such a novel policy review is underway in New York. According to an article in the New England Journal of Medicine (C.J. Sundram, Informed Consent for Major Medical Treatment of Mentally Disabled People: A New Approach, 318(21) New Eng. J. Med. 1368 (May 26, 1988), volunteer committees are empowered to make health care treatment choices for certain categories of mentally disabled people. Thus far, the results of the pilot project appear quite encouraging, and, indeed, they may serve as a model for other jurisdictions.

SEVEN

The Right to Refuse Treatment

§7.0   Introduction
A. Curable, Life-Threatening Illness
    §7.1   Religious and Philosophical Objections to Treatment
        §7.1.1   Treatment Compelled Over Religious Objections
        §7.1.2   Treatment Not Compelled Over Religious Objections
        §7.1.3   State Statutes and Religious Objections
        §7.1.4   Other Types of Litigation Involving Religious Objection
                 to Treatment
    §7.2   Incompetent or Incapacitated Persons
        §7.2.1   Incompetent Persons
        §7.2.2   Incapacitated Persons
        §7.2.3   State Statutes Authorizing Treatment
    §7.3   Emergency Life-Saving Treatment
        §7.3.1   Authority to Provide Treatment
        §7.3.2   Patients' Refusal of Treatment
        §7.3.3   Relatives' Refusal of Treatment
        §7.3.4   Disputes Among Family Members
        §7.3.5   Effects of Patients' Written Directives
        §7.3.6   Policy Considerations in Providing Treatment
B. Terminal Illness ·
    §7.4   Right to Refuse Terminal Care
        §7.4.1   Competent Persons
        §7.4.2   Incompetent Persons
    §7.5   Right to Withdraw Life-Sustaining Treatment
        §7.5.1   Competent Persons
        §7.5.2   Incompetent Persons
        §7.5.3   Practical Considerations Regarding Other Treatments
    §7.6   Orders Not to Resuscitate (DNRs)
        §7.6.1   Case Law
        §7.6.2   Rules and Regulations
        §7.6.3   Practical Considerations

437

§7.7   Orders Not to Hospitalize (DNHs)
       §7.7.1   What Is a DNH Order?
       §7.7.2   The Practical Significance of DNH Orders
§7.8   Living Wills, Patient Directives, and Durable Powers of Attorney
       §7.8.1   Living Wills
       §7.8.2   Patient Directives
       §7.8.3   Directives Generated by Health Facilities
       §7.8.4   Durable Powers of Attorney

§7.0   Introduction

If a patient has the right to *consent to* treatment, then it follows that she also has the right to *refuse* care. This process might be called negative consent: the decision involves a variety of alternative forms of care, including no treatment at all. The right to negative consent can be qualified by court orders and legislation.

In many instances a patient's decision to refrain from treatment runs contrary to the training and beliefs of health professionals. Doctors, nurses, health technicians, and others are imbued with the idea of effecting cures — not of allowing a curable or arrestable disease to run its course. When confronted by a patient who opts out of all care or some form of treatment (e.g., blood transfusions), the health professional often reacts by dismissing the decision as unwise. Sometimes the doctor decides the judgment was reached during an emotionally overwrought state. Sometimes the doctor rejects the decision made by a patient who is so ill that, if not legally incompetent, he is incapable of making a determination. The doctor may try to circumvent the patient's decision by calling upon family members to pressure the patient into doing the "right" thing or by going to court to have a guardian appointed.

On other occasions it is the health professional who champions the patient's right to decide. In these cases the family or friends have given up and cause the patient to refuse further treatment. In other circumstances the patient is unable to voice her decision and the family has decided what should be done.

Often the decision is based on a genuine belief of what should be done. The determination is based on what is perceived as being in the patient's best interest and on what he would have done had he been able to consent. There are instances, however, when family members decide that further treatment is unwarranted for selfish, emotional, or financial reasons.

Physicians and hospitals concerned about possible legal actions in these cases often consult lawyers for clarification. In a number of American jurisdictions this policy has resulted in health personnel going to court for orders compelling treatment, appointing a guardian to make decisions for a patient declared incompetent, or finding that the patient can decide what is to be done.

A variety of trends has emerged out of litigation in this area that is instructive to those involved in such matters. Further guidance has been provided by legislation in many states, including living wills, durable powers of attorney, and do-not-resuscitate legislation. Notwithstanding the voluminous case law and legislative inroads in this area, the law surrounding the right to refuse treatment is far from settled. As seen in this chapter, the right to decline treatment needs clarification, with many states carving out their own requirements through case law and legislation.

A. CURABLE, LIFE-THREATENING ILLNESS

§7.1 Religious and Philosophical Objections to Treatment

In many instances, patients may suffer from injuries or illnesses that are life threatening but curable. Most patients gladly accept treatment in such circumstances. The exception is those whose religious or philosophical beliefs are opposed to medical or surgical intervention. In this section, religious and philosophical objections to treatment are discussed. The rationale of courts that compel or do not compel treatment in these cases is examined, as is state statutory law on religious objections to treatment.

§7.1.1 Treatment Compelled Over Religious Objections

Many cases in which courts have been asked to order treatment have involved patients who refused to give consent based upon religious beliefs. By far the most common have involved Jehovah's Witnesses, whose religious beliefs forbid transfusions of any blood products or by-products. Faced with patients with internal hemorrhaging or in need of surgery requiring blood, doctors have often turned to the courts to overcome a patient's refusal to consent to transfusions.

Over the years the courts have developed legal theories in deciding such cases. The courts have also developed certain patterns of decision-making that turn on such factors as whether the patient is an adult or a minor, whether the patient is competent or incapacitated, and whether the patient is the chief provider for minor dependents.

In many of the cases, doctors or hospitals have gone to court seeking the appointment of a legal representative for the purpose of obtaining a consent to the transfusion of blood products. In other cases, the plaintiffs have sought court orders compelling the transfusion. Some of the hearings in these matters have been less than formal — with judicial proceedings conducted without the usual variety of pleading forms or conducted in a patient's hospital room.[1]

The basic legal premise for compelling treatment in the United States rests on the court-drawn distinction between religious beliefs and practices. In an 1879 case[2] involving polygamous marriage practices, the U.S. Supreme Court set a

---

§7.1   [1] Application of President & Directors of Georgetown College, Inc., 118 U.S. App. D.C. 80, 331 F.2d 1000 (D.C. Cir.), rehearing denied, 118 U.S. App. D.C. 90, 331 F.2d 1010, cert. denied, 377 U.S. 978 (1964).

[2] Reynolds v. United States, 98 U.S. 145 (1879) (a case involving a Mormon convicted of bigamy).

precedent that, while guaranteeing the free exercise of religious beliefs, permits the state in certain circumstances to limit religious practices. When the state can demonstrate a compelling interest in the preservation or promotion of health, life, safety, or welfare, religious practices may be curtailed. Thus the state has been able to force compulsory vaccination[3] and to stop ritual snake handling,[4] despite the existence of fervid religious beliefs. The following cases involving the Jehovah's Witnesses demonstrate these principles in the medical context.

In Application of President & Directors of Georgetown College, Inc.,[5] a 25-year-old woman with a ruptured ulcer was taken to a District of Columbia hospital for emergency care. She had lost approximately two-thirds of her total blood supply. The woman had a 7-month-old child at home. Both the woman and her husband were Jehovah's Witnesses and they rejected the suggestion of blood transfusions. Physicians attending the patient were alarmed: they believed death was imminent without such care. Lawyers for the hospital applied to the district court for an order authorizing blood transfusions. When this request was turned down, hospital counsel applied to the Court of Appeals for the District of Columbia for an appropriate writ.

Mr. Justice Skelley Wright authorized the transfusions after discussing the matter with the patient and her husband. They indicated that while they objected to the blood transfusions on religious grounds, should the court order it, they would not feel morally responsible. Doctors informed Judge Wright that with transfusion therapy the patient had a better than 50 percent chance of survival.

The factors that persuaded the judge to order treatment were fourfold. First, the state had a responsibility not to allow the patient to abandon her infant child by allowing herself to die. Her obligation to the community to look after her child

---

[3]Prince v. Massachusetts, 321 U.S. 158 (1944), rehearing denied, 321 U.S. 804 (1944).

[4]Hill v. State, 38 Ala. App. 404, 88 So. 2d 880 (1956), cert. denied, 264 Ala. 197, 88 So. 2d 887; Harden v. State, 188 Tenn. 17, 216 S.W.2d 708 (1948).

[5]Supra n.1.

provided the state with ample interest in preserving the woman's life.[6]

Second, the judge suggested that the patient's religious beliefs were not designed to cause her death: such a result would be only an unfortunate side effect of such beliefs. By coming to the hospital for treatment, she indicated a desire to live.[7]

A third set of factors that influenced the court involved the position of the doctors and the hospital.[8] Judge Wright questioned whether a patient could place the hospital and physicians in the position of civil and criminal liability for either forging ahead with treatment or allowing her to die. No clear authority could be found for the patient's right to direct her doctors to restrict the type of treatment she would receive to the point that death occurred.

Last, the judge suggested that a compelling factor was the key point that a life hung in the balance. Had he not ordered the transfusion "to preserve the status quo,"[9] death would have mooted the entire problem. He did not wish to gamble on not acting only to learn subsequently that the law required that the transfusion be ordered. He erred on the side of life.

In another Jehovah's Witness case,[10] a father of four was admitted voluntarily to a hospital for treatment of a bleeding ulcer. Doctors determined that he needed immediately at least five pints of blood. When the patient refused transfusion therapy, the attending physician went to court for a temporary restraining order. The court issued the order after interviewing the patient and hearing medical testimony that the transfusion was necessary to save the patient's life. The man informed the court that he would not resist a transfusion if the court granted the temporary restraining order. In issuing the order, the court relied upon the rationale voiced earlier in Application

---

[6]Id. at 88, 331 F.2d at 1008. See also In the Matter of the Application of Winthrop Univ. Hosp., 490 N.Y.S.2d 996 (Sup. Ct. 1985).

[7]Application of President & Directors of Georgetown College, Inc., 118 U.S. App. D.C. at 89, 331 F.2d at 1009.

[8]Id.

[9]Id. at 89-90, 331 F.2d at 1009-1010.

[10]United States v. George, 239 F. Supp. 752 (D. Conn. 1965).

of President & Directors of Georgetown College, Inc., supra. One additional factor was considered by the court: respect for the physician's oath and conscience.[11] A patient cannot seek out and demand medical attention and at the same time restrict the type of treatment he would accept to the point that it may amount to medical negligence. In short, patients cannot demand mistreatment or care that flies in the face of sound professional standards.

When a woman is pregnant and refuses blood transfusion therapy, thereby jeopardizing the well-being of the fetus, the state may have a compelling interest sufficient to warrant compulsory care. This point of law was discussed in the following two state court decisions.

In Raleigh Fitkin-Paul Morgan Memorial Hospital v. Anderson,[12] the court ordered a transfusion to save the life of an unborn fetus whose mother was well beyond her thirty-second week of pregnancy. The woman was at risk of hemorrhaging and she had informed hospital officials that she wished to decline transfusion care because of her beliefs as a Jehovah's Witness. The court refused to decide whether an adult could be compelled to undergo life-saving care. The state's interests in the welfare of the unborn child and of the mother were so interwoven that it was unnecessary to decide the issue.

In a Georgia case,[13] a hospital went to court seeking an order authorizing it to perform a caesarean section and transfusion upon a woman when she presented herself for childbirth. The woman was in her thirty-ninth week of pregnancy. While attending the hospital's outpatient clinic for prenatal care, physicians determined that she had a complete placenta previa; that is, the afterbirth was situated between the baby and the birth canal. Doctors indicated the unlikelihood of the condition resolving prior to delivery. They suggested that the risk of fetal mortality by vaginal birth in such circumstances is 99 percent. However, the mother had refused the suggestion of undergo-

[11] Id.
[12] 42 N.J. 421, 201 A.2d 537, cert. denied, 377 U.S. 985 (1964).
[13] Jefferson v. Griffin Spalding County Hosp., 277 S.E.2d 457 (Ga. 1981).

ing a caesarean section and blood transfusion prior to labor, which would have reduced greatly the risk of harm to the fetus and to herself. She based her decision on religious beliefs.

In a per curiam decision, the Supreme Court of Georgia handed down a two-part determination. First, it granted the hospital the power to administer all medical care deemed proper by the attending doctor to save the life of the unborn child. The order was limited, however, to when and if the woman sought voluntary admission for the emergency delivery of her child.[14]

The second portion of the decision was an almost open invitation to the state to intervene. Initially the court had been asked by the hospital to issue an order far broader in scope that would have compelled the woman to submit to a caesarean section prior to going into labor. The court was hesitant to do so but suggested it would consider such a request on the part of an appropriate state agency. The state accepted the "invitation" through the auspices of its Department of Family and Children Services and the Department of Human Resources.

As in the first part of the decision, the court found that the viable unborn child was entitled to the protection of the state. The state's interest was based upon what the U.S. Supreme Court described in Roe v. Wade as the potentiality of life in the unborn.[15] As a matter of law, the court indicated in this section of its decision that the unborn viable child was entitled to protection under the Georgia Juvenile Code. The parents, by refusing the caesarean section, were denying the child proper parental subsistence and care necessary for life and health. It was therefore ordered that the state be granted temporary custody of the child with full authority to consent to surgical delivery.[16]

What is particularly interesting here is that not only did the parents' religious interest give way to the state's interest in the child's life, but the mother's interests in bodily integrity and

[14] Id.
[15] Roe v. Wade, 410 U.S. 113 (1973).
[16] Jefferson v. Griffin Spaulding County Hosp., supra n.13.

freedom from undesired intrusion were overridden by the same state interest. The opinion suggests that the judiciary is willing to place limits on the right to refuse treatment in certain circumstances. That intrusive surgery upon one person for the benefit of another has now been compelled suggests that attorneys should reassess carefully their advice to medical and hospital clients in future matters.

This point has been reinforced in a New York case in which a woman who refused blood transfusions on religious grounds was compelled to have such treatment during a caesarean section. The court's ruling was based on the state's right to safeguard the health and safety of the unborn child as well as the state's interest in protecting the mother's welfare.[17] At least when the risks of death or serious permanent injury are high to both parties or to an unborn child without intervention, and the chances of survival are very good for both with blood transfusions or surgery, the courts may be inclined to order treatment. The state interest in preserving life and health cannot be minimized.

When, however, the mother is terminally ill with cancer and there is a slim chance that the fetus will survive if delivered by caesarean section, the basis for decision-making becomes difficult. Such was the situation in a District of Columbia case, in which there was a woman in the twenty-sixth week of pregnancy whose fetus was experiencing oxygen starvation and associated rapid heart rate.[18]

Prior to being sedated, the woman indicated that she would rather give up her life so that her baby could survive, should such an option arise in the twenty-eighth week of gestation. However, the woman apparently reversed her decision some time after being told of the trial court's ruling that a caesarean section be performed. The doctors had made it clear that the baby had a much better chance of survival if it reached 28 weeks' gestation. The doctors never discussed with the patient

[17]Crouse Irving Memorial Hosp. v. Paddock, 485 N.Y.S.2d 443 (Sup. Ct. 1985).
[18]In re A.C., 553 A.2d 611 (D.C. 1987).

what her choice would be if a decision had to be made prior to this benchmark. To compound the situation, there was a less than 20 percent chance that the infant would suffer permanent, severe disabilities such as cerebral palsy and blindness.

The hospital sought a declaratory judgment regarding what should be done in terms of performing a caesarean section. The trial court determined that the operation should proceed and an appeal was taken. The District of Columbia Court of Appeals denied a motion to stay the order. The operation proceeded and both the mother and child died soon thereafter.

In a written opinion that followed the situation, the court went to great lengths to distinguish the case from other decisions involving court-ordered care. In weighing the rights of the mother to bodily integrity against the interest of the state in preserving the health of her unborn child, the court determined that the complications arising from the caesarean section would not significantly alter the woman's condition because at best she had but two days left of "sedated life."[19] The child, however, had a chance of surviving the caesarean delivery despite the chance of being born handicapped. Thus the appellate court felt that the trial judge had acted properly to subordinate the interests of the mother to those of the child.

From a consent perspective, what is particularly troublesome about a court compelling treatment over religious objection is the procedure followed in authorizing care. Hospitals and physicians are often loath to become involved in protracted litigation or well-publicized adversarial proceedings. A more expedient means may be sought as a way of compelling treatment over religious objection.

One such method is to wait until the patient's situation becomes so critical that the situation degenerates into an "emergency," in which case administrative or medical personnel may think treatment is permissible. This is a misinterpretation of the medicolegal emergency exception to the general rules for a valid consent. A refusal of care, if properly made, survives the

[19]Id. at 617.

patient's lapsing into a state in which she is incapable of giving or declining consent to care.

Another route may be to obtain an ex parte order for appointment of a temporary guardian who is authorized to consent to the offensive treatment. This obviates the need for considerable inquiry and presentation of detailed evidence. According to one court there is no need for the courts to engage in the application of such legal theories as substituted judgment.[20]

The problem is particularly acute for Jehovah's Witnesses, who are often faced with court orders compelling administration of blood transfusions.[21] To counteract this problem, many, if not most, Jehovah's Witnesses carry a card that indicates their objection to such treatment. (See Appendix E.) As a Pennsylvania case demonstrates, however, executing such a document may not be the answer.[22]

In the Pennsylvania case, a 22-year-old man was injured in an automobile accident in New Jersey. After initial treatment in New Jersey, the man became comatose and was transferred to a trauma center in Pennsylvania. On his person at the time of his admission to the hospital in New Jersey was a medical alert card that indicated the patient's desire not to be treated with blood transfusions. In moving the patient to the trauma center this card was left behind along with other personal effects.[23]

On the day of his arrival at the trauma center the patient was scheduled for surgery. A brief, ex parte hearing was conducted over the telephone in which a verbal petition was made for authority to transfuse the patient. The court was told that the patient had an acute subdural hematoma and that he was already in the operating room. The court heard testimony from a

---

[20] In re Estate of Darrell Dorone, 349 Pa. Super. 59, 502 A.2d 1271 (1985).
[21] See University of Cincinnati Hosp. v. Edmond, 506 N.E.2d 299 (Ohio C.P., Hamilton County 1986), in which the court ordered blood and blood plasma for a patient who was unable to understand or give consent despite the fact that his adult children suggested it was against the man's religious beliefs.
[22] In re Estate of Darrell Dorone, supra n.20.
[23] Id. at 70, 502 A.2d at 1277.

doctor that while it was possible to conduct the surgery without blood, if bleeding occurred it would be necessary to transfuse the patient in order to save his life. The court accepted this opinion and appointed the hospital administrator as temporary guardian with the power to authorize a transfusion during the operation.[24]

Two days later, a second ex parte telephone hearing was carried out. Medical testimony indicated that the patient now had a blood clot in the brain that had to be removed immediately. The patient had a very low blood count and if a blood transfusion could not be carried out during the operation, the young man might die.[25] The administrator was once again appointed temporary guardian with the power to authorize blood transfusions during the surgery and during the patient's recovery.[26]

During the second ex parte proceeding the court received a telephone call from a lawyer entering an appearance on behalf of the patient. Like the young man, the lawyer was a Jehovah's Witness. With the judge's permission he read his own medical alert card over the telephone. The court indicated that it had not had the benefit of seeing a similar card executed by the patient because it had been left behind at the transferring facility.[27]

In affirming the action of the lower court, the Pennsylvania Superior Court discounted the value of the medical alert card in this case. As the court indicated: "While a medical alert card would be some evidence of what the patient would do if competent, it could not by itself support an application of the doctrine of substituted judgment."[28]

In order to engage in such an inquiry the court must review several factors, including:

1. when the card was executed;
2. the circumstances surrounding its execution;

[24] Id. at 68, 502 A.2d at 1276.
[25] Id. at 69, 502 A.2d at 1276.
[26] Id.
[27] Id. at 70, 502 A.2d at 1277.
[28] Id. at 73, 502 A.2d at 1278.

3. whether the card was executed as an "affirmation of faith"[29] or as a binding statement in a life-threatening situation; and
4. whether the situation had changed since the card was executed to the point that it no longer reflected the patient's desires and decision.[30]

Given the severity of the patient's condition the court did not have the time to conduct a review based on such criteria. Moreover, without the card, without knowing the circumstances surrounding its execution, and without testimony from witnesses regarding the strength of the patient's beliefs the court was not able to apply the theory of substituted judgment.[31]

In a footnote at the end of its opinion, it was noted that the court's decision should be read narrowly. The court did not address the issue of circumstances in which the trial court could delay its ruling without a risk of death or other severe harm. Moreover, it did not address the issue of clear and convincing evidence regarding what the patient would want done if competent.[32] In either instance, a different approach would be followed.

This decision, minimizing the importance of a medical alert card, casts significant doubts on living wills and durable powers of attorney. If all manner of evidence is necessary to substantiate the value of the medical alert card, what would it take for this same court faced with an emergency in which the patient had executed a living will or durable power of attorney? Would the court be as reluctant to accept such evidence as it was the medical alert card? Is it really a matter of religious objection that is at issue?

A Canadian decision suggests that a card carried on the person of the patient is an adequate refusal of treatment.[33] The case involved a patient who suffered extensive facial injuries in

[29] Id.
[30] Id.
[31] Id. at 73-74, 502 A.2d at 1278-1279.
[32] Id. at 74 n.8, 502 A.2d at 1279 n.8.
[33] Malette v. Shulman, 43 C.C.L.T. 62 (Ont. H.C. 1987).

a car crash. On her person was a card stating in French that she was a Jehovah's Witness and that she did not wish to have any blood or blood by-products. The card was not signed. Although the doctor who treated her was warned four times about the card, he chose to administer blood. The woman was unable to communicate verbally due to an airway impeding her ability to speak. Nonetheless, she did communicate through hand signals to a church elder her desire not to have the blood transfusions.

The court found that the doctor had committed a battery on the patient and that she should be awarded $20,000 in damages. Although this is by no means a great sum of money by American standards, the case does suggest the importance attributed by at least one court to written directives refusing treatment.[34]

The transfusion of a person over her specific objection is a troublesome issue. It is made all the more so by persons who are insensitive to religious beliefs. Perhaps the answer is state legislation in which the rights of patients are accorded greater awareness and application.

§7.1.2 *Treatment Not Compelled Over Religious Objections*

Over the years a number of American courts have refused to appoint a guardian for the purpose of either consenting to or directly ordering blood transfusions when the patient declined such treatment based on a religious belief. In many of these cases, the patient was childless — a key consideration in view of the state's interest in preventing the abandonment of minors in need of support. In each case the patient was fully aware of the consequences of his or her decision, a factor essential to informed consent. Each person's decision was made voluntarily. The two following cases illustrate this type of situation.

[34] Id.

In In re Melideo, a 23-year-old married woman had undergone a D & C and some twenty-four hours later had developed a serious uterine hemorrhage.[35] As a Jehovah's Witness she refused a blood transfusion. Legal proceedings were launched, and after hearing the case the court declined to order transfusion therapy. Since there were no dependent children and the patient was not pregnant, the state could not demonstrate a compelling interest sufficient to override the woman's constitutional guarantee of free exercise of religion.

Another matter also involved a patient who declined blood transfusion treatment based on religious belief.[36] The patient had knowingly chosen this option despite the fact that attending physicians thought death would occur without infusing blood. Unlike the *Melideo* case, the patient had two young children at home. The court was not persuaded, however, that this gave the state sufficient interest to overcome the patient's decision. The court had before it ample proof that both material and spiritual provision was available for the children.

It should be noted that when a patient is conscious and able to consent, his refusal to receive blood transfusions based on religious beliefs cannot be overridden by a court-appointed conservator when there is no demonstrable compelling state interest. In Holmes v. Silver Cross Hospital, the conservator's action led to a civil rights action by the patient.[37]

As the case law in this section suggests, unless the state can demonstrate an interest sufficient to prevail over the individual's religious beliefs, courts will be reluctant to order transfusion therapy.[38]

That dependent minors may survive the patient is not a sufficient state interest to warrant overriding the patient's ob-

[35] 88 Misc. 2d 974, 390 N.Y.S.2d 523 (1976).
[36] In re Osborne, 294 A.2d 372 (D.C. App. 1972). See also Erickson v. Dilgard, 44 Misc. 2d 27, 252 N.Y.S.2d 705 (1962).
[37] 340 F. Supp. 125 (N.D. Ill. 1965).
[38] See Mercy Hosp. v. Jackson, 62 Md. App. 409, 489 A.2d 1130 (1985), in which a patient in labor was not compelled to submit to a transfusion when fetus was never at risk. See also St. Mary's Hosp. v. Ramsey, 465 So. 2d 666 (Fla. Dist. Ct. App. 1985) (question certified to Supreme Court of Florida).

jection to blood transfusion therapy. Although concern may be expressed about the "quality" of the children's lives without the benefit of one parent's loving support,[39] this is not the true measure of the state's interest. Rather, the concern is whether the loss of the patient would result in abandonment of the individual's minor children. Besides the state-interest aspect of such cases, it must also be shown that a patient was aware of the consequences of her decision and that it was made voluntarily.

Perhaps the most unusual example of the right to refuse treatment based on religious objection occurred in a criminal case. A 47-year-old woman was shot and seriously injured. The woman's daughter was taken into custody and charged with aggravated assault on her mother and murdering her father.[40]

The victim authorized necessary surgery, but she refused any blood transfusions. She based her refusal on religious objections to the use of blood products. Believing that the victim was the only eyewitness the state had against the person in custody, the District Attorney obtained a court order authorizing the blood transfusions.[41]

Although the blood was administered, an emergency appeal was pursued. This appeal took on greater significance when it was learned that the victim would require additional surgery and additional blood transfusions.[42]

In vacating the lower court orders compelling the use of blood transfusions, the Supreme Court of Mississippi held:

> However, legitimate and important the State's interest may be in having available for testimony at trial an eyewitness, that interest is not within those so compelling as to entail Mattie Brown's rights to free exercise of her religious beliefs and to privacy.[43]

[39] For an interesting explanation of this principle, see Wons v. Public Health Trust of Dade County, 500 So. 2d 679 (Fla. Dist. Ct. App. 1987), in which the dissent argued that the "quality" of the surviving dependent children's lives along with the state's interest in preserving the patient's life should be sufficient to overcome the individual's right to refuse care.

[40] In re Brown, 478 So. 2d 1033 (Miss. 1985).

[41] Id.

[42] Id.

[43] Id. at 1039.

At the very least, the decision helps delineate just how far the state can go in compelling an individual to relinquish the exercise of his state or federal constitutional rights. To this court, in this case, the state had gone too far.

§7.1.3   State Statutes and Religious Objections

Not all the law relating to religious objection to life-saving treatment emanates from the courts. For example, according to legislation in Maryland, physicians cannot provide medical treatment to a patient who is known to have religious beliefs that prohibit such care.[44]

In anticipation of patients' presenting themselves with conditions necessitating treatment that is contrary to their religious beliefs, hospitals should develop a suitable policy. The health facility's legal advisor can alert the administration and staff to statutory requirements.

§7.1.4   Other Types of Litigation Involving Religious Objection to Treatment

Litigation involving religious objection to treatment is not restricted to requests for court orders compelling care or appointing a guardian to make such a decision for a patient. Religious objection to treatment can also find its way into wrongful death actions. A New York case[45] illustrates this point.

A 45-year-old woman gave birth by caesarean section to a healthy baby girl. However, when doctors attempted to remove the placenta, they found that the woman had placenta previa and placenta accreta, necessitating the removal of her uterus. During an emergency hysterectomy, the obstetrician-gynecologist lacerated the urinary bladder causing a massive hemorrhage.

---

[44]Md. Ann. Code 43 §135C (1980).
[45]Randolph v. City of New York, 117 A.D.2d 44, 501 N.Y.S.2d 837 (1986).

The woman was a practicing Jehovah's Witness who had advised the doctor prior to her hospitalization that she did not want any blood transfusions. This was also noted in her hospital admission record.[46]

Within approximately 40 minutes the patient lost about 80 percent of her blood. There was no indication that the hemorrhaging was being brought under control. As a result, the attending anesthesiologist, employed by the City Health and Hospitals Corporation at the hospital, requested that the City Corporation Counsel authorize a blood transfusion. When the authorization was received about 15 minutes later, a transfusion was initiated. Despite these efforts, the patient died.

Two wrongful death actions were instituted claiming negligence on the part of the obstetrician-gynecologist and the anesthesiologist. The case against the obstetrician-gynecologist was settled out of court, and the matter proceeded against the anesthesiologist and the City Health and Hospitals Corporation.

The plaintiff claimed that the defendants were liable for the patient's death for failing to start a blood transfusion when she began to hemorrhage. It was also claimed that the transfusion was administered in a negligent manner. Although the jury returned a verdict in favor of the plaintiff, the trial court granted a new trial on the issue of damages. An appeal followed.

The appellate court reversed the decision of the trial court. The claim that the anesthesiologist should have ignored the patient's religious beliefs and refusal of blood transfusion therapy was deemed to be without merit. Indeed, the court noted that New York specifically indicates that a patient has the right to decide her own medical care and that such a right ranks above the doctor's obligation to give necessary treatment.[47]

On the issue of negligent administration of the transfusion, the court also sided with the defendants. That the doctor did not act quickly to administer the blood transfusion was not a sufficient basis for holding him medically negligent. Expert

[46]Id.
[47]501 N.Y.S.2d at 841, citing N.Y. Pub. Health Law §§2504 and 2805-d.

medical testimony failed to establish that the blood transfusion supplied to the patient was the proximate cause of her death. The patient had a right to refuse the transfusion and therefore the doctor was not obliged to undertake "affirmative" action.[48] However, once he voluntarily intervened he was required to act with due care. The evidence in the case indicated that there was no lack of care on the part of the anesthesiologist. Rather, by the time the transfusion was started it was too late to save the woman's life.

This New York case shows the frustrations of respecting individual rights and exercising professional duties. If patients choose to follow a course that may lead to death, health professionals should not be held responsible for such outcomes. That seems to be in part the message of this case. As the court wrote:

> to require a physician to stand by helplessly, while a patient is dying, and, when it is too late to save the patient, the doctor is instructed to proceed to use his skills to save her, and, to then attempt to apply liability for his actions, is just unacceptable.[49]

§7.2 Incompetent or Incapacitated Persons

§7.2.1 Incompetent Persons

Competent persons may generally refuse curative, life-saving treatment. Exceptions include situations, as described earlier, in which a demonstrable state interest outweighs an individual's interest in free exercise of religion.

Treating incompetent persons poses a more complex question: how do medical personnel decide who is capable of making choices about his own health? A patient's refusal of a life-saving appendectomy that was recommended by physicians does not necessarily mean he is legally incompetent. Should the

[48] Id. at 842.
[49] Id. at 843.

same patient exhibit a disorientation to time, reality, and place, however, while at the same time demonstrating an overall inability to look after his own daily needs and personal hygiene, a court may reach a judgment of incompetence and appoint a guardian. In some cases the issue is quite clear, whereas in other instances it is not.

The case of Lane v. Candura illustrates this point.[1] A 77-year-old widow was hospitalized with gangrene of the lower right leg and foot. Doctors advised her to undergo amputation of a portion of the limb in order to save her life. On two occasions she agreed to the operation but each time withdrew her consent. Thereafter, her daughter went to court seeking appointment as temporary guardian of her mother with power to authorize the amputation. The patient's reasons for declining treatment were the unhappy state of her life since her husband's death, a concern about becoming a burden to her children, and a fear of becoming an invalid institutionalized in a nursing home. She was confused about certain matters and her conception of time was distorted. Her mind had a tendency to wander and she refused to discuss the proposed procedure with certain people, including one of the court-appointed psychiatrists.

Despite these considerations, the court refused to appoint the daughter as temporary guardian. It based its decision on the fact that the patient was at times lucid. At those times, she showed a high level of awareness about the implications of her choice. Moreover, the petitioner failed to prove that her mother's states of forgetfulness or confusion were related to or caused an inability to appreciate that declining the operation meant certain death. Her decision, while medically irrational, did not amount to legal incompetency.[2]

A New Jersey court reached the same conclusion in a similar case.[3] A 72-year-old divorced man who lived as a semi-recluse

§7.2 [1] 6 Mass. App. Ct. 377, 376 N.E.2d 1232 (1978).
[2] Shortly after the court rendered its decision, Mrs. Candura was visited by a family member who apparently discussed the need for surgery. She then consented to and underwent the operation.
[3] Matter of Quackenbush, 156 N.J. Super. 282, 383 A.2d 785 (1978).

was hospitalized with gangrene in both legs. Doctors recommended surgical removal of both limbs to save his life. Although at one point he signed a form authorizing the surgery, he later withdrew his consent. After hearing evidence, the court rejected the hospital's request to appoint a guardian with authority to consent to the amputations. The fact that he had changed his mind did not make the patient incompetent. Since the man was competent to decide his own future and any possible state interest was insufficient to overcome the patient's interest in an unwanted and extensive bodily intrusion, the court had no authority on which to appoint a guardian.

A person's confinement to a mental health facility does not mean she is incompetent to decide whether to undergo medical treatment. This principle has been set out in both statutory[4] and case law. The following Pennsylvania decision[5] demonstrates the judicial approach to the issue.

A woman had been committed to a state mental health facility for the treatment of a mental problem. During the course of a routine physical checkup, a physician found possible indicators of breast cancer. He recommended a breast biopsy. When she refused to undergo the recommended test, proceedings were launched to have a guardian appointed with authority to consent.

The court found that the patient was competent to decide whether she wanted to have the biopsy. In addition, it pointed out that no state interest would be served in appointing a guardian to provide consent to the procedure. Further, the patient had neither requested medical care from the mental health facility nor placed limitations on personnel restricting appropriate treatment.

Several cases have involved persons who *were* found to be

---

[4]See, e.g., R.I. Gen. Laws §40.1-5-5 (1977), wherein it is stated that: "A person shall not, solely by reason of his admission or certification to a facility for examination or care and treatment under the provisions of this chapter thereby be deemed incompetent to manage his affairs . . . or *for any other purpose*" (emphasis added).

[5]In re Yetter, 62 Pa. D. & C.2d 619 (1973).

incompetent or incapable of giving an informed consent.[6] One case that reflects the thinking of a court on the matter of competency is Matter of Schiller.[7] A 67-year-old widower with organic brain damage was hospitalized with a gangrenous right foot. Although antibiotic therapy had slowed the spread of infection, doctors advised amputation to avert death. At the request of the attending surgeon, a psychiatrist examined the patient on several occasions. He concluded that the patient did not understand that the amputation was necessary to save his life. An independent psychiatrist appointed by the court reached the same conclusion. Moreover, he found that the patient was disoriented as to place and time and lacked the capacity to make an informed judgment.

Based on the foregoing evidence and additional presentations to the court, a cousin of the patient was appointed special guardian with power to consent to the amputation. The court's judgment followed a comparison of the mental capacity required to give permission to surgery to that necessary for entering into a contract. More specifically, the court described the test for mental capacity as follows:

> Does the patient have sufficient mind to reasonably understand the condition, the nature and effect of the proposed treatment, attendant risks in pursuing the treatment, and not pursuing the treatment?[8]

Since the patient's mental ability did not meet this standard, the court appointed the special guardian in view of the patient's life-threatening condition and his good chances of cure with the recommended surgery.

Health facilities and personnel should not assume that treatment they perceive as curative or life-sustaining will always be ordered for incompetent patients. Moreover, procedural safe-

---

[6]See, e.g., In the Matter of Harvey "U," 501 N.Y.S.2d 920 (App. Div. 1986), in which on the basis of clear and convincing evidence a schizophrenic patient was found incompetent to either consent to or refuse amputation surgery on his feet.

[7]148 N.J. Super. 168, 372 A.2d 360 (1977).

[8]Id. at 181, 372 A.2d at 367.

guards imposed by statute[9] or judicial decisions[10] must be followed.

In a Washington case, the court ruled that a proposed laryngectomy could constitute an "amputation," thereby triggering certain statutory safeguards, including the necessity of judicial approval for the operation. The incompetent patient, a 66-year-old woman, had a malignant cancer of the larynx. Although unable to totally appreciate her problem, she repeatedly opposed the intended operation, opting instead for radiation therapy. As the Supreme Court of Washington suggested, the fact that the patient was incompetent did not mean that her express wishes should not be taken into consideration. Indeed, the court made it clear that the patient's wishes were to be given "substantial" weight in deciding what form of treatment was in her best interests.[11]

A more difficult issue for health personnel and the courts is the matter of nutritional therapy for those patients who cannot consume food in the usual manner. For example, at issue in a Massachusetts case was whether a 92-year-old woman suffering from severe mental illness should be forced to undergo surgery to restore a gastric feeding tube. The patient had repeatedly removed the tubing resulting in repetitive abdominal procedures to open a new entrance hole.[12] In applying the Massachusetts rule of substituted judgment the court determined that the operation should not be performed. The court based its decision on the patient's advanced age as it related to the risk factors of the procedure, the need for physical restraints for one week following the operation, the complications resulting from previous surgical procedures to establish an abdominal opening, and the inability to carry out important preoperative tests due to the patient's underlying hiatal hernia and cervical diverticulum conditions. The state's interest in preserving life was not sufficient to outweigh these considerations.[13]

[9]Guardianship of Ingram, 689 P.2d 1363 (Wash. 1984).
[10]Matter of Hier, 18 Mass. App. Ct. 200, 464 N.E.2d 959 (1984).
[11]Guardianship of Ingram, supra n.9, at 1370.
[12]Matter of Hier, supra n.10.
[13]Id.

Nutritional support and curative medical or surgical procedures may pose troubling medicolegal and ethical problems. Nonetheless, care should be taken to avoid decisions based on highly subjective values or single issue considerations such as age. As in the case of the terminally ill, consideration must be given to what would serve the best interests of the patient as well as applicable state interests. The difficulties posed by incompetent but nonterminally ill patients necessarily require careful, case-by-case determinations.

§7.2.2 Incapacitated Persons

At least one court has termed a person *incapacitated* rather than incompetent to the point that she could not give consent.[14] A guardian was appointed with authority to consent to amputation of both her feet — despite the fact that the patient had only a 50 percent chance of survival. Doctors predicted death without the operation. The patient's refusal to undergo care, as voiced by her guardian, was not upheld by the court. Her guardian described her as an intelligent, lucid, and articulate woman who simply refused to accept the seriousness of her condition. She neither refused nor consented to the amputation. Had she committed herself to refusing treatment overtly, her wish would have been respected. The court found that a person can have capacity to decide about some matters and an incapacity to decide about others. It placed the patient in this case within that category since her understanding was blocked when it came to discussing her possible death and the amputation. She exhibited delusional behavior about her condition that rendered her incapable of giving an informed consent on this question. These facts were sufficient for the appointment of the Tennessee Commissioner of Human Services as guardian, with authority to consent to surgery under the provisions of a state statute for the protection of the elderly.[15]

---

[14]State Dept. of Human Servs. v. Northern, 563 S.W.2d 197 (Tenn. Ct. App. 1978).
[15]Tenn. Code Ann. §14-5-106 (1978).

§7.2.3 State Statutes Authorizing Treatment

In some states legislation has been enacted that focuses on consent to treatment for incompetent and incapable persons who are without guardians or conservators of the person.[16] As the California Law Revision Commission noted, that state's law is intended to provide a quick way for health personnel to obtain an authorization for a patient's treatment while safeguarding his rights.[17]

According to the California law, a petition must be filed authorizing medical care and requesting that the petitioner be empowered to consent to medical treatment on behalf of the patient. The law specifies who may file such a petition, as well as the required contents of the documentation. The petition must provide the basic information required for informed consent, including a description of the patient's condition, the proposed course of care, the threat to the patient's health if treatment is delayed or denied, and the probable results of the proposed care as well as the medically available alternative forms of care. Any efforts to obtain the patient's consent must also be described.[18]

Prior to a hearing, the court may appoint a lawyer to represent the patient if she does not have counsel; provision is also made for notice of the place and time of the proceedings. A statutory alternative is also provided that dispenses with the requirement of a hearing, if both parties agree and stipulate that there is no remaining issue of fact.[19] The statute permits a court to order the recommended course of care and to appoint a person to give consent when the following evidence is established:

1. The patient's medical condition requires the recommended treatment.

---

[16] Cal. Prob. Code §§3200 et seq. (West 1981); Va. Code §37.1-134.2 (1981).
[17] See Cal. Prob. Code §3201 (West 1981), note.
[18] Cal. Prob. Code §3204 (West 1981).
[19] Cal. Prob. Code §§3205-3207 (West 1981).

2. Without treatment, the patient's life or physical well-being will probably be endangered.
3. The patient is unable to give informed consent.[20]

The California law does not permit the court to overrule a legally capable patient's decision to refuse treatment. Moreover, it does apply to those situations in which emergency treatment is necessary.[21]

Virginia also has a provision permitting a court to authorize treatment for an incompetent or incapable person who is without an available guardian or committee to give consent.[22] The court's decision must be based on clear and convincing evidence that the patient is incompetent or incapable and that the recommended treatment is medically necessary.[23]

Legislation like that in California or Virginia is not designed to authorize emergency treatment. It focuses on the chronically ill patient whose life or health is or may be threatened unless appropriate treatment is provided. The legislation does not preclude the need for court action, a requirement that may ultimately delay treatment.

In those states with similar legislation, it is important to expedite all required judicial proceedings. The necessary documentation and medical affidavits should be prepared promptly, with particular attention to showing the need for treatment. Getting a stipulation on the facts in urgent cases will also reduce the time factor involved.

This type of legislation will help to resolve cases involving the refusal of life-saving care. Where it fails, physicians and health institutions will have to turn for guidance to guardianship, conservatorships, and general consent provisions. The method for proceeding under these laws must be understood clearly so that the rights of the patient can be protected and necessary treatment be provided.

[20]Cal. Prob. Code §3208 (West 1981).
[21]Cal. Prob. Code §§3208, 3210 (West 1981).
[22]Va. Code §37.1-134.2 (1981).
[23]Id.

§7.3 Emergency Life-Saving Treatment

Physicians and nurses are often confronted in the emergency department with patients who are seriously injured and in shock. The patients are disoriented and perhaps incoherent or in severe pain. They shake their heads in disapproval of having treatment or voice a "No, no, no!" Does this constitute a decision not to have treatment, a negative consent?

On other occasions patients are brought to the hospital in an unconscious state. Sometimes they are accompanied by concerned family members who adamantly insist that if the patients could speak they would refuse the proposed treatment. Others arrive unconscious without family or friends, but with a card in their wallets or purses to the effect that, "I am a Jehovah's Witness. Do *not* use any blood or blood products in any medical treatment." (See Appendix E.) Should physicians and hospitals abide by family members' requests or those contained on wallet cards? What risks accompany a decision to accede to such requests or to ignore them?

Several sources of law affect this problem area of emergency department treatment. As discussed in detail in chapters 1 and 2, statutes and hospital policy are important in this area, as well as case decisions and the common law principle of implied consent. In some states a clear-cut judicial, legislative, or regulatory position has not been established on these issues. Physicians, hospitals, and free-standing emergency clinics in these states should therefore devise their own policy on meeting emergency situations.

§7.3.1 *Authority to Provide Treatment*

Both common law and legislation recognize the right to provide care in emergency situations. Consent is not necessary prior to health personnel's providing care, as long as the requirements are met for an emergency. The authority to administer treatment in these circumstances is based on a legal fiction. The law implies the consent of patients to reasonable care in the circumstances. The assumption being made is that if the patient were capable of consent, he would give authorization to treatment.[1]

The use of the emergency treatment rule is limited. The patient must need immediate attention to preserve life or health, and either the patient must be incapable of giving consent or the situation must make obtaining consent impractical.[2] Moreover, the physician is only justified in providing care that is reasonable in the context of the patient's condition.[3]

On the basis of factual proof of emergency conditions, courts have found that providing emergency treatment to patients of all ages — even to children without parental consent — is permissible.[4] One case involved the amputation of a badly injured arm.[5] However, precedent to the opposite effect exists where the courts determined that an emergency situation did not exist. In one case the amputation of a young boy's injured leg was not justified.[6]

Although a person may be legally and mentally capable of giving consent, the emergency nature of a situation may make it impractical or impossible to obtain this informed authorization. Severe allergic reactions, heart attacks, insect bites, or snake bites can create such situations.[7] By delaying treatment in order to go through the usual consent process the physician may actually cause the patient's condition to become irreversible. In this instance treatment may be provided that is reasonable in the circumstances. Still practitioners must be able to substantiate their judgment that conditions made consent impossible or impractical.

---

§7.3   [1] Restatement of Torts, §62 (1934).

[2] Wells v. McGehee, 390 So. 2d 196 (La. Ct. App. 1949). See also N.Y. Pub. Health Law §2504 (McKinney 1952).

[3] Rogers v. Sells, 178 Okla. 103, 61 P.2d 1018 (1936) (per curiam).

[4] See Wells v. McGehee, 390 So. 2d 196 (La. Ct. App. 1949); Jackovach v. Yocum, 212 Iowa 914, 237 N.W. 444 (1931); Luka v. Lowie, 171 Mich. 122, 136 N.W. 1106 (1912).

[5] Jackovach v. Yocum, supra n.4.

[6] Rogers v. Sells, supra n.3.

[7] Crouch v. Most, 78 N.M. 406, 432 P.2d 250 (1967).

§7.3.2   *Patients' Refusal of Treatment*

Health institutions are often faced with patients who refuse life-saving emergency treatment. The patients arrive in shock, with severe injuries, with the tell-tale signs of a stroke, or with the effects of alcohol or drug intoxication. Physicians are then faced with determining whether refusals of treatment from these patients are legally valid. Their resolution of this difficulty lies in the fundamental principles of consent (see chapter 1). When patients are capable of understanding the nature and consequences of their decisions and are legally capable of giving consent, their determination must be followed. When they lack mental or legal capacity, their refusal need not be heeded; consent must be obtained from someone authorized to act on their behalf. Even this step is not necessary when a medical emergency exists as recognized in state law.

Some health administrators would recommend obtaining court orders when seriously ill patients refuse treatment in a state of incoherence or confusion. For example, in John F. Kennedy Memorial Hospital v. Heston, a guardian was appointed with authority to consent to blood transfusions for an emergency patient.[8] The woman, a Jehovah's Witness, had been taken to the hospital with severe injuries following an automobile accident. In order to save her life, surgery and blood transfusions were required. At the time of her admission she was in shock, incoherent, and disoriented. During a subsequent action to vacate the guardianship order, she insisted that she had refused to accept blood because of her religious beliefs.

The New Jersey Supreme Court held that when a hospital and its staff are involuntarily faced with a patient whose religious beliefs preclude life-saving treatment, they can provide treatment consistent with prevailing medical standards. The court also noted that if time permits, a prior application to a court is appropriate. When no time can be spared for prior judicial approval, hospitals and their staffs should be able to rely upon an already established institutional policy. Health

[8] 58 N.J. 576, 279 A.2d 670 (1971).

facilities should develop such a policy in anticipation of these problems.

§7.3.3 Relatives' Refusal of Treatment

When the refusal of consent to emergency treatment comes not from the patient but from the family, another set of considerations comes into play. Generally speaking, when a patient is competent to make a decision regarding care, the consent of a spouse is neither relevant nor necessary.[9] When the patient is unconscious or incapable of consenting, however, an authorization from the patient's spouse or near relative may be sufficient in some states to permit treatment. This principle has been established by courts[10] and, in some jurisdictions, by legislation.[11]

Prevention of a lawsuit is the practical consideration behind securing the consent of an incompetent patient's relative. The son, daughter, or spouse who authorizes emergency surgery would have difficulty as the patient's legal representative suing the doctor or hospital for unauthorized treatment.

Obtaining a spouse's or relative's consent is not always possible or necessary. When contacting the spouse or relative is impractical or would delay care to the point of risking the patient's health or life, treatment may be provided without familial authorization.[12] When a relative refuses permission for what the doctor believes are measures necessary to save the patient's life, the relative's refusal may be overridden by a court of law. Such was the case in Collins v. Davis,[13] in which a county hospital in New York was able to obtain a court order permitting a surgical procedure on an incompetent patient. The man was in a coma

---

[9] See, e.g., Rosenberg v. Feigin, 119 Cal. App. 2d 783, 260 P.2d 143 (1955); Rytkonen v. Lojacono, 269 Mich. 270, 257 N.W. 703 (1934).

[10] See, e.g., Steele v. Woods, 327 S.W.2d 187, 198 (Mo. 1959).

[11] See Ark. Stat. Ann. §82-363 (1981); Ga. Code Ann. §88-2904 (1971).

[12] Fla. Stat. Ann. §743.064 (West 1979) (minors); Ga. Code Ann. §88-2905 (1971).

[13] 44 Misc. 2d 622, 254 N.Y.S.2d 666 (1964).

and his wife refused to give her consent. The court found that when the patient came into the hospital, the facility took on a legal duty of providing appropriate care. Neither the hospital nor the doctors treating him could then be put in the position of operating on the man or letting him expire due to lack of consent. The key issue was that the man required attention and the court was unwilling to take the chance of not ordering care only to find out subsequently that the law required care.

§7.3.4 Disputes Among Family Members

Another New York case demonstrates a frequent problem faced by hospitals: an incompetent patient requiring care and a dispute between next-of-kin over authorization of treatment. In Petition of Nemser, an 80-year-old woman was admitted as an emergency patient with diabetes and arteriosclerotic gangrene with infection of the right foot.[14] A staff psychiatrist determined that the patient was not capable of understanding the nature of an amputation nor of consenting to it. When one of her three children, a physician, refused to authorize surgical removal of the diseased foot, court proceedings were instituted by her other children. They sought the appointment of a temporary representative authorized to consent to the surgery.

The son who pressed for court action was convinced that the surgery would stop the spread of infection and prolong his mother's life. The son who opposed surgery had serious reservations about his mother's withstanding surgery: he urged a more conservative approach to treatment. The admitting physician described the proposed surgery as a choice between life and death. Two medical consultants disputed his statement; furthermore, they told the court that they could not assure the effectiveness of the amputation. They also noted that the patient's condition could return in the stump after the operation.

The court followed the advice of the guardian ad litem and declined to appoint a temporary guardian. It did so after mak-

[14]51 Misc. 2d 616, 273 N.Y.S.2d 624 (1966).

ing a finding, based on medical opinion, that the surgery was not a life-saving procedure. The court also addressed the petitioners' concern that since the court had declined to authorize the procedure at this point, should their mother take a "turn for the worse," the doctors and hospital might refrain from providing life-preserving surgical care without the written consent of the patient's next-of-kin or judicial approval. The court dismissed this argument, indicating that in an emergency, health care providers should not refrain from doing what their skilled judgment dictates regarding life-saving care because of the threat of a possible lawsuit. The decision to treat is a medical not a legal one.[15]

§7.3.5 Effects of Patients' Written Directives

Some patients arrive in the emergency department of a hospital carrying on their persons a card or a letter of instructions indicating allowable types of treatment. A common set of instructions asks that no blood or blood by-products be administered during the course of care. Whether a health institution is bound by these directives is open to debate.

Proponents of these instruction sheets or cards contend that the document is all that is necessary for a patient to refuse certain types of care. Written when the patient was legally and mentally capable of giving or refusing consent, the document should be treated as a legally binding authorization for designated forms of care.

Opponents to these cards or letters point out that the forms do not constitute a valid "informed" consent. When written in anticipation of a serious illness or injury, these documents do not reflect the patient's assessment of the actual condition at issue and any reasonable treatment options available. One could argue that without this information the patient's consent is not valid.

Whether health facilities and personnel should respect this

[15] Id.

type of documentation is a matter of institutional policy as well as of law. Since state law is sorely lacking in this area, with the exception of Maryland's, as noted earlier (§7.1.3), one of two possible options is available.

A conservative approach may be adopted, in which the cards or instruction sheets are considered invalid. Authorization for treatment could then perhaps be obtained from a relative of the patient. It is an open question whether that authorization would prove to be a sufficient defense to any subsequent challenge for unauthorized treatment by the patient. When, however, securing the consent of a relative is impractical or impossible, health personnel should proceed with treatment and err on the side of life. The prospect of a patient winning a substantial damages award because a physician ignored a statement on a card is rather remote. However, health facilities and health personnel must be prepared for such litigation, since actual physical harm is not a prerequisite to a lawsuit based on unauthorized treatment. Moreover, the tenor of the times is one of respect for the bodily integrity of the person.

The other tack to follow is to respect these cards or letters, particularly in the case of adults, who are presumed at law to be capable of giving or withholding consent. The families of patients should be contacted, not for their consent or assent, but to apprise them of the decisions that have been made regarding treatment. The fact that a family was contacted and voiced no objection is of great importance: should the patient die, they would be in a position to launch an action for wrongful death. Their lack of objection would then be significant evidence in such a case. To this end, notes in the patient's medical record should adequately document the statement refusing treatment, whether the patient's family was contacted, and whether they objected to the plan not to proceed with treatment. The notation should be dated and signed by the attending physician.

When, however, members of the patient's family do object to the lack of treatment, the better practice would be to initiate care. The interests of the patient must be balanced with the prospect of wrongful death litigation against the health institution in the event that she should die for lack of treatment.

At best, the refusal of treatment in these circumstances is a difficult question. As one judge has written:

> In this complicated life which we are now living, surrounded on every hand by complicated machinery and rapid transportation of all sorts, with more or less serious accidents occurring very frequently, with persons, young, middle-aged, and old, carried in great numbers daily into offices and hospitals, more or less injured and mangled, the rules of conduct on the part of trained and educated expert surgeons must be fixed to reasonably fit the conditions. If the surgeon, confronted by an emergency, is not to be permitted, after having fairly and carefully examined the situation, to exercise his professional judgment in his honest endeavor to save human life, then the public at large must suffer. If the surgeon is not to be permitted to honestly use his best judgment upon the necessity for an operation, without waiting to the consent of either the patient or his parents, then is the skilled hand of the expert stayed by an unreasonable rule, often to the detriment of the patient and humanity at large.[16]

§7.3.6 Policy Considerations in Providing Treatment

In most cases trying to obtain judicial approval for emergency treatment is impractical. Neither time nor resources can be allocated for judicial proceedings in each case. Most physicians and hospitals would be more comfortable if state legislation authorized treatment in urgent cases without patient consent. Such legislation will never, however, give physicians detailed or specific descriptions of what are and are not emergency patients. Nor will it ever resolve family disputes over treating patients incapable of consenting to medical care.

A more realistic approach is to plan for possible lawsuits: on what basis will they be filed — assault and battery or medical negligence? What damages can be claimed for saving the life of a person in danger of dying or being permanently disabled?

---

[16] Jackovach v. Yocum, 237 N.W. 444, 451 (1931).

Are the risks of successful litigation so great or will juries and judges find in favor of the health care providers? It is probably safe to say that as long as the health care team acts in a reasonable manner, in a fashion consistent with the appropriate standard of care required by the patient, suits for unauthorized care or lack of consent will be few — or at least end favorably for the doctor and hospital.

Problems can arise when the patient or a family member objects to the proposed treatment. Browbeating them may only strengthen their resolve not to consent. Talking to them as calmly as possible, while laying before them the facts and any reasonable alternatives to the proposed treatment, may sway them. If not, many jurisdictions offer at least three alternatives. Consulting with hospital counsel and looking at hospital organization guidelines should precede selecting a particular option.

a. Use of release forms. The first alternative is to get a release form signed that relieves the hospital, its employees, and staff from liability for not furnishing treatment. The form should be signed by the patient (if competent) or by the patient's next of kin (if not). A release form that has been executed properly is a good mechanism of protection from liability for health personnel when there has been a refusal to undergo treatment. It would not be effective, however, if signed by a patient whose degree of mental or physical incapacitation prevented appreciation of the nature of the proposed treatment or the risks of foregoing it. In those cases the form is not a valid consent to withhold treatment. Instead, the negative consent or release should be executed by a near relative who concurs with and is legally empowered to act for the patient.

b. Securing court orders for treatment. A second alternative is to go to court for a judicial order either appointing a legal representative to represent the patient or authorizing necessary care. This option is particularly attractive when a dispute among family members complicates the treatment process. It may also be a satisfactory option when a relative's decision to withhold authorization for treatment seems medically unsound or is based on personal interests. The courts can choose the path of appointing a legal representative or ordering treatment; they can decide not to intervene. Case-by-case analysis is integral to this process. When the court orders care, counsel should request that the order contain a statement releasing the health facility and personnel from civil or criminal liability in connection with providing that treatment. If such language is included, the order only immunizes those providing treatment in connection with the medical or surgical procedures authorized by the court. It does not extend to matters of substandard care or negligence. Such a clause, however, could be the basis for a defense to a legal action for unauthorized or substandard treatment or it may deter a lawsuit from being filed.

c. Treatment without authorization. The third alternative is to forge ahead with treatment despite the risk of potential liability. This choice may be the only practical solution when time limitations preclude persuading the next-of-kin or seeking a court order. Many states have set up special procedures for those emergency cases where judicial permission to treat or the appointment of a guardian is needed. Sometimes this machinery is not in place or the patient's condition does not permit any delay in treatment. In such cases erring on the side of care is better than opting for no treatment, which may lead to death and, possibly, wrongful death actions.

A detailed note should be written in the patient's chart explaining the situation and the reason for going ahead with treatment. Defending an unauthorized treatment suit launched by a patient who, in the doctor's medical judgment, was unable to appreciate his condition or formulate a decision is far easier than defending a suit based on wrongful death or abandonment. Health facilities must, however, be prepared for the prospect of litigation in these cases. Law and society usually support the preservation of life and the saving of any patients who can be cured.

B.   TERMINAL ILLNESS

§7.4   Right to Refuse Terminal Care

Unlike patients who are afflicted with a curable disease or who have injuries that, although life-threatening, can be corrected, a different set of considerations applies in the case of the terminally ill. The interests of the state are not as compelling as in the curable disease cases if, for example, the patient is a 25-year-old father of three with metastatic cancer who doctors believe has three months to live. Similarly, the state interest is not very compelling if the patient is a 63-year-old woman with end-stage renal disease, diabetes, and end-stage heart disease. Those who would seek an order to compel treatment for a patient in need of a blood transfusion are less likely to seek a judicial directive compelling treatment in the case of a terminally ill person.

The practical problems of consent for the terminally ill involve who may refuse care for the incompetent patient, when care may be withdrawn for competent or incompetent persons, and the methods available to give effect to a decision not to treat or to withdraw care.

Certain constitutional and common law principles apply here, for example the right to privacy and the concept of self-determination. Statutory enactments, particularly so-called living will laws, have also become available as legal mechanisms for effectuating the wishes of the dying patient. The law regarding terminally ill children has been included in chapter 5, on minors.

§7.4.1   Competent Persons

In a number of jurisdictions, the right of a competent person to refuse treatment has a common law basis, going back to the principle that a patient has a right to decide what will be done to her body.[1] In other jurisdictions, the judicially created right

---

§7.4   [1]Schloendorff v. Society of N.Y. Hosp., 211 N.Y. 125, 105 N.E. 92 (1914); Nolan v. Kechijian, 75 R.I. 165, 64 A.2d 866 (1949).

of privacy has formed the basis for a patient's right to decline treatment.[2] In these states, the courts must balance the person's privacy interest against the interests presented by the state as compelling. For the terminally ill, the privacy interest has usually prevailed over any demonstrated state interests. As the Massachusetts Supreme Judicial Court has explained in discussing this balance of individual versus state interest:

> There is a substantial distinction in the State's insistence that human life be saved where the affliction is curable, as opposed to the State interest where, as here, the issue is not whether but when, for how long, and at what cost to the individual life may be extended. . . . We believe it is not inconsistent to recognize a right to decline medical treatment in a situation of incurable illness.[3]

A competent, terminally ill person has the right to refuse all sorts of treatment, including such measures as CPR and artificial nutrition and hydration. The terminally ill person's decision to go without food or water may be problematic for some health professionals, who might seek to impose their wishes on the terminally ill.

Health facilities must address these potential points of confrontation. The rights of the terminally ill should be paramount — not the paternalistic attitudes or values of well-meaning staff. For those professionals who have difficulty with letting terminally ill persons die without aggressive interventions, it may be useful to provide practical in-service education programs or applied bioethics workshops.

Another possibility is to develop a practical policy and procedure on supportive care in which the limits of invasive measures for terminally ill persons are delineated. Obtaining consent to supportive care is paramount. Persons involved in such programs should be required to detail those measures they want taken during the terminal phase of their illness.

[2]Superintendent of Belchertown State School v. Saikewicz, 373 Mass. 728, 370 N.E.2d 417 (1977); Matter of Quinlan, 70 N.J. 10, 355 A.2d 647 (1976).
[3]Superintendent of Belchertown State School v. Saikewicz, 373 Mass. at 732, 370 N.E.2d at 425-426.

By establishing such a policy, much of the misunderstanding and tension surrounding the rights of the terminally ill and the responsibilities of well-intentioned caregivers can be eliminated. The major difficulty in recognizing a right to decline treatment in the case of the terminally ill is deciding who may make that decision for incompetent patients.

§7.4.2 Incompetent Persons

a. Overview of the law. The law is quite clear that incompetent, terminally ill individuals enjoy the same right accorded similarly situated competent persons in their ability to refuse terminal care. The major difference between the two groups is determining who can decline treatment on behalf of incompetent persons.

The answer is found in state legislation permitting execution of durable powers of attorney[4] and judicial opinions on the right of incompetent persons to decline terminal treatment.[5] Although the courts agree that incompetent individuals enjoy the right to refuse terminal treatment, they do not always agree on the means to the end.

Some decisions suggest the need for fairly extensive judicial involvement in the decision-making process for terminally ill, incompetent persons.[6] Other decisions suggest that judicial ap-

---

[4] Ark. Stat. Ann. §20-170-201 (1987); Me. Rev. Stat. Ann. tit. 18A, §§804-1 to 804-2 (1986).

[5] See, e.g., Foody v. Manchester Memorial Hosp., 40 Conn. Supp. 127, 482 A.2d 713 (1984); Severns v. Wilmington Med. Center, 425 A.2d 1565 (Del. 1980); John F. Kennedy Memorial Hosp. v. Bludworth, 452 So. 2d 921 (Fla. 1984); Matter of Spring, 380 Mass. 629, 405 N.E.2d 115 (1980); Superintendent of Belchertown State School v. Saikewicz, 373 Mass. 728, 370 N.E.2d 417 (1977); Conservatorship of Tores, 357 N.W.2d 332 (Minn. 1984); Matter of Quinlan, 70 N.J. 10, 355 A.2d 647 (1967); Matter of Storar, 52 N.Y.2d 363, 438 N.Y.S.2d 266, 420 N.E.2d 64 (1981); Leach v. Akron Gen. Med. Center, 68 Ohio Misc. 122, Ohio Op. 3d 49, 426 N.E.2d 809 (C.P. 1980); Guardianship of Hamlin, 689 P.2d 1372 (Wash. 1984).

[6] See, e.g., Severns v. Wilmington Med. Center, supra n.5; Superintendent of Belchertown State School v. Saikewicz, supra n.5.

proval is not always necessary.[7] However, certain conditions must be met before a decision can be made to withdraw treatment in the absence of judicial approval. These include:

1. a finding that the patient has no reasonable likelihood of ever recovering from a vegetative existence;
2. a determination that life-support measures are maintaining the person's life; and
3. a general agreement among the patient's immediate family, caregivers, and hospital ethics committees that it would be in the best interests of the patient to withdraw life-sustaining care.[8]

In those states in which judicial involvement has never been a requirement, in most if not all cases heavy reliance has been placed on hospital ethics committees.[9] In these situations, ethics committees have been asked to provide consultative opinions; they have not been asked to supplant the role of the appropriate decision maker.

Most of the courts now agree that consideration should be given to the declared wishes of the patient prior to becoming incompetent.[10] These courts hold that such statements provide guidance on what the patient would want done if capable of formulating a treatment choice.

The legal foundation for surrogate choice making is found in the fact that incompetent persons enjoy a right of privacy.[11] It is also found in the fact that incompetent persons possess the same protections derived from the common law principles of

[7]See John F. Kennedy Memorial Hosp. v. Bludworth, supra n.5; Matter of Spring, supra n.5; Conservatorship of Tores, supra n.5; Guardianship of Hamlin, supra n.5.

[8]See Guardianship of Hamlin, supra n.5.

[9]See Matter of Quinlan, supra n.5.

[10]See John F. Kennedy Memorial Hosp., supra n.5. See also In the Matter of Conroy, 98 N.J. 321, 486 A.2d 1209 (1985), which did away with the New Jersey Supreme Court's position in *Quinlan* banning consideration of previous statements of the incompetent person.

[11]Severns v. Wilmington Med. Center, supra n.5; Superintendent of Belchertown State School v. Saikewicz, supra n.5.

bodily integrity and self-determination as competent persons.[12] When the surrogate's decisions are made in a proper fashion, taking into account the right of privacy and the common law principle of individual choice making, there is little concern about civil or criminal liability in withdrawing or withholding terminal treatment from an incompetent individual. Thus, treatment involving CPR as well as artificial hydration and nutrition and antibiotic therapy can be withheld. Treatments can be withheld or discontinued if they interfere with the natural progression of the terminal disease and if the incompetent person through the surrogate decision maker views them as being contrary to his choice.

b. Dealing with family members. By far the most contentious issue surrounding surrogate decision-making involves the role of the family. At least one court has suggested that family members acting in good faith could fulfill the role of substituted decision makers.[13] However, as other judges have observed, how can the court be certain that a family's unanimous decision to discontinue life support is not generated by improper motives and that the determination reflects the wishes of the patient?[14] The judge's concern is well taken, particularly since caregivers may not be in a position to distinguish between proper motives and improper intent. Absent some type of formal safeguards, family members may act to "pull the plug" on a relative in order to hasten death. For such individuals, the motivation may not be money or securing possessions left to them in a will; it may be to ease their emotional pain in seeing a loved one linger in a terrible state. Whatever the family's motive, the rights and wishes of the patient must be respected and given full effect.

Another issue involves an all-too-familiar set of circumstances that confronts caregivers. A terminally ill, incompetent patient lies unconscious in a hospital bed. The three adult chil-

[12]See, e.g., Foody v. Manchester Memorial Hosp., supra n.5.
[13]Id.
[14]See Guardianship of Hamlin, supra n.5, at 1381 (dissenting opinion).

dren and spouse of the patient differ sharply over the choice that must be made: should life support be discontinued?

The wife and one child suggest to caregivers that the patient made some passing remarks about "dying with dignity" but never squarely addressed his own situation. The other children suggest that their father was a tough fighter all his life and that he would find it repugnant to discontinue life support.

The atmosphere becomes supercharged when one side or the other threatens to "see a lawyer" or "make trouble." In the middle of this dispute is the incompetent patient and attending caregivers. The question is what should be done.

By far the most sensible tactic is to avoid letting situations degenerate to such a level. This scenario is quite common and can be anticipated in a well-written policy and procedure manual on consent to treatment. For example:

1. Patients enrolled in hospice, palliative care, or support care programs should on admission be asked to complete a medical directive (living will) or to execute a durable power of attorney. The choice of a living will or durable power of attorney for health care will in part turn upon the legality of these anticipatory consent models in a given state.

2. Patients and their families should be involved in palliative care counselling and support programs that emphasize dialogue on treatment choices during terminal illness care.

3. Patients should be encouraged to discuss their wishes with family members, clergy or pastoral care workers, and attending physicians.

4. The wishes of all patients regarding treatment choices should either be documented on the treatment record as a detailed note or on a form of some sort that evidences that the individual made these choices when legally and mentally capable of doing so.

5. Provision should be made for surrogate choice making for adolescents and other children who are capable of appreciating the nature and consequences of treatment decisions.

6. The policy should be reviewed and updated periodically, taking into consideration the recommendations of legal counsel.
7. Consideration should be given to the recognition of living wills and other directives executed by patients in other jurisdictions since many states do not give legislative recognition to "foreign" medical directives.
8. The role of palliative care support workers, social workers, and patient representatives should be delineated in the policy and procedure.
9. The procedure should outline the role of health facility ethics committees.
10. The procedure should indicate the steps to take when there is need for judicial intervention or when litigation is anticipated.

In the above case, there is need for immediate crisis management to contain the threat of litigation and to avoid adverse publicity in the community served by the facility. A defensive posture is unwarranted. Rather, a conciliatory approach should be employed that diffuses pent-up hostility, anger, and anxiety. The goal should be to effect good communication and choice making. The facilitator for such discussions may be the attending physician, a patient representative, social worker, palliative care worker, or clergyman. Much depends upon the family's needs and who can best address the situation. In addition, legal counsel should be alerted to the problem and remain in the background providing pertinent advice to the health facility and health professionals. Discussions should be documented along with treatment choices that are made by those who stand in a position to give or refuse consent.

Judicial intervention may be unavoidable. Indeed, it may help to clear the air, particularly if the situation reaches an impasse and the decision is made to seek a declaration of incompetency and appointment of a guardian with the power to make treatment choices.

This scenario demonstrates the importance of being prepared for family disputes. It also suggests that there is no one pat formula for resolving such matters. Indeed, as the case law and legislation evolve on treatment of the terminally ill and, as seen later in this chapter, on management of patients in a persistent vegetative state (PVS), it is becoming clear that consent solutions are very state-specific. Caregivers must act accordingly.

§7.5   Right to Withdraw Life-Sustaining Treatment

As described earlier, courts have given effect to both competent and incompetent patients' right to refuse life-prolonging treatment. For some courts the question of withdrawing life-sustaining therapy presents a difficult issue. It is easier when the patient or resident is the one who is seeking the withdrawal of care: then there is no need to engage in the task of substituted judgment analysis. However, that type of analysis must be considered when the request for removing life support or withholding or withdrawing hydration or nutrition is made on behalf of an incompetent individual. The decisions discussed in the following two sections reflect the judicial approach to requests for the withdrawal of life-sustaining therapy.

§7.5.1   Competent Persons

a. Respiratory and cardiopulmonary function issues. A 73-year-old Florida man was hospitalized with amyotrophic lateral sclerosis, an incurable disease, commonly called Lou Gehrig's disease.[1] The disease had spread to the point that the patient was unable to breathe without the aid of a respirator. Even with the respirator his prognosis was death within a short period of time.

Despite his dependency upon the respirator, Mr. Perlmutter

---

§7.5   [1]Satz v. Perlmutter, 362 So. 2d 160 (Fla. Dist. Ct. App. 1978), affd., 374 So. 2d 359 (Fla. 1980).

remained in control of his mental faculties and was legally competent. On a number of occasions he requested that the respiratory be removed. When no one would fulfill his request, he removed it himself. After a few similar episodes, restraints were placed on his arms that, while allowing mobility, prevented Mr. Perlmutter from disconnecting the respirator.[2] Thereafter court proceedings were initiated.

The trial court issued an order authorizing the removal of the artificial measures sustaining Mr. Perlmutter's life. This order was appealed by the state of Florida. The Florida District Court of Appeal affirmed. In reaching its decision, the Florida appellate court followed the analysis outlined in the *Saikewicz* decision by the Massachusetts Supreme Judicial Court. It weighed Perlmutter's right to withdraw life-sustaining therapy against the state's interests in preserving life, preventing suicide, protecting innocent third parties, and maintaining the ethical integrity of the medical profession. In each instance the patient's right to discontinue further treatment was found superior to the interests of the state.[3]

The court held that the right to privacy as an expression of free choice and self-determination forms the basis for a person's right to withdraw from life-sustaining care. Since he understood completely the consequences of removing the respirator, and his family (none of whom were dependent minors) concurred fully in his decision, the court gave its approval to Mr. Perlmutter's request to discontinue further treatment. The court's holding was limited, however, to cases involving competent patients.[4]

The case then was reviewed by the Florida Supreme Court. In a very brief decision the court affirmed and adopted as its own the appellate court's opinion.[5] The Florida Supreme Court made it quite clear that the effect of the decision did not go beyond the facts of the present case. In other words, Perlmut-

---

[2]Perlmutter v. Florida Med. Center, No. 78-9747 (Fla. Cir. Ct., 17th Cir., July 11, 1978); Fort Lauderdale News, October 6, 1978 at 9a.
[3]Satz v. Perlmutter, 362 So. 2d 160, 162-164 (Fla. 1980).
[4]Id. at 162.
[5]Satz v. Perlmutter, 379 So. 2d 359 (Fla. 1980).

ter as a competent adult could withdraw from life-sustaining care since there were no minor dependents and all affected family members consented.[6] The court noted that the issues presented in this case were best addressed by the legislature so that all interests could be considered and accommodated. However, in the absence of legislation, it held, the courts must act to enforce constitutionally guaranteed rights. Until legislative action is taken in Florida, this means the courts will proceed on a case-by-case basis in these matters.[7]

In a case quite similar to *Perlmutter,* the California Court of Appeals ruled that a competent person has the right to refuse further life-prolonging treatment even though this will hasten death.[8] In that case, a 70-year-old man with emphysema, chronic respiratory failure, arteriosclerosis, an abdominal aneurysm, and a malignant lung tumor entered the hospital for treatment of depression. During a routine physical examination and chest X-ray, a lung tumor was discovered. A lung biopsy was performed that resulted in the lung's collapsing. When the lung would not reinflate, the patient was placed on a ventilator. Efforts to wean him from the machine proved unsuccessful. On several occasions the patient attempted to remove the ventilator tubes and, as in the *Perlmutter* case, hand restraints were placed on the patient.

Litigation followed seeking damages for battery, violation of state and federal constitutional rights, breach of fiduciary trust, intentional infliction of emotional distress, and conspiracy. In addition, the patient and his wife sought an injunction restraining the physicians and hospital from administering unauthorized medical care, including the use of the ventilator.[9]

The trial court denied the injunction, ruling that the right to remove life-support equipment was restricted to terminally ill, comatose patients, or those acting on their behalf. Prior to the California Court of Appeals hearing an appeal of the lower

[6] Id. at 360.
[7] Id. at 360-361.
[8] Bartling v. Superior Court, 163 Cal. App. 3d 186, 209 Cal. Rptr. 220 (1984).
[9] Id.

court ruling, the patient died. Despite the fact the case was moot, the court agreed to resolve the questions raised to prevent a recurrence.[10]

As the court noted, there was no question that the patient was legally capable of giving consent. The fact that due to severe depression the patient sometimes vacillated in his decision to disconnect the ventilator did not justify the conclusion that he was incapable of reaching a decision. The fact that the patient had executed a living will under the terms of the California Natural Death Act and a durable power of attorney for health care under other state legislation demonstrated that the patient understood the significance of his decision.[11] In addition, the patient and his wife executed documents releasing the hospital and doctors from civil liability if they decided to honor the patient's wishes.[12]

Having found that the patient was legally capable, the court next addressed the principal issue in the case: whether the interests of the patient outweighed demonstrable state interests in continuing the ventilator. The court concluded that given the patient's condition his interests in privacy guaranteed by the state and federal constitutions outweighed those of the state in the preservation of life. Moreover, the court pointed out that the fear of civil and criminal liability for carrying out the patient's wishes were unfounded. The case of Barber v. Superior Court, in which two physicians were found innocent of murder and conspiracy to commit murder in removing life-support equipment from a comatose patient at the written insistence of the family, answered the question of potential for criminal responsibility.[13] Moreover, there need be no concern about civil responsibility.[14]

The court went further, pointing out that in similar cases in the future there was no need to seek prior judicial approval

[10] Id.

[11] Cal. Civil Code §§2430-2443 (West 1983).

[12] Supra n.8.

[13] Barber v. Superior Court, 147 Cal. App. 3d 1006, 195 Cal. Rptr. 484 (1983).

[14] Supra n.8, 163 Cal. App. 3d at 198, 209 Cal. Rptr. at 227.

before carrying out the patient's wishes to withdraw treatment. The court based this conclusion on the absence of legislative guidance on the matter.[15]

A New Jersey court has also had occasion to review a request for withdrawal of life-sustaining care in the case of a woman afflicted with Lou Gehrig's disease.[16] In that case, the disease was quite advanced and had immobilized the patient to the point that she could only move her head. She required mechanical assistance to help her breathe. Deemed competent by the court to make an informed choice to withdraw from life-sustaining treatment, the court used the *Conroy* "guidelines" to conclude that the patient's right to terminate treatment outweighed identified state interests.[17]

The right to refuse life-sustaining care has also been recognized for competent adult patients of federal medical facilities.[18] The case in which this point arose involved a woman who was a patient at Walter Reed Army Medical Hospital. The patient had terminal adenocarcinoma of the pericardium. She also suffered from Adult Respiratory Distress Syndrome and lung tumors. It was this latter illness that led to the patient being placed on a respirator two days after her admission to the hospital. A petition was filed to have the respirator removed. This was done when it was made clear that army policy prohibited the withdrawal of a life-support system once it was in operation in army health facilities.

In granting an order for the removal of the life-support equipment, the court was aware that this would likely result in the patient's immediate death. However, as the court indicated:

> But while preservation of life in the abstract is no doubt a transcendent goal for any society which values human life, the state's interest in maintaining life must defer to the right to refuse treatment of a competent, emotionally stable, but termi-

---

[15]Id.

[16]See In re Farrell, 212 N.J. Super. 294, 514 A.2d 1342 (1986).

[17]Id.

[18]Tune v. Walter Reed Army Medical Hosp., 602 F. Supp. 1452 (D.D.C. 1985).

nally ill adult whose death is imminent and who is, therefore, the best, indeed, the only, true judge of how such life as remains to him may best be spent.[19]

In an effort to set guidelines and "clear the air" regarding the right of a competent patient to have life-sustaining medical equipment withdrawn, the Supreme Court of New Jersey rendered a decision involving a patient with Lou Gehrig's disease in Matter of Farrell.[20] Although the case involved a woman who was dying at home, the court made it clear that its requirements for determining competency extended to hospitals and nursing homes.[21]

The New Jersey court also made it clear that, absent "unusual circumstances," it was not necessary to seek judicial intervention in these cases. As long as the patient is determined to be competent, and is properly informed, the individual can decide to discontinue life-sustaining care. Such a choice must be made voluntarily and free of coercion.

To make certain that the patient is competent, the court indicated that two nonattending doctors must confirm that the patient is capable of reasoning and making judgments based on proper disclosure of pertinent information. This information includes details of the patient's prognosis, available medical alternatives, risk information, and the consequences of discontinuing medical care.[22]

The *Farrell* decision does not create a carte blanche for all competent patients to discontinue treatment. Rather, it is restricted to those terminally ill persons who are receiving life-sustaining care. Moreover, once the patient has made such a choice, the decision must be balanced against the state's interests in preserving life, preventing suicide, safeguarding the integrity of the medical profession, and protecting innocent third parties. Generally, however, these state interests would be out-

---

[19]Id. at 1455-1456.
[20]529 A.2d 404 (N.J. 1987).
[21]Id. at 415 n.8.
[22]Id. at 415.

weighed by the patient's interest in bodily integrity and freedom from unwanted intrusion.

The real question is whether the *Farrell* decision "clears the air" at all. This will be seen in future cases. The balancing required in weighing the interests of the patient against those of the state may make this impossible. Up until now in the death and dying case law, this balancing test has been carried out by the courts. *Farrell* suggests that this is no longer required. Who, then, will fill this void? The practical outcomes of the decision may answer this question.

   b.   Artificial nutrition and hydration issues.   Difficult situations can arise when competent patients afflicted with severe disabilities seek court orders that would effectively allow them to decline medical care and nourishment. One such case arose in New York.[23] A 54-year-old woman became a total quadriplegic following a fall. The woman required a ventilator to breathe and was totally dependent upon others for the most basic functions.

The woman asked the court to declare her competent to decide her own medical needs. Moreover, the patient wanted the court to order the defendants to comply with her written and stated wishes not to provide additional medical care other than pain medication. The woman also wanted the court to direct the defendants to comply with her requests should she become unable to communicate her desires.

The court declined to grant the relief requested, stating that the situation was not an actual and real dispute. The patient's request was seen as a petition for a declaratory judgment. The relief could not be granted since to do so in the absence of a genuine controversy would amount to an advisory opinion. However sympathetic the court was with the woman's condition, it noted nothing could be done until a real controversy existed. The court also pointed out that the best answer was a legislative solution to deal with this type of situation.[24]

[23] A.B. v. C., 124 Misc. 2d 672, 477 N.Y.S.2d 281 (Sup. Ct. 1984).
[24] Id.

§7.5.2 Incompetent Persons

Patients or residents in a persistent vegetative state (PVS) have become the focal point of considerable litigation. Removal of life-support equipment that sustains cardiopulmonary function has been the basis for some of the judicial action. However, the great preponderance of the case law deals with withholding or removing artificial hydration and nutrition from patients in a persistent vegetative state.

As seen in this section, the field is far from settled on what should be done with those people kept alive by medical technology. The outer limits of technology's ability to keep people alive have been pushed quite far thanks to such measures as nasogastric tubes, gastrostomies, and aggressive antibiotic therapy. The emotional and financial costs of such measures can be profound. Questions have arisen regarding the legal and ethical propriety of either using or withdrawing such treatment modalities. Even where it is agreed that "something" should be done to discontinue treatment, it must still be decided *who* should make the choice. While durable powers of attorney in health care and medical directives (living wills) can facilitate proper decision-making, there are and will always be questions regarding what should be done for those individuals who did not convey orally or in writing what they wanted done should they fall into a persistent vegetative state.

PVS requires practical solutions. Family concerns and disputes must be managed and the rights of the person in a persistent vegetative state must be addressed. Finding solutions, however, can be a difficult task.

   a. Respiratory and cardiopulmonary function issues. An elderly Massachusetts man developed end-stage renal disease and began receiving dialysis treatments three times a week at a private kidney center.[25] Thereafter, signs of mental disorientation began to occur and he became unable to care for himself. Physicians diagnosed his condition as chronic organic brain

[25] Matter of Spring, 9 Mass. App. Ct. 836, 399 N.E.2d 493 (1974).

syndrome, which eventually progressed to the point that he no longer recognized his wife or son. He was finally admitted to a nursing home when his wife became ill and could not care for his physical needs.[26]

During his stay at the nursing home, his mental condition deteriorated further. On occasion he became disruptive or wandered at night. While receiving dialysis he sometimes kicked nurses and pulled dialysis tubing from his arm. To control his behavior heavy sedation was administered. He was found not to know who or where he was and he did not understand the reason for his dialysis treatment.[27]

The patient's son petitioned and received appointment as conservator of his father's property. Subsequently, he was appointed temporary guardian. Along with the patient's wife, the son sought a court order prohibiting the administration to his father of life-prolonging medical care. After a hearing, the probate court issued such an order. The patient's guardian ad litem (who had been appointed for the hearing) appealed the probate court's decision. The Massachusetts Appeals Court affirmed and a further appeal was taken to the Supreme Judicial Court.

The Massachusetts high court reversed and remanded the appellate court's decision because that body had delegated control over the dialysis issue to the attending doctor, the temporary guardian, and the patient's wife.[28] This delegation was found to be erroneous in light of the *Saikewicz* decision, supra.

Mr. Spring had acquiesced to dialysis treatment. Prior to becoming incompetent he had not expressed preference for or against continuing such treatment. The proceedings before the probate court had been initiated properly. That court had applied correctly what the patient, if competent, would see as his interests and desires, as well as his present and future state of incompetency. The court had considered correctly the intrusiveness of the dialysis treatments, the life-prolonging na-

[26] Id.

[27] Matter of Spring, 380 Mass. 629, 405 N.E.2d 115 (1980), reversing 9 Mass. App. Ct. 836, 399 N.E.2d 493 (1979).

[28] Id. at 632, 405 N.E.2d at 117.

ture of the care, and the impossibility of cure of either the kidney disease or the organic brain syndrome. Evidence from the patient's wife and son, who enjoyed a close family relationship with the ward, had also been considered. They were concerned about what was in the patient's best interests and were in a good position to know his desires in the situation.[29] Pitted against the evidence supporting withdrawal of the dialysis care were the same state interests outlined in the *Saikewicz* case. As in that case, the state interests were found not to be so compelling as to require continuation of treatment.[30]

The shift of decision-making away from the court was held to be incorrect because the case had been presented correctly to the judiciary for resolution. Once it came before the court, the decision whether to withdraw treatment became a legal question. The methods for carrying out the decision to withhold care, especially those dealing with medical issues, were left as private medical decisions.[31]

The *Spring* case represents a clarification by the Massachusetts court of those instances in which prior judicial approval should be sought in cases involving terminally ill, incompetent patients. This "clarification," however, is only a list of factors that, if taken together in certain combinations, point in the direction of judicial review. The court declined to spell out what combinations necessitated or made it desirable to seek court approval. This it left to a case-by-case analysis.[32] Doubtful or disputed issues of law or fact could tip the scales in favor of court review.[33]

At bottom, the *Spring* case confirms once again that incompetent, terminally ill patients have the right to decline life-prolonging care. It points out, too, that such decisions may be effectuated by others under the substituted judgment test. The decision also goes one step further: it sets a precedent that

---

[29] Id. at 639, 405 N.E.2d at 122.
[30] Id. at 639, 405 N.E.2d at 123.
[31] Id. at 639, 405 N.E.2d at 122.
[32] Id. at 638, 405 N.E.2d at 121.
[33] Id. at 640, 405 N.E.2d at 122.

incompetent patients have the right, as do competent patients, to consent to the withdrawal of life-prolonging treatment.

b. Artificial nutrition and hydration issues. Years ago it would have been considered medically immoral to even suggest withholding or withdrawing nutritional support from a patient. In contemporary society, however, the issue has come to light as a treatment decision for the terminally ill.[34] The matter has also arisen with respect to incompetent patients for whom nutritional support constitutes life-sustaining care.[35] As the following cases suggest, there are several legal considerations involved in withdrawing nutritional care. State legislation, the doctrine of informed consent, and who should decide for incompetent persons whether to remove such treatment all constitute important concerns. One of the most interesting cases, In the Matter of Claire Conroy,[36] also reexamines portions of the *Quinlan* decision[37] resulting in what may be seen as a clarification of that case.

Ms. Conroy was an 84-year-old woman who suffered from organic brain syndrome. She was adjudicated an incompetent and her nephew was appointed her guardian. In 1979, Ms. Conroy was placed in a New Jersey nursing home. Although confused, she was able to converse and ambulate and was in relatively good physical health. However, her condition changed and she became more confused and physically dependent.

From 1979 until 1982, Ms. Conroy was hospitalized twice for medical problems. During her second hospitalization, a nasogastric tube was inserted to facilitate administration of medication and to feed the patient. The tubing remained in place

---

[34] Matter of Requena, 213 N.J. Super. 443, 517 A.2d 869 (Super. Ct. App. Div. 1986), affg. In re Requena, 213 N.J. Super. 475, 517 A.2d 886 (Super. Ct. Ch. Div. 1986); Corbett v. D'Alessandro, 487 So. 2d 368 (Fla. Dist. Ct. App. 1986); In the Matter of Claire C. Conroy, 98 N.J. 321, 486 A.2d 1209 (1985).

[35] See Brophy v. New England Sinai Hosp., 398 Mass. 417, 497 N.E.2d 626 (1986); Matter of Hier, 18 Mass. App. Ct. 200, 464 N.E.2d 959 (1984).

[36] Supra n.34.

[37] Matter of Quinlan, 70 N.J. 10, 355 A.2d 647 (1976).

when the patient was returned to the nursing home. Attempts to feed Ms. Conroy by hand failed since her ability to swallow was quite limited.[38]

The guardian requested permission to remove the nasogastric tube. This request was opposed by Ms. Conroy's guardian ad litem. At the time of the trial, Ms. Conroy suffered from a number of serious and irreversible ailments including arteriosclerotic heart disease, hypertension, diabetes, and gangrene of her left leg to the knee. She was unable to speak, had difficulty in swallowing, and she had no control of her excretory functions. Ms. Conroy was bedridden and unable to move from a semi-fetal position. Although awake, Ms. Conroy was described as having a very limited intellectual capacity. Moreover, it was unlikely that her mental condition would improve.[39]

The trial court granted permission for the removal of the tube. While an appeal was pending Ms. Conroy passed away. The appellate division decided to press ahead with a resolution of the case because the issues involved were of such public importance,[40] and reversed the trial court.

The Supreme Court of New Jersey, however, reversed the decision of the appellate division. In doing so, it delineated three different tests for surrogate decision-making on the issue of life-sustaining care. The court made it clear, however, that its holding was limited to nursing home patients like Ms. Conroy who would be likely to die within one year, even with treatment and who, though formerly competent, are now incapable of making decisions regarding life-sustaining care.[41]

The court began its analysis by reviewing the right to refuse or to accept treatment. The right to control of bodily integrity through informed consent to treatment and informed refusal of care was recognized by the court. Unlike the court's earlier decision in *Quinlan,* it did not involve itself in the application of the constitutional right of privacy. As the court pointed out, the

---

[38] Matter of Conroy, supra n.34, at 1217.
[39] Id.
[40] Id. at 1219.
[41] Id.

right to refuse care was a matter within the common law right of self-determination.[42]

The Supreme Court of New Jersey also evaluated the four principal state interests commonly cited in other death and dying cases. The court did so in the context of pointing out that the right to refuse life-sustaining treatment is not absolute. The four state interests addressed were the following:

1. Preserving life;
2. Preventing suicide;
3. Maintaining the integrity of the medical profession; and
4. Protecting innocent third parties.[43]

The facts in the *Conroy* situation and relevant case law made it clear that if the patient had been competent she would have requested that the nasogastric tube be removed. Moreover, this determination outweighed the state's interests in preserving life or safeguarding the integrity of the medical profession. This was not a situation in which the patient would be committing suicide, but rather would be exercising a determination to be free of medical intervention. If death were to occur, it would be the result of the patient's underlying condition. Removal of the tube would not pose a hazard to the public nor would the patient's death leave dependent minors without care and support.[44]

Having determined that Ms. Conroy's right to bodily integrity outweighed the state's perceived interests, the court then contrasted the present situation with that of Karen Ann Quinlan. In the *Quinlan* case the court dealt with a patient in a chronic, comatose, vegetative existence. The *Quinlan* decision left unanswered what principles would apply to those in a terminal state who had not necessarily lost their cognitive or sapient abilities.[45] The *Conroy* case involved just that issue.

The court ruled that life-sustaining care may be withheld or

[42] Id. at 1221.
[43] Id. at 1223.
[44] Id. at 1226.
[45] Id. at 1228.

withdrawn when it is clear that the patient, in the circumstances, would have declined care. The court developed three different means by which this determination could be made.

The first standard, the "subjective" test, gives effect to what the particular patient would have done if capable of making the determination. Under this test, evidence regarding the patient's intent may be discerned from various sources, including the following:

1. A written document or living will in which the patient directs that certain care not be given in particular circumstances;
2. An oral directive by the patient to family, friends, or health personnel;
3. A durable power of attorney or appointment of a proxy enabling another person to make decisions on behalf of the patient when he or she is incapable of doing so;
4. Statements voiced by the patient in reaction to care given to others;
5. Religious beliefs of the patient and the tenets of his or her faith; and
6. The pattern of the patient's conduct regarding earlier determinations about his or her health care.[46]

The court specifically stated that it had erred in the *Quinlan* case in disregarding statements made by the patient to her friends regarding artificial prolongation of life in the terminally ill.[47] The court cautioned, however, that the probative weight of these various sources of evidence depends upon the following factors:

1. Remoteness, consistency, and thoughtfulness of the patient's earlier statements or actions; and
2. The maturity of the patient at the time of the statements or acts.[48]

[46] Id. at 1229-1230.
[47] Id. at 1230.
[48] Id.

Under the "subjective" test, the surrogate decision maker must have adequate medical evidence regarding the care and prognosis of the patient. Moreover, the medical evidence should demonstrate that the patient is within the *Conroy* "pattern" of an incompetent, elderly nursing home resident who is experiencing both severe and permanent mental and physical disabilities and whose life expectancy is one year or less.[49]

In order for the surrogate to make an informed decision, it is important that the decision maker have as much information as would be necessary for a competent patient to make a decision, before consenting to or rejecting care. To this end, the court specified such information as:

1. the present level of physical, sensory, emotional, and cognitive function;
2. the level of pain associated with the patient's condition, with treatment, and with the discontinuation of care;
3. the extent of humiliation, dependence, and loss of dignity that is associated with the patient's condition and care; and
4. the patient's life expectancy and prognosis for recovery both with and without care.[50]

In addition, the court pointed out that the determination should take into account "the various treatment options; and the risks, side effects, and benefits of each of those options."[51]

Where the facts of a case do not lend themselves to the application of the subjective test, the court suggested two options: a "limited objective" test and a "pure-objective" standard.[52]

Under the "limited objective" test, care may be ended for an individual who has not clearly indicated her wishes before becoming incompetent. The test may be applied when in a *Conroy*-type situation treatment only prolongs the patient's suffering.[53] The decision maker must be "satisfied that it is clear that the

[49] Id. at 1231.
[50] Id.
[51] Id.
[52] Id. at 1232.
[53] Id.

burdens of the patient's continued life with the treatment outweigh the benefits of that life for him."[54]

The decision must be based on medical evidence. This would include the same type of evidence as used under the subjective standard as well as proof that treatment would only serve to prolong the patient's suffering and not supply the individual with any "net benefit."[55] The degree of pain, its duration, and constancy with or without treatment are also relevant factors. Similarly, the use of drugs to reduce pain is a consideration under the limited objective test.

In addition to medical evidence, the limited objective test requires "trustworthy" evidence that the patient would want care to be ended. The various forms of proof outlined under the subjective test that establish the patient's intent would be sufficient evidence. Similarly, evidence that would be too vague, casual, or remote to satisfy the requirements of the "subjective" test may be adequate under the limited objective standard.[56]

In the absence of trustworthy evidence or any proof at all that the individual would have refused care, life-sustaining treatment may still be terminated or withheld. This is possible in *Conroy*-type cases, under the "pure objective" test, if "the net burdens of the patient's life with the treatment . . . clearly and markedly outweigh the benefits the patient derives from life."[57] Moreover, life-sustaining treatment can be withheld if with the treatment the patient experiences such recurrent, severe, and unavoidable pain that administering life-sustaining care could be considered inhumane. That a patient suffers severe pain, however, does not permit the withdrawal of life-sustaining care if the incompetent patient had previously expressed the desire to be kept alive in such a condition.[58]

The court also pointed out that decision makers should exercise caution in authorizing the withholding or withdrawal of

[54]Id.
[55]Id.
[56]Id.
[57]Id.
[58]Id.

care unless "manifestly satisfied" that the patient has met the requirements of one of the three tests.[59] Furthermore, the court noted that decisions are not to be based on the social utility of the patient, the patient's personal worth or the value of the patient's life to others. The key is to focus on the patient's wishes and the pain and enjoyment experienced by that individual.

In utilizing any of the three tests developed in the case, the court rejected the distinction between ordinary and extraordinary care. Emphasis should be placed on the issue of proof sufficient to satisfy one of the tests. When such evidence is available, determinations can be made to withhold or withdraw artificial feeding techniques. In this regard, artificial feeding is to be treated just like any other form of care.[60]

The court indicated that the surrogate determination should be made by a guardian in accordance with a procedure outlined in the *Conroy* case. This necessarily requires a judicial decision that the patient is incompetent to make the treatment decision at issue. This is true even if the patient had previously been adjudicated an incompetent and a general guardian had been appointed.

The procedure outlined by the court included the following:

1. A person who believes that the withholding or withdrawal of life-sustaining care would give effect to the incompetent patient's desires or be in the patient's best interests, should notify the Office of the Ombudsman for the Institutionalized Elderly.
2. The patient's guardian or any other interested party can notify the ombudsman.
3. Anyone who believes that the contemplated decision would be an abuse of the patient should report this information to the ombudsman.
4. The ombudsman should treat every notification that life-sustaining care is to be withheld or withdrawn as a possible

---

[59] Id. at 1233.
[60] Id. at 1237.

abuse case and proceed with an investigation under applicable state legislation.

5. The attending physicians and nurses should supply evidence regarding the patient's condition.

6. Two doctors who are unaffiliated with either the nursing home or the attending doctor should be appointed and examine the patient to confirm the individual's condition and prognosis.

7. Based on the medical evidence supplied by the two doctors, the guardian, with the concurrence of the attending doctor, may withhold or withdraw life-sustaining care. The guardian may do so when "he believes in good faith, based on the medical evidence and any evidence of the patient's wishes, that it is clear that the subjective, limited-objective, or pure-objective test is satisfied."[61] The ombudsman must concur in this decision. Moreover, when the limited objective or pure objective test is used, the patient's family must concur in the determination.[62]

The procedure outlined by the court mentions a very specific role for the guardian of the patient. The court made it clear that a judicial determination must be made that the patient is incompetent to make the medical treatment decision. This is true whether or not the patient has a general guardian. If the patient already has a guardian the court should determine if he is a suitable person to represent the patient on this issue. For patients adjudicated incompetent, a guardian should be appointed.[63]

If the procedure outlined by the court is followed, and there is no evidence of bad faith, no one involved in the decision-making should be held civilly or criminally responsible.[64]

In applying these criteria, the Supreme Court of New Jersey found that the record in the *Conroy* case did not meet these

[61] Id. at 1242.
[62] Id.
[63] Id. at 1241.
[64] Id. at 1242.

standards.[65] Moreover, the court warned against using the process it established in resolving cases involving severely deformed newborns or the mentally alert quadriplegic who has given up on life. The court indicated it was far better to proceed slowly in this sensitive area and to permit the state legislature to devise a comprehensive plan for handling these issues.[66]

Are the tests developed in *Conroy* a practical answer to the difficult issues faced in this situation? Will *Conroy* be generalized to encompass other terminally ill patients or the defective newborn?

It is difficult at this stage to determine whether the *Conroy* case will become the benchmark for other courts. On the surface, the three different tests appear difficult to apply, and in the case of the limited objective and pure objective tests there may be some overlap. The environment in New Jersey is also unique in that the state has created the office of the ombudsman.

Conroy left many issues unanswered, and in 1987, in what has been described as a trilogy of cases, the New Jersey Supreme Court handed down decisions that clarified some of the points raised in their earlier case.[67] Matter of Jobes involved a non-elderly resident of a nursing home who was in a persistent vegetative state. The Supreme Court of New Jersey ruled that should the surrogate decision maker decline life-sustaining care, she must obtain the opinions of two independent physicians confirming that the patient is in a persistent vegetative state and that there is no hope of recovery. Moreover, the two doctors must be "knowledgeable" in neurology.[68]

The *Peter* case also served to fill in the gaps left after *Conroy*. In *Peter*, the New Jersey court dealt with an elderly nursing

[65] Id.
[66] Id. at 1244.
[67] See Matter of Jobes, 529 A.2d 434 (N.J. 1987); Matter of Peter by Johanning, 529 A.2d 419 (N.J. 1987). The third case in the trilogy, Matter of Farrell, 529 A.2d 404 (N.J. 1987), involved the right of a competent, terminally ill patient to discontinue artificial life support at home. It is discussed in §7.5.1.
[68] Matter of Jobes, supra n.67, at 448.

home resident who was in a persistent vegetative state with no hope of recovery. However, unlike Claire Conroy, Hilda Peter was not expected to die in the near future. For patients in this category, the court ruled that the "*Conroy* subjective test" should be employed. In effect this means that life-sustaining treatment can be withdrawn or withheld upon clear and convincing proof that the patient, if competent, would decline treatment. The court made it clear that this test applied to all "surrogate refusal of care cases" without regard to the patient's medical condition or life expectancy.[69] It remains to be seen whether these changes to New Jersey precedent really "clear the air" and resolve the lingering doubts left after *Conroy*.

The Massachusetts Supreme Judicial Court has also had occasion to review the issue of artificial tube feeding in the case of an incompetent patient.[70] The decision is of interest in that the Massachusetts court looked with some degree of favor upon the New Jersey *Conroy* opinion.[71] Furthermore, it dealt with the difficult issue of a hospital complying with a treatment decision with which it disagreed.

Paul Brophy, Sr., was a fireman and an emergency medical technician. From tragedies he had witnessed in his professional work he had concluded that he wished never to be maintained on life-support systems. Indeed, he had made this fact known to his family.[72] Late in March 1983 Mr. Brophy experienced a ruptured aneurysm at the apex of the basilar artery. He underwent surgery to correct this condition but never regained consciousness. Physicians considered Mr. Brophy to be in a persistent vegetative state. Although not brain dead, he had extensive, irreversible brain damage.

In December 1983 Mr. Brophy underwent surgery for the implantation of a gastrostomy tube. In February 1985 Mrs. Brophy, as legal guardian for her husband, petitioned the state

---

[69]Matter of Peter by Johanning, supra n.67, at 425.
[70]Brophy v. New England Sinai Hosp., 398 Mass. 417, 497 N.E.2d 626 (1986).
[71]Supra n.34.
[72]Brophy v. New England Sinai Hosp., 398 Mass. at 428, 497 N.E.2d at 631-632.

Probate Court for permission to discontinue all life-support measures, including artificial hydration and nutrition. Based on the evidence before it, the Probate Court concluded that Mr. Brophy, if competent, would refuse artificial nutrition and hydration. However, the court ordered continuation of such care and it enjoined both the guardian and the hospital from either removing or clamping the gastrostomy tube.[73]

On appeal, the Massachusetts Supreme Judicial Court set aside that portion of the Probate Court judgment that enjoined the removal or clamping of the tube. Moreover, it directed that a new order be issued in which the hospital was to help the guardian transfer Mr. Brophy to an appropriate facility or to his home. The guardian was also authorized to order such steps as she deemed necessary and appropriate.[74]

In reaching this determination, the court employed the substituted judgment standard. From the evidence adduced in the court below, it was clear that Mr. Brophy, if he were capable of doing so, would have requested that use of the gastrostomy tube be ended. The only inquiry left for the court to decide was whether the interests of the state necessitated overriding the substituted judgment.

In weighing the state's interest in preserving life against the individual's interests in autonomy and preservation of his humanity, the court was careful to avoid making a decision based on "quality of life" considerations. As the court stated:

> It is antithetical to our scheme of ordered liberty and to our respect for the autonomy of the individual for the State to make decisions regarding the individual's quality of life. It is for the patient to decide such issues. Our role is limited to ensuring that a refusal of treatment does not violate legal norms.[75]

The court felt that the trial judge had failed to take into account that Mr. Brophy would consider the gastrostomy tube highly invasive. Indeed, as a matter of law the court concluded

[73] Id. at 422, 497 N.E.2d at 629.
[74] Id. at 442, 497 N.E.2d at 640.
[75] Id. at 434, 497 N.E.2d at 635.

that long-term use of the tube was an invasive treatment. This, however, was but one factor to consider in weighing the interests of the individual against those of the State.[76] The court agreed with the Supreme Court of New Jersey that "the primary focus should be the patient's desires and experience of pain and enjoyment — not the type of treatment involved."[77]

The court also moved away from the distinction of ordinary versus extraordinary care it adopted in the *Saikewicz* decision.[78] As the court noted, although extraordinary versus ordinary care is a factor to be considered, in a case such as this the distinction is one without meaning.

The court concluded that the State interest in preserving life did not outweigh the individual interest in discontinuing artificial, life-sustaining care. Moreover, it was determined that discontinuing care would not be a death-producing step that would implicate the state's interest in preventing suicide. Rather, the patient's demise would occur from natural causes once life-sustaining therapy was withdrawn. Moreover, as long as the court did not compel the health facility to remove or clamp off the tube, there would be no violation of the ethical integrity of the medical profession. In reaching this last conclusion, the court relied upon pronouncements authored by the American Medical Association and the Massachusetts Medical Society regarding care refusal of gastrointestinal tube feedings for vegetative patients.[79]

The court was sympathetic to the interests of the hospital regarding its role in discontinuing artificial hydration and nutrition for incompetent patients. Nothing in state law, state legislation, or the principles of informed consent compelled a hospital to stop such measures at the request of a patient's guardian. The court concluded:

[76] Id. at 435-436, 497 N.E.2d at 636-637.
[77] Id. at 436, 497 N.E.2d at 637, quoting Matter of Conroy, 98 N.J. at 369, 486 A.2d at 1209.
[78] Superintendent of Belchertown State School v. Saikewicz, 373 Mass. 728, 370 N.E.2d 417 (1977).
[79] Brophy v. New England Sinai Hosp., supra n.72, at 439, n.37, 497 N.E.2d at 638, n.37.

It would be particularly inappropriate to force the hospital, which is willing to assist in a transfer of the patient, to take affirmative steps to end the provision of nutrition and hydration to him. A patient's right to refuse medical treatment does not warrant such an unnecessary intrusion upon the hospital's ethical integrity in this case.[80]

The Massachusetts court was by no means in complete agreement. Indeed, some blistering dissents followed the court's ruling. Nonetheless, it has established a precedent that when a patient, prior to becoming incompetent, makes his views known about life-sustaining measures, such care can be withdrawn on the basis of substituted judgment. This right extends beyond the terminally ill to those in a persistent vegetative state.[81]

The matter of discontinuing life-sustaining care while a patient is in a hospital does present administrative and ethical problems for health facilities. Should a health facility be compelled to assist or to permit a patient to carry out wishes that are contrary to hospital policy? What about the impact of such a choice on hospital staff?

The issue has arisen in a New Jersey case,[82] in which a 55-year-old woman with Lou Gehrig's disease wanted nasogastric tube feeding and other artificial life-sustaining measures stopped. In this case the patient was competent. However, she was severely debilitated, the disease having left her paralyzed from the neck down. She was fast approaching the point where she would require artificial feeding.

The hospital did not wish to comply with her request to not accept artificial tube feedings. The facility claimed that if it acquiesced in her decision it would be violating its own policy that stated it would not take part in withdrawing or withholding artificial feedings and fluids.[83]

[80]Id. at 441, 497 N.E.2d at 639.
[81]For an interesting commentary on the *Saikewicz* and *Brophy* cases, see Matuschak, The Right to Decline Medical Treatment After *Brophy*, 32 Boston B.J. No. 4 at 25 (Aug. 1988).
[82]Matter of Requena, 213 N.J. Super. 443, 517 A.2d 869 (Super. Ct. App. Div. 1986), affirming, per curiam, In re Requena, 213 N.J. Super. 475, 517 A.2d 886 (Super. Ct. Ch. Div. 1986).
[83]Id.

The hospital brought an action to compel the patient to leave the institution. In finding for the patient, the court noted that only if the hospital could provide a "convenient" and "suitable"[84] alternate facility would it be reasonable to compel the woman to leave the institution. Here, the alternate facility was 17 miles away. It was comparably equipped to care for the dying woman.

What tipped the scales in favor of the patient was the facility's failure to give adequate notice of its policy. Prior to becoming an inpatient, the woman had not been given notice of the hospital's policy. Furthermore, she had not been apprised of the hospital's stance for 15 months following her admission. Another important feature was that the patient did not want to leave the familiar surroundings and staff who had been caring for her. To move her then would have been a psychological and emotional trauma.

In the end, both the lower and appellate courts concluded that while the withholding or withdrawing of artificial feeding may offend hospital personnel and administration and run contrary to stated policy, these were "subordinate" considerations compared to the harm to the dying woman.[85]

Many courts might reach a different conclusion under similar circumstances. Here, the New Jersey court was concerned with the equities of each side. The court was also very mindful of the plight of the dying woman. Nonetheless, it is an instructive decision as it points out the need to inform patients "up front" about the limits of treatment options available at a health facility. If a health facility has particularly strong religious principles that run contrary to such measures as withholding or withdrawing artificial tube feeding and fluids, this should be made known at the outset to the patient and the family. This is the type of trying issue that should not become the object of litigation and unpleasant publicity.

A substantial body of case law continues to develop on the issue of withholding and removal of artificial hydration and

[84]Id.
[85]Id.

nutrition from persons in a persistent vegetative state.[86] It is clear that not all courts sanction the discontinuance of nasogastric tube feedings and hydration.[87] Similarly, there is a difference of opinion among the courts on the legal standard to be used in assessing proof of what the patient or resident would want done if capable of expressing an opinion on the matter. For example, the New York Court of Appeals requires clear and convincing evidence,[88] while the Massachusetts Supreme Judicial Court employs the "substituted judgment" approach.[89]

At the same time, legislation has begun to appear on the issue of discontinuing artificial nutrition and hydration,[90] and national professional organizations have issued position statements on the matter.[91] More litigation and legislative inroads should be anticipated.

Given the gap between the legal standards of proof and the differing judicial perspectives on discontinuing artificial sustenance, it is imperative that every health care facility obtain

---

[86]See, e.g., Rasmussen by Mitchell v. Fleming, 741 P.2d 674 (Ariz. 1987), affg. in part and revg. in part, 741 P.2d 667 (Ariz. Ct. App. 1986); In re Drabick, 245 Cal. Rptr. 840 (Cal. Ct. App. 1988); In re Estate of Prange, 520 N.E.2d 946 (Ill. App. Ct. 1988); Cruzan by Cruzan v. Harmon, 760 S.W.2d 408 (Mo. 1988) (en banc), cert. granted, 49 S. Ct. Bull. (CCH) B4467 (No. 88-1503 July 3, 1989); In re Terry, 523 A.2d 88 (N.H. 1986); Matter of Jobes, 529 A.2d 434 (N.J. 1987); Matter of Peter by Johanning, 529 A.2d 419 (N.J. 1987); O'Connor v. Hall, — N.E.2d — (N.Y. 1988); Delio v. Westchester County Med. Center, 516 N.Y.S.2d 677 (App. Div. 1987), revg., 510 N.Y.S.2d 415 (Sup. Ct. 1986); Workmen's Circle Home v. Fink, 514 N.Y.S.2d 893 (Sup. Ct. 1987); Vogel v. Forman, 512 N.Y.S.2d 622 (Sup. Ct. 1986); Application of Kerr, 517 N.Y.S.2d 346 (Sup. Ct. 1986); In the Matter of the Guardianship of Bayer, Case No. 4131, N.D. County Ct., Burleigh County, Dec. 11, 1987; In re Guardianship of Grant, 747 P.2d 445 (Wash. 1987).

[87]See Cruzan by Cruzan v. Harmon, supra n.86; O'Connor v. Hall, supra n.86; Vogel v. Forman, supra n.86; Application of Kerr, supra n.86. The Supreme Court decision in the *Cruzan* case is bound to have a profound impact on the issue of artificial hydration and nutrition of patients in a persistent vegetative state.

[88]O'Connor v. Hall, supra n.86.

[89]Brophy v. New England Sinai Hosp., 398 Mass. 417, 497 N.E.2d 626 (1986).

[90]See, e.g., Okla. Stat. Ann. tit. 63, §2902 (West 1987).

[91]See, e.g., Position of the American Dietetic Association: Issues in Feeding the Terminally Ill Adult, 10 ADA Reports 78-84 (January 1987).

specific legal advice. Perhaps more than any other area of the law dealing with death and dying issues, decisions involving artificial nutrition and hydration are state specific.

That state-specific legal advice is required should be taken into consideration when developing institutional guidelines or policies on initiating or withdrawing artificial nutrition and hydration of persons in a persistent vegetative state. The need is clear not only from a strict legal analysis but also as a means of assuring development of a practical policy that can handle intrafamily disputes and choice making in complicated situations.

§7.5.3   Practical Considerations Regarding Other Treatments

Whether decisions to withdraw treatment apply to competent or incompetent patients, the determination must be informed. The requirements for a valid consent must be met, including adequate disclosure of information about the likely consequences of the withdrawal of care. Patients, their families, or their legal representatives should be told about reasonable alternative forms of care. Unless these basic requirements are met, the decision against further treatment would be deficient.

Another important issue in the withdrawal of care involves proper documentation of the decision. Choices include a "consent" form for the withdrawal of treatment or a detailed notation in the patient's medical record that was written contemporaneously with the patient's decision. Documentation in these circumstances has a twofold purpose. First, it sets limits on permissible treatment for the patient. A patient's decision against chemotherapy, for example, may not preclude palliative care. The documentation in each case should specify what constitutes "withdrawal" of treatment and what treatment possibilities are still available.

The second purpose of documentation is legal defense. Having a duly executed consent form for the withdrawal of treatment, or a detailed note in the patient's chart to the same effect, can help prevent the health facility and its personnel from being sued successfully. No degree of documentation can prevent litigation. However, ample evidentiary proof in these cases makes it very difficult for the plaintiff to prevail.

Documentation should indicate that patients, their families, or their legal representatives have reached their decisions voluntarily, with full knowledge of the consequences. Any reasonable alternative forms of care disclosed to the patient should be recounted in writing.

The failure to obtain valid consent for either placing a patient on or removing a patient from life-support therapy can lead to litigation.[92] For example, in an Ohio case the survivors of a patient who had been placed on a respirator following cardiopulmonary arrest sued for damages for the time during which the patient was maintained on life-support therapy.[93] The Ohio Court of Appeals ruled that a cause of action did indeed exist based on wrongfully placing and maintaining a patient on a respirator. The plaintiffs presented questions of fact regarding the failure of the defendants to apprise the patient's family of the true nature of her illness and, allegedly, the administration of experimental drugs to the patient without the family's consent. The trial court was therefore in error for having dismissed the plaintiff's cause of action.[94]

Refusing further treatment is an issue that should not be taken lightly. Failure to follow a directive to withdraw care can constitute a cause of action for unauthorized treatment. Documentation in the patient's record is essential in this regard. Equally important, however, is a practical institutional policy governing the withdrawal of life-sustaining therapy in the face of a terminal illness. Such a policy should be based on practical legal advice. Authorizations for withdrawal of care should be

---

[92] See Strickland v. Deaconess Hosp., 735 P.2d 74 (Wash. Ct. App. 1987); McVey v. Englewood Hosp. Assn., 524 A.2d 450 (N.J. Super. Ct. App. Div. 1987); Estate of Leach v. Shapiro, 13 Ohio App. 3d 393, 469 N.E.2d 1047 (1984). It should be noted that, with the exception of Leach v. Shapiro, the courts granted summary judgment in favor of the defendants.

[93] Estate of Leach v. Shapiro, 13 Ohio App. 3d 393, 469 N.E.2d 1047 (1984).

[94] Id.

outlined in the policy statement, including the role of family in such decision-making. Withdrawal of care is a subject ripe for judicial review. This step may not be required, however, with careful planning, development, and implementation of a policy on withdrawal of care.

§7.6 Orders Not to Resuscitate (DNRs)

A related issue to refusals of life-prolonging therapy is orders not to resuscitate. For many years health professionals were reluctant to acknowledge the practice of instructing nurses not to attempt resuscitation of particular patients should they experience cessation of pulmonary or cardiac function. Health personnel feared possible criminal or civil liability for fulfilling these orders. In many institutions the orders were not written in the patient's chart. Rather, the directives were given verbally or removable symbols were affixed to the patient's chart that denoted a "DNR." Over time, however, health professionals have begun to acknowledge the use of DNRs in routine hospital practice. As they have done so, articles have been written that suggest the proper manner for issuing orders not to resuscitate.[1] In some states court action[2] and regulations[3] have also appeared that provide guidance for using DNRs.

As the Rabkin article suggests,[4] DNRs should be reserved for

§7.6 [1]See, e.g., Rabkin et al., Orders Not to Resuscitate, 295 New Eng. J. Med. 364 (1976); Optimum Care for Hopelessly Ill Patients: A Report of the Clinical Care Committee of the Massachusetts General Hospital, 295 New Eng. J. Med. 362 (1976).
[2]Matter of Dinnerstein, 6 Mass. App. Ct. 466, 380 N.E.2d 134 (1978). See also Hoyt v. St. Mary's Rehabilitation Center, No. 77-4555 (Hennepin County, Minn., Dist. Ct., February 13, 1981), wherein a patient was *removed* from a DNR list. Orders not to resuscitate were also considered in Severns v. Wilmington Med. Center, 425 A.2d 156 (1980). Finally, the application of an order not to resuscitate a terminally ill infant was considered in Custody of a Minor, 385 Mass. 697, 434 N.E.2d 601 (1982) (discussed in chapter 5, supra).
[3]Guidelines for "No Code" Orders in Los Angeles County, Department of Health Services Hospitals, Los Angeles County, California, 1979.
[4]Rabkin, Orders Not to Resuscitate, supra n.1.

a certain class of patients, specifically those who are terminally ill and whose deaths are imminent. Should they experience a sudden cessation of heart or lung function, resuscitation would not have any curative effect on the patients' underlying disease. The right to decline resuscitation would apply to both competent and incompetent patients; only the method of giving effect to such decisions would differ.[5]

With competent patients, when there is evidence of irreparable terminal illness and imminent death, Rabkin and his associates would have a nonattending staff physician and an ad hoc committee of physicians consult on the case. If they agreed with the attending physician's assessment (of terminal illness and imminency of death), then the informed consent of the patient would be sought to a DNR.[6]

The format for issuing DNRs for incompetent patients is somewhat different. Rabkin would require the same steps as those outlined for competent patients up to the point of securing the patient's consent. At that juncture, the proposed procedure would require the consent of an appropriate family member. Those who could authorize a postmortem examination would have the authority to consent to a DNR. For incompetents, the study carefully noted, the substitute consent must be based on the interests of the patient.

For both incompetent and competent patients certain documentation is required in the patient's chart. Notes for cognizant persons should include a review of the ad hoc and nonattending staff consultation, the information presented to the patient, the attending physician's assessment of the person's competence, and the patient's response or formal consent. For the incompetent, similar documentation is proposed — except that the authorization of the family is to be incorporated in the chart.[7]

The Rabkin proposal does not anticipate a number of possible situations. It does not suggest a response to a dispute among family members who cannot agree on a DNR for an incompe-

[5]Id.
[6]Id.
[7]Id.

tent relative. It also does not eliminate the possibility that the competent patient may be so depressed or in such pain that she would agree to almost anything — including a no-code order.

Proposals such as Rabkin's are useful in establishing hospital policy on orders not to resuscitate. A review of case law, however, is also instructive on the subject of DNRs.

§7.6.1 Case Law

A limited amount of reported case law exists on orders not to resuscitate. Of that number, the most well-known is a Massachusetts Appeals Court decision.

In Matter of Dinnerstein,[8] a 67-year-old woman with Alzheimer's disease was hospitalized following a massive stroke. Her condition was such that she was in a vegetative existence, immobile, unable to swallow without choking, and unable to speak. From time to time she opened her eyes, although she seemed unaware of her environment. In addition to the Alzheimer's disease, she had high blood pressure and life-threatening coronary artery disease. Physicians attending the woman termed her condition hopeless and her life expectancy less than one year. Death would likely come from another stroke. Cessation of cardiac or respiratory function could occur at any time.

The attending physician recommended that if the patient suffered an arrest, no resuscitation should be administered. The woman's two children agreed. The hospital, doctor, and the woman's two children filed a declaratory judgment action, seeking a determination that the physician could enter in the woman's medical chart an order prospectively not to resuscitate without court authorization. They asked that, alternatively, judicial approval be given if such authorization was determined to be a legal prerequisite to a no-code order.[9]

The Massachusetts Appeals Court held that prior judicial approval is not required for a legally valid order not to resuscitate. It found that the holding in *Saikewicz*, involving a life-

[8] 6 Mass. App. Ct. 466, 380 N.E.2d 134 (1978).
[9] Id.

prolonging treatment alternative, did not require resuscitation in all cases. Life-prolonging care was to be provided to those for whom there was ". . . some reasonable expectation of effecting a permanent or temporary cure of or relief from the illness or condition being treated."[10] Prolongation of life, the court added, "does not mean a mere suspension of the act of dying, but contemplates at the very least, a remission of symptoms enabling a return towards a normal, functioning, integrated existence."[11]

The court distinguished the instance case from the facts of the *Saikewicz* matter. In *Saikewicz,* a proposed series of chemotherapy treatments — which were not instituted — made it possible to extend the patient's life for a matter of months or years by causing a temporary remission of terminal leukemia. On the basis of substituted judgment, treatment was not undertaken. In the *Dinnerstein* case, there was no hope of effecting a remission. The patient was in the final stages of an unremitting, incurable disease and resuscitation would not cure or relieve the medical problems that led to the patient's terminal condition.[12] She would never be restored to a normal, integrated, knowing existence.

In stating that the present case did not involve a life-prolonging or life-saving treatment question like that involved in the *Saikewicz* case, the court held that what was involved was a medical question. The medical professional must determine what steps are proper "to ease the imminent passing of an irreversibly, terminally ill patient in light of the patient's history and condition and the wishes of her family." The only time the courts would become involved in such matters is in a negligence action in which it was argued that the doctor had not measured up to the appropriate standard of care.[13]

[10] Id. at 474, 380 N.E.2d at 138.
[11] Id.
[12] Id. at 474, 380 N.E.2d at 138-139.
[13] Id. at 476, 380 N.E.2d at 139. In Matter of Spring, 380 Mass. 629, 632, 405 N.E.2d 115, 120 (1980), the Massachusetts Supreme Judicial Court observed that the result reached in *Dinnerstein* was consistent with the holding in *Saikewicz.* See also Custody of a Minor, 385 Mass. 697, 434 N.E.2d 601 (1982).

Not all courts agree with the Appeals Court of Massachusetts in limiting judicial review in DNR matters. For example, in Hoyt v. St. Mary's Rehabilitation Center,[14] a Hennepin County, Minnesota, judge ordered the removal of a patient from a DNR list. The woman had undergone brain surgery five years before and she had emerged with the mental ability of a 2-year-old. Subsequent to the operation, the woman required total care of her physical needs, including artificial feeding. The woman's legal guardians, her mother and father, had apparently agreed with the attending physicians to remove her from the health facility's emergency care list. She was then placed on the DNR list.

A woman who had befriended the patient while visiting her relatives at the facility brought an action challenging the DNR order. The court found that a third party with a sincere interest in the incompetent patient may challenge the actions of a guardian.[15]

At a court hearing it was learned that only one of the patient's guardians had consented to the order not to resuscitate. The guardian who had consented to the DNR listing did not understand that in an emergency the patient would not receive any resuscitation. He had thought that DNR meant that his daughter would not be subjected to long-term life support machinery. At the close of the hearing, the court ordered that the patient be removed from the no-code (DNR order) list and returned to the list for emergency care.

In Delaware, a guardian of an incompetent patient was authorized by a court to order that a no-code blue entry be made in the patient's chart.[16] In that instance, the patient had suffered a broken neck and brain damage in an automobile accident. Doctors attending her held out no hope that she would ever regain consciousness or resume a normal life. Prior to the

---

[14]No. 77-4555 (Hennepin County, Minn., Dist. Ct., February 13, 1981).

[15]Id. The court indicated that third parties must make a prima facie showing of their interest and ability as well as of the failure of the guardian to use due consideration. Moreover, to avoid harassment, a decision should be subject to only one court challenge.

[16]Severns v. Wilmington Med. Center, 425 A.2d 156.

accident she had told her husband that, should she ever become unable to care for herself, she did not want to be kept alive in a vegetative state. Based on this and other evidence, the court allowed the no-code blue order.[17]

Although there is but a limited amount of case law on the subject, at least some judicial recognition has been given to orders not to resuscitate. The no-code or DNR is a medical procedure, an alternative to medical therapies that may be used in some instances. The actions of a physician in "no-coding" a patient in all likelihood will be measured by the appropriate standard of care in the circumstances. As long as the physician acts as a reasonable practitioner would have done in a similar situation, the law will not intrude from a medical negligence point of view. When there is evidence that consent to a no-code was obtained improperly, however, judicial intervention can be expected upon a proper challenge. Well-drafted procedures for ordering no-codes avoid such actions. Education of staff also reduces errors in coding and not coding patients for resuscitation. Careful attention should be paid to obtaining — where possible — the consent of the patient, or if this cannot be done, the consent of those who can authorize a DNR on his behalf. As in other aspects of medical care, the general steps for eliciting an informed consent should determine the actions of health personnel.

§7.6.2 *Rules and Regulations*

In at least two jurisdictions, steps have been taken to assist health care providers in issuing orders not to resuscitate. The guidelines issued by the Los Angeles County Department of Health apply only to patients in county hospitals or those who are conservatees or wards of the Los Angeles County Public Guardian's office.[18] New York state has enacted the Orders Not to Resuscitate Act.[19]

A no-code can, under the Los Angeles County guidelines, be

---

[17]Id.
[18]Supra n.3.
[19]See N.Y. Pub. Health Law §§2960-2978 (McKinney 1988).

issued when a patient has an incurable disease and death is expected, imminent, or inevitable. When the attending physician believes a no-code order is appropriate, she must consult with another member of the medical staff. If the consultant agrees, then the patient's consent to a no-code must be obtained. However, if the patient is not competent, his family, guardian, or conservator must consent. The order not to resuscitate must then be written on the physician's order sheet in the patient's chart and signed by both the attending and consulting physicians. Additional documentation in the patient's medical record should outline the findings of the doctors and the discussion of the no-code with the patient and/or his family, guardian, or conservator. The no-code must be reviewed periodically to determine if it remains appropriate to the patient's condition.[20]

Under the Los Angeles County guidelines, a no-code order may not be issued without a patient's consent. The same holds true in the case of an incompetent patient when the family, guardian, or conservator withholds consent. If the patient executed a valid declaration under the California living will law, this decision takes precedence over a no-code issued under the guidelines.[21]

The New York law creates a presumption in favor of resuscitation that can be overcome by a consent to the issuance of a DNR order.[22] The new law makes provision for determining competency regarding cardiopulmonary resuscitation, the way in which a capable adult may request the issuance of a DNR order, surrogate decision-making for incapable adults both with and without surrogate decision makers, and decision-making for minor patients. The New York law also requires physician review of the DNR order and a dispute mediation system for challenges to DNR orders. Judicial review is also possible under the new law.[23]

---

[20]Supra n.3.
[21]Id.
[22]See N.Y. Pub. Health Law §2962 (McKinney 1988).
[23]See N.Y. Pub. Health Law §2973 (McKinney 1988). It should be noted that courts can approve DNR orders in other circumstances as outlined in N.Y. Pub. Health Law §2976 (McKinney 1988).

The New York approach, at least on paper, is a welcome change from the anxiety and indecision that often accompanies orders not to resuscitate. The New York provision has seemingly anticipated the most common situations in which DNR problems are likely to occur. It remains to be seen whether the law is practical in its application. Moreover, only time will tell whether unanticipated difficulties will necessitate fine-tuning of the law. This is particularly important regarding interinstitutional and interagency transfers from nonspecified health facilities and home care programs that are not covered in the law. Notwithstanding these concerns, the New York law is a step in the right direction in terms of clearing up the ambiguities of consent to a DNR order.

§7.6.3 Practical Considerations

Unlike other medical treatment alternatives, the order not to resuscitate has evoked great concern, medically, legally, and ethically, among health care providers and those they serve. There is a fear that an individual who should be resuscitated will not be revived, or that a decision to no-code a patient will be made at the whim of a doctor without careful consideration. To overcome these concerns and to provide staff with criteria for no-coding a patient, it is advisable to develop a protocol for orders not to resuscitate. A sound and thoughtful plan could provide a certain degree of legal protection when a court challenge is based on negligence. Having a carefully devised standard of care that is applied consistently could assist defense counsel in establishing that the DNR constituted reasonable care in the circumstances.

The other consideration from a legal perspective is the matter of consent. An order not to resuscitate should not be issued without either the consent of the patient or the authorization of one legally empowered to act on her behalf. Civil actions for failure to obtain consent could result from such circumstances.

In the development of a no-code policy the importance of securing the advice of hospital counsel and the medical and nursing staff as well as of the administration of the health facility cannot be minimized. Recommendations of outside authorities, including accreditation bodies, should also be considered.[24]

§7.7   Orders Not to Hospitalize (DNHs)

If patients have the right to refuse resuscitation, the next question is whether they have a right to refuse hospitalization. This issue is of particular concern to residents of long-term and extended care facilities and clients of home health care programs.

As seen in this section, Do Not Hospitalize orders (DNHs) are on the cutting edge of the right to refuse treatment. There is no case law or legislative directives on the topic. Nonetheless, it is a consent issue that deserves consideration.

§7.7.1   What Is a DNH Order?

A DNH is a medical order issued by a licensed practitioner that indicates that a resident of a long-term care facility or a patient of a home care or extended care agency should not be hospitalized or receive certain types of hospital care. The concept has developed as a means of assuring the terminally ill and residents of long-term care centers that their wishes will be respected regarding highly intrusive forms of care. The developments in home care programs make DNHs equally important in those situations, particularly for patients enrolled in home-based palliative support treatment.

In many ways the DNH order tracks the framework of a Do Not Resuscitate directive (DNR). Eligibility criteria, consent,

[24]See, e.g., National Conference on Standards for Cardiopulmonary Resuscitation (CPR) and Emergency Cardiac Care (ECC), 227 J.A.M.A. 837 (1974). See also Ethics and Communication in Do-Not-Resuscitate Orders, 318(1) New Eng. J. Med. 43-46 (1988).

consent documentation, and revocation provisions should be built into a policy and procedure on Do Not Hospitalize orders.

The following is an example of such a policy and procedure framework:

1. To be eligible for a DNH order, a patient or resident must (a) be diagnosed as suffering from a terminal illness or (b) have determined that in the event of an acute episode, hospitalization or certain types of hospital care are not to be carried out.

2. To be effective, a DNH order must be based on the informed consent of the patient or resident or a duly authorized legal representative. The nature and consequences of a DNH order should be explained along with the alternatives (hospital care or certain types of hospital care) to it.

3. For those individuals who oppose certain types of hospital care (CPR, nasogastric tube feeding, cardiopulmonary life support, etc.), a written directive should be executed indicating the treatments to which they are opposed.

4. A DNH order shall be issued by the attending physician and placed on the medical record. For those patients or residents who authorize limited hospital care, the DNH order and the patient's written directive shall accompany the patient or resident in all transfers for hospitalization.

5. The patient or resident or duly authorized legal representative may verbally or in writing revoke consent for a DNH order.

6. Acute care facilities that regularly admit residents or patients from the transferring agency should be given a copy of this policy and procedure and should be requested to respect a duly executed DNH order and consent. In the event that such a policy is contrary to the philosophy of the acute care facility, patients and residents who might otherwise be sent to such a facility for hospitalization shall be informed of this fact. DNH orders and consents should be modified accordingly to remove such acute care facilities as likely acute care locations.

It should be noted that before a DNH policy is adopted, specific legal advice should be obtained on the legal propriety of such guidelines. It must be certain that the policy and procedure are not contrary to state law.

§7.7.2 The Practical Significance of DNH Orders

The primary purpose of DNH orders is to retain as much control as possible in the hands of terminally ill individuals and elderly persons who are loath to undergo aggressive, intrusive, life-prolonging measures. Moreover, a DNH order serves to "clear the air" for staff and family regarding what should and should not be done in an acute episode.

In an acute situation there is usually sufficient time to contact an ambulance or EMT unit for assistance. It is not the time, however, to decide the propriety of hospitalization. DNH orders provide a mechanism for honoring disinclinations toward hospital care on the part of the terminally ill or elderly persons. It is a practical, anticipatory device that permits good choice making and effective consents.

Until greater recognition is given to DNH orders, caution should be exercised in developing and implementing a policy and procedure on the topic. It is for this reason that sound legal advice should be obtained before embarking on such a policy. In at least 40 jurisdictions some form of legislation recognizes living wills or patient directives.[1] In the remaining states, pa-

§7.7 [1] See, e.g., Ala. Code §§22-8A-1 to 10 (1981); Del. Code Ann. tit. 16, §§2501 to 2509 (1982); D.C. Code Ann. §§6-2421 to 2430 (1982); Fla. Stat. ch. 84-58, §§765.01 to 765.15 (1984); Ga. Code Ann. §§31 to 32-1-12 (1986); Idaho Code §§39-4501 to 4509 (1988); Ill. Ann. Stat. ch. 110 1/2 §§701 to 710 (Smith-Hurd 1984); Kan. Stat. Ann. §§65-28, and 101 to 109 (1979); La. Rev. Stat. 40:1299.58.1 to 10 (1985); Mississippi Laws of 1984, Chapter 365; Nev. Rev. Stat. §449.540 to 690 (1987); N.M. Stat. Ann. §§24-7-1 to 11 (1984); N.C. Gen. Stat. §§90-320 to 322 (1983); Or. Rev. Stat. §§97.050 to 97.90 (1983); Tex. Stat. Ann. art. 4590h (1985); Vt. Stat. Ann. tit. 18, §§5251 to 5262 and tit. 13, §1801 (1982); Wash. Rev. Code Ann. §§70.122.010 to 70.122.905 (1979); W. Va. Code ch. 16, art. 30, §§1 to 10 (1984); Wisc. Stat. §§154.01 et seq. (1986); and Wyo. Stat. 33-26-144 to 33-26-152 (1984).

tients often provide family members or attending physicians with instructions for terminal care. Living wills or patient directives allow patients, while competent, to inform family and physician alike of their preferred kind of terminal care.

§7.8 Living Wills, Patient Directives, and Durable Powers of Attorney

Patients who are terminally ill have become more assertive of their rights in the hospital setting, indicating what types of medical interventions they will accept. In many states this change has been facilitated by so-called living will legislation. Where these documents have not received legal recognition, it is doubtful that the instructions contained in such written patient directives are legally enforceable. As noted in this section, however, the documents can be quite useful to physicians in considering treatment options for terminally ill patients.

§7.8.1 Living Wills

One means of giving effect to a patient's desires regarding terminal care is the so-called living will.

   a. Types of living wills.   Although there is similarity among the living will laws found throughout the country, there are some important distinctions to bear in mind. For example, in some states a minor[1] or an incompetent person[2] can have another execute a directive on his behalf.
   Some of the laws give recognition to living wills executed under the terms and conditions of similar provisions in other jurisdictions. This typically requires "substantial compliance"

---

§7.8 [1]See Ark. Stat. Ann. §20-17-214 (1987); N.M. Stat. Ann. §24-7-4 (1984).
   [2]Ark. Stat. Ann. §20-17-214 (1987).

with the law in the state giving recognition to a "foreign" living will.[3]

In some states a nonwritten directive can be issued, providing this is done in a prescribed fashion.[4] Living wills usually become operative when a person becomes terminally ill and can no longer participate in the decision-making process regarding treatment.[5]

Like other areas of the law dealing with the right to refuse care, living will legislation is usually quite state specific. Although as noted earlier some states do give recognition to living wills executed under the terms of legislation in other jurisdictions, this is not always the case. Therefore, particular attention should be given to the issue of what should be done regarding terminally ill persons who executed directives in other states.

For intrastate residents, it is equally important to make certain that living wills or patient directives conform to state requirements. By the same token, staff must be aware of the ways in which a living will can be amended or revoked.

It should also be noted that there has been considerable legislative activity in this area in the last few years, with many of the "old" living will laws undergoing modifications. As a result, it is important to make certain that health facilities review existing policies and procedures with a view toward amending internal guidelines to reflect these legislative changes.

b. Practical effect of living wills. Living wills remove much of the uncertainty surrounding treatment choices for terminally ill individuals. When properly executed, living wills eliminate indecision and family disputes. The legislation in place on the topic also goes a long way toward resolving concerns about civil and criminal liability, except of course for those who wrongfully and illegally tamper with patient directives.

As a preventive tool, living wills are an excellent mechanism for assuring "informed" treatment choices. As such, much

[3]See Haw. Rev. Stat. §327D-25 (1986); Alaska Stat. §18.12.090 (1986).
[4]Tex. Civ. Code Ann. art. 4590h (Vernon 1985).
[5]See, e.g., Alaska Stat. §18.12.010 (1986).

more should be done to make the documents "portable" so that a directive issued in one state will be accorded full recognition in another. By the same token more needs to be done in terms of staff education to make certain that the wishes of patients as set down in living wills are fully respected and implemented.

§7.8.2 Patient Directives

In the states without living will laws, patients often present their physicians with a list of instructions, informing them what treatments they want and do not want when they can no longer participate in the decision-making process. Sometimes these nonlegislative "directives" are verbal or handwritten; on other occasions the instructions are typewritten or drafted by a lawyer. The concern facing physicians and health care facilities is the legal effect of these instructions.

A person's consent to a particular form of treatment is not vitiated by her subsequent mental incompetency. Therefore, if a directive was written or given to the physician at a time when the patient was competent, it may be construed as part of the consent to treatment. When there is some question as to the patient's understanding and capability, or the voluntariness of the directive, the physician should proceed cautiously — just as he would do with any questionable "consent." Hospital policy should be in place to deal with dubious authorizations to treatment, and the same or a similar rule should apply to terminal care directives.

A source of uncertainty is the stance taken by the concerned family. Some may see the patient's instructions as ill advised; they jump at the opportunity to contradict the directive once the patient becomes incompetent. Other family members, however, may be highly supportive of the patient's requests. The resulting disagreement among family members forces the hospital and physician to make a decision either to follow or to ignore the family's requests in light of the patient's instructions.

One practical solution is to discuss patients' requests with them and their families while they are able to do so. In this way, any misunderstandings or disputes can be resolved while persons who are the focus of attention can elaborate on their treatment desires. Physicians and hospitals alike should make it clear that patients' wishes will be followed in a manner consistent with applicable standards of practice and law. When a patient requests a type of treatment that is illegal or against hospital policy, this factor should be communicated to her so that the directive might be altered. A detailed note should be entered in the patient's medical record following discussions with the patient and family. This policy provides evidence of the terminally ill "consent" process that might prove valid in any subsequent litigation and aid in terminal care.

On occasion a patient will arrive at a facility in the last throes of terminal illness. He is incapacitated and unable to communicate instructions regarding life-prolonging treatment. Either on the patient's person or in the possession of family members, however, is a living will or terminal care directive. Should the hospital or physician give effect to such a document, allegedly executed while the patient was competent, though in the absence of enabling legislation?

Unless hospitals or physicians were aware previously of a patient's instructions, it is unwise for them to rely upon documents of this type. Unlike the situation described earlier in which the patient could discuss the living will with the physician or hospital, here there is no way of telling whether the patient in fact signed the directive. Still, the physician can take the instructions into account in reaching a decision regarding the patient's treatment plan. They should be considered in light of prevailing standards of care in similar situations and the growing body of case law that suggests that extraordinary care or heroic measures are not required by law. Family disputes regarding treatment should be resolved in a fashion consistent with established hospital policy.

Even without legislative approval of living wills, patient directives can have a very useful function in designing a terminal care plan for dying patients. This fact has been made clear by at least one court in which a living will executed in the absence of enabling legislation was deemed in the nature of "an Informed

Medical Consent Statement."[6] As such it authorized either the refusal or removal of medical care provided by artificial means or devices when the patient was terminally ill and her death was imminent. It also applied when the patient experienced irreversible brain damage and could no longer communicate her treatment wishes.[7] Used wisely, with a patient and family aware of the instructions provided to the health facility and physician, a patient directive can preclude unfortunate disputes at a time of great emotional suffering.

§7.8.3 Directives Generated by Health Facilities

Another approach is development of a plan for terminally ill patients by the health facility. Such a policy might be incorporated into an ongoing palliative care program. Patients could be advised of alternate forms of life support methods available during the course of their illnesses. Families could also be advised so that they understand why and what is being done for their relatives. Patience and communication in such programs facilitate the process of patients' selecting the plan that best suits their needs.

In the case of incompetent patients, there are alternatives to obtaining prior judicial approval. For example, in New Jersey following the *Quinlan* case, a set of guidelines were developed for decision-making in the case of comatose patients.[8] The guidelines create the Ethics Committee (now Prognosis Committee) described in the *Quinlan* decision. The committee is composed of doctors representing general practice, surgery, medicine, neurosurgery or neurology, anesthesiology, and pediatrics (if a case requires it). At least two persons filling the designated specialty spots on the committee are to come from outside the facility's staff. Those attending or who have at-

---

[6]See Saunders v. State, 492 N.Y.S.2d 510 (Sup. Ct. 1985).
[7]Id.
[8]New Jersey Hospital Association, Guidelines for Health Facilities to Implement Procedures Concerning the Care of Comatose Non-Cognitive Patients.

tended the patient cannot serve on the committee. Once a written request is received to consider a case, the committee must meet and reach a conclusion either supporting or rejecting the diagnosis made by the attending physician. The committee, with the consent of the patient's family, may review pertinent patient records and obtain additional information regarding the patient from nursing and other health professionals. It must also determine which member or members of the committee will examine the patient.

Once a decision is reached by the committee, its findings are sent in writing to a number of people including the patient's family, the hospital administrator, and the attending physician. The group must specifically state whether there is "any reasonable possibility of the patient ever emerging from a comatose condition to a cognitive sapient state."[9] Thereafter, it is up to the attending physician, guided by the committee findings and with the concurrence of the patient's family, to take appropriate action. When a decision is made to withdraw life-support procedures, the attending physician must personally fulfill the duty.[10]

In Los Angeles County, guidelines have been developed regarding the use of respirators and ventilators for patients in irreversible coma.[11] Approved by the Los Angeles County Bar Association and the Los Angeles County Medical Association, the guidelines permit the withdrawal of life support when there is a written diagnosis based on adequate medical evidence that the patient is in irreversible coma. In addition, in the patient's medical record there must be no expressed intention by the patient regarding the commencing or sustaining of life-support procedures. The family must also concur in the disconnecting of life-prolonging ventilatory therapy.

The guidelines do not immunize physicians from civil actions or criminal charges. However, the Los Angeles County District

[9]Id.
[10]Id.
[11]Guidelines for Discontinuance of Cardiopulmonary Life-Support Systems Under Specified Circumstances, LACMA Physician, 4 May, 1981, pp. 30-31.

Attorney's office was consulted in the development of the policy. One striking feature about the guidelines is their creation of a standard of medical care in respiratory life-support situations. Theoretically, when a doctor or hospital measures up to the standards, the policy provides a sound defense in any civil action based on negligence or abandonment of a patient through the withdrawal of ventilatory life support.[12]

§7.8.4 Durable Powers of Attorney

In its report entitled Deciding to Forgo Life Sustaining Treatment,[13] the President's Commission for the Study of Ethical Problems in Medicine and Biomedical and Behavioral Research pointed out that durable powers of attorney may be a practical way of making treatment decisions for incompetent patients. As the Commission indicated, durable powers of attorney are statutory devices usually designed for handling the appointor's property and not medical treatment determinations. The Commission recommended that this statutory device be studied carefully with a view toward its application in the health care field.[14]

Since the Commission's report, several jurisdictions have enacted the so-called durable power of attorney in health care legislation.[15] Florida has also enacted legislation which permits a competent person to designate another to make treatment decisions for him. This is found in the Life-Prolonging Procedures Act.[16] As one commentator has pointed out, however, in other states the failure to expressly authorize the holder of the power of attorney to refuse life-sustaining care may prove

[12]Id.
[13]Publ. No. 1983 0-402-884. Superintendent of Documents, Washington, D.C.
[14]Id.
[15]See, e.g., Cal. Civ. Code §§2430-2513 (West 1987); D.C. Code Ann. §§21-2081 to 21-2085 (1987); Ill. Rev. Stat. Ann. ch. 110 1/2, §§804-1 to 12 (Smith-Hurd 1987); Me. Rev. Stat. Ann. tit. 18A, §§5-501 and 5-502 (1986); R.I. Gen. Laws §§23-4.10-1 to 23-4.10-2 (1986).
[16]Fla. Stat. Ann. §765.01 et seq. (West 1984).

problematic.[17] Strict interpretation of a statute vesting the power of attorney with authority to consent *to* treatment may not include the power to *withdraw* consent to treatment.

Court challenges are one way in which to test the scope of a durable power of attorney in the area of refusing treatment. Such an approach, however, is impractical, time-consuming, and expensive. States should study the feasibility of durable powers of attorney as a decision-making option for incompetent patients. If they find that this is a good means of determining the continuance of life-sustaining care, state legislation should be amended to clarify any ambiguities in current statutes on the subject.

[17]See Society for the Right to Die, Handbook of Living Will Laws, 1981-1984 p. 28 (1984).

EIGHT

Human Research and Experimentation

A. Scope of Federal Regulation
   §8.0   Historical Background
   §8.1   Overview of HHS Regulations
          §8.1.1   General Administrative Requirements
          §8.1.2   Role of Institutional Review Boards (IRBs)
          §8.1.3   Requirements for Consent
          §8.1.4   Documentation Requirements for Consent
          §8.1.5   General Applicability of HHS Regulations
   §8.2   Overview of FDA Regulations
          §8.2.1   Requirements for Consent
          §8.2.2   Standards for Consent Documentation
          §8.2.3   Waiver of Consent: Two Major Exceptions
   §8.3   Requirements of Other Federal Agencies and Departments
B. State Controls Over Human Research
   §8.4   Overview of State Requirements
          §8.4.1   The California Approach
          §8.4.2   The New York Approach
          §8.4.3   The Virginia Approach
          §8.4.4   General Statutory Provisions
          §8.4.5   Interplay with Federal Regulations
   §8.5   Overview of Drug Research Laws
          §8.5.1   Consent Requirements
C. Reproductive Research: Special Consent Considerations
   §8.6   Research Involving Pregnant Women: Federal Consent
          Requirements
          §8.6.1   IRB Responsibilities
          §8.6.2   Paternal Consent
          §8.6.3   Waiver of Consent Provisions

527

§8.7 Research Involving Pregnant Women: State Legislation
    §8.7.1 New Mexico: Strict Consent Requirements for Research
    §8.7.2 Dual Impact of State and Federal Laws
§8.8 Federal Constraints on Fetal Research
    §8.8.1 IRB Responsibilities
    §8.8.2 Fetal Research In Utero
    §8.8.3 Fetal Research Ex Utero
    §8.8.4 Exceptions to Federal Control
§8.9 State Laws on Fetal Research
    §8.9.1 The Massachusetts Example
    §8.9.2 The New Mexico Approach
    §8.9.3 Effect of Federal and State Fetal Research Laws
§8.10 Federal Laws Governing In Vitro Fertilization Research
    §8.10.1 Lack of Specific Consent Requirements
    §8.10.2 Authority of the Secretary and Ethical Advisory Boards
§8.11 State Laws Governing In Vitro Fertilization Research
§8.12 Impact of Governmental Controls on In Vitro Fertilization Research
D. Minors as Research Subjects
§8.13 1983 Federal Requirements
    §8.13.1 Relationship to Other HHS Regulations
    §8.13.2 Children and Permission for Research
    §8.13.3 Children's Assent to Research
    §8.13.4 Wards as Research Subjects
    §8.13.5 Additional Requirements
    §8.13.6 FDA Research and Children
§8.14 State Laws
    §8.14.1 General Provisions
    §8.14.2 Institutionalized and Mentally Handicapped Minors
    §8.14.3 Parental Consent as a Safeguard
    §8.14.4 Minors' Capability to Give Consent
§8.15 Impact of Federal and State Research Requirements
E. Research Involving the Mentally Ill, Handicapped, and Developmentally Disabled
§8.16 Federal Laws Governing Research
    §8.16.1 General Provisions
    §8.16.2 Consent Requirements
§8.17 State Laws Governing Research
    §8.17.1 General Requirements
    §8.17.2 Consent Provisions
    §8.17.3 Research Review Committees and Consent
    §8.17.4 Practical Considerations

§8.18   Effect of Federal and State Requirements
F. Prisoners as Research Subjects
    §8.19   Federal Regulations: HHS Regulations
            §8.19.1   Permissible Research
            §8.19.2   Responsibilities of the IRB
    §8.20   Federal Restrictions: FDA Regulations
            §8.20.1   Permissible Research
            §8.20.2   Responsibilities of the IRB
    §8.21   State Limitations
            §8.21.1   Legislative Constraints: Some State Examples
    §8.22   Effect of Federal and State Requirements
G. Elderly Persons as Research Subjects
    §8.23   Federal Regulatory Standards
            §8.23.1   Consent and Borderline Incompetent Subjects
            §8.23.2   Institutionalization and Competent Subjects
            §8.23.3   Duties of the IRB
    §8.24   State Legislative Requirements
            §8.24.1   Consent Process for Elderly Incompetent Persons
            §8.24.2   Consent Process for Questionably Competent Persons
    §8.25   Effect of Federal and State Requirements
H. Research With Other Vulnerable Populations
    §8.26   AIDS and ARC Victims
 I. Judicial Precedent in Human Research and Consent
    §8.27   The Need for Adequate Disclosure
            §8.27.1   Karp v. Cooley: Consent in Experimental Surgery
            §8.27.2   Novel Radiation Therapy: The Price of Inadequate
                       Disclosure
            §8.27.3   Consent to Experimental Use of Drugs
            §8.27.4   Experimental Surgery Upon a Prisoner: Consent
                       Without a Full Explanation
            §8.27.5   Documenting Consent to Research
 J. Practical Pointers for Consent to Human Research
    §8.28   Drug Company Sponsored Doctor's Office Trials: Consent
             Considerations
    §8.29   Commercial Use of Human Tissues Procured in the Research
             Setting
    §8.30   A Checklist of Management Considerations

A. SCOPE OF FEDERAL REGULATION

§8.0   Historical Background

For many years state and federal laws were silent on the issue of human research and experimentation. The situation changed, however, in 1971 with the first of a series of federal guidelines.[1] No single event or incident can be said to have precipitated this shift in policy. The Nazi experimentations brought to light at Nuremberg, the injection of live cancer cells beneath the skin of chronically ill patients at a New York hospital,[2] the Tuskegee syphilis work,[3] and other episodes surely had some influence.

In 1974, an act of Congress created a National Commission for the Protection of Human Subjects in Biomedical and Behavioral Research, which came up with recommendations on many aspects of human research.[4] Basic regulations for protection of human research subjects were published by HEW in 1974,[5] and regulations were subsequently published relating to fetuses, pregnant women, and prisoners.[6] In 1978, proposals were put forth to protect children[7] and the institutionalized mentally disabled;[8] however, no final regulatory action has been taken for the latter group of individuals.

The greatest change on the federal level occurred in 1981 when the Department of Health and Human Services (HHS), the successor to HEW, revamped the regulations protecting human subjects.[9] The new regulations basically retain the for-

---

§8.0 [1] The Institutional Guide to DHEW Policy on Protection of Human Subjects, DHEW Publication No. [NIH] 72-102 (1971).
[2] See J. Katz, Experimentation With Human Beings, ch. 1 (1972).
[3] Curran, The Tuskegee Syphilis Study, 289 New Eng. J. Med. 730 (1973).
[4] National Research Act, Pub. L. No. 93-348 (1974).
[5] 30 Fed. Reg. 18,914 (1974).
[6] 45 C.F.R. Part 46, Subparts B and C (1981).
[7] 43 Fed. Reg. 31,786 (July 21, 1978).
[8] 43 Fed. Reg. 53,950 (November 17, 1978).
[9] 46 Fed. Reg. 8,366 (January 26, 1981). See also amending provisions to

mer sections relating to fetuses, pregnant women, and prisoners. An interesting feature of the new regulations was to be a strong congruence with the Food and Drug Administration's (FDA) new regulations.[10] One commentator has suggested, however, that this similarity did not in fact reach the degree that had been hoped.[11] Another feature is an expedited review process for certain types of research.[12]

The U.S. government has not been the only source of law for the control of research and experimentation on human research subjects. Many states have become involved, legislating on such matters as fetal experimentation[13] and research on prisoners.[14] There have also been court cases in which it has been alleged that a person was the subject of unauthorized or negligent experimentation.[15]

In this chapter, discussion of both federal and state controls focuses on consent considerations. In view of both state and federal attention to special classes of research subjects, these groups receive particular consideration. When state and federal laws are silent on matters of consent in human research this is discussed with a view toward particular solutions. Case law is also examined where relevant to consent to research and experimentation. The specific regulations of federal agencies

---

correct errors in January 26, 1981 publication in 46 Fed. Reg. 19,195 (March 27, 1981).

[10] 46 Fed. Reg. 8,942 (January 27, 1981).

[11] Curran, New Ethical Research Policy for Clinical Medical Research, 304 New Eng. J. Med. 952, 953 (1981).

[12] 45 C.F.R. §46.110 (1981).

[13] Ill. Ann. Stat. ch. 38, §81-26 (Smith-Hurd 1985); Mass. Gen. Laws Ann. ch. 112, §12J (West 1976); Minn. Stat. Ann. §145.422 (West 1973); N.M. Stat. Ann. §§24-9A-1 et seq. (1979).

[14] Ariz. Rev. Stat. Ann. §31-321 (1973); Cal. Penal Code §§3500 et seq. (West 1985); Iowa Code Ann. §246.47 (1967).

[15] See, e.g., Karp v. Cooley, 493 F.2d 408, rehearing denied, 496 F.2d 878, cert. denied, 419 U.S. 845, 95 S. Ct. 79, 42 L. Ed. 2d 73 (1979); Cain v. United States, 643 F. Supp. 177 (S.D.N.Y. 1986); Whitlock v. Duke University, 637 F. Supp. 1463 (M.D.N.C. 1986); Zeller v. Greater Baltimore Med. Center, 67 Md. App. 75, 506 A.2d 646 (1986); Valenti v. Prudden, 58 A.2d 956, 397 N.Y.S.2d 181 (1977).

other than HHS and FDA pertaining to human research are not included here; they are of limited value in this general review of federal and state requirements.

§8.1 Overview of HHS Regulations

In referring to federal regulatory controls of human research, it is important to remember that two different groups of requirements exist. The newest HHS regulations promulgated in 1981 must be read in conjunction with subparts B and C of 45 C.F.R. Part 46 (1981). These subparts, as noted earlier, refer to pregnant women, fetuses, and prisoners as research subjects, and these subsections remain in force with some slight modification by the 1981 HHS action. The other source of federal control is found in the 1981 regulations put forth by FDA. For purposes of analysis, the HHS and FDA regulations are discussed separately.

§8.1.1 General Administrative Requirements

The HHS regulations apply to all research carried out or funded by the department, including research conducted or funded by it outside the United States.[1] Some exemptions may be granted with respect to projects conducted outside the United States.[2]

The regulations include a list of research activities that are exempted from coverage by the law. These include research on educational tests, observation of public behavior, the collection and study of existing data and specimens, as well as other activities.[3] Not exempted, however, are educational tests, survey and interview procedures, observations of public behavior, and col-

---

§8.1   [1] 45 C.F.R. §46.101(a) (1981).
[2] Id.
[3] 45 C.F.R. §46.101(b) (1981).

lections and studies of existing data and specimens in which research subjects are pinpointed directly or through identifiers.[4] Research in these situations falls within the category of regulated projects.

§8.1.2 Role of Institutional Review Boards (IRBs)

Institutions in which federally funded research is to be carried out must have a duly constituted institutional review board (IRB).[5] The regulations specify requirements for membership on an IRB, as well as the duties of the board in reviewing and certifying research projects.[6] Among these is the IRB's duty to require that subjects be given information consistent with the federal regulations and such other information as "in the IRB's judgment . . . would meaningfully add to the protection of the rights and welfare of subjects."[7]

In addition, the IRB is to require documentation of a subject's informed consent.[8] This requirement, however, can be waived in two instances. First, when the sole record linking the research subject with the researcher would be the consent document and the main threat of harm would be a breach of confidentiality, the decision whether to require documented consent is left up to the research subject.[9]

The other basis for waiving the requirement of documented consent occurs when the research presents no more than a minimal risk of harm to a research subject and involves no procedure for which written permission is required outside of the research setting. In either circumstance, the IRB may require the researcher to submit a written statement about the study to the subjects.[10] It should be pointed out that the IRB is

[4] Id.
[5] 45 C.F.R. §46.103 (1981).
[6] 46 C.F.R. §46.107 (1981).
[7] 45 C.F.R. §46.109 (1981).
[8] Id.
[9] 45 C.F.R. §46.117 (1981).
[10] Id.

not left without any direction about what constitutes "minimal risk." This term is defined in the regulations.[11]

§8.1.3 Requirements for Consent

A considerable portion of the regulations is devoted to the requirements for informed consent.[12] Consent must be obtained from the research subjects or their legally authorized representatives. No undue influence or coercion can be used to get subjects to participate. Information presented to patients must be in language understandable to them or their representatives. Neither written nor oral consent can contain exculpatory language that waives a subject's rights or releases the investigator, the institution, or the sponsor from liability for negligence.

Eight basic elements of informed consent have been identified under the regulations. Some or all of these elements do not apply in research projects approved by an IRB when it finds that:

1. a. The research is to evaluate or demonstrate benefit or service projects of the federal, state, or legal governments; or
    b. the project is to assess or show procedures for securing benefits or services under federal, state, or local programs; or
    c. the research is to demonstrate and weigh possible changes or alternatives in or to these procedures; and
    d. the project could not practicably be undertaken without waiving or altering the general consent requirements.
2. a. No more than minimal risk is involved for subjects;
    b. the subject will not incur an adverse effect to his or her

[11] 45 C.F.R. §46.102 (1981).
[12] 45 C.F.R. §§46.116-117 (1981).

rights or welfare from the waiver or alteration of consent requirements;

c. the research could not be carried out practically without the IRB grant of a waiver or alterations; and

d. when appropriate, following their participation in the research project, subjects will be given additional pertinent details.[13]

The eight consent elements are quite specific and are summarized below.

1. An explanation of the purpose of the study, including that it involves research with identification of those procedures to be used and those considered experimental; a description of the anticipated length of the subject's participation.

2. A statement of reasonably foreseeable risks or discomforts that the subject may experience.

3. An explanation of any benefits that might be received by the subject or others as a result of the research.

4. The disclosure of alternative procedures or treatment that might be beneficial to the subject.

5. The degree to which, if any, confidentiality of records identifying the subject will be kept.

6. The availability of compensation and medical care for injuries arising from procedures must be revealed, along with information regarding where further details may be obtained. This requirement only applies when a research project involves more than minimal risk.

7. The name or names of whom to contact regarding questions about the research and the rights of research subjects. A contact should also be supplied in the event of a research-related injury.

8. Subjects must be told that their participation is voluntary and that their refusal to participate will incur no penalty or loss of rights to which they are entitled. In addition, sub-

---

[13] 45 C.F.R. §46.116 (1981).

jects should be advised that they may discontinue their participation at any time without penalty or loss of benefits.[14]

In addition to the foregoing elements of consent, other requirements may be added when deemed appropriate. These include a further statement of (a) any risks of the research that are unforeseeable at the time, (b) any circumstances under which the subject may be withdrawn from the project by the investigator, (c) any additional costs that a subject may incur by reason of his participation in the research, (d) a subject's right to withdraw from a project and the mechanism for doing so in an orderly way, (e) any new findings made in the project that may affect the subject's willingness to participate, and (f) the approximate number of persons enrolled in the project.[15] It should be noted that the unforeseeable risk disclosure applies also to an embryo or fetus if the subject is or may become pregnant.[16]

§8.1.4   Documentation Requirements for Consent

The requirements for documentation of consent are quite detailed. With some exception, discussed earlier, written consent is required using a form approved by the IRB.[17] Subjects or their legally authorized representatives must sign one of the two types of consent documents that are permitted under the regulations. A so-called long form embodies all of the consent elements described above. Although this may be read to a subject or her representative, either one must be given the opportunity to read it before it is signed.

The other type of document is referred to as the short form. Rather than including all the prescribed elements of consent, this form states that the required information has been pre-

[14]Id.
[15]Id.
[16]Id.
[17]45 C.F.R. §46.117 (1981).

sented orally to the subject or his representative. Someone must witness the oral presentation. The IRB must approve a written summary of the verbal explanation. The consent document should be signed by either the subject or his authorized representative. The witness to the oral presentation must sign the short consent form, as well as a copy of the summary. The person who actually obtains the consent of the subject or his representative must also sign the summary. Both a copy of the summary and the short consent form must be given to the research subject or his authorized representative.[18]

§8.1.5 General Applicability of HHS Regulations

Pregnant women, in vitro fertilization of humans,[19] and fetal research[20] are singled out as special research subjects under the regulations. Prisoners also have been given special consideration under the regulations.[21] In 1983, HHS added a new subpart to its regulations governing minors as research subjects.[22] In addition to the general elements of consent noted above, other requirements are added for these groups of research subjects. Although these subjects are discussed in greater detail in §1.6 supra, it is important to note at this juncture that the general HHS requirements discussed in detail above remain applicable.

§8.2 Overview of FDA Regulations

One day after the Department of Health and Human Services promulgated its regulations, the Food and Drug Administration followed suit.[1] A new Subpart B was added to existing

[18]Id.
[19]45 C.F.R. §46.201 (1981).
[20]Id.
[21]45 C.F.R. §§46.301-306 (1981); 45 C.F.R. §§46.401-46.409 (1983).
[22]45 C.F.R. Part 46, Subpart D.
§8.2 [1]46 Fed. Reg. 8,942 (January 27, 1981).

FDA regulations relating to informed consent. As with the requirements imposed by HHS, an investigator who intends to use human research subjects must get their informed consent or the consent of the subjects' legally authorized representatives. The atmosphere in which consent is to be obtained should minimize potential coercion or undue influence. Information must be presented in language that is understandable to the subjects or their authorized representatives. No exculpatory language is permissible that waives subjects' legal rights or the liability of the investigator, the sponsor, the institution, or its agents.[2]

§8.2.1 Requirements for Consent

As with the HHS regulations, those of the FDA set forth eight basic elements as part of the requirements for informed consent.[3] The same is true of the additional consent requirements that may be provided to a subject when appropriate.[4] One major difference among the general elements of consent is that under the FDA regulations subjects must be informed that their records may be inspected by the FDA.[5]

The FDA has also issued guidelines on the emergency use of unapproved medical devices.[6] Among these guidelines are so-called patient protection procedures. These include obtaining the informed consent of the patient or the patient's legal representative. Once the unapproved device has been used in an emergency, the physician should notify the IRB and comply with existing informed consent regulations.[7]

[2] 21 C.F.R. §50.20 (1981).
[3] 21 C.F.R. §50.25 (1981).
[4] Id.
[5] Id.
[6] 50 Fed. Reg. 42,865 (October 22, 1985) and correction published in 50 Fed. Reg. 45,874 (November 4, 1985).
[7] 50 Fed. Reg. 42,867 (October 22, 1985).

§8.2.2 Standards for Consent Documentation

According to the FDA regulations, documentation of informed consent may be achieved in the same manner as that permitted by HHS. Provision is made for both long and short form consent.[8] The requirements of written consent, however, may be waived for research projects under the FDA regulations when it is determined that the research poses no more than a minimal risk of harm to subjects. Similarly, when the proposed procedure is one for which written permission is normally not required outside the research setting, that requirement may be waived.[9]

§8.2.3 Waiver of Consent: Two Major Exceptions

There are two major circumstances in which the general requirements for informed consent do not apply under the FDA regulations.[10] These exceptions are summarized below. It should be pointed out that the regulations' use of the term *test article* comprises any drug, medical device, electronic product, human food additive, or color additive.[11]

a. Feasibility. The first exception is created when there is not time to obtain informed consent prior to using the test article. This time conflict must be certified in writing by both the principal investigator and a physician who is not involved in the clinical investigation. They must certify *all* of the following:

1. The subject is faced with a life-threatening occurrence that requires employment of the test article.
2. Due to an inability to communicate with the subject or due

[8] 21 C.F.R. §50.27 (1981).
[9] 21 C.F.R. §56.109 (1981).
[10] 21 C.F.R. §50.23 (1981).
[11] 21 C.F.R. §50.3 (1981).

to his or her inability to give legally effective permission to use the test article, informed consent cannot be obtained.

3. Adequate time is lacking to secure consent from the subject's legal representative.

4. No other options of approved or generally recognized care are available that would afford an equal or greater opportunity of saving the subject's life.[12]

b. Preservation of life. The other exception to the general consent requirements permits immediate use of the test article by the principal investigator where it is necessary to preserve the subject's life and adequate time is not available to seek an independent assessment by another physician. Within five working days of using the test article, the clinical determination of the principal investigator must be reviewed and evaluated by a physician not engaged in the project. Her assessment must be in writing.[13]

Whether the independent assessment precedes or follows the use of the test article, under either exception the required documentation must be presented to the IRB. This information must be communicated within five working days following the use of the test article.[14]

§8.3 Requirements of Other Federal Agencies and Departments

It should not be forgotten that other agencies of the government may have occasion to conduct or sanction human research. This has been highlighted by the fact that proposed rule-making is underway to streamline federal policy on human research.[1] The intent is to develop one common policy or model for human research protection. If adopted, the model will cover a large cross section of federal agencies.

[12] Id. 21 C.F.R. §50.23.
[13] Id.
[14] Id.
§8.3 [1] See 53 Fed. Reg. 45,661 et seq. (November 10, 1988).

It is too soon to predict when the final rules will be put in place. However, for CEOs, risk managers, and others it is important to keep abreast of these changes, particularly if their facilities or agencies are involved in federally sanctioned or funded human research.

B. STATE CONTROLS OVER HUMAN RESEARCH

§8.4 Overview of State Requirements

Not all states have enacted legislation or promulgated regulations on human research. That area remains mostly under the auspices of the federal government. A number of notable exceptions can be found, however, including three large states.[1]

§8.4.1 The California Approach

The California human experimentation statute contains a research subjects' bill of rights, provisions on informed consent, and penalties for violating the applicable research laws.[2] It exempts those conducting a study in accordance with HEW (now HHS) regulations from the provision on subjects' rights and the penalty section. The exemption applies when the research is carried out in an institution holding a federal assurance.[3] Special provision is made for certain classes of persons to participate as research subjects. Among these are individuals under a conservatorship and developmentally disabled adults.[4] When

§8.4 [1]Cal. Health & Safety Code §§24170 et seq. (West 1978) (human experimentation); Cal. Penal Code §§3500 et seq. (West 1985) (biomedical and behavioral research); N.Y. Pub. Health Law §§2440 et seq. (McKinney 1975); Va. Code §§37.1-234 et seq. (1979).
[2]Cal. Health & Safety Code §§24172-24176 (West 1978).
[3]Id. at §24179.
[4]Id. at §24175 (West 1979).

consent to participate for individuals in these categories comes from someone other than the subject, the scope of permissible research is restricted. The experiments then have to relate to the maintenance or improvement of the subject's health or be geared toward collecting data regarding the pathological condition of the individual.[5] Another point of interest about the California law is that it does not apply to terminally ill patients who have executed a directive or living will.[6]

§8.4.2 The New York Approach

The New York law is not as detailed as the California provision; however, it does pay considerable attention to consent. The law contains a definition of informed consent and a requirement that the consent be subscribed to in writing.[7] Minors, incompetents, prisoners, and mentally disabled individuals may participate as research subjects.[8] For minors the consent of their parent or legal guardian is required, and for incompetents a person legally empowered to act for the subject must sign the consent.[9] In addition, consent must be obtained from both an institutional human research review committee and the commissioner for research on minors, incompetents, prisoners, and mentally disabled persons.[10] The state provisions do not apply, however, to research that is subject to and that complies with federal human research regulations.[11]

§8.4.3 The Virginia Approach

Virginia is another state with general provisions regarding human research. The law contains a definition of informed

[5] Id.
[6] Id. at §24179.5 (West 1979).
[7] N.Y. Pub. Health Law §§2441-2442 (McKinney 1975).
[8] Id. at §2444.
[9] Id. at §2442.
[10] Id. at §2444.
[11] Id. at §2445.

consent,[12] as well as a requirement that permission to participate in research be written.[13] Minors may participate in research and, providing they otherwise are capable of doing so, must indicate their consent in writing, as must their legally authorized representatives.[14] The authorized representative may not, however, consent to nontherapeutic research that is determined by a human research review committee to involve a hazardous risk to the subject.[15] As in the California and New York statutes, human research protocols that are subject to federal regulations are exempted from the Virginia requirement.[16]

§8.4.4 General Statutory Provisions

Other state human research requirements are not as elaborate as those discussed above. Many are part of state patients' rights laws; they require informed consent for those who participate in human research[17] or state that subjects may refuse to take part in research or experimentation.[18] Some states have laws protecting certain classes of potential research subjects. Prisoners are a good example of a group covered by this type of legislation. At least four states have laws on the subject.[19]

Many states have laws governing fetal research. Some ban the sale or distribution of live born or viable fetuses for purposes of research where the fetuses are the product of an abortion.[20]

---

[12]Va. Code §37.1-234 (1979).
[13]Id. at §37.1-235.
[14]Id.
[15]Id.
[16]Id. at §37.1-237.
[17]Fla. Stat. Ann. §393.13 (West 1979); Md. Pub. Health Code Ann. §43:565C (1980); Mo. Ann. Stat. §198.088 (Vernon 1979); Mont. Rev. Code Ann. §53-20-147 (1975); Wash. Rev. Code Ann. §74.42.040 (1979).
[18]Ark. Stat. Ann. §59-1416 (1979); Mass. Gen. Laws Ann. ch. 111, §70E (West 1979); Or. Rev. Stat. §441.605 (1981).
[19]Ariz. Rev. Stat. Ann. §31-321 (1966); Cal. Penal Code §§3500 et seq. (West 1985); Iowa Code Ann. §246.47 (West 1967); Tenn. Code Ann. §§41-2201 et seq. (1974).
[20]See, e.g., Ind. Code Ann. §35-1-58.5-6 (Burns 1977); Ky. Rev. Stat. §436.026 (1974); Okla. Stat. Ann. tit. 63, §1-735 (West 1978).

Exception is often made where the experimentation is necessary to protect the life or health of the fetus.[21] In some states failure to meet the statutory requirements with this type of legislation may result in criminal charges.[22]

§8.4.5 Interplay with Federal Regulations

As discussed in the previous section, the FDA and HHS are not the only governmental agencies engaged in research regulation. Many states or localities have laws on the subject. The federal regulations go to great lengths to avoid conflict among research laws at the various levels of government. As is mentioned in both the FDA[23] and HHS[24] regulations with respect to consent:

> . . . these regulations are not intended to preempt any applicable federal, state, or local laws which require additional information to be disclosed for informed consent to be legally effective.

Researchers, however, must still face the question of how to meet both federal and state consent requirements. In some circumstances that means dealing with a maze of regulatory and statutory interpretation.

§8.5   Overview of Drug Research Laws

Although the FDA is the principal U.S. authority for drug research and use, some states have enacted legislation on the matter.[1] Many statutes govern the use of laetrile and other

[21]See, e.g., La. Rev. Stat. Ann. §1299.35.13 (West 1981); Mo. Ann. Stat. §188.037 (Vernon 1979); Neb. Rev. Stat. §28-342 (1977).
[22]See, e.g., Ind. Code Ann. §35.1-58.5-6 (Burns 1977); Ky. Rev. Stat. §436.026 (1974); Neb. Rev. Stat. §28-342 (1981).
[23]21 C.F.R. §50.25 (1981).
[24]45 C.F.R. §46.116 (1981).
§8.5   [1]Fla. Stat. Ann. §458.333 (West 1979); Ga. Code §§84-901a et seq. (1980); Ill. Ann. Stat. ch. 56 1/2, §§1802 et seq. (Smith-Hurd 1977); Ky. Rev. Stat. §§311.950 et seq. (1980); Minn. Stat. Ann. §147.075 (West 1981).

controversial drug preparations,[2] and a few relate to controlled research with marijuana.[3] Oregon has an interesting statutory provision relating to experimental drug research that prescribes certain consent requirements.[4] Minors and incompetents may serve as research subjects providing that the requisite consent standards are met.[5]

§8.5.1 Consent Requirements

One common element found in state regulation of drug use or research with laetrile, marijuana, and other substances is the specific requirements one must meet in terms of consent. Some states have gone so far as to include a consent form in their statutes with which the actual documents should substantially agree.[6] The Oklahoma law provides an example of this statutory consent form:

WRITTEN INFORMED REQUEST FOR PRESCRIPTION OF AMYGDALIN (LAETRILE) FOR MEDICAL TREATMENT

Patient's Name: _____
Address: _____
Age: _____ Sex: _____

---

[2]Fla. Stat. Ann. §458.333 (West 1979) (laetrile); Fla. Stat. Ann. §458.335 (West 1981) (dimethyl sulfoxide [DMSO]); Ill. Ann. Stat. ch. 56 1/2, §§1802-1804 (Smith-Hurd 1977) (laetrile); Ill. Ann. Stat. ch. 56 1/2, §§1901-1906 (Smith-Hurd 1979) (chymopapain); Minn. Stat. Ann. §147.075 (West 1981) (DMSO); Okla. Stat. Ann. tit. 63, §§313.7 et seq. (West 1979) (lilium).

[3]Ga. Code §§84-901a et seq. (1980); Wash. Rev. Code Ann. §§69.51.010 et seq. (1979).

[4]Or. Rev. Stat. §§475.305 et seq. (1979).

[5]Id. at §§475.325, 475.335, 475.345, and 475.355.

[6]Ill. Ann. Stat. ch. 56 1/2, §1802.1 (Smith-Hurd 1977) (laetrile); Kan. Stat. Ann. §65-6b05 (1978) (laetrile); Okla. Stat. Ann. tit. 63 §§2-313.5, 2-313.11 (West 1977) (laetrile), and §2-31311 (West 1979) (lilium).

Name and address of prescribing physician:

_____

_____

Malignancy, diseases, illness or physical condition diagnosed for medical treatment by amygdalin (laetrile):

_____

_____

My physician has explained to me:
  (a) That the Federal Food and Drug Administration has determined amygdalin (laetrile) to be an "unapproved new drug" and that federal law prohibits the interstate distribution of an "unapproved new drug."
  (b) That neither the American Cancer Society, the American Medical Association, nor the Oklahoma State Medical Association recommends the use of amygdalin (laetrile) in the treatment of any malignancy, disease, illness or physical condition.
  (c) That there are alternative recognized treatments for the malignancy, disease, illness or physical condition from which I suffer which he has offered to provide for me including: (Here describe)

_____

_____

That notwithstanding the foregoing, I hereby request prescription and use of amygdalin (laetrile) in the medical treatment of the malignancy, disease, illness or physical condition from which I suffer.

_____
Signature of Patient

ATTEST:

_____
Prescribing Physician[7]

As seen in this brief discussion, many states have taken an active role in legislating controls for various aspects of human

[7]Okla. Stat. Ann. tit. 63, §2-313.5 (West 1979).

research. They have not been reluctant to legalize the limited use of drugs or substances which the FDA has not seen fit to approve. Yet they have imposed stricter requirements than the federal agencies in terms of certain classes of people who may participate in research projects. The federal and state activity in this field provides an interesting contrast. In the following sections of the chapter, these special groups of individuals are discussed in greater detail with an emphasis on state and federal consent requirements.

C. REPRODUCTIVE RESEARCH: SPECIAL CONSENT CONSIDERATIONS

§8.6 Research Involving Pregnant Women: Federal Consent Requirements

The HHS requirements are quite specific regarding pregnant women as research subjects. No study may be undertaken without prior work having been done on animals and nonpregnant individuals.[1] A pregnant woman is prohibited from taking part in a research study unless its purpose is the protection of the mother's health and the fetus will only be subject to the minimal risk necessary to meet the mother's health needs.[2] Alternatively, a pregnant woman may participate when the risk to the fetus is viewed as minimal.[3]

§8.6.1 IRB Responsibilities

The consent requirements for pregnant women are quite detailed and are imposed on top of the general consent regula-

§8.6 [1] 45 C.F.R. §46.206 (1980).
[2] 46 C.F.R. §46.207 (1980).
[3] Id.

tions. The institutional review board (IRB) must determine that sufficient attention has been given by the researcher to monitoring the consent process. This monitoring activity may take the form of the IRB or a subject advocate monitoring each individual's entrance into the study or random sampling. The monitoring focuses on the process of obtaining a woman's consent and may extend to on-site visits (to the source of the research activity). In this way the board determines whether any unforeseen risks have occurred.[4]

§8.6.2 Paternal Consent

Consent for a pregnant woman's participation in projects must come from both her and the biological father, if they are legally competent. They must be told of the possible effect the research will have on the fetus.[5] Exceptions are made concerning the father's consent when the purpose of the project is for the mother's health needs or the father is not available. In addition, consent of the father is not required when the pregnancy is the result of rape or when the identity or location of the father cannot be reasonably determined.[6]

§8.6.3 Waiver of Consent Provisions

The requirements for consent related to research on pregnant women may be waived or modified by the Secretary of Health and Human Services. Additional elements of the regulations' Subpart may also be avoided or amended in a given instance by the secretary.[7]

[4] 45 C.F.R. §46.205 (1980), as amended at 46 Fed. Reg. 8,386, January 26, 1981.
[5] 45 C.F.R. §46.207 (1980).
[6] Id.
[7] 45 C.F.R. §46.211 (1980).

§8.7   Research Involving Pregnant Women: State Legislation

In contrast to the federal controls relating to research directed at pregnant women, only a few state regulations refer to the subject. Most of the state legislation focuses on fetal research, leaving aside procedures carried out for the health needs of the mother. The silence of so many state laws on the issue should not be interpreted to mean that restrictions never apply. Investigators still have to meet applicable federal requirements when their work comes within the scope of HHS requirements. Otherwise they have to comply with applicable state consent laws, whether in statutory, regulatory, or case form. It is incumbent on investigators and the institutions in which they conduct their activities to familiarize themselves with applicable state and local requirements.

Massachusetts,[1] Michigan,[2] and North Dakota,[3] as part of their prohibitory fetal experimentation laws, expressly exempt diagnostic or treatment procedures that are necessary for the life or health of the mother. These exceptions do not specifically refer to clinical research of therapeutic benefit to the mother. One state law that does, however, is found in New Mexico.[4]

§8.7.1   *New Mexico: Strict Consent Requirements for Research*

Like its federal counterpart, the New Mexico statute sets forth specific requirements for consent.[5] Research can be conducted on a pregnant woman only when its purpose is to address her health needs and the fetus will be subject to the

§8.7   [1]Mass. Gen. Laws Ann. ch. 112, §12J (West 1976).
[2]Mich. Comp. Laws §333.2686 (1980).
[3]N.D. Cent. Code §14-02.2-01 (1975).
[4]N.M. Stat. Ann. §§24-9A-1 to 24-9A-7 (1979).
[5]Id. at §24-9A-5.

smallest degree of risk necessary to meet the objective. Alternatively, the research can be carried out when there is no significant risk of harm to the fetus. Due to the consent requirements in the law, the statute excludes legally incompetent pregnant women from participating as research subjects. The woman must be told of the possible effect the research may have upon the fetus prior to her giving informed consent.[6]

§8.7.2 Dual Impact of State and Federal Laws

Unlike the federal law, those state statutes that have taken a position on pregnant women as research subjects are not detailed in their consent requirements. New Mexico is an exception, but even that state does not require the consent of the father of the fetus prior to conducting research on the mother. To this extent, the federal law is more stringent than its state counterparts. This difference is perhaps a reflection of the fact that most _research_ directed at pregnant women — as distinct from diagnostic or therapeutic interventions — comes under federal regulations. When this is the case, researchers must be prepared to face considerable examination by an institutional review board.

The IRB is responsible for certifying that a research protocol meets minimum federal requirements. Two different sets of regulations on consent apply to pregnant women as research subjects.[7] All the requisite elements must be met prior to the IRB's approving the study. The IRB's role does not stop at this point. Through its own auspices or through the vehicle of subject advocates, it may monitor the consent process to be assured that the investigator is in compliance with applicable requirements.

The heightened regulatory intensity surrounding pregnant women as research subjects is a reflection of federal concern

---

[6]Id. at §24-9A-2.
[7]45 C.F.R. §46.116 (1981) and §46.207 (1980).

about one class of individuals. It is a signal to IRBs and investigators alike that they must be particularly diligent when pregnant women are involved as research subjects.

§8.8 Federal Constraints on Fetal Research

As for pregnant women, the HHS regulations have three sets of consent requirements that apply to fetal research. These include the general elements of consent[1] and other separate provisions found in the section on fetal experimentation.[2] No research activity can be carried out on a fetus unless prior adequate animal studies have been considered, along with research on nonpregnant individuals. Procedures may be carried out to meet the health needs of the fetus, but the risk to the fetus should be minimal or involve the least possible risk for reaching the purpose of the study.[3]

§8.8.1 IRB Responsibilities

The IRB has additional responsibilities when a project involves fetal research. It must determine that the investigator has made adequate arrangements for monitoring the consent process. This monitoring may take the form of participation by the IRB, or subject advocates may observe the consent process for each subject or sample the process in a number of instances. The IRB may also monitor the progress of the study and continue evaluation to determine if unanticipated risks have arisen.[4]

§8.8 [1]45 C.F.R. §46.116 (1981).
[2]45 C.F.R. §§46.208-209 (1980).
[3]45 C.F.R. §46.206 (1980).
[4]45 C.F.R. §46.205 (1980), as amended at 46 Fed. Reg. 8,386, January 26, 1981.

§8.8.2   *Fetal Research In Utero*

The use of fetuses in utero as research subjects is strictly limited. According to the HHS regulations, the only time a fetus in utero may be involved is when:

(1) The purpose of the activity is to meet the health needs of the particular fetus and the fetus will be placed at risk only to the minimum extent necessary to meet such needs, or (2) the risk to the fetus imposed by the research is minimal and the purpose of the activity is the development of important biomedical knowledge which cannot be obtained by other means.[5]

The federal regulations stipulate that the research can only be carried out when the parents of the fetus are legally competent and have given their informed consent. The consent of the father is not necessary when his identity or location cannot be reasonably determined or he is not reasonably available. The father's permission is also not necessary if the pregnancy is the result of rape.[6]

§8.8.3   *Fetal Research Ex Utero*

A different regulation governs research on fetuses ex utero. The requirements under this section are quite detailed and distinctions are drawn between viable and nonviable fetuses. Unless it is known whether a fetus ex utero is viable, it may not be involved in any research governed by the regulations. Two exceptions, however, provide partial relief from this total prohibition. Research may be conducted if:

(1) There will be no added risk to the fetus resulting from the activity, and the purpose of the activity is the development of important biomedical knowledge which cannot be obtained by

[5]45 C.F.R. §46.208 (1980).
[6]Id.

other means, or (2) The purpose of the activity is to enhance the possibility of survival of the particular fetus to the point of viability.[7]

a. Nonviable fetuses. Different requirements pertain to nonviable fetuses ex utero. Research may be carried out, but only when certain conditions are met: the vital functions of a fetus must not be sustained artificially, experimental activities that would stop the fetal heartbeat or respiration may not be used,[8] and the purpose of the research must be to develop "important biomedical knowledge which cannot be obtained by other means."[9]

b. Viable fetuses. When a fetus ex utero is found to be viable, it may be involved as a research subject — but only to the extent permitted by other provisions "in accordance with the requirements of other subparts of this part."[10] No further elaboration is provided in the regulation; what is permissible is left as a matter of interpretation.

c. Parental consent requirements. When it is uncertain whether a fetus ex utero is viable or when it is known that the fetus is nonviable, research may only be conducted if the mother and father are legally competent and they both give their informed consent. However, the provisions requiring the father's consent is excused in the three situations described above with respect to in utero fetal research.[11]

§8.8.4 *Exceptions to Federal Control*

Federal regulations do not control research activities involving dead fetuses or fetal material, cells, or tissue. This authority

---

[7] 45 C.F.R. §46.209 (1980).
[8] Id.
[9] Id.
[10] Id.
[11] Id.

is left to state and local governments.[12] Federal requirements for fetal research may be waived or modified by the Secretary of Health and Human Services. The conditions under which such action may be taken, however, are limited. Any modifications or waivers granted by the secretary must be published as notices in the Federal Register.[13]

§8.9   State Laws on Fetal Research

A great disparity separates state regulations for fetal research and experimentation. The most detailed requirements have been set by Massachusetts and by New Mexico as part of its Maternal, Fetal, and Infant law.[1] The New Mexico statutes are quite similar to the federal regulations on the subject, while the Massachusetts law is quite different. Other states have imposed far less exacting standards.

One common type of statute prohibits the sale, use of, or experimentation on any live or viable fetus who is or was the subject of an abortion.[2] An exception may be found where the proposed activity is to promote the life or health of the fetus[3] or its mother.[4] A few states do not base the permissibility of fetal research on whether or not an abortion is planned or was performed. The sale, use of, or experimentation on live human fetuses is often prohibited in these states.[5] However, exceptions are made for research or experimentation to protect the health or life of the fetus.[6]

---

[12]45 C.F.R. §46.210 (1980).

[13]45 C.F.R. §46.211 (1980).

§8.9   [1]Mass. Gen. Laws Ann. ch. 112, §12J (West 1976); N.M. Stat. Ann. §§24-9A-1 et seq. (1979).

[2]See, e.g., Ill. Ann. Stat. ch. 38, §81-26 (Smith-Hurd 1985); Mo. Ann. Stat. §188.037 (Vernon 1979); Okla. Stat. Ann. tit. 63, §1-735 (West 1978).

[3]Id.

[4]Mich. Comp. Laws §333.2685 (1980).

[5]See, e.g., Minn. Stat. Ann. §145.422 (West 1984); N.D. Cent. Code §14-02.2-01 (1975).

[6]Id.

In Illinois the same stringent controls regarding experimentation do not apply when the subject of the study is a fetus whose death did not result from an abortion.[7] Other states do not deny permission for research on the basis of fetal death resulting from abortion.[8] Consent, however, is still required prior to using fetal remains for research or experimentation. Depending on the state, that consent must come either from the mother[9] or from either of the parents of the fetus.[10]

Another notable point is that some jurisdictions do not distinguish between fetal research on live and dead fetuses. Consent remains, though, as a prerequisite to conducting such studies.[11] In contrast, some states do not generally require consent for routine pathological analysis.[12]

§8.9.1 The Massachusetts Example

As noted earlier, the most detailed state statutes on fetal research are found in Massachusetts and New Mexico. In Massachusetts fetal research procedures are not completely prohibited. Permitted activities are nevertheless limited to diagnostic and remedial procedures designed to determine the life or health status of the fetus or to preserve the life or health of either the fetus or its mother.[13] Procedures described as "incident to a study of a human fetus while it is in its mother's

---

[7]Ill. Ann. Stat. ch. 38, §81-26 (Smith-Hurd 1985) and §81-32.1 (Smith-Hurd 1980).

[8]See, e.g., Mass. Gen. Laws Ann. ch. 112, §12J (West 1976); N.D. Cent. Code §14-02.2 (1975).

[9]Mass. Gen. Laws Ann. ch. 112, §12J (West 1976); N.D. Cent. Code §14-02.2-02 (1975).

[10]Ill. Ann. Stat. ch. 38, §81-26 (Smith-Hurd 1979) and §81-32.1 (Smith-Hurd 1980).

[11]S.D. Codified Laws Ann. §34-23A-17 (1973); Tenn. Code Ann. §39-308 (1979).

[12]Ind. Code Ann. §35.1-58.5-6 (Burns 1977) (applies to aborted fetuses only); Mich. Comp. Laws §333.2688 (1980); N.D. Cent. Code §14-02.2-02 (1975).

[13]Mass. Gen. Laws Ann. ch. 112, §12J(a) I (West 1976).

womb"[14] are also allowed, providing the fetus is not a subject of a planned abortion. Moreover, the study should not substantially threaten the life or health of the fetus.[15]

  a. Criminal penalties and prior judicial review. Like the laws in some other states,[16] the Massachusetts statute provides for criminal sanctions for failure to meet its requirements.[17] A specific defense is provided in the law for research conducted with the written approval of an institutional review board.[18] Another mechanism built into the statute may avert criminal challenges. Under this provision, a determination may be sought from the state superior court as to whether the activity violates the statute. A judicial decision can be requested regardless of approval of the study by an IRB;[19] furthermore, an appeal is possible to the Supreme Judicial Court of Massachusetts.[20] If the court finds that the procedure violates the statute, notice of this fact is to appear in newspapers of general circulation and the district attorney is to send notification to each of the licensed hospitals and medical schools in the state by registered or certified mail.[21]

  b. Maternal consent to research on a dead fetus. The same type of restrictions do not apply with respect to experimentation on a dead fetus. Still, the consent of the mother must be obtained.[22] When a criminal challenge arises, the consent of the

[14]Id.
[15]Id.
[16]See, e.g., Ky. Rev. Stat. §436.026 (1974); Me. Rev. Stat. Ann. tit. 22, §1593 (1978); Tenn. Code Ann. §39-308 (1979).
[17]Mass. Gen. Laws Ann. ch. 112, §12J(a) V (West 1976).
[18]Id. at §12J(a) VI. The IRB must, however, meet other statutory requirements for its approval to serve as a complete defense. For example, the IRB must include a statement in its written approval that the procedure does not violate the terms of the statute, along with a reasonable ground for this conclusion, and that no judgment of a court was outstanding that held the procedure a violation of the statute.
[19]Id. at (b) II.
[20]Id. at (b) VI.
[21]Id. at (b) VII.
[22]Id. at (a) II.

mother is conclusively presumed to have been granted if the mother is at least 18 years old and the consent is in writing. Her authorization would take the form of an agreement to the use of the fetus "for scientific, laboratory, research or other kinds of experimentation or study,"[23] and it would also permit transfer of the dead fetus.[24]

§8.9.2 The New Mexico Approach

The statutory framework in New Mexico is quite different from that in Massachusetts. A fetus may serve as a research subject as long as the procedure fosters its health needs. Furthermore, the fetus can be subjected to only the minimal amount of risk required to carry out the activity. Research that imposes no significant risk is also permissible.[25] No activity can be undertaken, however, unless the mother of the fetus is legally competent and she has given informed consent for the research.[26]

A similar statutory provision applies to research on live-born infants. That research may only be carried out when adults or mentally competent persons are not suitable subjects and informed consent has been obtained from the mentally competent mother, father, or legal guardian of the infant.[27]

No research can be carried out on fetuses or live-born infants unless certain prerequisites are met.[28] Among these is that appropriate work must have been carried out on animals and nonpregnant human beings.[29]

The New Mexico statute also specifies requirements for consent.[30] The person from whom permission is to be obtained

---

[23] Id.
[24] Id.
[25] N.M. Stat. Ann. §29-9A-3 (1979).
[26] Id.
[27] Id. at §24-9A-4 (1979).
[28] Id. at §24-9A-5 (1979).
[29] Id.
[30] Id.

must be given an explanation of the procedures to be used and the purposes of each. Any experimental procedures must also be identified. Any discomforts or risks that can be reasonably expected and that are associated with the activity must be disclosed, along with any benefits. A description is to be given of any alternate procedures that may be advantageous to the subject. Whoever is obtaining the consent must offer to respond to any inquiries regarding the activity. Finally, the person giving consent must be told that he or she may withdraw consent and that participation in the project may be discontinued at any time without prejudice to the research subject.[31]

§8.9.3 *Effect of Federal and State Fetal Research Laws*

Unlike in other areas of human research, the state laws governing fetuses as subjects do not place limits on the scope of jurisdiction. For example, in California under its general human research statute, projects conducted in accordance with federal requirements are exempted from the state law.[32] On the other hand, the federal government *has* included such a limitation in its regulations, effectively giving the states wide discretion for imposing fetal research limitations.[33] In at least one instance this has proven problematic. Louisiana's abortion statute was declared unconstitutionally vague because it prohibited experimentation on unborn children or children born as a result of an abortion.[34] The court reasoned that the legislation failed to distinguish between medical experimentation and practice.

The state requirements, although concerned with consent to some degree, are more attentive to extraneous matters. Whether or not the fetus upon whom research is proposed is the subject of a planned abortion is an important consideration

---

[31] Id.
[32] Cal. Health & Safety Code §§24170 et seq. (West 1978).
[33] 45 C.F.R. §46.201 (1980).
[34] See Margaret S. v. Edwards, 794 F.2d 994 (5th Cir. 1986).

in some statutes. Criminal sanctions are another concern of some of the state laws, an element that is not often found in legislative controls on human research.

Both the federal and state laws reflect a deep sensitivity toward the vulnerability of fetuses as research subjects. Measured against that interest is a desire not to thwart all research activities involving fetuses. Balancing both interests is difficult, as evinced by the current body of state and federal laws on the subject.

An important task for institutional review boards and researchers alike is to become familiar with federal as well as state research requirements. All consent criteria must be met and no undue influence should be used or inducement offered to encourage participation.[35] The IRBs must also satisfy the additional federal requirements for monitoring or sampling the consent process. A policy should be developed for carrying out this responsibility.

There is no way of predicting whether the present set of controls will become more or less strict with the passage of time. Any serious research infractions, however, will likely motivate calls for further limitations. To the extent that this trend is valid, it should serve as a source of encouragement to researchers to meet applicable consent requirements and other criteria. Adherence to the laws may also be persuasive in relaxing the current state of legislative and regulatory controls.

Only Massachusetts has a built-in mechanism for determining whether a particular research activity would violate applicable state laws: a declaratory judgment issued by a court of law.[36] In states with criminal sanctions, it may be possible to seek declaratory judgments regarding the legality of a particular protocol. The courts, however, may be reluctant to intercede and make a determination. Furthermore, having to go to court for approval of research projects will only slow down or delay

---

[35] See, e.g., 45 C.F.R. §46.206 (1980); Mass. Gen. Laws Ann. ch. 112, §12J (West 1976); Mich. Comp. Laws §333.2689 (1980); N.M. Stat. Ann. §24-9A-5 (1979).

[36] Mass. Gen. Laws Ann. ch. 112, §12J (West 1976).

the research and it may be costly. The law also shifts a very important decision-making process out of an otherwise satisfactory arena.

No enterprise, be it medical or otherwise, can be guaranteed freedom from civil or criminal liability. Ultimately, the researcher or the IRB must still assume responsibility. On the federal level, prohibitory regulations may be waived or modified by the Secretary of the Department of Health and Human Services. To some extent such action will remove doubts about the applicability of the federal requirements. The researcher, however, is still not insulated from applicable legal obligations. His actions will be measured by state and federal requirements as well as by common law principles for human research. Adhering to these legislative and regulatory controls and case precedents is the best way to avoid legal entanglements. The issue of consent remains among the key elements of concern in this regard.

§8.10 Federal Laws Governing In Vitro Fertilization Research

The federal regulations on human research promulgated by the Department of Health and Human Services control research with human in vitro fertilization.[1] This regulation is part of the same subsection that governs research on pregnant women and fetuses. A distinction, however, is made among these categories: no specific section controlling consent is found in the regulations for in vitro fertilization. In vitro fertilization research is mentioned in the definition section of the regulations and includes:

> any fertilization of human ova which occurs outside the body of a female, either through admixture of donor human sperm and ova or by any other means.[2]

§8.10 [1]45 C.F.R. §46.201 (1980).
[2]45 C.F.R. §46.203 (1980).

§8.10.1 Lack of Specific Consent Requirements

The absence in the regulations of any specific consent requirements for in vitro fertilization does not mean that certain standards are not applicable. The general elements of consent found throughout the HHS regulations would apply to in vitro fertilization,[3] as would the general limitations found in the subpart on pregnant women, fetuses, and in vitro fertilization to the extent that these restrictions are relevant.[4]

§8.10.2 Authority of the Secretary and Ethical Advisory Boards

The Secretary of Health and Human Services may establish ethical advisory boards to advise him on ethical issues raised by research on pregnant women, fetuses, and in vitro fertilization. Their advisory capacity may extend to proposals for guidelines, general policies, and procedures. If the secretary approves, an advisory board can be empowered to establish categories of proposals that require advisory board review prior to federal funding.

Each in vitro fertilization must be reviewed by an ethical advisory board for ethical acceptability.[5] This limitation is the most exacting in the regulations for in vitro fertilization. Since the role of a board is advisory, its decision is not necessarily binding upon the secretary, but the ethical advisory board can be very persuasive since no in vitro fertilization research can be funded by HHS until it has been reviewed by such a body.[6]

Given the advisory board's potential role, it may advise the secretary on general policies, procedures, and guidelines for certain categories of applications. The advisory board may possibly exercise this power in the case of in vitro fertilization.

[3] 45 C.F.R. §46.116 (1980).
[4] 45 C.F.R. §46.206 (1980).
[5] 45 C.F.R. §46.204 (1980).
[6] Id.

Taken together with the board's responsibility for assessing from an ethical standpoint in vitro fertilization research, such projects could come under close scrutiny.

The major drawback to the present state of federal regulations on in vitro fertilization research is the ad hoc nature in which reviews are made by an advisory board. An applicant may have no idea as to the criteria upon which the board bases its assessment. There are no set criteria in the regulations and the board is not required to establish any. If the board should determine that a protocol does not measure up to its ethical standards, however, an applicant does have an avenue of relief. The final decision on whether to fund — and therefore to go ahead with — the project lies with the secretary. Since a board's opinion is advisory, the secretary could reject it. With the increasing interest surrounding in vitro fertilization it is possible that the secretary will recommend specific regulations. If this should occur, researchers should examine the proposals carefully and provide commentary and recommendations prior to the regulations becoming final.

§8.11   State Laws Governing In Vitro Fertilization Research

The states do not appear to be as interested in controlling in vitro fertilization as they do fetal experimentations. Only a small number of states have legislation on the subject.[1] The statutes in at least three states make reference to in vitro fertilization in their fetal experimentation laws.[2] There are no specific consent requirements attached to in vitro fertilization research in Illinois.

§8.11   [1] Ill. Ann. Stat. ch. 38, §81-26 (Smith-Hurd 1985); Minn. Stat. Ann. §145.421 (West 1983) (the statute includes in its definition of human conceptus "any human organism . . . produced in an artificial environment other than the human body . . . ," which seems to include in vitro fertilization); N.M. Stat. Ann. §24-9A-1 (1979).
[2] See references in n.1.

In Minnesota the restrictions on in vitro fertilization do not apply unless the human conceptus is living. As defined in the act, living means "the presence of evidence of life, such as movement, heart or respiratory activity, the presence of electroencephalographic or electrocardiographic activity."[3] Research or experimentation on a living human conceptus, as thus defined, can take place as long as scientific evidence has demonstrated the activity to be without risk of harm. An individual may not buy or sell a living human conceptus, but nothing in the law prohibits the purchasing or sale of cell culture from a nonliving human conceptus.[4] Nothing in the statute refers to specific consent requirements for in vitro fertilization research.

In its definition of clinical research the New Mexico law includes human in vitro fertilization.[5] As in the federal regulations, however, no specific consent provision applies. Once conceived, the product of in vitro fertilization by definition comes under the constraints for fetal research.[6] Consent requirements and other provisions relating to permissible research activities in this area would then apply.[7]

At least three states with general human research laws have not included in them specific references to in vitro fertilization.[8] For example, in California the closest reference to the subject is found in the requirements for research on fetal remains. Once an in vitro fertilization process results in conception, presumably the fetal legal requirements would apply.[9]

The absence in most states of statutory controls on in vitro fertilization research does not mean that certain standards are not applicable. When projects are federally funded, HHS regulations apply. When they are conducted without federal re-

[3] Minn. Stat. Ann. §145.421 (West 1973).
[4] Id.
[5] N.M. Stat. Ann. §24-9A-1 (1979).
[6] Id.
[7] Id. at §24-9A-3 and §24-9A-5 (1979).
[8] Cal. Health & Safety Code §§24170 et seq. (West 1978); N.Y. Pub. Health Law §§2440 et seq. (McKinney 1975); Va. Code §§37.1-234 et seq. (1979).
[9] Cal. Health & Safety Code §25956 (West 1973).

sources, the researcher has to conduct the studies in accordance with generally accepted standards of care for such research. In addition, she has to meet applicable requirements for consent. Into this category falls the disclosure to the prospective parents of the nature and purpose of the process and the likely results, benefits, risks, and availability, if any, of alternative means of achieving conception. The researcher then has to respond to any questions posed by the couple. Consent should come from both the prospective mother and father since both are contributing to the process.

Once in vitro fertilization becomes established as a common technique for human conception, its higher standards of care and consent requirement may be reduced. Until that time such a fertilization technique should be treated as a novel process, and the researcher should conduct himself accordingly.

§8.12 Impact of Governmental Controls on In Vitro Fertilization Research

Neither the federal nor state regulations governing in vitro fertilization research have any specific provisions regarding consent. Once the process has been completed successfully, however, it is possible that other regulations governing fetal research apply. As discussed in the sections on fetal research and experimentation, there are consent requirements that must be met.

In the absence of federal regulatory or state statutory controls that precisely govern in vitro fertilization, researchers should review other applicable consent laws. On the federal level, this search would include the general elements of consent set out by HHS in its regulations. On the state level might be found statutory consent requirements as well as pertinent case law.

Consent should be documented in accordance with either federal or state regulations. As opposed to the research that must follow federal consent regulations, studies under state jurisdiction may not be subject to any specified statutory or regulatory documentation requirements. Customary standards for documenting consent should then be followed, with any necessary modifications being added to take into consideration the experimental or research nature of the study.

Although some federal and state controls are becoming apparent in the field of in vitro fertilization research, further requirements should be anticipated. As certain practices become established as accepted medical procedures, however, these controls will not be applicable. In the interim, researchers must conduct themselves in accordance with applicable state and federal controls. Consent should be obtained carefully and documented in a manner that best ensures the rights of all concerned.

D. MINORS AS RESEARCH SUBJECTS

§8.13 1983 Federal Requirements

In June 1983 a new series of human research regulations governing minors was implemented by the Department of Health and Human Services.[1] The regulations represent a marked departure from the department's prior stance on the use of children in human research. In the past, the department's position on the subject was unclear, although a proposed set of rules had been put forth in 1978.[2] Based on the response to the 1978 proposals and the 1981 HHS policy implemented regarding adult human subjects, the new regulations were promulgated.[3]

The new regulations cover studies involving children as research subjects either conducted by HHS or funded by the department. The requirements have far-reaching effect, gov-

§8.13 [1] 45 C.F.R. Part 46, Subpart D.
[2] See 43 Fed. Reg. 31,786 (July 21, 1978).
[3] 48 Fed. Reg. 9,814, 9,815 (March 8, 1983).

erning studies carried out in the United States and abroad,[4] and recognize four possible categories in which children may participate as research subjects. These include:

1. Studies involving no more than minimal risk;[5]
2. Studies involving more than minimal risk with the prospect of direct benefit to the child;[6]
3. Studies involving more than minimal risk, with no direct benefit, but offering the prospect of "generalizable knowledge,"[7] and,
4. Studies that would otherwise not receive approval that could lead to the understanding, prevention, or alleviation of a "serious problem" affecting children's health or welfare.[8]

The new regulations affecting children also set forth provisions for permission by parents or guardians as well as the "assent" of the research subjects themselves.[9] Children who are wards of a state or an agency may also take part in human research activities in accordance with the requirements of a separate provision.[10]

The categories in which children may participate as research subjects require careful analysis and discussion by the membership of institutional review boards. Assessing what is minimal risk is no easy task. Meeting the conditions for research offering no direct benefit to a subject is equally difficult. HHS has spent considerable time developing the criteria for research in each of the four permissible categories, yet the terms of reference are vague and open to a variety of interpretations and applications, depending upon the type of studies involved and the philosophy of the institutional review boards. The new reg-

[4] 45 C.F.R. §46.401 (1983).
[5] 45 C.F.R. §46.404 (1983).
[6] 45 C.F.R. §46.405 (1983).
[7] 45 C.F.R. §46.406 (1983).
[8] 45 C.F.R. §46.407 (1983).
[9] 45 C.F.R. §46.408 (1983).
[10] 45 C.F.R. §46.409 (1983).

ulations may prove unworkable; institutional review boards across the country have their work cut out for them.

§8.13.1 Relationship to Other HHS Regulations

The regulations concerning children make it clear that certain exemptions applicable to adults also apply to minors.[11] Thus, research involving normal education practices, educational tests, and the collection or analysis of existing data are exempted from the requirements of the federal regulations, providing all conditions for these exclusions are met.[12] Research involving children that focuses on the observation of public behavior is also excluded, as long as the researcher or investigator does not take part in the activities under observation.[13]

In one instance, however, an exemption applicable to adults does not apply to children. Projects utilizing survey or interview techniques must be reviewed by an institutional review board in accordance with federal regulations.[14]

§8.13.2 Children and Permission for Research

A curious aspect of the regulations governing children is that parental or guardian authorization is cast in terms of "permission" rather than consent. Indeed, in the definition section, the terms *permission* and *assent* have been defined.[15] The significance of these definitions cannot be minimized, given the lengths to which consent requirements are spelled out for adults. The new subpart governing children as research subjects perhaps reflects a concern that children participate in the decision-making process. Whether the permission-assent provi-

[11]45 C.F.R. §46.401 (1983), referring to 45 C.F.R. §46.101 (1981).
[12]Id.
[13]Id.
[14]Id.
[15]45 C.F.R. §46.402 (1983).

sions are adequate to safeguard the rights of children against parental influence, and whether children have the ability to appreciate the nature and consequences of their assent, remains to be seen.

Permission for children to participate as research subjects must be obtained from parents or legal guardians.[16] The requirements for parental or guardian permission must be consistent with the regulations on consent found elsewhere in the rules relating to adult research subjects.[17] Each IRB must decide whether the authorization of one parent is sufficient for studies either involving minimal risk to the child or, when greater than minimal risk is involved, offering the prospect of direct benefit to the research subject.[18] Both parents must give their permission when a research study offers only the prospect of generalizable knowledge in the face of greater than minimal risk.[19] The same is true of studies that may lead to the understanding, prevention, or alleviation of serious difficulties affecting the welfare or health of children.[20] Even the requirement of permission from both parents, however, may be waived when one of them is incompetent, deceased, or not reasonably available, or when one parent has legal custody of the child.[21]

The requirement for parental permission may be waived in some cases when to do so is consistent with federal, state, and local law.[22] As stated in the regulations, this waiver would happen when an IRB finds that:

[a] research protocol is designed for conditions or for a subject population for which parental or guardian permission is not a reasonable requirement to protect the subjects (for example, neglected or abused children). . . .[23]

[16]45 C.F.R. §46.408 (1983).
[17]Id., referring to 45 C.F.R. §46.116 of Subpart A.
[18]45 C.F.R. §46.408 (1983).
[19]Id.
[20]Id.
[21]Id.
[22]Id.
[23]Id.

If the waiver is applied, a suitable substitute must be found to safeguard the children who will take part as research subjects. What is deemed a sufficient alternative will vary, depending upon the nature of the study and the anticipated risks and benefits, as well as the age, condition, maturity, and status of the subjects.[24]

§8.13.3 Children's Assent to Research

When an IRB determines that a child is capable of giving assent to participating in human research, provision must be made for obtaining the child's agreement.[25] The regulations do not specify *how* an IRB is to go about this task — and thus, considerable authority is left to each institutional review board. This lack of uniformity may also signal widespread variation in methods of obtaining the assent of minors, which could prove problematic in those studies involving a multitude of institutions. If each IRB has its own, unique requirements, interinstitutional differences could possibly frustrate or even thwart the research involving children. To avert such difficulties, each IRB must carefully consider what is required, at a minimum, to ensure that a child's assent is obtained. If, over time, institutional differences cannot be overcome, HHS may have to step in and promulgate regulations that provide for uniformity in seeking the assent of minors.

In considering whether minors are capable of giving their assent to human research, the regulations suggest that the IRB examine:

1. the age of the child;
2. the maturity of the child, and
3. the psychological state of the child.[26]

[24] Id.
[25] Id.
[26] Id.

This assessment may be made on an individual basis or for children as a group, depending on the determination of the IRB. When children are considered incapable of giving assent or when a procedure holds the prospect of direct benefit that is available only in a research setting, the regulations indicate that assent is not a necessary prerequisite.[27]

Even if children are deemed capable of giving assent, the requirement for obtaining their agreement may be waived under those circumstances recognized for waiver of consent for adults.[28] Included here are those projects that could not practicably be carried out without the waiver, in which no more than minimal risk is incurred by research subjects, and in which the waiver will not adversely affect the welfare or rights of the subjects.[29]

§8.13.4 *Wards as Research Subjects*

The HHS regulations make it clear that under certain circumstances, wards of a state, an agency, or institution may serve as research subjects.[30] They may be included in those studies involving greater than minimal risk that hold the prospect of generalizable knowledge or that offer the chance for an understanding or the prevention or alleviation of serious problems affecting children. However, research proceeding in these circumstances must either be related to the children's status as wards or be carried out in hospitals, institutions, or similar situations in which the majority of children serving as research subjects are *not* wards.[31]

When such a project receives IRB approval, an advocate must be appointed for each child who is a ward. This appointment must take place even when another person is serving as guardian or in loco parentis with a child.[32] The regulations go

[27] Id.
[28] Id., referring to 45 C.F.R. §46.116 of Subpart A.
[29] 45 C.F.R. §46.116 (1981).
[30] 45 C.F.R. §46.409 (1983).
[31] Id.
[32] Id.

further and set requirements for the advocate. An advocate must be able to act in the best interests of the ward during the course of the research. Moreover, the advocate cannot be associated with the research project, the investigators, or the guardian association of the ward.[33]

§8.13.5 Additional Requirements

In the 1981 revision of the adult human research regulations, provision was made for expedited review of projects involving certain types of procedures that entail no more than minimal risk.[34] Included in this category are collecting such material as hair and nail clippings, bodily excretions, and dental plaque.[35]

In at least two circumstances, however, expedited review clearly cannot be used with persons less than 18 years of age. These exceptions are venipuncture not exceeding stated amounts and certain types of noninvasive techniques such as EEGs and ECGs. However, it would not include the use of X-rays or microwaves.[36] Similar requirements are found in FDA regulations issued in 1981.[37]

Expedited review of protocols involving minors should not present any difficulty. The matter should be approached as it is with adults — except that, in the case of children, expedited review may not be used in the categories described above.

§8.13.6 FDA Research and Children

Unlike HHS, the FDA has not issued any specific regulations on human research involving children. This situation may

[33] Id.
[34] See 45 C.F.R. §46.110 (1981) and Notice, 46 Fed. Reg. 8,392 (January 26, 1981).
[35] Id.
[36] Id.
[37] See 21 C.F.R. §56.110 (1981) and Notice, 46 Fed. Reg. 8,390 (January 27, 1981).

change if FDA promulgates its own requirements. Until that time, however, care must be taken to apply all FDA requirements in a strict fashion. Of particular concern is the matter of consent and the recognized exceptions to these requirements.[38]

The FDA regulations are not designed to thwart human research involving any particular group of research subjects. Children are no exception in this regard. However, because a minor may not be capable of giving consent and because parents may not give a thoroughly *informed* consent or act in a child's best interests, there is cause for concern. Research protocols involving children should be reviewed carefully to make certain that adequate provision is made for consent and that the consent of research subjects or their legal representatives is obtained freely, without suggestion of undue influence or coercion. Care should also be taken in the documentation of consent, to substantiate that the authorization obtained met all applicable consent requirements.

§8.14   State Laws

Few states have statutes that explicitly apply to minors.[1] It is far more common to find references to minors as research subjects in laws relating to general experiment or research requirements,[2] or laws designed to protect certain categories of people.[3]

§8.14.1   General Provisions

In the general laws on human research, various approaches have been taken with respect to minors. California, for ex-

---

[38]See 21 C.F.R. §§50.20, 50.23, 50.25, and 50.27 (1981), and discussion supra at §8.2.

§8.14 [1]See, e.g., Cal. Health & Safety Code §26668.4 (West 1978).

[2]N.Y. Pub. Health Law §2444 (McKinney 1975); Va. Code §37.1-235 (1979).

[3]See S.D. Codified Laws Ann. §27B-8-20 (1975) (mentally retarded persons); Wyo. Stat. §9-6-672 (1981) (residents at a training school).

ample, requires that consent be obtained in accordance with its statutory requirements before prescription or use of an experimental drug.[4] The consent must be obtained from a parent or guardian of a minor, and in addition, the minor must also give consent if she is 7 years of age or older.[5] The consent, as well as the experimental activity, must be reviewed for acceptability by a human protection committee.[6]

In New York under that state's general human research laws, no specific consent provision applies to minors. They are treated as any other research subjects, except that consent for a minor must be subscribed to in writing either by a parent or legal guardian.[7] Prior to any research taking place involving minors, the human research review committee and the commissioner must also give their consent to activities involving minors.[8]

Under the Virginia provisions on human research, an approach is taken similar to that in California. Voluntary informed consent must be given in writing by both minors and their legally authorized representatives. Minors' consent is required if they are "otherwise capable of rendering voluntary informed consent."[9] Legally authorized representatives may not agree to nontherapeutic research unless the human research review committee finds that it will not represent a hazardous risk of harm to the subjects.[10]

§8.14.2 Institutionalized and Mentally Handicapped Minors

Of particular concern are children who are institutionalized and who are called upon to serve as research subjects. In the

[4]Cal. Health & Safety Code §26668.3 (West 1978), referring to §§24170 et seq.
[5]Cal. Health & Safety Code §26668.4 (West 1978).
[6]Cal. Health & Safety Code §26668.6 (West 1978).
[7]N.Y. Pub. Health Law §2442 (McKinney 1975).
[8]N.Y. Pub. Health Law §2444 (McKinney 1975).
[9]Va. Code §37.1-235 (1979).
[10]Id.

states without human research laws, protection for minors in this category may be found in statutory bills of rights[11] or other provisions that safeguard the well-being of such individuals.[12] In Wyoming, for example, in a statue regarding training school residents, a list of rights includes a reference to human research. It provides that a resident has:

> the right to refuse to be subjected to experimental medical or psychological research without the express and informed consent of the resident or his parent or guardian *if he is a minor.*[13] (Emphasis added.)

Similar provisions may be found in laws protecting the mentally ill and retarded as well as the developmentally disabled. However, these laws may or may not refer directly to minors. In South Dakota, minors are singled out in such legislation. When a mentally ill patient is less than 18 years of age, informed consent must be obtained from the parent who has legal custody prior to participation in any experimental research.[14] If any procedure intended to induce convulsions or coma is to be used and is considered advisable for the patient, a court may grant permission if no one eligible to consent is available.[15] Another provision states, however, that no experimental research may be carried out unless it has been approved by the board of charities and corrections.[16] A similar statutory scheme applies to mentally retarded persons, including minors.[17]

§8.14.3 Parental Consent as a Safeguard

Whether or not a state has legislation or regulations for the protection of minors in research, requiring parental or guard-

[11]Wyo. Stat. §9-6-672 (1981).
[12]S.D. Codified Laws Ann. §27A-12-20 (1975), §273-8-20 (1975).
[13]Wyo. Stat. §9-6-672 (1981).
[14]S.D. Codified Laws Ann. §27A-12-20 (1975).
[15]Id.
[16]S.D. Codified Laws Ann. §27A-12-21 (1975).
[17]S.D. Codified Laws Ann. §§27B-8-20 and 27B-8-21 (1975).

ian consent is not always an adequate safeguard. Parents are presumed at law to act in the best interests of their children, but this presumption does not apply in all cases. Parents may themselves be the subjects of undue incentives to permit their children to participate in research. Perhaps they see no reasonable alternative to trying a novel or untried technique. Alternatively they might allow an experimental procedure to be carried out on healthy children for the benefit of a sick sibling. At other times parents or guardians do not understand fully the nature or purpose of the experiment. Reasons such as these fall short of truly informed consent for a minor to participate in research. The rights of the minor thus go unprotected.

If in fact parents were not allowed to consent to their minor children's participation as research subjects, who would make the decision? Should a minor who is competent to make other decisions make the determination? Should it be left to a human subject research committee or a court? Should it be a combination of decision-making bodies?

§8.14.4 Minors' Capability to Give Consent

Minors may or may not be able to make a proper choice. They may be subject to peer pressure or other influences to participate. On the other hand, a minor suffering from leukemia at the age of 12 may be in a better position than his parents to decide whether he should take part in drug research. The research committee may be so bogged down in reviewing protocols that it would not adequately consider the peculiar aspects of each case. In an overseeing position, however, it may be able to pinpoint when flaws occur in the consent process and prevent participation by a minor. Courts would certainly be a fine forum for assuring a person of her procedural and substantive rights. But should research be subject to adversarial proceedings?

Attempts to resolve these issues should take into consideration the nature and purpose of the consent process in the human research setting. All the traditional criteria for consent must be met. A potential subject should be told about the purpose of the project, its attendant risks and benefits, reasonable alternative procedures (if it is therapeutic research), and any other information significant or material to the individual's decision. Disclosure should be in terms understandable to the subject. He must be legally and mentally capable of giving consent, and no undue influence or coercion should be used to obtain consent. The object of the consent process is a fully informed subject, with the degree of explanation required increasing with the potential risk of harm and novelty of the research. When minors are capable of assessing the requisite information and of appreciating the nature and consequences of taking part in the project, they should be able to make the decision themselves. The only impediment would be statutory laws requiring co-consent or sole consent from a parent or guardian.

Consent in the research setting is intended to make certain that the subject is fully aware of the experimental or novel aspect of the procedure. Thus greater disclosure is needed as the risk of harm escalates. Consent to research activities is also intended to prevent undue influence or coercion in the obtaining of research subjects. Consent procedures benefit researcher and subject alike by making certain that each understands his rights and responsibilities. As in traditional treatment settings, litigation for lack of informed consent is likely to flow from poor communication. The better informed the research subject, the less likely that lawsuits will follow on this ground.

Researchers should review applicable state consent statutes and case law if research legislation is silent on the matter of consent by minors. When decisions are made to involve minors as research subjects, the consent process should be followed strictly, bearing in mind its various purposes.

§8.15   Impact of Federal and State Research Requirements

The 1983 additions to the Health and Human Services regulations set a new standard for the use of children in human research. They represent a contrast with most state law on human research, in which few provisions relate specifically to children. The new federal provisions are not designed to discourage research involving children but are geared to protect such subjects. State law also does not dissuade researchers from conducting projects utilizing children. However, under federal and state regulations care must be taken to meet the requirements for consent, including such fundamental issues as a voluntary agreement to participate and a decision free of undue influence and coercion.

E. RESEARCH INVOLVING THE MENTALLY ILL, HANDICAPPED, AND DEVELOPMENTALLY DISABLED

§8.16 Federal Law Governing Research

Mental illness or developmental disability may impede a person's ability to give an informed consent. Authorizing participation in human research, where the subject may be exposed to serious risks, only heightens this concern. In this section, federal requirements are examined as they relate to this group of potential research subjects.

§8.16.1 General Provisions

As for minors, HEW, the predecessor of HHS, proposed specific regulations for institutionalized mentally disabled persons in 1978,[1] but no final rules have since been issued. Those who fall in this category, though, are still covered by the regulations promulgated in 1981 by FDA and HHS. Noninsti-

§8.16 [1]43 Fed. Reg. 53,950 (1978).

tutionalized mentally handicapped persons also come under these regulations as research subjects.

In other sets of regulations, provisions may apply to research involving legally or mentally incompetent people. For example, in the regulations for the Veteran's Administration, considerable attention is paid to the requirements for consent. Permission to proceed may be obtained from a legally authorized representative. Consent must be obtained for that part of the subject's care that is medically approved research, as well as for nonresearch portions.[2]

§8.16.2   Consent Requirements

The general elements for consent are spelled out in great detail in both the FDA and HHS regulations.[3] Although other regulatory provisions may apply in certain situations, most medical research comes under these rules. The regulations also contain specific requirements for documentation of informed consent.[4] Under both sets of regulations, consent may be obtained from a legally authorized representative.[5] Presumably, when mentally or developmentally disabled persons or mentally retarded individuals are without "legally authorized representatives" as defined in the regulations,[6] they cannot participate as research subjects — unless they can give legally effective informed consent themselves.

The institutional review boards that must assess protocols have additional burdens when mentally retarded, disabled, or developmentally disabled persons are proposed research subjects. One of the criteria for approval the IRB must apply is the following:

[2]38 C.F.R. §17.34 (1981).
[3]45 C.F.R. §46.116 (1981) (HHS) and 21 C.F.R. §§50.20 and 50.25 (1981) (FDA).
[4]45 C.F.R. §46.117 (1981) (HHS) and 21 C.F.R. §50.27 (1981) (FDA).
[5]Id.
[6]45 C.F.R. §46.102[d] (1981) (HHS) and 21 C.F.R. §50.3[m] (1981) (FDA).

Where some or all of the subjects are likely to be vulnerable to coercion or undue influence, such as persons with acute or severe physical or mental illness, or persons who are economically or educationally disadvantaged, appropriate additional safeguards have been included in the study to protect the welfare of these subjects.[7]

Under the HHS regulations additional safeguards may be imposed by the secretary when deemed necessary for the protection of subjects.[8] These added conditions may be imposed for any class of research projects. That coverage includes studies involving the mentally ill or retarded as well as the developmentally disabled.

Aside from these requirements, nothing in the current HHS or FDA regulations precludes or restricts human research on mentally retarded or disabled persons or the developmentally disabled. Safeguards or restrictions may nevertheless be imposed by the states, including additional consent requirements.

§8.17 State Laws Governing Research

Unlike their federal counterpart, the states have been active in controlling human research involving the mentally ill, mentally retarded, and developmentally disabled. As noted in this section, consent to participate in human research is singled out for particular attention.

§8.17.1 General Requirements

A few states have general statutes governing human research. California is such a state where provision has been made in the legislation for research involving such groups as

---

[7]21 C.F.R. §56.111 (1981) (FDA) and 45 C.F.R. §46.111 (1981) (HHS).
[8]45 C.F.R. §46.124 (1981) (HHS).

the adult developmentally disabled.[1] When a developmentally
disabled person is without a conservator and the individual is
mentally incapable of giving informed consent, then permission to involve the person as a research subject must be obtained through other statutory means.[2] When consent is
obtained from a person other than the patient, the statute limits
permissible medical research to those efforts designed to maintain or improve the subject's health. Activities to gather data
about the subject's pathological condition may also be carried
out.[3]

In New York, another state with general human research
legislation, mentally disabled or ill persons as well as developmentally disabled individuals may participate as research subjects. When they are unable to consent, however, authorization
must be obtained in writing from a person legally empowered
to act for them.[4] Additional safeguards are also imposed: the
consent of the human research review committee and the commissioner are required for human research on incompetent
and mentally disabled persons.[5]

Virginia has taken a slightly different approach. A legally
authorized representative can consent to research on behalf of
another.[6] The representative cannot agree to nontherapeutic
research unless a human research review committee finds that
the activity does not pose a hazardous risk to the subject. Furthermore, despite the consent of the legal representative, a
subject cannot be forced to take part in human research.[7]

§8.17.2 Consent Provisions

In addition to the states with general provisions governing
human research, some jurisdictions set requirements in their

§8.17 [1]Cal. Health & Safety Code §24175 (West 1979).
[2]Id.
[3]Id.
[4]N.Y. Pub. Health Law §2442 (McKinney 1975).
[5]N.Y. Pub. Health Law §2444 (McKinney 1975).
[6]Va. Code §37.1-235 (1979).
[7]Id.

mental health or developmental disability legislation. These laws usually are not as detailed as the general human research statutes, but consent is often a key consideration.

Some states have patients' bills of rights or similar legislation for the mentally ill, retarded, and developmentally disabled.[8] As part of these requirements, a provision may specify that a patient can refuse to participate in human research[9] or cannot be subjected to such activities without his consent.[10]

A number of states provide consent procedures within their legislation for the mentally ill, retarded, or developmentally disabled.[11] Although the procedural requirements vary from state to state, the person making the decision regarding research usually must be told of the nature, risks, benefits, and purposes of the procedure, as well as the availability of reasonable alternative activities. The fact that a person is considered mentally ill, retarded, or developmentally disabled does not automatically mean she is incapable for purposes of consent. When individuals are legally capable of giving informed consent, the determination is theirs alone. When, however, a subject is incapable of making a decision regarding research, the statutes provide for substituted consent. In some states the determination is to be made by the subject's parent or legal guardian,[12] whereas in others it is to be made by a court.[13] In addition to these safeguards, the type of research may be lim-

---

[8] Ark. Stat. Ann. §59-1416 (1979); Fla. Stat. Ann. §393.13 (West 1979) (bill of rights for retarded persons); Kan. Stat. Ann. §59-2929 (1986) (mentally ill patients); Mont. Code Ann. §53-20-147 (1975) (developmentally disabled).

[9] See, e.g., Ark. Stat. Ann. §59-1416 (1979).

[10] See, e.g., Kan. Stat. Ann. §59-2929 (1986).

[11] Fla. Stat. Ann. §393.13 (West 1979) (mentally retarded); Me. Rev. Stat. Ann. tit. 34B, §5605 (1984) (mentally retarded); Mont. Code Ann. §53-20-147 (1975) (developmentally disabled); N.J. Stat. Ann. §30:4-24.2 (West 1975) (mentally ill); N.D. Cent. Code §§25-01.2-09 and 25-01.2-11 (1981) (developmentally disabled).

[12] Fla. Stat. Ann. §393.13 (West 1979); Me. Rev. Stat. Ann. tit. 34, §2143 (1977); Mont. Code Ann. §53-20-147 (1975).

[13] N.J. Stat. Ann. §30:4-24.2 (West 1975); N.D. Cent. Code §§25-01.2-09, 25-01.2-11 (1981).

ited to those activities related to the specific objectives of the subject's treatment plan.[14]

§8.17.3 Research Review Committees and Consent

Besides the consent provisions sometimes found in the statutes, review of research protocols by special committees may be required.[15] These mechanisms are different than the court decisions made for consent. In North Dakota, for example, subjects are entitled to hearings at which they may proffer evidence and cross-examine witnesses and are entitled to counsel.[16] The court must find that the necessity for medical behavioral research or pharmacological research is established by clear and convincing evidence to be in the subject's best interest and that no less drastic means are available.[17]

By contrast, the review committees in Missouri are charged with the responsibility of assessing the appropriateness of the research subjects, the sufficiency of consent, and other criteria.[18] In Wisconsin, as in some other states, no research can be conducted upon a patient within the terms of the Mental Health Act without the patient's consent.[19] In addition, consent must be obtained from the patient's legal guardian. Both consents must come after consultation with the patient's legal counsel and independent specialists.[20] All research proposals must first be assessed and approved by the institution's research and human rights committee in which it is to take place. The committee and the department must determine that the research is in accordance with HEW (now HHS) regulations on human

[14]N.J. Stat. Ann. §30:4-24.2 (West 1975); N.D. Cent. Code §25-01.2-09 (1981).
[15]Mo. Stat. Ann. §630.194 (Vernon 1980); Wis. Stat. Ann. §51.61 (West 1986).
[16]N.D. Cent. Code §25-01.2-11 (1981).
[17]N.D. Cent. Code §§25-01.2-09 and 25-01.2-11 (1981).
[18]Mo. Ann. Stat. §630.194 (Vernon 1980).
[19]Wis. Stat. Ann. §51.61 (West 1986).
[20]Id.

research as well as with the statement on human research issued by the American Association on Mental Deficiency.[21]

§8.17.4 Practical Considerations

In jurisdictions without specific statutory research requirements, reviewing applicable state regulations is an important step. Even in states with human research legislation, further elaboration on consent and other research requirements can be discovered in regulations. California and Virginia are examples of states with additional regulatory controls.[22]

Where both statutes and regulations are silent on human research involving mentally ill, retarded, or developmentally disabled persons, consideration should be given to applicable case law as well as to general state provisions on consent. These provisions may set the standards for consent required for such persons, at least with respect to novel or therapeutic research. When the proposed subject group includes legally incompetent individuals, additional bodies of law may come into play. Possibilities include statutes on conservatorships, guardianships, or committees. The scope of authority vested in conservators or guardians may vary from case to case, and it is important to determine whether these court-appointed representatives have the authority to enroll their wards or conservatees in human research.

As with minors, the chief concerns relating to mentally ill or retarded persons as research subjects are competency to consent and the use of undue influence or coercion. Parents or guardians of the mentally ill or retarded may not appreciate the implications of involving their child or ward in research. Their decisions may not be based on the proposed subject's best interests. Those who are mentally ill or retarded may be competent

[21] Id.

[22] See, e.g., Cal. Acute Psychiatric Hospital Regulations 22, §71508 (1977); Va. Rules and Regs. to Assure Protection of the Subjects of Human Research (March 1981).

to consent, but the atmosphere in which permission is sought may be coercive or unduly influential in the subject's decision-making. With these considerations in mind, it is important that on the state level all the criteria for consent are met and that permission is obtained from those legally capable or authorized to act.

§8.18   Effect of Federal and State Requirements

The federal regulations on human research apply with equal weight to proposed subjects who are mentally ill, retarded, or developmentally disabled. Additional safeguards are provided by requiring IRBs to ensure that sufficient controls are in place to maintain the rights and well-being of these persons as potential research subjects.

On the state level, in some jurisdictions far more precise requirements are found. Choices include adversarial or other judicial proceedings, advice from independent experts and legal counsel, or review by institutional committees. Some states have specifically incorporated the requirement of consent or the individual's right to refuse to participate in the analysis of proposed research on the mentally ill, retarded, or developmentally disabled.

Research in which mentally handicapped people are asked to participate conjures up ethical and moral dilemmas for many people. From a legal perspective, the concern is to make certain that competent consent is obtained without undue influence or coercion. Just as mentally handicapped people should have the right to decline participation in research, so too should they have the opportunity to take part. The question is how either right should be exercised. Is judicial intervention necessary, or could the matter be handled as an internal institutional matter by a committee that would apply state and/or federal regulations? Are more stringent controls necessary for institutionalized subjects, as opposed to those in half-way homes, sheltered workplaces, or at home with parents or other relatives? Should a decision be based on the research involving nontherapeutic as opposed to therapeutic activities?

These and other related questions have not been fully addressed. It seems, however, that requiring judicial review in all cases is unnecessary. Adequate safeguards can be imposed through institutional review by a committee of the facility in which the protocol is to be carried out. Uniform criteria should be applied in each case to assess the participation by groups of subjects, the adequacy of consent, the necessity of the research, and the potential risks of harm and potential benefits. In this way a group in society could not be taken advantage of because of their mental or developmental deficiencies. Instead they would be given the same opportunities as others in society who have not been labelled as mentally or developmentally disabled. Under this system, any inadequacies in consent or the consent process would be dealt with in accordance with prevailing legal standards. Researchers would be liable for failing to meet the requisite criteria. No prior judicial review or declarations, however, would be available or required unless necessary under applicable state laws.

It is true that additional safeguards are necessary for the mentally ill, retarded, and developmentally disabled. Imposing the requirement of judicial consideration, though, as is the case in some states, seems a disproportionate and unwieldy response to the situation. More streamlined methods of assuming the rights of others are available and should be given serious consideration.

F.   PRISONERS AS RESEARCH SUBJECTS

§8.19   Federal Regulations: HHS Regulations

Both the FDA and HHS have special regulations governing prisoners as research subjects.[1] The requirements set forth in

§8.19   [1] 45 C.F.R. §§46.301-46.306 (1980) (HHS) and 21 C.F.R. Part 50, Subpart C.

each subpart are in addition to those found under the general provisions of the regulations. Thus the general elements for consent also apply to prisoners as research subjects.[2]

According to the HHS prisoner regulations, federal requirements do not authorize research that is barred by or to some degree limited by state law.[3] The stated purpose of the regulations is to provide added safeguards for prisoners:

> in as much as prisoners may be under constraints because of their incarceration which could affect their ability to make a truly voluntary and uncoerced decision whether or not to participate as subjects in research.[4]

§8.19.1 Permissible Research

The types of research activities permitted by the federal regulations are limited. General biomedical or behavioral research cannot be conducted on prisoners. Studies of the possible causes and effects of incarceration, however, may be conducted, provided that no more than inconvenience and minimal risk are involved. Studies of prisons as institutional structures are also permissible, again provided that no more than minimal risk and inconvenience to subjects are involved. Two types of permissible research require the Secretary of HHS to consult with experts in penology, medicine, and ethics prior to the research being conducted. These are projects on conditions affecting prisoners as a class and studies of practices that are intended and will likely improve the well-being and health of the subjects. The studies allowed of prisoners as a class have an interesting range: vaccine trials for hepatitis, as well as research on alcoholism, drug abuse, and sexual assaults.[5]

[2] 45 C.F.R. §46.116 (1981) (HHS) and 21 C.F.R. §§50.20, 50.25 (1981) (FDA).
[3] 45 C.F.R. §46.301 (1980).
[4] 45 C.F.R. §46.302 (1980).
[5] 45 C.F.R. §46.306 (1980).

§8.19.2   *Responsibilities of the IRB*

To ensure that prisoners make their decisions to participate without undue influence or coercion, the IRB is given additional responsibilities. It must make sure that any advantages from participating as compared to their general prison living conditions and other factors are not so great as to hamper the subjects' ability to consider risk factors. Risks attendant to the study should be similar to those accepted by nonprisoners. The disclosure of information must be put in terms that are understandable to the research subjects. The IRB must have adequate assurances that parole boards will not consider a prisoner's research participation in their parole decisions, and prisoners must know this prior to their participation in research activities. To prevent arbitrary intervention by other prisoners or prison officials in the selection of research subjects, the selection process should be fair, and random selection procedures should be used. Allowance is made for other selection procedures if justified in writing by the principal investigator. Should the board determine that follow-up examinations and care are necessary, it must make certain that sufficient measures have been taken for this purpose. Subjects enrolled in studies that may require follow-up examinations must be told of this fact.[6]

Aside from the limitations on permissible research activities and the additional responsibilities bestowed upon IRBs, federal prisoner regulations do not outline any other requirements. From a consent point of view, no additional elements are introduced — except those found in the section on the duties of the IRB. Prisoners must be informed that their participation in research will have no impact on parole and they must be told of the follow-up examinations and care available for certain research projects. The other consent-related element is the comparison between the general prison living conditions and the advantages derived from participation in research activities. If the latter are too great they will impede the subject's ability to assess the risks involved in the project.

[6]45 C.F.R. §46.305 (1980).

§8.20　Federal Restrictions: FDA Regulations

The federal Food and Drug Administration has also promulgated regulations governing the use of prisoners as research subjects. A principal focus of the regulations is to make certain that the consent of prisoners is obtained freely. To this end, as discussed in this section, IRBs must take steps to make certain that this and related requirements are met.

§8.20.1　Permissible Research

In the FDA regulations on human research, the types of projects in which prisoners may serve as subjects are limited. An IRB must certify that the project meets the requirements of the FDA regulations. The study must involve research on innovative or accepted practices that are intended to and likely to enhance the well-being and health of prison subjects. Where a project involves the assignment of prisoners to control groups in which benefit may not result, the FDA must first consult experts in penology, medicine, and ethics. Research on conditions relating to prisoners as a class can be carried out even when subjects are placed in control groups that are not likely to benefit from the study. The FDA must again consult with recognized experts on the proposed research prior to giving approval.[1]

Like the special HHS provisions on prisoners as research subjects, the FDA requirements do not include special provisions for informed consent. Instead, the regulations recognize that additional safeguards may be necessary for prisoners who are hampered in making a decision to participate by their incarceration. The purpose of the additional conditions is to make certain that a prisoner's decision to participate is voluntary and uncoerced.[2]

§8.20　[1] 21 C.F.R. §50.44 (1981).
[2] 21 C.F.R. §50.42 (1981).

§8.20.2 *Responsibilities of the IRB*

To meet the declared purpose of the FDA requirements on prisoners as research subjects, the regulations give further responsibilities to the IRB. That body must make certain that the difference between prisoners' general living situations and the advantages that may flow from taking part in research are not so great as to interfere with the ability to weigh the risks and benefits of participation. Risks that prisoners must take should be similar to those taken by nonprison subjects. Prisoners should be selected randomly as research subjects, unless the researcher justifies in writing the use of another selection method. As with the HHS requirements, this arrangement is designed to provide for a fair means of picking research subjects, free of arbitrary inroads by prisoners and prison officials. When information is presented to prisoners, it must be in terms understandable to them. The IRB must have assurance that the parole board will not consider a prisoner's participation in the study in their parole decisions. Prisoners must also be given this information in advance. Where the IRB determines that some follow-up examination and care may be necessary, it must be certain that sufficient preparations have been made for this purpose. Prisoners must also be told of the availability of follow-up examinations and care.[3]

The statements on participation not affecting parole decisions and the availability of follow-up examinations and care are the only additional disclosure requirements imposed by the FDA beyond its general elements of consent.[4] The assumption that the atmosphere in which a prisoner decides whether or not to participate in human research is free of coercion and undue influence is also part of the process of consent. In these respects, the regulations promulgated by FDA and HHS are quite similar.

Aside from the HHS and FDA prison research requirements, additional provisions may be found in the federal regu-

[3] 21 C.F.R. §50.48 (1981).
[4] 21 C.F.R. §50.20 (1981).

lations of other departments or agencies. The bulk of human research remains, however, subject to the rules imposed by either HHS or FDA.

§8.21 State Limitations

Among the state legislation that governs human research, it is not common to find statutes on prisoners as research subjects. This arrangement does not necessarily demonstrate a lack of state interest: governing controls may have been promulgated through regulations of various state agencies. An important step for researchers is to determine if state rules or regulations have been issued on the subject.

In those jurisdictions with legislation on prisoners as research subjects, the scope of the law varies from state to state. In New York, under general legislation relating to human research, prisoners may participate as subjects.[1] The provisions requiring consent and review by a human research review committee are the same for all subjects. Additional consent, however, is required from both the review committee and the commissioner for research involving prisoners.[2]

§8.21.1 *Legislative Constraints: Some State Examples*

Arizona,[3] California,[4] and Tennessee[5] are examples of states with specific prisoner legislation. Each of their laws refers to requirements for consent. In the Arizona law, any prisoner can participate in an approved medical research project, provided he has the written consent of both the prison superintendent and the prison physician. The prisoner must agree in writing to

§8.21 [1]N.Y. Pub. Health Law §§2440-2446 (McKinney 1975).
[2]N.Y. Pub. Health Law §2444 (McKinney 1975).
[3]Ariz. Rev. Stat. Ann. §§31.321 et seq. (1966).
[4]Cal. Penal Code §§3500 et seq. (West 1985).
[5]Tenn. Code Ann. §§41-2201 to 41-2207 (1974).

take part in the research, having been informed of the nature of the project and any dangers that might occur. In the written consent the prisoner must release the state, the superintendent, and the prison physician from liability arising out of his activities in the project.[6]

California permits only behavioral research on prisoners, and even then the scope of research is quite limited.[7] Studies are restricted to those that study the possible causes, effects, and processes of incarceration, prisons as institutional structures, or prisoners as incarcerated persons, and that present minimal or no risk and no more than mere inconvenience to the subjects of the research.[8]

The inmate research law in Tennessee permits prisoners to take part in medical experiments on a voluntary basis.[9] Prisoners must be given a written statement describing the nature and purpose of the experiment, why it is being done, present research on the subject matter of the test, procedures that prisoners must follow while participating in the study, and, for drug experiments, all known side effects.[10]

Other states have far less detailed statutory requirements for human research involving prisoners. In Iowa inmates may be sent to the medical college of the state university to participate in human research.[11] The prisoner must indicate in writing that she voluntarily wishes to participate. The statute also provides that a prisoner may withdraw this consent at any time.[12]

§8.22 Effect of Federal and State Requirements

The federal and state requirements all aim at voluntary, legally effective, informed consent. Whereas the federal regulations

[6]Ariz. Rev. Stat. Ann. §31-321 (1966).
[7]Cal. Penal Code §3505 (West 1985).
[8]Id.
[9]Tenn. Code Ann. §41-2201 (1974).
[10]Tenn. Code Ann. §41-2202 (1974).
[11]Iowa Code Ann. §246.47 (West 1967).
[12]Id.

stress the atmosphere in which consent is obtained, the states emphasize the elements of consent. This contrast is seen clearly in California, where three separate statutory provisions address the matter of consent by prisoners. The only disclosure requirements imposed by FDA and HHS, in addition to the general elements of consent, concern participation in research that has an impact on parole and involves possible follow-up examinations and care.

A genuine concern pertaining to prisoner research is undue influence and coercion, but the states with legislation on the subject have not directly addressed this important element of prisoner consent. It is one thing for a statute to stipulate that legally effective informed consent is required prior to conducting any research. It is quite another to permit financial compensation or perhaps early parole to prisoners who agree to take part in studies. Anticipation of financial reward or early parole may impair the prisoners' ability to weigh the risks and benefits of participating in research. The federal government, at least, seems to have put a limit on financial rewards in both the FDA and HHS regulations. IRBs under both sets of rules must determine that:

> (1) Any possible advantages accruing to the prisoner through his or her participation in the clinical investigation, when compared to the . . . opportunity for earnings in prison, are not of such a magnitude that his or her ability to weigh the risks of the investigation against the value of such advantages in the limited choice environment of the prison is impaired.[1]

Similarly, the two agencies insist upon assurances from parole boards that the latter will not take into account participation by prisoners in human research.[2]

The same type of limitations are not found in a statute such as that in Tennessee, which permits compensation of inmates "commensurate with payments for the same services to nonin-

§8.22 [1] 45 C.F.R. §46.305 (1980) (HHS) and 21 C.F.R. §50.48 (1981) (FDA).
[2] See references in n.1.

mates taking into consideration the special conditions of inmates."[3]

In states without specific statutes or regulations on prisoner research, review of applicable general consent laws and case law precedent becomes very important. These sources, along with provisions on the administration of correctional facilities, may supply guidelines for consent in the absence of federal regulations for research conducted or funded by that level of government. Whatever the controlling source of law, the chief concern in the prison setting remains the use of undue influence or coercion to coax a prisoner into participating in human research. This matter must be handled effectively in the event of possible litigation based on the absence of legally given, informed consent.

G. ELDERLY PERSONS AS RESEARCH SUBJECTS

§8.23 Federal Regulatory Standards

In their criteria for IRB approval of human research, both HHS and FDA regulations require a finding that:

> Where some or all of the subjects are likely to be vulnerable to coercion or undue influence, such as persons with acute or severe physical or mental illness, or persons who are economically or educationally disadvantaged, appropriate additional safeguards have been included in the study to protect the rights and welfare of these subjects.[1]

Elderly individuals, whether confined to a nursing home, extended care facility, or living alone could be in this catetory.

[3] Tenn. Code Ann. §41-2203 (1974).
§8.23 [1] 45 C.F.R. §46.111 (1981) (HHS) and 21 C.F.R. §56.111 (1981) (FDA).

No other specific references relating to the elderly are found in either set of federal regulations. The requirements for consent, documentation of consent, and other applicable provisions found in the general provisions' subparts, though, do apply.

§8.23.1   Consent and Borderline Incompetent Subjects

The difficult consent issue of the elderly concerns those who are borderline incompetent. Can such people give legally effective informed consent? Who is to decide? Is it sufficient to rely upon permission of a spouse or adult child? Is judicial intervention necessary?

If in the judgment of researchers an elderly person cannot give legally effective consent, that person cannot participate as a research subject. The only exception is when an incompetent person has a duly authorized legal representative who consents on the individual's behalf. According to the federal regulations, a legally authorized representative is:

> an individual or judicial or other body authorized under applicable law to consent on behalf of a prospective subject to the subject's participation in the procedure(s) involved in the research.[2]

Unless a state law or other applicable provision permits a spouse or adult child to act on behalf of a person who has not been declared incompetent, neither could agree to research involving the prospective subject. A judicial determination would be necessary. Without it, participation by persons of questionable competency is risky in terms of consent and legal responsibility.

§8.23.2   Institutionalization and Competent Subjects

Competent elderly people confined to institutional care also may be cause for concern. Does their institutionalization in a

---

[2]45 C.F.R. §46.102 (1981) (HHS) and 21 C.F.R. §50.3 (1981) (FDA).

nursing home or extended care facility impair their ability to reach an informed decision? Is the setting by itself a source of subtle coercion or undue influence? Do they feel compelled to take part in research for fear of retaliation if they were to refuse to do so?

§8.23.3 Duties of the IRB

In addition to its responsibilities for those susceptible to coercion and undue influence, the IRB must find that the selection of research subjects is equitable.[3] It must consider the purposes of the project, as well as the setting in which the study will be carried out. This duty definitely applies to elderly people who reside in nursing homes and similar institutions. If a selection process is considered unfair in light of research being conducted in a nursing facility, the protocol may not receive approval. The IRB may insist upon modifications to the selection process to bring it up to acceptable standards. Although this check does not guarantee that competent elderly residents will base their decisions on noninstitutional considerations, it does provide some assurance that participation will be more equitable. Taken together with added safeguards for those vulnerable to coercion and undue influence, the rights of the elderly as federal research subjects are afforded a number of important protections.

§8.24 State Legislative Requirements

In some states, statutory bills of rights have been enacted for elderly citizens in nursing homes and other residential facilities. Many of these lists of rights include a reference to research or medical experimentation. Some require prior informed consent for participation in research.[1] Others state that an elderly

---

[3] 45 C.F.R. §46.111 (1981) (HHS) and 21 C.F.R. §56.111 (1981) (FDA).

§8.24 [1] Md. Pub. Health Code Ann. art. 45, §565 C (1980); R.I. Gen. Laws §23-17.5-7 (1978); Wash. Rev. Code Ann. §74.42.040 (1981).

person has the right to refuse to take part in research or experiments.[2] These laws sometimes stipulate that a refusal to take part in human research will not jeopardize the individual's access to medical care or treatment.[3]

Whether or not a state has statutory or regulatory provisions for research involving the elderly, it is incumbent upon researchers to obtain legally effective informed consent. Applicable state requirements for consent would have to be met. At a minimum, this means disclosure of the nature, purpose, risks, and possible benefits of the research in language understandable to the potential subject. The surroundings in which consent is obtained should be free of undue influence or coercion. Subjects should be told that they are free to refuse to take part or that they may withdraw their consent at any time without jeopardizing their status as a resident in the facility.

§8.24.1   Consent Process for Elderly Incompetent Persons

Elderly residents who have been declared legally incompetent cannot take part in research unless permission has been obtained from duly authorized legal representatives. A related question is whether the representative's mandate is restricted to decisions affecting property or whether it includes matters involving the person of the incompetent individual. Only someone with the latter power would be permitted to authorize research.

§8.24.2   Consent Process for Questionably Competent Persons

For persons of questionable competency, consent is a difficult problem. Unless the spouse, adult child, or other next of kin is

---

[2] Mass. Gen. Laws Ann. ch. 111, §70E (West 1979) (part of a general patients' rights statute); N.J. Stat. Ann. §30:13-5 (West 1976); Ohio Rev. Code Ann. §3721.13 (Baldwin 1979); Or. Rev. Stat. §441.605 (1981).

[3] See, e.g., Ohio Rev. Code Ann. §3721.13 (Baldwin 1979).

legally authorized to act in such matters, it would be best to rely upon others as research subjects. The alternative is to seek a judicial declaration that would find the person competent or incompetent. When individuals are found to be unable to look after themselves, guardians may be appointed who may authorize research. However, the scope of a guardian's authority may be limited. For example, under California's human research law, a conservator may only consent to research:

> relating to maintaining or improving the health of the human subject or related to obtaining information about a pathological condition of the human subject.[4]

Other types of restrictive legislation may be found in different states.[5]

Researchers should be keenly aware of the impact of institutionalization upon subjects' ability to give effective legal consent. An elderly person may feel compelled to take part in research for fear of subsequently receiving inadequate medical care. These concerns may be unfounded, but should be anticipated prior to obtaining consent.

The more attention given to the elements of consent required in a given state, the more likely that the research protocol will be carried out smoothly. From a legal point of view, such efforts also ensure the rights of the subjects and of the research team.

§8.25 Effect of Federal and State Requirements

Unlike some state regulations, those promulgated by HHS and FDA do not contain specific provisions for the elderly as re-

[4]Cal. Health & Safety Code §24175 (West 1981).
[5]See, e.g., N.Y. Pub. Health Law §2444 (McKinney 1975), which requires consent from an incompetent individual's legal representatives as well as the consent of the human research review committee and the commissioner.

search subjects. However, the criteria for consent and IRB approval do apply to this segment of the population, thus providing some guarantee of their rights as human research subjects.

A chief concern on both the state and federal levels is how to obtain legally effective informed consent from those elderly citizens confined to nursing homes and other facilities. Is the setting likely to cause an elderly person to consent? Will they agree to research for fear of inadequate medical care if they refuse? Will they agree to take part as a welcomed change from their boring, idle routine, overlooking the risks involved? Do they see their participation as an easy way of making some much-needed money, ignoring the probable discomforts and possible risks involved? These and similar factors must be carefully assessed by the researcher, the IRB, or other reviewing bodies to make certain that the study or the institution does not unduly influence subjects' decisions.

Another cause for concern is the issue of competency to consent. Individuals do not necessarily lose the right to consent to care or research just because a guardian has been appointed to handle and manage their property interests. Guardianship of the person, including novel treatment, however, would necessitate permission of the guardian prior to involving the person in research.

Elderly persons of questionable competency should generally be avoided as research subjects. Their consent may not be reliable, given their overall inability to make competent decisions. Although consent may be obtained when they are competent, their tendency to slip in and out of states of lucidity may jeopardize the legal effectiveness of that consent. It is also unwise to rely upon permission granted by a spouse or next of kin in their circumstances. Unless they are legally authorized to act in these situations, their consent is not legally valid. Judicial relief may be possible, although a judge may not intervene in the absence of a life- or health-threatening emergency that necessitates compulsory care. These are some of the reasons why it is best to rely upon elderly persons who are capable of informed consent, as well as on those for whom a legally authorized representative has been appointed.

One final group deserves consideration. As noted earlier, the state legislation in place usually refers to elderly persons residing in nursing homes or other facilities. What rights do noninstitutionalized people have in this situation? To be sure, the benefits that accrue to an institutionalized person from participating in research, along with the setting itself, may be a source of undue influence or coercion. The same issues may affect elderly citizens living alone or with other family members. The prospect of financial remuneration in a study may unduly influence an elderly person of modest means. They may also misunderstand the purpose of the study, seeing it as a source of free health care. Institutionalization may play a significant role in the consent process, but other influential factors must not be overlooked for elderly subjects living outside structured residential facilities.

H.   RESEARCH WITH OTHER VULNERABLE POPULATIONS

Children, mentally disabled adults, elderly individuals, and prisoners are not the only individuals who are at risk of inadequate consent safeguards in human research. The terminally ill and others afflicted with devastating illnesses also need particular consideration. Many seriously ill individuals eagerly participate in human research in the hope that it might save them. Others participate in human research in order to help others prior to death.

Regardless of their motivation, the terminally and seriously ill are vulnerable groups to whom particular attention must be paid when seeking their consent to participate in human research. This area is bound to see considerable development as the scope of research widens into AIDS.

§8.26   AIDS and ARC Victims

Few would argue that a diagnosis of AIDS and even ARC is anything but a death sentence. Having been told that they are suffering from AIDS or ARC, many individuals may look to human research as the only hope they have of extending their lives or avoiding death.

Federal research regulations do not squarely address the sensitive legal and ethical issues associated with human research in this vulnerable population. Rather, this is the type of concern that might trigger the need for "additional safeguards"[1] envisaged in the HHS and FDA regulations.

What would constitute "additional safeguards"? The answer will largely turn on the purpose of the study and the human research requirements for it. Clearly, it would necessitate careful consideration of consent requirements to ensure that research subjects are well informed and that they are not exposed to undue influence or coercion in agreeing to take part in experimentation.

For IRBs and investigators it must be clear that research protocols do not trigger false hopes and expectations. The consent process and documentation should reinforce this principle. Indeed, in research in which participant vulnerability is acute, consideration should be given to concurrent monitoring and random sampling of the consent process to ensure investigator compliance.

On the state level there has been considerable legislative activity regarding AIDS. Some legislation, including laws in California,[2] specifically focus on human research and AIDS.

For investigators involved in AIDS research, it is imperative to keep abreast of state legislative developments. Laws that deal with consent to testing might well include discussion of consent to use test samples for research purposes. Legal counsel for health facilities and risk managers are often excellent resources for information about such state legislative developments.

---

§8.26   [1]See 45 C.F.R. §46.111 (1981) and 21 C.F.R. §56.111 (1981).
[2]See, e.g., Cal. Health & Safety Code §199.36 (West 1985).

I. JUDICIAL PRECEDENT IN HUMAN RESEARCH AND CONSENT

§8.27   The Need for Adequate Disclosure

Surprisingly, little case law has accumulated in the United States on the topic of consent and human research. What case law there is often addresses the requirements for consent to novel or experimental procedures. At a minimum, the case law suggests that the more novel or experimental the procedure, the greater the need for disclosure of information. Failure to meet what is perceived as the appropriate standard of consent will give rise to litigation. As seen in the past, this has sometimes proved costly to the defendant.

Perhaps the most well-known human experimentation case arose in Canada.[1] It involved an experimental procedure about which the research subject was not adequately informed. The United States has had only one highly publicized experimentation case — Karp v. Cooley — that involved medical care.[2]

§8.27.1   *Karp v. Cooley: Consent in Experimental Surgery*

In Karp v. Cooley, a 47-year-old man agreed to a type of cardiac surgery referred to as a wedge procedure.[3] In a signed consent document, the patient also agreed to the use of a mechanical heart substitute on a temporary basis and ultimately a human heart transplant if the patient's own cardiac function could not be restored following the operation.

When the wedge resectioning procedure proved unsuccessful, the patient's heart was removed and was replaced by the

§8.27   [1]Haluska v. University of Saskatchewan, [1966] 53 D.L.R.2d 436 (Sask. C.A.).
[2]Karp v. Cooley, 493 F.2d 408 (5th Cir. 1974).
[3]Id.

mechanical device. Later that was removed when a donor heart became available. The patient died some 32 hours after he received the transplanted human heart.[4] The cause of death was pneumonia and renal failure.[5]

A lawsuit was filed against the surgeon and others by the man's widow. The case raised issues of medical negligence, fraud, and experimentation as well as of consent. Of present concern are the allegations relating to consent and human experimentation.

The plaintiff claimed that her husband had not been given adequate information on which to make a decision. Among other things she alleged that her husband had not been told of a permanent risk of harm to his body from the mechanical implant, that it could cause renal failure, and that it was totally experimental. In affirming the trial court's directed verdict in favor of the defendants, the appellate court held that the plaintiff had not presented expert testimony regarding the appropriate standard of disclosure. Moreover, there was a lack of sufficient evidence on the causal link between the alleged lack of consent and the harm sustained.[6]

On the allegation of experimentation, the court, applying Texas law, held that the defendant's actions must be gauged by traditional medical negligence evidentiary standards.[7] The plaintiff failed to provide the substantial evidence required to make her case. There was no lack of consent, a prerequisite necessary to an allegation of experimentation. Furthermore, there was no proof of the type required for causation as well as proximate cause.[8]

The *Cooley* court did not directly take the stance that more disclosure is required with a novel or experimental procedure. It did acknowledge, however, the position taken by some commentators who were in agreement with this policy.[9] In Texas at

[4] Id. at 417.
[5] Id. at 418.
[6] Id. at 421.
[7] Id. at 423.
[8] Id. at 424.
[9] Id. at 424, n.23.

the time, as in many states today, the standard of disclosure was what a reasonable practitioner in the same field of expertise and locality would have disclosed to a patient under similar circumstances.[10] The standard could be established by expert witnesses. Even under this rule, a more stringent standard of disclosure may be applied to novel or experimental work, assuming that expert evidence was presented to support this requirement. It was on this issue perhaps more than any other that the plaintiff failed in the *Cooley* case. The situation illustrates once again the need for adequate disclosure of all material information that a patient needs to make an informed choice. Reason dictates that as the likelihood of risk becomes greater, the patient should be apprised of its significance. A patient who has been informed properly would be hard pressed to prove lack of adequate consent in subsequent litigation.

§8.27.2 Novel Radiation Therapy: The Price of Inadequate Disclosure

Defendants have not always been successful in cases involving alleged lack of consent where novel or experimental procedures were involved. For example, in a medical malpractice case against the Veterans Administration, a man won a judgment for negligence and for lack of informed consent.[11] The attending physicians felt that a drastic level of radiation was required to prevent a tumor from obstructing the man's colon. The prescribed preoperative radiation was given to reduce the size of the cancerous tumor in the man's rectum. Surgery was performed to remove the tumor once the radiation therapy was completed. The patient claimed that, as a result of the radiation he received, he experienced a number of complications, including various injuries to his urogenital tract. Applying New Mex-

---

[10]Id. at 420, referring to Wilson v. Scott, 412 S.W.2d 299, 301-304 (Tex. 1967).

[11]Ahern v. Veterans Administration, 537 F.2d 1098 (10th Cir. 1976).

ico law, the trial court held that the administration of 2.999 rads over a five-day period amounted to negligence. This finding was affirmed by the appellate court. That amount was well in excess of doses considered acceptable in the local medical community as well as across the country.[12]

On the issue of consent, the plaintiff claimed that he was told neither of the experimental nature of the radiation treatment nor of the possible hazards from such a high dosage of radiation. There was conflicting testimony on this issue, but the trial court found for the plaintiff. As the appellate court pointed out in affirming the lower court's decision:

> . . . in order for a physician to avoid liability by engaging in drastic or experimental treatment, which exceeds the bounds of established medical standards, his patient must always be fully informed of the experimental nature of the treatment and of the foreseeable consequences of the treatment.[13]

§8.27.3 Consent to Experimental Use of Drugs

The degree of disclosure is important, whether a novel or experimental procedure involves surgery[14] or drug therapy.[15] This relationship is illustrated in the two following cases, which involve allegedly experimental use of drugs.

---

[12] Id. at 1100.

[13] Id. at 1102.

[14] See, e.g., Schneider v. Revici, 817 F.2d 987 (2d Cir. 1987); Schwartz v. Boston Hosp. for Women, 402 F. Supp. 53 (S.D.N.Y. 1976); Hood v. Phillips, 537 S.W.2d 291 (Tex. Civ. App. 1976), affd., 554 S.W.2d 160 (Tex. 1977). Neither *Schwartz* nor *Hood* involved a final judgment. *Schwartz* concerned curettage as part of a caesarean section delivery. It was alleged that the curettage was performed without the patient's consent as part of an ongoing research project. *Hood* involved a controversial surgical procedure for the treatment of emphysema. The plaintiff alleged that the doctor did not inform him of attendant risks and the likelihood of failure to achieve intended results.

[15] Mink v. University of Chicago, 460 F. Supp. 713 (N.D. Ill. 1978); Blaxton v. United States, 428 F. Supp. 360 (D.D.C. 1977); Gaston v. Hunter, 588 P.2d 326 (Ariz. Ct. App. 1978).

In one case, a woman with Rh-negative blood was asked after the delivery of one of her children whether she would be willing to take Hyo-Rho-D as part of an experiment to determine its effectiveness beyond its FDA-designated shelf life.[16] In the past she had taken one of two drugs known to be effective in preventing Rh problems in subsequently conceived children. The woman declined to take part in the study and specifically requested the drug she had received in the past. Although a note was made in her chart that she was to receive the established drug, she was given an injection of the experimental preparation without her consent or knowledge as part of the study. The medical staff did not inform her of the mistake for several months and when they did she suffered a number of psychological and physical abnormalities. Tests showed, however, that the plaintiff experienced none of the problems with future pregnancies[17] that are linked to inadequate protection from possible Rh reactions.

In finding for the plaintiff, the court held that the hospital, a navy medical center, had violated acceptable standards of care. Use of the preparation beyond its established shelf life brought it within the meaning of "new drugs" under the Federal Food and Drug Act.[18] The hospital, along with its personnel, had failed to carry out their responsibilities under §505(i) of the act by permitting experimentation with non-FDA-approved drugs without the consent of the patient.[19] As the court pointed out, the act created a special duty of care for the hospital and the other defendants to prevent involuntary experimentation. Having failed to meet this responsibility, all of them were liable.[20]

In the other case a patient with an intervertebral disc herniation underwent injections of an investigational drug. Conservative treatment had failed to remedy her condition.[21] The

[16]Blaxton v. United States, 428 F. Supp. 360 (D.D.C. 1977).
[17]Id. at 362.
[18]21 U.S.C.A. §355 (West 1972).
[19]21 U.S.C.A. §505(i), as amended, 21 U.S.C.A. §355(i) (West 1972).
[20]Blaxton v. United States, supra n.16 at 362.
[21]Gaston v. Hunter, 121 Ariz. App. 33, 588 P.2d 326 (1978).

woman developed a number of complications from the drug therapy, including infection. She had to undergo several operations and was ultimately left with numbness in her feet and toes, bowel and urinary control problems, and constant pain as well as an abnormal gait.

The Arizona appellate court reversed in part a jury verdict for the defendants in the case. It affirmed the verdict, however, with respect to informed consent. The court pointed out that if the patient had agreed to the procedure with an appreciation of the nature of the procedure and its probable results, a lawsuit against the defendants could not be tried as battery. In this case the physician had met his obligation to disclose to the patient the novel or investigational nature of the treatment and therefore could not be found liable in battery.[22]

In another interesting case, the executor of a deceased mental health patient's estate successfully sued the United States Army under the Federal Torts Claim Act.[23] The army had an arrangement with a state mental health facility to conduct experiments with a mescaline derivative to test its potential use in chemical warfare. Although the patient was aware that the drugs he was given were experimental in nature, he did not understand that the substances were being given to him for purely experimental purposes. Some 25 years after his death from the experimental drugs, the estate was awarded $702,044.00 in damages.

§8.27.4 Experimental Surgery Upon a Prisoner: Consent Without a Full Explanation

At least one case has involved experimentation on a prisoner.[24] The plaintiff was an inmate at Sing Sing Prison when he along with others volunteered to take part in a surgical experiment. The purpose of the procedure was to test the value of

[22] Id.
[23] See Barrett v. United States, 660 F. Supp. 1291 (S.D.N.Y. 1987).
[24] Valenti v. Prudden, 58 A.D.2d 956, 397 N.Y.S.2d 181 (1977).

cartilage in healing. It required the making of two incisions in the plaintiff's chest, suturing of the wounds, and removal of the sutures one week later. The plaintiff executed a consent document absolving the physician and hospital from all claims. It also stated that "I have been advised and I understand that a small permanent scar may result from the experiment for which I have volunteered."

Following the operation, the prisoner was left with two rather large scars that could not be corrected by plastic surgery. In a lawsuit based on lack of adequate consent, the jury found for the plaintiff. The trial court set aside their verdict, but this decision was later modified by an appellate court. As the higher tribunal noted, the jury's findings were not against the weight of the evidence presented. There was some conflicting testimony over the expected results and what was meant by a small scar. There was proof, however, that the surgical experiment was not carried out as initially anticipated.[25]

§8.27.5   *Documenting Consent to Research*

Many schools of thought have arisen on the requirements for documentation of consent. Some hold that no consent forms are necessary and that a detailed note in a person's chart will suffice. Others claim that a short form is advisable — one that states "the risks of this procedure have been explained to me," and includes a brief description of the purpose of the treatment and anticipated results. Yet another group adheres to the belief that a detailed, highly descriptive consent form must be used. Choosing among these approaches, of course, is subject to legislative and regulatory provisions that mandate the use of certain forms.

Whatever format is used does not lessen the importance of properly informing a patient or research subject of the nature, purpose, possible risks, and expected results of the proposed procedure or therapy. Seemingly minor points should not be

[25] Id.

overlooked. What the researcher in *Valenti* thought was a "small scar" differed from the subject's perception. What the physicians in *Ahern* saw as novel radiation therapy was viewed as disastrous by the patient. Communication of significant information is vital, particularly where novel or experimental procedures are concerned. Although it is the patient to whom the information should always be directed, in some instances the involvement of the immediate next of kin is appropriate. Before doing so, permission should be obtained from the patient. Should the patient/subject die or be incapacitated as a result of the procedure, a well-informed relative will be hard pressed to sue successfully for lack of informed consent.

Documentation, whether in a patient's chart or in a consent form, should accurately reflect disclosed information. Lawsuits often stem from lack of communication, which when combined with a bad outcome may result in litigation for inadequate informed consent. At the least the communication gap can be closed.

J. PRACTICAL POINTERS FOR CONSENT TO HUMAN RESEARCH

There are a number of practical considerations that should be addressed regarding consent to human research that are not found in federal and state requirements. These concerns involve drug trials or research projects conducted in private physicians' offices and commercial use of human tissues obtained in research procedures. In this section, these matters are discussed. A practical checklist is also included dealing with human research management considerations.

§8.28 Drug Company Sponsored Doctor's Office Trials: Consent Considerations

Human research is not restricted to the sterile confines of health facilities. Research can be found in private doctors' offices in which clinicians carry out studies either sponsored by drug companies or conducted as a matter of interest by the physicians themselves.

The obvious concern about such research focuses on the lack of protocol review for the protection of human subjects. Without careful review by an IRB, how can it be certain that the research is ethically sound? Are the basic requirements for consent being met?

From a risk-prevention perspective, physicians should be cautious about conducting research for which there is not the independent evaluation that is routine with institutionally based trials. Care must be taken to ensure that the requirements for a valid consent to research are followed and that the threshold requirements found for therapeutic interventions are not lowered. To avoid liability, physicians should be sure they are insured against the consequences of human research carried out in their offices.

§8.29   Commercial Use of Human Tissues Procured in the Research Setting

Perhaps the most interesting issue in the area of consent and human research involves the need to disclose information regarding commercial use of tissues obtained in experimentation. Does a human research subject have a right to know that tissues or cells obtained in a study have potential commercial value? If so, does the subject have a right to share the profits or does the commercial potential belong to the investigator who makes the discovery and processes the raw material into a marketable item?

The issue is not simply a matter of speculation. The California Court of Appeal has ruled that a patient from whom a valuable commercial cell-line was derived had sufficiently stated a cause of action to permit his lawsuit to proceed to trial.[1]

---

§8.29   [1]Moore v. Regents of University of Cal., 249 Cal. Rptr. 494 (Cal. Ct. App. 1988).

The Office of Technology Assessment of the United States Congress has also published a report on the issue.[2]

There is little doubt that the issue of commercial use of human tissues raises serious ethical and moral concerns. From a legal perspective, however, commercial gain from human tissues obtained in research triggers concern about property rights, division of profits, and consent to tissue removal and use in this manner. For researchers and IRBs, it is important to secure expert legal advice on the matter. In particular, serious thought should be given to the ways in which the rights of research subjects can be protected and the need for adequate disclosure of information. Documentation of consent to commercial use of tissues procured in research trials must also be addressed.

§8.30   A Checklist of Management Considerations

Those involved in human research as well as those who administer institutions in which it is carried out should develop a checklist of matters that must be addressed. Resources within the institution, such as research committees, as well as outside consultants, such as legal counsel, should be involved. The following are a list of suggested topics for consideration. Further details may be added to tailor the checklist to individual needs.

1. Updating copies of current federal, state, and local research laws.
2. Legal interpretation of federal, state, and local requirements.
3. Constituting institutional review boards in accordance with federal and/or state or local laws.
4. Obtaining assurances from HHS and FDA.
5. Scheduling of IRB meetings and establishment of proper rules for IRB functions.

[2]See New Developments in Biotechnology: 1 Ownership of Human Tissues and Cells, Office of Technology Assessment, 1987.

6. Mechanism for expedited review procedures.
7. Proper documentation of consent and proper consent process.
8. Additional safeguards for special subjects such as minors, incompetents, prisoners, and the elderly.
9. Adequate institutional insurance and risk management for human research.
10. Policy for access to medical records for research purposes.
11. Compensation and/or treatment for injured subjects.
12. Policy for warning subjects of latent risks as information becomes available.

NINE

Organ Donation and Autopsy

§9.0   Introduction
A. Live Organ Donors and Consent
    §9.1   Basic Requirements of Consent
    §9.2   Competency of Live Organ Donors
           §9.2.1   Substituted Judgment and Incompetent Donors
           §9.2.2   Substituted Judgment and Best-Interest Theories
                    Combined
           §9.2.3   Little v. Little: The "Best" Interests of Mentally
                    Retarded Minors
           §9.2.4   Judical Denial of Permission to Remove Live Organs
                    from Incompetents
           §9.2.5   Judicial Review of Parental Decision-Making
           §9.2.6   Minors and Consent to Live Tissue Donation
    §9.3   Setting Standards for Donations by Incompetent Persons
           §9.3.1   Legislative Inroads: The Texas Example
           §9.3.2   Other Legislative Controls
    §9.4   The Issue of Forced Donation of Organs and Tissues
    §9.5   Commercial Use of Human Tissues
           §9.5.1   Moore v. Regents of the University of California: A
                    Case Example
           §9.5.2   Practical Considerations
B. Cadaver Organ Transplants and Consent
    §9.6   The Anatomical Gift Act and Consent
           §9.6.1   Cadaver Organ Transplants and Consent
           §9.6.2   Documentation of Cadaver Donations
           §9.6.3   Revoking Consent to Organ Donations
           §9.6.4   Other Important Provisions of Anatomical Gift Laws
           §9.6.5   Litigation Involving the Uniform Anatomical Gift
                    Laws

§9.7   Donor Designation Drivers' Licenses
     §9.7.1   Difficulties Associated with Donor Designation Programs
§9.8   The Moment of Death and Cadaver Organ Transplants
     §9.8.1   The Harvard Ad Hoc Committee Criteria
     §9.8.2   Judicial and Legislative Criteria for Death
     §9.8.3   Removal of Organs and Criminal Investigations
§9.9   Removal of Organs by Medical Examiners, Coroners, and Others
     §9.9.1   Corneal and Pituitary Gland Removal
     §9.9.2   Eye Enucleation Procedures
§9.10   Disposal and Use of Unclaimed Bodies
§9.11   Organ Procurement Legislation
     §9.11.1   Federal and State Requirements for Organ Procurement
     §9.11.2   Practical Considerations in Organ Procurement
C.   Autopsy and Consent
     §9.12   Statutory Authority to Conduct Medicolegal Autopsies
     §9.13   Power to Conduct Nonmedicolegal Autopsies
     §9.14   Judicial Action in Contested and Unauthorized Autopsies
       §9.14.1   Religious Objections to Autopsies
       §9.14.2   Unauthorized Autopsies
       §9.14.3   Medical Examiners' Power to Order Autopsies Sustained
       §9.14.4   The Need for Complete Disclosure
D.   Other Medical Uses for Dead Bodies
     §9.15   Dealing with the Newly Dead

§9.0   Introduction

Few subjects generate more medicolegal and ethical controversy than organ transplantation and donation. Questions have been raised regarding when the moment of death occurs, a prerequisite for excision of organs from a cadaver for purposes of transplantation. In other situations, the transplantation issue has involved live organ donation between siblings. How can a child of 7 "consent" to the removal of a kidney for the benefit of her brother? How can a mentally ill or retarded person authorize the donation of body parts? What safeguards exist for such people?

In a related area, concern has been expressed regarding autopsies. To be sure, in some instances, autopsies or postmortem examinations are required by law, particularly when death triggers a medicolegal investigation. Hospitals often want autopsies performed for various purposes. From whom should consent be obtained for such examinations? When consent is given for an autopsy, may the examiner or the facility retain fluids and tissues removed during the procedure or is additional consent required?

In some instances, the law regarding autopsies and organ donation overlap. When the deceased is the subject of a medicolegal investigation and an autopsy, how can the law give effect to a bequest of an anatomical gift? To an anatomical gift card? To a donation designated on a driver's license?

An additional complicating factor is the family. In some instances, the family may object to an anatomical gift — despite the fact that the deceased left a duly executed donor card. What takes precedence: the wishes of the family or the desires of the deceased? On other occasions, the deceased may not have left any indication of his wishes. When this is the case and there is a dispute within a family regarding organ donation, what should be the position of the hospital?

These and related issues are discussed in this chapter. Appendix G contains the Uniform Anatomical Gift Act. A thorough knowledge of this act is essential before proceeding with any matter involving organ donations.

A. LIVE ORGAN DONORS AND CONSENT

§9.1 Basic Requirements of Consent

Whether the prospective donor is an adult, a minor, or someone with a mental problem or deficiency, the key factor prior to the removal of body tissue is an informed consent given by the appropriate person. The principles outlined in chapter 1 for obtaining a consent apply here as in all other aspects of medical care. Applying the informed consent principles to live tissue or organ donation means a consideration of and discussion with the donor of the following:

1. Risks and possible consequences to donor.
2. Benefits to donor, if any.
3. Reasonable alternatives, if any.
4. Opportunity to question transplant physician.
5. Extent and scope of proposed surgery.
6. Length of recuperation.
7. Impairment of sexual function, if any, in adult donors particularly.
8. Extent of scarring.
9. Time out of work or time period of disability.
10. Special follow-up care required, if any.

Each of these factors should be covered carefully to foster informed decisions on the part of patients.

Failure to obtain a fully informed consent can lead to liability.[1] Steps to avoid such liability include following the procedures outlined above and documenting patients' consent. As discussed in chapter 1, this sequence does not necessarily require a consent form. A detailed note in the patient's chart, alone or in addition to the patient's written authorization, could suffice.

The failure to complete properly the consent process could be tried under the theory of assault and battery.[2] The challenge

§9.1 [1]Cf. Fleming v. Michigan Mut. Liab. Co., 363 F.2d 186 (5th Cir. 1966), in which the court discussed the issue of consent in a skin graft case. The donor contended that the physician had removed the tissue from the inside of her thighs allegedly contrary to her specific instructions. The court found that this was a factual dispute and that on the evidence the jury could find for the insurer. Despite the favorable finding for the defendant, the case does demonstrate the need for specific patient consent in a transplant situation. For a very thoughtful article on consent in transplantation, see Curran, A Problem of Consent: Kidney Transplantation in Minors, 34 N.Y.U.L. Rev. 891 (1959).

[2]See, e.g., Bang v. Miller, 251 Minn. 427, 88 N.W.2d 186 (Minn. 1958); Mohr v. Williams, 95 Minn. 26, 104 N.W. 12 (1905).

would be based on an unauthorized touching of a person's body. This legal response is more likely to occur when the physician has extended the operation beyond that to which the patient consented or when the wrong organ or other unauthorized tissue is removed. Problems such as the removal of incorrect organs can be avoided by proper surgical standards and dutiful operating room staffs. The process of consent, however, remains the responsibility of the surgeon.

§9.2 Competency of Live Organ Donors

As in other areas of health care, as long as an individual can render a fully informed consent, authorization for donation of body parts should come from the patient. The test for competency is the same as that required for consent to other medical and surgical procedures: the person must be of an age and possess the ability to exercise the mental faculties necessary to reach a reasoned judgment.

When prospective donors are minors or persons who are mentally retarded or ill, who can consent for them? And on what basis? In the United States, case law has been developed on these issues,[1] along with some statutory law.[2]

§9.2.1 *Substituted Judgment and Incompetent Donors*

The legal basis for some of the decisions involving incompetent persons is the principle of substituted judgment.[3] As it was

---

§9.2 [1]See unreported cases cited in Baron, Botsford & Cole, Live Tissue Transplants from Minor Donors in Massachusetts, 55 B.U.L. Rev. 159, 161-162, n.15 (1975); Hart v. Brown, 29 Conn. Supp. 368, 289 A.2d 386 (Super. Ct. 1972); In re Richardson, 284 So. 2d 185 (La. Ct. App. 1973), cert. denied, 284 So. 2d 338 (La. 1973); Strunk v. Strunk, 445 S.W.2d 145 (Ky. 1969).
[2]Colo. Rev. Stat. §13-22-104 (1963); Tex. Rev. Civ. Stat. Ann. art. 4590-2A (Vernon 1979).
[3]See discussion in Baron, Botsford & Cole, supra n.1.

originally developed, courts were authorized to transfer gifts from the estate of an incompetent person to another person on the basis that the individual would have done so if she were capable of making the gift.[4] As Professor Robertson has pointed out, under this theory all sorts of motives have been imputed to incompetent persons to justify gifts from their estates.[5] In these cases courts make subjective assessments of what individuals would do if competent. The difficulty of applying this principle to the transplant field is twofold. How does it relate to minors of tender years and to those who have never been in a state of competency, due to mental illness or mental retardation?

In response to the difficulties of assessing a prospective donor's charitable or altruistic feelings toward the intended donee, many courts have turned to the best-interest test. Unlike the substituted judgment doctrine, no subjective analysis is involved. Rather, the test turns on a consideration of what is objectively best for the prospective donor.[6]

§9.2.2 Substituted Judgment and Best-Interest Theories Combined

On occasion, the two theories have been applied together. In supposedly using the substituted judgment theory, some courts have based their decisions on what a reasonable person in the minor's position would do in the circumstances — an objective standard.[7] The two following cases illustrate this legal approach.

---

[4]The decision of Ex parte Whitebread, 35 Eng. Rep. 878 (Ch. 1816), is usually cited as the source of this theory. See Baron, Botsford & Cole, supra n.1, at 170, n.54.

[5]Robertson, Organ Donations and the Substituted Judgment Doctrine, 76 Colum. L. Rev. 48, 58 (1976). These motives include charity, altruism, and self-interest. See notes 55 and 56 at 58.

[6]Baron, Botsford & Cole, supra n.1, at 170, n.54.

[7]See, e.g., Strunk v. Strunk, 445 S.W.2d 145 (Ky. 1969); Hart v. Brown, 29 Conn. Supp. 368, 289 A.2d 386 (1972).

In Strunk v. Strunk,[8] a 27-year-old mentally retarded man became the subject of a court proceeding in which permission was sought to remove a kidney for transplantation. The prospective donor was a resident of a state institution for the mentally retarded. He had an I.Q. of 35 with a mental age of 6 years. His brother, who was married, had a fatal kidney disease, chronic glomerulus nephritis, and he required a kidney transplant. The only suitable donor in his family was the retarded sibling. Transplanting a kidney from a nonfamily member was considered to be medically unsound. The mother as committee applied to the lower courts of Kentucky for authority to go ahead with the kidney transplant and the tribunal authorized the procedure. Since the guardian ad litem questioned the court's authority to permit the surgery on a ward of the state, appeal was taken to the Kentucky Circuit Court and Court of Appeals.[9]

In reviewing the case, the Kentucky Court of Appeals pointed out that psychiatric and other evidence demonstrated that the brother's death would be detrimental to the ward's further treatment and rehabilitation. The sick brother served as a role model and a family link for the ward. Although retarded, the ward had emotional and personal reactions similar to those of a normal individual. Should his brother die without the ward's being given an opportunity to assist him, the ward could feel guilty.

The court found that the ward could give up a kidney for his brother's benefit. The decision was based on the substituted judgment theory as well as the best-interest test. It held that the risks to the donor did not outweigh the benefits to him of giving his brother a kidney.[10] It also found that a court of equity could authorize such a transplant and that the principle of substitution of judgment by a court of competent jurisdiction was broad enough to include not only property "but also to include

---

[8]445 S.W.2d 145 (Ky. 1969).
[9]Id.
[10]Id.

those factors which affected the well-being of the incompe-tent."[11]

In Hart v. Brown,[12] transplant surgeons and the facility in which the operation would take place refused to perform a kidney transplant between two identical twin minors without a judicial determination that the parents and/or the guardians ad litem had authority to consent to it. The case arose after physi-cians who were treating a young child of nearly 8 years of age for hemolytic uremic syndrome and malignant hypertension had to perform a bilateral nephrectomy (removal of both kid-neys). She was placed on dialysis, but doctors strongly recom-mended a kidney transplant for her long-term survival. The most suitable donor was her healthy twin sister. Using her kid-ney for the transplant rather than an organ donated by one of the parents increased the chances of success. It also eliminated the prospect of unpleasant side effects from immunosuppres-sive drugs. The short-term risks to the donor were termed "negligible," being no greater than the risk of anesthesia. The most serious risk in the long run was trauma to the donor's remaining kidney, which was described as "extremely rare in civilian life."[13]

A psychiatrist informed the court that the twins had a strong identification with one another and that giving up the kidney would be of great benefit to the donor.[14] He based this conclu-sion on the donor's enjoying a better family life with her sister living than one saddened by the death of the ill child. The court, however, termed the psychiatric evidence as being of limited value given the age of the children.[15]

The court pointed out that the prospective donor was told of the operation and, to the extent that she was capable of doing so, agreed to the operation. Additional support came from a clergyman who stated that the parents' decision to push ahead

[11] Id.
[12] 29 Conn. Supp. 368, 289 A.2d 386 (1972).
[13] Id. at 372, 289 A.2d at 389.
[14] Id.
[15] Id. at 374, 289 A.2d at 390.

with the surgery was both morally and ethically correct. The donor's guardian ad litem also voiced approval.[16]

The court authorized the operation in light of the foregoing testimony and evidence. From a legal perspective, it based its decision on the rationale employed in Strunk v. Strunk, supra, and the Massachusetts line of cases involving "grave emotional impact" to the donor if the kidney transplant was not permitted. It also based its decision on other American precedent in which minors could undergo nontherapeutic surgery on the basis of consent by parents or guardians.[17] Furthermore, the operation was in the best interests of the intended donor, due to her strong sibling affinity and family circumstance. The risks were small compared to the expected results. In applying the principle of substituted judgment, the court stated that:

> . . . natural parents of a minor should have the right to give their consent to an isograft kidney transplantation procedure when their *motivation* and *reasoning* are *favorably reviewed by a community representation* which includes a court of equity.[18] (Emphasis added.)

§9.2.3 Little v. Little: The "Best" Interests of Mentally Retarded Minors

The best-interest test has also been applied to the prospect of donation by a mentally retarded minor. In Little v. Little,[19] a 14-year-old girl with Down's syndrome was declared incompetent by a Texas court and her mother was appointed as her guardian. One week later, the mother-guardian filed an application seeking permission to authorize a kidney donation for the retarded child. A younger brother of the girl had end-stage renal disease and required a transplanted kidney. The only suitable donor was the retarded youngster.

---

[16]Id. at 373, 289 A.2d at 389.
[17]Bonner v. Moran, 75 U.S. App. D.C. 156, 126 F.2d 121 (1941), cited in, Hart v. Brown, supra n.12, at 374, 289 A.2d at 390.
[18]Supra n.14 at 375, 289 A.2d at 391.
[19]576 S.W.2d 493 (Tex. Civ. App. 1979).

As in the other cases described earlier, the incompetent child and her ill sibling shared a close familial tie. Although she could not understand the concept of death, the youngster could appreciate the idea of absence and she was not happy when her brother was away from home receiving dialysis treatments.[20] She also was aware that she could help her brother, something that could give her psychological benefit by raising her self-esteem. The donor was in good health and did not have respiratory problems or hypertension sometimes associated with Down's syndrome.[21] She also faced few risks in donating the kidney.

The guardian ad litem appointed to represent the youngster's interests objected to the removal of a kidney for transplantation. The objection was based on a lack of constitutional or statutory authority enabling the probate court to permit an operation on an incompetent for the benefit of another.[22] In the end, however, the Court of Civil Appeals sustained the trial court's authorization of the procedure, on the grounds of strong evidence that the donor would receive significant psychological benefits from giving up a kidney.[23]

The *Little* case points out some of the strengths and weaknesses in case law in the area of incompetent organ donors. Texas had a statute at the time that prohibited transplantation and other medical procedures on residents of state facilities for the mentally retarded.[24] The prospective donor in this case did not reside in a state mental health facility. It was argued that in the absence of similar legislation prohibiting transplantation procedures involving nonresidents, incompetents living outside state facilities could donate organs. This, the court said, was an untenable interpretation since it would allow guardians or the courts to authorize hazardous or nontherapeutic surgery on a ward. The statute dealing with state facility residents was de-

[20] Id. at 498.
[21] 576 S.W.2d 493 (Tex. Civ. App. 1979).
[22] Id.
[23] Id.
[24] Tex. Rev. Civ. Stat. Ann. art. 5547-300(E)24(c) (Vernon 1977).

signed to prevent the exploitation of incompetent persons. Statutory silence as to retarded persons living outside such facilities did not signal legislative approbation of nonbeneficial medical procedures.[25]

Having rejected this argument, however, the court went on to allow a nontherapeutic kidney transplant and, in doing so, limited its decision to the facts and circumstances before it. It concluded by urging a legislative solution to similar situations that would, on one hand, prevent the exploitation of minors and incompetents and, on the other, let them share some of the benefits of donating organs.[26]

§9.2.4 Judicial Denial of Permission to Remove Live Organs from Incompetents

Not all cases involving incompetent individuals result in orders authorizing removal of tissue or organs for transplantation. For example, a Louisiana court[27] turned down a request by a husband against his wife to compel her to consent to the donation of a kidney by one of their children for the benefit of the other. The case was brought in this manner as a procedural vehicle for getting it before the court. In actuality, the mother agreed to the proposed operation. The would-be donor was mentally retarded and had the mental age of a 3- or 4-year-old. He had Down's syndrome, but he was otherwise healthy. The intended donee, his sister, was 32 years old and divorced. She lived at home with her parents. In addition to her acute glomerulonephritis, she had other medical problems, one of which might adversely affect the transplanted organ.[28]

While the retarded brother was by far the most suitable donor in terms of "graph identity," he was not the only candidate.[29] The chances of success with the brother's kidney were

[25] Supra n.19.
[26] Id.
[27] In re Richardson, 284 So. 2d 185 (La. Ct. App. 1973).
[28] Id. at 186.
[29] Id. at 187.

far greater than they were if an organ from a cadaver donor or another relative were used. Still, there was no absolute necessity for the incompetent brother to give up a kidney to preserve his sister's life.

The Louisiana court distinguished this case from that of Strunk v. Strunk, supra, stating that the facts as well as the procedural and substantive considerations were different in each case. Louisiana law prohibited the intrusion of a minor's property for donation. Given this fact, it was no less protective of a minor's person, unless benefit to the minor could be established. Such benefit was not demonstrated; therefore the court held that neither the parents nor the court could authorize the proposed transplant.[30]

A similar result was reached in a Wisconsin case.[31] A 38-year-old mother of six with chronic glomerulonephritis was in need of a kidney transplant. Her own kidneys were removed as a means of controlling her condition. She had subsequently been treated with dialysis, but her condition deteriorated, necessitating a transplant. Although she had another brother and sister and her parents were alive, the only suitable candidate for donating a kidney was a brother who was a committed mental patient. He was diagnosed as being schizophrenic, of the chronic, catatonic type. His mental capacity was estimated at that of a 12-year-old.[32]

In denying the request for authority to permit the transplant, the court found that there was no evidence to indicate that it would be in the brother's best interest to donate a kidney. Furthermore, it declined to adopt the substituted judgment test as a basis for permitting the proposed surgery. It held that the doctrine of substituted judgment was developed for donation of gifts from the property of an incompetent. If applied literally, it would vest authority in the courts that is not permitted by statute, a position contrary to Wisconsin case law. There being no statutory authorization for the Wisconsin courts to

[30] Id. at 187.
[31] In re Guardianship of Pescinki, 67 Wis. 2d 4, 226 N.W.2d 180 (1975).
[32] Id.

permit the requested operation and no showing of its being in the ward's best interests, the petition was turned down.[33]

§9.2.5 Judicial Review of Parental Decision-Making

Not all transplant cases involving minors have relied on the best-interest or substituted judgment tests. According to Baron et al., one Massachusetts case simply involved judicial review of the parents' decision.[34] The matter involved bone marrow donation from a 6-year-old sibling for the benefit of another. The court ordered the transplant after terming psychological evidence of benefit to the donor as speculative, given his age. The parents were seen as having the chief right and duty to make the decision, with the court using its equity power to review the parents' decision for possible conflict of interest and to see if it was reasonable.[35] A similar approach was taken in Hart v. Brown, supra.

§9.2.6 Minors and Consent to Live Tissue Donation

In another Massachusetts bone marrow case, the minor's consent was deemed effective. The minor, however, was 17 years of age and the court's decision turned upon psychiatric evidence that he could make his own decisions regarding his welfare.[36] As can be seen in these cases, the overriding concern is the well-being of the donor. When she is incompetent, it is particularly important that steps be taken to prevent exploitation of the intended donor while allowing the individual to exercise the right of donation. An essential part of resolving

[33] Id.

[34] Supra n.1 at 171. The case referred to, Nathan v. Farinelli, Eq. No. 74-87 (Mass., July 3, 1974), is an unreported opinion.

[35] Supra n.1 at 172-173.

[36] Rappeport v. Stott, Civil No. J74-57 (Mass. August 28, 1974), discussed in Baron, Botsford & Cole, supra n.1, at 176-177.

these cases is to apply standards fairly and consistently to reach an equitable solution for those concerned.

§9.3 Setting Standards for Donations by Incompetent Persons

As suggested by the case review above, some courts have decided donation cases involving incompetents by relying on (a) best interest, (b) substituted judgment, and (c) judicial review of parental decision-making. A fourth standard has been to allow consent by minors on their own behalf. This criterion deserves further consideration.

The law traditionally held that a minor *could not* consent to his own medical treatment. Unless an emergency occurred, consent was required from a child's parent or legal guardian. (See chapter 5.) Gradually, however, this principle has begun to change. For example, in 1939 the First Restatement of Torts[1] stated that a minor who was sufficiently intelligent to appreciate the nature and consequences of his actions was capable of giving permission to treatment absent parental consent. More recently, a number of states have enacted statutes giving minors authority to consent to medical treatment and blood donation.[2] It is arguable that if a minor could consent to intrusions of his body for treatment and blood donation, the right should include the opportunity to donate body parts. The "benefit" that would accrue need not be limited to the harm that would follow if he were not allowed to donate. It should also include psychological benefits flowing from the giving of himself, including increased self-esteem and enhancement in family status.[3]

With children incapable of consent and those persons who

---

§9.3 [1]Restatement of Torts §59, Comment a (1939).
[2]Ariz. Rev. Stat. Ann. §44-132 (1962) (treatment), §44-134 (1970) (blood donation); Ark. Stat. Ann. §82-1606 (1977) (blood donation); Colo. Rev. Stat. §13-22-103 (1979) (treatment); Haw. Rev. Stat. §577A-2 (1979) (for purpose of certain forms of treatment).
[3]See, e.g., Little v. Little, 576 S.W.2d 493 (Tex. Civ. App. 1979).

are mentally incompetent, specific safeguards are necessary to protect their rights. Steps must be taken to avert psychological pressures, coercion, or exploitation for the benefit of another. The law should preserve their right to donate, however, as it does for those capable of consenting on their own behalf. Legislation is probably the best answer: it would strike a balance between procedural and substantive safeguards while preserving the right to donate.

§9.3.1 Legislative Inroads: The Texas Example

Some states have attempted to legislate in the field. As noted in the discussion of Little v. Little, supra, Texas had prohibited the transplantation of body tissues of residents of state mental health facilities. In 1979, probably in response to the court's suggestion in *Little,* Texas passed legislation regarding mentally retarded persons as kidney donors.[4]

The Texas statutes allow the guardians of certain mentally retarded persons to petition courts for permission to donate kidneys. The prospective donor must be "12 chronological years of age or more"[5] and the intended donee must be father, mother, son, daughter, sister, or brother of the ward.[6] The court must appoint both a guardian ad litem and an attorney ad litem for the incompetent person, neither of whom may be related to the donor within the second degree of consanguinity.

An order authorizing the donation can only be issued after a hearing in which the petitioner has the burden of proving good cause for the organ removal. The statute sets forth the following criteria:

1. The guardian of the ward must consent.
2. The ward must have given assent.
3. Proof must be shown that without the donated kidney, the

---

[4]Tex. Rev. Civ. Stat. Ann. art. 4590-2a (Vernon 1979).
[5]Id.
[6]Id.

donee would soon die or suffer a severe and progressive deterioration. With the transplanted kidney the donee must be shown to accrue substantial benefit.

4. There are no medically preferable options for the donee other than the transplant.

5. Both the operative and long-term risks of the transplant are minimal to the donor, who will not likely undergo psychological harm from donating a kidney.

6. The transplanting of the kidney promotes the donor's best interests.[7]

A number of other procedural requirements are set out in the law. Within seven days of the hearing, the court is to hold an in-chambers interview of the ward without her guardian in attendance. The purpose of the meeting is to decide whether the intended donor does assent to the procedure. To assist the court in deciding whether the prospective donor has the capacity to assent, a thorough evaluation and diagnosis can be ordered under the Texas Mentally Retarded Persons Act of 1977.[8] Additionally, at the time of hearing the attorney ad litem must advance the ward's interest, if any exist, in *not* participating as a donor. By statute, the tenor of the hearing is to be adversarial in nature.[9]

The Texas statute is quite novel for a number of reasons. It provides a wide array of procedural safeguards to prevent the exploitation of the ward. It incorporates the best-interest test, as well as generally accepted consent criteria. Not only does a ward have the benefit of a guardian ad litem and an attorney ad litem to promote her interests, but the court must conduct its own interview outside the presence of the ward's guardian. This provision, to assure the court that the ward has assented, is yet another check against possible exploitation, overreaching, or undue influence.

Another interesting aspect of the statute is the criteria that

[7] Id.
[8] Id.
[9] Id.

take into account the interests and needs of the intended donee. Such considerations have usually been implicit in court decisions regarding incompetent donors — or at minimum are mentioned by the court. In this statute, at least two criteria are set forth giving the donee status or weight in the decision-making process.

One of the criticisms of the Massachusetts cases involving minors as donors has been the lack of an adversarial approach expected in such proceedings.[10] Here, by legislation, an adversarial setting has been established for such proceedings when the rights of a mentally retarded individual are involved.

The Texas statute does have its failings. It only allows individuals 12 years of age and older to donate, and then only kidneys. It has left out a far less risky category of donation in bone marrow transplantation. No provision is made for a court to authorize a transplant when a guardian refuses to petition for an order authorizing the kidney donation. It is conceivable that a guardian could object on some unreasonable basis. Furthermore, the statute is silent on donations by those who are unable to assent to the kidney removal.

The Texas statute, despite its shortcomings, represents a valuable law for permitting organ donations by mentally retarded persons. Still, it is questionable that such an elaborate legislative scheme is necessary to protect the rights of the retarded in this one area of life. The situation is like dousing a lit match with a fire hose. Legislative guidelines are useful in this area of concern, but the Texas law seems to run to the extreme of protectionism.

§9.3.2 Other Legislative Controls

Texas is not alone in legislating in this area. Michigan, in fact, was the first state to act.[11] As the law of that state presently

---

[10]See Baron, Botsford & Cole, Live Organ and Tissue Transplants from Minor Donors in Massachusetts, 55 B.U.L. Rev. 159, 187 (1975).

[11]Mich. Stat. Ann. §27.3178 (19b) (Supp. 1974).

stands,[12] a person 14 years of age or older may donate a kidney to his father, mother, sister, brother, daughter, or son, when authorized to do so by a court. Unlike under the Texas law, the petition for an order may be instituted by the prospective donor's spouse, child, parent, other next of kin, or guardian. When the would-be donor is without a guardian, a guardian ad litem is appointed to protect his interests. When after a hearing it is determined that the donor is capable of appreciating the consequences of donating and agrees to make the donation, the court may authorize the gift.[13]

The Michigan statute, although less procedurally detailed than that of Texas, is a sound law. Admittedly, it deals with minors, *not* mentally retarded persons, as does the Texas statute. Still, the Michigan enactment does provide procedural protection to ensure an informed choice by the prospective donor. Where doctors and hospitals in Michigan are reluctant to proceed with a sibling bone marrow transplant without judicial approval, the law's limitation to kidney transplants does not facilitate a decision. The singling out of 14 as the age at which a minor can understand the nature and consequences of donating a kidney can also be criticized. Many children 12 years of age or younger are probably just as capable of such decision-making.

Colorado also has an organ transplant law relating to mentally retarded persons. When a mentally retarded person over 18 years of age desires to donate an organ, a court must decide if the individual is competent to consent. Two or more people expert in the field of mental retardation may be appointed by the court to examine the intended donor. Based on this and other evidence, the court must decide the issue of competency. If the court finds that the individual has given her consent, it must order that the organ be removed. If, however, the court reaches a decision of incompetency, it must order that no organ removal be performed.[14]

[12] Mich. Comp. Laws Ann. §700.407 (1979).
[13] Id.
[14] See Colo. Rev. Stat. §27-10.5-130 (1975).

The Colorado statute is quite narrow in focus, yet it does provide procedural protection for the retarded person. *No* provision, however, is made for organ donation by those who, although incapable of informed decisions, do have the desire to aid another. Then again, perhaps such statutory precision is impossible.

As these statutes suggest, legislative standards can be found in some states regarding organ transplantation that involves incompetents and minors. Rather than clearing up any uncertainty surrounding organ and tissue transplantation by such people, in many ways the enactments serve to restrict otherwise proper and needed donation procedures. The statutes described above nevertheless do point out some broad procedural safeguards that could be incorporated in more practical legislative or policy standards on incompetent donors.

§9.4 The Issue of Forced Donation of Organs and Tissues

In July 1978, a bone marrow transplant case received widespread publicity in the United States.[1] The case involved two adult cousins, one a 39-year-old with aplastic anemia and the other a 43-year-old with genetic compatibility sufficient for donating bone marrow to his stricken relative. Initially, the healthy cousin agreed to undergo tests to determine his suitability as a donor. When he was found to be a good match, additional confirmatory tests were ordered. He failed to appear for these tests and refused to donate the needed marrow to his cousin. Court proceedings were then commenced in an effort to force the bone marrow extraction.

---

§9.4 [1]McFall v. Shimp, No. 78-17711 in Equity (C.P. Allegheny County, Pa., July 26, 1978), cited in, Note, Coerced Donation of Body Tissues: Can We Live With McFall v. Shimp, 40 Ohio St. L.J. 409 (1979). As evidence of publicity the case received, see N.Y. Times, July 27, 1978, at A-10; Newsweek, Aug. 7, 1978, at 35.

The plaintiff, Mr. McFall, sought an injunction that would have forced the would-be bone marrow source, Mr. Shimp, to undergo the confirmatory tests. If the results proved that he shared a suitable degree of compatibility with his cousin, he would then be obliged to donate the bone marrow.[2]

In his arguments to the court, the plaintiff's lawyer advanced a number of points, including a duty on the part of the defendant to act and the authority of a court of equity to order the relief requested. As to the contention of a duty, the plaintiff's lawyer cited two cases[3] dealing with the rescue doctrine that is applicable to those standing in a special relationship to another. This was rejected by the court. As the defendant pointed out, Pennsylvania[4] follows the Restatement of Torts that it is not enough to impose a duty to act, but that one " . . . realizes or should realize that action on his part is necessary for another's aid or protection."[5]

The plaintiff's equity argument was based on thirteenth-century English law, the Second Statute of Westminster.[6] It was contended that the Pennsylvania courts, as descendants of this English tradition, were vested with the same equity powers. To this the judge responded quite negatively, saying:

> For a society, which respects the rights of *one* individual, to sink its teeth into the jugular vein or neck of one of its members and

[2] Coerced Donation of Body Tissues, supra n.1, at 411.

[3] Id. at 12, n.27. The cases cited are Hutchinson v. Dickie, 162 F.2d 103 (6th Cir. 1947), dealing with the owner of a boat and his guest, and Farwell v. Keaton, 396 Mich. 281, 240 N.W.2d 217 (1976), involving two people on a drinking binge.

[4] Id. at 13. The Pennsylvania case is Yania v. Bigan, 397 Pa. 316, 155 A.2d 343 (1959).

[5] Restatement of Torts (Second) §314 (1965), cited in Coerced Donation of Body Tissues, supra n.1, at 13, n.31.

[6] St. Westminster 2, 1285, 13 Edw. 1, c. 24., cited in Coerced Donation of Body Tissues, supra n.1, at 12, n.25:

> Whensoever from thenceforth a writ shall be found in the Chancery, and in a like case falling under the same right and requiring a like remedy, no precedent of a writ can be produced, the Clerks in Chancery shall agree in forming a new one; lest it happen for the future that the court of our lord the king be deficient in doing justice to the suitors.

suck from it sustenance for *another* member, is revolting to our
hard-wrought concepts of jurisprudence. Forcible extraction of
living body tissue causes revulsion to the judicial mind. Such
would raise the spectre of the swastika and the Inquisition, remi-
niscent of the horrors this portends.[7]

The injunction was denied and shortly thereafter, the plaintiff
died.[8]

It is unlikely that other courts would find differently from
the judge in McFall v. Shimp. Given the well-established principles of self-determination and personal privacy, jurists would
have difficulty holding that the powers of equity extend to forcible donation of body parts. A similar result could also be expected in a lawsuit for forcible donation of cadaver tissue. By
not compelling the aspiration of bone marrow, the court
reached a legally correct conclusion. Perhaps in the future a
different stance will be taken that will accommodate both legal
and ethical principles.

§9.5 Commercial Use of Human Tissues

Biotechnology is a thriving business that often depends upon
raw material obtained from volunteers. Seen as purely a business transaction, little can be found that obliges physicians and
other caregivers to obtain consent to removal and use of such
biotechnological products. However, as seen in this section, the
law of consent to treatment is highly relevant. The need for
patients to know that their tissues can be used to generate
considerable financial reward and the practical issue of documenting consent in such circumstances are the focal point of
this section of the chapter.

[7]McFall v. Shimp, supra n.1, at 2-3, quoted in Coerced Donation of Body
Tissues, supra n.1, at 413-414.
[8]Coerced Donation of Body Tissues, supra n.1, at 414.

§9.5.1 *Moore v. Regents of the University of California: A Case Example*

The most striking case in this area involved a Washington State man whose spleen was removed as part of treatment for hairy cell leukemia.[1] It was determined that the man's spleen tissue could be used to produce a valuable cell-line.

Without telling the patient, the defendants applied for a patent on the cell-line strain and arrangements were made with a large drug company to make a business venture out of the cell-line and its products. For their work, the doctors involved were given valuable stock options.

When the patient learned about the commercial use of his cells, he instituted legal proceedings involving conversion. The trial court granted the defendant's demurrer to the plaintiff's complaint. On appeal, the decision was reversed, the California Court of Appeal ruling that the plaintiff had adequately stated a cause of action.

The court's decision suggests that consent to surgical removal of the patient's spleen did not constitute an authorization for human research unrelated to treatment. Moreover, in the context of the conversion action, the surgical consent did not authorize commercial use of the patient's spleen tissue.

The *Moore* case is a long way from resolution. It is the type of case that could take years to reach a conclusion. Nonetheless, even at this stage it sends a clear message regarding the need for consent to commercial development of human cells and tissues.

§9.5.2 *Practical Considerations*

The *Moore* case demonstrates the importance of informed consent to commercial use of human tissue removed from pa-

---

§9.5 [1]Moore v. Regents of the University of Cal., 249 Cal. Rptr. 494 (Cal. Ct. App. 1988). This case is also discussed in the context of human research in §8.29 supra.

tients. Although the law is by no means completely settled on the issue, the following are some of the practical considerations which should be taken into account:

1. The ability of the patient to give or refuse consent;
2. Surrogate decision-making for patients unable to give or refuse consent;
3. Mechanisms in place and used to avoid undue influence or coercion of a patient from whom commercially viable materials may be obtained;
4. The scope of disclosure required in such cases; and
5. Documentation of consent to removal of tissues for commercial use.

This would include situations in which the patient is receiving payment for taking part in the business venture.

B. CADAVER ORGAN TRANSPLANTS AND CONSENT

§9.6 The Anatomical Gift Act and Consent

The law involving organ transplants from cadaver donors has been largely settled by the adoption throughout the 50 states and the District of Columbia of the Uniform Anatomical Gift Act. (See Appendix G.) Approved in 1968 by the National Conference of Commissioners on Uniform State Laws and the American Bar Association,[1] the act was designed to encourage anatomical gifts and to clarify the law. Since its adoption as a model law, many jurisdictions have enacted variations tailored to their individual needs. Additionally, a new means of effectuating anatomical gifts through donor cards on drivers' licenses has also come into effect in several jurisdictions.

§9.6 [1] Uniform Laws Annotated (West 1972) at 16, historical note.

The model law with its variations from state to state represents a well-considered plan for increasing the number of organs and tissues available for transplantation. Some of its individual provisions deserve discussion, particularly as regards consent.

§9.6.1   Cadaver Organ Transplants and Consent

In many enactments, a person must be at least 18 years of age and of sound mind in order to donate any part or all of his body.[2] Connecticut has taken the opposite tack, giving effect to anatomical gifts by persons who are 14 years of age but less than 18, and who have the consent of their parents or legal guardians.[3] Provision is also made in the law for persons, standing in order of priority, to make an anatomical gift on behalf of decedents. The usual order or priority is (a) spouse, (b) an adult son or daughter, (c) either parent, (d) an adult brother or sister, (e) a guardian of the person of the decedent at death, and (f) one authorized or under a duty to dispose of the decedent's body.[4] Persons in this list of priority are empowered to make the anatomical gift either immediately before or after death.[5]

A gift made by one of those specified above may be blocked if the donee has actual knowledge of opposition from either the decedent or from one of the same or prior class.[6] There is some actual statutory variation on this point, as in Florida where a gift by a spouse may be blocked by an adult son or daughter.[7] The law also states that the rights of the donee created by the gift take precedence over the rights of others, with the exception of laws regarding autopsies. At least one state has made provision for removal of organs designated for donation when

[2] See, e.g., R.I. Gen. Laws §23-18.5-2 (1979).
[3] Conn. Gen. Stat. Ann. §19-139d (1981).
[4] Supra n.1, §2 at 25.
[5] Id.
[6] Id.
[7] Fla. Stat. Ann. §732.912 (West 1984).

the decedent's body is the subject of a medicolegal investigation.[8]

Possible donees include hospitals, physicians and surgeons,
accredited medical or dental schools, storage banks and facilities, as well as specified individuals requiring gifts for therapy
or transplantation.[9] Some states have also included state anatomical boards as possible donees.[10]

§9.6.2 Documentation of Cadaver Donations

Gifts may be made by will or card. The card or document
other than a will must be executed by the donor in the presence
of two witnesses, who must sign it in her presence. Should the
donor be unable to sign, she can direct another to sign with the
same witnessing formalities just described. The gift, to be valid,
does not require delivery of the document during the donor's
lifetime. Provision is also made for those described earlier as
standing in priority to make gifts on behalf of the decedent.
They may do so by a signed document, telegram, or recorded
telephone or other recorded message.[11] The commissioners
also provided in a note on this section sample donor forms to be
used by living donors, their next of kin, or others authorized to
act.[12] The requirements for executing these documents vary
from state to state.

§9.6.3 Revoking Consent to Organ Donations

Provision is also made for the amendment of and revocation
of such gifts. Under the model law, after the document or gift

---

[8]See, e.g., Tex. Code Crim. Proc. art. 49.25 (Vernon 1987). See also Ohio
Rev. Code §2108.53 (Baldwin 1980), which permits the removal of a decedent's pituitary gland as an anatomical gift, providing it is not necessary for
the completion of an autopsy performed by a county coroner or as evidence.

[9]Supra n.1, §3 at 29.

[10]See, e.g., Okla. Stat. Ann. tit. 63, §2204 (West 1976).

[11]Supra n.1, §4 at 30-31.

[12]Id. at 32-33.

has been presented to a specific donee, it may be revoked or amended in any of four ways. First is a signed statement delivered to the donee. Second is an oral statement to the donee in the presence of two witnesses. If the donor is in a terminal state, he may also amend or revoke the gift in a statement addressed to the attending physician and then communicated to the donee. Last, by leaving cards or documents in their effects or on their persons, donors may revoke or amend a gift to a specific donee. When no delivery to a donee has yet occurred, the gift may be revoked or amended by following any of the four steps just described, as well as by destroying, cancelling, or mutilating the document and all copies of it.[13]

§9.6.4 Other Important Provisions of Anatomical Gift Laws

The last major section of the uniform law sets forth rights and duties at death.[14] The law permits the donee to either accept or reject the gift. When the gift is the donor's body, the donee may, subject to the conditions of the gift, permit embalming and funeral services. When the gift is a portion of the decedent's body, prior to embalming and without unnecessary mutilation, the donee may have the gift removed. Thereafter, the disposal of the donor's remains becomes the responsibility of his spouse or other family members.

Under the uniform act, the time of death is to be determined by the donor's attending physician. When there is no attending doctor, then the determination is to be made by the physician who certifies the death. The physician who determines death is also banned from participating in the removal or transplantation of organs from the donor. This arrangement has not been followed in all states.[15]

An immunity clause for civil actions and criminal proceed-

[13] Id., §6 at 37-39.
[14] Supra n.1, §7 at 39.
[15] See, e.g., Wyo. Stat. §35-5 (1978).

ings is also included. It applies to "a person who acts in good faith in accord with the terms of this Act or with the anatomical gift laws of another state [or a foreign country]. . . ."[16] Some states, in adopting this section, have deleted the bracketed reference to "a foreign country."[17]

The Uniform Anatomical Gift Act marks a major step in the law regarding cadaver organ donations. Some of the states, in enacting the law, have gone even further by lowering the age of consent to cadaver donation and by clarifying the use of organs from bodies that are the subject of medicolegal investigations.

§9.6.5   Litigation Involving the Uniform Anatomical Gift Laws

The Uniform Anatomical Gift Act has been put to the test in litigation. In a Wisconsin case,[18] a man brought suit for damages against transplant surgeons and the hospital in which his wife died. The woman had been taken to the hospital after experiencing an intracerebral hemorrhage. Following her admission, she was placed on life-support machinery, but her condition did not improve. The husband alleged that he was told by the physician attending his wife that she was dead. He then gave permission for his wife's kidneys to be removed for transplant purposes. It was only later that he learned, so he claimed, that his wife had remained "alive" for some 48 hours after he had been told she died. He also contended that his wife's death did not come until nearly half an hour after she had been pronounced dead and surgery had been started to remove her kidneys.

In a lawsuit, brought in his individual capacity, the husband alleged (a) willful and intentional mutilation of a corpse, (b) negligent mutilation of a dead body, and (c) negligence in re-

---

[16]Supra n.1, §7(c) at 39.
[17]See, e.g., Neb. Rev. Stat. §77-4807 (1981); N.H. Rev. Stat. Ann. §291-A:4 (1980).
[18]Williams v. Hofmann, 66 Wis. 2d 145, 223 N.W.2d 844 (1974).

porting incorrectly and prematurely a death message.[19] He also sought recovery of damages in his position as special administrator of his wife's estate, alleging assault and battery and negligence in actions occurring prior to his wife's death.[20]

As to the first set of claims, the Supreme Court of Wisconsin held that the alleged wrongdoing of the physicians and hospital came within the immunity clause included in §7 of the Uniform Anatomical Gift Act. The court found that §7(c) set up an affirmative defense immunizing those who acted in good faith in discharging their tasks under the act.

As to the allegations brought in his role as special administrator, the court pointed out that the grant of immunity in the act did not extend to care of the donor before death or to care of the live donee. It therefore overturned the lower court's order overruling the estate's demurrer to the defense of immunity in this aspect of the case.[21]

It should be noted that medical examiners and coroners can run afoul of state legislation governing anatomical gifts. Indeed, an attempt has been made to hold a hospital attorney legally accountable for dealing with authorization to remove organs for transplantation.[22] There is no certainty that the medical examiners or coroners will prevail in actions based on unauthorized removal of body tissues from a decedent. This point is well illustrated in a Florida case in which it was claimed that the medical examiner had authorized the removal of the decedent's corneas and eye globes despite the objections of the decedent's mother.[23] In reversing the trial court's dismissal, the appellate court noted that there was sufficient evidence — if proven — for a jury to conclude that the actions of the medical examiner were not protected under applicable Florida law.[24] The facts suggested that the mother's objection to the organ

[19] Id.
[20] Id.
[21] Id.
[22] See Brown v. Delaware Valley Transplantation Program, 539 A.2d 1373 (Pa. Super. Ct. 1988).
[23] See Kirker v. Orange County, 519 So. 2d 682 (Fla. Dist. Ct. App. 1988).
[24] Referring to Fla. Stat. Ann. §732.9185 (West 1985).

removal was charted in the patient record and that the medical examiner had falsified the autopsy report to cover his actions.

A quite different decision was reached in a New York case in which the court ruled that the hospital had acted in "good faith" in securing permission for the removal of the eyes of the decedent.[25] In this instance, the person who authorized the organ removal claimed to be the patient's wife. It turned out that while she had lived with the decedent for ten years and was the mother of his two children, the woman was not legally his wife. In ruling for the defendants, the court pointed out that the hospital had acted reasonably and in good faith in the situation.

Case law suggests that organ donation can prove to be the focal point of costly and time-consuming litigation. This need not be the case if legal requirements are followed and policies and procedures are developed for proper organ procurement.

§9.7 Donor Designation Drivers' Licenses

Other statutory enactments in the United States involve cadaver donation. In many states, those persons holding a driver's license may execute an organ donor card on the back of their operator's permit or chauffeur's license.[1] In other states, the license does not include the actual donor card.[2] In these states, the license bears a designation or decal indicating that the holder wishes to donate a portion of her body or that she has executed a donor card.[3] Some states have legislation requiring officials to cooperate with private groups in providing drivers with donor designation stickers.[4] At least two states,

---

[25] See Nicoletta v. Rochester Eye and Human Parts Bank, 519 N.Y.S.2d 928 (Sup. Ct. 1987).

§9.7 [1] See, e.g., Minn. Stat. Ann. §171.07 (West 1987); Va. Code §46.1-375 (1985).

[2] See, e.g., La. Rev. Stat. §32:410 (West 1983); Miss. Code Ann. §41-39-53 (1974); S.C. Code §44-43-40 (1984).

[3] See references in n.2.

[4] La. Rev. Stat. §32-410 (West 1983).

Massachusetts[5] and Arkansas,[6] have made provision for minors to express an intention to donate with permission of a parent or guardian. Mississippi has taken an approach slightly different from its sister states. State law requires officials to notify other jurisdictions of its donor program, including an explanation of donor markings on its drivers' licenses.[7]

Some jurisdictions have tied in driver's license donor cards to legislation on anatomical gifts.[8] Some of these states included the actual donor card,[9] whereas others adopted the decal or sticker program, simply designating the holder as a donor.[10]

The theory behind the driver's license donor program is that a number of possible organs for transplantation that come from automobile accident victims go to waste each year. With an anatomical gift card or a donor decal as part of the victim's driver's license, hospitals can identify would-be organ donors at a time when family members would otherwise be too distraught to make a decision. A decision to remove transplantable organs may also be made at an optimal time, prior to the deterioration of such tissues. Of course, the victim must be legally dead for organ removal, and the fatality must not be the subject of a medicolegal inquiry. When the decedent's demise does come within the scope of a coroner's or medical examiner's jurisdiction, it may be possible to obtain permission to remove those organs required for transplantation.

§9.7.1 Difficulties Associated with Donor Designation Programs

The donor designation program is another important step toward increasing the pool of cadaver organs for transplanta-

[5] Mass. Gen. Laws Ann. ch. 90, §8D (West 1981).
[6] Ark. Stat. Ann. §82-411.14 (1977).
[7] Miss. Code Ann. §41-39-53 (1974).
[8] See, e.g., Ga. Code Ann. §92A-465 (1979); Tenn. Code Ann. §53-42-105 (1973); Ark. Stat. Ann. §82-410.14 (1973); S.C. Code §32.715.1 (1981).
[9] Arkansas and Tennessee included the donor card on the reverse side of the driver's license.
[10] Georgia and South Carolina adopted the decal-notation method of designating the driver as an organ donor.

tion, but the method is not problem-free. In those states that specify only a decal or sticker on drivers' licenses, holders must also carry a duly executed anatomical gift card. If for some reason this card is not on the victim's person at the time he is brought to the hospital, cannot be found at his home, or is not duly executed, transplantable organs may go to waste. To be sure, permission to remove organs in this instance could be sought from the decedent's next of kin. Their objection, however, means no transplantation of cadaver organs.

Another drawback is the limited number of states that permit minors to execute a driver's license donor card or to put a decal on it. Many motor vehicle fatalities involve young persons between the ages of 16 and 25. People in this age group are ideal organ donors, yet the law in many ways thwarts the prospect of anatomical gifts by them. The only open avenue is reliance on distraught family members to consent to the donation, something that they may or may not wish to do.

§9.8 The Moment of Death and Cadaver Organ Transplants

Since the beginning of cadaver organ donation, there has been much discussion of the moment of death. Often the issues of organ transplantation and the time of the donor's demise are confused. Traditionally, the common law defined death as the total cessation of respiratory and cardiac function.[1] In the 1960s, with the development of modern life-support and life-saving techniques, questions began to be raised about the accuracy of this definition. It is possible for brain waves from electroencephalographic tracings to demonstrate no brain activity despite a patient's continued functioning with the aid of respirators and intravenous feedings. In 1968, a multidisciplinary group at the Harvard Medical School, chaired by Dr.

§9.8 [1] Black's Law Dictionary 488 (4th ed. 1957).

Henry K. Beecher, formulated new criteria for assessing death in the wake of advanced medical technology.[2]

§9.8.1 The Harvard Ad Hoc Committee Criteria

The Harvard committee's criteria, and other similar standards, basically rely upon clinical manifestations of death. Included here are an inability to breathe spontaneously, unresponsiveness to painful stimuli, unreactiveness of pupils to light, and as confirmation of these clinical signs, a flat electroencephalogram (EEG). The EEG test is performed twice over a time span of more than 24 hours, although that span may be shorter in some hospitals. It should reflect no change from one tracing to the next. The validity of the test excludes two conditions: hypothermia and central nervous system depressant intoxication.[3]

Brain death or, as the Beecher committee referred to it, irreversible coma means that those whose cardiac and respiratory functions are maintained artificially and who demonstrate clinical signs of death may be disconnected from life-support machinery when there is no evidence of brain activity. It also means that would-be donors in an irreversible coma (brain dead) can be declared dead, removed from life-support equipment, and undergo organ removal for transplantation.

§9.8.2 Judicial and Legislative Criteria for Death

A number of states have enacted statutory definitions of death or brain death.[4] Some state courts have taken action to

[2]See Harvard Medical School's Ad Hoc Committee to Examine the Definition of Brain Death, Report of the Ad Hoc Committee of the Harvard Medical School, 205 J.A.M.A. 337 (1968).

[3]Supra n.2 at 338.

[4]See, e.g., Kan. Stat. Ann. §77-202 (1979); Cal. Health & Safety Code §7180 (West 1974) (irreversible cessation of brain function); Ga. Code Ann. §88-1716.1 (1982) (irreversible cessation of brain function as determined by two physicians); Md. Ann. Code art. 43, §54F (1982); Mont. Code Ann. §50-22-101 (1983); N.M. Stat. Ann. §12-2-4 (1978).

adopt new definitions of death. For example, in Commonwealth v. Golston,[5] the Massachusetts Supreme Judicial Court recognized the Harvard Ad Hoc Committee criteria for irreversible coma, at least with respect to criminal convictions for homicide. Other courts have also adopted irreversible coma or brain death as the legal standard.[6]

When the irreversibly comatose or brain-dead patient is also an organ donor, a suspicion or fear may arise that the plug will be pulled before the patient is dead. In other cases, the irreversibly comatose patient, once dead, may become the subject of a homicide investigation and a medicolegal autopsy. If so, physicians may be reluctant to suggest organ removal from the decedent.

A number of state statutes on brain death specify that prior to an individual's disconnecting life-support equipment, the patient must first be declared dead.[7] Some go even further and state the obvious: no organ may be removed for transplantation until death has been pronounced.[8] To further protect the dying patient who may become a donor, some statutes prohibit a member of the transplant team from pronouncing the death of the would-be donor.[9] Aside from the various state statutes in the United States, some hospital policy guidelines and standards have been developed that would, in practice, preclude pulling the plug on a donor prior to her death. A departure from this standard raises the prospect of either civil or criminal proceedings or both.[10]

---

[5]373 Mass. 249, 366 N.E.2d 744 (1977).

[6]In re Bowman, 94 Wash. 2d 407, 617 P.2d 731 (1980); State v. Fierro, 124 Ariz. 182, 603 P.2d 74 (1979); Lovato v. Colorado, 198 Colo. 419, 601 P.2d 1072 (1979). See also People v. Eulo, 63 N.Y.2d 341, 472 N.E.2d 286 (1984), in which the New York Court of Appeals ruled that the definition of death includes cessation of cardiorespiratory function or cessation of brain activity.

[7]Haw. Rev. Stat. §327C-1 (1985); Tex. Rev. Civ. Stat. Ann. art. 4447t, §1-3 (Vernon 1979); W. Va. Code Ann. §16-19-1 (1980).

[8]See, e.g., Conn. Gen. Stat. Ann. §19-139i(b) (1980); Haw. Rev. Stat. §327C-1 (1985); Md. Code Ann. art. 43, §54F (1982); Okla. Stat. Ann. tit. 63, §1-301(g) (West 1975).

[9]Conn. Gen. Stat. §19-139i(b) (1980); La. Stat. Ann. §9:111 (West 1976).

[10]See, e.g., Fla. Stat. Ann. §382.085 (West 1980), which only provides pro-

In the criminal homicide area, cases have claimed that the physician's removal of life-support equipment — not the assailant's actions — precipitated the person's death.[11] These arguments uniformly have been rejected by the courts. The reasoning has been that the defendant's actions caused the victim's death and that the disconnecting of respirators or circulatory-support equipment was done only after the person was dead.

Some hospitals have been hesitant to excise organs for transplantation from homicide victims for other reasons. Sometimes uncertainty surrounds the law regarding removal of organs and the jurisdiction of coroners and medical examiners. The following New York case illustrates the problem.[12]

In 1975, a 21-year-old male was admitted to the Bronx Municipal Hospital Center with a gunshot wound to the brain. He was unconscious, unresponsive, and lacked spontaneous respiration. He was placed on life-sustaining equipment and put in the intensive care unit. He was found to be neurologically dead the following day. The patient's mother gave permission for removal of her son's kidneys for transplant purposes. Court proceedings were instituted by the New York City Health and Hospitals Corporation for a declaratory judgment to define the time of death for New York's Anatomical Gift Act. In the interim the patient suffered cardiovascular failure and was declared dead. His two kidneys were removed and transplanted successfully into two recipients.[13]

The court held that the petitioners stated a cause of action for a declaratory judgment. It also held that the New York Anatomical Gift law was enacted to encourage organ donations and that the term *death* as used in the statute suggested a

---

tection from civil or criminal liability for acting in compliance with legislative requirements.

[11] See, e.g., Commonwealth v. Golston, 373 Mass. 249, 366 N.E.2d 744 (1977).

[12] New York City Health & Hosps. Corp. v. Sálsona, 81 Misc. 2d 1002, 367 N.Y.S.2d 686.

[13] Id.

definition consistent with generally accepted medical standards.[14]

As a result of the court proceedings, a Memorandum of Understanding[15] emerged between the medical examiner, the district attorneys of the counties involved, and the Health and Hospitals Corporation. The memorandum outlines the steps that should be taken to notify the medical examiner when a potential donor is a homicide victim. It includes a form to be completed by the attending physician with such information as the circumstances of the patient's admission and injury, evidence of cardiac cessation and brain death, the name of the person from whom consent to donate was obtained, and signature by the attending physician. The agreement also provides for a biopsy of organs removed for transplant purposes.[16]

The stated policy of the agreement is to permit transplantation of organs from bodies within the jurisdiction of the medical examiner. Removal of organs is not allowed if it can be shown that it would impede the medical examiner in carrying out his duties under the law or it would interfere with the establishment of cause of death in court actions.[17]

§9.8.3 Removal of Organs and Criminal Investigations

Some states have anticipated difficulty between coroners or medical examiners and those seeking to remove organs for transplants. These states have struck a balance between the rights and duty of the coroner or medical examiner in carrying out his statutory obligation and the recognized need for cadaver organs. In Ohio, for example,[18] the anatomical gift law permits the coroner to waive the right to claim a donated organ

---

[14] Id.
[15] Id. at 1008-1010, 367 N.Y.S.2d at 691-693.
[16] Id.
[17] Id.
[18] Ohio Rev. Code Ann. §2108.02(E) (Page 1980).

when the organ is unnecessary for purposes of either autopsy or evidence.[19] Connecticut takes a different approach, making an anatomical gift contingent upon approval of the medical examiner when the donor's death is subject to his investigation.[20]

In Texas, once the cardiac transplant capital of the world, a statute was enacted that allows transplantation of organs from bodies under the jurisdiction of the medical examiner.[21] The law provides that a medical examiner or deputy go immediately to a transplant facility to conduct an inquest on the body of the deceased prospective organ donor. When a determination for an autopsy is reached, the medical examiner or deputy must examine the organ to be transplanted, as well as other clinical evidence on the condition of the organ. Upon completion of the examination, the organ is then released to the transplant team. The rest of the remains are transported to a suitable place for completion of the autopsy.

Death and organ transplantation are two distinct issues, yet from time to time these issues overlap or become confused. Hospitals should develop clear-cut guidelines on discontinuing respirators for brain-dead patients. These should be based on sound legal advice, taking into account medicolegal requirements of death investigation, potential organ transplants, and the emotional aspect of discussing organ removal with survivors. Effective communication is essential. The guidelines should avoid unnecessary delays in determining death and discontinuing life-support care. To do otherwise may open the door to unpleasant confrontations with surviving family members.[22]

---

[19] Id.

[20] Conn. Gen. Stat. Ann. §19-139i (1980).

[21] Tex. Code Crim. Proc. art. 49.25 (Vernon 1987).

[22] See Strachan v. John F. Kennedy Memorial Hosp., 209 N.J. Super. 300, 507 A.2d 718 (1986), in which the New Jersey Superior Court, Appellate Division, reversed and remanded a lawsuit based on the tort of outrage and inappropriate handling of a dead body. In this case it was claimed that unnecessary delays occurred following the determination of brain death involving a suicide victim. Although the court rejected the claim that the hospital should have had consent forms for pronouncement of brain death and for

In the absence of statutes defining death or empowering medical examiners to release organs for donation, policies can be developed among all interested parties to work out the release of transplantable organs. Hospitals, in particular, should work out a protocol for determining death, who may declare a person dead, and the excision of organs from donors who come within the jurisdiction of the coroner or medical examiner.

§9.9 Removal of Organs by Medical Examiners, Coroners, and Others

Aside from anatomical gift legislation, many states have statutes that authorize removal and disposal of body parts by medical examiners and coroners. The tissues most often referred to in the legislation are the pituitary gland and the cornea. Connecticut's statute[1] authorizes the chief medical examiner or the official performing an autopsy to remove pituitary and corneal tissues as long as certain requirements are met. There must be permission from the decedent's next of kin and the medical examiner (or the person doing the autopsy) must reasonably believe that removing the tissue would benefit a living person. Additionally, there must not be any disfigurement of the body caused by the tissue excision and the tissue removal should not impede subsequent investigation or autopsy of the deceased.

---

disconnecting life support, the case illustrates how a straightforward policy on such issues can avoid a confrontation with next of kin. It should be noted that on further appeal, the Supreme Court of New Jersey affirmed in part and reversed in part the appellate court's ruling. What is of particular interest is the New Jersey Supreme Court's determination that the hospital did not have a duty to the parents to have in place policies and procedures for removal of life-support systems. The court based its ruling on the hospital's duty to act in a reasonable fashion in handling the parents' request to release their son's dead body. The court's decision serves to put in proper focus the role of policies and procedures governing the discontinuance of life-support equipment. See Strachan v. John F. Kennedy Memorial Hosp., 538 A.2d 346 (N.J. 1988).

§9.9 [1]Conn. Gen. Stat. §19-139m (1982).

§9.9.1   Corneal and Pituitary Gland Removal

A number of state statutes specify removal of either corneal tissue or pituitary glands.[2] Unlike in the Connecticut enactment, these regulations do not require authorization of the decedent's next of kin. Rather, these statutes provide that there must be no objection by the next of kin. These laws apply to the bodies of decedents under the jurisdiction of a medical examiner or coroner. Many grant the medical examiner civil immunity[3] for carrying out the tissue removal in accordance with the statute. Some states also grant immunity from criminal liability.[4]

A few of the statutory laws take into account the religious beliefs of the decedent or the next of kin. New York,[5] for example, prohibits corneal tissue removal if it conflicts with the religious beliefs of the deceased. Other states, such as Ohio,[6] authorize the tissue removal unless there is a religious objection by the next of kin.

The legislatures of a few states have also enacted provisions that permit tissue removal even when next of kin are unavailable either to grant permission or to state that they have no objection. Virginia's statute authorizes eye and other tissue removal for transplantation without approval of next of kin when the viability of the tissue cannot be maintained for the amount of time it would require to contact the family of the decedent. It also requires that there be no known or foreseeable objection by the next of kin.[7]

Although statutes have been enacted regarding removal of corneal tissue, that has not blocked legal challenges to such practices. Indeed, in a Georgia case, that state's legislation au-

[2] See, e.g., Del. Code Ann. tit. 29, §4711 (1988); Ga. Code §§88-200-1 et seq. (1980) (cornea and eye tissue); Ohio Rev. Code Ann. §2108.53 (Baldwin 1978).
[3] See Del. Code Ann. tit. 29, §4712 (1988); N.Y. Pub. Health Law §4222 (McKinney 1978).
[4] Ga. Code Ann. §88-2010 (1980); Ky. Rev. Stat. §311.187 (1980).
[5] N.Y. Pub. Health Law §4222 (McKinney 1978).
[6] Ohio Rev. Code Ann. §2108.53 (Baldwin 1978).
[7] Va. Code §32.1-287 (1985).

thorizing corneal removal was challenged as being unconstitutional.[8]

The case arose following the demise of an infant from infant sudden death syndrome. The infant's corneas were removed during an autopsy by officials from the Georgia Lions Eye Bank. At no time were the parents notified of the intended removal of the tissue. Moreover, there was never any "realistic opportunity" to object to the procedure.[9] When the infant's mother learned what had occurred, she sued the hospital and eye bank for wrongful removal of the corneal tissue.

The trial court had found the Georgia statute unconstitutional on the ground that it denied due process. The law was characterized as depriving the next of kin her property right in the property of the deceased. It was also held that it failed to provide notice and an opportunity to object.[10]

In reversing the lower court's ruling, the Supreme Court of Georgia held that in Georgia there was no constitutionally protected right in the body of a decedent. It was better termed a common law quasi-property interest held by the survivors in taking possession and control of the decedent's body.

The court also found that the statute was constitutional. The legislature was deemed empowered to pass such legislation in the interest of the public welfare.[11] The Supreme Court of Florida has also upheld the constitutionality of corneal removal legislation.[12] Like the Georgia court before it, the Florida jurists ruled that the legislation furthers state objectives in restoring sight to those who are blind.

This Georgia case is instructive to eye bank personnel throughout the United States. Although the case was resolved in favor of the defendants, the need for communication with survivors is important. If cadaver organ procurement programs are to be increased, it is important to generate a positive

[8]Georgia Lions Eye Bank v. Lavant, 355 S.E.2d 127 (1985).
[9]Id. at 128.
[10]Id., interpreting O.C.G.A. §31-23-6(b)(1) (1978).
[11]Id. at 129.
[12]See State v. Powell, 497 So. 2d 1188 (Fla. 1986), interpreting Fla. Stat. Ann. §732.9185 (West 1983).

public image. That statutory law does not require notification of next of kin of organ or tissue removal does not preclude it from being done. It is a common sense approach that will foster better community relations.

§9.9.2 Eye Enucleation Procedures

Some states authorize persons who are not physicians to perform eye enucleation. Various jurisdictions designate licensed embalmers,[13] funeral service practitioners,[14] or individuals certified by a medical school as being qualified to perform the eye removal.[15]

§9.10 Disposal and Use of Unclaimed Bodies

Another series of statutes authorizes the state to distribute unclaimed bodies as anatomical specimens. Although each of the states has its own specific requirements for disposing of dead bodies, it is often necessary for public officials to notify the department of health or board of anatomy of the availability of unclaimed remains.[1] Usually the public official, department of health, or anatomy board must attempt to notify friends or relatives of the deceased. The notification time varies from 24 to 48 hours in most states.[2] Sometimes the notice goes out to fraternal organizations or persons of the same religious belief as that of the decedent.[3] When there is no response to the

---

[13]See, e.g., Miss. Code Ann. §41-39-11 (1984); Ohio Rev. Code Ann. §2108.60 (Baldwin 1984).

[14]N.M. Stat. Ann. §24-6-7(E) (1981).

[15]Mich. Comp. Laws Ann. §333.10105 (1978).

§9.10 [1]Ark. Stat. Ann. §82-404 (1959); Conn. Gen. Stat. §19-139 (1982).
[2]California requires a 24-hour notice period, Cal. Health & Safety Code §7200 (West 1970). Arkansas and Connecticut have set 48-hour notice periods, Ark. Stat. Ann. §82-404 (1959) and Conn. Gen. Stat. §19-139 (1982).
[3]Colo. Rev. Stat. §12-34-203 (1963).

notification or attempts to make contact fail, the unclaimed body may be scheduled for use in the advancement of science or medicine. In many jurisdictions this means retaining the body in a preserved state for a stated period of time.[4] In other states it means that the body may be distributed as soon as the original notification period has elapsed. When no one claims the body, it may be distributed to specific or unnamed medical schools,[5] dentistry schools,[6] schools of chiropractic studies[7] or embalming schools.[8] A body may also be distributed to hospitals, universities, or colleges.[9]

Certain categories of remains may not be used for anatomical research. Banned is the distribution of dead bodies with contagious disease,[10] of travelers,[11] of tramps,[12] of veterans,[13] and of those who requested prior to their deaths that they be buried.[14] Connecticut bans the use of those held in connection with a civil or criminal proceeding.[15] Similarly, if the decedent had been detained as a witness in a criminal proceeding, his body may not be used for anatomical research in Minnesota.[16] If the body

[4]Colo. Rev. Stat. Ann. §12-34-203 (1963) (body must be retained for 20 days); Cal. Health & Safety Code §7202 (West 1945) (body to be properly preserved and retained for 30 days).

[5]Connecticut, for example, specifies certain medical schools. Conn. Gen. Stat. Ann. §19-139 (1982) (University of Connecticut School of Medicine and Yale University School of Medicine). Other states just indicate that unclaimed bodies may be distributed for scientific advancement and educational purposes. See, e.g., Cal. Health & Safety Code §7202 (West 1945).

[6]See, e.g., Colo. Rev. Stat. Ann. §12-34-202 (1963); Fla. Stat. Ann. §245.12 (West 1977).

[7]Cal. Health & Safety Code §7203 (West 1939).

[8]Id.

[9]Ariz. Rev. Stat. §36-807 (1973) (hospitals, colleges, and universities); Me. Rev. Stat. Ann. tit. 22, §2884 (1954) (schools, including those of nursing and premedical study).

[10]E.g., Ariz. Rev. Stat. Ann. §36-806 (1956); Conn. Gen. Stat. Ann. §19-140 (1958).

[11]Conn. Gen. Stat. Ann. §19-140 (1958).

[12]Conn. Gen. Stat. §19-140 (1958).

[13]Mass. Gen. Laws Ann. ch. 113, §2 (West 1954).

[14]Ariz. Rev. Stat. Ann. §36-806 (1956) (those requesting burial within 24 hours prior to death); Conn. Gen. Stat. Ann. §19-140 (1958); Mass. Gen. Laws Ann. ch. 113, §2 (West 1954).

[15]Conn. Gen. Stat. Ann. §19-140 (1958).

[16]Minn. Stat. Ann. §145.15 (West 1969).

is claimed by a relative or friend,[17] or fraternal or religious organization,[18] it may not be used for scientific purposes.

Some jurisdictions have also enacted laws regarding disposal of fetal remains. In California,[19] fetal remains may be used for scientific or laboratory research as well as experimentation or study. Upon completion of the work, the fetal remains must be "promptly interred or disposed of by incineration."[20] Furthermore, during the course of the study or reasearch, the fetal tissues must be placed in an area away from public view.[21] The laws in California regarding fetal remains in research and study, as well as the storage of and disposal of same, do not apply to private or public educational institutions.[22]

The Mississippi Code[23] also includes a law regarding fetal tissues. The state board of health is authorized to promulgate regulations for the disposition of fetal remains. Massachusetts, in its statute regarding human fetal research, makes it a criminal offense to sell, transfer, distribute, or give away any fetus "for scientific laboratory research or other kind of experimentation."[24] Research and experimentation may be conducted upon a dead fetus with the mother's written consent. The consent would then constitute a lawful transfer of the fetal remains.[25] The law makes it clear, however, that the prohibitions on fetal research do not apply to routine pathology studies.

Lawful distribution of unclaimed bodies can provide useful information and training to a variety of health care students and professionals. Failure to comply with individual state requirements could lead to criminal[26] or civil liability. Health facilities should consult with their legal advisors for specific

---

[17] Ariz. Rev. Stat. Ann. §36-806 (1956) (friend or relative); Colo. Rev. Stat. Ann. §12-34-202 (1963) (friend or relative).
[18] Fla. Stat. Ann. §245.09 (West 1972) (charitable or religious organization).
[19] Cal. Health & Safety Code §§25956 (West 1973) and 25957 (West 1976).
[20] Id. at §25957(a).
[21] Id.
[22] Id. at §25957(b).
[23] Miss. Code Ann. §41-39-102.
[24] Mass. Gen. Laws Ann. ch. 112, §12J (West 1976).
[25] Id. at (a) II. The mother must be at least 18 years of age.
[26] See, e.g., Ariz. Rev. Stat. §36-808 (1973).

information concerning disposal of and scientific use of unclaimed bodies in their states.

§9.11 Organ Procurement Legislation

In 1986, in an effort to increase the available organ pool for
transplantation, Congress used its funding clout through Medicare and Medicaid to coerce hospitals into becoming more aggressive in organ procurement.[1]

Not to be left out, many states have also passed laws on the
topic.[2] As seen in this section, however, there are a number of
practical considerations which must be addressed, including a
practical yet effective way of dealing with distraught family
when requesting permission to procure organs for transplantation.

§9.11.1 Federal and State Requirements for Organ Procurement

The federal requirements governing organ procurement
were initially authorized under the Omnibus Budget Reconciliation Act of 1986.[3] The Department of Health and Human
Services issued regulations under the law in March 1988.[4]

On the state level, considerable legislative activity has oc-
cured. Under state law, hospitals are required to set up organ

§9.11 [1]See Pub. L. No. 99-509. It should be noted that there was subsequent legislative activity to defer the implementation date of the law. For this
information, see the ,Balanced Budget and Emergency Deficit Control
Reaffirmation Act of 1987, Pub. L. No. 100-119, and the Omnibus Budget
Reconciliation Act of 1987, Pub. L. No. 100-203.
[2]See, e.g., Ariz. Rev. Stat. §36-849 (1986); Ark. Stat. Ann. §20-17-502
(1987); Ga. Code §48-402 (1987); Ill. Ann. Stat. ch. 110 1/2, §752 (Smith-
Hurd 1987); Minn. Stat. Ann. §525.94 (West 1987); N.D. Cent. Code §23-
06.1-06.1 (1987).
[3]See n.1, supra.
[4]53 Fed. Reg. 6,526 (March 1, 1988).

procurement protocols[5] or policies or procedures[6] to facilitate acquisition of organs for transplantation.

Much of the state legislation focuses on approaching the family with a view toward securing consent to organ removal.[7] Some of the laws admonish caregivers to act with sensitivity when approaching family members.[8] Others suggest that the protocol or procedure for securing consent to organ procurement take into account religious opposition to such donation.[9]

For hospitals and other health facilities, organ procurement laws necessitate development of a practical policy and procedure. Such a procedure should address a number of key issues, including identification of potential organ donors, communication and reporting channels, documentation of organ donation intent on the patient's record, documentation of consent from family, and how the consent process is to proceed when approaching family members.

Although organ procurement is an important issue, the methods used to secure donated tissues and organs require careful thought. Through planning and well-developed policy and procedure manuals hospitals can develop a proper approach to organ procurement which takes into consideration federal and state requirements as well as the human side of the matter.

§9.11.2   Practical Considerations in Organ Procurement

For many health professionals, approaching a family with a request to harvest organs is a difficult task. It is seen as taking

[5] See Colo. Rev. Stat. §12-34-108.5 (1987); Kan. Stat. Ann. §65-3218 (1986); Ky. Rev. Stat. §311.241 (1986); Ohio Rev. Code Ann. §2108.021 (Baldwin 1987).

[6] Ark. Stat. Ann. §20-17-502 (1987); N.M. Stat. Ann. §24-6-10 (1987).

[7] Ga. Code §48-402 (1987); Mass. Gen. Laws Ann. ch. 113, §8 (West 1986).

[8] Colo. Rev. Stat. §12-34-108.5 (1987); Kan. Stat. Ann. §65-3218 (1986); Miss. Code Ann. §41-39-15 (1987).

[9] Ill. Ann. Stat. ch. 110 1/2, §752 (Smith-Hurd 1987); La. Rev. Stat. Ann. §17:2354.4 (West 1986).

advantage at a time of great personal stress. There is concern that family may not be able to give an effective consent or that they may react with hostility.

There is another side to the matter. For grief-stricken relatives, the opportunity to donate organs from a deceased loved one may be seen as a lasting memorial. Giving the "gift of life" to another person is interpreted as in some way perpetuating the life of the deceased.

Tact, good communication, and experience must be used when approaching a family with a view toward organ procurement. However, additional steps should be taken to minimize unpleasant situations. These include the following:

1. Develop screening programs to flag families who are unlikely to wish to donate based on religious or philosophical grounds;
2. For patients entering the hospital for elective procedures, build into the admitting process a request for consent to organ donation and document accordingly all authorizations;
3. Develop with hospital social workers and pastoral care workers a protocol for securing consent to organ procurement from family members;
4. Build into the program adequate training for those who must approach family for such requests, including role playing;
5. Ensure that all documentation and communication requirements are in place; and
6. Make certain that requests for organ donation do not run afoul of medical examiner and coroner jurisdiction requirements.

By taking an active approach, many of the difficulties encountered in organ procurement requests can be avoided. Sensitivity and tact as well as good communication skills are key issues in this regard.

C. AUTOPSY AND CONSENT

Autopsies are largely a legislative matter in the United States. Basically, two types of autopsy laws have been passed, those authorizing a medical examiner or coroner to conduct a post-mortem examination and those authorizing hospitals to perform autopsies with the consent of the decedent's next of kin. Several cases have also been reported regarding the authority of the medical examiner or coroner to carry out an autopsy when objections have been voiced by next of kin. The statutory and case law regarding autopsies is discussed below.

§9.12 Statutory Authority to Conduct Medicolegal Autopsies

Coroners and medical examiners are usually empowered to conduct an investigation into several categories of deaths. These include deaths due to violence, suicide, and suspicious or unexplained causes.[1] Some laws grant jurisdiction to a medical examiner or coroner when a person's death was due to criminal neglect or an unlawful act, or when an individual dies in an institution other than a hospital or nursing home.[2] Other statutes give the medical examiner or coroner jurisdiction in deaths caused by electrical, chemical, or thermal agents, as well as deaths resulting from occupational injury or disease.[3] Bodies of those who were sexually abused may also come within the scope of a coroner or medical examiner.[4] Children who are suspected to have died a sudden, unexplained death may

§9.12 [1] N.Y. County Law §673 (McKinney 1965). See also Tenn. Code Ann. §38-7-108 (1986).
[2] Id.
[3] Conn. Gen. Stat. Ann. §19-530 (1981).
[4] Mass. Gen. Laws Ann. ch. 38, §6 (West 1982).

fall under the medicolegal investigation laws in some states.[5] In some states, the authority to conduct a medicolegal inquiry may extend to cases in which death was sudden, unexpected, and not caused by any readily known illness or disease,[6] or deaths in which physicians are unable to certify the cause.[7]

A coroner's or medical examiner's jurisdiction over a dead body does not mean that she will perform an autopsy on it. Most of the laws on the subject authorize the use of such investigative methods — including autopsies — that are necessary to determine the cause of death.[8] In many states this investigation begins with an external postmortem examination, leaving autopsies as an additional step when the external check is not dispositive of the cause of death.[9] Some statutes authorize specific procedures short of autopsies. For example, the coroner or medical examiner may be authorized to draw blood and urine samples from the bodies of those killed while driving or riding in a motor vehicle. The samples are to be obtained prior to the body's being prepared for burial. The blood and urine are then subjected to a variety of tests, including those for alcohol, barbiturate, and amphetamine levels.[10] California permits a coroner to complete the certificate of death without an

---

[5]See, e.g., Cal. Govt. Code §27491.4 (West 1979), which states in part that:

> For purposes of inquiry the coroner shall, within 24 hours or as soon as feasible thereafter, where the suspected cause of death is sudden infant death syndrome unless the infant's physician of record certifies sudden infant death syndrome as the cause of death and a parent objects to an autopsy; and, in all other cases, the coroner may, in his or her discretion, take possession of the body, which shall include the authority to . . . make or cause to be made a postmortem or autopsy thereon. . . .

See also Mass. Gen. Laws Ann. ch. 38, §20 (West 1978).
[6]Conn. Gen. Stat. Ann. §19-530 (1981).
[7]N.Y. County Law §673 (McKinney 1965).
[8]Ala. Code §15-4-2 (1975); N.Y. County Law §674 (McKinney 1978).
[9]See, e.g., Ala. Code §15-4-2 (1975). In Alabama, an autopsy may be performed when the cause of death is not determined upon external examination of the body and the coroner has reasonable cause to believe that the person's death was due to unlawful means.
[10]Cal. Govt. Code §27491.25 (West 1974); N.Y. County Law §674 (McKinney 1978).

autopsy when available information provides sufficient evidence to establish the cause of death. This rule applies in those cases in which a peron died of natural causes and without medical attendance.[11]

Medical examiners or coroners may be required by courts to perform autopsies. For example, in Arizona,[12] a court may order a body exhumed and then autopsied when a person died under sudden, suspicious, or violent circumstances that were not investigated at the time.

Medicolegal autopsies fall into a category of very specific authority. Consent by relatives of the deceased is not an issue when the person's cause of death comes within the jurisdiction of the medical examiner or coroner. Such authority can be determined by reviewing applicable state law on the subject. Even in this aspect of law, however, there have been challenges to the scope of authority vested in medical examiners and coroners.

§9.13 Power to Conduct Nonmedicolegal Autopsies

Autopsies may be ordered by courts for reasons other than a medicolegal inquiry by a coroner or medical examiner. Wyoming, for instance, has a law that authorizes a court to order an autopsy when it is considered necessary in order to determine the exact cause of death.[1] The autopsy need not be performed by a coroner or medical examiner. Rather, the law specifies that it can be conducted by a physician who specializes in doing autopsies.[2]

[11]Cal. Govt. Code §27491.5 (West 1979). See also Conn. Gen. Stat. Ann. §19-530 (1981).
[12]Ariz. Rev. Stat. Ann. §11-598 (1975).
§9.13 [1]Wyo. Stat. §27-14-509 (1986).
[2]Id.

Some states have laws that authorize boards to order autopsies. New York has a statute that empowers the Mental Hygiene Review Board to order an autopsy of a dead patient or resident of a mental hygiene facility when the board determines that it is necessary in order to find the cause of death.[3]

A more common type of statute empowers hospitals or physicians to perform autopsies. Unlike those laws authorizing medical examiners or coroners to conduct such investigations, the nonforensic autopsy statutes do require consent. Consent typically comes from a relative of the decedent[4] or from instructions left by the person prior to death.[5] Many of the statutes set out a list of persons who may consent to an autopsy. The list is typically the same as that which designates who may assume custody of the body for burial.[6] In some jurisdictions the statute merely makes reference to those who may assume the legal duty of disposal or burial of the body.[7]

In some states there may not be specific statutory authority for nonforensic autopsies. It is then important to search the common law for judicial precedent authorizing relatives to consent to such procedures. Jurisdictions in this category include Georgia,[8] Massachusetts,[9] and Vermont.[10]

As a matter of sound judgment prior to performing an autopsy, physicians should determine with the aid of their legal advisors the legal requirements for securing permission to do such a procedure. Hospitals should also have guidelines on obtaining consent to autopsies. By identifying the statutory or common law criteria for authorizing autopsies, physicians and hospitals can avoid legal actions.

---

[3] N.Y. Mental Hyg. Law §45.17 (McKinney 1977).
[4] See, e.g., Conn. Gen. Stat. Ann. §19-143 (1981).
[5] See, e.g., Ark. Stat. Ann. §82-406 (1955).
[6] Id.; Conn. Gen. Stat. Ann. §19-143 (1981).
[7] See, e.g., N.Y. Pub. Health Law §4214 (McKinney 1953); N.Y. Pub. Health Law §4215 (McKinney 1967).
[8] Pollard v. Phelps, 56 Ga. App. 408, 193 S.E. 102 (1937).
[9] Vaughn v. Vaughn, 294 Mass. 164, 200 N.E. 912 (1936).
[10] Nichols v. Central Vermont Ry., 94 Vt. 14, 109 A. 905 (1919).

§9.14   Judicial Action in Contested and Unauthorized Autopsies

A number of cases have challenged the authority of coroners and medical examiners to perform autopsies. Many of these cases have been based on religious objection to autopsies. The following cases are illustrative of this type of challenge.

§9.14.1   Religious Objections to Autopsies

In a Maryland case,[1] the father of an 18-year-old man challenged the authority of the medical examiner to perform a postmortem examination on the body of his son. The father had picked his son up around 1:00 p.m. on the day of his death. They had returned to their home where they were in contact for the balance of the afternoon. Around 6:00 p.m. the father heard a thud in his son's room and went in to investigate. He found the young man did not respond and he called the rescue squad. The teenager was taken to the Holy Cross Hospital, but he died prior to his arrival.

There was no history of illness on the part of the young man and no evidence from interviewing the attending physicians, emergency personnel, and the family to explain this sudden, unexpected death. Under these circumstances the medical examiner assigned to the case ordered the body removed to Baltimore for a complete postmortem examination, pursuant to Maryland law.[2]

The father and his son were both Orthodox Jews. Their religious belief prohibited any molestation or mutilation of bodies after death, including autopsies. The father went to court seeking injunctive relief prohibiting the postmortem ex-

§9.14   [1]Snyder v. Holy Cross Hosp., 30 Md. App. 317, 352 A.2d 334 (1976).
[2]Md. Ann. Code art. 22, §6 (1980). Section 7 of the same article empowers the medical examiner to perform an autopsy whenever it is deemed necessary or desirable.

amination and an order directing release of his son's body for burial.[3]

In denying the injunction, the Maryland Court of Appeals noted that this was a medical examiner's case, since the young man had died suddenly while in apparent good health and while unattended by a physician. From the facts presented the only way the cause of death could be established was by conducting an autopsy. The father's First Amendment guarantee of freedom of religion was not absolute. The guarantee could be limited when religious practice (as opposed to religious belief) is at issue, if the state can demonstrate a sufficiently compelling interest. Here the state's interest outweighed that of the father. The state had a paramount right to learn the cause of death. Furthermore, the father could not assert his own constitutional rights regarding religious freedom with respect to an autopsy on the body of his son. While it was his right to provide a proper burial for his son, his property interest in the body was in the manner of a trust subject to applicable law.[4]

In three New York cases,[5] the courts prohibited the performance of autopsies. In one of these cases, the decedent was an Orthodox Jew. As noted in the *Snyder* case, supra, the Orthodox Jewish faith views autopsies as a mutilation of the dead. Unlike the *Snyder* case, though, there were no sudden, unexpected, or suspicious circumstances surrounding the cause of death.

In one case,[6] a 78-year-old woman was struck by a motor vehicle while crossing a street. She died one week later as the result of her injuries. The state had no plan to press criminal proceedings against the driver. Still the medical examiner

---

[3] Snyder v. Holy Cross Hosp., supra n.1.

[4] Id. Of interest is the amendment of the Maryland Code after this case to require the authorization of medical examiners or their agents for autopsies when there is a religious objection posed by the family of the deceased. See Md. Ann. Code art, 22, §7(b) (1982).

[5] Atkins v. Medical Examiner of Westchester County, 100 Misc. 2d 296, 418 N.Y.S.2d 839 (Supp. 1979); Weberman v. Zugibe, 90 Misc. 2d 254, 394 N.Y.S.2d 371 (Supp. 1977); Wilensky v. Greco, 74 Misc. 512, 344 N.Y.S.2d 77 (Supp. 1973).

[6] Atkins v. Medical Examiner of Westchester County, supra n.5.

wanted an autopsy performed to determine the cause of death. The son of the decedent went to court challenging the medical examiner's authority to conduct an autopsy. The court granted a permanent injunction banning the postmortem examination. The decision was based on the absence of any sound reason to warrant the procedure in the face of deeply held religious beliefs, just to satisfy the medical examiner's curiosity as to the cause of death.

A similar set of facts was the basis in Weberman v. Zugibe for enjoining the medical examiner from autopsying the victim of a pedestrian-automobile accident.[7] In this case, the woman was 66 years of age and she died within an hour of the accident. The medical examiner wanted to perform the autopsy to determine if her death was due to injury to one vital organ as opposed to another. The court held that, given the facts of the case and the reason advanced for the autopsy, it was neither a "necessary" procedure nor one sufficient to outweigh the religious beliefs of the woman's family.

In Wilensky v. Greco,[8] an autopsy was held not necessary under applicable state law in a case involving a 16-year-old victim of a highway accident. The young man had received a series of serious injuries and he died following surgery. The coroner wanted an autopsy to determine which of the injuries was the cause of death. This was held insufficient reason to overcome the religious beliefs of the young man's parents, absent any suspicion of criminality or foul play in connection with his death.

There have been other challenges to medical examiners and coroners who perform autopsies without the consent of the next of kin of the decedent. Unlike in the cases discussed above, these matters have not involved religious objections to autopsies. Rather, these cases have been brought on the basis of unauthorized postmortem examinations.

[7]Supra n.5.
[8]Supra n.5.

§9.14.2   Unauthorized Autopsies

In Rupp v. Jackson[9] and Scarpaci v. Milwaukee County,[10] relatives of two decedents challenged the authority of medical examiners to order autopsies without their consent. In *Rupp*, the Supreme Court of Florida dismissed a writ of certiorari filed by the medical examiner after the District Court of Appeals reversed and remanded a favorable trial court decision. The Supreme Court held that a state statute requiring the last attending doctor to complete a certificate specifying the cause of death did not empower the medical examiner to conduct an autopsy. When such an examination was desired, he had to follow statutory requirements regarding autopsies without the consent of surviving family.[11]

In *Scarpaci*,[12] the Supreme Court of Wisconsin affirmed the lower court's denial of a motion to dismiss an action brought by parents for an unauthorized autopsy on the body of their deceased child. The parents had made known that they did not want an autopsy, yet one was conducted without their permission upon the order of the medical examiner. The court noted that the power of the medical examiner to perform or order an autopsy is limited by statute; none may be conducted or authorized in the absence of legislative authority to do so.[13]

§9.14.3   Medical Examiners' Power to Order Autopsies Sustained

In other situations, the power of medical examiners to order autopsies has been sustained. For example, in Lee v. Weston,[14] a coroner ordered an autopsy to be conducted on the body of

[9]238 So. 2d 86 (Fla. 1970).
[10]96 Wis. 2d 663, 292 N.W.2d 816 (1980).
[11]Rupp v. Jackson, supra n.9.
[12]Supra n.10.
[13]Id.
[14]402 N.E.2d 23 (Ind. Ct. App. 1980).

an 18-year-old who had been found dead on the floor of his friend's apartment. His body was found next to a nearly empty bottle of whiskey. The court granted summary judgment in favor of the coroner in an action brought by the young man's parents. The court held that there was no malice or bad faith on the part of the coroner in ordering the autopsy, even though the order was issued after the body had been partially embalmed.

A similar result was reached in a federal court decision in Connecticut.[15] In that case a 16-year-old Florida boy was found dead in bed at a Connecticut boarding school. There was no external evidence as to the cause of death. Although the teenager was known to have Marfan's syndrome, the medical examiner concluded that an autopsy was necessary to determine the exact cause of death. An autopsy revealed that he had died of a ruptured saccular aneurysm due to the disease. The Second Circuit Court of Appeals affirmed the district court's dismissal of the action. It was pointed out that under Connecticut law, the medical examiner need not obtain the consent of a relative for an autopsy when, as here, the cause of death is obscure.

In an Illinois case,[16] relatives of a decedent filed suit against a hospital and coroner in connection with an allegedly wrongful autopsy. The decedent had been admitted with Hodgkin's disease and died in hospital. No physician was willing to sign the death certificate stating the reason for her death without an autopsy being performed. Under Illinois law,[17] the coroner needed information on the cause of the patient's demise in order to issue a death certificate. Illinois legislation authorized the coroner to order the autopsy, and applicable legislation authorized the hospital and its staff to perform the examination. On this basis the court denied the plaintiff's claim of an unauthorized autopsy.

---

[15] Donnelly v. Gerion, 467 F.2d 290 (2d Cir. 1972).

[16] Cybart v. Michael Reese Hosp. & Med. Center, 50 Ill. App. 3d 603, 365 N.E.2d 1002 (1977).

[17] Ill. Rev. Stat. ch. 31, §10.4 (1969), cited in Cybart v. Michael Reese Hosp. & Med. Center, supra n.16.

As the Illinois case suggests, coroners and medical examiners are not the only ones who may be sued for unauthorized autopsies. Hospitals or their staffs may liable for postmortems performed without permission. Lawsuits may also arise from cases in which consent is given for an autopsy but the scope of the procedure is unclear. The two cases following demonstrate this type of problem.

§9.14.4 The Need for Complete Disclosure

In Hendriksen v. Roosevelt Hospital,[18] the brother of the decedent brought a lawsuit for wrongful retention of internal organs and tissues removed at autopsy. The plaintiff had signed an authorization for an autopsy of his sister's body that granted permission for a complete autopsy, including a scalp incision to examine the brain.[19] When he learned that the hospital had retained his sister's brain and all her internal organs he sued. The U.S. District Court denied the defendant's motion to dismiss, stating that there was ample evidence for a jury question whether the hospital had exceeded the scope of the plaintiff's consent by retaining body parts following the autopsy. As the court suggested, nothing in New York's autopsy statute suggests that organ and tissue retention is part of a valid consent to a postmortem examination.[20]

The opposite conclusion was reached in a Kentucky case involving the alleged mutilation of the body of the plaintiff's son.[21] The plaintiff had signed a document authorizing the defendant to retain any body specimens of the decedent that the defendant considered necessary.[22] Upon learning that her son's heart was missing and that his brain had been placed in his stomach after autopsy, she sued the physician who performed the procedure. The trial court's directed verdict in

[18] 297 F. Supp. 1142 (S.D.N.Y. 1969).
[19] Id.
[20] Id.
[21] Lashbrook v. Barnes, 437 S.W. 502 (Ky. 1969).
[22] Id.

favor of the defendant was affirmed by the Kentucky Court of Appeals. Placing the brain in the abdomen and removing the heart was found to be in accordance with customary and usual practice. The procedure was not mutilation of the body since the mother had signed an authorization permitting the removal of body tissues.

Although consent to a medicolegal autopsy is not required, some families may object to particular aspects of such investigations. In an effort to assist such families, physicians may try to intervene between them and the coroner or medical examiner. As a Kansas case suggests,[23] great care should be exercised when intervening between families and coroners or medical examiners.

In that case, the death of a man was deemed a coroner's case, necessitating an autopsy. The physician who had attended the man contacted his mother and informed her that an autopsy was to be carried out. She indicated that she did not want her son's brain to be autopsied. Moreover, she did not want the Kansas Neurological Institute to examine his brain. The doctor never conveyed this information to the coroner and a complete autopsy was performed. The mother learned about it a few weeks later when a doctor contacted her to say that the Institute had her son's brain, and he wanted to know what she wanted done with it.

In the lawsuit that followed, the court pointed out that the woman had been misled by the doctor. He had not been under a legal duty to act, but once he had voluntarily involved himself in the situation, the doctor was then under the obligation to discharge his duty with care. Having not done so, he was held liable for the reasonable costs of exhuming the man's body so that the brain and the body could be buried together.[24]

The natural inclination is to help those in distress. Seeing a patient's loved ones grief-stricken may cause others to offer assistance. Nonetheless, care should be taken not to create inordinate expectations or to promise more than can be accomplished. Certainly, it is far better to let family and medical

[23] Burgess v. Perdue, 239 Kan. 473, 721 P.2d 239 (1986).
[24] Id.

examiners or coroners work out the details of an autopsy than to become an intervenor in the process. Well-intentioned intervention may actually disrupt the important communication of details and, as seen in this Kansas case, result in unwanted litigation.

Part of the difficulty in autopsy authorizations is making it clear to the surviving family what is to be done as part of the procedure. These situations involve people who may be terribly upset and emotionally overcome. They may not be thinking clearly or appreciate the scope of an autopsy. To avoid lawsuits for unauthorized postmortem studies, health personnel should explain carefully the nature of the examination. The disclosure need not be a detailed catalogue of each step in an autopsy, but the physician should disclose that information that is usually important to survivors, including the need to remove and retain organs, the possibility of a cranial autopsy, whether this or any other incision may leave a noticeable scar or whether it may be cosmetically hidden by the embalmer or the mortician, and the replacing of tissues removed during the procedure. Documentation of a family member's consent should be made and kept on file. When the physician feels that the family is emotionally unable to give an informed consent to the autopsy, she should not press the issue. Authorization obtained under these circumstances will not withstand close scrutiny by a court of law.

D. OTHER MEDICAL USES FOR DEAD BODIES

Cadavers offer medical students an excellent opportunity for learning anatomy and human body function. As noted earlier in the chapter, mechanisms are in place for donation of dead bodies for this purpose. Many medical schools have courses in place to sensitize students to dealing with death and demonstrating respect for dead bodies.

What is often overlooked, however, is the issue of students' using a newly dead patient as a training ground for practicing injections, intubation, and other procedures. As seen in this part of the chapter, not only are the ethics of the situation questionable, there is a real concern about the legality of such practices in the absence of informed consent.

§9.15 Dealing with the Newly Dead

In an excellent article, James P. Orlowski and others discussed the ethical aspects of using the newly dead for purposes of teaching medical students intubation.[1] Aside from the ethics of the situation, there is need to consider legal requirements governing mishandling of a corpse as well as the prospect of litigation.

For example, what would happen if a family came back into the patient's room having been told that their loved one had died, to find a group of medical students "practicing" on the body? Would there be sufficient ground for the tort of emotional distress or mental outrage? What is the likely outcome if the family complains to the press?

As Dr. Orlowski suggests, the best policy is to secure consent to such matters. Some families will object, based on religious or philosophical grounds. Pastoral care workers might be able to help identify which families should be approached for consent and which families should be avoided based on known religious affiliation. Objections should be respected. Other families, however, are likely to give consent when the process is handled appropriately. Documentation of an authorization should also be considered as part of a comprehensive consent policy and procedure.

The interests of health agencies in training future caregivers must be balanced against those of society and the grief-stricken family. Careful planning and consideration can help to avoid unpleasant circumstances.

§9.15 [1] See J. P. Orlowski, et al., The Ethics of Using Newly Dead Patients for Teaching and Practicing Intubation Techniques, 319(7) New Eng. J. Med. 439 (1988).

TEN

The Elderly and Consent

§10.0   Introduction
A.   The Misunderstandings of Aging and Consent
     §10.1   Aging and Its Effect on Capacity to Consent
B.   Competency and Consent to Treatment
     §10.2   Determinants of Competency for Purposes of Consent to Treatment
     §10.3   Lane v. Candura: The Inability to Identify Incompetency
     §10.4   Legislative Standards
     §10.5   "Incompetent" Persons Without Legal Guardians in Need of Care
C.   Elderly in Need of Protection
     §10.6   The Duty to Warn
     §10.7   The Duty to Protect
     §10.8   Refusing Assistance
     §10.9   Residents' Bill of Rights Legislation
D.   Refusing Treatment, Death, Dying, and the Elderly
     §10.10   Refusing Treatment
     §10.11   Consent Issues and Death and Dying

§10.0   Introduction

Consent to treatment presents important concerns for each special population. Elderly Americans represent a large segment of society with specific needs regarding consent to treatment. As seen in this chapter, society has responded to these needs by enacting protective legislation to safeguard the rights

671

of the elderly. Some of these laws deal with elder abuse and neglect; others deal with the rights of nursing home residents.

Although the elderly are a large segment of the population, legislators have been slow to develop practical statutory mechanisms to ensure adequate consent to treatment from incapacitated or incompetent older persons. In nursing homes and extended-care treatment facilities, choices have to be made for incompetent residents without a legal guardian or conservator to authorize or refuse treatment on their behalf.

Health care providers have also been slow to recognize the special consent needs of the elderly; they often share society's ignorance of the elderly and the results of aging. Residents of long-term care facilities and elderly patients in hospitals may be "written off" as incompetent due to slow responses to questions. Confusion as to time and place is often seen as a telltale sign of incompetency. If the patient is too embarrassed to admit that she cannot hear, or if the caregiver is insensitive to the possibility of a hearing loss, the false conclusion may be drawn that the person is incapable of understanding.

Developing the requisite ability to separate the normal effects of aging from mental incompetency takes training and experience. It also requires a sensitivity to the right of elderly persons to decline life-saving treatment that will necessitate amputation or will result in physical incapacitation. Caregivers sometimes find it difficult to accept a patient's decision to refuse life-saving or life-prolonging care. They cannot appreciate why an elderly person is so determined to go to the grave with a gangrenous leg rather than live confined to a wheelchair.

Consent requires caregivers to provide appropriate information for patients so that they can decide what should be done. Caregivers must not impose their own values or choices upon patients. This is a particularly important principle to bear in mind when caring for the elderly, who are often vulnerable to overbearing attitudes.

This chapter provides a practical perspective on consent issues facing the elderly. The primary emphasis is on developing useful strategies for dealing with consent to treatment for elderly individuals.

A. THE MISUNDERSTANDINGS OF AGING AND CONSENT

§10.1 Aging and Its Effect on Capacity to Consent

The stereotype is all too familiar: an older person hunched over and crippled with arthritis walking uncertainly down a hospital corridor. The frail individual has trouble hearing despite the use of bilateral hearing aids. The old man or woman also has trouble seeing due to advancing cataracts.

For young caregivers the stereotypic individual is dismissed as incapable of giving consent. Others perhaps see themselves 20 or more years later, and the discomfort of this thought compels them to hurry through consent. Still others avoid the consent process for purely economic considerations given the time required to secure an authorization for treatment from a frail, disabled, elderly person.

In the real world of modern health care, there is no room for convenient stereotypic models of consent. Caregivers should not use elderly patients' physical infirmities to gloss over the need for informed consent. Rather, their goal should be to obtain effective consent to treatment, taking into consideration the needs of elderly patients.

This approach requires practical initiatives in securing consent, including the following:

1. *Be Aware of Cognitive Capacity.* Elderly persons who are taking prescription medicine or who are chronically fatigued should not be asked to consent to treatment at the "low point" in their day. Rather, a time should be chosen that affords a good opportunity for full cognitive capacity.
2. *Be Mindful of Physical Deficits.* When working with elderly persons with a pronounced hearing disorder, staff should be certain that hearing aids are switched on and to speak loud enough for the hearing impaired person. Beware of speaking too swiftly or not looking at the individual

squarely while talking: lipreading can facilitate an effective consent.

3. *Set the Discussion at a Reasonable Level.* Caregivers should avoid oversimplifying important information when speaking with elderly patients. Older persons should not be treated like children. Absent a determination that it would be better to refrain from disclosing candid information, elderly persons should be informed of the material details that are necessary to consider in reaching an informed choice.

4. *Be Aware of Memory Loss and Inability to Understand Information.* A severe problem of short-term memory loss can compromise the consent process. When caregivers know or suspect such a problem, they must make certain that authorizations for treatment are carefully documented and include the name(s) of the person(s) present during the consent discussion. They must also assess the individual's ability to understand consent information. The length, speed, and content of disclosures should be adjusted to meet the needs of individual patients and residents.

By taking these matters into account, it is possible to accommodate some aspects of the aging process and the need for effective consent.

B. COMPETENCY AND CONSENT TO TREATMENT

§10.2 Determinants of Competency for Purposes of Consent to Treament

Competency, like dangerousness, is an elusive concept. Often applying generally accepted criteria will produce inappropriate results.

The patient's ability to appreciate his condition and the nature and consequences of a treatment choice; the ability to understand information; knowledge of place, self, and time; and coherent, lucid discussion are sometimes seen as the benchmarks of competency. When, however, patients give seemingly implausible or "irrational" explanations for refusing treatment, or when patients vacillate between agreeing to and declining "necessary" treatment, a warning signal is raised regarding competency to consent to treatment.

Great care must be exercised in designating a patient as incompetent to consent to treatment, especially when there is a conflict between the individual and the caregiver regarding "necessary" care. The caregiver's values should never be used to override an elderly patient's choice to decline life-saving or corrective surgery.

An 83-year-old woman may have a strong sense of self and personal integrity that compels her to decline a mastectomy. A 79-year-old man may have such an overwhelming fear of surgery that he refuses consent to a TURP procedure. A patient may vacillate between giving and revoking consent to a life-saving amputation of a gangrenous foot.[1]

In each instance, the patient should make the treatment choice, however much a caregiver or relative may disagree with the patient. Absent evidence that suggests an inability to understand and synthesize information, incoherence, or lack of lucidity, the choice should remain with the patient.

§10.3 Lane v. Candura: The Inability to Identify Incompetency

For caregivers, determining incompetency can be frustrating. A good example of this occurred in a Massachusetts case involving a 77-year-old woman with gangrene of the lower right leg and foot.[1] The woman was a widow who lived with her

§10.2 [1]See Lane v. Candura, 6 Mass. App. Ct. 377, 376 N.E.2d 1232 (1978).
§10.3 [1]Lane v. Candura, 6 Mass. App. Ct. 377, 376 N.E.2d 1232 (1978).

daughter. On two occasions the patient agreed to but then with-drew consent to an amputation. The woman's daughter sought a court order appointing her temporary guardian with the authority to consent to the surgery.

Psychiatrists evaluated the woman. Evidence suggested that the patient was confused about certain details and that she had a distorted concept of time. Her mind had a tendency to wander, and she refused to discuss the operation with certain individuals.

Despite this evidence, the court declined to appoint the daughter as temporary guardian. As the court noted, the woman's decision was medically irrational. Nonetheless, evidence of forgetfulness and periods of confusion could not be used as a basis for appointment of a guardian because the patient exhibited lucid periods in which she was fully aware of her treatment choice.[2]

The surprising twist in the case took place after the court's ruling when a relative visited the patient and discussed with her the need for the procedure. The patient then agreed to the operation.

The *Lane* case demonstrates the difficulty in assessing incompetency. In *Lane* the woman was able at times to understand treatment information and on occasion she was articulate in explaining that her decision was based on a fear of becoming a burden to her children and her desire to be free of institutional care in a nursing home. Moreover, she felt unhappy since her husband's death.

The case serves as an illustration of the difficulty in determining incompetency for purposes of consent and as a warning that cut-and-dried categories and evaluative norms will not always work in deciding who is able to give or refuse an informed consent to treatment.

Competency can turn on environmental and familial pressures or can shift with the presence of mind-altering drugs. As a result, great care must be exercised in assessing if a person is

[2]Id.

competent to make a treatment choice and, if not, whether steps can be taken to enable the incompetent person to make treatment decisions.

§10.4 Legislative Standards

Legislation can be found throughout the country for appointment of full or temporary guardians who are authorized to make treatment choices for incompetent individuals.[1] Each of these laws is state-specific, which means health agency administrators and caregivers must secure individualized legal advice on the steps to follow with patients or residents deemed incapable or incompetent to give consent.

In addition to the legislation governing appointment of guardians for purposes of consent, health facilities and professionals should keep in mind that elderly patients may have executed living wills or durable powers of attorney. Living wills tell caregivers what treatments the patient would want or refuse during incapacitation or incompetency. An individual with a duly executed durable power of attorney in health care can facilitate treatment decisions for the incompetent patient. (See §7.8 supra.)

It is wise to check for living wills and durable powers of attorney before going through the time and expense of seeking the appointment of a legal guardian. Indeed, for patients enrolled in palliative care programs, long-term care facility residents, and patients presenting themselves for elective procedures, it is wise to recommend execution of a legally valid living will or durable power of attorney, which could give patients and residents considerable peace of mind regarding treatment should they become incompetent.

---

§10.4 [1]See Ala. Code §26-2A-102 (1987); Idaho Code §15-5-312 (1982); Ind. Code Ann. §16-8-3-1 (Burns 1987) and §16-8-3-3 (Burns 1986); N.C. Gen. Stat. §35A-1241 (1987); Tenn. Code Ann. §34-4-112 (1981).

§10.5 "Incompetent Persons" Without Legal Guardians in Need of Care

Hospital personnel often encounter elderly "incompetent" individuals who require treatment. Many of these patients suffer from serious illness that requires invasive treatment. Incoherent or quite stubborn, such patients are often dirty and undernourished.

Do such patients have the right to refuse recommended therapy? Are they "incompetent," or do they retain the right to be free of unwanted, invasive care?

The answer depends upon the circumstances of each case. In a true medicolegal emergency (see chapter 2 supra), the patient presents herself with a life- or health-threatening condition requiring immediate care. She is unable to give consent and there is no time to secure an authorization from a duly authorized legal representative.

In most instances, however, the elderly person's condition does not fit the definition of a medicolegal emergency. Rather, the older person is in need of *necessary* care to avoid a life- or health-threatening episode. Nevertheless, the patient is uncooperative or flatly refuses recommended treatment.

At this juncture, health facilities or professionals could initiate legal proceedings to have the older individual declared incompetent in order to secure consent to treatment from a court-appointed guardian.

Courts will not simply rubber-stamp medical determinations of incompetency. Indeed, even when it is clear that an invasive treatment will save a patient's life, the courts will pay particular heed to the individual's decision to refuse care. Such was the case in New Jersey, where a 72-year-old man refused consent to amputation of his legs. As the court noted, the treatment was so invasive of the patient's right of privacy that it outweighed the state's interest in preserving life.[1]

From a practical perspective, similar cases should be antici-

---

§10.5   [1]Matter of Quackenbush, 156 N.J. Super. 282, 383 A.2d 785 (1978).

pated in a health agency's policy and procedure manual on consent. Staff should know how to respond to such matters, including, in some states, utilizing the judicial process for appointment of a legal guardian.

The motivation to secure consent from a legal guardian may not always reflect an abiding respect for personal integrity or autonomy; the decision may stem from fear of litigation. In some states this fear is unreasonable, particularly if legislation has removed the threat of liability for nonemergency treatment or diagnostic procedures performed when informed consent is "not reasonably possible."[2] Whether state law in a particular jurisdiction takes such a view is a matter requiring specific legal advice.

Acute care facilities are in a different position from long-term care agencies regarding competency to consent to treatment. In the long-term care setting, the agency has time to implement mechanisms for assuring a valid consent to treatment. Long-term and extended care facilities can avoid many consent problems by building into the admissions process a requirement that residents or patients designate a surrogate to make treatment choices on their behalf when they become incapable of doing so themselves. Patients and residents should be encouraged to write down their views and requests regarding treatment, which they might later be unable to convey. Not only does this provide guidance to a surrogate decision maker, but it helps reduce the likelihood of disputes among family members regarding appropriate treatment.

Such a procedure could be taken under existing legislation governing durable powers of attorney in health matters. Even in the absence of such laws, institutional policies can be developed and implemented on the matter.

This policy should encourage patients and residents to inform relatives and clergy of their desires regarding necessary care and the names of designated surrogate decision makers. Taking such a stand prior to incompetency or incapacity clears

---

[2]Matter of Merrill, 531 N.Y.S.2d 201 (Sup. Ct. 1988), referring to N.Y. Pub. Health Law §2805-d (McKinney 1975).

the way for smooth decision-making, and much of the intrafamilial squabbles and indecisiveness regarding treatment can be avoided.

It must be borne in mind that acute care facilities may hesitate to follow a long-term care agency's consent policy. This type of "systems" problem should be anticipated and ironed out through interagency discussions and policies. Staff education and effective communication are important in making sure that such an approach will work.

C. ELDERLY IN NEED OF PROTECTION

§10.6 The Duty to Warn

The needs of the elderly can be quite complicated when there is evidence or suspicion of abuse or neglect or when relatives, friends, and social workers believe older persons are having problems coping with the routine aspects of daily living.

The legal duty to warn described in chapter 1 has often been linked to specific victims of dangerous, mentally unbalanced individuals. The duty has also been addressed through legislation, particularly with respect to child abuse and neglect. In some states, protective laws have been enacted that focus specifically on abused, neglected, or exploited adults.[1]

Even in the absence of legislation, a case can be made that under common law principles a person who stands in a fiduciary relationship to an abused, neglected, or exploited adult is obliged to warn appropriate officials. The ever-expanding concept of the duty to warn coupled with the responsibilities of a fiduciary set the stage for such an argument.

§10.6 [1]See, e.g., Fla. Stat. Ann. §§415.105 to 415.107 (West 1986); N.C. Gen. Stat. §§108A-99 to 108A-111 (1981).

§10.7 The Duty to Protect

The duty to safeguard the elderly person who is unable to cope or who is in substantial danger or irreparable harm or death has a strong basis in state legislation.[1] Also, a person who owes a duty of care to another must take appropriate measures to safeguard that individual if he is at risk of harm.[2]

The duty to protect, however, can be a two-edged sword. For the elderly adult who is comfortable living in less-than-hygienic surroundings but who is suffering from severe sensory deficits that pose a serious risk of harm, "protection" could mean the end of such a lifestyle. What are the reasonable limits that society can impose on such an individual? How intrusive can protection be in terms of invasive surgery, diagnostic testing, or long-term medical management? What are the constraints on medical or nursing paternalism, which stifles individual decision-making? What safeguards are in place to ensure individual consent to treatment when an adult in need of protection is placed in a nursing home?

The answers to these questions are often quite difficult. No doubt individual liberties are at risk of loss with the implementation of protective measures.[3] It is difficult to balance individual liberties with the state's interest in preserving life and providing for the safety and welfare of less fortunate people. The challenge is bound to become more difficult with the ever-increasing number of older people in society and the many changes in the fabric of the family unit. Legislative inroads and court challenges are likely to occur as the limits of the duty to protect elderly individuals are defined.

---

§10.7 [1] See, e.g., Fla. Stat. Ann. §§415.105 to 415.107 (West 1986); N.C. Gen. Stat. §§108A-99 to 108A-111 (1981).
[2] Prosser and Keeton on Torts (5th ed. 1984).
[3] See, e.g., For the Elderly: Legal Rights (and Wrongs) Within the Health Care System, 20 Harvard C.R.-C.L.L. Rev. 426 (1985); G.J. Alexander, Remaining Responsible: On Control of One's Health Needs in Aging, 20 Santa Clara L. Rev. 13 (1980).

§10.8   Refusing Assistance

As noted earlier in the chapter, the courts do not automatically
rubber-stamp medical recommendations that would oblige elderly persons to submit to highly invasive treatment. Legislation dealing with protective services also imposes certain
limitations on what can be done for a person deemed abused,
neglected, or exploited.[1]

The laws make it clear that only "necessary" treatment can be
provided to the adult in need of protection. The laws do not
authorize that anything and everything be done for an unwilling individual. *Necessary* in this context suggests an urgent state
of affairs requiring action to correct a substantial risk of irreparable harm or death.[2]

That elderly persons have not bathed in weeks or cannot
hear well is not sufficient to justify extensive intervention on
their behalf. However, persons suffering from congestive heart
failure, life-threatening diabetic complications, or acute asth-
matic problems may be at sufficient risk to life or health to
warrant assessment and action.

Those involved in adult protection services need to be vigil-
ant about the disadvantages of intervening. The psychosocial
and emotional toll on the "rescued" party must be considered.
The fallout may not be immediate; indeed, it could occur over
the course of weeks or months and appear as depression,
malaise, or morbidity. However expressed, the right of the
individual to live her life as she chooses must be respected to
the extent permitted by law and reason.

§10.9   Residents' Bill of Rights Legislation

Many states have enacted laws specifying the rights of nursing
home residents.[1] These laws are often quite detailed, covering

§10.8 [1]See, e.g., Fla. Stat. Ann. §§415.105 to 415.107 (West 1986); N.C.
Gen. Stat. §§108A-99 to 108A-111 (1981).
 [2]Id.
 §10.9 [1]See, e.g., Kan. Stat. Ann. §28-39-78 (1982); Ohio Rev. Code Ann.

such issues as visitation, privacy, treatment, and payment. Provisions dealing with consent to treatment[2] and participation in human research[3] are often found in these laws. The legislation serves to reinforce the principles of personal autonomy and self-determination.

Residents' bill of rights legislation should not be treated as philosophical pronouncements or public relations statements. Although the language of the legislation may seem idealistic, patients' rights laws are enforceable standards of care. Failure to abide by such laws can be the basis for legal action.

Caregivers and health facility administrators should carefully consider the ways in which residents' rights laws are implemented and enforced. Quality assurance and risk management monitoring techniques can be useful in making certain that rights legislation is properly enforced.

D.   REFUSING TREATMENT, DEATH, DYING, AND THE ELDERLY

§10.10   Refusing Treatment

As discussed in chapter 7, considerable judicial approbation has been given to the right of both competent and incompetent individuals to refuse treatment. Many of the decisions favoring the individual's right to decline treatment have involved religious objections to care, highly invasive measures, and therapeutic interventions for terminally ill individuals.

For elderly people, particularly those who reside in nursing homes, the right to refuse treatment is often set forth in nurs-

---

§3721.13 (1979); Tenn. Code Ann. §68-11-901 (1987); Vt. Stat. Ann. tit. 18, §2101 (1985); Va. Code §32.1-138 (1987); Wash. Rev. Code Ann. §74.42.040 (1981).
   [2] Id.
   [3] Id.

ing home residents' bill of rights legislation.[1] Even in these laws, however, restrictions are sometimes imposed on the scope of the right to refuse care.

For example, in some states legislation permits the use of restraints in nursing homes.[2] Although residents may object to such measures, legislation allows the use of physical and chemical restraints in well-defined circumstances and upon the authorization of a physician.[3]

It is important that the residents or their duly authorized legal representatives make informed decisions regarding consent to or refusal of care. Residents or their legal representatives should be informed of the nature and purpose of proposed treatment, the probable risks and benefits of the care, available treatment options, and the risks of refusing care.

The same principle applies to elderly persons receiving hospital treatment or home care. Elderly persons should be told of the probable side effects associated with certain types of drugs and why a necessary operation is classified as "elective" so that they can make informed choices regarding what treatment best serves their needs.

Patients may well decide against treatment. Absent any indication of incompetency, caregivers should respect such decisions. Although health professionals may consider such choices unwise, they must remember that the patient must decide what is acceptable treatment.

§10.11   Consent Issues and Death and Dying

Honoring the wishes of chronically or terminally ill patients requires practical procedures. In chapter 7 many procedures

---

§10.10   [1]See, e.g., Kan. Stat. Ann. §28-39-78 (1982); Ohio Rev. Code Ann. §3721.13 (1979); Tenn. Code Ann. §68-11-901 (1987); Vt. Stat. Ann. tit. 18, §2101 (1985); Va. Code §32.1-138 (1987); Wash. Rev. Code Ann. §74.42.040 (1981).

[2]See, e.g., Kan. Stat. Ann. §28-39-78 (1982); Ohio Rev. Code Ann. §3721.13 (1979); Tenn. Code Ann. §68-11-901 (1987); Vt. Stat. Ann. tit. 18, §2101 (1985); Va. Code §32.1-138 (1987).

[3]Id.

were described, including living wills, durable powers of attorney in health care, and DNR and DNH orders.

Many of these devices can be employed to ensure that the treatment choices of the elderly are respected. The practical answers can be taken one step further by building into health care agency policy and procedure manuals on consent a requirement that elderly persons or their duly authorized legal representatives submit a medical directive or execute a durable power of attorney in health care. The exact approach taken will depend upon whether state law recognizes medical directives, living wills, or durable powers of attorney.

By requiring directives or durable powers of attorney, health agencies can avoid many of the difficult issues involved in providing treatment for incompetent individuals. Written directives give caregivers clear-cut guidance on what the elderly person deems acceptable treatment. Designating a durable power of attorney can facilitate treatment decisions, which might otherwise be difficult to make in the midst of family disputes or inaction.

It is important that legal counsel provide guidance on state law governing medical directives and durable powers of attorney, especially when elderly individuals indicate that they do not want artificial nutrition or hydration or that they do not want to be hospitalized in the event of an acute illness. Health care agency administrators should make clear to patients and residents the effect religious or philosophical position statements will have on their willingness to honor DNRs and DNHs and refusals of or requests for withdrawal of artificial nutrition and hydration. By putting patients and residents on notice, there is less likelihood of disagreements during the critical stages in the management of chronically or terminally ill individuals.

The best approach is to develop and implement a policy and procedure manual on the care of incompetent and terminally ill individuals. Such a document should address all the key points of consent to treatment with a view toward avoiding or minimizing risk exposure.

The following are some of the key consent issues that should be addressed in the policy and procedure manual:

1. Determinants of competency or capacity to give consent;
2. Documentation indicating appointment of a guardian or appointment of a durable power of attorney in health care;
3. Living will or medical directive incorporated in the treatment record;
4. Criteria for a DNR or DNH;
5. Medical order for DNR or DNH as well as documented consent from the patient, resident, or duly authorized legal representative;
6. Measures to be employed in the event of family disputes or disagreements regarding care to be given or withdrawn from an incompetent patient or resident;
7. Criteria to be used in implementing an order to withhold or withdraw artificial nutrition and hydration as well as other treatment measures that have the effect of prolonging the dying process;
8. Channels of communication to be used when problems arise dealing with treatment choices for incompetent individuals;
9. Documentation requirements to be used for recording treatment choices made for incompetent individuals;
10. The role of legal counsel;
11. Quality assurance and risk management measures to be used in educating staff as well as identifying, monitoring, and correcting consent problems; and
12. Regular review and updating of the policy and procedure manual to ensure that it is kept current in the light of legislative and case law developments.

As suggested in chapter 7, there is no clear-cut standard regarding withdrawal or withholding of artificial nutrition and hydration from individuals in a persistent vegetative state. Moreover, living wills executed in accordance with the requirements of legislation in one state may not be given effect in another jurisdiction. The lack of consensus reinforces the importance of obtaining specific legal advice on state law in the development and implementation of a practical policy and procedure manual on consent.

Health facilities should work closely with legal counsel in developing practical solutions to common consent problems involving incompetent, elderly individuals. By anticipating problems, such as the elderly person without a duly authorized legal representative or documented medical directive, health agencies can avoid making important choices without the benefit of adequate planning. On balance, anticipating key consent issues and developing reasonable responses offer an acceptable solution to many of the difficult choices that must be made for the care of incompetent, elderly patients and residents.

ELEVEN

AIDS and Consent

A. AIDS and the Law in Perspective
  §11.0   Overview of AIDS as a Legal Issue
  §11.1   AIDS and Consent: An Overview
B. Consent to AIDS Testing
  §11.2   Legislative Requirements
  §11.3   Case Law on AIDS Testing
C. Consent to AIDS Testing with Detainees and Prisoners
  §11.4   Testing of Detainees
  §11.5   Testing of Prisoners
D. Consent to AIDS Testing in Domestic Relations
  §11.6   Testing in Domestic Disputes
  §11.7   Testing and Determination of Visitation Rights
E. Confidentiality and the Duty to Disclose AIDS Test Results
  §11.8   Blood Banks and Centers
  §11.9   Health Facilities and Personnel
  §11.10   Family Members and Significant Others
  §11.11   Practical Limitations on the Duty to Disclose

A. AIDS AND THE LAW IN PERSPECTIVE

AIDS is an issue of global significance. A fatal illness that threatens young and old alike and that may well eliminate an entire generation in some African countries, AIDS has become the primary target of health officials around the world.

With efforts at education and prevention to contain the

689

spread of AIDS have come significant legal changes. At the federal and state levels considerable legislative activity has occurred. As seen in this chapter, much of this legislation involves consent issues, including authorizations for testing and permission to release AIDS test results. In addition, pertinent case law is discussed on the topic of AIDS and consent.

§11.0   Overview of AIDS as a Legal Issue

AIDS as a legal issue has many facets: employment, housing, access to health care, marriage, divorce, child custody and visitation rights, and death and dying issues. In part, these legal issues demonstrate society's inability to cope with a threat of pandemic proportions. Although AIDS is a disease that can affect a person of any age, the fact that so often its victims are young has struck an emotional chord. But society's attitudes toward AIDS are also affected by its prejudices against homosexuality and illicit drug use. The idea that "they" are getting what they deserve for being drug addicts or for being gay is a familiar undercurrent.

Some allege that government officials responded too slowly and inadequately to the AIDS threat. In part this "slow" response may be a reflection of social attitudes toward many of the victims of the disease. However, it may also reflect a decision to act cautiously on an issue that could easily allow authorities to garner considerable power at the expense of individual liberties.

Despite what may have appeared as needless delays to some individuals, AIDS legislative action has become quite extensive. There has also been considerable case law involving AIDS with much of it focusing on segregation in prisons[1] and other issues involving criminal law.[2]

§11.0   [1]See Glick v. Henderson, 885 F.2d 536 (8th Cir. 1988); Moenius v. Stevens, 688 F. Supp. 1054 (D. Md. 1988); Baez v. Rapping, 680 F. Supp. 112 (S.D.N.Y. 1988); Judd v. Packard, 669 F. Supp. 741 (D. Md. 1987).
[2]See United States v. Moore, 846 F.2d 1163 (8th Cir. 1988); Traufler v. Thompson, 662 F. Supp. 945 (N.D. Ill. 1987).

690

Given the amount of legislative activity and case law involving AIDS, it is likely that the field will continue to expand. More litigation can be anticipated dealing with individual rights of AIDS victims as well as those who are suffering from AIDS Related Complex (ARC). Through these legislative and litigation inroads, AIDS as a legal issue will become more clearly defined.

§11.1 AIDS and Consent: An Overview

AIDS is an illness that goes directly to the heart of consent law. The ability of an AIDS patient to give an authorization to treatment with experimental drugs raises a serious concern about coercion and undue influence. Faced with the prospect of certain death, is it possible for an AIDS patient to give a voluntary consent to participate in a novel treatment regimen?

The nature of the illness also raises concern about AIDS patients' ability to consent to treatment. Some AIDS patients manifest symptoms of dementia. Although this is a transient problem for some AIDS patients, it may become a permanent condition for others. Can an AIDS patient who experiences episodic periods of dementia give or refuse consent to treatment? How should staff determine when an AIDS patient is in a suitable state for giving or refusing consent?

Questions like these require practical answers, but practical solutions must be found to even more fundamental issues involving consent to AIDS testing. Although this is a matter now covered in some detail in a numer of states,[1] consent to AIDS testing is by no means a settled question. Although some legislative direction is in place governing confidentiality of AIDS testing, state law is not completely settled on this matter either. Indeed, questions still arise regarding the need for consent to disclose test results to the spouse or "significant other" of an AIDS patient.

§11.1   [1]See Cal. Health & Safety Code §199.22 and §199.27 (West 1987); Colo. Rev. Stat. §25-4-1405 (1987); Me. Rev. Stat. Ann. tit. 5, §19203-A (1987); Wis. Stat. Ann. §146.025 (West 1985).

691

Consent to treatment is but one piece of the larger mosaic of law concerning AIDS. Coercion, undue influence, competency, and authority to breach test confidentiality are the focal point of current discussions regarding AIDS and consent. The focus is likely to shift, however, as successful treatment modalities are brought into use and society and law struggle to achieve a balance between the need to take measures to protect the greater good and the rights of individual citizens.

B. CONSENT TO AIDS TESTING

A primary consideration with AIDS is the issue of testing those persons suspected of carrying HIV or suffering from the disease. Not only is it important to know for purposes of individual patient care, but also so that health care personnel can be alerted and take appropriate precautions. The latter point continues to be a frequent justification for AIDS testing, despite the insistence upon "universal precautions" in treating any patient.

As seen in this section, detailed legislative measures have been enacted governing AIDS testing. Moreover, considerable case law has been reported on the issue of testing patients for AIDS.

§11.2 Legislative Requirements

In those states with AIDS-testing legislation consent is a prerequisite to testing.[1] However, this basic premise is limited by a

§11.2 [1]See Cal. Health & Safety Code §199.22 (West 1987); Colo. Rev. Stat. §25-4-1405 (1987); Me. Rev. Stat. Ann. tit. 5, §19203-A (1987); Ind. Code Ann. §16-1-9.5-2.5 (Burns 1988); Mass. Gen. Laws Ann. ch. 111, §70F (West 1986).

series of exceptions that permit AIDS testing in the absence of consent of the patient.

For example, some laws permit testing without consent during an autopsy[2] or scientific research.[3] In Texas[4] and some other states, AIDS testing is permitted to screen whether tissues and fluids are suitable as donations.[5] Testing is also permitted when it is deemed a bona fide occupational qualification[6] and when it is considered important for proper management of a residential care facility.[7]

In some states, testing is permitted where caregivers or others are routinely exposed to the bodily fluids of another[8] or where a worker has been exposed to bodily fluids through a bite, needle prick, or splash.[9] In some states, testing of very young children without parental consent is also permitted.[10] The laws reflect a social attitude that the need to test far outweighs the individual's interest in refusing such intrusions: that in certain, well-delineated circumstances, society's need to know should prevail.

Even in those states that permit testing in the absence of consent, procedural safeguards are built into the laws. For example, in Rhode Island, if it is determined that there is a significant probability that a health care worker has been exposed to AIDS and the patient refuses consent to HIV testing, the worker can petition a state court to compel the patient to submit to a blood test.[11]

[2] Cal. Health & Safety Code §199.27 (West 1987).
[3] Id. See also Me. Rev. Stat. Ann. tit. 5, §19203-A (1987); Wis. Stat. Ann. §146.025 (1986). It should be noted that much of the "research" referred to in this category is carried out in blood banks or plasma centers where identifiers linking the sample to the subject have been removed. In other instances, the research is of the type approved by an IRB as described in chapter 8 supra.
[4] Tex. Rev. Civ. Stat. Ann. art. 4419b-1, §9.02 (Vernon 1987).
[5] Cal. Health & Safety Code §199.27 (West 1987).
[6] See Tex. Rev. Civ. Stat. Ann. art. 4419b-1, §9.02 (Vernon 1987).
[7] Id.
[8] R.I. Gen. Laws §23-6-14 (1989).
[9] Id. See also La. Rev. Stat. Ann. §40:1299.40 (West 1988).
[10] R.I. Gen. Laws §23-6-14 (1989).
[11] Id.

Where consent is required, legislation typically requires a "signed consent."[12] In many instances this document is in the nature of a signed release form. Provision also is made in some states for surrogate consents on behalf of those who are unable to give consent.[13]

The legislative trend is clearly in the direction of permitting nonconsensual AIDS or HIV testing in well-described situations. Further legislation on the topic should be anticipated. In the interim, for those caregivers in states without legislation or case law on the topic, it is important to secure sound legal advice on the issue of consent to AIDS testing. Such advice should anticipate problem cases involving refusals of consent to HIV testing and the inability of patients to give or refuse consent. Specific advice should also be secured on the way in which consent is documented for AIDS or HIV testing.

§11.3   Case Law on AIDS Testing

The issue of testing for AIDS or HIV has already resulted in some court decisions.[1] The case law that has appeared in the area suggests that mandatory testing requirements for the workplace trigger Fourth Amendment concerns regarding unreasonable searches and seizures.

In a Nebraska case, the U.S. District Court made it clear that a balance must be struck between the employee's reasonable expectation of privacy and the need of the employer to provide a safe environment for residents living in an agency for the developmentally disabled. The court noted that AIDS posed only a "theoretical risk" that did not merit invading the privacy of the workers. Moreover, the court noted that mandatory testing was not effective in preventing disease transmission. "Bet-

---

[12] Id. See also Me. Rev. Stat. Ann. tit. 5, §19203-A (1987).

[13] R.I. Gen. Laws §23-6-14 (1989). See also Me. Rev. Stat. Ann. tit. 5, §19203-A (1987).

§11.3   [1] See Health Ins. Assn. of America v. Corcoran, 531 N.Y.S.2d 456 (Sup. Ct. 1988); Glover v. Eastern Neb. Community Office of Retardation, 686 F. Supp. 243 (D. Neb. 1988).

ter safe than sorry" was not a sufficient basis for mandating HIV testing.[2]

Quite a different response came about in a New York case in which a group of insurance companies challenged a state regulation prohibiting HIV testing or considering evidence of AIDS to determine insurability.[3] In ruling that the regulation was invalid, the New York court found that the provision was not authorized by state legislation dealing with deceptive practices. The board powers granted to the state Superintendent of Insurance regarding unfair discrimination among individuals of the same class was deemed an insufficient basis for promulgating the HIV regulation. Indeed, the regulation was found to be arbitrary and capricious and lacking a rational or factual basis. As the court noted, statistically valid actuarial risk classifications could be derived from HIV testing, providing insurers with significant information regarding future medical costs. The fact that some social, financial, or psychological difficulties might arise from being denied health insurance was not a sufficient basis for upholding the regulation.[4]

Mandatory testing and blanket prohibitions are bound to trigger challenges in the AIDS context. Legislative or government workplace policies that are perceived as overreaching are good targets for such challenges. Unless the requirements can be shown to be a permissible intrusion on the individual's right of privacy or a valid exercise of government's prescriptive powers, all-encompassing provisions are certain to be the focal point of much litigation.

C. CONSENT TO AIDS TESTING WITH DETAINEES AND PRISONERS

One of the groups most at risk for AIDS transmission is the prison population. Intravenous drug users who end up in

---

[2]Glover v. Eastern Neb. Community Office of Retardation, supra n.1.
[3]See Health Ins. Assn. of America v. Corcoran, supra n.1.
[4]Id.

prison often carry the AIDS virus. In a prison with an illicit drug underground at work, the likelihood of disease transmission is increased. Added to this are unprotected homosexual practices that, in turn, facilitate the spread of HIV.

Prison officials recognize the immensity of the problem. Prison administrators sometimes feel that comprehensive testing of "at risk" populations can assist them in segregating AIDS-exposed individuals from those who are HIV-free. They also believe that such information is important to ensure the well-being of staff.

AIDS testing of detainees and prisoners has become the focal point of legislative and regulatory pronouncements, as well as some case law. As seen in this portion of the chapter, there is ample room for clearer direction on what should be done regarding AIDS testing of detainees and prisoners.

§11.4   Testing of Detainees

Case law suggests that the courts will pay particular attention to legislative requirements governing HIV testing of detainees.[1] Thus a court ruled that an affidavit in support of a search warrant for taking and testing a detainee's blood for HIV was inadequate since state law precluded disclosure of the test results.[2] Another court ruled that a detainee's release on bail could not be conditioned upon a negative AIDS test.[3]

Whether the issue is a search warrant for a blood test or setting the terms and conditions of pretrial release, concern about AIDS does not carve out an exception to the usual protections afforded pretrial detainees. Absent specific state law on

§11.4   [1]See Barlow v. Superior Court (People), 236 Cal. Rptr. 134 (Cal. Ct. App. 1987); People v. McGreevy, 514 N.Y.S.2d 622 (Sup. Ct. 1987).
[2]Barlow v. Superior Court (People), supra n.1. See also Haywood County v. Hudson, 740 S.W.2d 718 (Tenn. 1987) (testing permitted); Shelvin v. Lykos, 741 S.W.2d 178 (Tex. Ct. App. 1987) (testing denied).
[3]People v. McGreevy, supra n.1.

the subject, regular procedures should be followed in seeking AIDS testing of detainees.

§11.5 Testing of Prisoners

Like detainees, prisoners enjoy certain rights, including limitations on AIDS testing. However, prisoners' rights are more limited and some state legislation requires prisoners to submit to testing or treatment for sexually transmitted disease.[1] Since AIDS is considered a sexually transmitted disease, the right of a prisoner to decline HIV testing may in some states be moot.[2]

Legislation in some states squarely addresses the issue. For example, in Iowa testing is permitted for anyone confined to a jail[3] or correctional institution[4] who bites another or causes bodily fluids to be exchanged with or "cast upon" another. If such an individual refuses to submit to testing, officials of the jail or correction facility can go to court and obtain an order compelling submission to testing.[5]

On the federal level, the Federal Bureau of Prisons has issued an Operations Memorandum dealing with HIV testing, treatment, and education.[6] The policy is extensive, including testing of staff who suspect that they have been exposed to hazardous blood or bodily fluids.[7] Lawyers and health care providers working with federal prisoners should review the Operations Memorandum so that pertinent advice can be given on the issue of HIV testing.

Much of the case law on testing of prisoners for HIV has focused on gathering information for the victims of prisoners

§11.5 [1]See Fla. Stat. Ann. §384.32 (West 1986).
[2]Id.
[3]Iowa Code Ann. §356.48 (West 1987).
[4]Iowa Code Ann. §246.514 (West 1987).
[5]Id. See also Iowa Code Ann. §356.48 (West 1987).
[6]U.S. Department of Justice, Federal Bureau of Prisons, Operations Memorandum, Human Immunodeficiency Virus, No. 99-88 (6100), September 30, 1988.
[7]Id.

convicted of sexual assaults or rape.[8] In these situations, courts have usually held that testing and disclosure of results is permitted. The justification has been protecting the health and safety of the victim or relieving anxiety over the possibility of having contracted AIDS as the result of the attack.[9]

There is no doubt that prisoners retain certain rights despite their status. Nonetheless, prisoners' right to be free of AIDS testing is likely to give way when there is a demonstrated need to determine the presence or absence of HIV. This issue is bound to generate considerable legislative activity and litigation as the extent of AIDS in prison becomes better known.

D. CONSENT TO AIDS TESTING IN DOMESTIC RELATIONS

AIDS testing is sure to become an area of keen interest in the domestic relations field. Divorce based on a spouse's contracting AIDS or carrying HIV antibodies will become an important weapon in the arsenal of many family law experts. A related concern will be the right of divorced parents with AIDS to share custody or have visitation rights with their children. As seen in this section, the issues have already begun to emerge.

§11.6   Testing in Domestic Disputes

The limited case law in this area suggests a continuation of a strong judicial disinclination to order AIDS testing absent an appropriate basis for intruding upon an individual's privacy.

---

[8]See Matter of James L., 532 N.Y.S.2d 941 (App. Div. 1988); People v. Thomas, 529 N.Y.S.2d 429 (County Ct. 1988); People v. Toure, 523 N.Y.S.2d 746 (Sup. Ct. 1988).
[9]Id.

Such was the ruling in a New York case in which a husband sought to compel his wife to submit to a blood test for AIDS in an action involving custody determination.[1]

The husband claimed that his wife had been involved in a series of extramarital affairs. In rejecting the husband's request, the court pointed out that only in egregious cases that shock the conscience of the court is discovery permitted regarding marital fault. In this case, an unsubstantiated allegation was not enough to trigger an examination and test of the man's wife. For such testing to proceed, "The allegation must be relevant, material and substantiated and the reasons compelling for such an examination and test."[2]

The New York court's ruling reflects a very practical perspective on AIDS testing in divorce and custody proceedings. As the court noted, the emotionally charged background of marital litigation should not be used as a springboard for compelling a spouse to submit to invasive procedures. Nonetheless, it remains for other courts to determine what would constitute a "relevant" and substantiated claim sufficient to warrant an order compelling HIV testing in a divorce case.

§11.7   Testing and Determination of Visitation Rights

Aside from being a tactic in divorce proceedings, the issue of AIDS testing can arise in the sensitive area of custody and visitation rights. In a New York case the maternal grandparents of two minor children tried to secure custody from the father[1] and moved that he be forced to submit to HIV testing.

In denying the motion, the court noted that the father had informed various people that he had AIDS. When questioned about it while on the witness stand in the custody hearing, the father asserted his Fifth Amendment privilege against self-incrimination.

§11.6 [1] Anne D. v. Raymond D., 528 N.Y.S.2d 775 (Sup. Ct. 1988).
[2] Id. at 776.
§11.7 [1] Doe v. Roe, 526 N.Y.S.2d 718 (Sup. Ct. 1988).

The court noted that no claim had been made that the children would be in danger living with their father if he had AIDS. Rather, the grandparents' claim was based on the anticipated short life expectancy of a person with AIDS and the possibility that a person suffering from a terminal illness might commit suicide and take the lives of others.[2] These concerns were refuted by the court-appointed psychiatrist who noted a strong bond of love between the father and the children and the father's acceptance of AIDS. The psychiatrist felt that even if the father had AIDS he would not pose any danger to his children, and he found no inclination toward suicide.

The court concluded that there was no "compelling need" to order the AIDS test. Even on a less stringent test of "materiality and relevancy" there was no sufficient basis for compelling the father to submit to an AIDS test.[3]

Whether the less onerous standard of "materiality and relevancy" is used or the more exacting requirement of demonstrating a "compelling need," courts will closely scrutinize requests that parents submit to AIDS testing in custody disputes. As the *Doe* court noted:

> As an institution which is and should be a bulwark against discrimination of all kinds, the court system must be especially wary about attacks on individual and social rights made in the guise of health-related AIDS claims.[4]

E. CONFIDENTIALITY AND THE DUTY TO DISCLOSE AIDS TEST RESULTS

A distinction must be drawn between testing and disclosure of HIV test results. There is little doubt that both testing and disclosure of results of tests constitute invasions of individual

[2] Id. at 726.
[3] Id.
[4] Id.

rights and privacy. However, as many judicial opinions have shown, the right to be free from unwanted intrusions on privacy is not absolute. In certain instances — particularly where the life or health of others is in jeopardy — the individual's rights begin to erode in favor of concern for society.

As seen in this portion of the chapter, disclosure of HIV-positive test results has generated considerable legislative attention. Even with this legislative activity there is still considerable room for practical guidelines on the topic.

§11.8 Blood Banks and Centers

Legislation in some states allows blood banks and plasma centers to disclose HIV test results with the informed consent of test subjects.[1] Disclosure of test results is sometimes permitted without subject consent, providing the identity of the individual is not known and cannot be obtained by the researcher.[2] In some states, provision is made for individuals to designate to whom they want test results to be disclosed. This is usually done as part of a written informed consent governing disclosure.[3] Legislation in some states requires federally registered blood banks[4] and other institutions[5] to notify donors of HIV-positive test results.

Blood banks have also found themselves involved in litigation in which plaintiffs have sought to compel disclosure of the names of donors.[6] In most of the cases the plaintiff or his decedent fell victim to AIDS due to a blood transfusion. In the overwhelming majority of cases, the request to compel disclo-

---

§11.8   [1]See Wis. Stat. Ann. §146.025 (West 1986).
[2]Id.
[3]Id.
[4]See Ariz. Rev. Stat. Ann. §32-1483 (1987).
[5]Md. Ann. Code §18-334 (1988).
[6]See Gulf Coast Regional Blood Center v. Houston, 745 S.W.2d 557 (Tex. Ct. App. 1988); Rasmussen v. South Florida Blood Serv., 500 So. 2d 533 (Fla. 1987); Krygier v. Airweld, Inc., 520 N.Y.S.2d 475 (Sup. Ct. 1987).

sure of blood donors has been denied, particularly on the ground that confidentiality is needed to ensure adequate supplies of volunteer blood.[7]

To a large extent, the highly sensitive screening methods now used by blood banks eliminate a large measure of the risk of AIDS transmission through blood donation. Nonetheless, there are still cases in the judicial system involving "bad" blood transfusions that occurred prior to AIDS screening. These merit close watching in view of state law and judicial opinions on the matter.

Litigation aside, blood banks and plasma centers should closely monitor state legislative developments governing disclosure of HIV test results. AIDS is a "hot topic" for many state legislatures. As such, further initiatives should be anticipated dealing with consent to disclosure of HIV-positive test results.

§11.9   Health Facilities and Personnel

Many states indicate that health facilities and professionals cannot disclose HIV test results to anyone other than the patient except with the subject's informed consent.[1] However, in some jurisdictions, HIV test results can be released to the attending physician.[2]

In many states legislation authorizes disclosure of HIV test results for medical or epidemiological purposes, providing there is no identifying information linking the data to a specific patient.[3] Kentucky has a provision that permits disclosure to medical personnel in a medical emergency when to do so is necessary to "protect the health or life of the named party."[4]

Aside from those situations in which legislation carves out an

[7] But see Gulf Coast Regional Blood Center v. Houston, supra n.6, in which the court compelled disclosure of the names of blood donors.

§11.9   [1] See Mass. Gen. Laws Ann. ch. 111, §70F (West 1986).
[2] Ky. Rev. Stat. §214.420 (1986).
[3] Id. See also Ind. Code Ann. §16-1-9.5-7 (Burns 1988).
[4] Ky. Rev. Stat. §214.420 (1986).

exception, there is a general requirement to secure consent to release HIV test results. The failure to abide by this requirement can result in litigation. Indeed, litigation has resulted from the disclosure of an inmate's positive HIV test in casual discussion with nonmedical staff[5] and unauthorized publication of an HIV-positive patient's photograph.[6]

Absent a clear legislative mandate or a well-documented authorization from a patient, health facilities and personnel should never disclose confidential HIV or AIDS test results. To do otherwise is bound to set in motion considerable and unnecessary litigation.

§11.10 Family Members and Significant Others

Perhaps the most difficult issue involves disclosure of AIDS or HIV-positive tests to the loved ones of a patient. Although this legal issue involves the law of confidentiality and consent, it is a matter fraught with bioethical considerations.

Some states have chosen to legislate in the area. California law specifically removes any criminal or civil liability for disclosing to the person believed to be the spouse of the patient an HIV-positive test.[1] Other states have also enacted laws regarding disclosure to the spouse of a patient[2] and parents of minor children.[3]

Where state law is silent on the issue, health facilities and professionals should secure legal advice on disclosure of positive test result information. The need to keep patient information confidential must be balanced against society's concern for the welfare and safety of others who might fall "victim" to an infected individual who acts with reckless disregard toward

[5] Woods v. White, 689 F. Supp. 874 (W.D. Wis. 1988).
[6] Anderson v. Strong Memorial Hosp., 531 N.Y.S.2d 735 (Sup. Ct. 1988).
§11.10 [1] Cal. Health & Safety Code §199.27 (West 1987).
[2] R.I. Gen. Laws §23-6-17 (1989); Tex. Rev. Civ. Stat. Ann. art. 4419b-1 (Vernon 1987).
[3] Colo. Rev. Stat. §25-4-1405 (1987).

them. The evolving concept of the "duty to warn" may require a caregiver to notify the spouse of an AIDS or HIV-positive patient who refuses to take necessary precautions to prevent the spread of infection.

More legislation is anticipated in this area. Until the law is clear on the matter, health professionals and agencies should develop practical policies on disclosure of HIV positive test results. For health facilities, input is essential from legal counsel, the insurer, the risk manager, and the medical record administrator. Such policies require constant vigilance as legislative and regulatory directives are put in place on disclosure of AIDS and HIV-positive test results.

§11.11   Practical Limitations on the Duty to Disclose

In many instances concerns about confidentiality and the duty to disclose can be addressed early in the care and treatment of known or suspected HIV-positive patients. Staff education is essential to ensure that sensitive information is not "leaked" by casual conversation or sloppy storage of patient record information.

Staff issues aside, the caregiver-patient relationship should be based on trust and frank discussion. Caregivers should establish early in the treatment the reasons behind HIV testing and the need for disclosure to "essential" individuals any positive tests.

If the caregiver is candid and delineates the limits of anticipated confidentiality, patients will be better able to make choices regarding testing and releasing results. Such an approach can also avert potential confrontations that might arise over disclosure to a spouse or significant other.

For heath care agencies, the most prudent approach is development and implementation of a practical policy on AIDS testing. This policy should cover such issues as consent to testing, consent to disclosure, record access, and record handling. Legal counsel can provide valuable assistance in shaping the policy and procedure to conform with applicable state law.

Balancing the interests of staff who are at risk of exposure to HIV, the rights of the patient, and the needs of the family can be difficult. However, a practical policy or guide on the issue can help circumvent many of the common problems that arise with HIV testing and treatment of AIDS patients.

TWELVE

Documentation of Consent and Practical Rules for Consent

§12.0   Introduction
A. Documentation of Consent
    §12.1   Importance of Documentation
            §12.1.1   Forms of Documentation
            §12.1.2   Sample Long-Form Consent Document
            §12.1.3   Sample Short-Form Consent Document
            §12.1.4   Detailed Note in Patients' Records
            §12.1.5   Consent Checklist Form
            §12.1.6   Release Forms
    §12.2   Retention of Consent Documentation
B. Practical Rules for Consent
    §12.3   The Two-Stage Consent Process
    §12.4   Duty of Referral, On-Call, and Substitute Physicians
    §12.5   Duty of Health Care Facilities
            §12.5.1   Quality Assurance Audits and Preoperative
                       Nursing Routines
            §12.5.2   The Duty of the Health Agency When Consent
                       Processes Are Substandard
            §12.5.3   Effect of Diagnosis-Related Groups (DRGs) on
                       Consent Requirements
    §12.6   Mass Immunization and Consent
    §12.7   Nontreatment Situations and Consent
    §12.8   Telephone Consents
    §12.9   Videotaped Consents
    §12.10   The Role of the Family in Consent
    §12.11   Consent to Treatment and Risk Management
            §12.11.1   The Content of a Consent Policy

§12.11.2   Utilizing Risk Management and Quality Assurance
              Data
    §12.11.3   Preintervention History and Follow-up
§12.12   Contents of a Consent Policy and Procedure

§12.0   Introduction

As seen throughout earlier chapters, the legal principles regarding the law of consent span the spectrum from clearly to
poorly enunciated requirements. Health practitioners, however, need practical, concise guidance on their duties in the
consent process.

One fine practical source is not the courts, but the National
Council on Patient Information and Education (NCPIE).[1]
Through the auspices of this association, patients are being
encouraged to take a more active role in the consent process by
asking questions regarding prescription medication.

The FDA Drug Bulletin[2] suggests patients should ask about
the following:

1.   the name of the drug and its purpose;
2.   the way in which the drug is to be administered and for
     how long;
3.   the medications, foods, and drinks that should not be con-
     sumed when taking the medication;
4.   the types of activities to be avoided when using the medica-
     tion;
5.   the types of side effects that may occur and what should be
     done if they materialize; and
6.   to request written information that is available on the medi-
     cation.[3]

---

§12.0   [1]See Patients May Be Asking Questions About Prescriptions, FDA
Drug Bulletin, 16(2): 22 November 1986.
    [2]Id.
    [3]Id.

To many health professionals, these inquiries may seem less than earth-shattering. However, to patients, questions such as these and the responses to them help in the decision-making process regarding treatment. Such inquiries go directly to the basics of consent: nature, purpose, risk, benefit, and impact on lifestyle. Not only should these questions be asked by patients, but practitioners should use them as a guideline or checklist of matters to discuss when dispensing medication.

Other portions of this book discuss the need for proper documentation of consent and examine some of the more practical problems that arise in the consent process. Particular attention is directed in this concluding chapter to the reasons behind documentation of consent and the consequences of not recording a patient's authorization for treatment. Also considered are such issues as two-stage consent, the duty of the referral physician in the consent process, the role of the hospital in the consent process, consent in a mass immunization setting, and the need for consent to nontreatment procedures.

A. DOCUMENTATION OF CONSENT

§12.1 Importance of Documentation

Although a record of a patient's authorization to treatment may be important for many reasons, the chief legal reason is defense to a consent action. An authorization for treatment recorded in a form signed by the patient or described in a detailed note in the patient's chart may not be dispositive of an allegation based on lack of consent or a claim of inadequate disclosure of information. As evidence of consent, however, it may prove highly persuasive and tip the scales in favor of the defense. To a large extent the outcome depends on whether state law requires a written authorization for treatment and whether a signed authorization for treatment is considered to be consent. Some take the view that the document is merely evidence of consent.[1]

§12.1.1 Forms of Documentation

There are at least four basic ways in which consent may be documented. In some situations, an overlap may result in more than one format being used. The use of one type of documentation or another depends on the requirements of state law as well as institutional policy. When a written authorization signed by the patient is required, the need for a detailed note in the patient's medical record or a consent checklist is eliminated.

The first and most widely recognized type of documentation is the traditional long-form consent. This type of authorization is usually highly detailed, containing all pertinent information regarding risks, benefits, and reasonable alternatives associated with a particular procedure. It also contains other information considered relevant to the needs of a particular patient.

The second type of documentation is the so-called short-form consent. Unlike the more detailed form, the short-form consent document does not contain many specific details, including instead a statement that indicates that the risks and benefits have been explained to the patient.

The third type of documentation does not involve a consent form at all. Instead the practitioner who is to carry out a procedure documents the consent in the patient's medical record. She must summarize there the information disclosed to the patient during the consent process, including details regarding risks, benefits, and reasonable alternatives. The note should identify any questions asked by the patient and the answers given. The names of any witnesses to the consent should also be recorded. The note should be written as soon as the patient

§12.1 [1]See, e.g., Ga. Code §88-2906 (1971), in which a consent duly evidenced in writing is deemed to create a conclusive presumption of a valid authorization, absent fraudulent misrepresentation of material facts.

gives verbal authorization or within a reasonable time thereafter. It then should be dated and signed by the practitioner.

The fourth alternative is a so-called consent checklist, which contains a series of check-off spaces and short narrative components that must be completed by the person who obtains the patient's consent. The caregiver certifies that he has completed the consent process as noted by the form. The failure of the caregiver to properly complete the consent process as documented becomes a basis for privileges action.

The short-form and long-form consent documents can be used in combination with a detailed note in the patient's record or the consent checklist. Hospital policy may dictate this course to make certain that patients are indeed informed and they have given their consent to the proposed form of treatment. Individual practitioners who feel that the additional documentation serves as added protection from potential litigation may also choose this approach. Particular instances may call for this "double consent" to safeguard the interests of the patient and the institution. An example is a case in which the patient has refused consent to necessary treatment and has decided to leave the health facility against medical advice. Another is when a patient has been consuming drugs or alcohol, but not to a sufficient degree to render her mentally incapable of giving consent. If the double consent is used in these circumstances, the notation in the medical chart would emphasize that, although under the influence, the patient is not so impaired as to be considered mentally incapable of giving consent to treatment.

§12.1.2 Sample Long-Form Consent Document

The following is an example of a long-form consent document. It should be emphasized that this is *only* a sample and that physicians and health facilities should seek legal advice in developing their own forms. The legal requirements for consent in each state must be taken into account in the document.

CONSENT TO TREATMENT

1. I, _____, of _____, do hereby give my consent to the performance of (name of medical, surgical or diagnostic procedure). I understand that the procedure will involve (explanation of the procedure). I have made my decision voluntarily and freely.

2. I appreciate that there are certain risks associated with this procedure including (list of risks) and I freely assume these risks. I also understand that there are possible benefits associated with this procedure including (list of benefits). However, I appreciate there is no certainty that I will achieve these benefits and no guarantee has been made to me regarding the outcome of this procedure.

3. The reasonable alternative(s) to this procedure have been explained to me including (list of reasonable alternatives if any exist).

4. Any questions I have had regarding this procedure have been answered to my satisfaction.

5. In authorizing my physician, Dr. (name of doctor) to perform this procedure, I understand that he will be assisted by other health professionals of the (name of the health facility) and such others as he considers necessary in my care. I agree to their participation in my care.

6. To attest to my consent to this procedure, I hereby affix my signature to this authorization for treatment.

7. _____ Signature of patient

8. _____ Signature of witness

9. _____ Date and time

The long-form consent outlined above is fairly representative of this category of documentation. Clauses 1 through 4 meet the basic requirements for consent by describing the nature of the proposed procedure; the associated risks and benefits; information regarding alternative procedures, if any exist; and responses to patient inquiries regarding the proposed procedure. Clause 5 makes certain that the patient understands that other health professionals will be involved in the procedure. This paragraph could be phrased differently to read, "I agree to the performance of this procedure by my physician, Dr. _____, and such other persons of her choosing." Much depends upon the style and legal requirements perceived by hospital counsel. Realistically, however, those assisting a procedure performed in a hospital are assigned by their department heads so that the attending physician has little choice in the matter.

Clauses 6 through 9 involve attesting to the patient's authorization for treatment. The signature of the patient and that of any witnesses are important where a signed, written consent is required by law. The witnesses attest to the patient's signing the document, not necessarily to the consent process. To do the latter, the witnesses must actually be present for the consent process in which the attending doctor explained the proposed procedure.

When patients are legally incapable of giving consent, the form should be altered to permit the signature of a legal representative, providing that individual is authorized to act for the patient in matters of health care. State legislation may also designate who may act for a patient when he is incapable of giving consent. (See chapters 1 and 2 supra.)

The date and time are important in the event that allegations are raised that the form was signed *after* the procedure was done or *after* the patient had been medicated so that she was not mentally capable of giving consent.

Other clauses should be added as necessary. For example, when the proposed procedure is an abdominal exploratory operation, another paragraph could be included that states:

> Since this procedure is an exploratory operation, I hereby authorize my physician to take such steps as he considers necessary in his medical judgment, including the removal of specimens for examination or the removal of diseased tissue or organs.

Such a clause may prove important as protection against claims that the doctor went beyond the scope of authorized treatment.

The written clause cannot, however, replace the dialogue between patient and physician that should precede the signing of the consent form. During this exchange, the physician should explain the intended operation.

§12.1.3 Sample Short-Form Consent Document

The following is an example of a short-form consent document. It must be kept in mind that, like the long form, this consent document is not a substitute for the consent process in which the patient is informed by her attending doctor of relevant details associated with the intended intervention.

CONSENT TO TREATMENT

1. I, _____, of _____, do hereby agree to the performance of (name of procedure) by my doctor, Dr. (name of physician) and such others as he considers necessary.

2. The nature and consequences of the procedure have been explained to me. I understand that it will involve (brief explanation of the procedure).

3. The risks and benefits of this procedure have been explained to me. I also understand that there are certain medical and surgical alternatives to this procedure and I have been given information regarding other medically or surgically feasible forms of care.

4. I hereby freely and voluntarily give my signed authorization for this procedure.

5. _____ Signature of patient

6. _____ Signature of witness

7. _____ Date and time

The difference between the long- and short-form consent documents are readily discernible. The short form does not contain specific risk, benefit, or reasonable alternative information. The document simply acknowledges in paragraph 3 that the patient has been informed of these details.

Clause 1 identifies who will perform the operation or intervention, and clause 2 points out what is involved in the procedure. Paragraph 4 notes that the patient gives her consent voluntarily, and clauses 5 through 7 deal with considerations important from a defensive point of view, as outlined above.

The evidentiary importance of the short-form consent document rests heavily on the testimony of the plaintiff, the defendant, and witnesses. A patient could claim that he signed the form out of a desire not to "make any trouble" — even though the physician did not inform him of the procedure or of the risks involved. The same could be said of the long form, but in that case, the information disclosed in the consent process is also incorporated in the document, making it more likely that one way or another the patient was "informed." Of course, a patient could always claim that he never read the document before signing it. The patient does bear a certain responsibility in the consent process, and the fact that he signed a document may raise considerable doubts in the minds of a jury or a judge as to the veracity of his claims of ignorance.

When the short-form document is used, good policy may require a detailed note in the patient's chart, outlining the information disclosed to the patient before she signed the written consent. It should also include the names of any witnesses to the consent process, who may or may not be the same individuals who witness the patient sign the document. The note should be dated and timed. This added measure of documentation may prove important in subsequent litigation when the trier of facts must decide who should be believed: the patient or the physician. When the physician has taken the time to write the detailed note in the patient's record, it may sway the case in the doctor's favor, since it demonstrates diligence in completing consent requirements.

§12.1.4   Detailed Notes in Patients' Records

Some health facilities may opt out from the use of consent forms, relying instead on detailed notes in patients' health records. The advantage of such a practice is that it does not permit a form to become the substitute for the time and care involved in the actual consent process between the patient and the attending physician. It places a considerable burden upon the practitioner to make certain that the consent process is complete. He must then recount what transpired during the discussion. Since each patient's condition is different, each note will be tailored to reflect these distinctions. Risk, benefit, and reasonable alternative information is particularly apt to vary. (See Appendix C.)

The detailed note should never be used alone to document the consent process where state or federal law requires a signed, written authorization from the patient. When this is the case, however, there may be sound justification for requiring a consent form in conjunction with a detailed note in the patient's health record.

At a minimum, the detailed note should include the following information:

1. A description of the proposed procedure as given to the patient.
2. A list of the risks and benefits disclosed to the patient.
3. A list of any reasonable alternative forms of care, if any exist; this information should have also been disclosed to the patient.
4. That the patient was told that others would participate in the performance of the procedure.
5. That the patient was told that there was no guarantee of the procedure's success.
6. When the procedure is exploratory in nature, that the patient understood and agreed to its extent and the possible removal of tissue for pathological assessment or excision, if diseased.

7. That the patient posed certain questions regarding the proposed operation, and that these were answered.

8. That the patient was informed of additional information that the doctor considered important in his or her case — such as probable discomfort, the impact the procedure would have on his ability to resume his normal lifestyle and work, the length of recuperation as well as the period the patient will be unable to resume his employment.

9. That in the physician's estimation, the patient was mentally capable of giving consent and that, insofar as he or she knew, the patient was also legally competent to give consent. It should also be noted that the patient agreed that the decision was made freely.

10. The names of any witnesses to the consent process should be written in the detailed note. The note should then be signed by the doctor, timed, and dated.

Of the various types of documentation, the preferable form from a patient's point of view is the detailed note in the patient's chart. This method avoids the use of standardized forms and it reduces the probability of the consent document's being used as a substitute for the consent process. From a legal point of view it is also preferable. Both the hospital in which the procedure is to be performed and the attending physician can no longer depend upon the consent form as sufficient proof of the patient's authorization. Doctors have to take additional time with patients to make certain that they understand what will be done. Having to sit down and write a summary of conversations with patients will also impress on doctors the importance of the consent process and the notes that are included in medical records. When enforced as hospital policy, the documentation in the patient's chart alters the image of consent in the minds of health professionals. The shift in policy will hopefully mean a change from viewing consent as a burdensome part of hospital bureaucracy to a greater concern for the rights and needs of patients. As a result, the risks of legal actions based on lack of or inadequate consent will be reduced.

Some may argue that detailed notes in patients' medical records are self-serving documents, and thus of little defensive value. While this concern may be true for some types of documentation, it is not so in the case of detailed notes. Allegations of drafting a self-serving note would likely arise when one is written in anticipation of litigation after a patient has suffered injury. When, however, the detailed note is written at the time the patient gave authorization and it is timed and dated, the plaintiff is hard-pressed to prove such an allegation.

§12.1.5   Consent Checklist Form

To deal with complaints that it takes too long to write a detailed note in the patient's record, the fourth option is to develop a consent checklist. (See Appendix D.) Such a document includes a series of check-off spaces documenting each step of the consent process. Space should also be available following each check-off item to permit caregivers to expand on a given category of information.

The consent checklist should require the caregiver to certify that she has completed each of the noted items by signing and dating the completed form. The failure to complete each consent step as checked off would form the basis for staff privileges action.

The consent checklist serves as a reminder to caregivers of their responsibilities in the consent process. If well designed, the system should ease quality assurance and risk management.

§12.1.6   Release Forms

Release forms have been discussed in the context of legal defense and refusing care. In some legal quarters release forms are seen as a valuable tool in dealing with patients who decline or withdraw from care. However, use of release forms to exculpate a facility or a health professional *prior to treatment* and without giving the patient adequate time to reflect upon such a choice is quite another matter. The law looks with considerable disfavor upon "signing away" the right to litigate. This is particularly so when the language of the document is ambiguous. A New York case illustrates this point.[2]

The plaintiff, a teacher and student at New York University, went to the New York University College of Dentistry clinic for some dental reconstruction. In the midst of a dental examination, he was given a paper to sign entitled "Registration Form." There was no opportunity to review the document. The plaintiff was simply told that his signature was needed on an official registration form. In fact, the document contained several subparts including the following:

> IN CONSIDERATION OF the reduced rates given to me by the New York University I hereby release and agree to save harmless NEW YORK UNIVERSITY, its doctors and students from any and all liability arising out of or in connection with any injuries or damages which I may sustain while on its premises, or as a result of any treatment in its infirmaries.[3]

The plaintiff subsequently brought action for dental malpractice. The lower court granted a defense request for summary judgment on the ground that the language of the release was clear and barred the plaintiff's action.[4]

On appeal, the court reinstated the plaintiff's complaint and dismissed the release as an affirmative defense. As the court pointed out, a release form must contain "express and unmistakable language"[5] to the effect that the parties wish to exempt themselves from the consequences of negligent activity. There must not be any ambiguity, and the meaning of the document must be understandable.[6]

In this case, the court ruled that the language of the release form failed to measure up to these requirements. The word "negligence" was never used. As the court pointed out, even if the plaintiff had been able to read the language carefully, he might have reasonably concluded that the defendant was not to

---

[2]Abramowitz v. New York Univ. Dental Center, 110 A.D.2d 343, 494 N.Y.S.2d 721 (1985).
[3]494 N.Y.S.2d at 722.
[4]494 N.Y.S.2d at 723.
[5]Id.
[6]Id.

be held accountable for minor injuries and discomforts that might arise from the work of sufficiently supervised post-graduate dental students. It would be an error to conclude that he understood it would exculpate the defendant from all liability for harm that occurred by failing to exercise ordinary care.[7]

The practical point of this case is clear: release forms require careful drafting and patients must have a clear understanding of the import of such documents. Simply telling patients that they are "registration" forms or "administrative formalities" will not suffice. Moreover, such forms should not be given to a patient without a proper explanation and ample time to review them. Certainly, it is inappropriate to request that a patient sign such a form in the midst of treatment.

The release form is an important form of consent documentation. However, because the right to litigate may be signed away with such a form, careful use of language and strict adherence to the consent process is required in securing a proper execution of the document.

§12.2   Retention of Consent Documentation

Regardless of how consent is documented, a common concern is how long the authorization should be retained. The best rule of thumb is to determine the primary purposes of the document. When it is being used for continuous forms of care, such as dialysis, it should be retained for the duration of the treatment.

From a legal perspective, documentation should be retained for as long as the practitioner or health facility may be subject to litigation regarding the care given. Applicable statutes of limitation determine the longest period of exposure to liability. This statutory review would include such considerations as tolling of the statutes of limitation, in the case of minors or the mentally disabled, and the time of discovery rule in some jurisdictions. The period of liability will differ for some health facili-

---

[7] 494 N.Y.S.2d at 724-725.

ties, such as children's hospitals and mental health facilities, in view of tolling provisions. The best policy is to keep consent documentation on file for the longest period of time of potential liability calculated under these limitation periods.

For many health facilities it would be unduly burdensome or even impossible to keep patient records in the usual form for several years. The move to computerized medical records and the widespread use of microfilm and other photographic copies has gone a long way toward solving these difficulties. Providing that state evidence laws permit the use of such copies of handwritten original forms, no difficulty should arise from retaining patient consent documents in this way.

A more difficult issue is the computerization of medical records, including patient consent forms. The acceptability of this method is doubtful since the information on computer files can be easily tampered with in a self-serving fashion. The signatures of the patient or a witness, and the date and time at which the document was complete may be key issues in a consent action. For this reason, unless state law permits otherwise, so-called hard-copy consent forms should not be put on computers. The documents should be retained in their original form or in any other manner acceptable under the laws of evidence in a particular state.

B. PRACTICAL RULES FOR CONSENT

§12.3 The Two-Stage Consent Process

Some practitioners prefer to disclose to a patient all relevant risk, benefit, and reasonable alternative information in their offices rather than in a hospital. The two-stage consent process, it is suggested, permits practitioners to take more time with their patients. Discussing the merits of proposed procedures in doctors' offices is more conducive to the consent process than the unfamiliar atmosphere of a hospital.

In a two-stage consent, patients receive information from

their physicians days or even weeks in advance of hospitalization for a diagnostic, medical, or surgical procedure. Once in the hospital, nurses or ward clerks may present patients with forms that authorize procedures based on the information provided by the physicians. A hospital employee may ask if a patient understands what is going to happen or if she has any questions regarding the procedure. If at this point the patient indicates a lack of understanding or a need to ask questions, the consent process has been shown to be incomplete. The attending physician should be contacted and asked to see the patient before the authorization form is signed.

The difficulty with the two-stage consent is one of time. The lapse between the consent process in a doctor's office and the document being executed in a hospital is conducive to patients' either forgetting what they were told or developing a list of questions that must be answered before they can give consent. That patients may have several questions is not necessarily bad, but their inability to remember what they were told undermines the value of the two-stage consent. A second session is then necessary with the physician, who may be pressed for time and, as a result, not discharge his consent responsibilities properly. Shortening the time between the office session and the execution of the consent document may alleviate the forgetful patient problem, but it will do nothing to eliminate questions. Since physicians are responsible for the consent process, they should not delegate this duty to someone else. If they do, and patients rely on misinformation from others to their detriment, the doctors may be implicated in subsequent consent litigation. Based on these considerations, the two-stage consent is not recommended.

§12.4 Duty of Referral, On-Call, and Substitute Physicians

One area of the law that is less than clear is the responsibility of the referral, on-call, or substitute physician for obtaining informed consent. How extensive is this duty? Can the referral or on-call doctor rely upon a consent or disclosure carried out by the attending physician? Questions such as these require considered responses. It is particularly important in group practices as well as in situations in which physicians leave a substitute physician in place while they are on vacation. Moreover, when the substitute physician is asked to carry out a continuing form of therapy, the need for disclosure and "screening" questions to detect side effects from treatment is another key concern.

The specialist or consulting physician, psychologist, or other health professional should not depend upon the referring physician to complete the consent process with the patient. This duty rests squarely with the consultant, not the referring physician. Case law on the duty of the referring physician in these circumstances reinforces this principle.[1]

An example of this principle is found in a Pennsylvania case in which a man lost his ability to walk following an exploratory laminectomy.[2] At the time of his admission to the hospital by an orthopedic surgeon, the patient had signed a consent form. Later the defendant, a neurosurgeon, was called in as a consultant. After running some tests he recommended the operation. Rather than obtaining consent himself, the neurosurgeon relied upon the admitting consent form. The Supreme Court of Pennsylvania pointed out that the defendant should not have relied upon the consent obtained before he was called in as a consultant. In this case, even if the defendant had been entitled to rely upon the consent, the patient's authorization was not informed, as evinced by the man's continued questioning of nurses and residents.[3] A similar finding was made in a Montana case on the duty of the referring physician.[4]

Imposing the responsibility for obtaining consent on the specialist or consultant rather than on the referring physician re-

---

§12.4 [1]Liera v. Wisner, 171 Mont. 254, 557 P.2d 805 (1976); Gray v. Grunnagle, 423 Pa. 144, 223 A.2d 663 (1966).
[2]Gray v. Grunnagle, supra n.1.
[3]Id.
[4]Liera v. Wisner, supra n.1.

affirms the basic requirements of the law of consent. It is the duty of the person who is to perform a diagnostic, surgical, or medical intervention to obtain the patient's authorization for treatment. This principle can be extended to other health professionals, such as physiotherapists who actually work with patients in rehabilitation programs. Although referring doctors may indicate in general terms what type of therapy they want for patients, obtaining the patient's authorization remains the duty of the physiotherapist.

For referring physicians to be liable for failure to obtain a valid consent, they must retain more than a "degree of participation" in the care of patients.[5] Merely visiting a patient in the hospital is not enough to trigger such a duty.[6] However, according to at least one court, when referring doctors order tests or procedures or participate in treatment, the duty to inform does apply.[7] The rationale is that in these instances the referring physicians have taken an active role in patient care.

To prevent consent difficulties in this regard, health facilities should clearly indicate to staff physicians and allied health personnel who is responsible for obtaining patients' authorization. This can be accomplished through policy statements, guidelines, and in-service training.

The issue of consent is of importance not only to referral physicians, but to those who are "on-call" or who agree to "cover" for another doctor who is on vacation.

In group practices, in which the physicians are employees of a professional medical corporation, the issue of consent can be an important factor. For example, in a Rhode Island case,[8] two urologists were employed by a corporation known as Urologic Services, Inc. One physician in the group had advised the plaintiff that he would require both a cystoscopy and a urethroscopy. The plaintiff was assured by the physician that he would not require an external surgical incision.

---

[5]Nisenholtz v. Mt. Sinai Hosp., 126 Misc. 2d 658, 483 N.Y.S.2d 568 (1984).
[6]Id.
[7]Id.
[8]Sousa v. Chaset, 519 A.2d 1132 (R.I. 1987).

The physician was called out of town on an urgent family matter and he asked another doctor employed by the corporation to contact the plaintiff. This doctor advised the plaintiff of the situation and asked him whether he wished to postpone his hospitalization or to go ahead with his scheduled tests and be treated by him. The plaintiff agreed that the second physician should admit him and carry out the tests.

When the physician was unable to pass a urethroscope through the area of the plaintiff's meatus, he performed a meatotomy to enlarge the area. This was a procedure separate from the diagnostic tests. Postoperatively, the plaintiff developed complications and litigation followed.

The plaintiff claimed that the operation was conducted without his consent and that the first physician was vicariously liable for the second doctor's decision to procede with surgery. As the court pointed out, the first doctor never departed from his promise to refrain from making an external surgical incision. Moreover, there was no evidence that either physician was the agent or employee of the other. Hence, the Supreme Court of Rhode Island ruled that the lower court properly directed a verdict on this issue.[9]

When the relationship is one in which the "covering" or substitute physician is an independent contractor, the result may be different. For example, in a New York case,[10] the attending physician had begun a period of treatment known as gold therapy on the plaintiff. The doctor noted in his office chart on the patient that he had advised her of the possible complications associated with such therapy and that the plaintiff had agreed to it. When he decided to go off on vacation, the attending physician arranged with another doctor to cover for him.

The substitute doctor met with the plaintiff in his office, interviewed her about her condition, and carried out some tests. He also gave her a gold injection. This was repeated one week later. When the patient appeared for her third injection, she had a rash. The substitute physician advised her that the

[9]Id.
[10]Sangiuolo v. Leventhal, 505 N.Y.S.2d 507 (Sup. Ct. 1986).

treatments must stop, and he gave her some medications and carried out some tests. There was one additional session the following week in which the substitute doctor adjusted her medications.

The plaintiff sued the substitute physician for malpractice and lack of informed consent. In a motion for summary judgment brought by the defendant, the court granted the request as to the issue of malpractice. However, on the matter of consent, the court noted that there was a genuine issue of material fact whether the attending doctor had apprised the plaintiff of the risks of gold therapy.

The defendant claimed that he was entitled to rely upon the notation in his colleague's records regarding disclosure of risk information. As the court noted, the substitute physician, as an independent caregiver, was obliged to inform the plaintiff of the risks, benefits, and alternative forms of treatment. It was also noted that this duty *may* have been met by the first doctor. This was a matter for the trier of fact to resolve at trial. If at trial it was determined that the first physician did not make an adequate disclosure of risk information, then the substitute doctor would have relied in error on the entry in the records.[11]

The substitute physician also raised another point. He argued that a ruling such as this would make it more difficult for physicians going on vacation to obtain substitute coverage for their patients. The court responded by saying that "most 'covering' situations involve handling whatever new problems arise, and the covering physician's duty to inform with respect to new problems is unaffected. Furthermore, the burden of advising of the risks of a continuing course of treatment is minimal."[12]

Many physicians would take strong exception to the New York ruling. They would argue that they are entitled to rely upon a notation in a colleague's chart. However, there is something slightly different in this case: that the patient was undergoing a continuing form of therapy. Although there may not be a need to secure consent for each treatment session, it is

[11] Id. at 510.
[12] Id.

important to screen patients for risks that may have arisen subsequent to the last intervention. According to the opinion, this was done at the outset of the third office visit.[13]

Perhaps the emphasis on the "burden of advising"[14] about risks in such cases is better placed at the outset of the treatment relationship. When a doctor takes over in the midst of a continuing course of therapy, perhaps to satisfy himself that the patient does indeed understand the risks of therapy, he should question the individual. This does, however, seem to go beyond what the rules of consent require. Absent any reason to believe that the patient does not appreciate the risks and benefits of ongoing therapy, as well as reasonable alternatives to it, it does not seem necessary to reopen the matter of consent. This is particularly so when the office records of the attending doctor indicate that the patient has been apprised of the risks associated with therapy. However, when a patient begins to question the need for ongoing treatment or expresses reservations regarding the risks incident to such care, then it would be advisable to reopen the matter of consent. At this point the consent to continuous treatment may be in doubt and therefore deserves reexamination.

On-call and substitute doctors work within the gray area of the law of consent. As a result, they should seek specific legal advice on preventive measures to follow. At the very least, they should be diligent in reviewing office records and hospital charts for documentary evidence of consent. If they believe that such records are lacking, it may be prudent to explore the matter with patients prior to embarking on a course of therapy. Moreover, they should be diligent in documenting discussions of consent with patients. This is particularly true when there is a need to alter the course of treatment. The on-call arrangement should be made clear to patients of all doctors in the coverage plan, to make certain that they agree to treatment by the on-call doctor. The same is true of hospitals in which the on-call doctor will provide coverage for patients.[15]

---

[13] Id. at 508.
[14] Id. at 510.
[15] See Kenner v. Northern Ill. Med. Center, 517 N.E.2d 1137 (Ill. App. Ct.

§12.5   Duty of Health Care Facilities

In an era in which corporate responsibility on the part of health care facilities is commonplace, it is logical that some would argue that health care agencies have a legal duty in the consent process. Although most case law suggests that hospitals and other institutions are not responsible for securing consent,[1] the responsibility question becomes more interesting when facilities immerse themselves in the consent process. Similarly, legal obligations and vicarious responsibility might well arise when staff know or ought to know that consents to treatment are substandard.

In this section preoperative quality assurance audits or routines are described as one mechanism that can be used to alert health facilities to substandard consent processes. This is followed by a discussion of what steps the facility should take when it is clear that patients have not been afforded an adequate consent process. Finally, the impact of DRGs on consent will be described.

§12.5.1   *Quality Assurance Audits and Preoperative Nursing Routines*

It is quite common for hospitals to perform quality assurance audits that monitor patient care and standards compliance. As part of this function, audits or nursing routines are completed to ensure preoperatively that patients understand prepping and postsurgical measures. In many ways these routines constitute an important aspect of patient education. The dialogue with the nurse can also help to lessen the patient's anxiety about surgery.

1987), in which the court reversed a summary judgment in favor of the defendants. According to the court there was a material issue of fact whether the patient had given consent to treatment by the on-call doctor, and this prevented the granting of summary judgment in favor of the defendants.

§12.5   [1]See §1.14.4 supra.

This process is not without legal danger. A strong argument can be made that if a nurse knows or should know from her quality assurance or preoperative routine that the patient is not well informed, the hospital is on notice and should act accordingly. The failure to take action — such as stopping the intended operation until the patient's understanding of the procedure is adequate — resulting in reasonably foreseeable injury or death, might constitute negligence. Such an obligation could be imposed on the basis of the facility's independent duty of care to patients.

Veteran nurses are in an excellent position to identify substandard consents. The patient's understanding of a procedure, when coupled with a few questions about the individual's knowledge of the intervention, can determine if the patient has given an informed consent.

As part of a comprehensive consent policy and procedure a mechanism can be put in place to correct such situations. Once a caregiver knows or should know that a patient has a poor understanding of a proposed intervention, the professional who is to carry out the treatment should be notified and come in to discuss the matter with the patient. The procedure should be placed on hold to ensure that nothing is done until the consent problems are corrected.

There is no doubt that such a procedure can cause administrative headaches. Doctors might complain about having to see the patient again or they might want to get residents or interns to see the patient to "straighten things out." Nonetheless, once operational, the practice will have a salutary effect on the quality of patients' consents. It also gives important risk management support to caregivers who might otherwise proceed with invasive procedures without adequate consent.

§12.5.2 The Duty of the Health Agency When Consent Processes Are Substandard

As noted in §1.14.4, supra, a health agency is generally viewed as not having a legal duty of care in the consent process.

The courts usually hold that consent is a matter between patient and caregiver.

This prevailing view is not without its exceptions. Hospitals are duty bound to prevent harm to patients that they know or ought to know is likely to occur as the result of substandard performance on the part of a caregiver. The same is true of substandard consent practices known to the health agency.[2]

Given the fact that health agencies do incur a duty of care once on notice of substandard consent practices, it is incumbent on the facilities to act to protect patients. For invasive diagnostic or surgical procedures this may mean having an automatic hold on the procedure pending satisfaction of the consent process.

If hospitals discern that incomplete or substandard consent practices are part of a pattern of professional performance, it may be prudent to consider such information when clinical privileges are next under review. Indeed, if the problem is serious enough, it may be necessary to suspend or revoke privileges. Much would depend, however, upon the content of health agency bylaws and whether privileges action could be taken for substandard consent practices.

Physicians are not the only professionals responsible for securing consent. A technician who is to carry out a test or procedure also has a duty to secure consent. Once again, if quality assurance or risk management monitoring demonstrates a pattern of substandard consent practices by a caregiver, such information should be included in performance appraisals with a view toward education, discipline, or job action.

§12.5.3   Effect of Diagnosis-Related Groups (DRGs) on Consent Requirements

It is impossible to state with statistical precision the impact of diagnosis-related groups (DRGs) on consent practices. Studies would be necessary to determine what if any effect DRGs have had and continue to have on the way in which consents to treatment are obtained by caregivers.

[2]Fiorentino v. Wenger, 19 N.Y.2d 407, 280 N.Y.S.2d 373, 227 N.E.2d 296 (1967). See also discussion at §1.14.4.

Statistical analysis notwithstanding, there is a more immediate, practical concern. If DRGs motivate doctors to recommend one form of care over another in an effort to avoid a treatment method that might extend hospitalization beyond the permissible limit, it may be the case that the patient should be apprised of this information. In many states, patients have a right to material information. Details about reasonable treatment options are considered part of the material information that should be imparted to the patient.

Caregivers must be careful to separate personal considerations regarding DRGs from decisions regarding appropriate treatment alternatives. Patients need to have sufficient information to make treatment choices. The bottom line is that it is not acceptable to hold back details about treatment options which might cause administrative inconvenience for physicians.

§12.6 Mass Immunization and Consent

The difficulties encountered in the Swine Flu Immunization Program have resulted in a considerable body of litigation,[1] but the swine flu situation is by no means representative of what ordinarily occurs in a mass immunization setting. Indeed, Congress passed special legislation to cover the situation.[2]

The swine flu outbreak was not the first time that a mass immunization program resulted in litigation.[3] Nor is Congress the only legislature in the United States to have passed legislation relating to mass vaccinations. Pennsylvania, for example, has done so with respect to liability on the part of physicians and nurses in such treatment situations.[4]

One common issue found in all mass immunization programs is how to make certain that a patient gives informed

---

§12.6 [1]See, e.g., Petty v. United States, 679 F.2d 719 (8th Cir. 1982), and cases cited therein at 726, n.7. See also Mills v. United States, 765 F.2d 373 (1985).
[2]42 U.S.C. §§247b(j)-247b(l) (1976).
[3]Reyes v. Wyeth Laboratories, 498 F.2d 1264 (5th Cir. 1974); Davis v. Wyeth Laboratories, 399 F.2d 121 (9th Cir. 1968).
[4]Pa. Stat. Ann. tit. 35, §10151 (Purdon 1976).

consent. Unlike the usual treatment situation, the patient may not know who administers the medication he receives. To require the health professional to go through the usual consent process with each and every patient would be terribly time-consuming and impractical. Some other method of making certain that the patient has been informed must be found.

One reasonable suggestion is to have large signs displayed throughout the pretreatment and treatment areas. The signs would contain pertinent information for patients, including possible risks, benefits, the availability of any reasonable forms of care, and what the patient should do if any listed side effects occur. As patients enter they should be given a pamphlet that reiterates what is found on the wall displays. In areas in which the population is multilingual, both the sign boards and pamphlets should be printed in the languages spoken in the area. Just before patients reach the treatment area, they should be asked if they understand the information provided and whether they have any questions. If they indicate that they do not understand, cannot read, or have questions, they should be placed in a separate line in which they may receive more individualized attention. Services that should be available include interpreters and assistance for the visually or hearing impaired.

Should any question remain regarding an individual's capacity to give consent in these circumstances, she should not be immunized and instead should be referred to the family physician. A similar tack may be taken with those who are present with underlying health problems or who are on medication that makes immunization inadvisable.

Requiring a signed, written consent in these circumstances is impractical and of doubtful legal value. The more practical way in which to deal with the problem is to use signs, pamphlets, and interchange with a qualified health professional.

§12.7   Nontreatment Situations and Consent

Various procedures to which a person may be subjected do not involve treatment. Some are undertaken for religious purposes, such as ritual circumcision, or for educational purposes, such as taking photographs of various parts of a person's body. Unless state law requires otherwise, the consent of the patient or legal representative should be obtained prior to carrying out any nontreatment procedures. Because the procedure may be invasive either of the patient's body or the right of privacy, consent is an important prerequisite.

In the case of photographs taken for scientific or educational purposes, patients should be told whether they will be readily identifiable and whether the photographs will be published. If they limit the scope of the photos or the right to publish the pictures, their decision must be respected. Adequate documentation in a patient's health record should support the taking and using of photos; a detailed note in the patient's record or a short-form consent document are possible choices. The type of documentation used will depend on institutional policy as well as the requirements of state law.

§12.8   Telephone Consents

Health facilities often accept authorizations for treatment over the telephone, by telegram, or from some other telecommunication. This practice typically involves situations in which patients are incapable of authorizing care and consent from next of kin or a guardian is deemed necessary.

There are a number of key issues in the use of telephone or telegraphic consents. For example, are these authorizations permissible under state law? What information should be conveyed to the third party? Who should speak to next of kin or the patient's guardian? What type of institutional policy on documentation should be employed?

Health facilities and personnel should obtain specific legal advice regarding state requirements on telephone or telegraphic consents. This advice should include a survey of applicable state legislation and regulations as well as case law on consent.

The information conveyed during a telephone consent

should follow the basic criteria for a valid authorization out-lined in chapter 1. If possible, the caregiver should obtain rele-vant medical history information about the patient from the third party: for example, the patient's history of cardiac or respiratory diseases, the medications currently being used by the patient, prior history of surgery, and known allergies.

The health professional who is to provide treatment to the patient should speak with the person who is giving an authori-zation. This responsibility should not be delegated to a ward clerk, medical student, intern, or nurse. The attending physi-cian should carry out this task since he is in the best position to inform the third party and to ask pertinent questions about the patient's history.

Documentation of telephone consents should include such information as the following:

1. Date, time, and telephone number called.
2. Name and position of the person who spoke to the patient's relatives or legal guardian.
3. Name and relationship of the third party to the patient.
4. A summary of the information conveyed to the third party.
5. A brief account of questions posed to the third party along with a summary of the answers to these questions.
6. Date and time of entry in patient record as well as the writer's signature.

Documentation of telephone consents is important for pur-poses of a legal defense. A proper entry in the patient's record is also significant for treatment. In some hospitals another em-ployee listens to the conversation as a witness to the telephone consent. This practice is of dubious value, particularly if the requirements of the consent process have not been met. It is far better to develop a practical policy on telephone consents and to apply them in a uniform manner than to depend on a tele-phone witness.

From a legal prevention point of view, careful thought should be given to when telephone consents may be used and the requirements for who may obtain such an authorization.

Documentation of such authorizations should be incorporated in a comprehensive policy governing telephone consents.

§12.9 Videotaped Consents

The age of VCRs, CD ROMs, and other technology has sparked considerable interest in the use of advanced audiovisual material in the consent process. Indeed, as a defensive measure, some caregivers videotape their discussions with patients and keep the videotapes on file. If they are subsequently sued for negligent consent, these physicians believe that the videotaped consent will serve as a strong defense.

Whether or not a videotaped consent is admissible as evidence is a matter of state law. Even where it is permitted, the videotape must be made and maintained in a manner consistent with the rules of evidence.

A more important and practical issue is the use of videotaped information as an *adjunct to* the consent process. Legislation in Georgia permits videotapes to be used in this manner.[1]

Well-designed videotapes should be an excellent adjunctive tool in the consent process. It would assist caregivers in conveying important information of a general nature. However, videotapes can never replace the individualized discussion of relevant risk, benefit, and treatment option information between a caregiver and patient.

Specific legal advice is important before moving to a consent process utilizing videotape material. Indeed, it is essential to secure permission for such materials in human research trials where the consent requirements are governed by exacting federal and state law on the topic of disclosure.

§12.10 The Role of Family in Consent

Although the law requires that an authorization for treatment be obtained from the patient, there are situations in which it is

§12.9 [1]See Ga. Code §88-2904 (1986).

advisable to involve the patient's family in the consent process. This may occur when legislation authorizes next of kin to consent on behalf of an incompetent patient. It may also happen when patients are legally and mentally capable of authorizing care, but the assistance of a family member may facilitate the consent process.

One such typical circumstance is that of a patient hospitalized in an intensive care unit. The patient may have visual or hearing impairment. The patient may also be receiving conflicting and sometimes highly technical information from a variety of health care personnel. Considering the deficits of the patient, the flood of incoming information, and the hectic atmosphere of the intensive care setting, it may be useful to involve a trusted family member to assist in the consent process.

Family involvement can take many forms. It may result in the family member's meeting regularly with the health care team or attending doctor. It may mean the family member will assist doctors in putting the patient's condition and treatment options in a way she can understand. The scope of such involvement will depend upon the nature of the patient's condition, the willingness of the family to become involved, and the patient's agreement to family interaction in the consent process.

Before embarking on a "family-oriented" consent process, it is important to obtain the patient's permission to involve specific individuals. If the patient is reluctant to do so, his decision should be respected.

When patients do agree to permit family to help the consent process, this should be documented in the patient's record. The name and relationship of interested family should be noted in the chart. Moreover, the note should indicate what information has been conveyed to the interested family member as well as to the patient.

Allowing family members to assist in the consent process can prove quite helpful. However, it should be remembered that the ultimate determination regarding one form of care over another rests with the competent patient. The role of family must be kept in perspective: next of kin should act as "facilitators." The only time this role will change is if family members are empowered either by statute or court order to authorize care for the patient.

Case law in the field of consent and the terminally ill demonstrates a return to greater family involvement in treatment decisions. This trend may permeate nonterminal care situtations. As a result, it is important for health facilities and personnel to develop practical policies governing family-oriented consents. Care must be taken to prevent situations in which families acting in bad faith or on the basis of inadequate information consent to inappropriate care. Policies should also provide for eliciting pertinent patient history information from concerned family so that proposed treatment is based on a good understanding by the family.

Family-oriented consents may prove highly practical and avert the need for the appointment of guardians or judicial action. However, health facilities and professionals should delineate how and under what circumstances the family-oriented consent process should be utilized. It is an area ripe for preventive legal action as well as practical health care delivery.

§12.11 Consent to Treatment and Risk Management

As can be seen throughout this book, consent actions form a large part of medicolegal litigation. In many instances, however, consent lawsuits are avoidable. Breakdowns in communication, inadequate documentation, substandard policy and procedure manuals, or the total absence of such directives contribute to what may be described as avoidable consent issues.

Amidst the calls for tort reform, the Joint Commission on Accreditation of Healthcare Organizations (JCAHO) has embarked upon developing risk management standards in its accreditation material. The current materials already contain specific standards on consent for use in general hospitals[1] as

---

§12.11   [1]See JCAHO, Accreditation Manual for Hospitals (AMH) (1988).

well as facilities caring for mentally ill and retarded and the developmentally disabled.[2] Such a practice is quite standard throughout the accreditation materials developed by JCAHO and this has been the case for quite some time.

The Joint Commission's risk management standards, which took effect in January 1989, do not deal specifically with the matter of consent to treatment. Rather, the focus is on the medical staff privileging and credentialing process, as well as the involvement of the medical staff in hospital risk management activities. In this context, it can be argued that doctors have a new task in terms of risk management and consent to treatment. Doctors must now help develop the means for identifying specific instances involving potential risk in the clinical aspects of patient care and safety. Moreover, they must assist in the correction of these matters.[3] To the extent that doctors can help pinpoint consent-related clinical risks, they will be much involved in the risk management side of hospital practices.

JCAHO is not, however, the only professional group or agency to express interest in risk management. Indeed, there has been much renewed interest in the concept of institutional risk management programs. What is often overlooked in such initiatives is the development of consent guidelines in a comprehensive risk management program. Sometimes these attempts focus on the issue of consent forms, thereby overlooking the more important aspects of the consent process.

In this section a preventive program on consent is examined, utilizing data readily available from dedicated risk management and quality assurance sources.

§12.11.1   The Content of a Consent Policy

The health facility or agency should have a practical policy and procedure on consent to treatment. The document should

[2] See JCAHO, Consolidated Standards Manual (CSM) (1988).
[3] See AMH Standards Revised, Perspectives 8:7-9, January/February 1988, referring to M.S.6.1.7.1.2 and M.S.6.1.7.1.3 in the Accreditation Manual for Hospitals 1989.

be written in clear, easy to understand terminology. It should be based on the needs of the health facility and the patients it serves. Prototypes should be avoided, as these standardized documents often do not make it possible to tailor the document to meet the requirements of the institution.

The policy and procedure should contain boilerplate provisions including the following:

1. criteria for a valid consent;
2. guidance on disclosure of information as specified in §1.12.1;
3. guidance on what need not be disclosed;
4. who is to inform the patient and who is to obtain consent;
5. when disclosure-consent is to take place;
6. exceptions to the rules as delineated in chapter 2;
7. documentation of consent; and
8. education of staff regarding the consent policy and procedures to be followed.

The content of the manual should be based on applicable state legislation, regulations, and case law. Thus, if a state has one age of consent for psychiatric care and another for sexual abuse treatment, this information should be incorporated in the manual. It is not necessary or advisable, however, to include the *actual* law in the guide. Since legislation and regulations are often modified, incorporating the actual law in the manual may make it quickly outdated. A far better approach is to incorporate the essence of the law in the document.

The consent policy and procedure manual should reflect the types of problem situations that arise in the health facility. The problem issues should be delineated along with the approach to be followed in reaching a resolution. This would include who should be contacted in administration, involvement of the facility's lawyer when necessary, and the documentation to be completed.

The manual should be reviewed periodically and updated as necessary. This process should involve the services of the institution's lawyer who can advise on changes in the law that should be reflected in the manual.

The focus of the manual should be on avoiding consent problems, anticipating where problems are likely to occur and how these difficulties can be averted. The manual should also reflect a considered approach to minimizing the severity of problems that do occur. This requires the active participation of personnel in risk management, quality assurance, claims management, and patient relations. Communications between staff and patients as well as among personnel is essential.

§12.11.2   Utilizing Risk Management and Quality Assurance Data

The health facility should use pertinent risk management and quality assurance data to identify actual or potential risk management consent problems. This can be accommodated in integrated quality assurance/risk management programs.

Generic outcome screening, concurrent record review, and occurrence screening are all useful methods for pinpointing flaws in the consent process. Records that have been flagged should be reviewed carefully to determine if staff physicians are meeting their obligation to inform patients. Similarly, records should be examined closely for new types of consent problems that are not part of the current consent policy and procedure manual. If these issues are likely to recur, the manual should be amended to reflect these additional problems and provide appropriate responses to them. Staff should also be apprised of these changes through in-service education and orientation programs.

If patients undergo prediagnostic or preoperative nursing education audits, care should be taken to review the consent components. If discussions with patients indicate that they do not understand the nature and purpose or the risks and benefits of the proposed intervention, this fact should be communicated to the physician immediately. It should not be filed in the audit cabinet for subsequent review. The failure to act promptly on such information may be a source of potential litigation.

If it can be shown that through its quality assurance and patient education audit the hospital knew or should have known that the patient's consent was flawed, the failure to take corrective action may result in litigation. Although the hospital usually is not responsible for securing a patient authorization to treatment, if it can be shown that the hospital was "on notice" of an impediment in the consent process that could reasonably and foreseeably result in harm, the ground for negligence may be firmly established. Such a predicament is not farfetched given the growing trend toward corporate liability and the types of information generated in quality assurance and nursing audits of patient awareness.

§12.11.3 Preintervention History and Follow-up

One of the most important tools in tailoring the consent process to meet the needs of patients is a thorough history. The failure to take an accurate history for evaluation of risks has been discussed in consent litigation.[4]

If the patient history reveals a significant likelihood of risks coming to fruition, a determination should be made whether to proceed with the proposed intervention. Careful thought should be given to the availability of less risky procedures. If, however, there is no reasonable option, steps should be taken to put in place the personnel, equipment, and medication needed to *minimize* the severity of a bad outcome. Moreover, the patient should be apprised of these risks and what can and cannot reasonably be done to prevent their occurrence or minimize their severity. If the patient accepts these risks and authorizes the proposed intervention, this information should be documented in accordance with the consent policy and procedure manual. As with other aspects of risk management and con-

---

[4]See, e.g., Brown v. Dahl, 41 Wash. App. 565, 705 P.2d 781 (1985), in which an expert witness pointed out the inadequacies of the preanesthetic history taken by the defendant and the resultant failure to properly assess the patient for the use of a general anesthetic.

sent, the focus should be on communication and anticipation of problems *before* they occur.

§12.12   Content of a Consent Policy and Procedure

A policy and procedure on consent to treatment should address a number of issues including:

1. Pertinent legislation and regulations;
2. Requirements for a valid consent;
3. Persons responsible for securing consent;
4. Use of interpreters when necessary;
5. Situations in which telephone consents can be used;
6. Exceptions to the rules;
7. Recurrent problem cases;
8. Routine responses to anticipated problem cases;
9. Measures to be taken in unanticipated situations;
10. Provision for consent to continuing treatment situations such as dialysis or chemotherapy;
11. Authorization for photographs, organ procurement, and autopsy;
12. Documentation of consent to treatment;
13. Concurrent identifiers to be used for quality assurance and risk management in assessing consent to treatment;
14. Reporting channels and methods of communication; and
15. The names and telephone numbers of legal counsel and risk managers who can be contacted when problems arise.

The policy and procedure should begin with a clear-cut policy on the need for consent to treatment, and should be written in a manner that avoids ambiguity and gives staff good direction for handling consent issues. It should also be reviewed at least annually to ensure that provisions in it do not become outdated. For this purpose, legal counsel should be requested to review the policy and procedure to ensure that cases and legislative developments are incorporated into the document.

APPENDIX A

Long Consent Form

The following is an example of a long consent form, as described in §12.1.2.

CONSENT TO TREATMENT

1. I, _____, of _____,
do hereby give my consent to the performance of (name of medical,
surgical or diagnostic procedure). I understand that the procedure
will involve (explanation of the procedure). I have made my decision
voluntarily and freely.

2. I appreciate that there are certain risks associated with this procedure including (list of risks) and I freely assume these risks. I also
understand that there are possible benefits associated with this procedure including (list of benefits). However, I appreciate there is no
certainty that I will achieve these benefits and no guarantee has been
made to me regarding the outcome of this procedure.

3. The reasonable alternative(s) to this procedure have been explained to me including (list of reasonable alternatives if any exist).

4. Any questions I have had regarding this procedure have been
answered to my satisfaction.

5. In authorizing my physician, Dr. (name of doctor) to perform
this procedure, I understand that he will be assisted by other health
professionals of the (name of the health facility) and such others as he

considers necessary in my care. I agree to their participation in my care.

6. To attest to my consent to this procedure, I hereby affix my signature to this authorization for treatment.

7. _____ Signature of patient

8. _____ Signature of witness

9. _____ Date and time

APPENDIX B

Short Consent Form

The following is an example of a short consent form, as described in §12.1.3.

CONSENT TO TREATMENT

1. I, _____, of _____, do hereby agree to the performance of (name of procedure) by my doctor, Dr. (name of physician) and such others as he considers necessary.

2. The nature and consequences of the procedure have been explained to me. I understand that it will involve (brief explanation of the procedure).

3. The risks and benefits of this procedure have been explained to me. I also understand that there are certain medical and surgical alternatives to this procedure and I have been given information regarding other medically or surgically feasible forms of care.

4. I hereby freely and voluntarily give my signed authorization for this procedure.

5. _____ Signature of patient

6. _____ Signature of witness

7. _____ Date and time

APPENDIX C

Detailed Note in Medical Record

As explained in chapter 12, a detailed note in the medical record may be viewed more favorably as evidence of consent than a boilerplate consent form. A well-written note is a more credible piece of evidence than a standardized form, since the fact that the caregiver took the time to write a patient-specific note in the health record suggests that he also took time to obtain consent.

However, the detailed note in the record can backfire, particularly if the content fails to demonstrate that all the required elements of the consent process were completed. Instead of being a valuable defensive tool, the detailed note may help the plaintiff's case.

Caregivers may complain that they do not have the time to write a detailed note in the record. This suggestion indicates that caregivers do not understand how a detailed note should be written in the record. It is not necessary to write a treatise or even a four-page note. Rather, as seen in the following examples of the wrong way and the right way to document consent in the patient's record, the note should be clear, concise, and to the point.

THE WRONG WAY

3-2-89. Pt. told of risks and rewards. Pt. agreed to angioplasty. No questions. Scheduled for 0945 hrs tomorrow.

This note is inadequate since it fails to demonstrate that all the required elements of a valid consent had been accomplished. Standing alone, the note would be of little value for defense purposes in any consent litigation.

THE RIGHT WAY

3-2-89, 1430 hrs. Mr. Josten was told that the purpose of the angioplasty was to try to open his blocked coronary arteries. Dr. Ress and I showed Mr. Josten and his wife a diagram, demonstrating the blockage and how we propose to proceed. The pt. and his wife were told of the risks associated with the procedure, including the possibility of heart attack and death. They were told that a failed angioplasty may necessitate cardiac bypass surgery. Since med. mgt. has failed, there are no other reasonable treatment options to recommend. Pt. understands what may happen without angioplasty. Mr. Josten did not have any questions. He was alert, able to comprehend, and appeared confident. Procedure scheduled for 0945 hrs tomorrow.

This note contains references to the important elements of the consent process. It also contains a reference to the fact that another physician and the patient's wife were in attendance. This is useful since it indicates that there were witnesses present during the consent process. From an evidentiary perspective, the note provides an important defensive weapon to any litigation based on lack of informed consent.

Even this note, however, could stand some improvement. The note should include reference to all the probable risks and benefits associated with angioplasty that the doctor discussed with the patient and his wife. Similarly, the specific risk information conveyed about foregoing treatment should be described in the note. Notwithstanding these suggestions, the note represents a good example of a detailed notation of consent in the patient record.

APPENDIX D

Consent Checklist Form

The following is an example of a consent checklist form, as described in §12.1.5.

CONSENT TO TREATMENT
CERTIFICATION DOCUMENT

I, _____ M.D., informed _____ of the following information.

[Check off the following where appropriate:]

[] Nature and purpose of procedure:
_____ (specify procedure).

[] Probable risks and probable benefits of procedure:
_____.

[] Reasonable treatment options (if any exist):
_____,
and their probable risks and probable benefits:
_____.

[] The risks of foregoing treatment, including:
_____.

[] An explanation of what the patient should anticipate following the procedure in terms of pain, discomfort, disability, and disfigurement.

751

[] Answers to all questions posed by the patient using language the patient could understand.

Condition of patient at time of consent process:

[] Lucid and coherent.
[] Receiving analgesics but mentally capable of giving consent.
[] Receiving analgesics and mentally incapable of giving consent.
[] Mentally incapable of giving consent due to other factors:

_____,

and an authorization was obtained from _____
_____, who was permitted to give consent on behalf of patient.

[] Interpreter assisted in securing consent of patient:
_____ (specify name of interpreter).

[] Family who assisted in securing consent of patient:

_____

(specify names of family members).

Names of those present during the consent process:

_____

I certify that the consent process described above occurred as stated.

| _____ | _____ | _____ |
| *Date* | *Time* | *Signature of caregiver* |

NOTE: The failure to properly complete the consent process constitutes sufficient basis for revoking medical staff privileges or otherwise taking appropriate disciplinary procedures.

APPENDIX E

Jehovah's Witness Cards and Release Forms

The following are reproductions of the American Jehovah's Witness Medical Directive/Release card and the Canadian Jehovah's Witness Medical Alert card in French and English, as described in §7.1. Also included are Canadian Jehovah's Witness release forms in French and English. The American card is reprinted here with the permission of the Watchtower Bible and Tract Society of New York, Inc., and the Canadian cards and forms with the permission of the Watchtower Bible and Tract Society of Canada.

MEDICAL DIRECTIVE/RELEASE

I,   , direct that **no blood transfusions** be given to me, even though physicians deem such vital to my health or my life. I accept non-blood expanders (such as Dextran, saline or Ringer's solution, hetastarch). I am   years old and execute this document of my own initiative. It accords with my rights as a patient and my beliefs as one of Jehovah's Witnesses. The Bible commands: "Keep abstaining . . . from blood." (Acts 15:28, 29) This is, and has been, my religious stand for   years. I direct that I be given no blood transfusions. I accept any added risk this may bring. **I release doctors, anesthesiologists, hospitals and their personnel from responsibility for any untoward results caused by my refusal, despite their competent care.** In the event that I lose consciousness, I authorize either witness below to see that my decision is upheld.

_____   _____
Signature   Date

_____ _____ _____
Witness   Relationship   Phone

_____ _____ _____
Witness   Relationship   Phone

Printed in U.S.A.

Allergies:_____

Current medication: _____

Medical problems:_____

IN CASE OF EMERGENCY, PLEASE CONTACT:

_____   _____
Name   Phone

_____
Address

_____

— —

MEDICAL DOCUMENT
(see inside)

NO BLOOD

American Jehovah's Witness Medical Directive/Release Card

754

MEDICAL ALERT

I direct that *no blood transfusions* be administered to me, even though others deem such necessary to preserve my life or health. *I will accept non-blood expanders.* This is in accord with my rights as a patient and the beliefs of Jehovah's Witnesses. I release the doctors and hospital of any liability for damages caused by my refusal. My position will not change even if I am unconscious, and I hold these directions as binding upon my heirs, legal representatives, or guardians.

SIGNATURE

PRINT NAME   DATE

WITNESS   WITNESS   (over)

Allergies: _____

Current medication: _____

_____

Medical problems: _____

_____

IN CASE OF EMERGENCY, PLEASE CONTACT:

Name: _____ Phone: _____

Address: _____ _____

The Bible commands: 'Keep abstaining from blood.'—Acts 15:29.

Printed in Canada   (over)

Canadian Jehovah's Witness Medical Alert Card

À L'ATTENTION DES MÉDECINS

Je demande instamment qu'on ne m'administre *pas de transfusion sanguine*, même si des tierces la jugent indispensable pour préserver ma vie ou ma santé. Néanmoins, *j'accepte des restaurateurs non sanguins du volume plasmatique.* Ma décision est conforme aux droits du patient et aux croyances des Témoins de Jéhovah. Je décharge les médecins et l'hôpital de toute responsabilité qui pourrait découler des conséquences dommageables causées par mon refus. Ma position ne changera pas même si je suis inconscient, et je considère que ces instructions obligent mes ayants droit, représentants légaux ou tuteurs.

_____
SIGNATURE

_____
NOM EN CARACTÈRES D'IMPRIMERIE   DATE

_____
TÉMOIN   TÉMOIN   (voir au verso)

Allergies: _____

Traitement médical en cours: _____

_____

Problèmes de santé: _____

_____

EN CAS D'URGENCE, VEUILLEZ JOINDRE:

Nom: _____ Tél.: _____

Adresse: _____

La Bible nous ordonne: 'Abstenez-vous de sang.' — Actes 15:29.

Imprimé au Canada   (voir au recto)

Canadian Jehovah's Witness Medical Alert Card in French

756

CANADIAN JEHOVAH'S WITNESS RELEASE FROM LIABILITY:

RELEASE FROM LIABILITY

To _____ Hospital and the medical and nursing personnel having anything to do with the case of _____:

You are hereby notified and instructed that I do not accept any transfusion of blood, blood products, or blood fractions to be used in the treatment of this patient. I accept non-blood expanders and other forms of alternative management. I do not want this patient to suffer the harmful and lethal effects of transfusion.

I make this medical/religious directive as one of Jehovah's Witnesses.

I understand that the attending physicians may feel that blood transfusions are necessary. I do not share their opinion, but, rather, adhere to the instructions given in this notice.

This matter has been carefully considered by me, and my instructions are not going to change because I, or the above-named patient, is unconscious.

I release doctors, hospitals, and hospital personnel from liability for any damages caused by their compliance with this directive. This directive shall be binding on my heirs, executors, and assigns.

DATED this _____ day of _____, 19____.

_____
Patient, Parent, or Guardian

_____
WITNESS

[The following section should be completed when the patient is a minor who has made his own decision:]

I, _____, am the patient described above. I am _____ years of age. I fully agree with and support the above direction and release.

DATED this _____ day of _____, 19____.

_____
NAME

757

CANADIAN JEHOVAH'S WITNESS RELEASE FROM LIABILITY, IN FRENCH:

DECHARGE DE RESPONSABILITÉ

A l'hôpital _____ et aux membres du personnel médical et l'infirmier ayant quelque intérêt que ce soit dans le cas de _____:

Veuillez prendre acte par le présente de mon refuse de toute transfusion de sang, de dérivés sanguins ou de fractions de sang a cours du traitement dudit patient. Néanmoins, j'accepte des restaurateurs non sanguins du volume plasmatique, ainsi que d'autres thérapeutiques de remplacement. Je ne veux pas que ce patient subisse les effets nuisibles ou même mortels d'une transfusion.

Je donne ces instructions médicales/religieuses en tant que Témoin Jéhovah.

Je me rends compte que les médicins traitants puissent être d'avis que des transfusions sanguines sont nécessaires. Je ne partage pas leur opinion, mais je m'en tiens au contraire aux instructions données dans le présent avis.

J'ai soigneusement réfléchi à cette question, et mes instructions ne changeront pas même si moi ou le patient susnommé sommes inconscients.

Je décharge les médecins, les hôpitaux et le personnel hospitalier de la responsabilité de tout dommage causé parce qu'ils auront respecté ces instructions. Celles-ci lieront mes héritiers, mes exécuteurs testamentaires et mes ayants droit.

DATÉ ce _____ jour de _____ 19____.

_____
Patient, parént ou tuteur

_____
TÉMOIN

[Il faut remplir la section suivante si le patient est un mineur qui a pris sa propre décision:]

758

Canadian Jehovah's Witness Release from Liability, in French

Je soussigné, ——————————————————, suis le patient décrit plus haut. J'ai ———— ans. Je suis entièrement d'accord avec les instructions et la décharge ci-dessus, et je les soutiens.

DATÉ ce ———— jour de ———————— 19————.

—————————————————
NOM

APPENDIX F

*Uniform Brain Death Act**

For legal and medical purposes, an individual who has sustained irreversible cessation of all functioning of the brain, including the brain stem, is dead. A determination under this section must be made in accordance with reasonable medical standards.

Commissioners' Note
Between 1970 and 1978, nineteen states enacted legislation recognizing the concept of brain death. This was a new legislative undertaking, for death had always been determined before by common law principles. The common law criterion for death was: "an absence of spontaneous respiratory and cardiac function."

The technology of medical care can now overcome the natural cessation of both breathing and heartbeat. That technology creates a concern among medical practitioners that legal liability might be imposed when life-support systems are withdrawn, even though the case is hopeless and acceptable medical practice sanctions the withdrawal, and though the continuation of artificial means of life support offends even those most morally and emotionally committed to "the preservation of human life." This Act expresses community approval of withdrawing artificial life-support systems when the whole brain has irreversibly ceased to work.

*The Uniform Brain Death Act was approved by the National Conference of Commissioners on Uniform State Laws in August 1978.

This Act is silent as to acceptable diagnostic tests and medical procedures. It addresses the concept of brain death, not the criteria used to reach the medical conclusion that brain death has occurred. The medical profession should formulate over time the acceptable practices, taking into account new knowledge of brain function and new diagnostic equipment.

The "time" of death is an overriding concern of anyone contemplating the occurrence of brain death. Upon reflection, the Special Committee concluded that, in those instances in which time of death affects legal rights, this Act should simply state the facts constituting brain death and thus provide the basis for whatever inquiry is necessary to fix the time of death.

Some other questions and subjects not addressed by this narrow Act are: living wills, death with dignity, euthanasia, rules on death certificates, maintaining life-support beyond brain death in cases of pregnant women or of organ donors, and protection accorded the dead body.

Commissioners' Comment

This section legislates the concept of brain death. The Act does not preclude a determination of death under other legal or medical criteria, including the traditional criteria of cessation of respiration and circulation. Other criteria are practical in cases where artificial life-support systems are not utilized. Even those criteria are indicative of brain death.

"Functioning" is a critical word in the Act. It expresses the idea of *purposeful* activity in all parts of the brain, as distinguished from random activity. In a dead brain, some meaningless cellular processes, detectable by sensitive monitoring equipment, could create legal confusion if the word "activity" were substituted for "functioning."

APPENDIX G

*Uniform Anatomical Gift Act**

An act authorizing the gift of all or part of a human body after death for specified purposes.

Section 1 [Definitions]

(a) "Bank or storage facility" means a facility licensed, accredited or approved under the laws of any state for storage of human bodies or parts thereof.

(b) "Decedent" means a deceased individual and includes a stillborn infant or fetus.

(c) "Donor" means an individual who makes a gift of all or part of his body.

(d) "Hospital" means a hospital licensed, accredited or approved under the laws of any state and includes a hospital operated by the United States government, a state, or a subdivision thereof, although not required to be licensed under state laws.

(e) "Part" includes organs, tissues, eyes, bones, arteries, blood, other fluids and other portions of a human body, and "part" includes "parts."

(f) "Person" means an individual, corporation, government or governmental subdivision or agency, business trust, estate, trust, partnership or association or any other legal entity.

*The final draft of the Uniform Anatomical Gift Act was approved by the Commissioners on Uniform State Laws on July 30, 1968.

(g) "Physician" or "surgeon" means a physician or surgeon licensed or authorized to practice under the laws of any state.

(h) "State" includes any state, district, commonwealth, territory, insular possession, and any other area subject to the legislative authority of the United States of America.

Section 2 [Persons Who May Execute an Anatomical Gift]

(a) Any individual of sound mind and 18 years of age or more may give all or any part of his body for any purposes specified in Section 3, the gift to take effect upon death.

(b) Any of the following persons, in order or priority stated, when persons in prior classes are not available at the time of death, and in the absence of actual notice of contrary indications by the decedent, or actual notice of opposition by a member of the same or a prior class, may give all or any part of the decedent's body for any purpose specified in Section 3:

(1)   the spouse,
(2)   an adult son or daughter,
(3)   either parent,
(4)   an adult brother or sister,
(5)   a guardian of the person of the decedent at the time of his death,
(6)   any other person authorized or under obligation to dispose of the body.

(c) If the donee has actual notice of contrary indications by the decedent, or that a gift by a member of a class is opposed by a member of the same or a prior class, the donee shall not accept the gift. The persons authorized by subsection (b) may make the gift after death or immediately before death.

(d) A gift of all or part of a body authorizes any examination necessary to assure medical acceptability of the gift for the purpose intended.

(e) The rights of the donee created by the gift are paramount to the rights of others except as provided by Section 7(d).

Section 3   [Persons Who May Become Donees, and Purposes for Which Anatomical Gifts May Be Made]

The following persons may become donees of gifts of bodies or parts thereof for the purposes stated:

(1)   any hospital, surgeon, or physician, for medical or dental education, research, advancement of medical or dental science, therapy or transplantation; or

(2)   any accredited medical or dental school, college or university for education, research, advancement of medical or dental science or therapy; or

(3)   any bank or storage facility, for medical or dental education, research, advancement of medical or dental science, therapy or transplantation; or

(4)   any special individual for therapy or transplantation needed by him.

Section 4   [Manner of Executing Anatomical Gifts]

(a) A gift of all or part of the body under Section 2(a) may be made by will. The gift becomes effective upon the death of the testator without waiting for probate. If the will is not probated, or if it is declared invalid for testamentary purposes, the gift, to the extent that it has been acted upon in good faith, is nevertheless valid and effective.

(b) A gift of all or part of the body under Section 2(a) may also be made by document other than a will. The gift becomes effective upon the death of the donor. The document, which may be a card designed to be carried on the person, must be signed by the donor, in the presence of 2 witnesses who must sign the document in his presence. If the donor cannot sign, the document may be signed for him at his direction and in his presence, and in the presence of 2 witnesses who must sign the document in his presence. Delivery of the document of gift during the donor's lifetime is not necessary to make the gift valid.

(c) The gift may be made to a specified donee or without specifying a donee. If the latter, the gift may be accepted by the attending physician as donee upon or following death. If the gift is made to a specified donee who is not available at the time and place of death, the attending physician upon or following death, in the absence of any expressed indication that the donor desired otherwise, may accept the gift as donee. The physician who becomes a donee under this subsection shall not participate in the procedures for removing or transplanting a part.

(d) Notwithstanding Section 7(b), the donor may designate in his will, card or other document of gift the surgeon or physician to carry out the appropriate procedures. In the absence of a designation, or if the designee is not available, the donee or other person authorized to accept the gift may employ or authorize any surgeon or physician for the purpose.

(e) Any gift by a person designated in Section 2(b) shall be made by a document signed by him, or made by his telegraphic, recorded telephonic or other recorded message.

Section 5   [Delivery of Document of Gift]

If the gift is made by the donor to a specified donee, the will, card or other document, or an executive copy thereof, may be delivered to the donee to expedite the appropriate procedures immediately after death, but delivery is not necessary to the validity of the gift. The will, card or other document, or an executed copy thereof, may be deposited in any hospital, bank or storage facility or registry office that accepts them for safekeeping or for facilitation of procedures after death. On request of any interested party upon or after the donor's death, the person in possession shall produce the document for examination.

Section 6   [Amendment or Revocation of the Gift]

(a) If the will, card or other document or executed copy thereof, has been delivered to a specified donee, the donor may amend or revoke the gift by:

(1)   the execution and delivery to the donee of a signed statement, or
(2)   an oral statement made in the presence of 2 persons and communicated to the donee, or
(3)   a statement during a terminal illness or injury addressed to an attending physician and communicated to the donee, or
(4)   a signed card or document found on his person or in his effects.

(b) Any document of gift which has not been delivered to the donee may be revoked by the donor in the manner set out in subsection (a) or by destruction, cancellation, or mutilation of the document and all executed copies thereof.

(c) Any gift made by a will may also be amended or revoked in the manner provided for amendment or revocation of wills, or as provided in subsection (a).

Section 7   [Rights and Duties at Death]

(a) The donee may accept or reject the gift. If the donee accepts a gift of the entire body, he may, subject to the terms of the gift, authorize embalming and the use of the body in funeral services. If the gift is of a part of the body, the donee, upon the death of the donor and prior to embalming, shall cause the part to be removed without unnecessary mutilation. After removal of the part, custody of the remainder of the body vests in the surviving spouse, next of kin or other persons under obligation to dispose of the body.

(b) The time of death shall be determined by a physician who attends the donor at his death, or, if none, the physician who certifies the death. This physician shall not participate in the procedures for removing or transplanting a part.

(c) A person who acts in good faith in accord with the terms of this Act, or under the anatomical gift laws of another state [or a foreign country] is not liable for damages in any civil action or subject to prosecution in any criminal proceeding for his act.

(d) The provisions of this Act are subject to the laws of this state prescribing powers and duties with respect to autopsies.

Section 8 [Uniformity of Interpretation]

This Act shall be so construed as to effectuate its general purpose to make uniform the law of those states which enact it.

Section 9 [Short Title]

This Act may be cited as the Uniform Anatomical Gift Act.

Section 10 [Repeal]

The following acts and parts of acts are repealed. . . .

Section 11 [Time of Taking Effect]

This Act shall take effect. . . .

APPENDIX H

*Proposed Uniform Donation Card**

DONOR CARD OF

_____

(print or type name of donor)

In the hope that my gift may help others, I hereby make this anatomical gift to take effect upon my death. The words and marks below indicate my desires.

I give:

       (a) _____ any needed organs or parts

       (b) _____ only the following organs or parts

       _____

       (specify the organ(s) or part(s))

       (c) _____ my entire body for anatomical study

For the purposes of transplantation, therapy, medical research or education.

Limitations: _____

(specify limitations, if any)

This is a legal document under the Uniform Anatomical Gift Act or similar laws.

----

*A card of this type may be used to effect a gift under the Uniform Anatomical Gift Act.

(Other side of card)

Signed by the Donor in the presence of the following two witnesses:

_____   _____
       Witness   *Signature of donor*

_____   _____
       Witness   *Date of birth*

                      _____
                         Date signed

This space available to refer to the group distributing the card and the telephone number and/or address where further information may be obtained.

TABLE OF CASES

A.B. v. C., 7.5
Abortion Coalition of Mich. v. Michigan Dept. of Health, 5.6
Abramowitz v. New York Univ. Dental Center, 12.1
A.C., In re, 7.1
Adams v. El-Bash, 1.15
Aden v. Younger, 6.3
Ahern v. Veterans Admin., 8.27
Akron Center for Reproductive Health v. Rosen, 5.6
Akron Center for Reproductive Health v. Slaby, 5.6
Akron, City of, v. Akron Center for Reproductive Health, 3.5, 5.5, 5.6
Alexander v. Gosner, 1.12, 1.14
American College of Obstetricians and Gynecologists, Pa. Section, v. Thornburgh, 5.6
American Hosp. Assn. v. Heckler, 5.16
Anderson v. Strong Mem. Hosp., 11.9
Anne D. v. Raymond D., 11.6
Application of _____.
See name of party.
Arena v. Gingrich, 1.15
Atkins v. Medical Examiner of Westchester County, 9.14
Avila v. New York City Health and Hosps. Corp., 6.8
Azzolino v. Dingfelder, 3.9

B., In the Matter of Hospitalization of, 6.4

Baez v. Rapping, 11.0
Baird v. Attorney General, 5.6
Baker, People ex rel., v. Strautz, 2.5
Bakker v. Welsh, 5.2
Baltzell v. Baptist Med. Center, 1.14
Bang v. Miller, 9.1
Barber v. Superior Court, 7.5
Barclay v. Campbell, 6.4
Barlow v. Superior Court (People), 11.4
Barrett v. United States, 8.27
Barry, In re Guardianship of, 5.17
Bartling v. Superior Court, 7.5
Bates v. Jensen, 5.16
Bayer, Matter of Guardianship of, 7.5
Beal v. Hamilton, 1.15
Beck v. Lovell, 3.2
Becker v. Schwartz, 3.9
Bee v. Greaves, 4.6
Bellotti v. Baird (U.S. 1976) (Bellotti I), 5.6
Bellotti v. Baird (U.S. 1979) (Bellotti II), 5.6
Bennett v. Graves, 3.2
Berman v. Allen, 3.9
Blackmon v. Langley, 1.12
Blaxton v. United States, 8.27
Blefare v. United States, 4.12
Bloskas v. Murray 1.12
Blue v. Blue, 5.2
Bonner v. Moran, 9.2
Bothman v. Warren B., 5.16
Bourgeois v. Davis, 3.10
Bowden v. State, 4.12
Bowen v. American Hosp. Assn., 5.16

Bowers v. Garfield, 1.15
Bowman, In re, 9.8
Boyd, In re, 6.4
Brooklyn Hosp., Application of, 5.16
Brophy v. New England Sinai Hosp., 7.5
Brown, In re, 7.1
Brown v. Dahl, 1.12, 1.18, 12.11
Brown v. Delaware Valley Transplantation Program, 9.6
Brown v. Sisters of Mercy, 4.11
B.S., Matter of Commitment of, 6.2
Buck v. Bell, 6.7
Burgess v. Purdue, 9.14
Burton, In re, 6.4
Butler v. Brown, 1.12
Buzzell v. Libi, 1.7

Cage v. Wood, 5.6
Cain v. United States, 8.0
Campbell v. Pitt County Memorial Hosp., 1.14
Canterbury v. Spence, 1.3, 1.15, 1.16
Cardwell v. Bechtol, 5.2
Carey v. Population Services Intl., 5.5
Carmen v. Dippold, 3.9
Carmichael v. Reitz, 3.1
Carter v. Cangello, 5.3
Cavitt, In re, 5.9
Chambers v. Nottebaum, 1.7, 1.16
Chambers v. G.D. Searle, 3.1
Charles v. Carey, 3.5
Cicero, Application of, 5.16
Clark, In re, 5.16
Cobbs v. Grant, 1.3, 1.12, 1.13, 1.15, 1.16, 3.2, 3.12, 3.13
Coe v. Gerstein, 3.6
Coleman v. Coleman, 3.6
Collins v. Itoh, 1.13, 1.15
Commissioner of Corrections v. Myers, 4.4, 4.6
Commonwealth v. Bowen, 3.5
Commonwealth v. Golston, 9.8
Conrod v. Imatani, 1.18
Conroy, Claire, In the Matter of, 7.4, 7.5

Cooper v. Curry, 1.14
Corbett v. D'Alessandro, 7.5
Crawford v. Wojnas, 2.6
Cross v. Trapp, 1.12, 1.15
Crouch v. Most, 2.2, 7.3
Crouse Irving Memorial Hosp. v. Paddock, 7.1
Cruzan v. Harmon, 7.5
Curlender v. Bio-Science Laboratories, 3.9
Custody of a Minor (Mass. 1978), 5.17
Custody of a Minor (Mass. 1979), 5.17
Custody of a Minor (Mass. 1982), 5.17, 7.6
Cybart v. Michael Reese Hosp. & Med. Center, 9.14

Danielson, Matter of, 6.4
Darling v. Charleston Community Memorial Hosp., 1.13
Darrah v. Kite, 1.7
Davidson v. Shirley, 3.10
Davis v. Charter-By-the-Sea, Inc., 2.2
Davis v. United States, 1.12
Davis v. Wyeth Laboratories, 12.6
D.D., Matter of, 5.9
Delio v. Westchester County Med. Center, 7.5
Demers v. Gerety, 1.7
Department of Health and Rehabilitation Servs. v. Straight, Inc., 5.7
Dicenzo v. Berg, 1.10
Dinnerstein, Matter of, 7.6
Doe, In re, 6.9
Doe v. Bolton, 3.4, 3.6, 5.6
Doe v. Deschamps, 3.5
Doe v. Doe, 3.6
Doe v. Irwin, 5.5
Doe v. Roe, 11.7
Doe (McGaskill) v. State, 4.12
Donnelly v. Gerion, 9.14
Dorone, Darrell, In re Estate of, 7.1
Drabick, In re, 7.5
Duffy v. Fear, 3.1
Dulke v. Upjohn, 3.1
Dumer v. St. Michael's Hosp., 3.9

E.G., In the Interest of, 5.18
Eiser v. Feldman, 3.1
Eleanor R. v. South Oaks Hosp., 6.4
Eric B. v. Ted B., In re, 5.16
Erickson v. Dilgard, 7.1
Estate of _____. See name of party.
Ex parte _____. See name of party.

Fadley, In re, 6.3
Fain v. Smith, 1.15
Farrell, Matter of, 7.5
Farwell v. Keaton, 9.4
Felix v. Hoffman-LaRoche, Inc., 1.14
Ferebee v. Chevron Chem. Co., 3.1
Festa v. Greenberg, 3.2
Fiorentio v. Wenger, 1.14
Fleming v. Michigan Mut. Liab. Co., 9.1
Fiorentino v. Wenger, 12.5
Flores v. Flushing Hosp. & Med. Center, 1.15
Foody v. Manchester Memorial Hosp., 7.4
Forlana v. Hughes, 1.2
Frazier v. Levi, 6.8
Freiman v. Ashcroft, 3.5
Funke v. Fieldman, 1.19

Garst v. Cullum, 1.19
Garzione v. Vassar Bros. Hosp., 1.14
Gaskin v. Booth, 1.18
Gaston v. Hunter, 8.27
Gates v. Jensen, 1.12, 5.16
Georgia Lions Eye Bank v. Lavant, 9.9
Gerben v. Holslaw, 5.17
German v. Nichopoulos, 1.18
Gildiner v. Thomas Jefferson Union Hosp., 3.9
Gleitman v. Cosgrove, 3.9
Glick v. Henderson, 11.0
Glick v. McKay, 5.6
Glover v. Eastern Neb. Community Office of Retardation, 11.3

Goedecke v. State Dept. of Institutions, 6.4
Goldberg v. Ruskin, 3.9
Grady, In re, 5.9, 6.8
Grant, In re Guardianship of, 7.5
Gray v. Grunnagle, 12.4
Green, In re, 5.16
Gregory S., In re, 5.10
Grieves v. Superior Court, 3.2
Guardianship of _____. See name of party.
Gulf & Ship Island R.R. v. Sullivan, 5.2
Gulf Coast Reg. Blood Center v. Houston, 11.8
Gundy v. Pauley, 6.3
Gust, In Interest of, 6.4

Haley v. United States, 1.12
Haluska v. University of Saskatchewan, 8.27
Hamilton v. Hardy, 3.1
Hamlin, Guardianship of, 7.4
Hand v. Krakowski, 1.14
Hanks v. Ranson Swan & Burch, Ltd., 3.12
Harden v. State, 7.1
Harnish v. Children's Hosp. Med. Center, 1.12
Harrigan v. United States, 1.19
Harris v. State, 3.6
Hart v. Brown, 9.2
Hartman v. May, 5.10
Harvey "U," In the Matter of, 7.2
Hayes, Guardianship of, 5.9, 6.8
Haymon v. Wilkerson, 3.9
Haywood County v. Hudson, 11.4
H.B. v. Wilkinson, 5.6
Hedgecorth v. Group Health Plan, Inc., 1.12
Health Ins. Assn. of America v. Corcoran, 11.3
Hefty v. Comprehensive Care Corp., 5.8
Hendriksen v. Roosevelt Hosp., 9.14
Hernandez v. United States, 1.10
Hickman v. Group Health Plan, Inc., 3.9

Hier, Matter of, 7.2, 7.5
Hinkelman v. Burgess Med. Center, 2.6
Hill v. State, 5.16, 7.1
Hillstrom, Matter of Welfare of, 6.7
H.L. v. Matheson, 5.5, 5.6
Hodgson v. State of Minnesota, 5.6
Hoe v. Brown, 5.6
Hofbauer, Matter of, 5.16, 5.17
Holmes v. Powers, 6.8
Holmes v. Silver Cross Hosp., 7.1
Holt v. Nelson, 1.15, 1.16, 2.6
Hondroulis v. Schuhmacher, 1.16
Hood v. Phillips, 8.27
Hook v. Rothstein, 1.12
Howard v. Leecher, 3.9
Hoyt v. St. Mary's Rehab. Center, 7.6
Hudson, In re, 5.1
Huffman v. D.C., 2.5
Huguez v. United States, 4.12
Hutchinson v. Dickie, 9.4
Hutton v. Craighead, 1.16

Iafelice v. Zarafu, 1.12
In re _____. See name of party.
In the Matter of _____. See name of party.
Inderbitzen v. Lane Hosp., 1.2
Ingram, Guardianship of, 7.2
Ingram v. Hook's Drugs, Inc., 1.14
Ipock v. Gilmore, 3.10
Ipock for Hill v. Gilmore, 1.2

Jackovach v. Yocum, 5.1, 5.12, 7.3
Jacksonville Clergy Consultation Serv. v. Martinez, 5.6
Jacobs v. Theimer, 3.9
Jacobson v. Massachusetts, 5.10
James L., Matter of, 11.5
Jamison v. Lindsay, 3.13
Jane Does v. State of Utah Dept. of Health, 5.5
Jarvis v. Levine, 6.4
Jeffcoat v. Phillips, 3.3
Jefferson v. Griffin Spaulding County Hosp., 7.1

Jehovah's Witnesses in the State of Washington v. King County Hosp., 5.16
J.L. v. Parham, 5.8
Jobes, Matter of, 7.5
Jocza v. Hottenstein, 1.18
John F. Kennedy Memorial Hosp. v. Bludworth, 7.4
John F. Kennedy Memorial Hosp. v. Heston, 7.3
Johnson v. Solomon, 5.8
Johnson, Matter of, 5.9
Jones, State ex rel. v. Gerhardstein, 6.4
Jones v. Irvin, 1.14
Jones v. North Carolina Prisoners' Labor Union, 4.6
Jones v. Smith, 3.6
Jones v. Walgreen, 1.14
Joswick by Joswick v. Lenox Hill Hosp., 5.16
Judd v. Packard, 11.0

Kaimowitz v. Department of Mental Health, 6.5
Karp v. Cooley, 8.0, 8.27
Kemp, Guardianship of, 5.9, 6.8
Kenner v. Northern Ill. Med. Center, 12.4
Keogan v. Holy Family Hosp., 1.12
Kerr, Application of, 7.5
Keyhea v. Rushen, 4.6
Kirby v. Spivey, 1.11
Kirk v. Michael Reese Hosp. and Med. Center, 2.6
Kirker v. Orange County, 9.6
Kissenger v. Lofgren, 1.15
K.K.B., In the Mental Health of, 6.4
Klink v. G.D. Searle & Co., 3.1
Kohouteck v. Hafner, 3.9
Kolocontronis v. Ritterbusch, 6.4
Krane v. Saint Anthony Hosp. Sys., 1.14
Krueger v. San Francisco Forty-Niners, 1.3
Krygier v. Airweld, Inc., 11.8

Landeros v. Flood, 2.6, 5.13
Lane v. Candura, 7.2, 10.2, 10.3
Lane v. United States, 1.7
Large v. Superior Court, 4.6
Largey v. Rothman, 1.13, 1.15
Lashbrook v. Barnes, 9.14
Latham v. Hayes, 1.15, 1.16
Leach v. Akron Gen. Med. Center, 7.4
Leach, Estate of, v. Shapiro, 7.5
Lee v. Weston, 9.14
Lee v. Winston, 4.12
Leesley v. West, 1.14
Leiva v. Nance, 1.3
Leonard v. New Orleans Orthopedic Clinic, 1.15
Liera v. Wisner, 12.4
Linda, Guardianship of, 6.4
Lillian F. v. Superior Court, 6.3
Lininger v. Eisenbaum, 3.9
Little v. Little, 9.2, 9.3
Lipscomb v. Memorial Hosp., 1.7, 1.17
Lloyd v. Kull, 1.7
Logan v. Greenwich Hosp. Assn., 1.12
Longmire v. Hoey, 3.10
Lovato v. Colorado, 9.8
Luka v. Lowrie, 2.2, 5.2
Luna v. Nering, 1.18
Lynch v. Bay Ridge Obstetrical and Gynecological Assocs., 3.1

MacDonald v. Ortho Pharmaceutical Corp., 1.14, 3.1
McEwen v. Ortho Pharmaceutical Corp., 3.1
McFall v. Shimp, 9.4
McGrady v. Wright, 1.12
McIntosh v. Milano, 2.6
McPherson v. Ellis, 1.12, 1.15
McVey v. Englewood Hosp. Assn., 7.5
Madsen v. Park Nicollet Med. Center, 1.20
Mahannah v. Hirsch, 1.12
Maier v. Bessler, 5.10
Maine Med. Center v. Houle, 5.16

Malette v. Shulman, 7.1
Margaret S. v. Edwards, 3.5, 8.9
Marshall v. Clinic for Women, P.A., 3.1
Martin v. Lowney, 1.15
Maskripodis v. Merrell-Dow Pharmaceuticals, 1.14
Matter of _____. See name of party.
Melideo, In re, 7.1
Mercy Hosp. v. Jackson, 7.1
Meretsky v. Ellenby, 1.7
Merrill, Matter of, 10.5
Miller v. Kennedy, 1.15
Mills v. Rogers, 6.4
Mills v. United States, 12.6
Milton, In re, 6.9
Mink v. University of Chicago, 8.27
Mitchell v. Davis, 5.16, 7.5
M.K.R., In re, 5.9
Moe, Mary, Matter of (Mass. 1982), 6.7, 6.8
Moe, Mary, Matter of (Mass. App. 1981), 5.6
Moe, Mary, Matter of (Mass. App. 1984), 5.6
Moenius v. Stevens, 11.0
Mohr v. Williams, 1.2, 1.7, 1.16, 9.1
Moore v. Preventive Medicine Med. Group, Inc., 1.11
Moore v. Regents of Univ. of Cal., 8.29, 9.5
Moore's Sterilization, In re, 5.9
Morrison v. State, 5.16
Moser v. Stallings, 1.2
Moss v. Rishworth, 5.1
M.P., In re Mental Commitment of, 6.4
Mroczkowski v. Straub Clinic & Hosp., Inc., 1.16
Murray v. University of Pa. Hosp., 3.2
Murray v. Vandevander, 3.3

Nathan v. Farinelli, 9.2
Nelson v. Hayne, 5.8
New York City Health & Hosps. Corp. v. Salsona, 9.8

New York City Health & Hosps.
  Corp. v. Stein, 6.3
New York, State of, v. Heckler, 5.5
Nichols v. Central Vermont Ry.,
  9.13
Nicoletta v. Rochester Eye and Human Parts Bank, 9.6
Niccoli v. Thompson, 1.18
Nickell v. Gonzalez, 1.12
Nisenholtz v. Mt. Sinai Hosp., 1.12,
  12.4
Nolan v. Kechijian, 1.10, 7.4
North Carolina Assn. for Retarded
  Children v. State, 5.9
Nutting v. Associates in Obstetrics
  and Gynecology, 3.1

O'Connor v. Hall, 7.5
Orford v. Orford, 3.7
Osborne, In re, 7.1
Ostergard v. United States, 3.2

Pardy v. United States, 1.13, 1.15
Parham v. J.R., 5.8
Parker v. St. Paul Fire & Marine Ins.
  Co., 3.10
Pauscher v. Iowa Methodist Med.
  Center, 1.13, 1.14
Peck v. Counseling Serv. of Addison
  County, Inc., 2.6
Pegram v. Sisco, 3.11
Pena v. New York State Div. of
  Youth, 5.8
People v. Coe, 1.2
People v. Gauntlett, 4.6
People v. Eulo, 9.8
People v. Jones, 4.12
People v. McGeevy, 11.4
People v. Medina, 6.4
People v. Rodriguez, 4.12
People v. Sargent, 1.19
People v. Smith, 4.12
People v. Stockton Pregnancy Control Med. Clinic, 2.6
People v. Thomas, 11.5
People v. Toure, 11.5

Perlmutter v. Florida Med. Center,
  7.5
Perreira v. State, 2.6
Perry v. Hodgson, 1.2
Pescinki, In re Guardianship of, 9.2
Peter by Johanning, Matter of, 7.5
Petition of Nemser, 7.3.4
Petty v. United States, 12.6
P.F. v. Walsh, 5.8
Pharmaceutical Mfrs. Assn. v. FDA,
  3.1
Phillip B., In re, 5.16
Phillips v. Hull, 1.15, 3.2
Pierluisi v. E.R. Squibb & Sons, 3.1
Pizzalotto v. Wilson, 3.10
Planned Parenthood Assn. of Kansas City v. Ashcroft, 3.5
Planned Parenthood Assn. of Utah
  v. Matheson, 5.5
Planned Parenthood Fedn. of Am.
  v. Bowen, 3.5
Planned Parenthood Fedn. of Am.
  v. Heckler, 5.5
Planned Parenthood League of
  Mass. v. Bellotti (1st Cir. 1981),
  3.5, 5.6
Planned Parenthood League of
  Mass. v. Bellotti (Mass. 1981), 5.6
Planned Parenthood of Cent. Mo. v.
  Danforth, 3.5, 3.6, 5.6
Pollard v. Phelps, 9.13
Ponter v. Ponter, 3.3
Porter v. Powell, 5.2
Prange, Estate of, 7.5
Pratt v. Davis, 2.2
Pratt v. University of Minn.
  Affiliated Hosps. and Clinics, 3.9
Precourt v. Frederick, 1.13
President & Directors of
  Georgetown College, Application
  of, 7.1
Prince v. Massachusetts, 7.1
Proffitt v. Bartolo, 3.9
Pugsley v. Privette, 1.2

Quackenbush, Matter of, 7.2, 10.5
Quinlan, In re, 6.8
Quinlan, Matter of, 7.4, 7.5, 7.8

R.A.J. v. Miller, 6.4
Raleigh Fitkin-Paul Morgan Memorial Hosp. v. Anderson, 7.1
Ramirez v. Richardson-Merrell, 1.14
Randolph v. City of New York, 7.1
Rappeport v. Stott, 9.2
Rasmussen v. South Fla. Blood Service, 11.8
Ray v. Wagner, 1.12
Raynor v. Richardson-Merrell, 1.14
Reil v. Weinberger, 1.4
Rennie v. Klein, 6.4
Reproductive Health Servs. v. Webster, 3.3, 3.4, 3.5
Requena, In re, 7.5
Requena, Matter of, 7.5
Reyes v. Wyeth Laboratories, 12.6
Reynolds v. McNichols, 4.7
Reynolds v. United States, 5.16, 7.1
Richardson, In re, 9.2
Riedisser v. Nelson, 1.12, 1.15, 3.10
Riese v. St. Mary's Hosp. & Med. Center, 6.4
Riff v. Morgan Pharmacy, 1.14
Ritz v. Florida Patient's Compensation Fund, 6.9
Rivers v. Katz, 6.4
Roberson v. Menorah Med. Center, 1.14, 3.10
Roberts v. Patel, 3.9
Roberts v. Woods, 2.4
Robinson v. Parrish, 3.2
Roe v. Wade, 3.3, 3.4, 3.5, 3.6, 3.9, 5.6, 7.1
Roe, In the Matter of the Guardianship of, 6.4
Rogers v. Commissioner of Dept. of Mental Health, 6.4
Rogers v. Lu, 1.18
Rogers v. Okin, 6.4
Rogers v. Sells, 5.2, 7.3
Rosenberg v. Feigin, 7.3
Rothenberger v. Doe, 3.6
Rook v. Trout, 1.18
Rubino v. Fretias, 1.2
Ruby v. Massey, 5.9
Runnels v. Rosendale, 4.4, 4.6

Rupp v. Jackson, 9.14
Rytkonen v. Lojacono, 7.3

Sagala v. Taveres, 1.18
Saint Mary's Hosp. v. Ramsey, 7.1
Salisbury, Matter of, 6.9
Sallmaier, In re, 6.8
Sampson, Re, 5.16
Sangiuolo v. Leventhal, 12.4
Sard v. Hardy, 1.12, 1.13, 1.15, 1.16, 1.18, 3.2
Satz v. Perlmutter, 7.5
Saunders v. State, 7.8
Savastano v. Saribeyoglu, 6.4
Scaria v. St. Paul Fire & Marine Ins. Co., 1.15
Scarpaci v. Milwaukee County, 9.14
Schiller, Matter of, 7.2
Schloendorff v. Society of New York Hosp., 1.2, 6.4, 7.4
Schmerber v. California, 4.12
Schneider v. Revici, 8.27
Schuoler, In re, 6.3
Schuster v. Altenberg, 2.6
Schwartz v. Boston Hosp. for Women, 8.27
Sconiers v. Jarvis, 4.6
Scott v. Plante, 6.4
Seals v. Pitman, 1.7
Secretary of Public Welfare of Pa. v. Institutionalized Juveniles, 5.8
Seiforth, In re, 5.16
Severns v. Wilmington Med. Center, 7.4, 7.6
Shack v. Holland, 3.9
Sheahan v. Dexter, 1.16
Shelter v. Rochelle, 1.15
Shelvin v. Lykos, 11.4
Shenefield v. Greenwich Hosp. Assn., 1.14
Sherlock v. Stillwater Clinic, 3.2
Sherr v. Northport-East Northport Univ. Free School Dist., 5.10
Shin v. St. James Mercy Hosp., 1.13
Shirley C., Matter of, 6.9
Short v. Downs, 1.19
Smith v. Cote, 3.9

Smith v. Reisig, 1.12, 3.10
Smith v. Seibly, 5.2
Snyder v. Holy Cross Hosp., 9.14
Sousa v. Chaset, 12.4
Spencer by and Through Spencer v. Seikel, 3.9
Spikes v. Health, 1.2, 1.3, 3.1
Spring, Matter of, 7.4, 7.5, 7.6
Stafford v. Louisiana State Univ., 2.2
Stager v. Schneider, 1.12
Stallings v. Ratliff, 1.18
State v. Bryant, 4.10
State v. Fierro, 9.8
State v. Haynie, 4.12
State v. Koome, 5.6
State v. Overstreet, 4.12
State v. Perricone, 5.16
State v. Powell, 9.9
State v. Wood, 4.10
State Dept. of Human Services v. Northern, 7.2
State of New York v. Heckler, 5.5
Steele v. St. Paul Fire & Marine Ins. Co., 1.12, 3.10
Steele v. Woods, 7.3
Storar, Matter of, 7.4
Strachan v. John F. Kennedy Mem. Hosp., 9.8
Strickland v. Deaconess Hosp., 7.5
Strunk v. Strunk, 9.2
Sullivan v. Montgomery, 5.2, 5.12
Superintendent of Belchertown State School v. Saikewicz, 5.17, 7.5, 7.5, 7.6
Swayze v. McNeil Laboratories, Inc., 1.14
Swenson v. Swenson, 5.2

Tabor v. Scobee, 5.1, 5.2, 5.12
Tarasoff v. Regents of the Univ. of Cal., 2.6
Tatro v. Lueken, 1.13, 3.10
Terry, In re, 7.5
T.—H.— v. Jones, 5.5
Thimatariga v. Chambers, 3.2
Thornburgh v. American College of Obstetricians and Gynecologists, 3.5

Tores, Conservatorship of, 7.4
Tower v. Hirschorn, 2.6
T.P., In re, 5.6
Traufler v. Thompson, 11.0
Tresemer v. Barke, 3.1
Troy v. Long Island Jewish-Hillside Med. Center, 1.12, 1.15
Truan v. Smith, 3.12
Truesdell, Matter of, 6.7
Truman v. Thomas, 1.11, 3.13
Tune v. Walter Reed Army Med. Hosp., 7.5

United States v. Charters, 6.4
United States v. George, 7.1
United States v. Leatherman, 6.4
United States v. Moore, 11.0
University of Cincinnati Hosp. v. Edmond, 7.1

Valdez v. Percy, 3.12
Valenti v. Prudden, 8.0, 8.27
Valerie N., Conservatorship of, 6.7
Vasko, In re, 5.16
Vaughn v. G.D. Searle & Co., 3.1
Vaughn v. Vaughn, 9.13
Vogel v. Forman, 7.5

Washington Healthcare Corp. v. Barrow, 1.12
Weberman v. Zugibe, 9.14
Webster v. Reproductive Health Servs., 3.4, 3.5
Weekly v. Solomon, 1.18
Weiss v. Missouri Dept. of Mental Health, 6.4
Welch v. Shepard, 4.7
Wells v. McGehee, 5.2, 5.12, 7.3
Wells v. Ortho Pharmaceutical Corp., 1.14, 3.1
Wheeler v. Barker, 2.2
Whitebread, Ex parte, 9.2
Whitlock v. Duke Univ., 8.0
Wilensky v. Greco, 9.14
Wilkinson v. Vesey, 1.3, 1.12, 1.13, 1.15, 1.16, 1.18
Williams v. Hofmann, 9.6

Williams v. United States, 2.6
Willmann, In re, 5.16
Wilson v. Kuenzi, 3.9
Wilson v. Lehman, 1.6
Wilson v. Lockwood, 1.14, 1.18
Wilson v. Scott, 8.27
Winfrey v. Citizens Southern Natl. Bank, 1.7, 3.10
Winston v. Lee, 4.12
Winters v. Miller, 6.4
Winthrop Univ. Hosp., In the Matter of the Application of, 7.1
Wolfe v. Schroering, 3.5
Women's Services, P.C. v. Thone, 3.5
Wons v. Public Health Trust of Dade County, 7.1
Woods v. White, 11.9
Woolley v. Henderson, 1.16

Workmen's Circle Home v. Fink, 7.5
Wright v. DeWitt School Dist., 5.10
W.S., Matter of, 6.3
Wyatt v. Alderholt, 5.8
Wynn v. Carey, 5.6

Yania v. Bigan, 9.4
Yetter, In re, 7.2
Young v. United States, 1.13
Youngberg v. Romeo, 6.4, 6.6
Younts v. St. Francis Hosp. & School of Nursing, 5.2

Zeller v. Greater Baltimore Med. Center, 3.15, 8.0
Zoslei v. Gaines, 5.1

TABLE OF STATUTES

All references are to sections.

FEDERAL

Public Laws

Pub. L. No. 93-348	8.0 n.4
Pub. L. No. 98-457	5.16.3 n.59
Pub. L. No. 99-272, §9121	1.4.3 n.5
Pub. L. No. 99-509	9.11 n.1
Pub. L. No. 100-119	9.11 n.1
Pub. L. No. 100-203	9.11 n.1

United States Code

21 U.S.C. §355	8.27.3 nn.18, 19
21 U.S.C. §355(i)	8.27.3 n.19
21 U.S.C. §505	8.27.3 n.19
29 U.S.C. §794	5.16.3 n.61
42 U.S.C. §§247b(j)-(l)	12.6 n.2
42 U.S.C. §300	5.5.2 n.13
42 U.S.C. §300a-6	3.5.4 n.41

Federal Register

30 Fed. Reg. 18,914	8.0 n.5
42 Fed. Reg. 26,317	6.5 n.1
43 Fed. Reg. 31,786	8.0 n.7; 8.13 n.2
43 Fed. Reg. 53,950	8.0 n.8; 8.16.1 n.1
46 Fed. Reg. 8,366	8.0 n.9
46 Fed. Reg. 8,390	8.13.5 n.37
46 Fed. Reg. 8,392	8.13.5 n.35
46 Fed. Reg. 8,942	8.0 n.10; 8.2 n.1
46 Fed. Reg. 19,195	8.0 n.9
48 Fed. Reg. 9,814, 9,815	8.11 n.3
50 Fed. Reg. 42,865	8.2.1 n.6
50 Fed. Reg. 42,867	8.2.1 n.7
50 Fed. Reg. 45,874	8.2.1 n.6
53 Fed. Reg. 45,661 et seq.	8.3 n.1

Code of Federal Regulations

21 C.F.R. §5.11	3.1.4 n.27
21 C.F.R. Part 50, Subpart C	8.19 n.1
21 C.F.R. §50.3	8.2.3 n.11; 8.23.1 n.2
21 C.F.R. §50.3(m)	8.16.2 n.6
21 C.F.R. §50.20	8.2 n.2; 8.13.6 n.38; 8.16.2 n.3; 8.19 n.2; 8.20.2 n.4
21 C.F.R. §50.23	8.2.3 nn.10, 12
21 C.F.R. §50.25	8.2.1 n.3; 8.4.5 n.23; 8.16.2 n.3; 8.19 n.2
21 C.F.R. §50.27	8.2.2 n.8; 8.16.2 n.4
21 C.F.R. §50.42	8.20.1 n.2

21 C.F.R. §50.44	8.20.1 n.1	8.1.3 n.12;
21 C.F.R. §50.48	8.20.2 n.3;	8.1.4 n.17;
	8.22 n.1	8.16.2 n.4
21 C.F.R. §56.109	8.2.2 n.9	45 C.F.R. §46.124	8.16.2 n.8
21 C.F.R. §56.110	8.13.5 n.37	45 C.F.R. §46.201	8.1.5 n.19;
21 C.F.R. §56.111	8.16.2 n.7;		8.9.3 n.33;
	8.23 n.1;		8.10 n.1
	8.23.3 n.3;	45 C.F.R. §46.203	8.10 n.2
	8.26 n.1	45 C.F.R. §46.204	8.10.2 n.5
28 C.F.R. §549.65	4.6.3 n.33	45 C.F.R. §46.205	8.6.1 n.4;
38 C.F.R. §17.34	8.16.1 n.2		8.8.1 n.4
42 C.F.R. §59.5(a)(4)	5.5.2 n.14	45 C.F.R. §46.205.35	3.2 n.3;
42 C.F.R. §59.8(a)(1)	3.5.4 n.42		3.2.3 n.28
42 C.F.R. §431.107	2.6.3 n.12	45 C.F.R. §46.206	8.6 n.1;
45 C.F.R. Part 46,	8.0 n.6		8.8 n.3;
Subparts B & C			8.9.3 n.35;
45 C.F.R. Part 46,	8.13 n.1;		8.10.1 n.4
Subpart D	8.15 n.22	45 C.F.R. §46.207	8.6 n.2;
45 C.F.R. §46.101	2.6.3 n.13;		8.6.2 n.5
	2.9.2 n.1;	45 C.F.R. §46.208	8.8 n.2;
	8.13.1 n.11		8.8.2 n.5
45 C.F.R. §46.101(a)	2.9.2 n.2;	45 C.F.R. §46.209	8.8 n.2;
	8.1.1 n.1		8.8.3 n.7
45 C.F.R. §46.101(b)	8.1.1 n.3	45 C.F.R. §46.210	8.4.4 n.12
45 C.F.R. §46.102	2.9.2 n.5;	45 C.F.R. §46.211	8.6.3 n.7;
	8.1.2 n.11;		8.4.4 n.13
	8.23.1 n.2	45 C.F.R. §46.301	8.19 nn.1, 3
45 C.F.R. §46.102(d)	8.16.2 n.6	45 C.F.R. §§46.301	8.1.5 n.21
45 C.F.R. §46.103	8.1.2 n.5	to 306	
45 C.F.R. §46.107	8.1.2 n.6	45 C.F.R. §46.302	8.19 n.4
45 C.F.R. §46.109	8.1.2 n.7	45 C.F.R. §46.305	8.22 n.1;
45 C.F.R. §46.110	8.0 n.12;		8.19.2 n.6
	8.13.5 n.34	45 C.F.R. §46.306	8.19.1 n.5
45 C.F.R. §46.111	8.16.2 n.7;	45 C.F.R. §46.401	8.13 n.4;
	8.23 n.1;		8.13.1 n.11
	8.23.3 n.3;	45 C.F.R. §§46.401	8.1.5 n.21
	8.26 n.1	to 409	
45 C.F.R. §46.116	2.9.2 n.6;	45 C.F.R. §46.402	8.13.2 n.15
	8.1.3 nn.12, 13;	45 C.F.R. §46.404	8.13 n.5
	8.4.5 n.24;	45 C.F.R. §46.405	8.13 n.6
	8.7.2 n.7;	45 C.F.R. §46.406	8.13 n.7
	8.8 n.1;	45 C.F.R. §46.407	8.13 n.8
	8.10.1 n.3;	45 C.F.R. §46.408	8.13 n.9;
	8.13.2 n.17;		8.13.2 nn.16, 18
	8.13.3 nn.28, 29;	45 C.F.R. §46.409	8.13 n.10;
	8.16.2 n.3;		8.13.4 n.30
	8.19 n.2	45 C.F.R. §84.55(d)	5.16.3 n.62
45 C.F.R. §46.117	8.1.2 n.9;	45 C.F.R. §84.55(e)	5.16.3 n.63

STATE STATUTES

Alabama

Code

§6-5-482	1.17 n.4
§15-4-2	9.12 nn.8, 9
§22-8-1	2.2 n.2
§22-8-4	5.3.1 n.2
§22-8-5	5.3.6 n.46
§22-8-7	5.3.3 n.30
§§22-8A-1 to 10	7.7.2 n.1
§22-16-9	5.4.1 n.5
§22-20-3	5.11.1 nn.1, 8
§26-2A-102	10.4 n.1
§32-5-192	4.11 nn.2, 4, 5

Alaska

Statutes

§09.55.546	1.16.4 n.11
§09.55.556	1.3 n.8;
	1.12 n.2;
	1.12.1 n.7;
	1.13.3 nn.15, 17, 19;
	1.15 nn.1, 4;
	1.15.4 n.15;
	1.16 n.1;
	1.16.2 n.5;
	1.19 nn.5, 8;
	2.3 nn.1, 3;
	2.4 n.1;
	2.4.1 nn.2, 5, 9;
	2.7 n.2
§09.65.100	5.2.3 n.30;
	5.3.1 n.1;
	5.3.3 nn.30, 31;
	5.3.6 n.46
§18.12.010	7.8.1 n.5
§18.12.090	7.8.1 n.3
§47.30.690	5.8 n.1

Arizona

Revised Statutes Annotated

§11-598	9.12 n.12
§31-321	8.0 n.14;
	8.4.4 n.19;
	8.21.1 nn.3, 6
§32-1483	11.8 n.4
§36-512	6.9 nn.4, 9, 10
§36-526	6.2.1 n.7
§36-551.01	6.4.2 nn.10, 11, 12, 13,
	17
§36-560	6.2.1 n.12
§36-806	9.10 nn.10, 14, 17
§36-807	9.10 n.9
§36-808	9.10 n.26
§36-849	9.11 n.2
§44-132	5.2.3 n.30;
	5.3.1 n.16;
	5.3.3 nn.32, 33;
	9.3 n.2
§44-132.01	5.4.1 n.2

Arkansas

Statutes Annotated

§20-9-602	1.5.3 n.2;
	2.2 n.4;
	2.2.2 n.8;
	5.3.1 n.21
§20-17-214	7.8.1 n.1
§20-17-502	9.11 n.2;
	9.11.1 n.6
§34-2614	1.15 n.1;
	1.15.2 n.7;
	1.19 nn.3, 4
§41-44-3	1.6.2 nn.2, 3
§59-1415	6.4.1 n.7
§59-1416	6.2.2 n.19;
	6.4.2 nn.9, 11, 12, 17;
	6.5.2 n.6;
	6.9 n.2;
	8.4.4 n.18;
	8.17.2 nn.8, 9

§82-363	5.3.5 n.42;
	5.3.6 n.46;
	7.3.3 n.11
§82-411.14	9.7 nn.6, 8;
	9.10 nn.1, 2;
	9.13 n.5
§82-629	5.4.1 n.8
§82-1606	9.3 n.2

California

Business and Professions Code

§2257	3.12 n.2

Civil Code

§25.6	5.3.3 nn.32, 33
§25.8	5.3.5 n.43
§25.9	5.8 n.1;
	5.8.2 nn.8, 10, 12, 13, 15,
	16, 17, 18
§34.9	5.12.1 nn.10, 12, 13, 15
§34.10	5.7 nn.1, 3, 8, 9
§62	5.2.3 n.30
§§2430 to 2443	7.5.1 n.11;
	7.8.4 n.15
§7005	3.7.2 nn.3, 5, 6;
	3.7.3 n.9

Civil Procedure Code

§340.5	1.17 nn.1, 6, 8

Government Code

§27491.4	9.12 n.5
§27491.5	9.12 n.11
§27491.25	9.12 n.10

Health & Safety Code

§199.22	11.1 n.1;
	11.2 n.1

§199.27	11.1 n.1;
	11.2 nn.2, 5;
	11.10 n.1
§199.36	8.26 n.2
§303.5	5.10.1 n.11
§1530.6	5.14 n.7
§1704.5	13.2 n.2;
	3.12.1 n.3
§7180	9.8.2 n.4
§7202	9.10 nn.2, 4, 5, 7
§§24170 et seq.	2.9.2 n.8;
	8.4 n.1;
	8.9.3 n.32;
	8.11 n.8;
	8.14.1 n.4
§24172	2.9.2 n.11
§§24172-24176	8.4.1 n.2
§24173	2.9.2 n.12
§24175	8.17.1 n.1;
	8.24.2 n.4
§24179	8.4.1 n.3
§24179.5	8.4.1 n.6
§25956	8.11 n.9;
	9.10 n.19
§25957	9.10 n.19
§25957(a)	9.10 n.20
§25957(b)	9.10 n.22
§26668.3	8.14.1 n.4
§26668.4	8.14 n.1;
	8.14.1 n.5
§26668.6	8.14.1 n.6

Penal Code

§§3500 et seq.	8.0 n.14;
	8.4 n.1;
	8.4.4 n.19;
	8.21.1 n.4
§3505	8.21.1 n.7

Probate Code

§§3200 to 3211	1.6.2 n.4;
	7.2.3 n.16
§3201	7.2.3 n.17
§3204	7.2.3 n.18
§§3205 to 3207	7.2.3 n.19

| §3208 | 1.6.2 n.5; |
| | 7.2.3 nn.20, 21 |

Welfare & Institutions Code

§§5000 et seq.	4.6.1 n.7
§5006	5.16.1 n.1
§5325	6.1 n.1;
	6.2.2 n.20;
	6.5.2 nn.6, 8
§5326.85	6.3.1 n.5
§7518	6.9 n.7
§14191	3.2 n.2

§27-10-103	5.8 n.1
§27-10.5-109	6.2.1 n.13
§27-10.5-114	6.4.2 nn.10, 17;
	6.9 nn.1, 2, 18
§27-10.5-115	6.6.1 nn.1, 4;
	6.6.2 nn.5, 7, 8, 9, 12;
	6.6.3 nn.19, 22
§27-10.5-128	6.7 nn.5, 8, 10
§27-10.5-130	6.6.2 n.10;
	6.7 nn.6, 8, 12;
	9.3.2 n.14
§45-78 et seq.	6.7 n.11

Colorado

Revised Statutes

§12-34-108.5	9.11.1 nn.5, 8
§12-34-202	9.10 nn.6, 17
§12-34-203	9.10 nn.3, 4
§13-20-402	6.3 n.3;
	6.3.1 n.13
§13-20-403	5.8.2 n.18
§13-22-102	5.7 nn.2, 7
§13-22-103	5.3.1 n.3;
	5.3.1 n.29;
	5.3.3 n.32;
	9.3 n.2
§13-22-105	5.5 n.1;
	5.5.3 nn.24, 25, 30
§13-22-106	1.5.3 n.4;
	2.6.2 n.10;
	5.12.1 nn.10, 12, 15
§13-80-105	1.15 n.2;
	1.17 n.6
§23-23-103	5.14 n.1
§25-1-311	2.5 nn.7, 11
§25-4-402	5.4.2 n.13
§25-4-903	5.10.1 nn.5, 6, 7
§25-4-908	5.10.1 n.8
§25-4-1405	11.1 n.1;
	11.2 n.1;
	11.10 n.3
§25-6-102	5.5 n.1;
	5.5.3 n.35

Connecticut

General Statutes

§10-204a	2.5 nn.9, 15;
	5.10.1 nn.5, 6
§17-205f	5.8 nn.5, 9, 12;
	5.8.2 n.11
§17-205h	5.8.2 nn.16, 22
§17-206d	6.4.2 nn.9, 23;
	6.5.2 n.9
§19-66g	3.4 n.7
§19-89	2.6.1 n.2
§19-92	5.11.1 n.10
§19-139	9.10 nn.1, 2, 5
§19-139(b)	9.8.2 n.8
§19-139d	9.6.1 n.3
§19-139i	9.8.3 n.20
§19-139i(b)	9.8.2 n.9
§19-139m	9.9 n.1
§19-140	9.10 nn.10, 11, 14, 15
§19-143	9.13 nn.4, 6
§19-216	5.11.1 nn.1, 3, 8
§19-530	9.12 nn.3, 6, 11
§45-69g	3.7.2 n.6
§45-69i	3.7.2 n.7;
	3.7.3 n.10
§§45-78q to 45-78y	6.7 nn.7, 8
§45-78y	6.7 nn.7, 13
§45-78z	6.7 n.7;
	6.9 n.19
§46b-26	2.5 n.18
§53a-90	2.5 nn.2, 3

Delaware

Code Annotated

tit. 14, §131	5.10.1 nn.5, 8, 10
tit. 16, §§2501 to 2509	7.7.2 n.1
tit. 16, §4765	4.8 n.3
tit. 18, §707	1.5.3 n.6
tit. 18, §6801	1.12.1 n.4
tit. 18, §6852	1.12 n.2;
	1.12.1 n.8;
	1.13.3 nn.15, 19;
	1.15 nn.1, 4;
	1.15.2 n.7;
	1.15.4 n.15;
	1.16.2 n.5;
	1.16.4 n.10;
	2.4 n.1;
	2.7 n.2
tit. 18, §6854	1.18.1 nn.8, 10
tit. 29, §4711	9.9.1 n.2
tit. 29, §4712	9.9.1 n.3

District of Columbia

Code Annotated

§6-1690	6.6.2 nn.5, 8, 9, 11, 12;
	6.6.3 n.21
§§6-2421 to 2430	7.7.2 n.1
§§21-2081 to 2085	7.8.4 n.15

Florida

Statutes

§232.032	5.10.1 nn.4, 5
§245.09	9.10 n.18
§245.12	9.10 n.6
§381.382	5.5.2 n.26;
	5.5.3 nn.24, 33
§382.085	9.8.2 n.10
§383.04	5.11.1 nn.10, 11
§383.08	3.8 nn.1, 2
§384.061	5.4.1 nn.2, 4
§384.32	4.7.1 n.1;
	11.5 n.1

§390.001	5.6.3 n.52
§393.12	6.2 n.2
§393.13	6.1 nn.1, 2, 3;
	6.2.2 nn.21, 22;
	6.4.2 nn.10, 11, 12, 16, 18;
	6.6.2 nn.5, 9;
	6.9 nn.1, 8;
	8.4.4 n.17;
	8.17.2 nn.8, 11, 12
§394.459	6.4.2 n.24;
	6.9 nn.1, 5
§396.082	5.7 nn.1, 4, 8
§397.052	5.7 n.12
§§415.105 to 107	10.6 n.1;
	10.7 n.1;
	10.8 n.1
§458.324	3.12 n.2
§458.325	6.3 n.3;
	6.3.1 nn.8, 11;
	6.5.2 nn.9, 11;
	6.5.3 n.16
§458.333	8.5 nn.1, 2
§458.335	8.5 n.2
§459.0125	3.12 n.2
§732.912	9.6.1 n.7
§732.9185	9.6.5 n.24;
	9.9.1 n.12
§743.064	5.12 nn.1, 4;
	7.3.3 n.12
§743.065	5.3.6 n.46
§§765.01 to 15	7.7.2 n.1;
	7.8.4 n.16
§768.45	1.3 n.8
§768.46	1.10 n.1;
	1.12 n.2;
	1.12.1 nn.7, 8;
	1.12.2 n.24;
	1.15.4 n.17;
	1.19 n.11
§827.07	2.6.1 n.1

Georgia

Code Annotated (Michie)

§3-1101	1.17 n.1
§§31 to 32-1-12	7.7.2 n.1
§31-23-6(b)(1)	9.9.1 n.10

§32-911	5.10.1 nn.1, 5, 9
§48-402	9.11 n.2
§48-408	9.11.1 n.7
§53-215	2.5 n.19
§53-216	2.5 n.20
§68A-902.1	4.11 nn.3, 9
§74-101.1	3.7.2 n.4
§74-104.3	5.4.1 nn.2, 4, 5; 5.4.2 n.16
§§84-901a et seq.	8.5 nn.1, 3
§84-933	6.7 n.13
§84-935.1	6.9 n.19
§§88-200-1 et seq.	9.9.1 n.2
§88-403.1	5.7 nn.1, 2, 3, 10
§88-502.6	6.9 nn.3, 8, 10
§88-1201.1	5.11.1 n.4
§88-1203	2.5 n.10
§88-1204	2.5 n.17
§88-1604	2.5 nn.1, 4
§88-1606	2.5 n.8
§88-1716.1	9.8.2 n.4
§88-2010	9.9.1 n.4
§88-2904	2.2 n.4; 2.2.2 n.8; 5.3.5 n.41; 5.3.6 n.46; 7.3.3 n.11; 12.9 n.1
§88-2905	1.13.3 n.16; 2.2 nn.2, 3, 5; 7.3.3 n.12
§88-2906	1.12.1 n.12; 12.1 n.1
§92A-465	9.7 n.8
§99-223	5.10.1 nn.3, 5

Hawaii

Revised Statutes

§286-152	4.11 n.9
§286-181	4.11 n.2
§298-42	5.10.1 n.1
§321-52.5	5.11.1 nn.2, 8
§325-32	5.10.1 n.4
§325-34	5.10.1 n.6
§327C-1	9.8.2 nn.7, 8
§327D-25	7.8.1 n.3
§334-59	6.2.1 n.5
§334-60	6.1 n.5; 6.2.1 n.4
§577A-2	9.3 n.2
§657-7.3	1.17 n.2

1980 Session Laws

Act 272	6.6.2 n.5; 6.6.3 n.23

Idaho

Code

§5-219	1.17 nn.6, 7
§15-5-312	10.4 n.1
§16-1616	5.16.1 nn.4, 7, 9, 11
§32-412	2.5 n.20; 3.9.4 n.24
§32-414	2.5 n.21
§37-3102	5.7 n.2
§39-136	2.2 n.2
§39-604	4.7.1 n.1
§39-1001	3.8 n.1
§39-1004	3.8 n.5
§39-1005	3.8 n.7
§39-3801	5.4.1 nn.2, 5, 7, 8
§§39-3901 et seq.	5.9.1 n.1
§39-3903	5.9.1 n.2; 6.7 n.13
§39-3908	6.9 n.19
§39-4303	1.6.2 n.2; 1.10.2 n.9; 2.2 nn.2, 4
§39-4304	1.12 n.1
§39-4305	1.16.5 nn.17, 19
§§39-4501 to 4509	7.7.2 n.1
§66-345	6.6.2 n.5; 6.6.3 n.24

Illinois

Annotated Statutes (Smith-Hurd)

ch. 23, §233	5.11.2 n.15
ch. 23, §2054	2.6.1 n.1
ch. 23, §2229	5.11.2 n.16
ch. 23, §2336	5.11.2 n.19
ch. 31, §10.4	9.14.3 n.17
ch. 38, §81-23.2	3.4 nn.7, 8
ch. 38, §81-26	8.0 n.13;
	8.9 nn.2, 7, 10;
	8.11 n.1
ch. 38, §81-32.1	8.9 nn.7, 10
ch. 38, §1003-6-2	4.3 n.1
ch. 56 1/2, §§1802 et seq.	8.5 n.1
ch. 56 1/2, §1802.1	8.5.1 n.7
ch. 56 1/2, §§1901 to 1906	8.5 n.2
ch. 91 1/2, §2-107	6.4.2 nn.10, 21, 26
ch. 91 1/2, §2-110	6.5.2 n.9
ch. 91 1/2, §§3-501 to 3-504	5.8 n.1
ch. 91 1/2, §3-501	5.8.2 nn.8, 11
ch. 91 1/2, §3-502	5.8.2 nn.9, 11, 12
ch. 91 1/2, §4-500	6.2.1 n.9
ch. 110 1/2, §§701 to 710	7.7.2 n.1
ch. 110 1/2, §752	9.11 nn.2, 9
ch. 110 1/2, §§804-1 to 12	7.8.4 n.15
ch. 111, §4501	5.3.1 n.7
ch. 111, §4502	5.3.5 n.44
ch. 111, §4503	5.12 nn.1, 3
ch. 111, §4504	5.4.1 nn.5, 6
ch. 111, §4505	5.4.2 n.16
ch. 111 1/2, §22.12	2.5 n.15
ch. 111 1/2, §53.31	3.4.1 n.1
ch. 111 1/2, §§4503 et seq.	3.14.3 n.7
ch. 111 1/2, §4801	3.8 nn.2, 4
ch. 111 1/2, §4802	3.8 n.7
ch. 111 1/2, §4903	5.11.1 n.2
ch. 111 1/2, §4904	5.11.1 n.2
ch. 111 1/2, §4905	5.11.1 n.8
ch. 122, §27-8.1	5.11.2 n.13

Indiana

Statutes Annotated Code (Burns)

§16-1-9.5-2.5	11.2 n.1
§16-1-9.5-7	11.9 n.3
§16-1-11-20	3.8 n.4
§16-8-3-1	6.9 n.1;
	10.4 n.1
§16-13-6.1-23	5.7 nn.1, 2, 5, 7
§16-14-1.6-6	6.6.2 n.14;
	6.6.3 n.25
§31-1-1-7	2.5 n.21
§35-1-58.5-6	8.4.4 nn.20, 22;
	8.9 n.12

Iowa

Code Annotated (West)

§139.9	5.10.1 nn.1, 3
§140.12	3.8 nn.1, 7
§140.13	5.11.1 nn.10, 11
§140.9	5.4.1 nn.2, 3
§147.137	1.12.1 n.14
§246.47	8.0 n.14;
	8.4.4 n.19;
	8.21.1 n.11
§246.514	11.5 n.4
§321B.5	4.10 n.1;
	4.11 n.4
§356.48	11.5 n.3
§614.1	1.17 nn.1, 7

Kansas

Statutes Annotated

§23-128	3.7.2 n.6
§28-39-78	10.9 n.1;
	10.10 nn.1, 2
§38-122	5.3.6 n.46
§38-123b	5.3.2 nn.23, 28;
	5.3.3 n.32
§38-843	5.14 nn.3, 4
§38-845	5.14 n.5

Table of Statutes

§59-2910	6.4.1 nn.2, 3, 6
§59-2916d	6.4.1 n.3
§59-2917a	6.2.1 n.8
§59-2929	5.8.2 nn.15, 16, 23;
	6.2.2 nn.20, 22;
	8.17.2 nn.8, 10
§65-28	7.7.2 n.1
§65-153b	5.11.1 nn.10, 11
§65-153f	3.8 n.1
§65-180	5.11.1 n.1
§65-448	5.12.1 nn.10, 15
§65-2836	3.12 n.2
§65-2891	5.12 nn.4, 6
§65-2892	5.4.1 nn.3, 9;
	5.4.2 n.14
§65-3218	9.11.1 nn.5, 8
§65-6b05	8.5.1 n.7
§§65-101 to 109	7.7.2 n.1
§72-5205	5.11.2 n.16
§77-202	9.8.2 n.4

Kentucky

Revised Statutes Annotated (Baldwin)

§65-448	5.12.1 n.12
§202A.180	6.1 n.1;
	6.2.2 n.20;
	6.5.2 n.6
§208A.230	5.14 n.3
§214.036	5.10.1 n.9
§214.185	5.3.3 nn.30, 33;
	5.4.1 n.1
§214.185(2)	5.3.1 n.17
§214.420	11.9 nn.2, 4
§216B.400	5.12.1 nn.10, 15, 16
§222.440	5.7 n.1
§304-40-320	1.13.3 n.16;
	1.16.2 n.6
§311.187	9.9.1 n.4
§311.241	9.11.1 n.5
§311.935	3.12 n.2
§§311.950 et seq.	8.5 n.1
§436.023	3.4 n.8
§436.026	8.4.4 nn.20, 22;
	8.9.1 n.16

Louisiana

Revised Statutes Annotated (West)

§9:111	9.8.2 n.9
§13:1583	5.14 n.1
§15:860	4.6.1 n.2
§17:2354.4	9.11.1 n.9
§28:171	6.4.2 nn.9, 11;
	6.9 nn.1, 3, 9, 10
§28:390	5.8 n.2;
	5.8.2 n.23
§32:410	9.7 nn.2, 4
§40:1065.1	5.4.1 n.4;
	5.4.2 n.16
§40:1299	5.11.1 n.3
§40:1299.1	5.11.1 n.3
§40:1299.35.13	8.4.4 n.21
§40:1299.40	11.2 n.9
§40:1299.53	5.3.1 n.8;
	5.3.5 n.42;
	5.12 nn.1, 2, 5
§40:1299.54	2.2 n.7
§40:1299.58	5.8.2 n.22
§40:1299.58.1-10	7.7.2 n.1
§661	4.11 n.2
§1095	5.3.4 n.35
§1096	5.7 n.5

Maine

Revised Statutes Annotated

tit. 18A, §§5-501, 502	7.8.4 n.15
tit. 18A, §804-1 to	7.4.2 n.4
804-2	
tit. 20, §1194	5.10.1 n.8
tit. 20, §6451	5.11.2 n.15
tit. 20A, §6351	5.10.1 n.12
tit. 22, §3-B	5.14 n.3
tit. 22, §1021	2.5 nn.5, 11
tit. 22, §1189	3.8 n.3
tit. 22, §1231	3.8 n.1
tit. 22, §1593	8.9.1 n.16
tit. 22, §1598	3.4 nn.7, 8
tit. 22, §1908	5.5 n.1;
	5.5.2 n.27;
	5.5.3 nn.24, 34

tit. 22, §2884	9.10 n.9
tit. 22, §4070	5.16.1 n.8
tit. 22, §4071	5.16.1 nn.5, 10
tit. 25A, §6351	5.10.1 n.12
tit. 32, §2595	5.4.2 n.16
tit. 32, §3817	5.7 n.5
tit. 32, §6221	5.7 n.5
tit. 32, §7004	5.7 n.5
tit. 34, §2143	8.17.2 n.12
tit. 34, §2144	6.1 n.2
tit. 34B, §5477	6.2.1 nn.10, 11
tit. 34B, §5605	5.8.2 n.23;
	6.2.2 n.19;
	6.6.2 n.9;
	8.17.2 n.11

Maryland

Annotated Code

art. 18, §334	11.8 n.5
art. 20, §113	3.12 n.2
art. 22, §6	9.14.1 n.2
art. 22, §7	9.14.1 n.2
art. 22, §7B	9.14.1 n.4
art. 27, §700F	4.8 n.1
art. 43, §31B	3.8 nn.2, 4
art. 43, §54F	9.8.2 nn.4, 8
art. 43, §135	5.3.1 n.9;
	5.4.1 n.1; 5.7 n.6
art. 43, §135B	1.5.3 n.4
art. 43, §135C	7.1.3 n.44
art. 43, §565C	8.4.4 n.17
art. 43, §556F	3.14.1 n.2
art. 45, §566C	8.24 n.1

Education Code Annotated

§7-403	5.11.12 nn.15, 16

Massachusetts

General Laws

ch. 38, §6	9.12 n.4
ch. 38, §20	9.12 n.5

ch. 71, §54B	5.15 n.3
ch. 71, §55A	5.15 n.2
ch. 76, §15A	5.11.2 n.17
ch. 90, §8D	9.7 n.5
ch. 90, §24	4.11 n.8
ch. 111, §70E	3.12 n.2;
	3.12.1 n.5;
	8.4.4 n.18;
	8.24 n.2
ch. 111, §70F	11.9 n.1
ch. 111, §117	5.4.1 n. 1
ch. 112, §12E	5.7 nn.3, 8
ch. 112, §12F	5.3.1 n.4;
	5.3.3 n.30;
	5.3.4 n.40;
	5.3.6 n.46
ch. 112, §12J	8.0 n.13;
	8.7 n.1;
	8.9 nn.1, 8, 9;
	8.9.3 nn.35, 36;
	9.10 n.24
ch. 112, §12J(a)I	8.9.1 n.13
ch. 112, §12J(a)II	8.9.1 n.22;
	9.10 n.25
ch. 112, §12J(a)V	8.9.1 n.17
ch. 112, §12J(a)VI	8.9.1 n.18
ch. 112, §12J(b)II	8.9.1 n.19
ch. 112, §12J(b)VI	8.9.1 n.20
ch. 112, §12J(b)VII	8.9.1 n.21
ch. 112, §12S	5.6.1 n.17
ch. 113, §2	9.10 n.13
ch. 113, §8	9.11.1 n.7
ch. 123, §22	6.3.1 n.8
ch. 123, §23	6.5.2 n.6

Michigan

Compiled Laws

§330.1716	6.3.1 n.15
§333.2685	8.9 n.4
§333.2686	8.7 n.2
§333.2688	8.9 n.12
§333.2689	8.9.3 n.35
§333.6501	4.5 nn.1, 13
§333.10105	9.9.1 n.15
§380.11787	5.15 nn.1, 4

§700.407	9.3.2 n.12	§41-41-7	1.13.3 n.16;
§771.3(4)	4.6.5 n.39		2.2 n.2;
			5.12 nn.1, 2, 5
		§41-41-9	5.12 n.5
	Statutes Annotated	§41-42-7	5.5 n.1;
			5.5.3 nn.24, 28, 31
§27.3178(19b)	9.3.2 n.11	§41-45-1	6.7 n.4
		§41-45-19	6.9 n.19
		§43-23-21	5.14 n.1
		§63-11-5	4.11 n.2
	Minnesota	§63-11-7	4.10 n.1
		§63-11-9	4.11 n.9
	Statutes Annotated (West)	§63-11-11	4.11 n.11

§123.70	5.10.1 nn.1, 2,		
	4, 6, 7		*General Laws*
§144.346	5.3.4 n.36;		
	5.7 n.1	ch. 365	7.7.2 n.1
§144.651	6.1 n.3		
§145.15	9.10 n.16		
§145.421	8.11 nn.2, 3		
§145.422	8.0 n.13;		*Missouri*
	8.9 n.5		
§147.075	8.5 nn.1, 2		*Annotated Statutes (Vernon)*
§169.123	4.11 nn.5, 9		
§171.07	9.7 n.1	§53-20-147	8.17.2 n.11
§253A.17	6.9 nn.1, 3, 5, 9	§105.700	4.3 n.2;
§254.09	2.5 n.6		4.8 n.5
§260.191	5.13 n.7	§167.181	5.10.1 n.7
§525.94	9.11 n.2	§188.037	8.4.4 n.21;
			8.9 n.2
		§188.039	3.4 n.7
		§191.225	5.12.1 nn.10, 12, 15
	Mississippi	§198.088	8.4.4 n.17
		§210.030	3.8 n.3
	Code Annotated	§431.061	5.3.1 n.10;
			5.3.3 n.30;
§15-1-36	1.17 n.1		5.3.6 n.46
§41-21-201	5.11.1 n.1	§431.062	5.3.4 n.34
§41-21-203	5.11.1 n.1	§431.063	5.12 nn.5, 3
§41-23-37	5.10.1 nn.1,	§516.105	1.17 n.7
	2, 6	§630.115	5.8.2 n.23
§41-24-1	5.11.2 n.17	§630.130	5.8.2 n.15;
§41-39-11	9.9.2 n.13		6.3 n.3;
§41-39-15	9.11.1 n.8		6.3.1 nn.5, 6, 9, 16
§41-39-53	9.7 n.7	§630.133	5.8.2 nn.16, 19
§41-39-102	9.10 n.23	§630.183	6.9 nn.1, 5
§41-41-3	5.3.1 n.22;	§630.194	8.17.3 nn.15, 18
	5.3.5 n.42	§632.110	5.8.1 nn.4, 6

Montana

Code Annotated

§20-5-405	5.10.1 n.8
§27-2-205	1.17 nn.2, 6
§41-1-102	1.5.3 n.5
§41-1-402	1.5.3 n.3; 5.2.3 n.30; 5.3.1 n.5; 5.4.1 n.3
§41-1-403	5.3.4 n.37; 5.4.2 n.14
§41-1-406	5.8.2 nn.8, 14
§41-1-407	5.3.3 nn.31, 32
§50-19-103	3.8 nn.1, 2
§50-20-107	5.6.2 n.33
§50-22-101	9.8.2 n.4
§53-20-145	6.4.2 nn.15, 17
§53-20-146	6.3.1 n.10; 6.6.1 nn.1, 2; 6.6.2 nn.8, 9; 6.6.3 nn.20, 27
§53-20-147	8.9.4 n.17; 8.17.2 nn.8, 12
§53-21-145	6.4.2 nn.9, 11, 12, 14, 16, 17
§53-21-148	6.2.2 n.20; 6.5.2 nn.9, 12
§53-23-104	5.9.1 nn.4, 5

Nebraska

Revised Statutes

§28-342	8.4.4 nn.21, 22
§39-669.08	4.11 n.2
§39-669.10	4.10 n.1
§39-669.12	4.11 n.14
§44-2816	1.12 n.1; 1.12.1 n.8; 1.15.2 n.6
§44-2820	1.15.4 n.13
§71-604.03	5.11.1 n.1
§71-1116	3.8 nn.2, 5, 7
§71-1121	5.4.1 nn.10, 12; 5.4.2 n.15
§71-5041	5.7 n.7

§77-4807	9.6.4 n.17
§79-444	5.11.2 n.13
§83-1066	5.8.2 n.24; 6.1 n.3

Nevada

Revised Statutes

§62-240	5.14 n.2
§129.030	5.3.1 n.6
§129.060	5.4.1 n.2
§392.420	5.11.2 nn.15, 16, 18, 19
§392.435	5.10.1 nn.1, 2, 4
§392.437	5.10.1 n.5
§392.446	5.10.1 n.8
§433.484	5.8.2 n.21; 6.6.2 n.14
§442.010	3.8 n.1
§442.050	5.11.1 n.10
§442.255	5.6.2 nn.38, 40
§§449.540 to 690	7.7.2 n.1
§484.383	4.11 nn.3, 4, 5, 8, 9

New Hampshire

Revised Statutes Annotated

§14.11-a	5.4.1 n.7
§262-A:69d	4.10 n.1; 4.11 nn.3, 6, 8
§291-A:4	9.6.4 n.17
§318-B:12d	5.7 n.14
§507-C:2	1.15 n.1; 1.19 nn.3, 4
§507-C:3	1.18 n.1
§457:23	2.5 n.19

New Jersey

Statutes Annotated (West)

§9:1-1.1	5.16.1 n.1
§9:6-1.1	5.16.1 n.2
§9:6-8.31	5.13 n.6

§18A:40-4	5.11.2 nn.15, 16, 19
§18A:40-4.1	5.15 n.2
§26:1A-66	5.16.1 nn.1, 2
§26:2-111	5.11.1 n.2
§26:4-32	4.7.1 nn.5, 6
§26:4-49.7	2.5 nn.1, 2, 3;
	4.7.1 nn.2, 9
§26:4-49.8	2.5 n.1
§26:4-48.1	4.4.7 n.4
§30:4-7.2	4.3 n.4;
	4.8 n.5
§30:4-7.6	5.16.1 n.1
§30:4-24.2	6.1 n.3;
	6.2 n.2;
	6.2.2 nn.19, 20, 21;
	6.3.1 n.9;
	6.4.2 nn.7, 10,
	12, 13, 14, 18;
	6.7 n.8;
	8.17.2 nn.11, 13, 14
§30:6D-5	6.7 n.8
§30:13-5	8.24 n.2
§37:1-20	2.5 n.19
§45:9-22.2	3.12 n.2

New Mexico

Statutes Annotated

§12-2-4	9.8.2 n.4
§24-1-10	3.8 n.1
§24-3-1	5.11.2 n.17
§24-6-7(E)	9.9.1 n.14
§24-6-10	9.11.1 n.6
§24-7-1	7.7.2 n.1
§24-7-4	5.18 n.2;
	7.8.1 n.1
§§24-9A et seq.	8.0 n.13;
	8.7 n.4;
	8.9 n.1
§24-9A-1	8.11 nn.1, 5
§24-9A-2	8.7.1 n.6
§24-9A-3	8.11 n.7
§24-10-1	5.2.3 n.30;
	5.3.1 n.18;
	5.3.3 n.33
§29-9A-3	8.9.2 n.25
§29-9A-4	8.9.2 n.27

§24-9S-5	8.7.1 n.5;
	8.9.2 n.28;
	8.9.3 n.35;
	8.11 n.7
§30-9-5	2.5 nn.1, 3;
	4.7.4 n.7
§43-1-15	6.3 n.3;
	6.3.1 n.8;
	6.5.2 nn.9, 13
§43-1-16	5.8.2 nn.9, 10, 15
§43-1-17	5.8 n.1;
	5.8.2 nn.16, 17, 18, 19
§66-8-107	4.10 n.1;
	4.11 n.3

New York

Civil Procedure Law

§214-a	1.17 n.7

County Law

§673	9.12 nn.1, 7
§674	9.12 nn.8, 10

Domestic Relations Law

§73	3.7.2 nn.4, 6

Mental Hygiene Law

§9.13	5.8 n.1;
	5.8.2 n.9;
	6.1.1 n.8
§15.13	5.8 n.2;
	6.1.1 n.9
§15.15	6.1 n.4
§45.17	9.13 n.3

Penal Law

§265.25	2.6.2 n.11

Public Health Law

§12-b	1.2 n.4
§2164	5.10.1 n.13
§2302	4.7.1 n.5
§2306	2.6.1 n.2
§2404	3.12 n.2
§§2440 et seq.	8.4 n.1;
	8.11 n.8
§§2440 to 2446	2.9.2 n.9;
	8.21 n.1
§2441	2.9.2 n.13;
	8.4.2 n.7
§2442	8.4.2 n.9;
	8.14.1 n.7;
	8.17.1 n.4
§2444	8.4.2 n.8;
	8.14 n.2;
	8.14.1 n.8;
	8.17.1 n.5;
	8.21 n.2;
	8.24.2 n.5
§2500-a	5.11.1 nn.4, 6, 7
§2504	5.3.1 n.11;
	5.3.3 n.30;
	5.3.6 n.46;
	7.1.4 n.47;
	7.3.1 n.2
§2805-d	1.3 n.8;
	1.12.1 n.7;
	1.12.2 n.34;
	1.13.3 n.15;
	1.15.4 nn.13, 15;
	1.16 n.1;
	1.16.2 n.5;
	1.16.4 n.10;
	2.3 n.2;
	2.4 n.1;
	2.4.1 nn.6, 9;
	2.7 n.2;
	7.1.4 n.47
§§2960 to 2978	7.6.2 n.19
§2962	7.6.2 n.22
§2973	7.6.2 n.23
§2976	7.6.2 n.23
§4214	9.13 n.7
§4215	9.13 n.7
§4222	9.9.1 nn.3, 5

Social Service Law

§383-b	5.13 n.8

North Carolina

General Statutes

§7A-732	5.16.1 nn.6, 9
§20-139.1	4.11 n.10
§35A-1241	10.4 n.1
§35-37	5.9.1 n.3
§90-21.4	5.3.4 n.34
§§90-320 to 322	7.7.2 n.1
§§108A-99 to 108A-11	10.6 n.1;
	10.7 n.1;
	10.8 n.1
§122-55.6	6.4.2 nn.9, 17
§130-87	5.10.1 n.11
§148-46.2	4.6.1 n.3

North Dakota

Century Code

§14-02.1-03	3.4 n.8
§14-02.2	8.9 n.8
§14-02.2-01	8.7 n.3;
	8.9 n.5
§14-02.2-02	8.9 nn.9, 12
§12-10-17	5.4.1 n.7;
	5.7 n.4
§23-06.1-06.1	9.11 n.2
§23-07-07.1	3.8 n.3
§23-07-07.3	3.8 nn.5, 7
§23-07-08	4.7.1 n.1
§23-07-17.1	5.10.1 nn.1, 3
§25-01.2-09	8.17.2 nn.11, 13, 14;
	8.17.3 n.17
§25-01.2-11	5.8.2 n.18;
	5.9.2 n.6;
	6.5.2 nn.13, 15;
	6.7 nn.7, 13;
	8.17.2 n.11;
	8.17.3 nn.16, 17
§25-01.2-15	5.8.2 n.24

§25-03.1-40	6.5.2 n.7;	tit. 43A, §346	6.9 n.19
	6.9 n.2	tit. 47, §751	4.11 n.3
§39-20-03	4.10 n.1	tit. 63, §1-301	9.8.2 n.8
§39-20-14	4.11 n.8	tit. 63, §1-515	3.8 nn.1, 2
		tit. 63, §1-516	3.8 nn.5, 7
		tit. 63, §1-524	2.5 nn.1, 4
		tit. 63, §1-735	8.4.4 n.20;

Ohio

			8.9 n.2
		tit. 63, §2-313.5	8.5.1 n.8
Revised Code Annotated (Baldwin)		tit. 63, §2-313.7	8.5 n.2
		tit. 63, §2-313.11	8.5.1 n.7
§2108.02(e)	9.8.3 n.18	tit. 63, §2204	9.6.1 n.10
§2108.53	9.6.1 nn.6, 8;	tit. 63, §2602	5.3.1 n.12;
	9.9.1 n.2		5.3.3 n.31;
§2108.60	9.9.1 n.13		5.3.4 n.38;
§2305.11	1.17 n.5		5.3.6 n.46;
§2317.54	1.10 n.1;		5.4.1 n.3;
	1.16.5 nn.14, 16, 18, 19		5.4.2 n.15
§2907.27	2.5 n.2;	tit. 63, §2902	7.6 n.90
	4.7.1 n.5	tit. 70, §1210.192	5.10.1 n.7
§2907.29	5.12.1 nn.10, 12, 15, 16	tit. 76, §18	1.17 n.5
§3313.671	2.5 nn.9, 15;		
	5.10.1 nn.1, 2, 7		
§3701.60	3.14.1 n.3		
§3701.501	5.11.1 nn.3, 6	**Oregon**	
§3709.241	5.4.1 nn.3, 5		
§3719.012	5.7 nn.7, 8	*Revised Statutes*	
§3721.13	8.24 nn.2, 3;		
	10.9 n.1;	§§97.050 to 97.90	7.7.2 n.1
	10.10 nn.1, 2	§109.650	5.4.2 nn.14, 16
§5122.271	6.7 n.8;	§418.307	5.14 n.6
	6.9 n.14	§426.220	5.8.1 nn.5, 7;
§5123.86	6.6.1 nn.1, 4;		6.1.1 n.11
	6.7 n.11	§426.385	6.1 n.2;
			6.6.2 nn.7, 14
		§426.715	6.5.3 n.16
		§434.170	4.7 n.1
Oklahoma		§434.200	3.8 nn.1, 3
		§435.305	3.3.3 n.3
Statutes Annotated (West)		§441.605	8.4.4 n.18;
			8.24 n.2
tit. 10, §170.1	5.3.5 n.45	§§475.305 et seq.	8.5 n.5
tit. 10, §170.2	5.12 nn.1, 4	§475.325	8.5 n.6
tit. 10, §413	5.10.1 n.7	§475.335	8.5 n.6
tit. 10, §1130	5.16.1 n.3	§475.345	8.5 n.6
tit. 43A, §4-104	6.9 n.8	§475.355	8.5 n.6
tit. 43A, §4-404	6.9 n.3	§677.365	3.7.2 n.6;
tit. 43A, §5-204	6.4.1 nn.2, 5, 7		3.7.4 n.13

Pennsylvania

Consolidated Statutes Annotated
(Purdon)

tit. 18, §3205	3.5.1 n.17
tit. 18, §3205(a)	3.5.1 n.15
tit. 18, §3205(c)	3.5.1 n.16
tit. 18, §3208(a)(2)	3.5.1 n.19
tit. 24, §14-1419	5.16.1 n.1
tit. 35, §521.13	3.8 nn.1, 8
tit. 35, §621	5.11.1 n.2
tit. 35, §5218	4.7.1 nn.6, 8
tit. 35, §5641	3.12 n.2
tit. 35, §5642	3.12 n.2
tit. 35, §10102	5.3.1 n.13
tit. 35, §10104	2.2 n.2
tit. 35, §10151	12.6 n.4
tit. 40, §1301.103	1.12.1 nn.1, 9;
	1.12.2 n.24;
	1.13.3 nn.15, 16;
	1.16.4 n.10;
	1.19 n.10;
	2.4 n.1;
	2.4.1 n.7
tit. 50, §720	5.8.2 n.11
tit. 50, §7204	5.8.2 n.12

Rhode Island

General Laws

§9-1-14.1	1.17 n.5
§15-2-3	2.5 n.20
§23-4.6-1	5.3.2 nn.24, 26
§23-4.7-1	3.4 n.7
§23-4.7-2	3.4 n.7
§23-4.10-1	7.8.4 n.15
§22-4.10-2	7.8.4 n.15
§23-6-14	11.2 nn.8, 10, 11
§23-6-17	11.10 n.2
§23-11-3	1.5.4 n.7
§23-13-4	5.11.1 n.10
§23-17.5-7	8.24 n.1

§31-27-2.1	4.11 n.3
§40.1-5-5	1.5 n.1;
	6.1 n.4;
	6.2.1 n.5;
	7.2.1 n.4
§40.1-22-23	6.9 nn.3, 7

South Carolina

Code of Laws

§15-3-545	1.17 n.7
§20-7-280	5.3.2 nn. 25, 27
§32-715-1	9.7 n.8
§44-23-1020	6.6.2 n.7
§44-29-90	2.5 n.17
§44-29-100	2.5 n.1;
	4.7.1 n.1
§44-29-120	2.5 n.8;
	3.8 n.1
§44-43-40	9.7 n.2
§44-53-760	5.7 n.9
§56-2950	4.11 n.2

South Dakota

Codified Laws Annotated

§13-28-7.1	5.10.1 nn.2, 5
§27A-12-6	6.4.2 n.22;
	6.6.2 n.13
§27A-12-19	6.9 nn.3, 8
§27A-12-20	8.14.2 nn.12, 14
§27A-12-21	8.14.2 n.16
§27B-8-20	8.14 n.3;
	8.14.2 nn.12, 17
§27B-8-21	8.14.2 n.17
§32-23-13	4.11 nn.14, 15
§32-23-14	4.11 n.9
§32-23-15	4.11 n.10
§34-23-10	3.8 n.1
§34-23-12	3.8 nn.5, 7
§34-23-16	5.4.1 nn.8, 11
§34-23A-17	8.9 n.11
§34-24-6	5.11.1 n.12

Tennessee

Code Annotated

§14-5-106	7.2.2 n.15
§29-26-115	1.18 n.1
§29-26-118	1.3 n.8;
	1.12.1 n.8;
	1.15.2 n.6;
	1.19 n.3
§33-320	5.8.2 nn.15,
	16, 18, 19
§34-4-112	10.4 n.1
§36-502	2.5 nn.18, 21
§37-1-128	5.14 n.2
§38-7-108	9.12 n.2
§39-302	3.4 nn.7, 8;
	5.6.2 n.33
§39-308	8.9 n.11;
	8.9.1 n.16
§41-41-138	4.9 n.1
§41-2201	8.21.1 n.9
§§41-2201 et seq.	8.4.4 n.19
§§41-2201 to 2207	8.21.1 n.5
§41-2202	8.21 n.10
§41-2203	8.22 n.3
§49-6-5001	5.10.1 n.3
§53-42-105	9.7 n.8
§53-4067	5.5.3 n.31
§§53-4604 to 4607	5.5.3 n.29
§53-4608	5.5.3 n.36
§55-10-406	4.11 n.3
§63-6-220	5.7 n.5
§68-5-301	5.11.1 n.1
§68-5-302	5.11.1 n.1
§68-10-10	5.4.1 n.1
§68-11-901	10.9 n.1;
	10.10 nn.1, 2
§68-34-104	5.5.3 n.24

Texas

Criminal Procedure Code Annotated

§49.25	9.6.1 n.8;
	9.8.3 n.21

Education Code Annotated

§2.09	5.10.1 n.4

Family Code Annotated

§35.04	5.13 n.1

Revised Civil Statutes Annotated

art. 4419b-1, §9.02	11.2 nn.4, 6;
	11.10 n.2
art. 4447t, §§1 to 3	9.8.2 n.7
art. 4590h	7.7.2 n.1;
	7.8.1 n.4
art. 4590i	1.2 n.14;
	1.12.1 n.16;
	1.15.2 n.10;
	1.16.5 n.13
art. 4590-2a	9.3.1 n.4
art. 5547-300, §24(c)	9.2.3 n.24

Utah

Code Annotated

§26-6-19	4.7.1 n.1
§26-15-86	5.16.1 nn.1, 2
§55-22a-2	5.10.1 n.2
§§62A-6-101 to 116	5.9.1 n.8
§62A-6-103	5.9.1 n.9
§62A-6-108	5.9.1 n.10
§76-70-304	5.6.2 n.33
§78-14-5	1.12 n.2;
	1.12.1 n.7;
	1.13.3 nn.15, 17, 19;
	1.15 n.1;
	1.15.4 nn.13, 15;
	1.16 n.1;
	1.16.2 n.5;
	1.16.4 n.10;
	1.16.5 nn.13, 15, 19;
	1.19 nn.2, 8;
	2.4 n.1;
	2.4.1 n.8;

	2.7 n.2;
	5.3.1 n.14;
	5.3.5 n.42

Vermont

Statutes Annotated

tit. 12, §1908	1.19 n.3
tit. 12, §1909	1.12 n.2;
	1.13.3 nn.17, 19;
	1.15.2 n.6;
	1.15.4 n.15;
	1.16 n.1;
	1.19 nn.3, 9;
	2.3 n.2;
	2.7 n.2
tit. 13, §1801	7.7.2 n.1
tit. 18, §1102	3.8 nn.1, 2
tit. 18, §1121	2.5 n.9
tit. 18, §1122	2.5 n.15
tit. 18, §2101	10.9 n.1;
	10.10 nn.1, 2
tit. 18, §4226	5.4.1 nn.5, 6;
	5.4.2 n.16
tit. 18, §5134	2.5 n.18
tit. 18, §§5251 to 5262	7.7.2 n.1
tit. 18, §7503	5.8.2 nn.9, 11;
	6.1 n.6
tit. 18, §8702	5.9.1 n.4
tit. 18, §8711	6.7 n.13

Virginia

Code Annotated

§7.1-235	8.14 n.2
§16.1-275	5.14 n.2
§22.1-270	5.11.2 n.13
§32.1-46	5.10.1 n.5
§32.1-59	4.7.1 n.1
§32.1-60	3.8 n.1
§32.1-138	10.9 n.1;
	10.10 nn.1, 2

§32.1-287	9.9.1 n.7
§37.1-134.2	1.6.2 nn.4, 5;
	7.2.3 nn.16, 22
§37.1-234	2.9.2 n.14
§§37.1-234 et seq.	2.9.2 n.10;
	8.4 n.1;
	8.4.3 n.12;
	8.11 n.8
§37.1-235	2.9.2 nn.10. 15;
	8.4.3 n.13;
	8.14.1 n.9;
	8.17.1 n.6
§37.1-237	2.9.2 n.10;
	8.4.3 n.16
§46.1-375	9.7 n.1
§54-325.9	5.9.1 n.6;
	6.7 n.8
§54-325.12	6.7 nn.8, 9, 13
§54-325.15	6.9 n.19
§54-325.21	6.9 n.8
§54.1-2971	3.12 n.2

Washington

Revised Code Annotated

§7.70.050	1.12.1 nn.5, 7;
	1.12.2 n.24;
	1.13.3 n.17;
	1.15.4 n.13
§7.70.060	1.16.5 nn.13, 14, 19
§11.92.040	6.5.2 n.13
§26.26.50	3.7.2 n.4;
	3.7.3 nn.9, 12
§28A.31.106	5.10.1 n.7
§28A.31.134	5.11.2 n.18
§46.20.308	4.11 n.2
§§69.51.010 et seq.	8.5 n.3
§69.54.060	5.7 nn.4, 10
§70.24.090	3.8 n.1
§70.24.110	5.4.1 nn.7, 8
§74.42.040	8.4.4 n.17
§§70.122.010 to 905	7.7.2 n.1
§71.05.370	6.1 n.1
§74.42.040	8.24 n.1;
	10.9 n.1;
	10.10 n.1

West Virginia

Code

§16-3-4	5.10.1 n.4
§§16-4-4 to 5	4.7.1 nn.5, 8
§16-4-10	5.4.1 n.3
§16-4A-4	3.8 nn.5, 7
§16-19-1	9.8.2 n.7
§§16-30-1 to 10	7.7.2 n.1
§27-4-3	6.1.1 n.8
§27-5-9	6.1 n.1;
	6.2 nn.1, 2
§27-16-1	5.9.1 n.7
§48-1-6	2.5 nn.18, 19
§49-7-27	5.3.1 n.19
§60-6-23	5.7 n.7

Wisconsin

Statutes Annotated (West)

§51.47	5.7 nn.2, 3, 7, 10
§51.59	6.2 n.2
§51.61	5.8.2 n.23;
	6.4.1 nn.2, 4, 5;
	6.4.2 nn.20, 21, 25;
	6.5.2 n.7;

	8.17.3 nn.15, 19
§146.02	5.11.1 nn.3, 5
§146.025	11.1 n.1;
	11.2 n.3;
	11.8 n.1
§§154.01 et seq.	7.7.2 n.1
§343.305	4.11 n.3
§891.40	3.7.2 n.4;
	3.7.3 nn.9, 11
§893.55	1.17 n.6

Wyoming

Statutes

§9-6-672	8.14 n.3;
	8.14.2 nn.11, 13
§14-1-101	5.2.3 n.30;
	5.3.1 nn.15, 20
§24-1-309	5.10.1 n.8
§25-3-109	5.8.5 n.41
§25-3-125	6.2 n.2
§27-14-509	9.13 n.1
§§33-26-144 to 152	7.7.2 n.1
§35-4-134	4.7.1 n.1
§35-4-138	5.11.1 n.10
§35-4-502	3.8 n.1
§35-5	9.6.4 n.15

INDEX

All references are to sections.

Abortion
  illegitimate father and consent,
    3.6
  impermissible disclosures, 3.5.1
  information to be disclosed, 3.5.1
  spousal consent, 3.6
  Supreme Court rulings, 3.5
  waiting periods, 3.5.2
  who may obtain consent, 3.5.3
  written consent, 3.5.1
AIDS
  confidentiality
    blood banks, 11.8
    family members, 11.10
    health facilities, 11.9
    personnel, 11.9
    significant others, 11.10
  consent, generally, 11.1
    case law, 11.3
    legislative requirements, 11.2
  human research, 8.26
  testing
    detainees, 11.4
    divorce, 11.6
    prisoners, 11.5
    visitation rights, 11.7
Artificial insemination
  adultery, 3.7.5
  A.I.D., 3.7
  A.I.H., 3.7
  disclosure requirements, 3.7.1
  donor, status of, 3.7.3
  spousal consent, 3.7.2
  unmarried recipients, 3.7.4

Assault and battery
  consent actions based on, 1.2
  negligence theory distinguished
    from, 1.3
Autopsy
  case law
    authority to order autopsy,
      9.14.3
    disclosure of scope of autopsy,
      9.14.3
    disposal and retention of tis-
      sues, 9.14.3
    religious objections, 9.14.3
    unauthorized autopsies, 9.14.2
  forensic investigations
    collecting tissues and fluids,
      9.12
  medicolegal autopsies
    consent unnecessary, 9.12
    court orders, 9.12
    statutory authority, 9.12
  nonmedicolegal autopsies
    court action, 8.14
    power to conduct, 9.13

Birth defects
  duty to disclose risk of, 3.9, 3.9.1,
    3.9.2, 3.9.3
  genetic counselling, 3.9.2
  inadequate disclosure of risks,
    3.9.1
    Down's syndrome, 3.9.1

Birth defects, inadequate disclosure
of risks (*continued*)
maternal rubella exposure,
3.9.3
polycystic kidney disease, 3.9.1
Tay-Sachs, 3.9.1
Brain death. *See* Death
Breach of contract as basis for suit,
1.3
Burden of proof
defendant's duty, 1.19
plaintiff's responsibility, 1.19

Cadaver. *See* Organ donation, Unclaimed bodies
Cancer. *See also* Mastectomy
cervical
duty to disclose information,
1.12.3
Child abuse. *See* Minors
Child birth
practical considerations, 3.9.6
required disclosure of information, 3.9, 3.9.5
unauthorized examination, 1.2
Civil rights actions
restraints, 6.6.2
unauthorized examination or
treatment, 4.7.2
Commitment. *See* Mentally ill and
mentally retarded
Compulsory treatment
consent, 2.5
constitutional considerations of,
2.5
immunization, 2.5
premarital screening, 2.5
preschool screening, 2.5
venereal disease, 2.5
Consent actions
assault and battery, 1.2
defenses, 1.16, 1.17
negligence theory, 1.2
causality, 1.15.5
duty to disclose, 1.15.3
elements, 1.3, 1.15
fiduciary relationship, 1.15.1

nondisclosure, unjustified,
1.15.4
policy justification, 1.3.1
proximate cause, 1.15.5
Consent forms
abortion and, 3.5.1
conclusive presumptions and,
1.16.5
general admission forms, 1.7
general consent forms, 1.7.3
human research, 8.5.1
policy considerations, 1.14.2
rebutting presumptions and,
1.16.5
retention, 12.2
samples, 12.1.2, 12.1.3
Consent process. *See also* Express
consent, Implied consent,
Consent forms, Withdrawal,
Written consent
answering patients' questions, 1.9
attending physician, responsibility of, 1.9
health facility, role in, 12.5
patients' questions, significance
of, 1.9
authorization for specific care, 1.7
general admission forms, 1.7
general consent forms, 1.7.3
instructions from patient, 1.7.1
patient history, importance of,
1.7
compulsory treatment and, 2.5
disclosure of information, 1.8
basic information, 1.12
diagnostic tests, 1.12.3
interpreters, use of, 1.8
language used, 1.8
level of discussion, 1.8
medical community rule,
1.11.3, 1.13, 1.13.1
not required, when, 1.13, 2.7
patient need rule, 1.11.3, 1.13.2
reasonable alternatives, 1.12.2
remote risks, 1.12.1
risk-benefit information, 1.12.1
talking down to patient, 1.8
withholding information, 1.12.2

health facility role in, 12.5
informed refusal, 1.11.2, 3.13.2
legal capacity
  conservatorships, 1.5.1
  duty of health administrator,
    1.5.1
  duty of health care provider,
    1.5.1
  duty of health facilities, 1.5.2
  guardianships, 1.5.1
  legislative incapacity, 1.5.4
  mentally ill, 1.5
  minors, 1.5.3
  objections to treatment by pa-
    tient, 1.5.2
  presumption of capacity, 1.5
mental capacity
  delusions, 1.6.1
  intoxication, 1.6
  irrational behavior, 1.6.1
  lucid phases, 1.6.1
  medical emergency, 1.6.2
  nonemergency care, 1.6.2
  physical injury, 1.6
  presumption of competency,
    1.6
  refusal of care, 1.6.3
  shock-trauma, 1.6
  terminal illness, 1.6.1
  withdrawal of consent, 1.6.1
nontreatment situations
  circumcision, ritual, 12.7
  educational pursuits, 12.7
  religious practices, 12.7
two-stage process, 12.3
voluntary, 1.4
  financial coercion, 1.4.3
  hospital consents, voluntariness
    of, 1.4.1
  medicare antidumping provi-
    sions, 1.4.3
  personnel and coercive behav-
    ior, 1.4.2
  sterilization consents, 1.4.2
  "take it or leave it" approach,
    1.4.2
  ultimatums, 1.4.2
undue influence, 1.4

written consent, when necessary,
  1.10.2
Continuous or repetitive treatment
  allergy desensitization, 2.8
  consent requirements, 2.8
  chemotherapy, 2.8
  cobalt treatment, 2.8
  documentation of consent, 2.8
  renal dialysis, 2.8
Contraception. *See also* Minors
  "Dear Doctor" letters, 3.1.4
  disclosure, 3.1.4
  IUDs, 3.1
  manufacturer's duty, 3.1.1
  minimizing litigation, 3.1.5
  physician's duty, 3.1
  the "Pill," 3.1
  package inserts, effect of, 3.1.2

Death, determination (brain death)
  case law, 9.8.2
  criminal defenses, 9.8.2
  disconnecting life support as pre-
    requisite, 9.8.1, 9.8.2
  Harvard Ad Hoc criteria, 9.8.1
  organ transplantation and, 9.8.2,
    9.8.3
Deception and consent
  human research, 2.9.2
  policy considerations, 2.9.3
  related to therapeutic privilege,
    2.9.1
  when permitted, 2.9.1
Defenses
  disclosure unnecessary
    authorization regardless of
      risks, 1.16.2
    common risks, 1.16.1
    remote risks, 1.16.1
  documentation of consent, impor-
    tance of, 1.16.5
  emergency situation, 1.16.3
  negligence actions, defenses to,
    1.16.6
  signed consent, 1.16.5
    conclusive presumptions, 1.16.5
    presumptions rebuttable, 1.16.5

Defenses (*continued*)
  statutes of limitation, 1.17
    discovery rule, 1.17
    proof, 12.2
    tolling of, 1.17
  therapeutic privilege, 1.9, 1.16.4
Derivative liability, 3.9.5
Detainees
  compulsory medical examina-
    tions, 4.7.1
  drug abuse
    examination and treatment, 4.8
    legislation, 4.8
  physical and surgical searches, 4.9
    collecting samples, 4.9
    communicable disease, 4.9
    consent, 4.9
    emergency treatment, distin-
      guished from, 4.12.1
    emetics, 4.12.1
    hospital policy, 4.9
    physician's duty, 4.9, 4.12.1,
      4.12.2
    rectal examinations, 4.12.1
    stomach pumping, 4.12.1
    surgical removal of bullet,
      4.12.2
    surgical removal, when imper-
      missible, 4.12.2
    unauthorized examinations or
      treatment, 4.7.2, 4.12.1
Developmentally disabled. *See* Mentally retarded
Diagnostic procedures
  cervical cancer, 1.12.3
  ventriculogram, 1.7.3
Disclosure
  basic information required, 1.12
  diagnostic procedures, 1.12.3
    cervical cancer, 1.12.3
    Pap smear, 1.12.3, 3.13.2
  interpreters, use of, 1.8
  language used, 1.8
  level of discussion, 1.8
  medical community rule, 1.12.1
  nondisclosure
    authorization, regardless of
      risks, 1.15.2
    common risks, 1.15.1

continuous or repetitive care,
  2.8
deception and, 2.9.1
documentation, 1.16.2, 2.7.2
emergency treatment, 1.13.3,
  1.16.3, 2.2.1
evidence, 1.16.1
majority view, 1.13.1
minority view, 1.13.2
pathology studies, 3.13.1
placebo and, 2.9.1
policy considerations, 1.16.2,
  2.7.1
practical considerations, 2.7.2
reasonable alternatives, 1.12.2
remote risks, 1.13.3, 1.15.1
risk-benefit information, 1.12.1
statutory standards, 1.13.3
talking down to patients, 1.8
therapeutic privilege, 1.15.4,
  2.4
when permitted, 1.13, 2.7
withholding information,
  1.16.4
patient need rule, 1.12.1
to third parties
  child abuse, 2.6.1
  duty to disclose, 2.6
  parental notification of child's
    treatment, 2.6.2
  patient's permission, 2.6.3
  psychiatric patients, 2.6.1
  venereal disease, 2.6.1
  when impermissible, 2.6.3
Documentation. *See also* Consent
  forms
  consent checklists, 12.1.5
  consent policy and procedure,
    12.12
  content of, 12.11.1
  continuous or repetitive treat-
    ment, 2.8
  duty of health care facilities, 12.5
    quality assurance audits, 12.5.1
    risk management, 12.11.2
    substandard performance,
      12.5.2
  forms of, 12.1.1
    samples, 12.1.2, 12.1.3

human research, 8.1.4, 8.2.2,
  8.27.5
patient's chart
  contents, 12.1.4
  purpose, 12.1.1
purpose, 12.1
retention, 12.2
  legal reasons for, 12.2
  statutes of limitation, 12.2
telephone consents, 12.8
therapeutic privilege, 2.4.3
videotaped consents, 12.9
Drunk driving
blood samples, 4.10
conscious driver, refusal of tests,
  4.11
implied consent, 4.10
legislation, 4.11
tests
  consent, 4.11
  disclosure of information, 4.11
  duty of health personnel, 4.11
unconscious driver
  blood and fluid samples from,
    4.10
  liability of health personnel,
    4.10
urine samples, 4.10
Duty to obtain consent
caregivers, 1.14.1
danger of delegating duty, 1.14.2
drug manufacturers', 1.14.3
health facilities', 1.14.4
pharmacists', 1.14.5

Elderly persons
capacity to consent, 10.1
competency and consent, 10.2
death and dying, 10.10, 10.11
duty to protect, 10.7
duty to warn, 10.6
incompetent persons, 10.5
legislative standards, 10.4
refusing assistance, 10.8
residents' bill of rights legislation,
  10.9
Emergency treatment
consent, 1.7.4, 2.2

determination of, 2.2.2
disclosure unnecessary, 1.15.3
implied consent, 1.10.1
impossibility of obtaining consent,
  distinguished from, 2.3
legislative standards, 2.2.1
mentally ill or retarded, of, 6.9
minors, of, 5.1, 5.2, 5.2.1, 5.12,
  5.15
policy considerations, 2.2.4
prisoners, of, 4.4
refused by patient, 7.3.2
scope of permissible care, 2.2.4,
  7.3, 7.3.1
unauthorized care, when permitted, 1.7.4, 2.2.2
Eugenics. *See* Mentally ill
Expert testimony
when not required, 1.18.1
when required, 1.18.1
Exploratory surgery, 1.7.3
Express consent. *See also* Implied
  consent
defined, 1.10.1
implied consent, distinguished
  from, 1.10.1
Evidence
burden of proof, 1.19
common risks, 1.16.1
remote risks, 1.16.1
standard of proof, 1.19

Forms. *See* Consent forms
Fraud as basis for suit, 1.3

Gynecology. *See also* Abortion, Prenatal screening
cervical conization, 3.11
DES screening, 3.14.3
D & C, 3.10.2
hysterectomy, 1.7.3, 3.10-3.10.4
  consent to, 3.10
  inadequate disclosure, 3.10.2,
    3.10.3
  necessary disclosure of informa-
    tion, 3.10.4
  unauthorized, 3.10.1
  ureterovaginal fistula, 3.10.3

Gynecology (*continued*)
  obstetrical examination, 1.1
  Pap smear, 3.13.2, 3.14.1, 3.14.2
  radium implants, 3.11
    disclosure requirements, 3.11.1

HMOs, 1.1.2
Human research
  case law
    consent actions, 8.27, 8.27.1,
      8.27.2
    drug therapy, 8.27.3
    heart transplantation, 8.27.1
    radiation therapy, 8.27.2
    surgery, experimental, 8.27.1,
      8.27.3, 8.27.4
  checklist, 8.30
  commercial use of human tissues,
    8.29
  dimethyl sulfoxide (DMSO), 8.5.1
  documenting consent, 8.27.5
  drug company sponsored, 8.28
    conducted in doctor's office,
      8.28
  elderly
    competent, institutionalized,
      8.23.2
    consent, requirements for,
      8.23.1, 8.24, 8.24.1, 8.24.2
    federal regulations, 8.23
    IRBs, duties of, 8.23.3
    legal representative and con-
      sent, 8.23.1, 8.24.2
    possibly incompetent persons,
      8.23.1, 8.24.2
    state laws, 8.24
  FDA regulations
    consent documentation, 8.2.2
    consent requirements, 8.2.1
    waiver of consent require-
      ments, 8.2.3
  fetal research
    co-consent, when required,
      8.8.3
    consent requirements, 8.9.1,
      8.9.2
    criminal responsibility, 8.4.4,
      8.9.1
    ex utero research, 8.8.3
    father's consent, 8.8.2
    in utero research, consent for,
      8.8.2
    IRBs, duties in, 8.8.1, 8.9.1
    judicial review, 8.9.1
    Massachusetts example, 8.9.1
    New Mexico example, 8.9.2
    nonregulated fetal research,
      federal, 8.8.4
    nonviable fetus, 8.8.3, 8.9.1
    remains of, research with, 9.9
    "sale or use of" legislation, 8.9
    state legislation, 8.4.4, 8.9
    viable fetus, 8.8.3
  historical background, 8.0
  HHS regulations
    administrative requirements,
      8.1.1
    application, 8.1.1, 8.1.5
    consent documentation, 8.1.2,
      8.1.4
    consent requirements, 8.1.3
    IRBs, 8.1.2
    waiver of consent require-
      ments, 8.1.2
  in vitro fertilization research
    consent requirements, 8.10.1
    ethical advisory boards, 8.10.2
    federal law, 8.10
    HHS, Secretary's duties, 8.10.2
    state law, 8.11
  laetrile, research on, 8.5.1
  marijuana, research on, 8.5.1
  mentally ill, mentally retarded,
    and developmentally disabled
    California law, 8.17.1
    consent requirements, 8.16.2,
      8.17.1, 8.17.2
    conservator, consent of, 8.17.4
    general provisions for, 8.16.1
    IRBs, role in, 8.16.2
    legal guardian, consent of,
      8.17.2, 8.17.4
    New York law, 8.17.1
    parental consent, 8.17.2
    research review committees,
      8.17.3
    state law, 8.17, 8.17.1

subject's consent, 8.17.2
substituted judgment, 8.17.2
Virginia law, 8.17.1
minors
 as research subjects, 8.4.2,
  8.4.3, 8.13
 consent requirements, 8.13.1
 exempted activities, 8.13.4
 expedited review, 8.13.2
 FDA requirements, 8.13.3
 institutionalized and mentally
  handicapped minors, 8.14.2
 minors' consent to research,
  8.14.4
 parental consent, 8.14.3
 policy considerations, 8.13.5
 state laws, 8.14, 8.14.1
pregnant women, federal law
 as research subjects, 8.6
 consent process, 8.6.1
 father's consent, 8.6.2
 IRBs, duties in, 8.6.1
 waiver of consent, 8.6.3
pregnant women, state law
 as research subjects, 8.7
 consent requirements, 8.7.1
 New Mexico example, 8.7.1
prisoners
 compensation for activities,
  8.22
 consent requirements, 8.19.2,
  8.20.1, 8.21.1
 FDA regulations, 8.20, 8.20.1
 federal research regulations,
  8.19
 IRBs, duties of, 8.19.1, 8.20.2
 limitations, 8.21.1
 New York example, 8.21
 parole, effect on, 8.19.2
 permissible research activities,
  8.19.1
 state laws, 8.21, 8.21.1
 surgery, experimental, 8.26.4
state and federal requirements
  compared
 elderly, 8.25
 fetal research, 8.9.3
 generally, 8.4.5
 in vitro fertilization, 8.12

 mentally ill, retarded and developmentally disabled, 8.18
 pregnant women, 8.7.2
 prisoners, 8.22
state statutes and regulations
 California example, 8.4.1
 drug research, 8.5
 minors as research subjects,
  8.15
 New York example, 8.4.2
 types of research subjects,
  8.4.1, 8.4.2, 8.4.3, 8.4.4
 Virginia example, 8.4.3

Immunization
 implied consent, 1.10.1
 mass or public immunization programs, 12.6
 communication techniques,
  12.6
 consent procedures, 12.6
 swine flu, 12.6
Implied consent. *See also*
  Impossibility
 defined, 1.10.1
 drunk driving, 4.10
 emergency care, 1.10.1
 express consent, distinguished
  from, 1.10.1
 intoxicated persons, 4.10
 minors, 5.2.1
 unconscious persons, 4.10
 blood samples from, 4.10
 drunk driving laws, 4.10, 4.11
 legislation, 4.10
 liability of health personnel,
  4.10
Impossibility of obtaining consent,
  2.3
 asthma, 2.3
 elements, 2.3
 heart attack, 2.3
 severe allergy reactions, 2.3
 snake bites, 2.3
Informed refusal. *See* Refusing
  treatment
Interpreters, use of, 1.8

JCAHO and consent, 1.13.4

Legislation
assault and battery actions repealed, 1.2
legislative incapacity to consent,
1.5.4
reform measures, 1.2
Living wills. *See* Refusing treatment

Mastectomy
breast biopsy, unauthorized extension of, 3.12.3
frozen section biopsy, duty to disclose, 3.12.4
physician's duty to warn, 3.12.2
statutory requirements, 3.12.1
Medical emergencies. *See* Emergency treatment
Mental capacity. *See also* Mentally ill
and mentally retarded
conservatorship, 1.6.2
emergency care, 1.6.2
guardianship, 1.6.2
incapacity, 1.6.2
intoxication, 1.6
irrational behavior, 1.6.1
lucid phases, 1.6.1
mental illness, 1.6
nonemergency care, 1.6.2
physical injury, 1.6
presumption of competency, 1.6
refusal of care, 1.6.3
shock-trauma, 1.6
terminal illness, 1.6.1
withdrawal of consent, 1.6.1
Mentally ill and mentally retarded.
See also Mental capacity
aversive stimuli, 6.6, 6.6.1
consent requirements, 6.6.1
legislation, 6.6.1
behavioral modification, 6.6, 6.6.1
consent requirements, 6.6.1
legislation, 6.6.1
commitment
basis for, 6.1, 6.2.1
consent requirements, 6.1

due process considerations, 6.1,
6.2
involuntary patients, 6.2
legal incapacity, 6.2
legislation, 6.1
voluntary, 6.1
electroshock treatment
benefits, 6.3
case law, 6.3.4
competency to give consent,
6.3.1
constitutional arguments, 6.3.4
court orders for, 6.3.1
documentation, 6.3.3
elements of informed consent
for, 6.3, 6.3.2, 6.3.5
emergency use, 6.3.3
legislation controlling, 6.3.1
minors and, 6.3.1
practical legal rules for, 6.3.5
refusing consent, 6.3.1
risks, 6.3
role of next of kin, 6.3.1
human research on, 8.17.1-8.17.3
isolation and seclusion
documentation, 6.6.3
legislative controls, 6.6.3
limitations, 6.6.3
medical and surgical care
emergency treatment, 6.9
legislation, 6.9
patient's consent, 6.9
permissible treatment, 6.9
sterilization, incidental, 6.9
medication
case law, 6.4.4
competent patients and, 6.4.4
consent requirements, 6.4.2,
6.4.3
constitutional considerations,
6.4.4, 6.4.5
developmentally disabled, recognized treatment for, 6.4.2
documentation, 6.4.1
immunity from liability for administering, 6.4.1
incompetent patients and, 6.4.4
involuntary treatment with, 6.4,
6.4.4

legislative controls, 6.4.1, 6.4.2
liberty interests, 6.4.4
precommitment use, 6.4.1
prohibited uses, 6.4.2
punishment with, 6.4.2
religious objections, 6.4.5
right to refuse, 6.4.1, 6.4.2
risks, 6.4
standard of proof, involuntary
   patients, 6.4.4
substituted judgment theory,
   6.4.4
minors, 5.8
psychosurgery
   capacity to consent, 6.5.4
   case law, 6.5.4
   co-consent requirements, 6.5.2
   consent requirements, 6.5.2
   defined, 6.5.1
   experimental practices, 6.5.4
   factors influencing, 6.5.3
   liberty interests, 6.5.3
   procedural requirements, 6.5.2
   right of privacy, 6.5.4
   standard of proof, 6.5.2
   state legislation, 6.5.2
   third party authorizations, 6.5.2
   voluntariness of consent, 6.5.4
release
   retention over patient's objec-
      tion, 6.1.1
   temporary absences, 6.1.1
   voluntary patients, 6.1.1
restraints
   case law, 6.6.2
   factors influencing, 6.6.2
   legislation, 6.6.2
   liberty interest, 6.6.2
   limitations, 6.6.2
   presumed validity in use of,
      6.6.2
   punishment, as, 6.6.2
rights
   bill of rights, 6.1, 6.2.2
   informed consent, 6.2.2
   institutionalized persons, 6.2.2
sterilization
   authorization without enabling
      legislation, 6.8.1, 6.8.2

capacity to consent, 6.7
case law, 6.7, 6.8.1, 6.8.2
co-consent, 6.7
consent requirements, 6.7
court orders for, 6.8
due process considerations,
   6.8.2
enabling legislation authorizing
   procedure, 6.8.1, 6.8.2
eugenic, 6.7
factors influencing, 6.8.2
legislation, 6.7
legislative silence on, 6.8.2,
   6.8.3
parens patriae power, 6.8
procedural requirements, 6.8.2
standard of proof, 6.7, 6.8.2
voluntariness of consent, 6.7
treatment, 6.4.2, 6.9
Minors
abortion
   constitutional arguments, 5.6.1
   maturity to give informed con-
      sent, 5.6.1
   parental consent, 5.6.1
   parental notification, 5.5.2,
      5.6.2
   spousal consent and notifica-
      tion, 5.6.3
child abuse
   case law, 5.13
   court orders for examination,
      5.13
   minors' consent to care, 5.13
   legislative requirements, 5.13
common law view, 5.1
contraception
   case law, 5.5
   consent standards, 5.5.1
   legislation, 5.5, 5.5.3
   medical considerations, 5.5.2
   parental consent and notifica-
      tion, 5.5.2
   right to obtain, 5.5.1
   state interests, 5.5.2
delinquent and deprived children
   authorization for treatment,
      5.14
   immunity from litigation, 5.14

Minors, delinquent and deprived
children (*continued*)
parental objections to treatment, 5.14
scope of permissible care, 5.14
drug and alcohol treatment statutory requirements, 5.7
emancipated minor, 1.5.3
tests, 5.2.3
emergency treatment, 5.1, 5.2.1
common law approach, 5.12
exemption from liability, 5.12
legislation, 5.12
minors' consent, 5.12
school children, 5.15
immunization
case law, 5.10.2
consent for, 5.10.1
exceptions to rules, 5.10.2
legislative standards, 5.10.1
medical exemptions, 5.10.1
personal beliefs exemptions,
5.10.1
religious exemptions, 5.10.1,
5.10.2
school immunizations, 5.10.1
implied consent, 5.2.1
legal capacity, 1.5.3, 5.1
legislative standards, 5.3.1-5.3.7
mature minor, 1.5.3, 5.2.2
mentally ill and mentally retarded, 5.8, 6.3.1
minor parents, 1.5.3, 5.3.6
organ donation, 9.2.2, 9.2.3,
9.2.6
parental consent for treatment,
generally, 5.1
refusing treatment
best-interest test, 5.16.2
birth and genetic defects,
5.16.3
blood transfusions, 5.16.2
child neglect, distinguished
from, 5.16.2
court orders for care, 5.16.1
defective newborns, 5.16.3
elective procedures, 5.16.2
Jehovah's Witnesses, 5.16.2

lifesaving care, 5.16.2
minors' refusing care, 5.18
orders not to resuscitate, 5.17.1
parens patriae power, 5.16.2
parental refusal of care, 5.16
philosophical beliefs, 5.16.2
religious beliefs, 5.16.1, 5.16.2
spiritual treatment, distinguished from, 5.16.1
state interests, 5.16.2
statutory limits on parental
power, 5.16.1
surgery, corrective, 5.16.2
terminally ill children, 5.17,
5.17.1
schoolchildren
authorization for treatment, 5.15
drug treatment, 5.15
emergency care, 5.15
immunity from litigation, 5.15
legislative requirements for
care, 5.15
medical care, 5.15
screening and treatment
consent, how obtained, 5.11.3
galactosemia, 5.11.1
homocystinuria, 5.11.1
hypothyroidism, 5.11.1
maple syrup urine disease,
5.11.1
newborns, 5.11.1
ophthalmia neonatorum, 5.11.1
PKU, 5.11.1
religious exemptions, 5.11.1,
5.11.2
school age children, 5.11.2
scoliosis, 5.11.2
sickle cell anemia or trait,
5.11.1, 5.11.2
tuberculosis, 5.11.2
tyrosinemia, 5.11.1
visual disorders, 5.11.2
sexual assault treatment, 1.4.3,
5.12.1
disclosure of information to
minors, 5.12.1
minors' consent, 5.12.1
statutes, 5.12.1

sexually transmitted disease,
   1.5.3, 5.4
   authority to treat minors, 5.4.1
   confidentiality of treatment,
      5.4.2
   parental notification, 5.4.2
   spousal notification, 5.4.2
   specific legislation, 5.4.1
sterilization, 5.2.3
   capacity to consent, 5.9.2
   guidelines, 5.9.2
   institutionalized minors, distin-
      guished, 5.9.2
   judicial limitations, 5.9.2
   jurisdictional limitations, 5.9.2
   mentally incompetent minors,
      5.9
   right of privacy, 5.9.2
   standard of proof, 5.9.2
   statutory law, 5.9.1
unauthorized treatment, 5.1
Misrepresentation as basis for suit,
   1.3

Negligence
   assault and battery distinguished
      from, 1.3
   consent actions, 1.2
   elements, 1.3
   policy justification, 1.3.1
Nondisclosure. *See* Disclosure

Obstetrics. *See* Gynecology
Organ donation. *See also* Death
   cadaver donors
      anatomical gift acts, 9.6
      consent requirements, 9.6
      consent, from whom, 9.6.1
      death, time of, 9.6.4
      donees' rights, 9.6.4
      donor card, 9.6.2
      duties, at time of death, 9.6.4
      immunity provisions, 9.6.4
      litigation, 9.6.5
      physicians, duties of, 9.6.4
      revoking consent, 9.6.2

cadaver organs
   corneal tissue removal, 9.9,
      9.9.1
   criminal cases, 9.8.2, 9.8.3
   eye enucleation, 9.9.2
   family of decedent, disputes
      among, 9.11.2
   funeral service practitioners,
      9.9.2
   medical examiners and coroners
      in, 9.8.3, 9.9, 9.9.1
   pituitary gland removal, 9.9.1
commercial use of human tissues,
   9.5, 9.5.1
driver's licenses, donor designation, 9.7, 9.7.1
live organ donors
   best interest theory, 9.2.2
   competency to donate, 9.2
   compulsory donation, 9.4
   consent requirements, 9.1
   court action, 9.2.2, 9.2.3, 9.2.4,
      9.2.5
   documentation of consent, 9.1
   factors influencing, 9.1, 9.2.2
   incompetent donors, 9.2.1
   legislation, 9.3.1, 9.3.2
   mentally retarded donor, 9.2.2,
      9.2.3, 9.2.4
   minors, 9.2.2, 9.2.3, 9.2.6
   minors, consent from, 9.2.6
   organ procurement legislation,
      9.11, 9.11.1
   parental consent, 9.2.4, 9.2.5
   permission denied, 9.2.4
   standards for decision-making,
      9.3
   substituted judgment theory,
      9.2.1, 9.2.2
use of the newly dead, 9.15

Physician
   case law, 12.4
   consultant physician, duty of,
      12.4
   duty of, in consent, 1.14.1

Placebo
consent for use, 2.9.1
human research, 2.9.2
policy considerations, 2.9.3
therapeutic privilege, 2.9.1
Prenatal screening
exceptions to required screening, 3.8
mandatory screening, 3.8
need for, 3.8
venereal disease, 3.8
Prisoners
capacity to consent, 1.5.4, 4.1.3
communication with, 4.2
compulsory examination or treatment
legislative requirements, 4.7.1
venereal disease, 4.7.1
drug abuse
examination and treatment, 4.8
legislation, 4.8
refusing care, 4.8
hunger strikes
federal regulations, 4.6.3
state interests, 4.6.3
inadequate disclosure of information, 4.1.3
incapacity to consent
duty of correctional officials, 4.4
emergency treatment, 4.4
intoxication, 4.5
parens patriae power, 4.5
right of privacy, 4.4, 4.5
state legislation, 4.3
model prisoner syndrome, 4.1.1
physical and surgical searches
collecting samples, 4.9
communicable disease, 4.9
consent, 4.9
emergency treatment, distinguished from, 4.12.1
emetics, 4.12.1
hospital policy, 4.9
physician, duty of, 4.9, 4.12.1, 4.12.2
rectal examinations, 4.12.1
removal of bullet, 4.12.2
stomach pumping, 4.12.1

surgical intervention, when impermissible, 4.12.2
treatment and criminal investigation combined, 4.9
refusing treatment
case law, 4.6.2
contagious diseases, 4.6.1
drugs, forcible administration, 4.6.2
emergency care, 7.3, 7.3.1
hemodialysis, 4.6.2
legislative limits, 4.6.1
life-threatening situation, 7.3
prison security and, 4.6.2
religious objections, 4.6.4
right to refuse, 4.6
state interests, 4.6.2
venereal disease, 4.6.1
unauthorized examination or treatment, 4.6.2, 4.12.1
voluntariness of consent, 4.1
coercive institutional setting, 4.1.2

Prostitutes
compulsory medical examinations, 4.7.1
unauthorized examination or treatment, 4.7.2
venereal disease, 4.7.1

Refusal of treatment
competent persons, 7.2.1, 7.4.1, 7.5.1
durable powers of attorney, 7.8.4
emergency life-saving care, 7.3
family disputes, 7.3.4
patients' refusal, 7.3.2
relatives' refusal, 7.3.3
written directives, effect of, 7.3.5
incapacitated persons, 7.2.2
incompetent persons, 7.2, 7.4.2, 7.5.2
artificial nutrition and hydration, 7.5.2
life-sustaining care, 7.5.2

life-threatening illness, 7.2.1
respiratory and cardiopulmonary function, 7.5.2
terminal illness, 7.4.2
informed refusal, 1.11.2
living wills, 7.8, 7.8.1
orders not to hospitalize (DNH),
  7.7
orders not to resuscitate (DNR),
  7.6
patient directives, 7.8.2
philosophical objections, 7.1
religious objections, 7.1
  compelled care, 7.1.1
  legislation, 7.1.3
  treatment not compelled, 7.1.2
terminal illness, withdrawing care
  competent patients, 7.5.1
  consent requirements, 7.5.3
  documentation, 7.5.3
  incompetent patients, 7.5.2
  practical issues, 7.5.3
  right of privacy, 7.5.1
  state interests, 7.5.1, 7.5.2
Release forms. *See also* Consent
  forms
  legal defense, 1.11.1
  refusing treatment, 1.11.1, 7.3.6
  withdrawing consent, 1.11.1

Schoolchildren. *See* Minors
Searches. *See* Prisoners
Spousal consent
  abortion, 3.6
  artificial insemination, 3.7.2
  sterilization, 3.3, 3.3.1, 3.3.2
Statutes of limitation. *See* Defenses
Standard of proof
  clear and convincing, 1.19
  preponderance of evidence, 1.19
Sterilization
  consent criteria, 3.2
  disclosure of information re-
    quired, 3.2.2
  invalid consent, consequences of,
    3.2.1
  practical considerations, 3.2.3
  spousal consent, 3.3, 3.3.1

right of privacy, 3.3.2
spousal consultation, 3.3.4
statutory law, 3.3.3
Surgery
  disclosure of pathology studies,
    3.13.1
  operation on different body part,
    1.2, 1.7.2
  specific procedures
    amputation, 7.2.1, 7.2.2
    amniotomy, 3.9.5
    appendectomy, 5.2.1
    caesarean section, 3.2.1
    cleft palate, 5.16.2
    ear, 1.7.2, 5.2.2
    eye, 5.16.2
    exploratory, 1.7.3
    harelip, 5.16.2
    hysterectomy, 1.7.3, 3.10,
      3.10.1, 3.10.2, 3.10.3, 3.10.4
    ileostomy, 1.7.4
    knee, 1.7.2
    mastectomy, 3.12
    mole, removal of, 1.7.4
    oophorectomy, 1.7.4
    "pinch-graft," 5.2.2
    rhinoplasty, 1.7.1
    spinal anesthetic, 1.7.1
    thyroidectomy, 2.4.1
    tonsillectomy, 5.2.2
    tubal ligation, 1.13.2, 3.2.1
    tracheotomy, 1.6.4
    ulcer surgery, 1.13.2
    vasectomy, 3.2.2, 5.2.3
  unauthorized procedures, 1.2,
    3.12.3

Therapeutic privilege
  defense to consent action, 1.15.4
  documentation required, 1.15.4,
    2.4.3
  prescribing medication, 6.4.3
  when inapplicable, 2.4.2
  when justified, 1.16.2, 2.4, 2.4.1

Unanticipated circumstances
  consent unnecessary, 1.7.4

Unauthorized procedures
 extension of surgery, 1.2
 mastectomy, 3.12.3
 obstetrical examination, 1.2
 operation on different body part,
  1.2
Unclaimed bodies
 anatomical research, 9.10
 disposal, 9.10
 fetal remains, 9.10
 research with, 9.10

Withdrawal of consent
 capacity, 1.11
 documentation, 1.11.1
 informed withdrawal, 1.11.2
 legal defense, 1.11.1
 medication, effect of, 1.11
 release forms, use of, 1.11
 patient's right to, 1.11
Withholding information. *See* Therapeutic privilege
Written consent
 consent process, distinguished
  from, 1.10.2
 legal defense, 1.10.2
 when necessary, 1.10.2